Red Hat® Linux® All-in-One Desk Reference For D[...]

D1409382

Bash Shell

- Pipe:
  - command1 | command2

- Redirections:
  - command > file (output goes to file)
  - command < file (input from file)
  - command > file (append to file)
  - command 2> file (errors go to file)

- Commands:
  - alias (Defines shortcut for a long command)
  - apropos (Searches the manpages for keywords)

- history (Displays most recent commands)
- locate (Finds files)
- whereis (Finds executable files for a command)
- which (Shows full pathname for a command)
- man (Displays online help)
- printenv (Displays the environment variables)

- Environment variables:
  - HOME (User's home directory)
  - PATH (Directories to search for commands)
  - TERM (Name of terminal type)

File System

- Key directories in the file system:
  - /   Root directory (base of file system)
  - /   (Executable programs)
  - /boot   (Linux kernel and boot loader)
  - /dev   (Special device files)
  - /etc   (System configuration files)
  - /home   (Home directories of all users)
  - /lib   (Library files for programs)
  - /mnt   (Mount points forCD-ROM, floppy)
  - /root   (Home directory of the root user)
  - /sbin   (System-administration commands)
  - /tmp   (Temporary directory)
  - /usr   (Many important programs)
  - /var   (Various system files, such as logs)

- Commands:

cat	Copies a file to the standard output
cd	Changes current directory
chmod	Changes file permissions
chown	Changes file ownerships
cp	Copies files
dd	Copies blocks of data
df	Reports disk space usage by device
diff	Compares two text files
du	Reports disk space usage by directory
file	Displays the type of data in a file
find	Finds files based on specified criteria

grep	Searches for text in a file
ln	Links a file name to a link name
ls	Displays the contents of a directory
mkdir	Creates a directory
more	Displays a text file, one page at a time
mount	Mounts a file system
mv	Renames or moves file
pwd	Displays the current directory
rm	Deletes files
rmdir	Deletes directories
sort	Sorts lines in a text file
split	Splits a file into smaller parts
umount	Unmount a file system
wc	Counts words and lines in a file

- File permissions:
  - rwxrwxrwx   3 groups of rwx, leftmost is for owner, middle for group, rightmost for others; rwx stands for read (r), write (w), execute (x); dash (-) means no permission
  - rwx——   Only owner can read, write, execute
  - rw-r—r—   Everyone can read, owner can write
  - rw——-   Only owner can read and write
  - r—r—r—   Read-only file (everyone can read)

Red Hat® Linux® All-in-One Desk Reference For Dummies®

Cheat Sheet

Red Hat Linux Installation

1. Resize disk partition using partitioning tool such as PartitionMagic or get a second hard disk.
2. Boot PC from first CD-ROM or create boot disk and boot from the boot disk.
3. Go through graphical installation steps.
4. Configure other hardware when system first boots up.

Red Hat Linux Configuration

- Run graphical Red Hat configuration tools from Main Menu⇨System Settings
- To configure the X Window System, run

    ```
    redhat-config-xfree86
    ```

- Printer setup: Main Menu⇨System Settings⇨Printing
- Sound card setup: Main Menu⇨System Settings⇨Soundcard Detection

GNOME and KDE Desktops

- Click the Main Menu button in GNOME or the K button in KDE and then select applications to run
- Always right-click for a pop-up menu of options
- Right-click on the GNOME panel to add applets to the panel
- OpenOffice.org applications: Main Menu⇨Office

System Administration

Manage user accounts: Main Menu⇨System Settings⇨Users and Groups

Manage packages: Main Menu⇨System Settings⇨Packages

Configure services: Main Menu⇨Server Settings⇨Services

Install RPM packages: `rpm -ivh packagefile`

Check if RPM is installed: `rpm -q rpmname`

Unpack compressed tar files: `tar zxvf filename.tgz`

Network Configuration

- **Network configuration:** Main Menu⇨System Tools⇨Network Device Control
- **Internet connection:** Main Menu⇨System Tools⇨Internet Configuration Wizard

Commands:

- `ping`   Checks network connectivity
- `ifconfig`   Configures network interface
- `netstat`   Displays network status

For Dummies: Bestselling Book Series for Beginners

Red Hat® Linux®
ALL-IN-ONE DESK REFERENCE
FOR
DUMMIES®

Red Hat® Linux®
ALL-IN-ONE DESK REFERENCE
FOR
DUMMIES®

by Naba Barkakati

WILEY

Wiley Publishing, Inc.

Red Hat® Linux® All-in-One Desk Reference For Dummies®

Published by
Wiley Publishing, Inc.
909 Third Avenue
New York, NY 10022
www.wiley.com

Copyright © 2003 by Wiley Publishing, Inc., Indianapolis, Indiana

Published by Wiley Publishing, Inc., Indianapolis, Indiana

Published simultaneously in Canada

For general information on our other products and services or to obtain technical support, please contact our Customer Care Department within the U.S. at 800-762-2974, outside the U.S. at 317-572-3993, or fax 317-572-4002.

Wiley also publishes its books in a variety of electronic formats. Some content that appears in print may not be available in electronic books.

Library of Congress Control Number: 2002111061

ISBN: 0-7645-2442-9

Manufactured in the United States of America

10 9 8 7 6 5 4 3 2 1

1B/SQ/RS/QS/IN

About the Author

Naba Barkakati is an electrical engineer and a successful computer-book author who has experience in a wide variety of systems, ranging from MS-DOS and Windows to UNIX and Linux. He bought his first personal computer — an IBM PC-AT — in 1984 after graduating with a PhD in electrical engineering from the University of Maryland at College Park. While pursuing a full-time career in engineering, Naba dreamed of writing software for the emerging PC software market. As luck would have it, instead of building a software empire like Microsoft, he ended up writing successful computer books. Currently, Naba is a Senior Level Technologist at the Center for Technology and Engineering in the U.S. General Accounting Office.

Over the past 15 years, Naba has written over 25 computer books on a number of topics ranging from Windows programming with C++ to Linux. He has authored several best-selling titles, such as *The Waite Group's Turbo C++ Bible, Object-Oriented Programming in C++, X Window System Programming, Visual C++ Developer's Guide, Borland C++ 4 Developer's Guide,* and *Linux Secrets*. His books have been translated into many languages, including Spanish, French, Polish, Greek, Italian, Chinese, Japanese, and Korean. Naba's most recent books are *Red Hat Linux 7.2 Weekend Crash Course* and *Red Hat Linux 7.3 Secrets*.

Naba lives in North Potomac, Maryland, with his wife Leha, and their children, Ivy, Emily, and Ashley.

Dedication

I would like to dedicate this book to my wife Leha, and daughters Ivy, Emily, and Ashley.

Acknowledgments

I am grateful to Terri Varveris for getting me started on this book — a set of eight quick reference guides on all aspects of Red Hat Linux. As the project editor, Andrea Boucher guided me through the manuscript-submission process and kept everything moving. I appreciate the guidance and support that Terri and Andrea gave me during this project.

I would like to thank Jason Luster for reviewing the manuscript for technical accuracy and providing many useful suggestions for improving the book's content.

Thanks to everyone at Wiley Publishing for transforming my raw manuscript into this well-edited and beautifully packaged book.

Of course, there would be no reason for this book if it were not for Linux. For this, we have Linus Torvalds and the legions of Linux developers around the world to thank. Thanks to Red Hat for providing beta copies of Red Hat Linux and the publisher's edition CDs that are bundled with this book.

Finally, and as always, my greatest thanks go to my wife, Leha, and our daughters, Ivy, Emily, and Ashley — it is their love and support that keeps me going. Thanks for being there!

Publisher's Acknowledgments

We're proud of this book; please send us your comments through our online registration form located at www.dummies.com/register/.

Some of the people who helped bring this book to market include the following:

Acquisitions, Editorial, and Media Development

Project Editor: Andrea C. Boucher

Acquisitions Editor: Terri Varveris

Technical Editor: Jason Luster

Editorial Manager: Carol Sheehan

Permissions Editor: Carmen Krikorian

Media Development Specialist: Megan Decraene

Media Development Manager: Laura VanWinkle

Media Development Supervisor: Richard Graves

Editorial Assistant: Amanda Foxworth

Cartoons: Rich Tennant (www.the5thwave.com)

Production

Project Coordinator: Ryan Steffen

Layout and Graphics: Beth Brooks, Amanda Carter, Carrie Foster, LeAndra Johnson, Kristin McMullan, Tiffany Muth, Heather Pope, Jacque Schneider, Julie Trippetti, Jeremey Unger, Erin Zeltner

Proofreaders: Melissa D. Buddendeck, John Tyler Connoley, Andy Hollandbeck, Carl W. Pierce, Dwight Ramsey, Charles Spencer

Indexer: Ty Koontz

Publishing and Editorial for Technology Dummies

Richard Swadley, Vice President and Executive Group Publisher

Andy Cummings, Vice President and Publisher

Mary C. Corder, Editorial Director

Publishing for Consumer Dummies

Diane Graves Steele, Vice President and Publisher

Joyce Pepple, Acquisitions Director

Composition Services

Gerry Fahey, Vice President of Production Services

Debbie Stailey, Director of Composition Services

Contents at a Glance

Table of Contents

Introduction

Red Hat continues to improve its version of Linux. The recently released Red Hat Linux 8 comes with many new system components including the Linux 2.4.18 kernel, XFree86 4.2.0, GNOME 2.0, KDE 3.0, GCC 3.2 compiler, and the glibc 2.2.93 system libraries. This version supports USB hard disks and includes many new system configuration tools.

Red Hat Linux 8 also includes the recently released OpenOffice.org office suite. To top it off, Red Hat Linux 8 comes with a new and improved graphical installation program that's truly new!

About Red Hat Linux All-in-One

Red Hat Linux All-in-One Desk Reference For Dummies follows the successful model of the All-in-One Desk Reference and gives you eight different quick-reference guides in a single book. Taken together, these eight books provide detailed information on installing, configuring, and using Red Hat Linux.

What you'll like most about this book is that you don't have to read it sequentially chapter by chapter, or, for that matter, even the sections in a chapter. You can pretty much turn to the topic you want and quickly get the answer to your pressing questions about Red Hat Linux, be it about using the OpenOffice.org word processor or setting up the Apache Web server.

Here are some of the things you can do with this book:

✦ Install and configure Red Hat Linux from the CD-ROMs included with the book.

✦ Connect the Red Hat Linux PC to the Internet through a DSL or cable modem.

✦ Set up dial-up networking with PPP.

✦ Get tips, techniques, and shortcuts for specific uses of Red Hat Linux, such as

- Setting up and using Internet services such as Web, Mail, News, FTP, NFS, NIS, and DNS

- Setting up a Windows server using Samba

- Using Red Hat Linux commands

- Using Perl, shell, and C programming on Red Hat Linux

- Using the applications that come with Red Hat Linux

+ Understanding the basics of system and network security
+ Performing system administration tasks

Conventions Used in This Book

I use a simple notational style in this book. All listings, filenames, function names, variable names, and keywords are typeset in a `monospace` font for ease of reading. I italicize the first occurrences of new terms and concepts and then provide a definition right there. The output of commands follows the typed command and the output is shown in a monospace font.

What You Don't Have to Read

Each mini reference book zeros in on a specific task area such as using the Internet or running Internet servers and then provides hands-on instructions on how to perform a series of related tasks. You can jump right to a section and read about a specific task. You don't have to read anything but the few paragraphs or the list of steps that relate to your question. Use the Table of Contents or the Index to locate the pages that are relevant to your question.

You can safely ignore text next to the Technical Stuff icons as well as the sidebars.

Who Are You?

I assume that you are somewhat familiar with a PC — you know how to turn it on and off and you have dabbled a bit with Windows. Considering that most new PCs come preloaded with Windows, this should be a safe assumption, right?

When it comes to installing Red Hat Linux on your PC, if you want to retain your Windows 2000 or Windows XP installations intact, I assume you won't mind investing in a good disk-partitioning tool such as PowerQuest's PartitionMagic, available at `www.powerquest.com/partitionmagic` (no, I don't have any connections with PowerQuest).

I also assume that you are willing to accept the risk that when you try to install Red Hat Linux, some things may not quite work. This can happen if you have some uncommon types of hardware. If you are afraid of ruining your system, try finding a slightly older spare Pentium PC that you can sacrifice and then install Red Hat Linux on that PC.

How This Book Is Organized

Red Hat Linux All-in-One Desk Reference For Dummies has eight books, each of which focuses on a small set of related topics. If you are looking for information on a specific topic, check the book names on the spine or consult the Table of Contents.

This desktop reference starts with a minibook that explains the basics of Red Hat Linux and guides you through the installation process (this is a unique aspect of this book because you typically do not purchase a PC with Red Hat Linux preinstalled). The second minibook serves as a user's guide to Red Hat Linux — it focuses on exploring various aspects of a Red Hat Linux workstation, including the GNOME and KDE GUIs and many of the applications that come bundled with Red Hat Linux. The third minibook covers networking and Book IV goes into using the Internet. Book V introduces system administration. The sixth minibook turns to the important subject of securing a Red Hat Linux system and its associated network. Book VII teaches how to run a variety of Internet servers from mail to Web server. The eighth and final minibook introduces you to programming.

Here's a quick overview of the eight books and what they contain:

Book I: Red Hat Basics: What is Red Hat Linux? Installing, configuring, and troubleshooting Red Hat Linux. Taking Red Hat Linux for a test drive.

Book II: Workstations and Applications: Exploring GNOME and KDE. Learning how to use the shell (what's a shell anyway?). Learning to navigate the Red Hat Linux file system. Exploring the applications such as OpenOffice.org as well as the text editors (vi and Emacs).

Book III: Networking: Connecting the Red Hat Linux PC to the Internet through a dial-up connection or a high-speed always-on connection such as DSL or cable modem. Configuring and managing TCP/IP networks.

Book IV: Internet: Using various Internet services such as e-mail, Web surfing, and reading newsgroups. Transferring files with FTP.

Book V: Administration: Learning to perform basic system administration. Managing user accounts and the file system. Installing applications. Working with devices and printers. Upgrading and customizing the Linux kernel.

Book VI: Security: Understanding network and host security. Learning the techniques to secure the host and the network. Performing security audits.

Book VII: Internet Servers: Managing the Internet services. Configuring the Apache Web server. Setting up the FTP server (including anonymous FTP). Configuring the mail and news servers. Providing DNS and NIS. File sharing with NFS. Using Samba to set up a Windows server.

Book VIII: Programming: Learning the basics of programming. Exploring the software development tools in Red Hat Linux. Writing shell scripts. Learning C and Perl programming.

Appendix: About the CDs: Summarizes the contents of the book's companion CD-ROMs.

What's on the CDs?

The CDs contain the Publisher's Edition of Red Hat Linux 8 from Red Hat, Inc. You may use the CDs in accordance with the license agreements accompanying the software. To learn more about the contents of the CDs, please consult the appendix.

Icons Used in This Book

Following the time-honored tradition of the *All-in-One Desktop Reference For Dummies* series, I use icons to help you quickly pinpoint useful information. The icons include the following:

The Remember icon marks a general interesting fact — something that I thought you'd like to know and remember.

The Tip icon marks things that you can do to make your job easier.

The Warning icon highlights potential pitfalls. With this icon, I'm telling you: "Watch out! This could hurt your system!"

The Technical Stuff icon marks technical information that could be of interest to an advanced user (or those of us aspiring to be advanced users).

Sidebars

I use sidebars throughout the book to highlight interesting, but not critical, information. Sidebars explain concepts you may not have encountered before or give a little insight into a related topic. If you're in a hurry, you can safely skip the sidebars.

Where to Go from Here

It's time to get started on your Red Hat Linux adventure. Take out the CDs and install Red Hat Linux. Then, turn to a relevant chapter and let the fun begin. Use the Table of Contents and the Index to figure out where you want to go. Before you know it, you'll become an expert at Red Hat Linux!

I hope you enjoy consulting this book as much as I enjoyed writing it!

Book I

Red Hat Basics

"When we started the company, we weren't going to call it 'Red Hat'. But eventually we decided it sounded better than 'Beard of Bees Linux'."

Contents at a Glance

Chapter 1: Introducing Red Hat Linux

In This Chapter

✔ Explaining what Red Hat Linux is

✔ Going over what Red Hat Linux includes

✔ Discovering how Red Hat Linux helps you manage

✔ Getting started

I bet you have heard about Linux, and you probably know the Red Hat name as well. If you're wondering what exactly Red Hat Linux is and what it can help you do, this chapter is all about answering those questions. I provide a broad-brushstroke picture of Red Hat Linux and tell you how you can start using Red Hat Linux. By the way, this book covers Red Hat Linux for Intel 80x86 and Pentium processors (basically any PC that can run any flavor of Windows).

What Is Red Hat Linux?

Trying to describe Red Hat Linux is a bit like that story of six blind men trying to describe an elephant. You know the one — one blind man touches the elephant's side and says that the elephant is like a wall. The other checks out the tusk and concludes that an elephant is like a spear, and so on. Along those lines, Red Hat Linux appears to be many different things depending on what you experience. You can think of it as the graphical user interface or just a PC to run your e-mail program, but, at its heart, it's an operating system. The following sections explain what I mean by this statement.

Operating systems and Linux

You know that your PC is a bunch of *hardware* — things you can touch like the system box, the monitor, the keyboard, and mouse. The system box contains the most important hardware of all — the central processing unit (CPU) that runs the *software* (these are the things you cannot touch). In a typical Pentium 4 PC, the Pentium 4 microprocessor is the CPU. Other important hardware in the system box are the memory and the disk.

Does Linux really run on any computer?

Linux runs on many different types of computer systems, and it does seem like it runs on nearly any type of computer. Linus Torvalds and other programmers originally developed Linux for the Intel 80x86 processor. Nowadays, Linux is also available for systems based on other processors, such as Intel's new 64-bit IA-64 architecture Itanium processor; Motorola 68000 family; Alpha AXP processor; Sun SPARC and UltraSPARC processors; Hewlett-Packard's HP PA-RISC processor; the PowerPC and PowerPC64 processors; and the MIPS R4x00 and R5x00 processors. More recently, IBM has announced Linux for its S/390 mainframe. This book covers Red Hat Linux for Intel 80x86 and Pentium processors (these are known as the IA-32 architecture processors).

The *operating system* is the software that manages all the hardware and runs other software at your command. You, the user, provide those commands by clicking menus and icons or by typing some cryptic text. Linux is an operating system, just as UNIX, Windows 98, Windows 2000, and Windows XP are operating systems. The Linux operating system is modeled after UNIX and it also goes by the name *Linux kernel*.

It's the operating system that gives a computer its personality. For example, you can run Windows 98 or Windows XP on a PC. On that same PC, you can also install and run Linux. That means, depending on the operating system installed on it, a PC can be a Windows 98, Windows XP, or a Linux system.

The primary job of an operating system is to load software — computer programs — from the hard disk (or other permanent storage) into the memory and get the CPU to run those programs. Everything that you do with your computer is possible because of the operating system. So if the operating system somehow messes up, the whole system freezes up. You know how infuriating it is when your favorite operating system — maybe the one that came with your PC — suddenly calls it quits just as you were about to click the Send button after composing that long e-mail to your friend. You try the three-finger salute of Ctrl+Alt+Del, but nothing happens. And then it's time for the Reset button. Luckily, that sort of thing almost never happens with Linux — it has a reputation for being a very reliable operating system.

In technical mumbo jumbo, Linux is a multiuser, multitasking operating system. All this means is that Linux enables multiple users to log in, and Linux can run more than one program at the same time. Nearly all operating systems are multiuser and multitasking, but when Linux first started in 1994, being multiuser and multitasking was a big selling point.

Linux distributions

Red Hat Linux is a specific Linux distribution. A *Linux distribution* is essentially a package consisting of the Linux kernel — the operating system — and a collection of applications, together with an easy-to-use installation program.

There are many Linux distributions, and each includes the Linux operating system: the XFree86 X Window System that provides the graphical user interface; one or more graphical desktops, such as GNOME and KDE; and a huge selection of other computer programs (the applications). Everything comes in the form of ready-to-run software, but the source code and documentation are also included. By now, each Linux distribution includes so much software that it comes on multiple CD-ROMs (which this book includes).

Like many other Linux distributions, Red Hat Linux is a commercial distribution. You can buy Red Hat Linux in computer stores and bookstores. If you have heard about Open Source and the GNU *(GNU's Not UNIX)* license, you may assume that no one can sell Linux for profit. Luckily for companies such as Red Hat, the GNU license, called the GNU General Public License (GPL), does allow for commercial, for-profit distribution, but requires that the software be distributed in source-code form, and stipulates that anyone may copy and distribute the software in source-code form to anyone else. This means that my publisher may include the Red Hat Linux CD-ROMs with this book and you may make as many copies of the CDs as you like.

Making sense of version numbers

Both the Linux kernel and Red Hat Linux have their own version numbers, not to mention the many other software programs (such as GNOME and KDE) that come with Red Hat Linux. The version numbers for the Linux kernel and Red Hat Linux are unrelated, but each has particular significance.

Linux kernel version numbers

After Linux kernel version 1.0 was released on March 14, 1994, the loosely knit Linux development community adopted a version-numbering scheme. Version numbers such as 1.X.Y and 2.X.Y, where X is an even number, are considered to be the stable versions. The last number, Y, is the patch level, which is incremented as problems are fixed. For example, 2.4.18 is a typical stable version of the Linux kernel. Notice that these version numbers are in the form of three integers separated by periods — Major.Minor.Patch — where Major and Minor are numbers denoting the major and minor version numbers, and Patch is another number representing the patch level.

Version numbers of the form 2.X.Y with an odd X number are beta releases for developers only; they may be unstable, so you should not adopt these versions for day-to-day use. For example, 2.5.37 is a beta release of the Linux kernel. Developers add new features to these odd-numbered versions of Linux.

You can find out about the latest version of the Linux kernel online at www.kernel.org.

Red Hat Linux version numbers

Red Hat assigns the Red Hat Linux version numbers, such as 7.3 or 8.0. They are of the form X.Y, where X is the major version and Y the minor version. Unlike with the Linux kernel version numbers, there is no special meaning associated with odd and even minor versions. Each version of Red Hat Linux includes specific versions of the Linux kernel and other major components, such as GNOME, KDE, and various applications.

Red Hat releases new versions of Red Hat Linux on a regular basis. For example, Red Hat Linux 6.0 came out in April 1999 and 7.3 in May 2002. Typically, each new major version of Red Hat Linux provides significant new features.

What Red Hat Linux Includes

Red Hat Linux comes with the Linux kernel and a whole lot more software. These software packages include everything from the graphical desktops to Internet servers and programming tools to create new software. In this section, I briefly describe some of the major software packages that come bundled with Red Hat Linux. Without this bundled software, Red Hat Linux wouldn't be as popular as it is today.

What is the GNU Project?

GNU is a recursive acronym that stands for *GNU's Not UNIX.* The GNU Project was launched in 1984 by Richard Stallman to develop a complete UNIX-like operating system. The GNU Project developed nearly everything needed for a complete operating system except for the operating system kernel. All GNU software was distributed under the GNU General Public License (GPL). GPL essentially requires that the software is distributed in source-code form and stipulates that any user may copy, modify, and distribute the software to anyone else in source-code form. Users may, however, have to pay for their copy of GNU software.

The Free Software Foundation (FSF) is a tax-exempt charity that raises funds for work on the GNU Project. To find out more about the GNU Project, visit its home page at www.gnu.org. There you can find information about how to contact the Free Software Foundation and how you may help the GNU Project.

GNU software

I'll start with a collection of software that came from the GNU Project. You get to know these GNU utilities only if you use your Red Hat Linux system through a text terminal (or a graphical window that mimics a text terminal), but the GNU software is one of the basic parts of Red Hat Linux.

As a Red Hat Linux user, you may not realize the extent to which Red Hat Linux (and, for that matter, all Linux distributions) relies on GNU software. Nearly all tasks you perform in a Red Hat Linux system involve one or more GNU software packages. For example, the GNOME graphical user interface (GUI) and the command interpreter, Bash shell, are both GNU software. If you rebuild the kernel or develop software, you do so with the GNU C and C++ compiler that is part of the GNU software that accompany Red Hat Linux. If you edit text files with the ed or Emacs editor, you are again using a GNU software package. The list goes on and on.

Table 1-1 lists some of the well-known GNU software packages that come with Red Hat Linux. I show this table only to give you a feel for all the different kinds of things you can do with GNU software. Depending on your interests, you may never need to use many of these packages, but it's good to know they are there in case you ever need them.

Table 1-1	Well-Known GNU Software Packages
Software Package	*Description*
Autoconf	Generates shell scripts that automatically configure source-code packages.
Automake	Generates `Makefile.in` files for use with Autoconf.
Bash	The default shell — command interpreter — in Red Hat Linux
Bc	An interactive calculator with arbitrary precision numbers
Binutils	A package that includes several utilities for working with binary files: `ar`, `as`, `gasp`, `gprof`, `ld`, `nm`, `objcopy`, `objdump`, `ranlib`, `readelf`, `size`, `strings`, and `strip`
Gnuchess	A chess-playing program
GNU C Library	For use with all Linux programs
Cpio	Copies file archives to and from disk or to another part of the file system.
Diff	Compares files, showing line-by-line changes in several different formats.
Ed	A line-oriented text editor
Emacs	An extensible, customizable full-screen text editor and computing environment

(continued)

Table 1-1 *(continued)*

Software Package	Description
Fileutils	A package that implements the following Linux commands: `chgrp`, `chmod`, `chown`, `cp`, `dd`, `df`, `dir`, `dircolors`, `du`, `install`, `ln`, `ls`, `mkdir`, `mkfifo`, `mknod`, `mv`, `rm`, `rmdir`, `sync`, `touch`, and `vdir`
Findutils	A package that includes the `find`, `locate`, and `xargs` utilities
Finger	A utility program designed to enable users on the Internet to get information about one another
Gawk	The GNU Project's implementation of the AWK programming language
GCC	Compilers for C, C++, Objective C, and other languages
Gdb	Source-level debugger for C, C++ and Fortran
Gdbm	A replacement for the traditional `dbm` and `ndbm` database libraries
Gettext	A set of utilities that enables software maintainers to internationalize (that means make the software work with different languages such as English, French, Spanish, etc.) a software package's user messages
Ghostscript	An interpreter for the Postscript and Portable Document Format (PDF) languages
Ghostview	An X Window System application that provides a graphical front end to Ghostscript, and enables users to view Postscript or PDF files in a window
The GIMP	The GNU Image Manipulation Program is an Adobe Photoshop-like image-processing program
GNOME	Provides a graphical user interface (GUI) for a wide variety of tasks that a Linux user might perform.
Gnumeric	A graphical spreadsheet (similar to Microsoft Excel) that works in GNOME
grep package	Includes the `grep`, `egrep`, and `fgrep` commands that are used to find lines that match a specified text pattern
Groff	A document-formatting system similar to `troff`
GTK+	A GUI toolkit for the X Window System (used to develop GNOME applications)
Gzip	A GNU utility for compressing and decompressing files
Indent	Formats C source code by indenting it in one of several different styles.
Less	A page-by-page display program similar to `more`, but with additional capabilities
Libpng	A library for image files in the Portable Network Graphics (PNG) format

Software Package	Description
m4	An implementation of the traditional UNIX macro processor
Make	A utility that determines which files of a large software package need to be recompiled, and issues the commands to recompile them
Mtools	A set of programs that enables users to read, write, and manipulate files on a DOS file system (typically a floppy disk)
Ncurses	A package for displaying and updating text on text-only terminals
Patch	A GNU version of Larry Wall's program to take the output of diff and apply those differences to an original file to generate the modified version
RCS	The Revision Control System is used for version control and management of source files in software projects.
Sed	A stream-oriented version of the ed text editor
Sharutils	A package that includes `shar` (used to make shell archives out of many files) and `unshar` (to unpack these shell archives)
Shellutils	A package that includes the following utilities, which are part of the Bash shell: `basename`, `chroot`, `date`, `dirname`, `echo`, `env`, `expr`, `factor`, `false`, `groups`, `hostname`, `id`, `logname`, `nice`, `nohup`, `pathchk`, `printenv`, `printf`, `pwd`, `seq`, `sleep`, `stty`, `su`, `tee`, `test`, `true`, `tty`, `uname`, `uptime`, `users`, `who`, `whoami`, **and** `yes`
Tar	A tape archiving program that includes multivolume support; the capability to archive sparse files, handle compression and decompression, and create remote archives; and other special features for incremental and full backups
Texinfo	A set of utilities that generates printed manuals, plain ASCII text, and online hypertext documentation (called Info), and enables users to view and read online Info documents
Textutils	A set of utilities such as `cut`, `join`, `nl`, `split`, `tail`, `wc`, and so on, for manipulating text
Time	A utility that reports the user, system, and actual time that a process uses

GUIs and applications

Let's face it — typing cryptic Linux commands on a terminal is boring. For average users like us, it's much easier if we can use the system through a graphical user interface (*GUI*, pronounced "gooey"). This is where the X Window System, or X, comes to our rescue.

X is kind of like Microsoft Windows, but the underlying details of how X works is completely different from Windows. Unlike Windows, X provides the basic features of displaying windows on the screen, but it does not come with any specific look or feel for graphical applications. That look and feel comes from GUIs, such as GNOME and KDE, which make use of the X Window System.

Red Hat Linux comes with the X Window System in the form of XFree86 — an implementation of X Window System for 80x86 systems. XFree86 works with a wide variety of video cards available for today's PCs.

As for the GUI, Red Hat Linux includes two powerful GUI desktops: KDE (K Desktop Environment) and GNOME (GNU Object Model Environment). If both GNOME and KDE are installed on a PC, you can choose which desktop you want as default or switch between the two. KDE and GNOME provide desktops similar to the ones in Microsoft Windows and the Macintosh OS. GNOME also comes with the Nautilus graphical shell that makes it easy to find files, run applications, and configure your Red Hat Linux system. With GNOME or KDE, you can begin using your Red Hat Linux workstation without having to learn cryptic Linux commands. However, if you should ever need to use Linux commands, all you have to do is open a terminal window and type the commands at the prompt.

Red Hat Linux also comes with many graphical applications. The most noteworthy program is GIMP *(GNU Image Manipulation Program),* a program for working with photos and other images. GIMP's capabilities are on a par with Adobe Photoshop.

Providing common productivity software — such as word-processing, spreadsheet, and database applications — is an area in which Linux used to be lacking. This situation has changed, though. Both GNOME and KDE come with some office-productivity applications. In addition, there are several prominent, commercially available office-productivity applications for Linux that are not included on the companion CD-ROMs. Applixware Office — now called Anyware Desktop for Linux — is a good example of productivity software for Linux (`www.vistasource.com`). Other well-known productivity-software packages include WordPerfect Office 2000 for Linux from Corel Corporation (`linux.corel.com`) and StarOffice from Sun Microsystems (`www.sun.com/staroffice`).

Networks

Red Hat Linux comes with everything needed to use the system in networks so that the system can exchange data with other systems. On networks, computers that exchange data have to follow well-defined rules or protocols. A *network protocol* is the method the sender and receiver agree upon for exchanging data across a network. Such a protocol is similar to the rules that you might follow when you are having a conversation with someone at a party. You typically start by saying hello, exchanging names, and then taking turns talking. That's about the same way network protocols work.

The two computers use the protocol to send bits and bytes back and forth across the network.

One of the most well-known and popular network protocols is Transmission Control Protocol/Internet Protocol *(TCP/IP)*. TCP/IP is the protocol of choice on the Internet — the "network of networks" that now spans the globe. Red Hat Linux supports the TCP/IP protocol and any network applications that make use of TCP/IP.

Internet servers

Some of the popular network applications are specifically designed to deliver information from one system to another. When you send electronic mail (e-mail) or visit Web sites using a Web browser, you use these network applications (also called Internet services). Here are some of the common Internet services:

✦ Electronic mail (e-mail) that you use to send messages to any other person on the Internet using addresses like `joe@someplace.com`.

✦ World Wide Web (or simply, Web) that you browse using a Web browser.

✦ News services, where you can read newsgroups and post news items to newsgroups with names such as `comp.os.linux.networking` or `comp.os.linux.setup`.

✦ File transfers that you can use to download files.

✦ Remote login that you can use to log in to another computer (the remote computer) on the Internet, assuming that you have a user name and password to access that remote computer.

Any Red Hat Linux PC can offer these Internet services. To do so, the PC must be connected to the Internet and it must run special server software that we call the *Internet servers*. Each of the servers uses a specific protocol for transferring information. For example, here are some common Internet servers that you'll find in Red Hat Linux:

✦ `sendmail` is the mail server for exchanging e-mail messages between systems using SMTP *(Simple Mail Transfer Protocol)*.

✦ Apache `httpd` is the Web server for sending documents from one system to another using HTTP *(Hypertext Transfer Protocol)*.

✦ `vsftpd` is the server for transferring files between computers on the Internet using FTP *(File Transfer Protocol)*.

✦ `innd` is the news server for distribution of news articles in a store-and-forward fashion across the Internet using NNTP *(Network News Transfer Protocol)*.

✦ `in.telnetd` allows a user on one system to log into another system on the Internet using the TELNET protocol.

Software development

Red Hat Linux is particularly well suited to software development. Straight out of the box, it's chock-full of software-development tools such as the compiler and libraries of code needed to build programs. If you happen to know UNIX and the C programming language, you will feel right at home programming in Red Hat Linux.

As far as the development environment goes, Red Hat Linux has the same basic tools (such as an editor, a compiler, and a debugger) that you might use on other UNIX workstations, such as those from IBM, Sun Microsystems, and Hewlett-Packard (HP). What this means is that if you work by day on one of these UNIX workstations, you can use a Red Hat Linux PC in the evening at home to duplicate that development environment at a fraction of the cost. Then you can either complete work projects at home or devote your time to software you write for fun and to share on the Internet.

Just to give you a sense of Linux's software-development support, here's a list of various features that make Linux a productive software-development environment:

✦ GNU C compiler, `gcc`, which can compile ANSI-standard C programs

✦ GNU C++ compiler (g++), which supports ANSI-standard C++ features

✦ The GNU `make` utility, which enables you to compile and link large programs

✦ The GNU debugger, `gdb`, which enables you to step through your program to find problems and to determine where and how a program has failed. (The failed program's memory image is saved in a file named core; `gdb` can examine this file.)

✦ The GNU profiling utility, `gprof`, which enables you to determine the degree to which a piece of software uses your computer's processor time

✦ Concurrent Versions System (CVS) and Revision Control System (RCS), which maintain version information and control access to the source files so that two programmers don't modify the same source file inadvertently

✦ The GNU Emacs editor, which prepares source files and even launches a compile-link process to build the program

✦ The Perl scripting language, which you can use to write scripts that tie together many smaller programs with Linux commands to accomplish a specific task

✦ The Tool Command Language and its graphical toolkit (Tcl/Tk), which enable you to build graphical applications rapidly

✦ The Python language, an interpreted language comparable to Perl and Tcl (the Red Hat Linux installation program, called `anaconda`, is written in Python)

✦ Dynamically linked shared libraries, which allow the actual program files to be much smaller because all the library code that several programs may use is shared, with only one copy loaded in the system's memory

Online documentation

As you become more adept at using Red Hat Linux, you may want to look up information quickly — without having to turn the pages of this great book, for example. Luckily, Red Hat Linux comes with enough online information to jog your memory in those situations when you vaguely recall a command's name, but can't remember the exact syntax of what you are supposed to type.

If you use Linux commands, you can view the manual page — commonly referred to as the *man page* — for a command by using the `man` command. (You do have to remember that command in order to access online help.)

You can also get help from the GUI desktops. Both GNOME and KDE desktops come with help viewers to view online help information. In GNOME, select Main Menu⇨Help. You then see two broad categories of information:

✦ **GNOME - Desktop** is information on how to use the GNOME desktop and some GNOME applications.

✦ **Additional documents** include online documentation for the GNU software (primarily for the software development tools) and the set of online manual pages (called man pages for short).

You can then browse the information by clicking the links on the initial help window. Figure 1-1 shows a typical help file in GNOME.

In KDE desktop, you can start KDE Help by clicking the lifebuoy icon. The KDE Help application looks similar to the GNOME help browser (Figure 1-2).

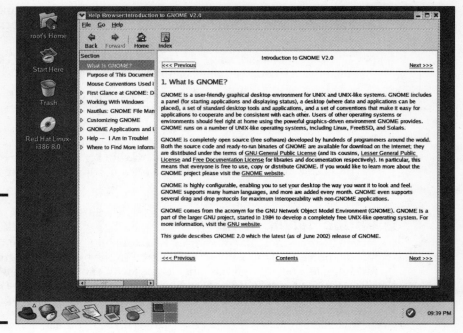

Figure 1-1:
Here's a
typical
sample of
online help
in the
GNOME
desktop.

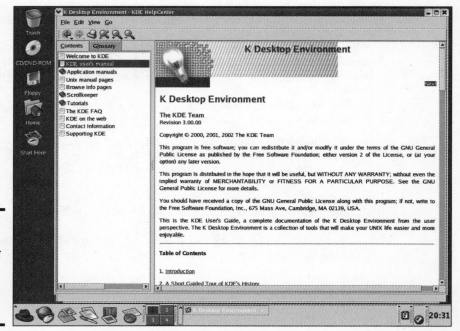

Figure 1-2:
The KDE
Help Center
provides
online help
in the KDE
desktop.

You can then click the links to view specific online help information. There are links to learn how to use KDE and obtain information about the KDE Project. Another set of links provides access to the man pages and GNU info pages, just as the GNOME Help browser does.

What Red Hat Linux Helps You Manage

As an operating system, Red Hat Linux acts as the intermediary through which you, as the "lord of the system," manage all the hardware. The hardware includes the system box, the monitor, the keyboard, the mouse, and anything else connected to the system box. The catch-all term *peripheral* refers to any equipment attached to the system.

Inside that system box is the system's brain — the microprocessor (Intel Pentium 4, for example) or the central processing unit (CPU) — that performs the instructions contained in a computer program. When the microprocessor is running a computer program, that program's instructions are stored in the memory or RAM. RAM stands for *Random Access Memory* (that means any part of the memory can be accessed randomly — in arbitrary order).

The system box has another crucial component — the disk. The disk is the permanent storage space for computer programs and data. It's permanent in the sense that the contents don't disappear when you power off the PC. The disk is organized into files, which are in turn organized in a hierarchical fashion into directories and subdirectories (somewhat like organizing paper folders into the drawers in a file cabinet).

To keep a Red Hat Linux system running properly, you or someone else has to make sure the hardware is working properly and the files are backed up regularly. There is also the matter of security — making sure only legitimate people can access and use the system. These tasks are what we call *system administration*.

If you are using Red Hat Linux at a big facility with many computers, there's probably a full-time system administrator who takes care of all system administration tasks. On the other hand, if you are running Red Hat Linux on a home PC, you are the system administrator. Don't let the thought frighten you. You don't have to learn any magic incantations or prepare cryptic configuration files to be a system administrator. Red Hat Linux includes many graphical tools such as GNOME's Nautilus graphical shell that makes system administration a "point-and-click" job just like running any other application.

So what kinds of things do you do to manage the hardware and files? Let's take a look.

Disks and CD-ROMs

Red Hat Linux comes on two or more CD-ROMs and, after installation, the Linux kernel as well all the applications are stored on the hard disk. So the hard disk and the CD-ROM drive are very important parts of your PC.

Typically, the hard disk is prepared for use in Red Hat Linux during the installation process. After that, you typically leave the hard disk alone except to back up the data stored on the disk. You also occasionally install new applications on the hard disk.

Using CD-ROMs in Red Hat Linux is easy. While you are logged in at the GNOME or KDE desktop, just pop in a CD in the CD-ROM drive and the CD's contents should automatically appear in a window. This whole process of accessing the files on a CD from Red Hat Linux is called *mounting the CD*.

Of course your PC may have other disk drives — floppy disk or Zip drive — besides the hard disk and CD-ROM drive. Using floppy disks or Zip disks in Red Hat Linux is also simple. You insert a disk and double-click an icon for the disk drive on the GUI desktop. That mounts the disk, and you can begin using the disk.

Peripheral devices

Anything connected to your PC is a peripheral device, and so are some components like sound cards that are installed inside the system box. You can configure and manage these peripheral devices in Red Hat Linux.

One of the common peripherals is a printer, typically hooked up to the parallel port of your PC. Red Hat Linux comes with a graphical Printer Configuration tool that you can use to configure the printer.

Another peripheral device that needs configuration is the sound card. Unlike Windows, you have to perform a configuration step in Red Hat Linux before the sound will work. Again, you can run a graphical sound card configuration utility to configure the sound card (select Main Menu⇨System Settings⇨ Soundcard Detection from the graphical desktop). This utility runs from a text-mode menu, but it's still fairly easy to use.

Red Hat Linux configures other peripheral devices such as the mouse and keyboard at the time of installation. You basically leave them alone.

File systems and sharing

The whole organization of directories and files is called the *file system*. You can, of course, manage the file system using Red Hat Linux. When you browse the files from the GNOME or KDE graphical desktop, you work with the familiar folder icons.

A key task in caring for a file system is to back up important files. In Red Hat Linux you can use the `tar` program to archive one or more directories on a tape (if you have a tape drive).

Red Hat Linux can also share parts of the file system with other systems on a network. For example, you can use the Network File System (NFS) to share files with other systems on the network. To a user on the system, the remote system's files appear to be in a directory on the local system.

Another interesting feature of Red Hat Linux is its support for Microsoft Windows file sharing. Red Hat Linux comes with the Samba package that basically makes the Red Hat Linux system work just like another Windows file or print server.

Network

Now that most PCs are either in a local area network or connected to the Internet, you need to manage the network as well. Red Hat Linux comes with a Network Configuration tool to set up the local area network. For connecting to the Internet using a modem, you use the Internet Configuration Wizard.

If you connect to the Internet using DSL (that's the fast Internet connection from the phone company) or cable modem, you need a PC with an Ethernet card and then connect that Ethernet card to the cable or DSL. This means that connecting to the Internet with DSL or cable modem requires you to set up the local area network and configure the Ethernet card. These steps are typically done during Red Hat Linux installation. Of course, you can do the configurations later on by using the Network Configuration tool.

Red Hat Linux also includes tools to configure a firewall to make the system somewhat secure from anyone attempting to snoop over the Internet connection. You can configure the firewall by running the Firewall Configuration tool (select Main Menu⇨System Settings⇨Security Level from the graphical desktop).

How Do I Get Started?

Based on my personal experience in learning new subjects, I prescribe a four-step process to get started with Red Hat Linux:

1. **Install** Red Hat Linux on your PC.

2. **Configure** Red Hat Linux so everything works to your liking.

3. **Explore** the GUI desktops and the applications.

4. **Learn** the details of specific subjects such as Internet servers.

In the following sections, I explain the prescription a bit more.

Install

Microsoft Windows comes installed on your new PC, but Red Hat Linux usually doesn't. So your first hurdle is to get Red Hat Linux onto your PC.

After you overcome your initial fear of the unknown, I bet you'll find it fairly easy to install Red Hat Linux. Where do you get Red Hat Linux? Well, the good news is that it's free — available just for the downloading. For example, visit the Linux Online Web site at www.linux.org and click the Download button.

Because Red Hat Linux is HUGE — it takes several CDs to hold the complete distribution, your best bet is to buy a book (such as this one) that comes with Red Hat Linux on CD-ROMs. You can then install Red Hat Linux by following the instructions in the book.

Just to pique your curiosity, installation involves creating space on the hard disk for both Windows and Linux. Then there is a step to create the Linux partitions and install Red Hat Linux from the CDs. Along the way, you configure many items from the Ethernet card, if any, to the X Window System.

Configure

When you have finished installing Red Hat Linux, you need to configure many things that aren't done during installation; for example, the sound card and the printer.

If you aren't getting a graphical login screen, you have to troubleshoot that problem. Typically, the troubleshooting involves configuring the X Window System using some tools that come with Red Hat Linux.

You also want to configure your GUI desktop of choice — GNOME or KDE. Each has configuration tools. You can use these tools to select the look and feel of the desktop from the background to the entire color scheme.

After you're through with the configuration step, all the hardware on your system and the applications should be running to your liking.

Explore

With a properly configured Red Hat Linux PC at your disposal, you'll be ready to explore Red Hat Linux. You can begin the exploration from the GUI desktop that you get after logging in.

Explore the GUI desktops — GNOME and KDE — and the folders and files that make up the Linux file system. You can also try out the applications from the desktop. You'll find office and multimedia applications and databases to explore.

You should also try out the *shell* — the command interpreter application that accepts typed commands and runs other programs. You can also explore the text editors that work in text mode. It's good to know how to edit text files without the GUI just in case the GUI is not available. At least you won't be helpless.

Learn

After you have explored the Red Hat Linux landscape and know what is what, you can then dig in deeper and learn specific subject areas. For example, you may be interested in setting up Internet servers. You can then learn the details of setting up individual servers such as sendmail for e-mail, Apache for Web server, and the INN server for news.

There are many more areas you can choose to learn about, for example, security, programming, and system administration.

Of course, you can expect this step to continue on and on. After all, learning is a lifelong journey.

Bon voyage!

Chapter 2: Installing Red Hat Linux

In This Chapter

- ✔ Making a list of your PC's hardware
- ✔ Creating a Red Hat install boot disk
- ✔ Setting aside disk space for Red Hat Linux
- ✔ Starting the Red Hat Linux installation
- ✔ Creating hard disk partitions for Red Hat Linux
- ✔ Setting up key system parameters
- ✔ Selecting packages to install
- ✔ Completing the installation

PCs come with Microsoft Windows preinstalled. If you want to use Red Hat Linux, you have to first install it. This book comes with the Red Hat Linux CD-ROMs — all you have to do is follow the steps explained in this chapter to install Red Hat Linux.

You may feel worried about installing a new operating system on your PC. You may feel that it's like brain surgery — or, rather, more like grafting on a new brain because you can install Red Hat Linux in addition to Microsoft Windows. When you install two operating systems like that, you can choose to start one or other as you power up the PC. The biggest headache in adding Red Hat Linux to a PC with Windows is creating a new disk partition — basically setting aside a part of the disk — for Red Hat Linux. The rest of the installation is fairly routine, just a matter of following the instructions. I explain everything in this chapter.

Following the Installation Steps

Installing Red Hat Linux involves a number of steps. I want to briefly walk you through the steps without the details. Then you can follow the detailed steps and install Red Hat Linux from this book's companion CD-ROMs.

The very first step is to take a quick inventory of some key hardware components in your PC and make sure that everything works in Red Hat Linux.

If you are buying a new PC, you can make sure that the PC you buy has components that work in Red Hat Linux. If you plan to install Red Hat Linux on an older PC, you can gather information about the hardware and check against the list of hardware that Red Hat Linux supports (this list is available on the Web at `hardware.redhat.com/hcl`). If you find that some of the required components of a PC don't work in Red Hat Linux, you're better off not installing Red Hat Linux on that PC.

The second step is to prepare a Red Hat install boot disk you need when you start the installation (this step is not necessary if your PC can boot from the CD-ROM drive). The first companion CD-ROM has a program that you can run in Windows and use to prepare the boot disk for Red Hat installation.

The third step is to make room for Red Hat Linux on your PC's hard disk. This step can be easy or hard, depending on whether you want to replace Windows with Red Hat Linux or you want to keep both Windows and Red Hat Linux. If you want to install Red Hat Linux without removing Windows, you have to partition or divide the hard disk, which can be one of the scary steps because you run the risk of ruining the hard disk and wiping out whatever is on the disk. When you start, the entire hard disk is used by the existing operating system, which, I assume, is one of the versions of Microsoft Windows — 95, 98, Me, NT, 2000, or XP. To install Red Hat Linux without disturbing the existing Windows, you have to divide the disk into two parts and create a new part that the Red Hat Linux installation program can use. For peace of mind, you may want to invest in a commercial hard-drive partitioning product such as PartitionMagic. For Windows 95/98/Me systems, you can use a program called FIPS that's included on this book's first CD-ROM.

After you set aside a hard disk partition for Red Hat Linux, you can begin the final step — boot the PC from the Red Hat install boot disk and start the Red Hat Linux installation. There are quite a few steps during installation, but, when you've come this far, it should be smooth sailing. Just switch the CDs when asked to and you should be done in an hour or two. The Red Hat installer brings up a graphical user interface (GUI) and guides you through all the steps. One key step involves partitioning the hard disk again, but this time you simply split the extra partition you created earlier. After a few configuration steps such as setting up the network and the time zone, you select the software packages to install and then let the installer complete the remaining installation chores.

Checking Your PC's Hardware

Before you do anything else, you first need to check to see if your PC's hardware works with Red Hat Linux. You could jump right in and begin installing, but if Red Hat Linux fails to recognize some hardware in your PC, the installation may not be successful. So check out the hardware for compatibility with Red Hat Linux before you begin installation.

Note: Not every piece of hardware needs to be compatible with Red Hat Linux. For example, you can install Red Hat Linux on a PC with an unsupported sound card as long as you don't care about playing any audio CDs in Red Hat Linux.

Here, then, is a short list of PC hardware that must work in Red Hat Linux or else you can't proceed:

✦ Processor

✦ Hard disk drive

✦ CD-ROM drive

✦ Keyboard

All of these must be compatible with Red Hat Linux. For the GUI desktops such as GNOME and KDE to work, the PC must also have a compatible mouse, video card, and monitor.

Making a list, checking it twice

Before you can check if Red Hat Linux supports the hardware in your PC, you have to find out what's in your PC. To make a list of your PC's hardware, follow these steps:

1. **From Windows (any version), open the Control Panel and double-click the System icon.**

The System Properties window appears. The initial window shows some important information such as the version of Windows, the processor type (for example, GenuineIntel Pentium II Processor), and the amount of memory (for example, 128.0MB RAM). Write down that information.

2. **In Windows 95/98/Me, click the Device Manager tab. In Windows NT/2000/XP, click the Hardware Tab and then click the Device Manager button.**

Information about all the PC's devices appears.

3. **Browse the information from the treelike hierarchical organization that shows the devices by type.**

For example, you'll see labels such as CDROM, Disk drives, Display adapters, and so on. Click the plus sign (+) next to a label to see the details for that device type. For example, When I click the plus sign next to the Display adapters, I see the name *ATI Xpert98 AGP 2X,* which is the name of the display adapter (video card) on my PC.

4. Write down the make, model, and any other information about the following devices to create your hardware inventory:

- CD-ROM drive
- Disk drives
- Video card
- Monitor
- Keyboard
- Mouse
- Any network card, SCSI controller, sound card, and modem

After you complete these steps, you need to install Red Hat Linux. To summarize, you typically need to gather information about some or all of the following key components in your PC before you start the Red Hat installation:

✦ **Processor:** A Pentium or better is best. The processor speed, expressed in MHz (megahertz) or GHz (gigahertz), is not that important, but the faster the better. Red Hat Linux can run on other Intel-compatible processors such as AMD K5, K6, and Cyrix and IBM processors.

✦ **RAM:** This is the amount of memory. As with process speed, the more RAM, the better. You need at least 64MB to install Red Hat Linux and run a GUI desktop.

✦ **CD-ROM:** The exact model does not matter. What matters is how the CD-ROM drive is connected to the PC. Most new PCs have CD-ROM drives that connect to the hard disk controller (called IDE for *integrated drive electronics*). Any IDE CD-ROM works in Red Hat Linux.

✦ **Hard disks:** If you see the word *IDE* in the disk drive name, then it's an IDE drive and should work in Red Hat Linux. Another type of hard disk controller is SCSI, which Red Hat Linux supports. You also need to know the size of the hard disk. To find the disk size, double-click the My Computer icon on the Windows desktop and then right-click the disk drive icon (for example, labeled C:), and select Properties from the pop-up menu. A window then shows information about the disk drive, including the total capacity and the amount of free space. To comfortably install and play with Red Hat Linux, you need about 3GB of disk space.

✦ **Keyboard:** All keyboards should work with Red Hat Linux. All you need to write down is the type of keyboard (such as Standard 101/102-key keyboard).

✦ **Mouse:** You need the type of mouse (such as PS/2 or USB) and model (such as Microsoft Intellimouse) to configure the X Window System.

✦ **Video card:** Also known as *display adapter,* you need the video card's make and model to configure the X Window System. Red Hat Linux works fine with all video cards in text mode, but you need X to work with the video card so that you can have the GUI.

✦ **Monitor:** The kind of monitor is not particularly critical except that it must be capable of displaying the screen resolutions that the video card uses. The screen resolution is expressed in terms of the number of picture elements, or pixels, horizontally and vertically (for example, 1024 x 768). Write down the make and model of the monitor (you can find this on the back of the monitor).

✦ **Network card:** Not all PCs have network cards, but if yours does, jot down the make and model (such as 3Com Etherlink XL 3C900-B Ethernet card). If the installation program fails to detect the network card, you need this information to set up the network.

✦ **SCSI controller:** Some high-performance PCs have SCSI *(Small Computer System Interface)* controllers that connect disk drives and other peripherals to a PC. If your PC happens to have a SCSI controller, write down the name of the controller.

✦ **Sound card:** If your PC has a sound card and you want to have sound in Red Hat Linux, you have to know the make and model of the sound card. Then you can configure the sound card after successfully installing Red Hat Linux.

✦ **Modem:** If you plan to dial out to the Internet, you need the modem information (such as Sportster 56k).

In addition to this hardware, you should also find out the make and model of any printer that you plan to use in Red Hat Linux.

Checking for Red Hat compatibility

With your hardware inventory in hand, visit Red Hat's Web site at `hardware.redhat.com/hcl`. Click the Hardware Compatibility List (HCL) link. From the search form on that Web page you can look up your hardware to see if it's supported or not.

Red Hat lists the status of each hardware component using one of the following legends:

✦ **Certified:** Hardware has been tested and certified by Red Hat. This type of hardware is fully supported. The installation program automatically detects certified hardware and installs the appropriate drivers.

✦ **Compatible:** Hardware has been reviewed by Red Hat and is supported. Such hardware is generally known to work, but Red Hat has not certified the hardware. The installation program should be able to detect and use compatible hardware.

✦ **Community Knowledge:** Hardware is not tested or supported by Red Hat. To use this hardware, you may perform some explicit steps, such as manually loading the driver and editing configuration files.

✦ **Not Supported:** Hardware has been tested by Red Hat and found not to work properly in Red Hat Linux.

If you're lucky, most of your PC's hardware such as video card, monitor, and network card will be certified or compatible.

Creating the Red Hat Install Boot Disk

To boot your PC and start the Red Hat Linux installation program, you need a Red Hat install boot disk (you can skip this step if your PC can boot directly from the CD-ROM). You prepare the boot disk in Windows.

This book comes with the Publisher's Edition version of Red Hat Linux 8.0, provided by Red Hat. Unfortunately, the CDs don't include the DOSUTILS directory. If you have full Red Hat Linux distribution, use the following directions to repartition your hard disk with FIPS. Otherwise, download `rawrite.exe` from one of the FTP sites listed at `www.redhat.com/download/mirror.html`. Click one of the *Distribution* links and look in the directory corresponding to the Red Hat Linux version number. For example, `rawrite.exe` for Red Hat Linux 8.0 should be in the `8.0/en/os/i386/dosutils` directory. Use a browser to download the `rawrite.exe` file. Then follow the steps below, but run the version of `rawrite.exe` that you downloaded from the FTP site.

To create the boot disk, follow these steps:

1. **In Windows 95/98/Me, open an MS-DOS Prompt window by selecting Start⇨Run and then typing the word** Command **in the text field.**

2. **In Windows NT/2000/XP, select Start⇨Run. Click the Browse button and go to the WINNT folder; then open the SYSTEM32 folder, and select the CMD.EXE file in that folder. Click OK to run that program.**

3. **Put the first companion CD-ROM in the CD-ROM drive. Then type the following commands in the window you opened in Step 1 or 2 (my comments are in parentheses, and your input is in boldface):**

```
d:    (use the drive letter for your CD-ROM drive)
cd \dosutils
rawrite
Enter disk image source file name: \images\boot.img
Enter target diskette drive: a
Please insert a formatted diskette into drive A: and
press -ENTER- :
```

As instructed, put a formatted disk into your PC's A drive and then press Enter. That disk will become the Red Hat install boot disk.

4. **After you see the command prompt again, take the Red Hat install boot disk out of the A drive and (if you haven't done so already) label it or mark it so you know what that disk is.**

Setting Aside Space for Red Hat Linux

Windows is sitting on a big partition taking over the whole disk. You want to shrink that partition and create room for Linux. During Linux installation, the installation program uses that free space for the Linux partitions.

The challenge is to resize the current partition without destroying anything on the hard disk. I cover tools that help you resize the partition, but first you have to make sure that all used areas of the disk are contiguous, or as tightly packed as possible. This is where defragmenting comes in.

Defragmenting your hard disk

"Defrag your disk" is the magic chant of many a help desk. It's the help desk's prescription for all PC ailments. Well, for once they are right. You do need to defragment your hard disk to make room for Red Hat Linux. What defragmenting does is move all the files to the beginning of the partition and pack them tight. The result is free space at the end of the partition, so the partition can be shrunk without destroying any data.

To defragment the hard disk:

1. **Double-click My Computer from the desktop and then right-click the disk icon and select Properties from the pop-up menu.**

2. **In the Properties window, click the Tools tab and then click the Defragment Now button.**

3. **And wait. And wait. And wait.**

   You'll hear lots of noise from the disk drive and after a couple of hours, the defragmenting should be complete.

There are some *gotchas* with these instructions. First, don't use your PC or other programs while defragmenting the hard disk. Close all programs, including the ones in the system tray. One good way is to hit Ctrl+Alt+Del, click which program you want to stop, and then click the End Task button.

The second *gotcha* is that the defragmenter does not move hidden files, and there are plenty of such files in your system. You don't see them in the folders because, guess what, they are hidden. You may have to manually find the hidden files and see if you can delete the ones that seem to be junk.

You can find all the hidden files in your PC with a simple command. Open an MS-DOS window and then type the following commands:

```
cd \
dir /a:h /s > hidden.txt
```

After the command is finished, you'll have a list of all hidden files in the text file called `hidden.txt`. Open the file in Microsoft Word or just type **edit hidden.txt** to browse that file in a text editor. When I tried this, I noticed a whole lot of files with names like `~WRL0004.TMP` that clearly seemed like temporary files created by some Microsoft software, probably Word. Who knows why they were hidden. Anyway, I had to change the file attribute by using MS-DOS incantations like `ATTRIB -H ~WRL0004.TMP` and then typing **ERASE ~WRL0004.TMP** to finally delete the file. I had to repeat this for many more junk files. What a bummer!

Another option for dealing with the hidden files is to just unhide them and then run the defragmenter. To unhide all files in the PC, type the following command in an MS-DOS window:

```
attrib -h *.* /s
```

Sit back and after a long time, this unhides all files. You can then run the defragmenter.

Resizing your hard disk partition

After defragmenting the hard disk, you're ready to shrink the existing hard disk partition. You want to do this without damaging the current contents of the hard disk. You have two choices:

✦ **PartitionMagic:** This is a commercial product that can resize hard disk partitions and create new partitions on any version of Microsoft Windows.

✦ **FIPS:** This is a free program that runs in MS-DOS mode and can split an existing partition into two. FIPS works only with Windows 95/98/Me systems. More accurately, FIPS does not work with the NTFS file system that's often used in Windows NT/2000/XP systems. For those systems, your best bet is PartitionMagic.

I'll quickly go over repartitioning with both PartitionMagic and FIPS.

Repartitioning with PartitionMagic

PartitionMagic, from PowerQuest, can resize and split disk partitions in all Microsoft operating systems from Windows 95/98/Me to Windows NT/2000/XP. It's a commercial product, so you have to buy it to use it. At the time I'm writing this, the list price of PartitionMagic 7.0 is $69.95. You can read about it and buy it at `www.powerquest.com/partitionmagic`.

When you run PartitionMagic, it shows the current partitions in a window. You probably have just one partition. You have to reduce the size of that existing disk partition, which creates unused space following the first partition. Then, during Red Hat Linux installation, the installation program can create new Linux partitions in the unused space.

To reduce the size of the partition, follow these steps:

1. **In the partition map in PartitionMagic's main window, right-click the partition and select Resize/Move from the menu.**

   The Resize Partition dialog box appears.

2. **In the Resize Partition dialog box, click and drag the right edge of the partition to a smaller size. For a large hard disk (anything over 8GB), reduce the Windows partition to 5GB and leave the rest for Red Hat Linux.**

3. **Click Apply and then Yes to apply the changes. After PartitionMagic has made the changes, click OK.**

4. **Reboot the PC.**

5. **Select Start➪Programs➪Accessories➪System Tools➪ScanDisk to run ScanDisk.**

Repartitioning with FIPS

The first companion CD-ROM includes a utility program called FIPS (the *First Nondestructive Interactive Partition Splitting Program*) that can split an existing disk partition into two partitions. FIPS cordons off the unused part of a hard disk and makes a new partition out of that unused part without destroying any existing data. FIPS cannot split partitions with the NTFS file system that's often used in Windows NT/2000/XP systems.

Some words of caution before you proceed to repartition your hard disk with FIPS. In the words of the FIPS author Arno Schaefer, "FIPS is still somewhat experimental, although it has been used by many people successfully and without serious problems." That tells you in a nutshell that you are on your own when it comes to using FIPS. Neither I nor the publisher can accept responsibility or liability for damages resulting from the use or misuse of FIPS. There is a chance that FIPS could damage your hard disk, making it unusable. You should try FIPS only after making sure that you have backed up everything in the hard disk and that your backup is usable.

This book comes with the Publisher's Edition version of Red Hat Linux 8.0, provided by Red Hat. Unfortunately, the CDs don't include the DOSUTILS directory. If you have full Red Hat Linux distribution, use the following directions to create the boot disk. Otherwise, download fips.exe from one of the FTP sites listed at www.redhat.com/download/mirror.html. Click one of the *Distribution* links and look in the directory corresponding to the Red Hat Linux version number. For example, fips.exe for Red Hat Linux 8.0 should be in the 8.0/en/os/i386/dosutils directory. Use a browser to download the fips.exe file. Then follow the steps below, but run the version of fips.exe that you downloaded from the FTP site.

You have to defragment the hard disk before you can use FIPS. Also, you have to run FIPS stand-alone by booting from a startup disk, not from inside Windows. To use FIPS, follow these steps:

1. **Open the Control Panel by selecting Start⇨Settings⇨Control Panel.**

2. **Double-click the Add/Remove Programs icon in the Control Panel window.**

3. **Click the Startup Disk tab and then click the Create Disk button and follow the instructions.**

4. **Insert this book's first companion CD-ROM in the CD-ROM drive.**

5. **Use Explorer to view the contents of the DOSUTILS folder. Then copy FIPS.EXE and RESTORRB.EXE to the startup disk in the A drive.**

   FIPS.EXE is the program that splits partitions. RESTORRB.EXE is a program that can restore parts of your hard disk from a backup of the areas created by FIPS (you use RESTORRB if something goes wrong).

6. **Go to the FIPSDOCS folder that's inside the DOSUTILS folder in the CD. Copy the ERRORS.TXT file to the startup disk.**

   ERRORS.TXT is a list of FIPS error messages. You consult this list for an explanation of any error messages displayed by FIPS.

7. **Leave the startup disk in the A drive, and restart the PC.**

   The PC boots from A and displays the A:\> prompt.

8. **Type FIPS.**

   The FIPS program runs and shows you information about your hard disk. FIPS gives you an opportunity to save a backup copy of important disk areas before proceeding. After that, FIPS displays the first free cylinder where the new partition can start (as well as the size of the partition, in megabytes). Ignore the cylinder number and focus on the megabytes.

9. **Use the left and right arrow keys to adjust the size of the new partition — the one that results from splitting the existing partition.**

Pressing the left arrow shrinks the existing partition; pressing the right arrow leaves more room in the existing partition, but reduces the size of the new partition you are creating.

10. When you are satisfied with the size of the new partition, press Enter.

FIPS displays the modified partition table and prompts you to enter C to continue or R to reedit the partition table.

11. Press C to continue.

FIPS displays some information about the disk and asks whether you want to write the new partition information to the disk.

12. Press Y.

FIPS writes the new partition table to the hard disk and then exits.

13. Remove the disk from the A drive and reboot the PC.

When the system comes up, everything in your hard disk should be intact, but the C drive will be smaller. You have created a new partition from the unused parts of the old C drive.

14. Select Start⇨Programs⇨Accessories⇨System Tools⇨ScanDisk to run ScanDisk.

This ensures that Windows gets adjusted to the new size of the C drive.

You needn't do anything with the newly created partition under DOS. Later, during Red Hat Linux installation, you will create two or more Linux partitions out of this new partition.

After you use FIPS, Windows may assign different drive letters to other disk and CD-ROM drives on your PC. For example, your D drive may become E. FIPS does make sure that the C drive remains C so you should be able to boot your system after FIPS splits the partitions. You have to remember to look at different drive names (for example, E instead of D) to get to programs and files on drives other than C.

Starting the Red Hat Linux Installation

To install Linux, insert the first CD in the CD drive, put the Red Hat install boot disk in your A drive, and restart your PC (in Windows select Start⇨Shutdown and then select Restart from the dialog box). The install boot disk contains a smaller version of the Linux kernel and the installation program.

After your PC powers up, it loads the Linux kernel from the boot disk and the Linux kernel starts running the Red Hat installation program. For the rest of the installation, you work with the installation program's GUI screens.

If the CD-ROM is not in the drive when you reboot the PC, the installer starts in text mode and prompts you for the CD-ROM. Only then will it start the X Window System and switch to a graphical installation screen.

After a few moments, text screen displays a welcome message and a `boot:` prompt. The welcome message tells you that help is available by pressing one of the function keys F1 through F5. To start installing Red Hat Linux immediately, press Enter.

Installing Red Hat Linux from the companion CD-ROMs on a fast (200MHz or better) Pentium PC should take about an hour, even if you install nearly all packages.

The Red Hat installation program *probes* — attempts to determine the presence of — specific hardware and tailors the installation steps accordingly. For example, if the installation program detects a network card, the program automatically displays the screens where you can configure the network. This means that you may see a different sequence of screens than what I show in this chapter. The exact sequence depends on your PC's specific hardware configuration.

If you run into any problems during the installation, please turn to Book I, Chapter 3. That chapter shows how to troubleshoot common installation problems.

Selecting Keyboard, Mouse, and Installation Type

This is the first phase of the installation where you go through a number of steps before moving on to create the disk partitions for Red Hat Linux. Here are the steps in the first phase:

1. **The installation program displays a list of languages that you can use for the rest of the installation. The list includes languages such as English, French, German, Icelandic, Italian, Norwegian, Romanian, Slovak, Russian, and Ukrainian. Use your mouse to select the language you want and then click Next to proceed to the next step.**

Each screen has online help available on the left side of the screen. You can read the help message to learn more about what you are supposed to do in a specific screen.

2. **The installation program displays a list of keyboard layouts, as shown in Figure 2-1.**

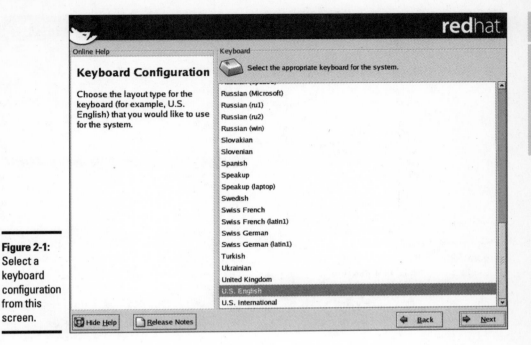

Figure 2-1:
Select a
keyboard
configuration
from this
screen.

Select a keyboard layout suitable for your language's character set
(for example, U.S. English in the United States).

3. **The installation program displays a screen (see Figure 2-2) from
which you can configure the mouse in your system.**

A treelike list shows the mouse types, organized alphabetically by manufacturer. You should know the mouse type and whether it is connected
to the PC's serial port or the PS/2 port (the small round connector). If
the name of your mouse appears in the list, select it. Otherwise, select
a generic mouse type. Most new PCs have a PS/2 mouse. Finally, for a
two-button mouse, select the Emulate 3 Buttons option. Because many
X applications assume that you are using a three-button mouse, you
should go ahead and select this option. On a typical two-button mouse,
you can simulate a middle-button click by pressing both buttons simultaneously. On a Microsoft Intellimouse, the wheel acts as the middle
button.

If you select a mouse with a serial interface, you have to specify the
serial port where the mouse is connected. For COM1, specify
/dev/ttyS0 as the device; for COM2, the device name is /dev/ttyS1.

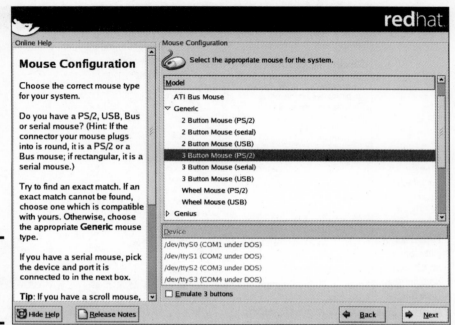

Figure 2-2:
Configure
your mouse
in this
screen.

4. **The installation program displays a screen (see Figure 2-3) asking if you want to install a new system or upgrade an older Red Hat installation.**

   For a new installation, you have to select the installation type — Personal Desktop, Workstation, Server, or Custom. The Personal Desktop, Workstation, and Server installations simplify the installation process by partitioning the disk in a predefined manner. The Personal Desktop installation creates a Red Hat Linux system for home, laptop, or desktop use. A graphical environment is installed along with productivity applications.

   A Workstation-class installation installs a graphical environment as well as software development tools. This type of installation also deletes all currently existing Linux-related partitions and creates a set of new partitions for Linux. A Server-class installation deletes all existing disk partitions, including any existing Windows partitions, and creates a whole slew of Linux partitions. Server-class installation does not install the graphical environment.

   For maximum flexibility, select the Custom installation. That way you can select all the packages you want to try out.

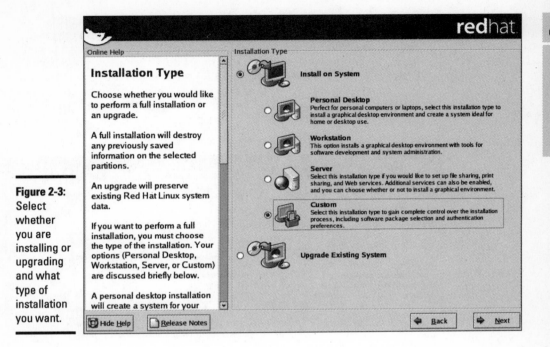

Figure 2-3:
Select
whether
you are
installing or
upgrading
and what
type of
installation
you want.

The next major phase of installation involves partitioning the hard disk for use in Red Hat Linux.

Partitioning the Disk for Red Hat Linux

The Red Hat installer displays a screen (see Figure 2-4) from which you can select a partitioning strategy.

The screen gives you three options for partitioning and using the hard disk:

✦ **Automatically partition** — This option causes the Red Hat installation program to create new partitions for installing Linux based on your installation type, such as workstation or server. After the automatic partitioning, you get a chance to customize the partitions. This is the option most users choose.

✦ **Manually partition with Disk Druid** — With this option, you can use the Disk Druid program that lets you partition the disk and, at the same time, specify which parts of the Linux file system are to be loaded on which partition.

✦ **Manually partition with fdisk (experts only)** — If you select this option, you use the Linux fdisk program that requires you to type cryptic one-letter commands to manipulate disk partitions. After you learn the commands, however, you may find fdisk more powerful than Disk Druid. For example, Disk Druid does not easily let you change the partition type, which indicates the type of file system to be stored on the partition, but you can easily change the partition type with fdisk. Because fdisk is harder to use, the option is labeled "experts only."

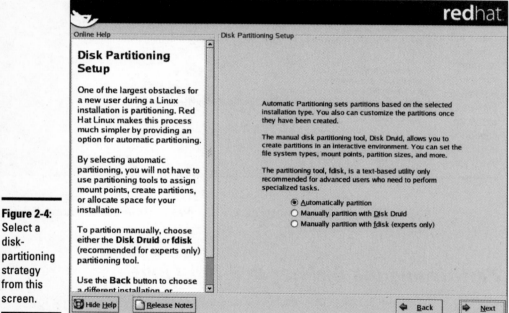

Figure 2-4:
Select a disk-partitioning strategy from this screen.

From the disk-partitioning strategy screen (refer to Figure 2-4), select the first option to have the installer automatically partition the disk for you. The Red Hat installer then displays another screen (see Figure 2-5) that asks you how you want the automatic partitioning to be done.

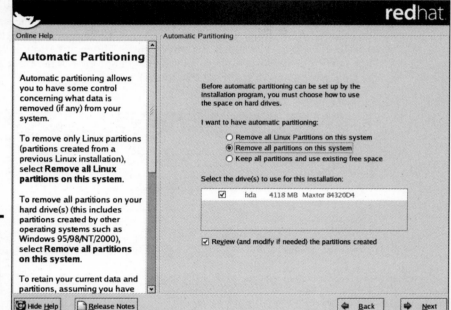

Figure 2-5:
Select an
automatic
partitioning
option from
this screen.

You can select from three options:

✦ **Remove all Linux Partitions on this system** — This option causes the
Red Hat installer to remove all existing Linux partitions and to create
new partitions for installing Red Hat Linux. You can use this option if
you already have any version of Linux installed on your PC and want
to wipe it out and install the latest version of Red Hat Linux.

✦ **Remove all partitions on this system** — This option is similar to the
first option, except that the installation program removes all partitions,
including those used by other operating systems such as Microsoft
Windows. Use this only if you want Red Hat Linux as the only
operating system for your PC.

✦ **Keep all partitions and use existing free space** — If you have created
space for Linux by using PartitionMagic or the FIPS utility, select this
option to create the Linux partitions using the free space on the hard
disk. If you are installing Red Hat Linux on a new PC after resizing the
partition, this is the option to choose.

Select the appropriate option and click Next. For example, if you select the first option, the Red Hat Linux installation program displays a dialog box to confirm your choice and to point out that all data in the existing Linux partitions will be lost. Click Yes to continue. The installation program shows the partitions it has prepared, as shown in Figure 2-6. The exact appearance of this screen depends on your hard disk's current partitions.

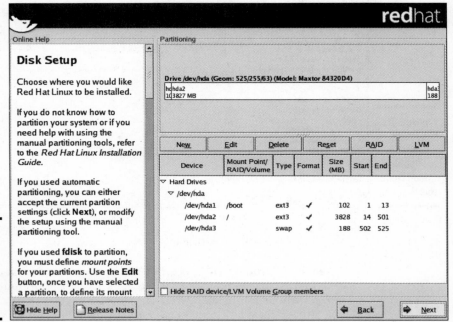

Figure 2-6:
Disk partitions created by the Red Hat installer.

This Disk Setup screen displays a list of disk drives and the current partition information for one of the drives. If you want to accept these partitions as is, click Next to proceed.

Setting Up Key System Parameters

With the disk partitioning out of the way, you're almost ready to begin installing the software packages. First, the Red Hat installer prompts you to set up some key system parameters. Specifically, you have to do the following:

✦ Install the boot loader

✦ Configure the network

◆ Configure the firewall

◆ Select languages to support

◆ Set the time zone

◆ Set the root password and add user accounts

◆ Configure password authentication

You can go through these steps fairly quickly.

Installing the boot loader

You can install one of two boot loaders — GRUB or LILO. GRUB stands
for *GRand Unified Bootloader,* and LILO stands for *Linux Loader.* The *boot
loader* is a tiny program that resides on the hard disk and starts an operating system when you power up your PC. If you have Windows on your hard
disk, you can configure the boot loader to load any of these operating
systems as well.

The Red Hat installer displays the boot loader installation screen
(see Figure 2-7) that prompts you to select the boot loader you want to
install and where you want to install the boot loader.

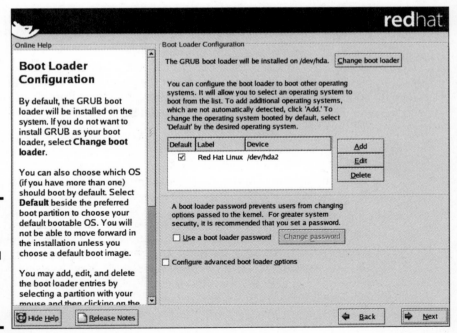

Figure 2-7:
Indicate
whether or
not to install
a boot
loader and
where to
install it.

The top part of the screen explains that GRUB is the default boot loader and that it's installed by default. If you want, click Change Boot Loader to select the older LILO boot loader. You can also skip the boot loader installation entirely. If you choose not to install any boot loader, you should definitely create a boot disk later on. Otherwise, you won't be able to start Red Hat Linux when you reboot the PC. You get a chance to create the boot disk at the very end of the installation.

The middle of the boot loader installation screen lists the disk partitions from which you can boot the PC. A table lists the Linux partition and any other partitions that may contain another operating system (such as Windows XP or 2000). Each entry in that table is an operating system that the boot loader can load and start. The default operating system is the one with a check mark in the Default column in Figure 2-7 (in this case, Red Hat Linux is the default operating system).

For greater security (so no one can boot your system without a password), select the Use a Boot Loader Password checkbox. The installer displays a dialog box where you can specify a password for GRUB.

If you select the Configure Advanced Boot Loader Options checkbox (Figure 2-7) and click Next, the next screen gives you the option to install the boot loader in one of two locations:

✦ *Master Boot Record* (MBR), which is located in the first sector of your PC's hard disk (the C drive)

✦ First sector of the Linux boot partition

You should install the boot loader in the Master Boot Record unless you are using another operating system loader, such as BootMagic or Windows NT/2000/XP Boot Manager. After making your selections, click Next to continue.

Configuring the network

Assuming the Linux kernel detected a network card, the Red Hat installer displays the network configuration screen (Figure 2-8).

From this screen, you can set up your network card's IP address (so that other PCs in the network can talk to your PC). This screen displays a list of the network devices (for example, Ethernet cards) installed in your PC. For each network device, you can indicate how the IP address is set. Click the Edit button next to the list and a dialog box appears (Figure 2-9) from which you can specify the options.

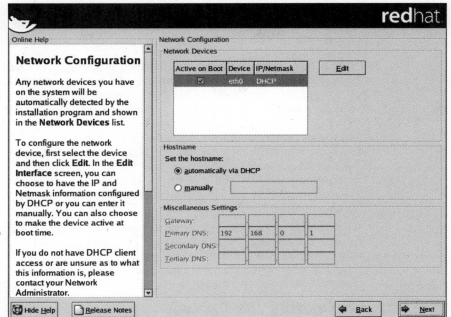

Figure 2-8:
Configure
the network
options from
this screen.

Figure 2-9:
Configure
each
network
interface
from a
dialog box
like this one.

You have two choices for specifying the IP *(Internet Protocol)* address for the
network card:

✦ **Configure using DHCP** — Enable this option if your PC gets its
IP address and other network information from a *Dynamic Host
Configuration Protocol* (DHCP) server. This is often the case if your
PC is connected to a DSL or cable modem router.

✦ **Activate on boot** — Enable this option to turn on the network when
your system boots.

Select DHCP only if a DHCP server is running on your local area network. If you choose DHCP, your network configuration is set automatically, and you can skip the rest of this section.

If you do not select the Configure Using DHCP option, you have to provide an IP address and other network information. Do this by entering the requested parameters in the text input fields that appear in the dialog box (refer to Figure 2-9). Make the selections and click OK to close the dialog box.

In the rest of the Network Configuration screen (Figure 2-8), you have to specify how to set the host name. You have two options to set the host name:

✦ **automatically via DHCP** — Enable this option to assign a host name automatically using DHCP (the name is of the form `dhcppc1`, `dhcppc2`, and so on).

✦ **manually** — Use this option to manually specify a host name and type the name in the text field next to the radio button.

Enter the requested parameters and click Next to continue.

Configuring the firewall

In this step, select a predefined level of security from the Firewall Configuration screen (see Figure 2-10) and customize these security levels to suit your needs.

From this screen you can set the security levels of your Red Hat Linux PC. You have to select from one of the following predefined security levels:

✦ **High security** means your system does not accept any connections other than those that you explicitly enable. By default, a system with high security allows only domain name lookups and DHCP requests that your PC needs to get an IP address.

✦ **Medium security** means the system accepts only a handful of well-defined network connections.

✦ **No firewall security** means your system accepts all types of connections and does not perform any security checking. Use this option only if your system runs in a trusted network or if you plan to set up a more elaborate firewall configuration later on.

After you select a predefined security level, you can click the Customize button and select other services that you may want to enable. When you're done configuring the firewall, click Next to continue.

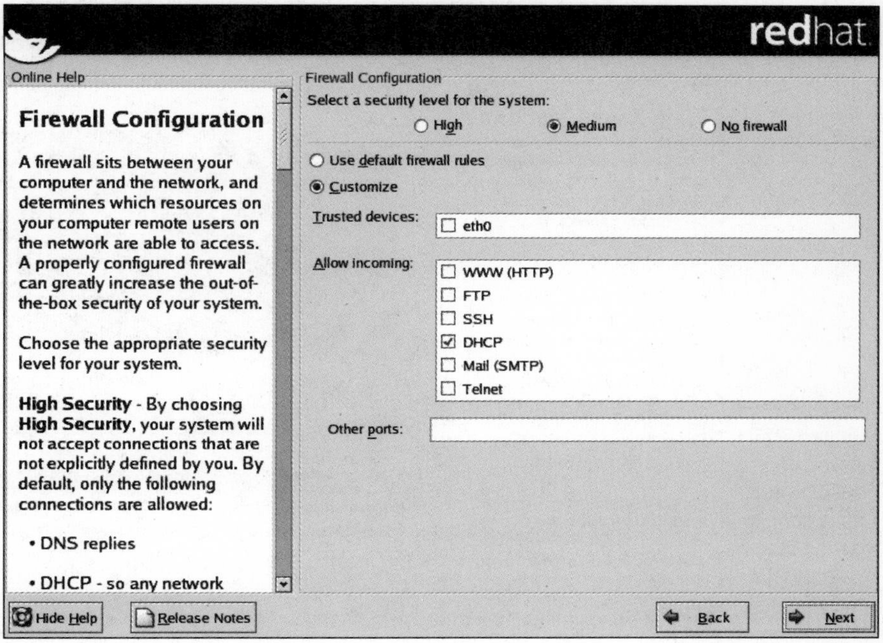

Figure 2-10:
Select a
security
level from
this screen.

Selecting languages to support

In this step, select one or more languages that your Red Hat Linux system needs to support when the installation is complete. These are the languages the system will support when you reboot the PC after completing the Red Hat Linux installation. From the Language Support Selection screen, select one or more languages to support. You must also select a default language. Then click Next to continue.

Setting the time zone

After completing the network configuration, select the time zone — the difference between the local time and the current time in Greenwich, England, which is the standard reference time (also known as *Greenwich Mean Time* or GMT as well as UTC or *Universal Coordinated Time*). The installer shows you a screen (Figure 2-11) from which you can select the time zone, either in terms of a geographic location or as an offset from the UTC.

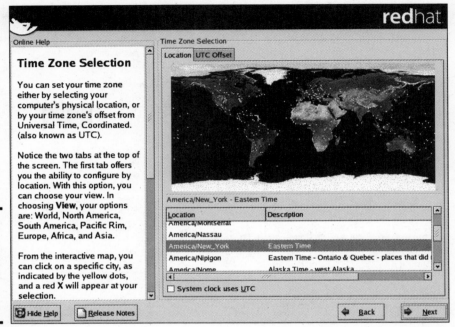

Figure 2-11:
You can
select your
time zone in
terms of a
geographic
location.

Notice the two tabs — Location and UTC Offset — from which you can set the time zone. Initially, the screen shows the Location tab. This tab lets you pick a time zone by simply clicking your geographic location. As you move the mouse over the map, the currently selected location's name appears in a text field. If you want, you can also select your location from a long list of countries and regions. If you live on the East Coast of the United States, for example, select USA/Eastern. Of course, the easiest way is to simply click the eastern United States on the map.

If the World view of the map is too large for you to select your location, click the View button on top of the map. A drop-down list of views appears with the following options: World, North America, South America, Pacific Rim, Europe, Africa, and Asia. You can then click the view appropriate for your location.

The other way to set a time zone is to specify the time difference between your local time and UTC. Click the UTC Offset tab to select the time zone this way. For example, if you are in the eastern part of the United States, select UTC-05:00 as the time zone. This tab also allows you to enable daylight saving time, which applies to the United States only.

After you select your time zone, click Next to continue.

Setting the root password and adding user accounts

The installer displays the Account Configuration screen (see Figure 2-12) from which you can set the root password and add one or more user accounts.

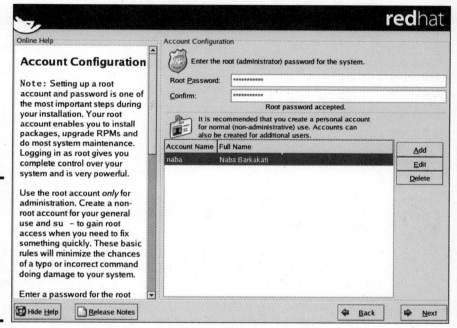

Figure 2-12:
Set the
`root`
password
and add
other user
accounts
from this
screen.

The *root user* is the super user in Linux. Because the super user can do anything in the system, you should assign a password that you can remember but that others cannot guess easily. Make the password at least eight characters long, include a mix of letters and numbers, and, for good measure, throw in some special characters, such as + or *.

Type the password on the first line and reenter the password on the next line. Each character in the password appears as an asterisk (*) on the screen. You have to type the password twice, and both entries must match before the installation program accepts it. This ensures that you do not make any typing mistakes. After you type the `root` password twice, you may also want to add one or more user accounts.

To add a user account, click the Add button, and fill in the user name, password, and full name fields in the resulting dialog box (Figure 2-13). The new account information then appears in the table to the left of the Add button in the Account Configuration screen (refer to Figure 2-12).

Figure 2-13:
Add a user account by filling in information in this dialog box.

 Even if you are the only user on the system, go ahead and add yourself as a user. That way, you can log in as yourself for normal work and use the `root` password only when necessary.

You must enter the `root` password before you can proceed with the rest of the installation. After you have done so and have added any other user accounts you need, click the Next button to continue with the installation.

Configuring password authentication

The installer displays a screen from which you can configure password authentication. There are several options that you can enable or disable. You should use the default settings for increased system security. Click Next to continue with the installation.

Selecting and Installing the Package Groups

After you set up the key system parameters, the installer displays a screen from which you can select the Red Hat Linux package groups that you want to install. That way, after you have selected the package groups, you can take a coffee break and the Red Hat installation program can format the disk partitions and copy all selected files to those partitions.

A *package group* is made up of several Red Hat packages. Each Red Hat package, in turn, includes many files that make up specific software.

Figure 2-14 shows the screen with the list of package groups or components that you can choose to install. An icon, a descriptive label, and a checkbox prefix identify each package group.

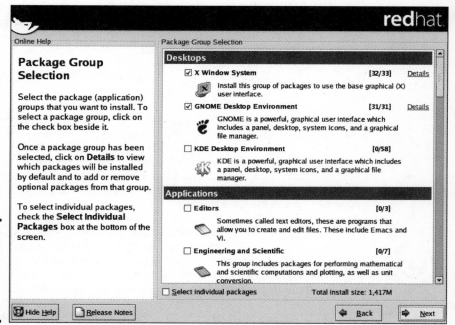

Figure 2-14:
Select the package groups to install from this screen.

Some of the package groups are already selected, as indicated by the check marks in the checkboxes. You can think of the selected package groups as the minimal set of packages recommended by Red Hat for installation for the class of installation (workstation, server, or custom) you have chosen. You can, however, choose to install any or all of the components. Use the mouse to move up and down in the scrolling list and click the mouse on a checkbox to select or deselect that package group.

In an actual production installation of Red Hat Linux, you would install exactly those package groups that you need. However, when you are trying to learn everything about Red Hat Linux you need many different packages. If you have enough disk space (at least 3GB) for the Linux partition, go ahead and select the package group labeled Everything — this installs all the package groups. Being able to install everything makes it easy for you to try out everything.

In addition to the package groups that you select from the screen shown in Figure 2-14, the Red Hat installer automatically installs a large number of packages that are needed to run the Linux kernel and the applications you select. In other words, even if you do not select any of the package groups on this screen, the installation program installs a large number of packages that are needed simply to run the core Linux operating system and a minimal set of utilities.

Each package group requires specific packages to run. The Red Hat installation program automatically checks for any package dependencies and shows you a list of packages that are required but that you have not selected. In this case, you should install the required packages.

After you have selected the package groups you want to install, click Next to continue.

The installer then displays a screen informing you that installation is about to begin. Click Next to proceed with the installation. The Red Hat installer formats the disk partitions and installs the packages. As it installs packages, the installation program displays a status screen showing the progress of the installation, including information such as total number of packages to install, number installed so far, estimated amount of disk space needed, and estimated time remaining to install.

The hard disk formatting and installation can take quite a bit of time — so you can take a break and check back in 15 minutes or so (don't take too long a break, though, or you may come back to find the installer waiting for you to insert CD #2). When you come back, you should be able to get a sense of the time remaining from the status screen, which updates continually.

After all the packages are installed, the installation program displays a screen (Figure 2-15) that asks you to insert a blank floppy into your PC's A drive. This floppy is the boot disk that you can use to start Red Hat Linux if something happens to the hard disk or if you have not installed the boot loader.

Insert a blank floppy into your PC's A drive, and click Next (note that all data on the floppy is destroyed). The installation program copies the Linux kernel and some other files to the floppy.

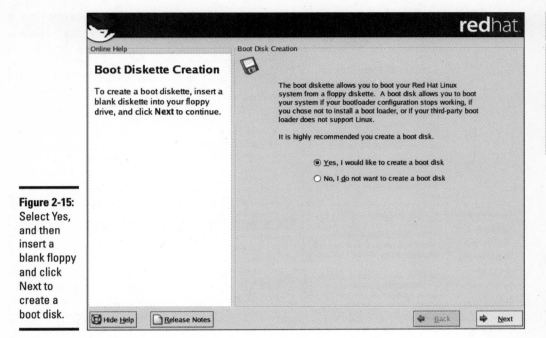

Figure 2-15:
Select Yes,
and then
insert a
blank floppy
and click
Next to
create a
boot disk.

Completing the Installation

The installer configures the X Window System after copying files from the CD-ROM to the hard disk. To enable the graphical installation, the installer runs a version of the X Window System with minimal capability that can work on all video cards. In this step, the installer prepares the configuration file to be used by the X Window System when you reboot the PC.

The installer tries to detect the video card and displays the result in a screen. The detected card appears as the selected item in a long list of video cards, as shown in Figure 2-16.

If you know the exact name of the video card, or the name of the video chipset used in the video card, select that item from the list. Also select the amount of video memory from the drop-down list at the bottom of the screen. Click Next to continue.

Next, the installer tries to detect the monitor, displaying a screen with the results, whether successful or not (see Figure 2-17).

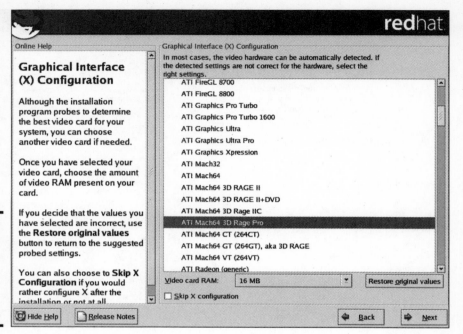

Figure 2-16:
This screen displays the result of detecting the video card.

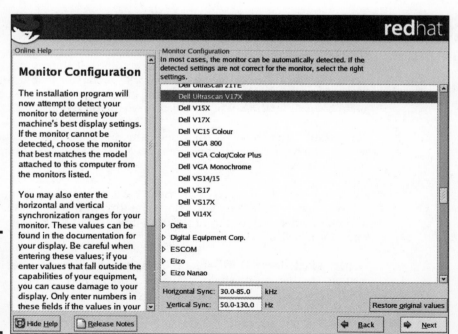

Figure 2-17:
This screen shows the result of detecting the monitor.

If the Red Hat installer displays a wrong monitor or a generic one as the choice, scroll through the list and pick your monitor from the list. One good thing about monitors is that you can always look up the make and model number on the back of the monitor.

If your monitor's make and model is not on the list, you have to select a generic monitor and then enter a range of values for the two parameters that appear along the bottom of the screen:

✦ **Horizontal Sync** — This is the number of times per second that the monitor can display a horizontal line in kilohertz (kHz). A typical range may be 30 – 64 kHz.

✦ **Vertical Sync** — This is how many times a second the monitor can display the entire screen in Hertz (Hz). Also known as *vertical refresh rate,* the typical range is 50–90 Hz.

Typically, the monitor's documentation includes all this information. If you bought your PC recently, you may still have the documentation. If you have lost your monitor's documentation, one way to find the information may be to visit your computer vendor's Web site and look for the technical specification of the monitor. I was able to locate useful information about my system's monitor from the vendor's Web site.

Do not specify a horizontal synchronization range beyond the capabilities of your monitor. A wrong value can damage the monitor.

Next, the Red Hat installer displays a screen from which you can customize the system's GUI (see Figure 2-18).

Select the color depth and screen resolution from the drop-down lists. Select from the checkboxes — Text and Graphical — to specify whether you want a text or a graphical login screen when the system restarts. Most users prefer a graphical login.

After you finish configuring the GUI, click Next. The installer displays a message informing you that installation is complete and tells you to visit Red Hat's Web site at www.redhat.com/errata for information on any updates and bug fixes. The message also reminds you to remove the floppy from drive A before exiting the installation program. Do so, label the floppy appropriately, and save it for future use. Then click the Exit button to reboot your PC.

Congratulations! You're now the owner of a brand new Red Hat Linux system!

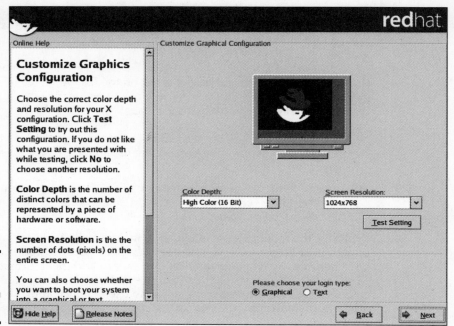

Figure 2-18:
Customize
the GUI from
this screen.

Chapter 3: Troubleshooting and Configuring Red Hat Linux

In This Chapter

✔ **Troubleshooting the installation**

✔ **Configuring X**

✔ **Setting up printers**

✔ **Turning on sound**

✔ **Adding user accounts**

✔ **Managing CD-ROMs**

✔ **Installing RPM packages**

During Red Hat Linux installation, the installer attempts to automatically detect key hardware components such as the SCSI controller and network card. The installer takes you through a sequence of installation steps that depend on what hardware the installer detects. For example, if the installer cannot detect the network card, it skips the network configuration step.

Another installation problem crops up when you restart the PC and, instead of a graphical login screen, you get a text terminal. This means that there is something wrong with the X Window System (or X) configuration.

Also, Red Hat kept the installation simple and did not include configuration of all hardware in your PC. For example, the installation does not set up printers or configure the sound card.

In this chapter, I show you some alternate ways to install Red Hat Linux so that you can force it to configure some key hardware such as the network card and the SCSI controller (if you have one). I also show you how to reconfigure X and perform a few other configuration steps, such as adding a user account, setting up a printer, and configuring the sound card.

You may also need to install additional software packages from the companion CD-ROMs. I show you how to install Red Hat Packages (RPMs) — the format in which you get most of this software.

Using Text Mode Installation

The Red Hat installer attempts to use a minimal X Window System (X) to display the graphical user installation screens. If the installer fails to detect a video card, X does not start. If — for this reason or any other reason — it fails to start X, you can always fall back on a text mode installation. Then you can specify the video card manually.

To use text mode installation, type **text** at the boot: prompt after you start the PC from the Red Hat install boot floppy. From then on, the basic sequence of installation is similar to that of the graphical installation described in Chapter 2. You should be able to respond to the prompts and perform the installation.

In text mode, when the installer fails to detect the video card, it displays a list of video cards from which you can select one. By selecting the video card, X may work when you reboot the PC. If it does not, you can configure X by using Xconfigurator (I show this later in this chapter).

Using the linux isa Command

If the Red Hat installer does not detect the SCSI controller or network card, you can specify these devices manually by typing **linux isa** at the boot: prompt.

To see if the installer deleted the hardware, look for any indication of SCSI or network devices in the messages the Linux kernel displays as it boots. To view these messages during installation, press Ctrl+Alt+F4. This switches the display to a text-mode virtual console on which the messages appear. (A *virtual console* is a screen of text or graphical information stored in memory that you can view on the physical screen by pressing the appropriate key sequence.)

Another sign of undetected hardware is when the installation program skips a step. For example, if the Linux kernel does not detect the network card, the installation program skips the network configuration step.

To manually install devices, type **linux isa** at the boot: prompt in the initial text screen. The installer then displays a dialog box that gives you the opportunity to add devices. Press Tab to highlight the Add Device button; then press Enter. The installer displays a dialog box that prompts for the type of device — SCSI or Network.

If you have any SCSI device, such as an SCSI hard drive, select SCSI and press Enter. The installer displays a list of SCSI controllers from which you can select the one on your system and press Enter. The installer then loads that driver module. The SCSI driver automatically probes and determines the SCSI controller's settings.

After you add any SCSI controllers, you are back at the initial dialog box from which you can add network cards. If you select Network from the list and press Enter, the installation program displays a list of network cards from which you can select your network card.

When you press Enter, the installation program loads the driver module for the selected network card. That driver probes and determines the network card settings.

If you need a Linux device driver that does not come with Red Hat Linux, try checking the vendor's Web site or a search engine such as Google (`www.google.com`). Many hardware vendors provide Linux device drivers for download, just as they do Windows drivers.

After you finish adding the SCSI controllers and network cards, the installer switches to graphics mode and guides you through the rest of the installation.

Troubleshooting X

I have this problem on an older PC every time I install Red Hat Linux. During installation, the X configuration step seems to be fine. But when I reboot the PC for the first time after installation, the graphical login screen does not appear. Instead, the boot process seems to hang just as it starts something called `firstboot`. If this happens to you, here's how you can troubleshoot the problem.

That `firstboot` process happens to be a special step where, if all went well, the Red Hat Setup agent would have started and enabled you to perform one-time setups such as date and time configuration as well as install any other CDs. The reason `firstboot` may get stuck is because the graphical X environment is not working on your system. You have to get around the `firstboot` process to configure X again and continue with the normal course of events that Red Hat has planned for you. Here's what you should do:

1. **Press Ctrl+Alt+F1 to get back to the boot screen.**

    You see the text display with the boot messages that stop at a line displaying information about `firstboot`.

2. **Press Ctrl+Alt+Del to reboot the PC.**

    The PC starts to boot and you get to a screen where the GRUB boot loader prompts you to press Enter to boot Red Hat Linux.

3. Press a **to add an option for use by the Linux kernel.**

The GRUB boot loader then displays a command line for the Linux kernel and prompts you to add what you want.

4. Type a space followed by the word single **and then press Enter.**

The Linux kernel boots in a single-user mode and displays a prompt that looks like the following:

```
sh-2.05b#
```

Now you're ready to configure X.

X uses a configuration file, called XF86Config, to figure out the type of display card, monitor, and the kind of screen resolution you want. The Red Hat installer prepares the configuration file, but sometimes the configuration is not correct.

Use the utility program called xf86config (the full pathname is /usr/bin/X11/xf86config) to generate a usable XF86Config file. The xf86config program is a text mode program that asks you questions. You need to have some information about your PC's video card and monitor to answer these questions.

To run xf86config, type the following command at the command prompt:

```
/usr/bin/X11/xf86config
```

The xf86config program displays a screen of text with some helpful information. Press Enter to continue.

The xf86config program asks you to specify a mouse protocol that determines how the X server communicates with the mouse. The program shows you the following list of options:

```
1.   Microsoft compatible (2-button protocol)
2.   Mouse Systems (3-button protocol)
3.   Bus Mouse
4.   PS/2 Mouse
5.   Logitech Mouse (serial, old type, Logitech protocol)
6.   Logitech MouseMan (Microsoft compatible)
7.   MM Series
8.   MM HitTablet
9.   Microsoft IntelliMouse
```

Type the number that corresponds to your mouse type. If your mouse is connected to a PS/2-style port, for example, select 4. Type the appropriate number, and press Enter.

The `xf86config` program then asks the following:

```
Please answer the following question with either 'y' or 'n'.
Do you want to enable Emulate3Buttons?
```

If your mouse has two buttons, `xf86config` suggests that you enable `Emulate3Buttons`. Type y. If you enable `Emulate3Buttons`, you can simulate a middle-button click by pressing both buttons simultaneously. Many X applications assume that the mouse has three buttons, so this feature comes in handy in the PC world, where a mouse typically has only two buttons.

Next you have to specify the full device name for the mouse. During Red Hat Linux installation, the installer creates a link between your mouse device and the standard name `/dev/mouse`. Therefore, you can press Enter.

The `xf86config` program displays a list of keyboard types and prompts you for the one that matches your keyboard. Enter the number from the list. If none of the types matches, you can always select 1, which represents the Generic 101-key PC keyboard.

The `xf86config` program then asks you for the country for which the keyboard should be configured. Again, you have to pick from a list the program displays. After you select the country, the `xf86config` program gives you the option of setting a few more keyboard options.

Next, `xf86config` informs you that it needs the horizontal and the vertical synchronization rates (or frequencies) of your monitor. These two critical parameters of your monitor have the following meanings:

✦ **Horizontal synchronization frequency** — The number of times per second that the monitor can display a horizontal raster line, in kilohertz (kHz)

✦ **Vertical synchronization rate or vertical refresh rate** — How many times a second the monitor can display the entire screen

Press Enter to continue. The `xf86config` program offers you the following options for the horizontal synchronization frequency:

```
  hsync in kHz; monitor type with characteristic modes
1  31.5; Standard VGA, 640x480 @ 60 Hz
2  31.5 - 35.1; Super VGA, 800x600 @ 56 Hz
3  31.5, 35.5; 8514 Compatible, 1024x768 @ 87 Hz interlaced
  (no 800x600)
4  31.5, 35.15, 35.5; Super VGA, 1024x768 @ 87 Hz interlaced,
  800x600 @ 56 Hz
5  31.5 - 37.9; Extended Super VGA, 800x600 @ 60 Hz, 640x480
  @ 72 Hz
6  31.5 - 48.5; Non-Interlaced SVGA, 1024x768 @ 60 Hz,
  800x600 @ 72 Hz
```

```
 7  31.5 - 57.0; High Frequency SVGA, 1024x768 @ 70 Hz
 8  31.5 - 64.3; Monitor that can do 1280x1024 @ 60 Hz
 9  31.5 - 79.0; Monitor that can do 1280x1024 @ 74 Hz
10  31.5 - 82.0; Monitor that can do 1280x1024 @ 76 Hz
11  Enter your own horizontal sync range

Enter your choice (1-11): 11
```

You can enter the number that corresponds to your monitor or type 11 to specify a range.

Do not specify a horizontal synchronization range beyond the capabilities of your monitor. An incorrect value can damage the monitor.

Many monitor manuals provide a range of values for the horizontal synchronization rate. To enter a range of values, type 11, and press Enter. The program prompts you for the range. Enter the range as two values separated by a hyphen (-). My monitor's documentation, for example, says that the horizontal synchronization range is 30–69 kHz, so I enter the following:

```
Horizontal sync range: 30-69
```

Next xf86config prompts you for the vertical synchronization rate and gives you the following options:

```
1  50-70
2  50-90
3  50-100
4  40-150
5  Enter your own vertical sync range

Enter your choice: 5
```

If you know the range, type 5 and press Enter. At the next prompt, enter the range for the vertical synchronization. My monitor's documentation shows this range to be 50–120 Hz, so I enter the following:

```
Vertical sync range: 50-120
```

Next you have to enter an identifier for your monitor's definition. Typically, you enter your monitor's make and model, but you can enter anything here. This identifier is used to refer to the monitor in another part of the XF86Config configuration file. For my system's monitor, I respond as follows:

```
Enter an identifier for your monitor definition: Micron700FGx
```

The next task is to configure the video card settings. The xf86config program displays an explanatory message and asks this question:

```
Do you want to look at the card database? y
```

Type **y,** and press Enter. The program then displays a list of video cards one screen at a time. Press Enter after each screen to see the entire list. The make, model, and chipset of the video card are crucial pieces of information you need to configure XFree86 properly.

One of my PCs, for example, has a Diamond Stealth 3D 2000 PRO video card with the S3 ViRGE/DX chipset. I notice the following line on one of the screens:

```
206   Diamond Multimedia Stealth 3D 2000 PRO        S3 ViRGE/DX
```

I type 206 — the number corresponding to my video card — and press Enter.

After you enter your selection, xf86config displays some information (and any appropriate instructions) about the video card you selected. When I select card 206, for example, xf86config displays the following:

```
Your selected card definition:

Identifier: Diamond Multimedia Stealth 3D 2000 PRO
Chipset:    S3 ViRGE/DX
Driver:     s3virge
Do NOT probe clocks or use any Clocks line.

Press enter to continue, or ctrl-c to abort.
```

After you press Enter to continue, xf86config asks how much video memory your video card has. Most current video cards have anywhere from 4MB (4,096KB) to 64MB (65,536KB) of video memory. You need at least 1MB of video memory to display 256 colors at 1,024 x 768 resolution (1,024 pixels horizontally by 768 pixels vertically). Type the number that corresponds to the amount of memory in your video card, and press Enter.

Now you have to provide an identifier for your video card. The following is what I enter for my PC's video card:

```
Enter an identifier for your video card definition: Diamond
    Stealth 3D 2000 PRO
```

The program next displays a list of video modes (resolutions and number of colors) that the monitor and card can support. You can enter 4 to accept the modes.

The xf86config program then asks you to enter the default color depth in terms of number of bits per pixel. The choices range from monochrome (1 bit per pixel), to millions of colors (24 bits per pixel). Enter the number corresponding to the depth you want, and press Enter.

This step completes your session with xf86config. The program displays a message asking whether or not it can write the configuration file to /etc/X11/XF86Config file. Type y and press Enter. The xf86config program writes the configuration file and exits.

If you are lucky, the X configuration file that xf86config generates may be all you need to run X with your PC's video card and monitor.

Restart the PC and see if you get a graphical login screen — just type **reboot** at the prompt. If all goes well, you'll go through the normal Red Hat Linux initial setup screens and, finally, get the graphical login screen.

Setting Up Printers

The Red Hat installer does not include a printer configuration step, but you can easily configure a printer from a graphical utility program. To set up printers, follow these steps:

1. **From the graphical login screen, log in as** root.

2. **From the GNOME desktop, select Main Menu (the Red Hat logo icon)⇨ System Settings⇨Printing.**

   The printer configuration tool is called printconf-gui. Figure 3-1 shows its main window.

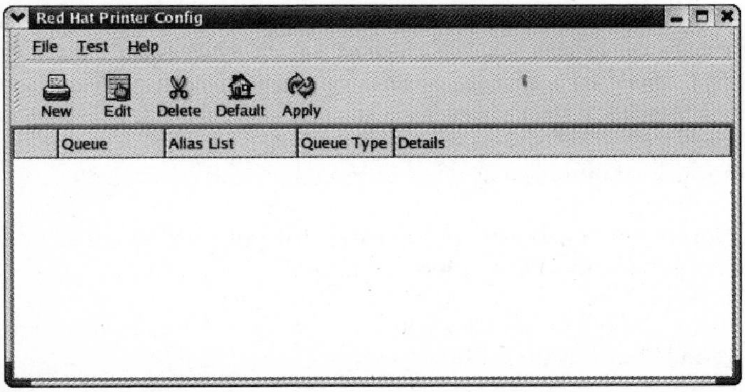

Figure 3-1: Configure and manage printers from the print conf-gui main window.

3. **Click the New button to configure a new printer.**

   This starts Red Hat's printer configuration wizard. The initial screen displays a message. Click Forward to continue.

4. **In the next screen (see Figure 3-2), enter the name for the print queue and select the type of print queue.**

To set up a printer connected to your PC's parallel port, select the Local Printer checkbox.

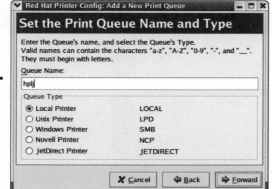

Figure 3-2:
Enter the print queue name and set the type of printer connection.

You can select from five types of print queues:

- **Local Printer** — Refers to a printer connected directly to a parallel or serial port of your PC.

- **Unix Printer** — Refers to a printer connected to another Linux system on the local network.

- **Windows Printer** — Refers to a printer connected to a Windows PC on the local network.

- **Novell Printer** — Refers to a printer connected to a Novell Netware server on your local area network.

- **JetDirect Printer** — Refers to a HP JetDirect printer that's connected directly to the local network.

Select the print queue type that applies to your situation. For example, if you want to print on a shared Windows printer, select the Windows Printer checkbox. Click Forward after you're done with this step.

5. **If you select the Local Printer, the next screen displays information about the detected parallel port. Click Forward to continue.**

6. **Select a print driver for your printer from the screen shown in Figure 3-3.**

Scroll down the list of printers until you find your printer's manufacturer, click the triangle arrow next to the name, and then select the driver. Click Forward to continue.

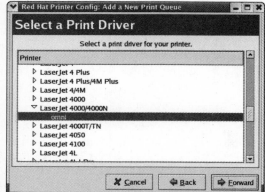

Figure 3-3:
Select a print driver for your printer from this screen.

7. **The last screen (Figure 3-4) shows the information about the new print queue. Check all the information to make sure it's correct and then click Apply to create the print queue.**

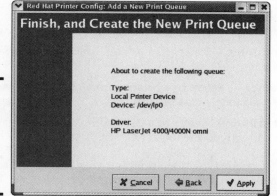

Figure 3-4:
Check the information for accuracy, and then click Apply.

8. **If all goes well, you'll see the new printer listed in the `printconf-gui` main window, as shown in Figure 3-5. Select File⇨Save Changes to save the new printer information.**

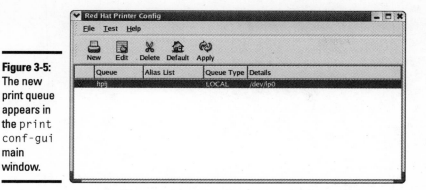

Figure 3-5:
The new
print queue
appears in
the `print`
`conf-gui`
main
window.

**9. Print a test page to make sure that the printer is properly configured.
From the `printconf-gui` menu bar, select Test⇨ASCII Text Testpage
to make sure that plain text files print correctly. Then select Test⇨US
Letter PostScript Testpage to confirm that pages with images and
graphics print properly.**

Turning On Sound

Your PC must have a sound card and speakers to play audio CDs. If your
PC has a sound card, go ahead and hook up the speakers according to the
instructions from the PC's manufacturer.

When you first boot your PC with Red Hat Linux, a utility called Kudzu
detects the sound card and gives you the option to install the driver. If
you have gone through that step, you're set to try out the sound card.
Otherwise, you can set up the sound card using the following steps:

**1. At the graphics login screen, log in as `root`. When you get to the
GNOME desktop, select Main Menu⇨System Settings⇨Soundcard
Detection.**

This runs the Red Hat sound card configuration utility.

**2. The sound card configuration utility gets information about the sound
cards from another program called Kudzu and displays information
about the detected sound card (Figure 3-6).**

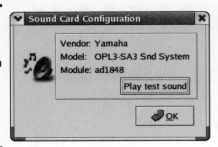

Figure 3-6:
The sound
card
configuration
utility
displays
information
about the
sound card.

3. **Click the Play Test Sound button to play a test sound clip.**

4. **If all goes well, you should hear the sound. Click OK to quit the sound card configuration utility.**

After you configure the sound card, you can play audio CDs and other sound files in Red Hat Linux.

Adding User Accounts

If you installed Red Hat Linux yourself, you know that during installation, the Red Hat installer prompts for the `root` user's password. At the same time, you can also add more user accounts — for yourself, family members, neighbor, or anyone else. If you did not add other user accounts during installation, you can do so now. You can use the Red Hat User Manager to add a new user account on your system.

It's a good idea to set up other user accounts besides `root`. The problem with `root` is the absolute power of that super user account — you can literally do anything, including destroy critical system files with ease. It's better to log in as an ordinary user. When you must do something as `root`, simply type the `su -` command. You'll be prompted for the `root` password and after you enter that password you'll become `root`. When you're finished with your super user duties, type **exit** to return to your mere mortal self.

To add user accounts using the Red Hat User Manager, follow these steps:

1. **Select Main Menu (Red Hat logo)⇨System Settings⇨Users and Groups from the GNOME desktop.**

   If you're not logged in as `root`, the Red Hat User Manager prompts you for the `root` password (see Figure 3-7).

Figure 3-7:
You have to
enter the
`root`
password to
run the Red
Hat User
Manager.

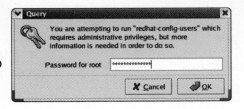

2. **Enter the password and click OK.**

3. **The Red Hat User Manager window appears, as shown in Figure 3-8.**

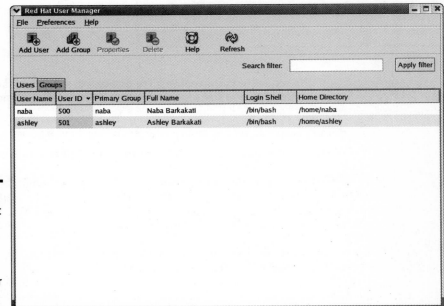

Figure 3-8:
The Red Hat
User
Manager
window
shows the
current user
accounts.

The window in Figure 3-8 shows two tabs: Users and Groups. The Users
tab displays the current list of user accounts. The Groups tab lists the
current list of groups. Figure 3-8 shows the list of users on my Red Hat
Linux system; the list will be different on your system.

4. **To add a new user, click the Add User button on the toolbar.**

The Create New User dialog box appears, as shown in Figure 3-9.

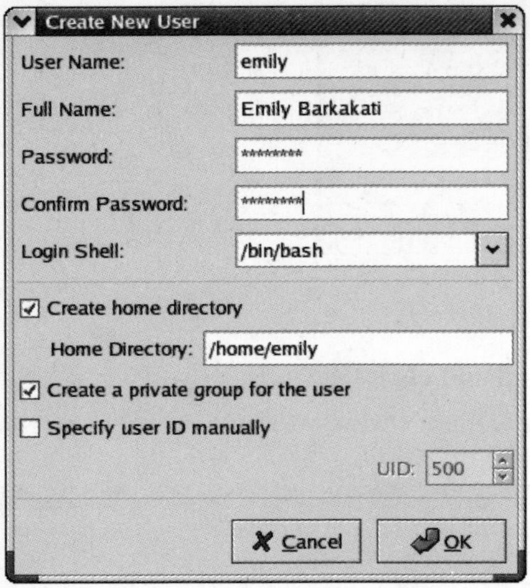

Figure 3-9:
Enter
information
about a new
user
account in
the Create
New User
dialog box.

Fill in the requested information. Then click OK. The new user now appears in the list on the Users tab in the Red Hat User Manager window.

5. **Repeat Step 4 to add as many user accounts as you want.**

6. **When done, choose Action⇨Exit to quit the Red Hat User Manager.**

To edit existing user account information, click the user name from the list in the Users tab and then click the Properties button on the toolbar. That user's information appears in a User Properties dialog box. You can then edit the information and click OK to make the changes.

If you want to remove a user account, click the user name in the Users tab. Then click the Delete button on the toolbar.

Managing CD-ROMs

The GNOME desktop makes it easy to use CD-ROMs in Red Hat Linux. Just place a CD-ROM in the drive, and an icon appears on the desktop. Behind the scenes a special utility called Magicdev is always running, waiting to detect when a CD-ROM is inserted or removed. When you insert a CD that has an `autorun` file, Magicdev prompts you if you want to run that file (Figure 3-10).

Figure 3-10:
Magicdev
prompts you
if you want
to run the
`autorun`
file on a CD.

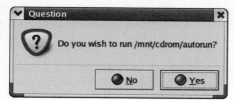

Typically, running the `autorun` file starts an installer that can install the software that's on the CD.

Magicdev also automatically starts the Nautilus file manager that shows the contents of the CD-ROM (Figure 3-11).

Figure 3-11:
When you
insert a CD,
Nautilus
displays the
CD's
contents.

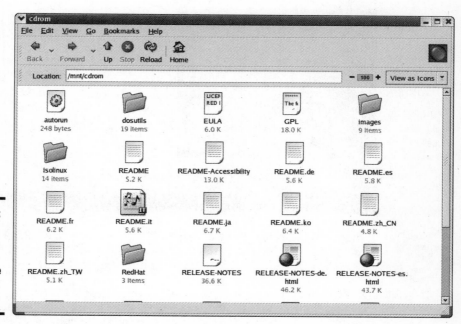

Finally, Magicdev puts a CD-ROM icon on the GNOME desktop. You can then use the CD either through the Nautilus file manager or through the icon on the desktop. To access the files and folders, you simply double-click the icons in the Nautilus window.

The CD-ROM icon is better for some other tasks, such as ejecting the CD when you're done with it. If you right-click the CD-ROM icon, a pop-up menu appears with a list of things you can do with the CD-ROM (Figure 3-12).

Figure 3-12: Right click on the CD-ROM icon to use it.

When you are done with the CD, select Eject from the pop-up menu to eject the CD-ROM from the drive and automatically remove the icon as well.

If there is a CD in the CD-ROM drive and you don't see a CD-ROM icon on the GNOME desktop, just eject the CD (press the button on the CD-ROM drive). Insert the CD again and Magicdev should recognize the CD.

The KDE desktop does not automatically open the CD-ROM's contents in a file manager. Instead, KDE provides a CD/DVD-ROM icon on the desktop. After inserting a CD into the CD-ROM drive, you can simply double-click the CD/DVD-ROM icon to view the CD's contents in a file manager (Figure 3-13).

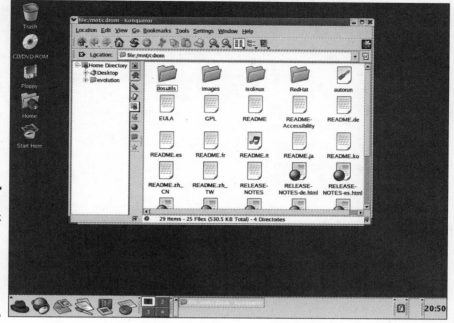

Figure 3-13:
Double-click
the
CD/DVD-
ROM icon in
KDE to view
a CD's
contents.

Installing RPM Packages

Sometimes you have to install or remove software to troubleshoot or configure your Red Hat Linux system. Most Red Hat Linux software comes in the
form of Red Hat Package Manager (RPM) files. An RPM file is basically a
single package that contains everything — all the files and configuration
information — needed to install a software product. In this section, I show
you how to install RPM packages.

From the GNOME desktop, use Red Hat's Package Management utility —
a graphical utility for installing and uninstalling RPMs. To start the Package
Management utility, choose Main Menu⇨System Settings⇨Packages. If you
are not logged in as root, a dialog box prompts you for the root password.
Enter that password and press Enter. The Package Management utility starts
and gathers information about the status of packages installed on your
system (Figure 3-14).

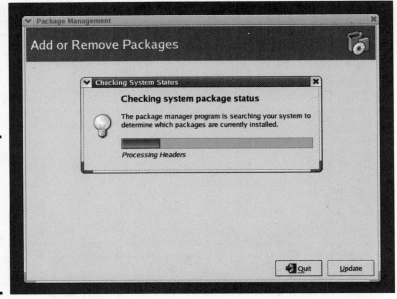

Figure 3-14:
The
Package
Manage-
ment utility
gathers
information
about
installed
packages.

After it sorts through the information about all the installed packages, the
Package Management utility displays a list of all the packages (Figure 3-15).

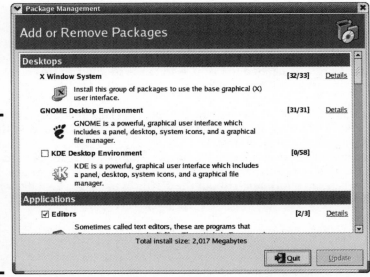

Figure 3-15:
The
Package
Manage-
ment utility
shows
information
about the
package
groups.

The Package Management window displays information about the packages organized into package groups such as Desktops and Applications (a *package group* is a collection of related RPMs). Each package group has a graphical icon, a label such as X Window System or GNOME Desktop Environment, and a brief description as well. A checkbox precedes each package group name. If the package is already installed, a check mark appears in the checkbox. For example, in Figure 3-15, the X Window System and GNOME Desktop Environment package groups are installed, but the KDE Desktop Environment is not yet installed.

For the installed package groups (the ones with check marks), notice the hypertext link labeled Details on the right-hand side of the package's name and description. If you click Details, the Package Management utility brings up a new window in which it displays further details about the contents of that package group. For example, Figure 3-16 displays the detailed content of the GNOME Desktop Environment package group.

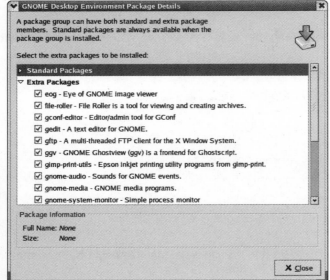

Figure 3-16:
Clicking the
Details for a
package
group brings
up its
detailed
contents.

Click Close after you finish examining the details of a package group.

To install an uninstalled package group, simply click the checkbox so that a check mark appears there. Then click the Update button to proceed with the installation. The Package Management utility figures out what specific files have to be installed for that package group. (Because of interdependencies among package groups, installing one package group may require installing quite a few other package groups.) After it completes gathering information, a dialog box informs you what will be installed and how much disk space will be needed. For example, Figure 3-17 shows the information about package and space requirements for the KDE Desktop Environment (56 packages and about 178MB of disk space).

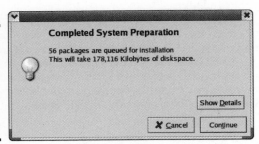

Figure 3-17: Clicking the Details for a package brings up its detailed contents.

Click Continue to proceed. The Package Management utility then updates the system and displays the progress as it installs files (Figure 3-18).

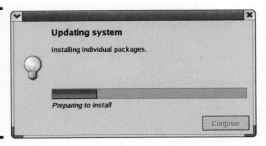

Figure 3-18: Package Management utility displays progress as it updates the system.

If a new CD is needed, the Package Management utility prompts you for the next CD (Figure 3-19). Insert the requested CD and click OK.

Figure 3-19:
You will be
prompted
for CDs, as
necessary.

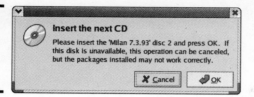

Insert the next CD

Please insert the 'Milan 7.3.93' disc 2 and press OK. If
this disk is unavailable, this operation can be canceled,
but the packages installed may not work correctly.

✗ Cancel   OK

To remove one or more package groups, uncheck the check marks for those
package groups in the Package Management window and then click the
Update button. A dialog box shows you the details of what will be removed.
Click Continue and the packages are history!

Chapter 4: Trying Out Red Hat Linux

In This Chapter

✔ Booting Red Hat Linux

✔ Logging in

✔ Checking out the GUI desktops

✔ Playing with the shell

✔ Shutting down

You're sitting in front of your PC about to turn it on. You know that the PC has Red Hat Linux installed (maybe you did the installing yourself, but who's keeping track?). You're wondering what to expect when you turn it on and what you should do afterward. Not to worry. If this is your first time using Red Hat Linux, this chapter shows you how to log in, check out the graphical desktops, try out some cryptic Linux commands, and finally, shut down the PC.

Those of you who already know something about Red Hat Linux, flip through the pages to see if anything is new. You never know what you may not know!

Booting Red Hat Linux

When you power up the PC, it goes through the normal power-up sequence and loads the boot loader — GRUB or LILO, depending on which one was selected during Red Hat Linux installation. The *boot loader* is a tiny computer program that loads the rest of the operating system from disk into the computer's memory. These programs are now called *boot loaders* (once known as bootstrap loader). The whole process of starting up a computer is called *booting*.

Whether the boot loader is LILO or GRUB doesn't matter much. In either case, a graphical screen appears with the names of operating systems that the boot loader can load. For example, if your PC has Windows and

Red Hat Linux, you see both names listed. You can then press the up and down arrow keys to select the operating system you want to use. If the PC is set up to load Red Hat Linux by default, wait a few seconds and then the boot loader starts Red Hat Linux. To be more precise, the boot loader loads the *Linux kernel* — the core of the Linux operating system — into the PC's memory.

As the Linux kernel starts, you should see a long list of opening messages often referred to as the *boot messages*. These messages include the names of the devices that Linux detects. One of the first lines in the boot messages reads `Calibrating delay loop... 421.23 BogoMIPS` — the number that precedes BogoMIPS depends on your PC's processor speed, whether it's an old 200 MHz Pentium or a new 1 GHz Pentium 4. *BogoMIPS* is Linux jargon that refers to a measure of time. The kernel uses the BogoMIPS measurement when it has to wait a small amount of time for some event to occur (like getting a response back from a disk controller when it's ready).

When you boot Red Hat Linux for the first time after installation, you get the Red Hat Setup Agent that displays a welcome screen and then takes you through date and time setup (Figure 4-1), gives you a chance to register with Red Hat Network, and install any additional CDs.

If the screen goes dark and there is no activity, the first-time configuration utility may be having trouble starting the X Window System. Unfortunately, you cannot try out Red Hat Linux without fixing this problem. Sometimes the graphical environment fails even though the graphical interface seems to work fine during installation. There are ways to fix this problem. Go to Book I, Chapter 3 for more information on how to troubleshoot this problem.

What is BogoMIPS?

As Red Hat Linux boots, you get a message that says `Calibrating delay loop... 421.23 BogoMIPS`, with some number before the word *BogoMIPS*. BogoMIPS is one of those words that confounds new Linux users, but it's just jargon with a simple meaning.

BogoMIPS is Linus's invention (yes, the same Linus Torvalds who started Linux) and it means bogus MIPS. As you may know, MIPS is an acronym for *millions of instructions per second* — a measure of how fast your computer runs programs. Unfortunately, MIPS is not a very good measure of performance because comparing the MIPS of different types of computers is difficult. BogoMIPS is basically a way to measure the computer's speed that's independent of the exact processor type. Linux uses the BogoMIPS number to calibrate a delay loop, in which the computer keeps running some useless instructions until a specified amount of time has passed. Of course, the reason for killing valuable processor time like this is to wait for some slowpoke device to get ready for work.

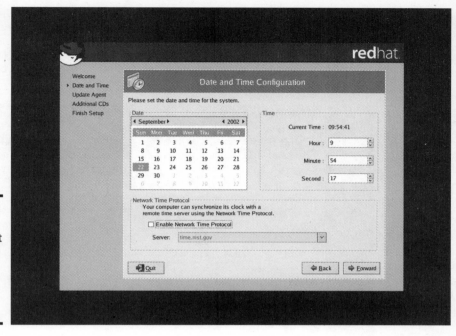

Figure 4-1:
Red Hat
Setup Agent
displays the
Date and
Time Con-
figuration
window.

The Red Hat Setup Agent's first configuration step is for date and time. You can set the date and time from the screen in Figure 4-1.

If your system is connected to the Internet, click the checkbox labeled Enable Network Time Protocol and then select a server from the drop-down list labeled Server. That way, the system is going to get its time directly from one of the super-accurate time servers on the Net.

After setting the date and time, click Forward. The Red Hat Setup Agent then prompts you if you want to register with Red Hat Network (Figure 4-2). To register, click Forward and respond to the requested information. After that step is done, click Forward again.

The Red Hat Setup Agent then displays a window from which you can install additional CDs (Figure 4-3). If you have additional CDs to install, click the appropriate icon. Otherwise, click Forward.

When you're done with the Red Hat Setup Agent, you're really done for good because it runs only once when you boot for the first time. If, for some reason, you want to go through these steps again, here's the scoop on how to run the Red Hat Setup Agent again. Log in as `root` and type the following command in a terminal window (to open a terminal window select Main Menu⇨System Tools⇨Terminal):

```
chkconfig --level 5 firstboot on
```

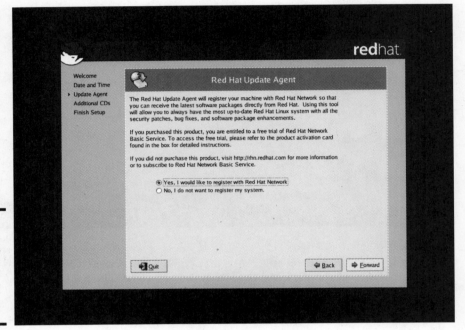

Figure 4-2:
You get an opportunity to register with Red Hat Network.

That's it! Next time you reboot the PC, you'll have the pleasure of meeting the Red Hat Setup Agent again.

When you're through with the Red Hat Setup Agent, you should get the graphical login screen (Figure 4-4).

The login window in the middle of the screen displays a welcome message with your PC's name — it's called the *host name*. The name is assigned when the network is configured. If the network is not configured, `localhost.localdomain` is the host name. If your PC gets its network address (the IP address) from a Dynamic Host Configuration Protocol (DHCP) server, then that server provides a cryptic host name for your PC. The login window also has a text input field that prompts you for your user name.

Figure 4-3:
You can install any other CDs that you may have.

You can log in using any of the accounts you define during or after the installation. There is always the `root` user name, which happens to be the super user or the administrator account. Whether you installed Red Hat Linux yourself or someone installed it for you, you should know the `root` password. Without that, you cannot do many of the tasks necessary to learn how Linux works.

For example, to log in as user spiderman, type **spiderman** in the first text field and press Enter (move the mouse over the login dialog box before you begin typing). Then type spiderman's password and press Enter. You should then see the initial graphical user interface (GUI — pronounced *gooey* for short) appear. What you get depends on your choice of GUI — GNOME or KDE. If someone made the choice for you, don't worry, GNOME and KDE are both quite good and versatile.

Figure 4-4:
The
Welcome
screen is
where you
log in as
a user.

Exploring GUI Desktops

Red Hat Linux comes with two GUI desktops — GNOME and KDE. If you have installed both, you can try them out one by one. It's easy to select one of these desktops just before you log into the system — I show you how.

GNOME is typically the default GUI in Red Hat Linux, so you can start with GNOME. Then log out and log back in, but select KDE as the GUI. That way you can try out both desktops.

GNOME

GNOME stands for *GNU Network Object Model Environment,* and GNU, as you probably know, stands for *GNU's Not UNIX.* GNOME is a graphical user inter-face (GUI) and a programming environment. From the user's perspective, GNOME is like Microsoft Windows. Behind the scenes, GNOME has many features that allow programmers to write graphical applications that can work together well. In this chapter, I point out only some key features of the GNOME GUI, leaving the details to you to explore on your own at your leisure.

If you are curious, you can always find out the latest information about GNOME by visiting the GNOME home page at `www.gnome.org`.

Typically, GNOME is the default in Red Hat Linux. After you log in, you see the GNOME GUI desktop. Figure 4-5 shows the GNOME desktop after you log in as `root`.

When you log in as root, you could accidentally damage your system because you can do anything when you are `root`. Always log in as a normal user (except when you log in for the first time so you can create other user accounts).

Figure 4-5:
Initial
GNOME GUI
desktop
after logging
in as root.

The exact appearance of the GNOME desktop depends on the current *session* (the set of applications that is running at that time). As you can see, the initial GNOME desktop, shown in Figure 4-5, is very similar to the Windows desktop. It has the GNOME Panel, or simply the panel (similar to the Windows taskbar) along the bottom and icons for folders and applications appear directly on the desktop. This is similar to the way you can place icons directly on the Windows desktop.

You can move and resize the windows just as you do in Microsoft Windows. Also, as in the window frames in Microsoft Windows, the right-hand corner of the window's title bar includes three buttons. The leftmost button reduces the window to an icon, the middle button maximizes the window to fill up the entire screen, and the rightmost button closes the window.

The GNOME panel

The GNOME panel is a key feature of the GNOME desktop. The panel is a separate GNOME application. As Figure 4-6 shows, it provides a display area for menus and small panel applets. Each panel applet is a small program that is designed to work inside the panel. For example, the clock applet on the panel's far right displays the current date and time.

Figure 4-6:
You can start programs from the GNOME panel.

The panel includes several other applets besides the clock applet at the far right edge:

✦ **The GNOME Pager applet:** Provides a virtual desktop that's larger than the physical dimensions of your system's screen. In Figure 4-6, the pager displays four pages in a small display area. Each page represents an area equal to the size of the display screen. To go to a specific page, click that page in the pager window. The GNOME Pager applet displays buttons for each window being displayed in the current virtual page.

✦ **Launcher applets:** The buttons to the right of the Red Hat icon are launcher applets. Each of these applets displays a button with the icon of application. Clicking a button starts (launches) that application. Try clicking each of these buttons to see what happens. The mouse and earth button launches the Mozilla Web browser whereas clicking the pen and paper icon opens the OpenOffice.org word processor. Move the mouse over an icon and a small help message appears with information about that icon.

✦ **The GNOME weather applet:** Displays the local weather. You don't see this applet until you start it. You can start it from the menu that appears when you right-click the panel window.

The Main Menu button, or the "Red Hat Logo"

In Figure 4-6, the leftmost edge of the panel shows a button with the familiar Red Hat logo. That "red hat" is the Main Menu button — the most important part of the GNOME panel. Just like the Start button in Microsoft Windows, you can launch applications from the menu that pops up when you click the left mouse button on the red hat. Figure 4-7 shows a typical view of the Main Menu on a Red Hat Linux PC.

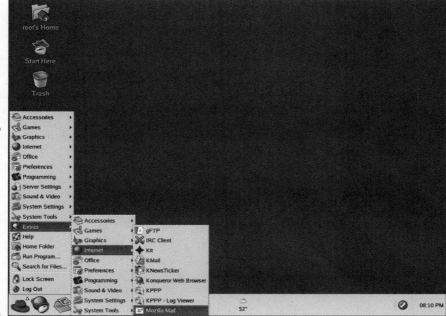

Figure 4-7:
Click the red hat (Main Menu) and move the mouse pointer from menu to menu to start the program you want.

Typically, the Main Menu and its submenus list items that start an application. Some of the menu items have an arrow; move the mouse pointer on an item with an arrow and another menu pops up. In this case, the menu selection is Main Menu⇨Extras⇨Internet⇨Mozilla Mail.

You can start applets such as the weather applet from the menu that appears when you right-click the GNOME panel. To start the weather applet, right-click the panel and select Add to Panel⇨Accessories⇨Weather Report (Figure 4-8). In the Add to Panel menu, you find many more categories of applets that you can try out.

Figure 4-8:
Right-click
the panel
and click
Add to
Panel to see
the applets
such as
GNOME
Weather
that you can
add to the
panel.

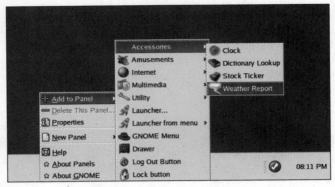

Explore all the items in the Main Menu to see all the tasks you can perform
from this menu. In particular, move the mouse over the Main Menu⇨
Preferences item to see your options (Figure 4-9) for changing the appearance of the desktop. For example, you can change the desktop's background
from this menu.

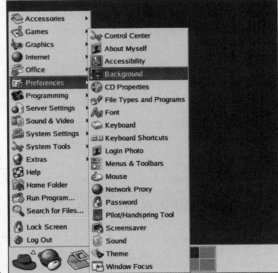

Figure 4-9:
Main
Menu⇨
Preferences
has options
to customize
the desktop.

Customizing GNOME

By now you may be itching to do a bit of decorating. No one likes to stick to
the plain blue GNOME desktop. After all, it's your desktop. You should be

able to set it up any way you want it. You can configure most aspects of the GNOME desktop's *look and feel* — the appearance and behavior — by selecting various options from the Main Menu⇨Preferences menu.

Changing the background

To see how the desktop decorating business works, start by selecting Main Menu⇨Preferences⇨Background and a dialog box appears, as shown in Figure 4-10.

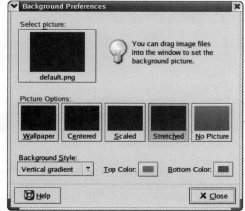

Figure 4-10:
Changing
the GNOME
desktop's
background.

From this dialog box you can select a background of solid color or color gradient background or pick *wallpaper* (an image to be used as the background). A *color gradient* background starts with one color and gradually changes to another color. The gradient can be in the vertical direction (top to bottom) or horizontal (left to right).

To select a horizontal color gradient, try these steps:

1. **Click the Background Style drop-down box — the one that currently says Vertical gradient (see Figure 4-10). From the list, select Horizontal gradient.**

2. **Click the button that shows a color next to the label Left Color.**

    This brings up a color selection dialog box (see Figure 4-11) from which you can pick a color.

3. **Repeat the same process to select the Right Color.**

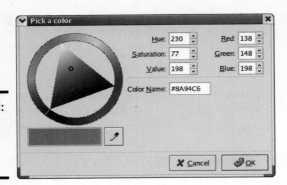

Figure 4-11:
The dialog box where you pick a color.

After you complete these steps, the image of the monitor in the dialog box shows you a preview of the new background color.

If you want to use an image as wallpaper, click the Select picture box in the upper-left corner of the dialog box. A dialog box displays the contents of the /usr/share/backgrounds/images directory, which is where you'll find some background images that you can select (for more wallpaper images, check out the directory /usr/share/backgrounds/wallpapers as well). As you click on an image file's name, you see a preview of the image (Figure 4-12). You can select any *Joint Photographic Experts Group* (JPEG) or *Portable Network Graphics* (PNG) format image file as wallpaper. After selecting an image, click OK.

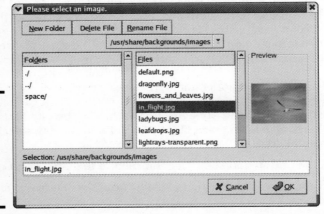

Figure 4-12:
Select an image to use as wallpaper from this dialog box.

The new wallpaper should immediately appear on the desktop (Figure 4-13). When you are done making the changes, click the OK button to close the dialog box and apply the changes.

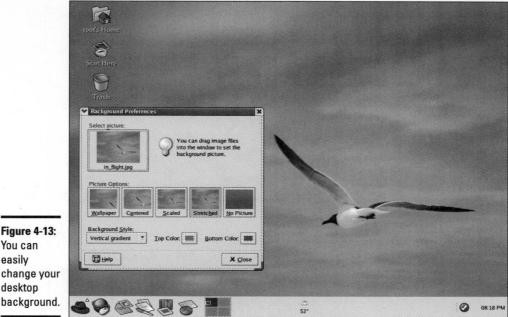

Figure 4-13:
You can easily change your desktop background.

Selecting a theme

Another more exciting customization is to select a new theme for the entire user interface. A *theme* refers to a collection of appearance and behavior (look and feel) for all the user interface components such as buttons, checkboxes, scrollbars, and so on.

To try out some new themes, choose Main Menu⇨Preferences⇨Theme. From the Theme Preferences dialog box (see Figure 4-14) you can try out different themes and select one that you like. The default theme is called Bluecurve. To try another theme, select the theme from the list and the window's appearance changes to match the theme. You can select the theme from the Application tab and a window border look and feel from the Window Border tab. For example, Figure 4-14 shows the result of selecting the Raleigh application and the Atlanta border.

Go ahead and try out some of the available themes. When you select a theme, you can see the results in the Theme Preference window itself. If you like a theme, click the Close button to use that theme. Otherwise, select the Bluecurve theme before clicking Close.

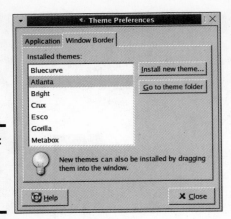

Figure 4-14:
Selecting a new theme for the desktop.

Logging out of GNOME

If you want to try out the KDE GUI, you have to log out. Select Main
Menu⇨Log out. Click Yes when a dialog box asks you if you really want to
log out.

KDE

KDE stands for the *K Desktop Environment*. The KDE project started in
October 1996 with an intent to develop a common GUI for UNIX systems
that use the X Window System. The first beta version of KDE version was
released a year later in October 1997. KDE version 1.0 was released in July
1998; KDE 2.0 on October 23, 2000; and the latest version — KDE 3.0 — was
released on April 3, 2002.

From the user's perspective, KDE provides a graphical desktop environment
that includes a window manager, the Konqueror Web browser and file manager, a panel for starting applications, a help system, configuration tools,
and many applications, including the OpenOffice.org office suite, image
viewer, PostScript viewer, and mail and news programs.

From the developer's perspective, KDE has class libraries and object models
for easy application development in C++. KDE is a large development project
with many collaborators.

You can always find out the latest information about KDE by visiting the KDE
home page at www.kde.org.

To try the KDE GUI, you have to have KDE installed on your system. If you
do not have KDE installed, you probably did not want the KDE GUI in the

first place. If your system has only KDE installed, you get the KDE GUI as soon as you log in.

If you have both GNOME and KDE installed on your system, you can select the GUI just before you log in. From the login window (see Figure 4-15), click Session and from the pop-up dialog box, choose KDE for a KDE session and then log in as usual.

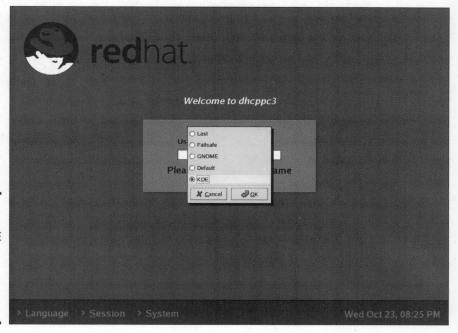

Figure 4-15:
You can select a KDE GUI by clicking Session in the login window.

When you log in and make this selection, you get the KDE desktop for this session. The next time you log in again, the system continues to use KDE until you switch back to GNOME.

After you select KDE as the GUI for the session and log in, you should see an initial KDE desktop similar to the one shown in Figure 4-16.

You will find that KDE is very easy to use and has many similarities with the Windows GUI. You can start applications from a menu that's similar to the Start menu in Windows. As in Windows, you can place folders and applications directly on the KDE desktop.

Figure 4-16:
The initial
KDE desktop
for a typical
user.

KDE panel

The KDE panel appearing along the bottom edge of the screen is meant for starting applications. The right end of the panel shows an arrow pointing to the right. You can click on this arrow to hide the panel and make more room on the desktop for applications. When the panel is hidden, it still shows a small bar with an arrow. To view the entire panel again, click that arrow and the panel slides out.

The most important component of the panel is the Red Hat button on the left-hand side of the panel (In default KDE installations, the menu appears as a large letter K, but Red Hat has replaced it with the Red Hat logo). That button is like the Start button in Windows. When you click the Red Hat button, a pop-up menu appears. From this menu, you can get to other menus by moving the mouse over items with a rightward pointing arrow. For example, Figure 4-17 shows a typical menu selection for changing the desktop background.

You can start applications from this menu. That's why the KDE documentation calls the Red Hat button (of course, the KDE documentation refers to the button as the K button) the *Application Starter*.

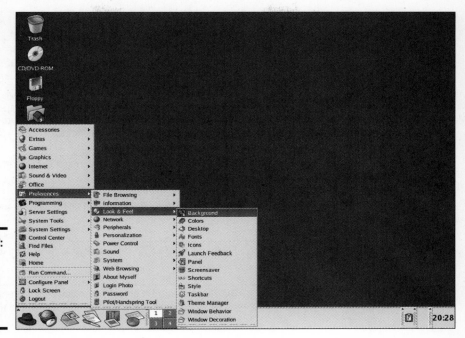

Figure 4-17:
Click the
Red Hat
button for
the KDE
menus.

Next to the Red Hat button, the panel includes many more buttons. If you don't know what a button does, simply move the mouse over the button and a small pop-up window displays a brief message about that button.

Table 4-1 gives you an idea of what happens when you click each of the major buttons on the KDE panel. When you have some time, try out each of these buttons one by one to get a feel for what you can do in KDE.

Table 4-1	KDE Panel Buttons
When You Click This Button	*It Does This*
	Shows the application menu from which you can start any application.
	Starts the Mozilla Web browser.
	Starts the Ximian Evolution e-mail and calendaring software.

(continued)

Table 4-1 *(continued)*

When You Click This Button	It Does This
	Runs OpenOffice.org Writer, a Microsoft Word-like word processor.
	Runs the OpenOffice.org Impress slide presentation program that's similar to Microsoft PowerPoint.
	Runs OpenOffice.org Calc, a Microsoft Excel-like spreadsheet program.
	Switches to the desktop whose number you have clicked.
	Runs Klipper, the KDE clipboard utility for cutting and pasting information.
19:50	Displays the current time. Click to view the current month's calendar. Right click for menu to adjust date and time.

Customizing the KDE desktop

KDE makes it very easy to customize the look and feel of the KDE desktop. Everything you need to decorate the desktop is in one place: the KDE Control Center. To start the KDE Control Center, select K⇨Control Center.

When the KDE Control Center starts, it displays the main window with a tree menu on the left-hand side and some summary information about your system in the workspace to the right, as shown in Figure 4-18.

The KDE Control Center's tree menu shows the items that you can customize with this program. The tree menu is organized into categories such as File Browsing, Information, Look & Feel, Network, and Sound. Click the plus sign (+) to the left of an item to view the subcategories for that item. To change an item, go through the tree menu to locate the item and then click it. That item's configuration options then appear in a tabbed dialog box on the right side of the window.

Changing the background

To change the desktop's background, choose Look & Feel⇨Background. A tab appears (see Figure 4-19) that shows the options for customizing the desktop's background.

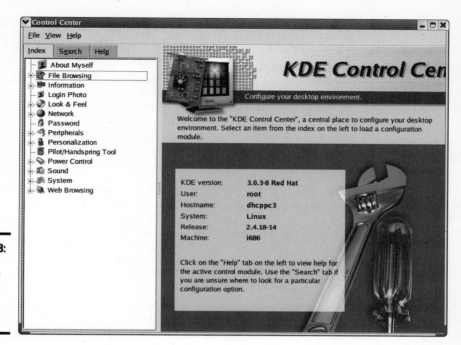

Figure 4-18:
Initial
window of
the KDE
Control
Center.

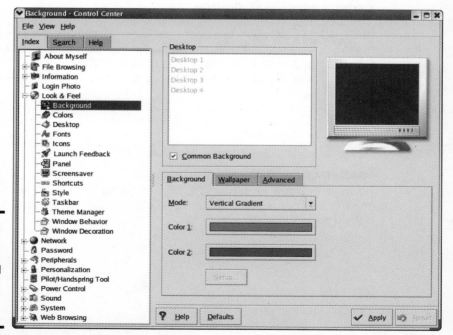

Figure 4-19:
Changing
the desktop
background
with KDE
Control
Center.

If you want to change the background of a specific desktop, click the Common Background button to turn off the check mark. Then, from the list of desktops, you can select the desktop whose background you want to change.

You can select either a solid color background with a variety of gradients (meaning the color changes gradually from one color to another) or wallpaper (an image used as a background). For solid color backgrounds, you can select the gradient from the Mode drop-down menu. You can then pick the two colors by clicking the Color 1 and Color 2 color buttons. After making your selections, click Apply to try out the background. If you don't like it, click Reset to revert back to the previous background.

If you want to use wallpaper as background, click the Wallpaper tab for the wallpaper selections. Then click the Browse button. This brings up a dialog box showing the JPEG images in the `/usr/share/backgrounds/wallpapers` directory. You can select any one of these images and click OK. Then click the Apply button in the KDE Control Center to apply this wallpaper to the desktop. If you don't like the appearance, click Reset.

Selecting a theme

As you can see from the menu items in the Look & Feel category of the KDE Control Center (refer to Figure 4-19), you can customize a number of aspects of look and feel, from colors and fonts to icons. I won't go through all the items here, but you should experiment with some of these items to see what you want for your KDE desktop.

One quick and easy way to select a packaged look and feel is to use one of the themes offered by the Theme Manager. To pick a theme, choose Look & Feel⇨Theme Manager. This brings up the Theme Manager selections from which you can click the name of a theme and see a preview of that theme, as shown in Figure 4-20.

To try out a theme, click Apply. If you don't like it, click Reset to revert back to the current look and feel.

Logging Out of KDE

When you're done exploring KDE, log out. To log out of KDE, select K⇨Logout. You can also right-click empty areas of the desktop and select Logout from the pop-up menu.

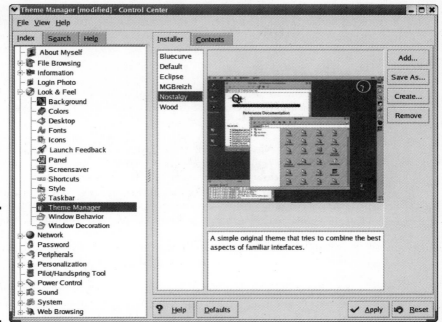

Figure 4-20:
Selecting
and
previewing
a theme in
KDE Control
Center.

Playing with the Shell

Red Hat Linux is basically UNIX, and UNIX just doesn't feel like UNIX unless
you can type cryptic commands in a text terminal. Although GNOME and
KDE have done a lot to bring us into the world of *w*indows, *i*cons, *m*ouse,
and *p*ointer (affectionately known as *WIMP* :-), sometimes you're stuck with
nothing but a plain text screen with a prompt that looks like this:

```
[root@dhcppc4 etc]#
```

This is most often the case when something is wrong with the X Window
System, which is essentially the machinery that runs the windows and
menus you normally see. In those cases, you have to work with the Shell
and learn some of the cryptic Linux commands.

You can prepare for unexpected encounters with the shell by trying out
some Linux commands in a terminal window while you are in the GNOME
or KDE GUI. After you get the hang of it, you might even keep a terminal

window open, just so you can use one of those cryptic commands simply because it's faster than trying to point and click (those two letter commands do pack some punch!).

Starting the Bash shell

Simply put, the *shell* is the Linux command interpreter — it's a program that reads what you type, interprets that text as a command, and does what the command is supposed to do.

Before you start playing with the shell, open a terminal window. In both GNOME and KDE, select Main Menu ⇨System Tools⇨Terminal. What appears is a window with a prompt, like the one shown in Figure 4-21. That's a terminal window, and it works just like an old-fashioned terminal. A shell program is running and ready to accept any text that you type. You type text, press Enter, and something happens depending on what you typed.

The prompt that you see depends on the shell that runs in that terminal window. The default Linux shell is called *Bash*.

Bash understands a whole host of standard Linux commands with which you can look at files, go from one directory to another, see what programs are running, who else is logged in, and a whole lot more.

In addition to the Linux commands, Bash can run any program stored in an executable file. Bash can also execute text files, called *shell scripts,* that contain Linux commands

Understanding shell commands

Because a shell interprets what you type, it is important to know how the shell figures out the text that you enter. All shell commands have this general format:

```
command option1 option2 ... optionN
```

A single line of commands is commonly referred to as a *command line*. On a command line, you enter a command followed by one or more options (or arguments) known as *command-line options* (or command-line arguments).

One basic rule is that you have to use a space or a tab to separate the command from the options. You also must separate options with a space or a tab. If you want to use an option that contains embedded spaces, you have to put that option inside quotation marks. For example, to search for two words of text in the password file, I enter the following `grep` command (`grep` one of those cryptic commands that is used to search for text in files):

```
grep "Font Server" /etc/passwd
```

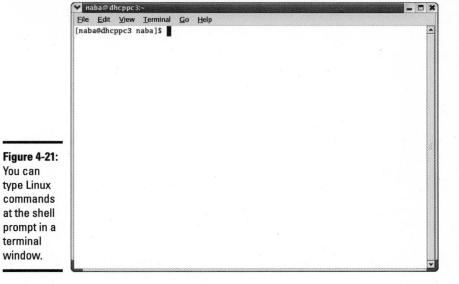

Figure 4-21: You can type Linux commands at the shell prompt in a terminal window.

When `grep` prints the line with those words, it looks like this:

```
xfs:x:43:43:X Font Server:/etc/X11/fs:/sbin/nologin
```

If you created a user account in your name, go ahead and type the `grep` command with your name as an argument, but remember to enclose the name in quotes.

Trying a few Linux commands

While you have the terminal window open, go ahead and try a few Linux commands just for fun. I guide you through some random examples to give you a feel for what you can do at the shell prompt.

To see how long the Red Hat Linux PC has been up since you last powered it up, type the following. (*Note:* I show the typed command in bold, followed by the output from that command.)

```
uptime
```

```
 7:13pm  up 29 days, 55 min,  3 users,  load average: 1.00,
    1.00, 1.00
```

The part up 29 days, 55 min tells you that this particular PC has been up for nearly a month. Hmmm... can Windows do that?

To see what version of Linux kernel your system is running, use the uname command like this:

```
uname -srv
```

```
Linux 2.4.18-12.5 #1 Mon Aug 26 08:51:52 EDT 2002
```

In this case, the system is running Linux kernel version 2.4.18.

To read a file, use the more command. Here's an example:

```
more /etc/passwd
```

```
root:x:0:0:root:/root:/bin/bash
bin:x:1:1:bin:/bin:/sbin/nologin
daemon:x:2:2:daemon:/sbin:/sbin/nologin
adm:x:3:4:adm:/var/adm:/sbin/nologin
... lines deleted ...
```

To see a list of all the programs that are currently running on the system, use the ps command, like this:

```
ps ax
```

```
 PID TTY       STAT   TIME COMMAND
   1 ?          S     0:04 init
   2 ?          SW    0:00 [keventd]
   3 ?          SW    0:00 [kapmd]
   4 ?          SWN   0:00 [ksoftirqd_CPU0]
   5 ?          SW    0:44 [kswapd]
   6 ?          SW    0:00 [bdflush]
   7 ?          SW    0:00 [kupdated]
   8 ?          SW    0:00 [mdrecoveryd]
  12 ?          SW    0:17 [kjournald]
  91 ?          SW    0:00 [khubd]
 194 ?          SW    0:00 [kjournald]
```

```
604 ?          S          0:04 syslogd -m 0
609 ?          S          0:00 klogd -x
629 ?          S          0:00 portmap
657 ?          S          0:00 rpc.statd
... lines deleted ...
```

Amazing how many programs that can run on a system even when there's only you logged in as a user, isn't it?

As you can guess, you can do everything from a shell prompt, but it does take some getting used to.

Shutting Down

When you are ready to shut down Red Hat Linux, you must do so in an orderly manner. Even if you are the sole user of a Red Hat Linux PC, several other programs are usually running in the background. Also, operating systems such as Linux try to optimize the way that they write data to the disk. Because disk access is relatively slow (compared with the time needed to access memory locations), data generally is held in memory and written to the disk in large chunks. Therefore, if you simply turn the power off, you run the risk that some files will not be updated properly.

Any user (you do not even have to be logged in) can shut down the system from the desktop or the graphical login screen. If you are at the KDE or GNOME desktop, first log out. You can do so by selecting Log Out from the main menu in either GNOME or KDE.

When you see the graphical login screen, the System menu in the login window provides menu options for rebooting or halting the system. To shut down the system, simply click System (from the bottom of the screen) and then choose Shut down the computer from the menu, as shown in Figure 4-22.

Then another dialog box asks you to confirm if you really want to halt the system. Click the Yes button. The system then shuts down in an orderly manner.

Figure 4-22:
Click
System
and then
select Shut
down the
computer
to halt your
Red Hat
Linux
system.

As the system shuts down, you see messages about processes being shut down. You may be surprised at how many processes there are, even though no one is explicitly running any programs on the system. If your system does not automatically power off on shut down, you can manually turn off the power.

Book II

Workstations and Applications

"Think of our relationship as a version of Red Hat Linux — I will not share a directory on the love-branch of your life."

Contents at a Glance

Chapter 1: Exploring GNOME

In This Chapter

- ✔ **Taking stock of GNOME**
- ✔ **Using the GNOME panel**
- ✔ **Examining the Main Menu**
- ✔ **Running applets**
- ✔ **Using the Nautilus shell**
- ✔ **Configuring GNOME**

GNOME (pronounced *Guh-NOME*) is a GUI for Red Hat Linux. GNOME is similar to Microsoft Windows, but does have its differences. Unlike Microsoft Windows, you can pick your GUI in Red Hat Linux. If you don't like GNOME, just log out and log back in with the KDE, the other GUI. Try doing that with Microsoft Windows!

The best way to get a feel for GNOME is to explore it as a user. I give you a brief guided tour of GNOME in this chapter. Then you can continue to explore and learn more as you continue to use GNOME.

By the way, GNOME is developed independent of Linux. In fact, GNOME runs on other UNIX operating systems besides Linux. Visit the GNOME home page at `www.gnome.org` to learn the latest about GNOME.

Taking Stock of GNOME

When you use GNOME, all that you see and experience is the GUI desktop. There is, however, much more to GNOME than the GUI desktop. For example, here are some key facts about GNOME:

- ✦ GNOME provides a development environment for GUI applications. It comes with a programming toolkit that programmers can use to create GUI applications.

- ✦ GNOME supports an object model — it defines the structure of software components so that they can communicate with one another.

- ✦ The GNOME GUI is modular, so it works with any window manager designed for the X Window System. For example, Red Hat Linux comes with several window managers such as Sawfish, MWM, and TWM. Each window manager has its own look and feel. GNOME works with any of these window managers.

✦ All GNOME documentation is written using the *Standard Generalized Markup Language* (SGML). This means that you can view the manual for a GNOME application on any Web browser.

✦ GNOME comes with a set of office applications called OpenOffice.org. It includes the Writer word processor, the Calc spreadsheet, the Impress presentation program, and the Draw drawing program.

Okay, I think you get the idea. GNOME is a mighty workhorse underneath that pretty exterior.

GNOME desktop

If you have both GNOME and KDE installed on your system, you can select which GUI you want just before you log in. From the graphical login window, select Session⇨GNOME to select a GNOME session and then log in as usual. Typically, GNOME is the default GUI in Red Hat Linux, so you get the GNOME desktop if you log in without selecting a specific GUI.

The initial GNOME desktop (Figure 1-1) looks like any other popular GUI such as Microsoft Windows or Apple's Mac.

Figure 1-1:
The GNOME desktop looks like other popular GUI desktops.

The desktop shows icons for your folder, the trash can for deleted files, and an icon for any CD-ROM in the CD-ROM drive. Double-clicking the Start Here icon (on the upper-left corner of the desktop) starts the Nautilus file manager.

The other major feature of the GNOME desktop is the bar along the bottom, which is called the *GNOME panel* or just *panel*. The panel is similar to the Windows taskbar. It has buttons on the left that are shortcuts to various programs and a date and time display to the right. The middle part of the panel shows buttons for applications that you may be running.

Desktop pop-up menus

Right-click on a clear area on the GNOME desktop and a menu pops up (Figure 1-2).

Book II
Chapter 1

Exploring GNOME

Figure 1-2:
Right-click
on the
GNOME
desktop for
this pop-up
menu.

You can use these menu options for a number of tasks — from opening a Nautilus window to changing the desktop background. Table 1-1 explains what each menu option does. The menu items that do not apply are grayed out. Go ahead and give some of these menu options a try.

Table 1-1	GNOME Desktop Menu Options
When You Select This Option	*It Does the Following*
New Window	Opens a new Nautilus window that shows your home directory (folder).
New Folder	Creates a new folder on the desktop and waits for you to edit the folder's name.

(continued)

Table 1-1 *(continued)*

When You Select This Option	*It Does the Following*
New Launcher	Brings up a dialog box from where you can set up a new launcher — an icon on the desktop that acts as a shortcut to an application.
New Terminal	Opens a terminal window where you can type Linux commands.
Scripts	Opens a Nautilus window showing the contents of the .gnome2/nautilus-scripts subdirectory of your home directory.
Clean up by Name	Arranges the desktop icons alphabetically by name.
Cut File	Cuts a selected file.
Copy File	Copies a selected file.
Paste Files	Pastes a file onto the desktop (the icon would appear).
Disks	Brings up a menu of removable drives and CD-ROM drives from which you can select a drive to access.
Use Default Background	Resets the desktop background to the default.
Change Desktop Background	Brings up a dialog box from which you can select a new background.

Icon pop-up menus

Right-clicking on any desktop icon causes another menu to appear. This pop-up menu has some options that are the same for any icon, but the last option depends on the icon being clicked. For example, Figure 1-3 shows the menu that appears when you right-click on the trash can icon.

Notice that the last option is Empty Trash, which is appropriate for the trash can icon. Table 1-2 gives an overview of the common menu options in the icon pop-up menus. As you'd expect, the menu items that do not apply to an icon are grayed out.

Okay. Do you see the pattern here? I bet you do. Whenever you are exploring GNOME or, for that matter any GUI, always right-click before you pick. You'll be amazed at all kinds of things you can do from the menus that pop up when you right-click!

Table 1-2	**GNOME Icon Menu Options**
When You Select This Option	*It Does the Following*
Open	Opens the file (usually in a Nautilus window).
Open With	Opens the file with a viewer or an application (you choose).

When You Select This Option	It Does the Following
Scripts	For folders, all executable items appear in a Nautilus window from which you can run the scripts.
Cut File	Cuts selected files.
Copy File	Copies selected files.
Paste Files	Pastes the files previously cut.
Duplicate	Creates a duplicate copy of the icon.
Make Link	Creates a link to that icon (a link is a shortcut).
Rename	Renames the icon (you have to enter the new name).
Move to Trash	Moves the icon to the trash.
Remove Custom Icon	Removes the custom image that you had selected for the icon.
Stretch Icon	Stretches the icon (you have to drag the mouse to indicate the new size).
Restore Icon's Original Size	Returns the icon to its earlier size.
Show Properties	Displays information about the icon.
Empty Trash	Permanently deletes items in the trash (you get a chance to say yes or no) — this item appears only when you right click the Trash icon.

**Book II
Chapter 1**

Exploring GNOME

Figure 1-3:
Right-click on an icon on the GNOME desktop for this type of pop-up menu.

Using the GNOME Panel

The GNOME panel, or simply panel, is the long rectangular window that stretches across the bottom of the GNOME desktop. Figure 1-4 shows a typical view of the panel.

Figure 1-4:
This is a typical view of the GNOME panel.

The panel is a parking place for icons. Some of them start programs when you click them. Some show status such as what programs are currently running, as well information such as the date and time.

Starting at the left, the Red Hat icon is GNOME's Main Menu button — it's like the Start button in Microsoft Windows. Then comes a few icons that start various programs. Table 1-3 briefly explains what these icons do.

By the way, if you move the mouse pointer on top of an icon, a small balloon help pops up and gives you a helpful hint about the icon.

Table 1-3	Icons on the GNOME Panel
When You Click This Icon	*It Does the Following*
	Brings up the Main Menu from which you can select applications to run.
	Runs the Mozilla Web browser.
	Starts the Ximian Evolution e-mail and calendaring software.
	Runs OpenOffice.org Writer, a Microsoft Word-like word processor.

When You Click This Icon	It Does the Following
	Runs the OpenOffice.org Impress slide presentation program that's similar to Microsoft PowerPoint.
	Runs OpenOffice.org Calc, a Microsoft Excel-like spreadsheet program.

To the right of these icons is a workspace switcher icon that shows four rectangular areas, each representing a virtual desktop. You can click one of these rectangles to switch to a different virtual desktop. This feature makes it seem like you have four separate desktops to work with. To be honest, I seem to stay stuck in one virtual screen, but it's nice to know the other virtual desktops are there, if I ever need them.

The area to the right of the pager icon displays buttons for the programs you have started so far. This area is blank if you have not yet started any programs.

There may be other icons next to the pager, but the date and time is what always appear at the rightmost edge of the panel.

Now a little bit of technical detail about these icons on the panel. The panel itself is a GNOME application and each of these icons is called *applets* (for little applications). These panel applets can do things like launch other programs or display the date and time.

If you right-click any icon or anywhere on the panel, you get a pop-up menu from which you can learn more or perform some task. For example, if you right-click the second icon from the left, the menu shown in Figure 1-5 pops up. As you can see, you can perform tasks such as remove the icon from the panel, move the icon the panel, and look at its properties from the pop-up menu. If you right-click an empty area of the panel, you can even access the menus to start any program.

Figure 1-5:
Right-click on an icon in the GNOME Panel to view its pop-up menu.

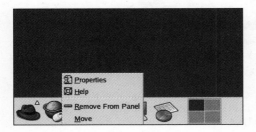

Main Menu

The Red Hat icon on the GNOME Panel is the Main Menu button for Red Hat Linux. That's where you'll find everything you want to run in Red Hat Linux. I am not going to bore you with a lengthy listing of everything in the Main Menu; rather, I provide an overview and point out some interesting items. You can do the exploring yourself.

Click the Main Menu button to bring up the initial menu. Then move the pointer to an arrow next to a menu item to bring the next menu, and so on. You can go through a menu hierarchy and make selections from the final menu. If you position the cursor on a menu item, a small balloon help may give you more information about that item. Figure 1-6 shows a typical menu hierarchy showing the selection of the Web browser. Note the balloon help that appears in the small rectangular window next to the Web Browser menu item.

You'd have guessed it anyway, but here goes. I use the notation Main Menu⇨Internet⇨Web Browser to denote the menu selection sequence that you use to select the Web browser, as shown in Figure 1-6.

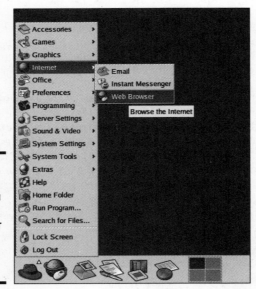

Figure 1-6:
Click the Main Menu button and mouse over to view the program menus.

In the first menu in the hierarchy, the Programs item gives you access to all the applications and utilities in Red Hat Linux. These are organized into several menu categories that you see in the next menu pane:

✦ **Accessories** menu gives you access to utilities such as a calculator, dictionary, a file archive manager, text editor, and a tool for synchronizing with a Palm or Handspring personal digital assistant (PDA).

✦ **Games** menu has a selection of, what else, games.

✦ **Graphics** menu has programs such as the GIMP (an Adobe Photoshop-like program), a digital camera interface, a scanner interface, and an Adobe Acrobat viewer.

✦ **Internet** menu is for Internet applications such as the Mozilla Web browsers, the Ximian Evolution e-mail and personal information management (PIM) software, and the Gaim AOL Instant Messenger client.

✦ **Office** menu brings up a menu of the OpenOffice.org office applications that include Write word processor, Calc spreadsheet, Draw drawing program, Impress slide presentation program, and several other applications.

✦ **Preferences** menu has utilities that you can use to configure various aspects of the GNOME desktop.

✦ **Programming** menu lets you start some software development tools such as a programmer's editor (Emacs).

✦ **Server Settings** menu lets you configure and manage the servers such as the Web server, Domain Name System (DNS) server, and Network File System (NFS) server.

✦ **Sound & Video** menu has multimedia applications such as CD player, sound recorder, and volume control.

✦ **System Settings** menu has system configuration utilities that you can use to perform many system administration tasks such as add user accounts and set the date and time.

✦ **System Tools** menu lists system management utilities such as floppy formatter, system monitor, Internet configuration wizard, system log viewer, and a terminal.

The Main Menu➪Extras menu item is an interesting menu. It gives you access to all the menus that are in the KDE desktop. This means that you can run the KDE applications from the GNOME desktop (assuming, of course, that both GNOME and KDE are installed on your system).

The other menu items on Main Menu are for some commonly performed tasks. Here's what they do:

✦ Main Menu➪Help brings up the GNOME help browser.

✦ Main Menu➪Home Folder opens your home directory in the Nautilus file manager.

✦ Main Menu⇨Run Program displays a dialog box where you can enter the name of a program to run and click Run to start that program.

✦ Main Menu⇨Search for Files runs a search tool from which you can search for files.

✦ Main Menu⇨Lock Screen starts the screen saver and locks the screen.

✦ Main Menu⇨Log Out logs you out (you get a chance to confirm whether you really want to log out or not).

Okay. That's all I am going to tell you. You'll use the Main Menu a lot as you use Red Hat Linux. Even if it seems too much initially, it'll all become very familiar as you spend more time with Red Hat Linux.

Applets

Applets are small programs that run inside the GNOME Panel. What that means is that the applets do some useful tasks and then display some interesting information on the panel. For example, the date and time display on the right edge of the panel is the output of the Clock applet. You can launch an applet from the menus that appear when you right-click on an empty area of the panel. Applets are really handy when you want to monitor some information or just want a convenient way to run some application.

One of the interesting utility applets is Weather Report. Assuming that your Red Hat Linux PC has an Internet connection, this applet downloads the weather and displays it. You can set up your geographic location in the applet.

To add the Weather Report applet to the panel, right-click on an empty area of the panel and select Add to Panel⇨Accessories⇨Weather Report. Figure 1-7 shows the menu from which you select GNOME Weather.

Figure 1-7:
You can select applets by right-clicking on the GNOME panel and selecting Add to Panel.

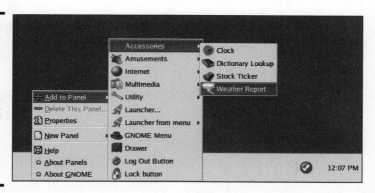

After the Weather Report applet runs, it initially appears in the middle of the empty area in the panel. Right-click the icon and select Move. Then you can position it where you want it on the panel.

To set the geographic location in the weather applet, right-click and select Preferences. The Weather Preferences menu appears, as shown in Figure 1-8.

Figure 1-8:
Set the geographic location from the Weather Preferences menu.

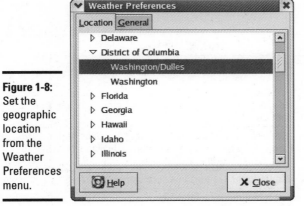

For U.S. locations, scroll down to your state and click the plus sign. Then select your location from the list and click OK. Then right-click the GNOME Weather applet icon and select Update. The applet should now display the weather for your location. Figure 1-9 shows a typical weather display by the Weather Report applet.

Figure 1-9:
The Weather Report applet displays weather information on the panel.

If you don't want the applet anymore, right-click and select Remove From Panel from the menu.

GNOME has many more applets (over 20, if you want to count) that you can try out. There is almost a cottage industry of applets. For example, refer to Figure 1-7. The first menu shows five categories of applets and a number of button applets such as the Log Out button and the Lock button. Table 1-4 gives you an overview of the applets in these categories.

If any of the applets listed in Table 1-4 strikes your fancy, go ahead and try it out. To find an applet, right-click an empty area of the panel and select Add to Panel and then look in the appropriate category menu.

Table 1-4	GNOME Applets
Applet	*What It Does*
Accessories	
Clock	Displays the current time (and date, when you mouse over the applet).
Dictionary Lookup	Displays a small text input area and a Lookup button so you can type a word and look up its meaning by using the GNOME Dictionary program.
Stock Ticker	Displays stock quotes in a scrolling stock ticker.
Weather Report	Displays weather information.
Amusements	
Fish	Displays a small fish.
Geyes	A pair of eyes that follows your mouse around the screen.
Internet	
Inbox Monitor	Checks for e-mail and lets you know when you have new mail.
Modem Lights	Provides an interface for dialing out with the modem and viewing status information about the modem when you are using it.
Multimedia	
CD Player	Provides the user interface for a CD player.
Volume Control	Provides an interface for controlling sound volume and launching an audio mixer application.
Utility	
Battery Charge Monitor	Displays the charge status of your laptop's battery (so this applet is for laptops only).
Character Palette	Shows accented versions of a character (you type the character) so that you can copy and paste it into documents.
Command Line	Adds a small command line where you can type Linux commands.
Disk Mounter	Displays a disk drive icon that you can click to access a drive.
Keyboard Layout Switcher	Displays an icon through which you can switch the keyboard layout from one country to another.

Applet	What It Does
Notification Area	Sets up an area where notification icons appear.
System Monitor	Shows you how busy your PC is.
Window List	Displays buttons for each of the running applications.
Workspace Switcher	Displays a rectangle that contains four small rectangular areas, each representing a virtual desktop that you can click to switch to that virtual desktop.
Launchers	
Launcher...	Brings up a dialog box from where you can set up a new launcher — an icon on the panel that acts as a shortcut to an application.
Launcher from menu	Provides access to the entire Main Menu hierarchy from which you can pick a program and create a launcher for that program on the panel.
Other	
Log Out Button	Adds a button to the panel that you can click to log out.
Lock Button	Adds a button to the panel that you can click to lock the screen.

Book II
Chapter 1

Exploring GNOME

Using the Nautilus Shell

The Nautilus file manager, or more accurately graphical shell, is intuitive to use — it is similar to the Windows Active Desktop. You can manage files and folders and also manage your system with Nautilus.

Viewing files and folders

When you double-click a file or a folder, Nautilus starts automatically. For example, double-click the home icon in the upper-left corner of the GNOME desktop. Nautilus runs and displays the contents of your home directory (think of a directory as a folder that can contain other files and folders). If you want to see the folders you are browsing, select View⇨Side Pane from the Nautilus menu. Figure 1-10 shows a typical user's home directory in the Nautilus file manager after you select View⇨Side Pane.

With the side pane open, the Nautilus window is vertically divided into two parts. The left window shows different views of the file system and other objects that you can browse with Nautilus. The right window shows the files and folders in the currently selected folder in the left window. Nautilus displays icons for files and folders. For image files, it shows a thumbnail of the image.

Figure 1-10:
You can
view files
and folders
in Nautilus.

The Nautilus window's title bar shows the name of the currently selected folder. The Location text box along the top of the window shows the full name of the directory in Linuxspeak — in this case, Figure 1-10 is showing the contents of the /home/ashley directory.

If you have used Windows Explorer, you can use Nautilus in a similar manner. To view the contents of another directory, do the following:

1. Right-click in the left window and click Tree in the pop-up menu.

A tab labeled Tree appears at the bottom edge of that window.

2. Click the Tree tab in the left window.

A tree menu of directories appears in that window.

3. Click the right arrow next to the folder labeled /. In the resulting tree view, locate the directory you want to browse.

For example, to look at the /etc directory, click the right arrow next to the /etc directory. This causes Nautilus to display the subdirectories in /etc and to change the right arrow to a down arrow. X11 is one of the subdirectories in /etc that you'd view in the next step.

4. To view the contents of the X11 subdirectory, click X11.

The right-hand window now shows the contents of the /etc/X11 directory, as shown in Figure 1-11.

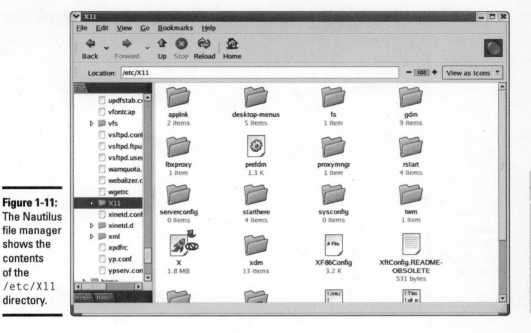

Figure 1-11:
The Nautilus
file manager
shows the
contents
of the
/etc/X11
directory.

Nautilus displays the contents of the selected directory using different types of icons. Each directory appears as a folder, with the name of the directory shown underneath the folder icon. Ordinary files, such as XF86Config, appear as a sheet of paper. The file named X is a link to an executable file. The prefdm file is another executable file.

The Nautilus window has the usual menu bar and a toolbar. Notice the button labeled View as Icons in Figure 1-11 on right side of the toolbar. That means Nautilus is displaying the directory contents using large icons. Click the button, and a drop-down list appears. Select View as List from the list; this causes Nautilus to display the contents by using smaller icons in a list format, along with detailed information such as the size of each file or directory and the time when each was last modified, as shown in Figure 1-12.

If you click any of the column headings — File Name, Size, Type, or Date Modified — along the top of the list view, Nautilus sorts the list according to that column. For example, click the Date Modified column heading. Nautilus now displays the list of files and directories sorted according to the time of their last modification. Clicking the File Name column heading sorts the files and folders alphabetically.

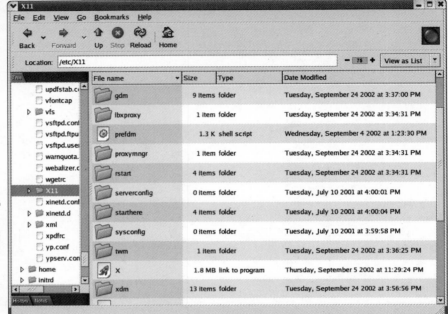

Figure 1-12:
The Nautilus file manager shows a list view of the `/etc/X11` directory.

Not only can you move around different folders using Nautilus, you can also do things like move a file from one folder to another or delete a file. I won't outline each step, because they are intuitive and similar to what you'd do in any GUI such as Windows or Mac. Here are some of the things you can do in Nautilus:

✦ To move a file to a different folder, drag and drop the file's icon on the folder where you want the file.

✦ To copy a file to a new location, select the file's icon and select Edit⇨Copy File from the Nautilus menu. You can also right-click the file's icon and select Copy File from the pop-up menu. Then move to the folder where you want to copy the file and select Edit⇨Paste Files.

✦ To delete a file or directory, right-click the icon, and select Move to Trash from the pop-up menu (you can do this only if you have permission to delete the file). To permanently delete the file, right-click the Trash icon on the desktop, and select Empty Trash from the pop-up menu. Of course, do this only if you really want to delete the file. If you need to retrieve a file from Trash, double-click the Trash icon and then drag the file's icon back to the folder where you want to save it. You can retrieve a file from Trash up until you empty the Trash.

✦ To rename a file or a directory, right-click the icon and select Rename from the pop-up menu. Then you can type the new name or edit the name.

✦ To create a new folder, right-click in an empty area of the right-hand window and select New Folder from the pop-up menu. After the new folder icon appears, you can rename it by right-clicking and selecting Rename from the pop-up menu. If you don't have permission to create a folder, that menu item is grayed out.

Configuring GNOME

To configure GNOME (as well as other parts of Red Hat Linux), simply double-click on the map and compass Start Here icon (yes, the icons are hard to identify, but you can see the label). Figure 1-13 shows the resulting Nautilus window.

**Book II
Chapter 1**

Exploring GNOME

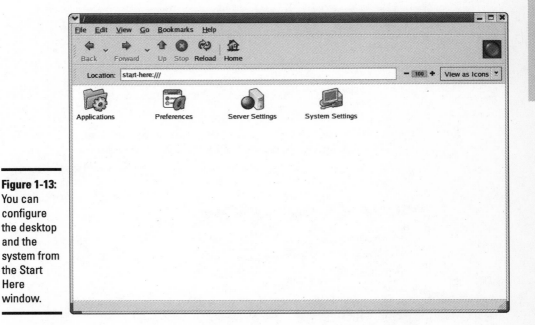

Figure 1-13:
You can configure the desktop and the system from the Start Here window.

This Nautilus window looks somewhat like the Control Panel in Microsoft Windows. As in the Windows Control Panel, you do many things from the Start Here window.

To configure the GNOME desktop from the window shown in Figure 1-13, do the following:

1. Double-click the Preferences icon.

Nautilus displays the Preferences window, as shown in Figure 1-14.

Figure 1-14:
From the
Control
Center
window you
can indicate
your
preferences.

2. **You can configure many different items from the Control Center. To select a background, double-click the Background icon.**

Nautilus launches the Background selection dialog box (Figure 1-15).

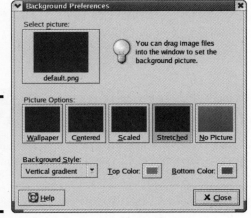

Figure 1-15:
Select a
background
color or
wallpaper
from this
dialog box.

You can now select a background color or wallpaper (an image used as background) for the desktop. To pick wallpaper, click the Select picture button on the upper-left corner of the window (refer to Figure 1-15) and go through the directories to select any JPEG file as the wallpaper. Pick one of the images in the /usr/share/wallpaper directory. Then click OK in the Background dialog box. Figure 1-16 shows the GNOME desktop after I selected the alien-night.jpg file as the background.

Figure 1-16:
The GNOME desktop looks more appealing with new wallpaper.

If you want to configure other aspects of the GNOME desktop or Red Hat Linux, simply double-click on one of the icons in Figure 1-14 and give it a try.

Chapter 2: Exploring KDE

In This Chapter

✔ **Taking stock of KDE**

✔ **Using the KDE panel**

✔ **Examining the KDE Main Menu**

✔ **Running KDE applets**

✔ **Using Konqueror**

✔ **Configuring KDE**

KDE (pronounced *kay-dee-ee*) is a GUI for Red Hat Linux. KDE is like Microsoft Windows, but different. Unlike Microsoft Windows, which is also the operating system, KDE is just a GUI that runs on the Linux operating system. From your perspective, this means that if you don't like KDE, all you have to do is log out and log back in with the other GUI — GNOME. Try doing that with Microsoft Windows!

The best way to get the feel for KDE is to explore it as a user. I give you a brief guided tour of KDE in this chapter. Then you can continue to explore and learn more as you continue to use KDE.

By the way, KDE is developed independent of Linux. In fact, KDE runs on other UNIX operating systems besides Linux. Visit the KDE home page at www.kde.org to keep up with KDE news.

Taking Stock of KDE

KDE is a complete desktop environment for users, but it is also a programming environment for developers. Here are some key facts about KDE:

✦ KDE is written in C++ and uses object-oriented development.

✦ KDE includes a GUI toolkit so that developers can write GUI applications using the toolkit.

✦ KDE supports an object model — software components that can interact with each other.

✦ KDE includes an office application suite. The office suite, KOffice, includes a spreadsheet (KSpread), a FrameMaker-like word processor (KWord), a presentation application (KPresenter), and a drawing program (KIllustrator). Red Hat has decided, however, to install and set up only the OpenOffice.org applications in KDE.

✦ KDE supports internationalization, and most KDE applications have been translated into over 25 languages.

Okay, you get the idea. KDE is not just a pretty face — there's some pretty powerful machinery underneath that polished exterior.

KDE desktop

If you have both GNOME and KDE installed on your system, you can select which GUI you want just before you log in. To select a KDE session, follow these steps:

1. **Click Session at the bottom of the graphical login screen (Figure 2-1).**

A dialog box appears with a list of sessions.

2. **Click the KDE radio button in the dialog box and then click OK to continue.**

3. **Type your user name and password to log in as usual.**

Figure 2-1: Click Session and then click KDE to get a KDE desktop.

After you type your password, the display manager prompts you if you want to make KDE the default GUI. You can click Yes or No depending on what you want. After that a screen (Figure 2-2) shows the progress as KDE starts up.

Figure 2-2: This screen shows progress as the graphical desktop gets ready for business.

The initial KDE desktop (Figure 2-3) looks like any other popular GUI such as Microsoft Windows or Apple's Mac. More importantly, if you have seen GNOME, you'd be surprised to see that the KDE desktop now looks surprisingly similar to the GNOME desktop. This is no accident — Red Hat wanted to make it easier on us poor users by adopting a similar look and feel for both GNOME and KDE.

The KDE desktop shows icons for your folder, a trash can for deleted files, and icons for floppy and CD/DVD drives and shortcuts to files or Web sites. You also find the Start Here shortcut that you can use to configure the KDE desktop and much more.

The other major feature of the KDE desktop is the bar along the bottom. It's the KDE panel, or simply, *panel*. The panel is similar to the Windows taskbar. It has buttons for various applications as well as a date and time display on the right-hand side. The middle part of the panel shows buttons for any applications that you have started (or that were automatically started).

Desktop pop-up menus

Right-click on a clear area on the KDE desktop and a menu pops up (Figure 2-4).

Figure 2-3:
The KDE
desktop
looks like
other
popular GUI
desktops.

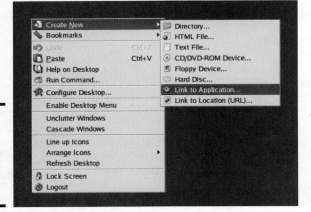

Figure 2-4:
Right-click
on the KDE
desktop for
this pop-up
menu.

From this desktop menu, you can do a whole lot of things. You can create items on the desktop — from directories and documents to icons for accessing the CD-ROM drive. You can also arrange the icons, lock the screen (if you are stepping away from the PC for a while), and log out.

Desktop menu options with a right arrow have other menus that appear when you mouse over the arrow. For example, Figure 2-4 shows the menu that appears when you mouse over Create New. You get to select what exactly you want to create on the desktop.

Table 2-1 explains what each menu option does. The menu items that do not apply are grayed out. Go ahead and click some of these menu options and see what happens. Even if you create some folders and other icons on the desktop, you can always delete them later on.

Table 2-1	KDE Desktop Menu Options
When You Select This Option	*It Does the Following*
Create New	Pops up another menu from which you can select what you want to create — a directory, various types of documents, a shortcut for a device, or a Web site.
Bookmarks	Starts the bookmark editor.
Undo	Reverses a previous move, cut, or paste operation that you performed on a desktop item.
Paste	Paste a previously cut or copied item.
Help on Desktop	Opens the KDE Help Center window.
Run Command	Prompts for a Linux command to run and then runs it (if you click Run).
Configure Desktop	Starts the KDE Control Center from where you can customize the desktop (including what menu pops up when you click each of the mouse buttons).
Enable Desktop Menu	Adds a menu bar to the desktop (the menus on the menu bar have similar options as this pop-up menu).
Unclutter Window	Makes an attempt to unclutter the windows that are currently open on the desktop by moving them apart (doesn't do much good if you have too many open windows).
Cascade Windows	Puts all currently open windows on top of one another (this does seem to clear up the clutter some).
Line up Icons	Lines up all the icons.
Arrange Icons	Brings up a menu with options for arranging icons by name, size, or type.
Refresh Desktop	Redraws the desktop (gets rid of any glitches such as a badly behaved program that leaves behind a mess on the desktop).
Lock Screen	Starts the screen saver and locks the screen (you have to type the password to get out of the screen-saver mode).
Logout	Lets you log out.

Try clicking the middle button on an empty area of the KDE desktop. If your mouse has three buttons (or a wheel) and it's set up correctly in the X Window System, you should see another menu. By default, a middle-click brings up a menu with a list of currently open windows and the desktops. You can then click an item to switch to that window or desktop. If nothing happens when you double-click, don't worry — you can still get to everything in KDE.

Icon pop-up menus

Right-clicking any desktop icon causes another menu to appear. Most items on this pop-up menu are the same no matter what icon you click. Right-clicking the Trash icon, for example, produces a somewhat different menu. Figure 2-5 shows the menu that appears when you right-click the Home folder icon.

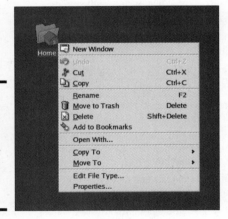

Figure 2-5: Right-click an icon on the KDE desktop for this type of pop-up menu.

Table 2-2 gives an overview of the common menu options in the icon pop-up menus. As you'd expect, any menu option that does not apply is grayed out.

I bet you see a pattern here. It's the right-click. No matter where you are in KDE, always right-click before you pick. You're bound to find something useful when you right-click!

Table 2-2	KDE Icon Menu Options
When You Select This Option	*It Does the Following*
New Window	Opens the file in a new Konqueror window (Konqueror is the file manager-cum-Web browser in KDE).
Undo	Reverses the last copy, cut, or paste operation, assuming you had just performed one of these operations.
Cut	Cuts information about the icon and displays a menu with options such as e-mail the item or edit the contents.
Copy	Copies information about the icon and displays a menu with options such as e-mail the item or edit the contents.
Rename	Renames the icon (you have to enter the new name).
Move to Trash	Prompts you if you want to move the icon to Trash and does so if you say yes.
Delete	Prompts you if you really want to delete the icon and does so if you say yes.
Add to Bookmarks	Adds information about the icon to the bookmarks.
Open With	Opens a dialog box from where you can select an application that you want to use to open the item represented by the icon.
Copy To	Displays another menu from which you can select the location where you want to copy the item represented by the icon.
Move To	Displays another menu from which you can select the location where you want to move the item represented by the icon.
Edit File Type	Brings up a file type editor where you can edit some information about the icon.
Properties	Displays the properties of the icon.

Book II
Chapter 2

Exploring KDE

Using the KDE Panel

The KDE panel is the long bar that stretches across the bottom of the KDE desktop. Figure 2-6 shows a typical view of the panel.

Figure 2-6:
This is a typical view of the KDE panel.

The panel has a lot of icons. Some of these icons start programs when you click them. Some show status information such as what programs are currently running, as well other information such as the date and time.

Starting at the left, the Red Hat icon is what KDE documentation calls the K button — it's like the Start button in Microsoft Windows. Then come quite a few icons that start various programs.

When you mouse over an icon a small balloon help pops up and gives you a helpful hint about the icon. For some icons, the balloon help hint is quite useful. For others, it may be just the name of a KDE application (all of which usually start with a K). The name may or may not tell you something useful. After you use KDE for a while, you recognize the names, so with time the balloon help becomes very useful as gentle reminders of what each icon does.

To the right of these application icons you see the desktop pager icon. That icon shows four small rectangles, numbered 1 through 4. Each rectangle represents a virtual desktop. Click a number to switch to that virtual desktop. This feature makes it seem like you have four separate desktops to work with. To be honest, I end up using only one desktop, but it's nice to know that the other virtual desktops are there, if I ever need them. On the other hand, if you are writing code and preparing the user's guide, you could use one desktop for all the coding work and a second desktop for writing the user's guide. You can, of course, switch from one desktop to the other with a single mouse click.

The panel taskbar appears to the right of the virtual desktop pager icon. The taskbar displays a button for each running application in a rectangular area on the panel. You can click on a button to alternately reduce that application to an icon or to switch to that application.

The rightmost item on the panel is a digital clock that displays the current time. If you move the mouse over the time and pause, the date appears in a small pop-up window. Right-clicking the clock brings up a menu from which you can adjust the date and time.

Now a little bit of technical detail about the panel and the icons. The panel itself is a KDE application called the Kicker. Each of the icons is either a button or an applet. The buttons start applications or perform special functions such as hiding all open windows. The applets are little applications, also called *plugins*. The applets run in the panel and do useful things like display the current date and time.

If you right-click on any icon or anywhere on the panel, you get a pop-up menu from which you can do something relevant to that icon. For example, you can typically move the icon or remove it entirely. You can also set some preferences and add more buttons and applets to the panel.

The Main Menu

The Red Hat icon on the KDE panel is what KDE documentation calls the K Menu button (now that Red Hat made both GNOME and KDE panels look about the same, I call this the *Main Menu* button). That's where you'll find everything you want to run in Red Hat Linux. I am going to provide an overview of the Main Menu and point out some interesting items. You can then do the exploring yourself.

Click the Main Menu button to bring up the first level menu. Then mouse over any menu item with an arrow to bring the next level menu and so on. You can go through a menu hierarchy and make selections from the final menu.

Book II
Chapter 2

Exploring KDE

A word about the way I refer to a menu selection. I use the notation Main Menu⇨Internet⇨Email to indicate the menu selection sequence that you'd use to select the mail reader (Figure 2-7). Similarly, I would say select Main Menu⇨Internet⇨Web Browser to start the Mozilla Web browser. You get the idea.

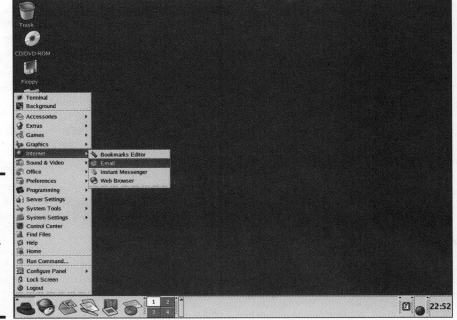

Figure 2-7:
Click the Main Menu button and mouse over items to view the menu hierarchy.

In the first menu in the hierarchy, the first dozen or so items (from the top) give you access to all the applications and utilities in Red Hat Linux. Moving the mouse over each of these brings up other menus from where you can pick the application or utility you want to run. Here are the menu categories that you see in the first menu pane of the Main Menu:

✦ **Accessories** menu has a host of utility programs such as a scientific calculator, character selector, floppy formatter, dictionary, Palm Pilot or Handspring sync, and so on.

✦ **Extras** menu provides access to many other KDE tools and utilities that have been moved out of the Main Menu to make the Main Menu consistent with what's in GNOME.

✦ **Games** menu brings up a menu of what else, games (and a whole of them at that).

✦ **Graphics** menu has programs such as the GIMP (an Adobe Photoshop like program), a digital camera interface, a scanner interface, a screen capture program, and an Adobe Acrobat viewer.

✦ **Internet** menu (refer to Figure 2-7) is for Internet applications such as the Web browser, e-mail reader, and Instant Messenger.

✦ **Sound & Video** menu has multimedia applications such as CD player, sound mixer, and volume control.

✦ **Office** menu brings up a menu of applications from the OpenOffice.org office suite (includes Writer word processor, Calc spreadsheet, Impress slide presentation program, Draw drawing program, and much more).

✦ **Preferences** menu brings up another menu from which you can configure many aspects of the system. In particular, Preferences⇨Look & Feel menu gives you the option to customize the appearance and the behavior of the KDE desktop. You can also view information about your system hardware from the Preferences⇨Information menu.

✦ **Programming** menu lets you run software development tools such as the Emacs editor and the KDE development environment (KDevelop).

✦ **Server Settings** menu provides access to tools for configuring the Web server, Domain Name System (DNS) server, and Network File System (NFS) server. You can also turn various services on or off from this menu.

✦ **System Tools** menu has a number of tools for performing tasks such as configure the Internet connection, view the system logs, register with Red Hat Network, and open a terminal window where you can type Linux commands.

✦ **System Settings** menu lists over 15 tools for setting up your Red Hat Linux system. It includes tools for managing user accounts, configuring printers, and changing your password.

✦ **Control Center** opens the KDE Control Center window from which you can configure the KDE desktop (in addition to what you can do from the Preferences menu).

✦ **Find Files** brings up the Find Files tool from which you can search for files in your system.

✦ **Help** starts the KDE Help Center — the online help in KDE.

✦ **Home** displays the contents of your home folder in a Konqueror file manager window.

✦ **Run Command** displays a dialog box where you can enter the name of a program to run.

✦ **Configure Panel** menu provides options to configure the KDE panel. In particular, Configure Panel⇨Add⇨Applet brings up a menu of *applets* — small programs that run inside the KDE panel. Applets do some useful tasks and then display some interesting information on the panel. For example, the time display on the right edge of the panel is the output of the Clock applet.

✦ **Lock Screen** starts the screen saver and locks the screen so you can leave your workstation temporarily. When you want to return to the desktop, KDE prompts you for your password (Figure 2-8).

✦ **Logout** does what it says, logs you out (of course, only after you confirm that you really want to log out).

**Book II
Chapter 2**

Exploring KDE

Figure 2-8:
KDE
prompts for
a password
before
opening a
locked
screen.

Okay. That's all I am going to tell you about KDE's Main Menu. You'll use the Main Menu a lot as you use Red Hat Linux. Even if it seems a bit much initially, you'll become very familiar with the menus as you spend more time using Red Hat Linux.

Applets

Applets are small programs that run inside the KDE panel. You can launch an applet from the menus that appear when you select Main Menu⇨Configure

Panel➪Add➪Applet. Applets are really handy when you want to monitor some information or just want a convenient way to run some applications.

TIP

To quickly get to the applet menu, right-click an empty area of the KDE panel and select Add➪Applet from the pop-up menu.

One of the interesting applets is Dictionary. This applet displays a text entry area on the panel. You can type a word and press Enter to look up its definition. Assuming that your Red Hat Linux PC has an Internet connection, this applet connects to the server dict.org and downloads a definition for the word you typed and displays it in a new window.

To add the Dictionary applet to the panel, select Main Menu➪Configure Panel➪Add➪Applet➪Dictionary. Figure 2-9 shows the menu hierarchy from which you select Dictionary.

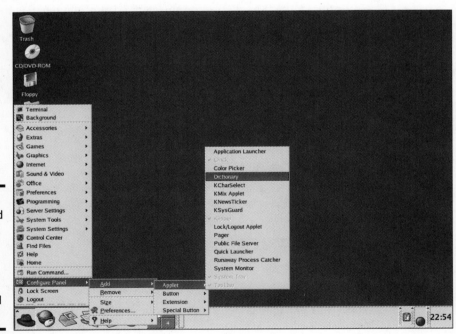

Figure 2-9:
You can add applets to the panel from Main Menu➪ Configure Panel➪Add ➪Applet.

The Dictionary applet starts and displays a text-entry area (Figure 2-10) on the panel.

Figure 2-10:
The
Dictionary
applet
displays a
text-entry
area on the
panel for
looking up
definitions
of words.

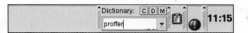

To look up a word in the dictionary, click the text entry area and type the word. Then press Enter. The Dictionary applet downloads the definition of the word from `dict.org` and displays the results in a new window. For example, Figure 2-11 displays the result of looking up the word *proffer*.

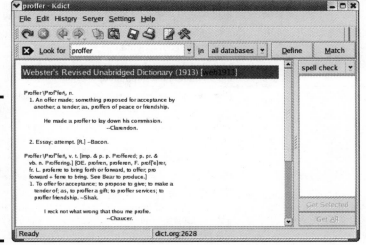

Figure 2-11:
The
Dictionary
applet
displays the
definition
of words
in a new
window.

If you don't want the applet anymore, select Main Menu⇨Configure Panel⇨ Remove⇨Applet⇨Dictionary.

KDE has many more applets (over 15, but who's counting) that you can try out. You can see their names in the Applet menu in Figure 2-9. The grayed-out items are the applets that are already running. For example, the Clock applet is already running. Clock is responsible for the time display at the right edge of the panel. Table 2-3 gives you an overview of the applets in KDE.

TIP

If any of the applets listed in Table 2-3 strikes your fancy, go ahead and try it out. To find an applet, select Main Menu⇨Configure Panel⇨Add⇨Applet and then click on the applet's name.

Table 2-3	KDE Applet Overview
Applet	*What It Does*
Application Launcher	Adds a small command line where you can type a Linux command and run it.
Clock	Displays the current time in a small digital clock and shows the date underneath.
Color Picker	Shows a dropper icon that you can use to pick a color from anywhere on the desktop (you can then copy that color value to other configuration files).
Dictionary	Adds a small text-entry area where you can type a word and look it up in a dictionary (results appear in a new window).
KCharSelect	Shows accented versions of characters that you can copy and paste it into documents.
KMix Applet	Provides an interface for controlling sound volume and launching an audio mixer application.
KNewsTicker	Displays latest news from various sources (such as www. slashdot.org and dot.kde.org) in a scrolling ticker.
KSysGuard	Gathers and plots CPU and memory usage information from one or more systems on a network (used to monitor servers).
Klipper	Provides a clipboard utility for cutting and pasting information.
Lock/Logout Applet	Provides two icons — a lock icon to lock the screen and an off switch to log out.
Pager	Shows a view of the virtual desktops that you can use to navigate around the desktops (this applet is already running when you first log in).
Public File Server	Provides a public Web server (you can configure the directory that is being shared and the rate of data transfer).
Quick Launcher	Holds small icons for many applications (clicking an icon launches that application).
Runway Process catcher	Shows a smiley face that turns angry when any process starts using too much CPU time or memory.
System Monitor	Graphically shows how much system resources (memory, CPU time) are being used.

Applet	What It Does
System Tray	Provides an area that can hold special applications such as Klipper.
Taskbar	Displays buttons for each of the running applications (this applet is already running when you first log in).

Using Konqueror

Konqueror is a file manager as well as a Web browser. It's intuitive to use — somewhat similar to the Windows Active Desktop. You can manage files and folders and also view Web pages with Konqueror.

Book II
Chapter 2

Viewing files and folders

When you double-click on a folder icon on the desktop, Konqueror starts automatically. For example, double-click the home icon in the upper-left corner of the KDE desktop. Konqueror runs and displays the contents of your home directory (think of a directory as a folder that can contain other files and folders). Figure 2-12 shows a typical user's home directory in the Konqueror.

Exploring KDE

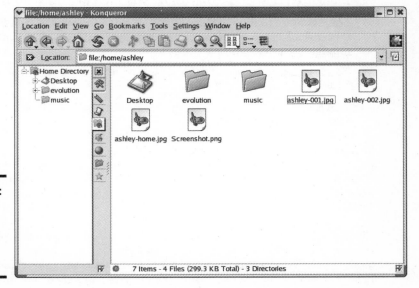

Figure 2-12:
You can
view files
and folders
in
Konqueror.

If you have used Windows Explorer, you can use Konqueror in a similar manner.

The Konqueror window is vertically divided into two parts. The left window shows a tree view of the current folder. The right window shows the files and folders in the current folder using icons. Konqueror uses different types of icons for different files.

The Konqueror window's title bar shows the name of the currently selected directory. The Location text box along the top of the window shows the full name of the directory using Konqueror terminology — in this case, Figure 2-12 is showing the contents of the /home/ashley directory.

The vertical row of buttons between the left and right windows is for selecting other things to browse. When you click one of these buttons, the left window displays a tree menu of items you can browse. For example, to browse other parts of the file system, do the following:

1. **From the vertical column of icons in the Konqueror window (refer to Figure 2-12), click the Folder icon (the one that appears just above the star-shaped icon).**

A tree menu of directories appears in the left window.

2. **In the tree view, locate the folder you want to browse.**

For example, to look at the etc folder, click the plus sign next to the etc folder. This causes Konqueror to display the other folders in etc and to change the plus sign to a minus sign.

3. **To view the contents of the X11 subdirectory, scroll down and click X11.**

The right-hand window now shows the contents of the /etc/X11 directory, as shown in Figure 2-13.

Konqueror displays the contents of a folder using different types of icons. Each directory appears as a folder, with the name of the directory shown underneath the folder icon. Ordinary files, such as XF86Config, appear as a sheet of paper. The file named X is a shortcut to an executable file. The prefdm file is another executable file.

The Konqueror window has the usual menu bar and a toolbar. You can view the files and folders in other formats as well. For example, select View⇨View Mode⇨Detailed List View. Konqueror now displays the folder's contents using smaller icons in a list format (Figure 2-14), along with detailed information such as the size of each file or directory, and the time when each was last modified.

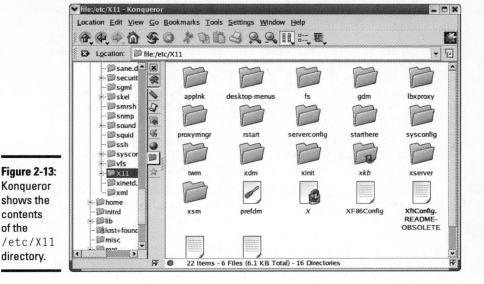

Figure 2-13:
Konqueror
shows the
contents
of the
/etc/X11
directory.

Figure 2-14:
Konqueror
shows a
detailed list
view of the
/etc/X11
directory.

If you click any of the column headings — Name, Size, File Type, or
Modified — along the top of the list view, Konqueror sorts the list
according to that column. For example, click the Modified column heading. Konqueror now displays the list of files and folders sorted according
to the time of last modification. Clicking the Name column heading sorts
the files and directories alphabetically.

Not only can you move around different folders using Konqueror, you can also do things like move a file from one folder to another or delete a file. I won't outline each step, because they are intuitive and similar to what you'd do in any GUI such as Windows or Mac. Here are some of the things you can do in Konqueror:

✦ To view a text file, click the file name and Konqueror displays the file in the right window. To get back to the detailed list of files, right-click and then select Back.

✦ To copy or move a file to a different folder, drag and drop the file's icon on the folder where you want the file. A menu pops up and asks you whether you want to copy, move, or simply link to that directory.

✦ To delete a file or directory, right-click the icon, and select Move to Trash from the pop-up menu. To permanently delete the file, right-click the Trash can icon on the desktop, and select Empty Trash from the pop-up menu. Of course, do this only if you really want to delete the file. If you want to recover a file from the trash, double click the Trash icon on the desktop and from that window drag and drop the file icon into the folder where you want to save the file. When asked whether you want to copy or move, select move. You can recover files from the trash up until the moment you empty the trash.

✦ To rename a file or a directory, right-click the icon, and select Rename from the pop-up menu. Then you can type the new name or edit the old name.

✦ To create a new folder, right-click in an empty area of the right-hand window and select Create New➪Directory from the pop-up menu. Then type the name of the new directory and click OK. If you don't have permission to create a directory, you'll get an error message.

Viewing Web pages

Konqueror is much more than a file manager. With it, you can view a Web page as easily as viewing a folder. Just type a Web address in the Location box and see what happens. For example, Figure 2-15 shows the Konqueror window after I typed www.irs.gov in the Location text box on the toolbar and pressed Enter.

Konqueror displays the Web site on the right-hand window. The left window still shows whatever it was displaying earlier.

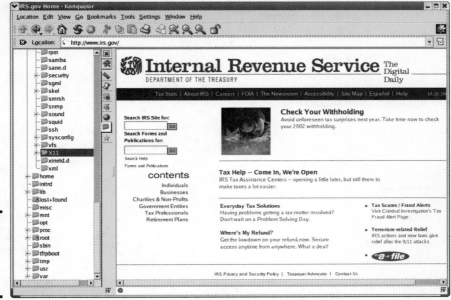

Figure 2-15:
Konqueror
can browse
the Web
as well.

Configuring KDE

There are many ways to configure the KDE desktop, but for one-stop-shopping KDE configuration I use the KDE Control Center. Select Main Menu⇨Control Center. The Control Center starts and shows summary information about the Red Hat Linux system in a window (Figure 2-16).

The Control Center window is vertically divided into two parts. The narrower left window shows a tree menu with 10 or so top-level categories of customization that you can perform. The wider right window is where you enter information.

To customize a specific category such as Look & Feel, click the plus sign (+) to the left of the label. The plus sign changes to a minus sign (–) and you get a list of all the items that you can specify. For example, to change the KDE desktop's background from the window shown in Figure 2-16, do the following:

1. **Click the plus sign next to Look & Feel. From the new items that appear, double-click Background. The Control Center displays the choices for desktop background on the right window. You can select a background color or wallpaper (an image used as background) for the desktop. To select wallpaper, click the Wallpaper tab (Figure 2-17).**

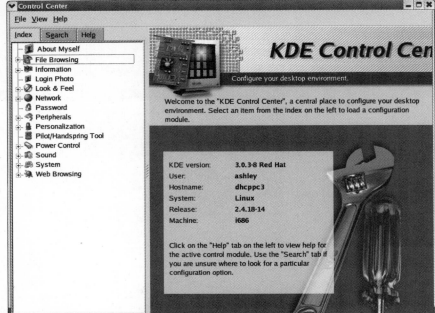

Figure 2-16:
You can
configure
the KDE
desktop
from the
KDE Control
Center.

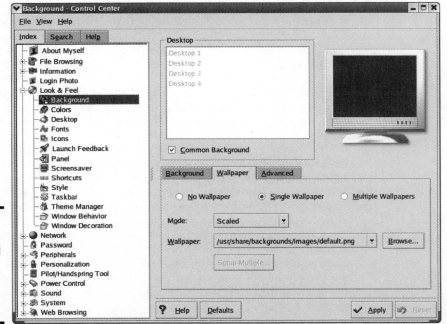

Figure 2-17:
Select a
background
color or
wallpaper
from this
window.

2. Click the Browse button next to the name of the current Wallpaper.

The Control Center brings up the Select Wallpaper dialog box (Figure 2-18).

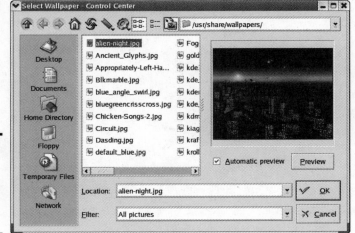

Figure 2-18:
Select a
wallpaper
image from
this dialog
box.

3. Pick one of the JPEG image files from the list of files. Then click OK. When you get back to the Control Center window, click Apply to put the new change into effect.

Figure 2-19 shows the KDE desktop after I selected the `alien-night.jpg` file as the wallpaper.

If you want to configure other aspects of the KDE desktop, simply select other items in the Look & Feel list in Figure 2-17 and give it a try. Click Apply to try out a new configuration, but if you don't like the result, click Reset to revert to the old settings.

Figure 2-19:
The KDE
desktop
looks
positively
sci-fi with
the right
wallpaper.

Chapter 3: Learning the Shell

In This Chapter

✓ Opening terminal windows and virtual consoles

✓ Using the Bash shell

✓ Learning some Linux commands

✓ Writing shell scripts

Sometimes things just don't work. What would you do if the GUI desktop stops responding to your mouse clicks? What if the GUI won't start at all? You can still tell your Red Hat Linux system what to do, but you have to do it by typing commands in a text screen. In these situations, you'd be working with the shell — the Linux command interpreter. I introduce the Bash shell — the default shell in Red Hat Linux — in this chapter.

After you learn to work with the shell, you may even begin to like the simplicity and power of the Linux commands. And then, even if you are a GUI aficionado, someday soon you may find yourself firing up a terminal window and making the system sing and dance with two- or three-letter commands strung together by strange punctuation characters. Hey, I can dream, can't I?

Opening Terminal Windows and Virtual Consoles

First things first. If you are working in GNOME or KDE where do you type commands for the shell? Good question.

The easiest way to get to the shell is to open a *terminal* (also called *console*) window. Both GNOME and KDE panels have an icon to open a terminal window. The icon looks like a monitor. Click that icon to get a terminal window. Now you can type commands to your heart's content.

If for some reason the GUI seems to be hung (you click and type but nothing happens), you can turn to the virtual consoles. The *physical console* is the monitor and keyboard combination. The idea of virtual consoles is to give the appearance of several consoles even though you have only one physical console.

To get to the first virtual console from the GNOME or KDE desktop, press Ctrl+Alt+F1. Press Ctrl+Alt+F2 for the second virtual console, and so on. Each of these virtual consoles is a text screen where you can log in and type Linux commands to perform various tasks. When you're done, type **exit** to log out.

You can use up to six virtual consoles. The seventh one is used for the GUI desktop. To get back to the GUI desktop, press Ctrl+Alt+F7.

Using the Bash Shell

If you have used MS-DOS, you may be familiar with COMMAND.COM, the DOS command interpreter. That program displays the infamous C:\> prompt. In Windows, you can see this prompt if you open a command window.

Red Hat Linux comes with a command interpreter that resembles COMMAND.COM in DOS, but can do a whole lot more. The Red Hat Linux command interpreter is called *shell*.

The default shell in Red Hat Linux is Bash. When you open a terminal window or log in at a text console, the Bash shell is what prompts you for commands and, when you type a command, the shell executes that command.

In addition to the standard Linux commands, Bash can execute any computer program. So you can type the name of an application (the name is usually more cryptic than what you see in GNOME or KDE menus) at the shell prompt, and the shell starts that application.

Learning the syntax of shell commands

Because a shell interprets what you type, it is important to know how the shell processes the text that you enter. All shell commands have this general format that starts with a command followed by options (some commands have no options):

```
command option1 option2 ... optionN
```

A single line of command commonly is referred to as a *command line*. On a command line, you enter a command followed by zero or more options (or arguments). These strings of options are called *command-line options* (or command-line arguments).

The shell uses a blank space or tab to tell the command and options apart. Naturally, you should help it out by using a space or a tab to separate the command from the options and the options from one another.

You can have an option that contains spaces. All you have to do is put that option inside quotation marks. For example, to search for my name in the password file, I enter the following grep command (grep is used for searching for text in files):

```
grep "Naba Barkakati" /etc/passwd
```

When grep prints the line with my name, it looks like this:

```
naba:x:500:500:Naba Barkakati:/home/naba:/bin/bash
```

If you created a user account with your user name, go ahead and type the grep command with your user name as an argument.

In the output from the grep command, you can see the name of the shell (/bin/bash) following the last colon (:).

The number of command-line options and their format, of course, depends on the actual command. Typically, these options look like -X , where X is a single character. For example, the ls command lists the contents of a directory. You can use the -l option to see more details, like this:

```
[ashley@dhcppc4 ashley]$ ls -l
total 8
drwxrwxr-x   2 ashley    ashley    4096 Jun 29 13:35 Directory
drwx------   7 ashley    ashley    4096 Jun 29 11:44 Mail
```

The [ashley@dhcppc4 ashley]$ part is the shell prompt for the user named ashley. On your system, the prompt depends on your user name. When showing examples, I omit the prompt.

If a command is too long to fit on a single line, you can press the backslash (\) key, followed by Enter. Then, continue typing the command on the next line. For example, type the following command (press Enter after each line):

```
cat \
/etc/passwd
```

The cat command then displays the contents of the /etc/passwd file.

You can concatenate several shorter commands on a single line. Just separate the commands by semicolons (;). For example, the following command

```
cd; ls -l; pwd
```

changes the current directory to your home directory, lists the contents of that directory, and then shows the name of that directory.

Combining shell commands

You can combine simple shell commands to create a more sophisticated command. Suppose you want to find out whether a device file named sbpcd resides in your system's /dev directory because some documentation tells you that for a Sound Blaster Pro CD-ROM drive, you need that device file. You can use the command ls /dev to get a directory listing of the /dev directory and browse through it to see whether that listing contains sbpcd. Unfortunately, the /dev directory has a great many entries, so you find it hard to find any item that has sbpcd in its name. You can, however, combine the ls command with grep and come up with a command line that does exactly what you want. Here's that command line:

```
ls /dev | grep sbpcd
```

The shell sends the output of the ls command (the directory listing) to the grep command, which searches for the string sbpcd. That vertical bar (|) is known as a *pipe* because it acts as a conduit (think of a water pipe) between the two programs — the output of the first command is fed into the input of the second one.

Controlling command input and output

Most Linux commands have a common feature — they always read from the standard input (usually, the keyboard) and write to the standard output (usually, the screen). Error messages are sent to the standard error (usually, the screen also). These three devices often are referred to as *stdin, stdout,* and *stderr.*

You can make a command get its input from a file and have the command send its output to a file. Just so you know, the highfalutin' term for this feature is input and output redirection, or *I/O redirection.*

Getting command input from a file

If you want a command to read from a file, you can redirect the standard input to come from that file instead of the keyboard. For example, type the following command:

```
sort < /etc/passwd
```

This command displays a sorted list of the lines in the /etc/passwd file. In this case, the less than sign (<) redirects stdin so the sort command reads its input from the /etc/passwd file.

Saving command output in a file

To save the output of a command in a file, redirect the standard output to a file. For example, type **cd** to change to your home directory and then type the following command:

```
grep typedef /usr/include/* > typedef.out
```

This command searches through all files in the /usr/include directory for the occurrence of the text typedef and then saves the output in a file called typedef.out. The greater-than sign (>) redirects stdout to a file.

This command also illustrates another feature of Bash. When you use an asterisk (*), Bash replaces the asterisk with a list of all the filenames in the specified directory. Thus, /usr/include/* means all the files in the /usr/include directory.

**Book II
Chapter 3**

Learning the Shell

Saving error messages in a file

Sometimes you type a command and it generates a whole lot of error messages that scroll by so fast you can't tell what's going on. One way to see all the error messages is to save the error messages in a file. You can do that by redirecting stderr to a file.

For example, type the following command:

```
find / -name isapnp -print 2> finderr
```

This command looks throughout the file system for files named isapnp, but saves all the error messages in the file named finderr. The number 2 followed by the greater-than sign (2>) redirects stderr to a file.

If you want to simply discard the error messages instead of saving them in a file, use /dev/null as the filename, like this:

```
find / -name isapnp -print 2> /dev/null
```

That /dev/null is a special file, often called the *bit bucket* and sometimes glorified as the *Great Bit Bucket in the Sky,* that simply discards whatever it receives. So now you know what they mean when you hear phrases like, "Your mail probably ended up in the bit bucket."

Typing less with automatic command completion

Many commands take a filename as an argument. To view the contents of the text file named /etc/modules.conf, for example, type the following command:

```
cat /etc/modules.conf
```

That `cat` command displays the file `/etc/modules.conf`. For any command that takes a filename as an argument, you can use a Bash feature to avoid having to type the whole filename. All you have to type is the bare minimum — just the first few characters — to uniquely identify the file in its directory.

To see an example, type **cat /etc/mod** but don't press Enter; press Tab instead. Bash automatically completes the filename, so that the command becomes `cat /etc/modules.conf`. Now press Enter to run the command.

Whenever you type a filename, press Tab after the first few characters of the filename. Bash probably can complete the filename so that you don't have to type the entire name. If you don't enter enough characters to uniquely identify the file, Bash beeps. Just type a few more characters and press Tab again.

Going wild with asterisks and question marks

There's another way to avoid typing long filenames. (After all, making less work for users is the idea of computers, isn't it?)

This particular trick involves using the asterisk (*) and question mark (?) and a few more tricks. These special characters are called *wildcards* because they match zero or more characters in a line of text.

If you know MS-DOS, you may have used commands such as `COPY *.* A:` to copy all files from the current directory to the A drive. Bash accepts similar wildcards in filenames. As you'd expect, Bash provides many more wildcard options than the MS-DOS command interpreter does.

You can use three types of wildcards in Bash:

✦ The **asterisk (*)** character matches zero or more characters in a filename. That means * denotes all files in a directory.

✦ The **question mark (?)** matches any single character. So if you type `test?` that matches any five-character text that begins with `test`.

✦ A **set of characters in brackets** matches any single character from that set. The string `[aB]*`, for example, matches any filename that starts with `a` or `B`.

Wildcards are handy when you want to do something to a whole lot of files. For example, to copy all the files from the `/mnt/cdrom` directory to the current directory, type the following:

```
cp /mnt/cdrom/*
```

Bash replaces the wildcard character * with the names of all the files in the /mnt/cdrom directory. The period at the end of the command represents the current directory.

You can use the asterisk with other parts of a filename to select a more specific group of files. Suppose that you want to use the grep command to search for the text typedef struct in all files of the /usr/include directory that meet the following criteria:

✦ The filename starts with s.

✦ The filename ends with .h.

**Book II
Chapter 3**

Learning the Shell

The wildcard specification s*.h denotes all filenames that meet these criteria. Thus, you can perform the search with the following command:

```
grep "typedef struct" /usr/include/s*.h
```

The string contains a space that you want the grep command to find, so you have to enclose that string in quotation marks. That way Bash does not try to interpret each word in that text as a separate command-line argument.

The question mark (?) matches a single character. Suppose that you have four files — image1.pcx, image2.pcx, image3.pcx, and image4.pcx — in the current directory. To copy these files to the /mnt/floppy directory, use the following command:

```
cp image?.pcx /mnt/floppy
```

Bash replaces the single question mark with any single character, and copies the four files to /mnt.

The third wildcard format — [...] — matches a single character from a specific set of characters enclosed in square brackets. You may want to combine this format with other wildcards to narrow down the matching filenames to a smaller set. To see a list of all filenames in the /etc/X11/xdm directory that start with x or X, type the following command:

```
ls /etc/X11/xdm/[xX]*
```

Repeating previously typed commands

To make it easy for you to repeat long commands, Bash stores up to 500 old commands. Bash keeps a command history (a list of old commands). To see the command history, type **history**. Bash displays a numbered list of the old commands, including those that you entered during previous logins.

If the command list is too long, you can limit the number of old commands you want to see. To see the last 10 commands only, type this command:

```
history 10
```

To repeat a command from the list that the `history` command shows, simply type an exclamation point (!), followed by that command's number. To repeat command number 3, type **!3**.

There is a way to repeat an old command without knowing its command number. Suppose you typed `more /usr/lib/X11/xdm/xdm-config` a few minutes ago, and now you want to look at that file again. To repeat the previous `more` command, type the following:

```
!more
```

Often, you may want to repeat the last command that you just typed, perhaps with a slight change. For example, you may have displayed the contents of the directory by using the `ls -l` command. To repeat that command, type two exclamation points as follows:

```
!!
```

Sometimes, you may want to repeat the previous command but add extra arguments to it. Suppose that `ls -l` shows too many files. Simply repeat that command, but pipe the output through the `more` command as follows:

```
!! | more
```

Bash replaces the two exclamation points with the previous command and then appends | `more` to that command.

Here's the easiest way to recall previous commands. Just press the up arrow key and Bash keeps going backward through the history of commands you previously typed. To move forward in the command history, press the down arrow key.

Learning Linux Commands

You type Linux commands at the shell prompt. By Linux commands I mean some of the commands that the Bash shell understands as well as the command-line utilities that come with Linux. In this section I'll introduce you to a few major categories of Linux commands.

I can't possibly cover all the Linux commands in this chapter, but I want to give you a feel for the breadth of the commands by showing you a list of the common Linux commands. Table 3-1 lists the common Linux commands organized by categories. Before you start learning any Linux commands, you should browse through these commands by category.

Table 3-1	Overview of Common Linux Commands
Command Name	*Action*
Getting Online Help	
apropos	Finds online manual pages for a specified keyword.
info	Displays online help information about a specified command.
man	Displays online help information.
whatis	Similar to apropos, but searches for complete words only.
Making Commands Easier	
alias	Defines an abbreviation for a long command.
type	Shows the type and location of a command.
unalias	Deletes an abbreviation defined using alias.
Managing Files and Directories	
cd	Changes the current directory.
chmod	Changes file permissions.
chown	Changes file owner and group.
cp	Copies files.
ln	Creates symbolic links to files and directories.
ls	Displays the contents of a directory.
mkdir	Creates a directory.
mv	Renames a file as well as moves a file from one directory to another.
rm	Deletes files.
rmdir	Deletes directories.
pwd	Displays the current directory.
touch	Updates a file's time stamp.
Finding Files	
find	Finds files based on specified criteria such as name, size, and so on.
locate	Finds files using a periodically updated database.
whereis	Finds files based in the typical directories where executable (also known as *binary*) files are located.
which	Finds files in the directories listed in the PATH environment variable.

(continued)

Book II
Chapter 3

Learning the Shell

Table 3-1 *(continued)*

Command Name	Action
Processing Files	
cat	Displays a file on standard output (can be used to concatenate several files into one big file).
cut	Extracts specified sections from each line of text in a file.
dd	Copies blocks of data from one file to another (used to copy data from devices).
diff	Compares two text files and finds any differences.
expand	Converts all tabs into spaces.
file	Displays the type of data in a file.
fold	Wraps each line of text to fit a specified width.
grep	Searches for regular expressions within a text file.
less	Displays a text file, one page at a time (can go backward also).
lpr	Prints files.
more	Displays a text file, one page at a time (goes forward only).
nl	Numbers all nonblank lines in a text file and prints the lines to standard output.
paste	Concatenates corresponding lines from several files.
patch	Updates a text file using the differences between the original and revised copy of the file.
sed	Copies a file to standard output while applying specified editing commands.
sort	Sorts lines in a text file.
split	Breaks up a file into several smaller files with specified size.
tac	Reverses a file (last line first and so on).
tail	Displays the last few lines of a file.
tr	Substitutes one group of characters for another throughout a file.
uniq	Eliminates duplicate lines from a text file.
wc	Counts the number of lines, words, and characters in a text file.
zcat	Displays a compressed file (after decompressing).
zless	Displays a compressed file one page at a time (can go backward also).
zmore	Displays a compressed file one page at a time.
Archiving and Compressing Files	
compress	Compresses files.
cpio	Copies files to and from an archive.

Command Name	Action
gunzip	Decompresses files compressed with GNU ZIP (gzip).
gzip	Compresses files using GNU ZIP.
tar	Creates an archive of files in one or more directories (originally meant for archiving on tape).
uncompress	Decompresses files compressed with compress.
Managing Processes	
bg	Runs an interrupted process in the background.
fg	Runs a process in the foreground.
free	Displays the amount of free and used memory in the system.
halt	Shuts down Linux and halts the computer.
kill	Sends a signal to a process (usually used to terminate a process).
ldd	Displays the shared libraries needed to run a program.
nice	Runs a process with lower priority (referred to as nice mode).
ps	Displays a list of currently running processes.
printenv	Displays the current environment variables.
pstree	Similar to ps, but shows parent-child relationships clearly.
reboot	Stops Linux and then restarts the computer.
shutdown	Shuts down Linux.
top	Displays a list of most processor- and memory-intensive processes.
uname	Displays information about the system and the Linux kernel.
Managing Users	
chsh	Changes the shell (command interpreter).
groups	Prints the list of groups that includes a specified user.
id	Displays the user and group ID for a specified user name.
passwd	Changes the password.
su	Starts a new shell as another user or root (when invoked without any argument).
Managing the File System	
df	Summarizes free and available space in all mounted storage devices.
du	Displays disk usage information.
fdformat	Formats a diskette.
fdisk	Partitions a hard disk.
fsck	Checks and repairs a file system.

(continued)

**Book II
Chapter 3**

Learning the Shell

Table 3-1 *(continued)*

Command Name	Action
mkfs	Creates a new file system.
mknod	Creates a device file.
mkswap	Creates a swap space for Linux in a file or a disk partition.
mount	Mounts a device (for example, the CD-ROM) on a directory in the file system.
swapoff	Deactivates a swap space.
swapon	Activates a swap space.
sync	Writes buffered (saved in memory) data to files.
tty	Displays the device name for the current terminal.
umount	Unmounts a device from the file system.
Working with Date and Time	
cal	Displays a calendar for a specified month or year.
date	Shows the current date and time or sets a new date and time.

Becoming root (super user)

When you want to do anything privileged like administering your system, you have to become root. Normally you log in as a regular user with your normal user name. When you need the root privileges, though, use the following command to become root:

```
su -
```

That's su followed by the minus sign (or hyphen). The shell then prompts you for the root password. Type the password and press Enter.

After you're done with whatever you wanted to do as root (and you have the privilege to do anything as root), type **exit** to return to your normal self.

Managing processes

Every time the shell executes a command that you type, it starts a process. The shell itself is a process. So are any scripts or programs that the shell runs.

Use the ps ax command to see a list of processes. When you type **ps ax**, Bash shows you the current set of processes. Here are a few lines of output from the ps ax command (I also included the −cols 132 option to ensure that you can see each command in its entirety):

```
ps ax --cols 132
   PID TTY      STAT    TIME COMMAND
     1 ?        S       0:04 init
     2 ?        SW      0:00 [keventd]
     3 ?        SW      0:00 [kapmd]
     4 ?        SWN     0:00 [ksoftirqd_CPU0]
     5 ?        SW      0:30 [kswapd]
... lines deleted ...
28550 pts/0    R       0:00 ps ax --cols 132
```

In this listing, the first column has the heading `PID` and shows a number for each process. PID stands for *process ID* (identification), which is a sequential number assigned by the Linux kernel. If you look through the output of the `ps ax` command, you see that the `init` command is the first process and that it has a PID or process number of 1. That's why `init` is referred to as the "mother of all processes."

The `COMMAND` column shows the command that created each process.

The process ID or process number is useful when you have to forcibly stop an errant process. Look at the output of the `ps ax` command and note the `PID` of the offending process. Then, use the `kill` command with that process number. To stop process number 28550, for example, type the following command:

```
kill -9 28550
```

Working with date and time

You can use the date command to display the current date and time or set a new date and time. Type the `date` command at the shell prompt and you get a result similar to the following:

```
date
Sat Sep 28 12:08:57 EDT 2002
```

As you can see, the `date` command alone displays the current date and time.

To set the date, log in as `root` and then type **date** followed by the date and time in the `MMDDhhmmYYYY` format where each character is a digit. For example, to set the date and time to December 31, 2002 9:30 PM, you would type:

```
date 123121302002
```

The `MMDDhhmmYYYY` date and time format has the following meaning:

+ `MM` is a two-digit number for the month (01 through 12).
+ `DD` is a two-digit number for the day of the month (01 through 31).

✦ hh is a two-digit hour in 24-hour format (00 is midnight and 23 is 11:00 PM).

✦ mm is a two-digit number for the minutes (00 through 59).

✦ YYYY is the 4-digit year (such as 2002) .

The other interesting date-related command is cal. If you type cal without any options, it prints a calendar for the current month. If you type cal followed by a number, cal treats the number as the year and prints the calendar for that year. To view the calendar for a specific month in a specific year, provide the month number (1 = January, 2 = February, and so on) followed by the year. Thus, to view the calendar for January 2003 type the following and you'll get the calendar for that month:

```
cal 1 2003
      January 2003
Su Mo Tu We Th Fr Sa
             1  2  3  4
 5  6  7  8  9 10 11
12 13 14 15 16 17 18
19 20 21 22 23 24 25
26 27 28 29 30 31
```

Processing files

You can search through a text file with grep and view a text file, a screen at a time, with more. For example, to search for my user name in the /etc/passwd file, I use

```
grep naba /etc/passwd
```

To view the /etc/inittab file a screenful at a time, I type

```
more /etc/inittab
```

As each screen pauses, I press the space bar to go to the next page.

There are many more Linux commands that work on files — mostly on text files, but some commands also work on any file. I describe few of the file processing tools.

Counting words and lines in a text file

I am always curious about the size of files. For text files, the number of characters is basically the size of the file in bytes (because each character takes a byte of storage). What about words and the number of lines, though?

The Linux wc command comes to the rescue. The wc command displays the total number of characters, words, and lines in a text file. For example, try the following command:

```
wc /etc/inittab
     57      244     1756 /etc/inittab
```

The second line shows the output. In this case, `wc` reports that there are 57 lines, 244 words, and 1756 characters in the `/etc/inittab` file. If you simply want to see the number of lines in a file, use the `-l` option, like this:

```
wc -l /etc/inittab
     57 /etc/inittab
```

As you can see, in this case `wc` simply displays the line count.

If you don't specify a filename, the `wc` command expects input from the standard input. You can use the pipe feature of the shell to feed the output of another command to `wc`. This can be handy sometimes.

Suppose you want a rough count of the processes running on your system. You can get a list of all processes with the `ps ax` command, but instead of manually counting the lines, just pipe the output of `ps` to `wc` and you can get a rough count, like this:

```
ps ax | wc -l
     76
```

That means the `ps` command produced 76 lines of output. Because the first line simply shows the headings for the tabular columns, you can estimate that there are about 75 processes running on your system (of course, this count probably includes the processes used to run the `ps` and `wc` commands as well, but who's counting).

Sorting text files

You can sort the lines in a text file using the `sort` command. To see how the `sort` command works, first type **more /etc/passwd** to see the current contents of the `/etc/passwd` file. Now type **sort /etc/passwd** to see the lines sorted alphabetically. If you want to sort a file and save the sorted version in another file, you have to use the Bash shell's output redirection feature like this:

```
sort /etc/passwd > ~/sorted.text
```

This command sorts the lines in the `/etc/passwd` file and saves the output in a file named `sorted.text` in your home directory.

Substituting or deleting characters from a file

Another interesting command is `tr` — it substitutes one group of characters for another (or deletes a selected character) throughout a file. Suppose that

Book II
Chapter 3

Learning the Shell

you occasionally have to use MS-DOS text files on your Red Hat Linux system. Although you may expect to use a text file on any system without any problems, there is one catch: DOS uses a carriage return followed by a line feed to mark the end of each line, whereas Red Hat Linux uses only a line feed.

On your Red Hat Linux system, you can get rid of the extra carriage returns in the DOS text file by using the `tr` command with the `-d` option. Essentially, to convert the DOS text file `filename.dos` to a Linux text file named `filename.linux`, type the following:

```
tr -d '\015' < filename.dos > filename.linux
```

In this command, `'\015'` denotes the code for the carriage-return character in octal notation.

Spilling a file into several smaller files

The `split` command is handy for those times when you want to copy a file to a floppy disk, but the file is too large to fit on a single floppy. You can then use the split command to break up the file into smaller files, each of which can fit on a floppy.

By default, `split` puts 1,000 lines into each file. The files are named by groups of letters like `aa`, `ab`, `ac`, and so on. You can specify a prefix for the filenames. For example, to split a large file called `hugefile.tar` into smaller files that fit into several high-density 3.5-inch floppy disks, use `split` as follows:

```
split -b 1440k hugefile.tar part.
```

This command splits the `hugefile.tar` file into 1440K chunks so each can fit into a floppy disk. The command creates files named `part.aa`, `part.ab`, `part.ac` and so on.

To combine the split files back into a single file, use the `cat` command as follows:

```
cat part.?? > hugefile.tar
```

Writing Shell Scripts

If you had ever used MS-DOS, you may remember MS-DOS batch files. These are text files with MS-DOS commands. Similarly, shell scripts are also text files with a bunch of shell commands.

If you are not a programmer, you may feel apprehensive about programming. But shell programming can be as simple as storing a few commands in a file. Right now you won't be able to write complex shell scripts, but you can certainly try out a simple shell script.

To try your hand at a little shell programming, type the following text at the shell prompt exactly as shown and then press Ctrl+D when done:

```
cd
cat > simple
#!/bin/sh
echo "This script's name is: $0"
echo Argument 1: $1
echo Argument 2: $2
```

The `cd` command changes the current directory to your home directory. Then the `cat` command displays whatever you type; in this case I am sending the output to a file named `simple`. After you press Ctrl+D the `cat` command ends and you should again see the shell prompt. What you have done is created a file named `simple` that contains the following shell script:

```
#!/bin/sh
echo "This script's name is: $0"
echo Argument 1: $1
echo Argument 2: $2
```

The first line causes Linux to run the Bash shell program (its name is `/bin/bash`). The shell then reads the rest of the lines in the script.

Just as most Linux commands accept command-line options, a Bash script also accepts command-line options. Inside the script, you can refer to the options as `$1`, `$2`, and so on. The special name `$0` refers to the name of the script itself.

To run this shell script, you have to first make the file executable with the following command:

```
chmod +x simple
```

Now run the script with the following command:

```
./simple one two
This script's name is: ./simple
Argument 1: one
Argument 2: two
```

The ./ prefix to the script's name indicates that the `simple` file is in the current directory.

This script simply prints the script's name and the first two command-line options that the user types after the script's name.

Next, try running the script with a few arguments, as follows:

```
./simple "This is one argument" second-argument third
This script's name is: ./simple
Argument 1: This is one argument
Argument 2: second-argument
```

The shell treats the entire string within double quotation marks as a single argument. Otherwise, the shell uses spaces as separators between arguments on the command line.

Most useful shell scripts are more complicated than this simple script, but this simple exercise gives you a rough idea of how to write shell scripts.

Place Linux commands in a file and use the `chmod` command to make the file executable. Voilá! You have created a shell script!

Chapter 4: Navigating the Red Hat Linux File System

In This Chapter

✔ Understanding the Red Hat Linux file system

✔ Navigating the file system with Linux commands

✔ Understanding file permissions

✔ Manipulating files and directories with Linux commands

To use files and directories well, you need to understand the concept of a hierarchical file system. Even if you use the GUI file managers to access files and folders (folders are another name for directories), you can benefit from a lay of the land of the file system.

In this chapter I introduce you to the Linux file system. Then you learn to work with files and directories with several Linux commands.

Understanding the Red Hat Linux File System

Like any other operating system, Red Hat Linux organizes information in files and directories. Directories, in turn, hold the files. A *directory* is a special file that can contain other files and directories. Because a directory can contain other directories, this method of organizing files gives rise to a hierarchical structure. This hierarchical organization of files is called the *file system*.

The Red Hat Linux file system gives you a unified view of all storage in your PC. The file system has a single root directory, indicated by a forward slash (/). Then there is a hierarchy of files and directories. Parts of the file system can reside in different physical media, such as hard disk, floppy disk, and CD-ROM. Figure 4-1 illustrates the concept of the Red Hat Linux file system (which is the same in any Linux system) and how it spans multiple physical devices.

If you are familiar with MS-DOS or Windows, you find something missing in the Red Hat Linux file system. There are no drive letters in Red Hat Linux. All disk drives and CD-ROM drives are part of a single file system.

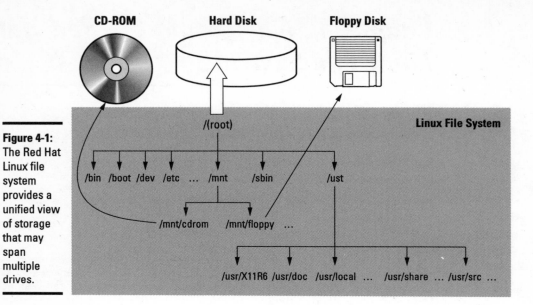

Figure 4-1:
The Red Hat Linux file system provides a unified view of storage that may span multiple drives.

In Red Hat Linux, you can have long filenames (up to 256 characters), and filenames are case-sensitive. Often, these filenames have multiple extensions, such as `sample.tar.Z`. Some UNIX filenames include the following: `index.html`, `Makefile`, `kernel-smp-2.4.18-3.i686.rpm`, `.bash_profile`, and `httpd_src.tar.gz`.

To locate a file, you need more than just the file's name. You also need information about the directory hierarchy. The full hierarchy of directories leading to the file is called the *pathname*. Just like the name implies, it's the path to the file through the maze of the file system. Figure 4-2 shows a typical pathname for a file in Red Hat Linux.

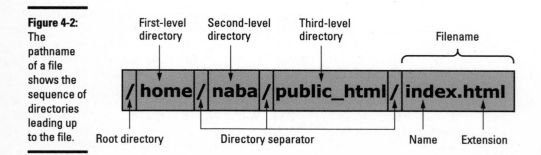

Figure 4-2:
The pathname of a file shows the sequence of directories leading up to the file.

As Figure 4-2 shows, the pathname has the following parts:

✦ The root directory, indicated by a forward slash (/) character

✦ The directory hierarchy with each directory name separated from the previous one by a forward slash (/) character. A / appears after the last directory name.

✦ The filename, with a name and one or more optional extensions. A period appears before each extension.

The Red Hat Linux file system has a well-defined set of top-level directories, and some of these directories have specific purposes. You find it easier to find your way around the file system if you know the purpose of these directories. You'll also become adept at guessing where to look for specific types of files when you face a new situation. Table 4-1 briefly describes the top-level directories in the Red Hat Linux file system.

Table 4-1	Top-Level Directories in Red Hat Linux File System
Directory	*Description*
/	Root directory that forms the base of the file system. All files and directories are contained logically in the root directory, regardless of their physical locations.
/bin	Contains the executable programs that are part of the Linux operating system. Many Linux commands, such as cat, cp, ls, more, and tar, are located in /bin.
/boot	Contains the Linux kernel and other files that the LILO and GRUB boot managers need (the kernel and other files can be anywhere, but it is customary to place them in the /boot directory).
/dev	Contains special files that represent devices attached to the system.
/etc	Contains most system configuration files and the initialization scripts (in the /etc/rc.d subdirectory).
/home	Conventional location of the home directories of all users. User naba's home directory, for example, is /home/naba.
/lib	Contains library files for all programs stored in /sbin and /bin directories, including the loadable driver modules, needed to start Red Hat Linux.
/lost+found	Directory for lost files. Every disk partition has a lost+found directory.
/mnt	A directory for temporarily mounted file systems, such as CD-ROM drives, floppy disks, and Zip drives. Contains the /mnt/floppy directory for mounting floppy disks and the /mnt/cdrom directory for mounting the CD-ROM drive.

(continued)

Table 4-1 *(continued)*

Directory	Description
/opt	Provides a storage area for large application software packages.
/proc	A special directory that contains information about various aspects of the Red Hat Linux system.
/root	The home directory for the root user.
/sbin	Contains executable files representing commands typically used for system-administration tasks and used by the root user. Commands such as halt and shutdown reside in the /sbin directory.
/tmp	Temporary directory that any user can use as a scratch directory, meaning that the contents of this directory are considered unimportant and usually are deleted every time the system boots.
/usr	Contains the subdirectories for many important programs, such as the X Window System (in the /usr/X11R6 directory), and the online manual. Table 4-2 shows some of the standard subdirectories in /usr.
/var	Contains various system files (such as logs), as well as directories for holding other information, such as files for the Web server and anonymous FTP server.

The /usr directory also contains a number of standard subdirectories. Table 4-2 lists the important subdirectories in /usr.

Table 4-2	**Important /usr Subdirectories**
Subdirectory	Description
/usr/X11R6	Contains the XFree86 (X Window System) software.
/usr/bin	Contains executable files for many more Linux commands, including utility programs commonly available in Linux, but is not part of the core Linux operating system.
/usr/games	Contains some old Linux games.
/usr/include	Contains the header files (files with names ending in .h) for the C and C++ programming languages; also includes the X11 header files in the /usr/include/X11 directory and the Linux kernel header files in the /usr/include/linux directory.
/usr/lib	Contains the libraries for C and C++ programming languages; also contains many other libraries, such as database libraries, graphical toolkit libraries, and so on.
/usr/local	Contains local files. The /usr/local/bin directory, for example, is supposed to be the location for any executable program developed on your system.

Subdirectory	Description
/usr/sbin	Contains many administrative commands, such as commands for electronic mail and networking.
/usr/share	Contains shared data, such as default configuration files and images for many applications. For example, /usr/share/gnome contains various shared files for the GNOME desktop; and /usr/share/doc has the documentation files for many Linux applications (such as the Bash shell, the Sawfish window manager, and the GIMP image-processing program).
/usr/share/man	Contains the online manual (which you can read by using the man command).
/usr/src	Contains the source code for the Linux kernel (the core operating system).

Navigating the File System with Linux Commands

Although GUI file managers such as Nautilus (in GNOME) or Konqueror (in KDE) are easy to use, you can use them only if you have a working GUI desktop. Sometimes, you may not have a graphical environment to run a graphical file manager. For example, you may be logged in through a text terminal, or X may not be working on your system. In those situations, you have to rely on Linux commands to work with files and directories. Of course, you can always use Linux commands, even in the graphical environment — all you have to do is open a terminal window and type the Linux commands.

I briefly show some Linux commands for moving around the Red Hat Linux file system.

Command for directory navigation

In Red Hat Linux, when you log in as root, your home directory is /root. For other users, the home directory is usually in the /home directory. My home directory (when I log in as naba) is /home/naba. This information is stored in the /etc/passwd file. By default, only you have permission to save files in your home directory, and only you can create subdirectories in your home directory to further organize your files.

Linux supports the concept of a current directory, which is the directory on which all file and directory commands operate. After you log in, for example, your current directory is the home directory. To see the current directory, type the pwd command.

To change the current directory, use the cd command. To change the current directory to /usr/share/doc, type the following:

```
cd /usr/share/doc
```

Then, to change the directory to the `bash-2.05b` subdirectory in `/usr/share/doc`, type this command:

```
cd bash-2.05b
```

Now, if you use the `pwd` command, that command shows `/usr/share/doc/bash-2.05b` as the current directory.

These two examples show that you can refer to a directory's name in two ways:

✦ An *absolute* pathname (such as `/usr/share/doc`) that specifies the exact directory in the directory tree

✦ A *relative* directory name (such as `bash-2.05b`, which represents the `bash-2.05b` subdirectory of the current directory, whatever that may be)

If you type `cd bash-2.05b` in `/usr/share/doc`, the current directory changes to `/usr/share/doc/bash-2.05b`. However, if I type the same command in `/home/naba`, the shell tries to change the current directory to `/home/naba/bash-2.05b`.

Use the `cd` command without any arguments to change the current directory back to your home directory. No matter where you are, typing **cd** at the shell prompt brings you back home!

By the way, the tilde character (~) refers to your home directory. Thus, the command `cd ~` also changes the current directory to your home directory. You can also refer to another user's home directory by appending that user's name to the tilde. Thus, `cd ~superman` changes the current directory to the home directory of `superman`.

Wait, there's more. A single dot (.) and two dots (. .) — often referred to as *dot-dot* — also have special meanings. A single dot (.) indicates the current directory, whereas two dots (. .) indicate the parent directory. For example, if the current directory is `/usr/share`, you go one level up to `/usr` by typing

```
cd ..
```

Commands for directory listings and permissions

You can get a directory listing by using the `ls` command. By default, the `ls` command — without any options — displays the contents of the current directory in a compact, multicolumn format. For example, type the next two commands to see the contents of the `/etc/X11` directory:

```
cd /etc/X11
ls
```

The output looks like this (on the console you'd see some items in different colors):

```
applnk          prefdm          sysconfig   XftConfig.README-OBSOLETE   xserver
desktop-menus   proxymngr       twm         xinit                       xsm
fs              rstart          X           xkb
gdm             serverconfig    xdm         Xmodmap
lbxproxy        starthere       XF86Config  Xresources
```

From this listing (without the colors), you cannot tell whether an entry is a file or a directory. To tell the directories and files apart, use the -F option with ls and you'll get more clues:

```
ls -F
applnk/          prefdm*          sysconfig/   XftConfig.README-OBSOLETE   xserver/
desktop-menus/   proxymngr/       twm/         xinit/                      xsm/
fs/              rstart/          X@           xkb@
gdm/             serverconfig/    xdm/         Xmodmap
lbxproxy/        starthere/       XF86Config   Xresources
```

The output from ls -F shows the directory names with a slash (/) appended to them. Plain filenames appear as is. The at sign (@) appended to the file named X indicates that that file is a link to another file (in other words, this filename simply refers to another file; it's a shortcut). An asterisk (*) is appended to executable files (see, for example, the prefdm file in the listing). The shell can run any executable file.

You can see even more detailed information about the files and directories with the -l option:

```
ls -l
```

For the /etc/X11 directory, a typical output from ls -l looks like the following:

```
total 80
drwxr-xr-x  4 root  root  4096 Sep 24 15:52 applnk
drwxr-xr-x  2 root  root  4096 Sep 24 14:59 desktop-menus
drwxr-xr-x  2 root  root  4096 Sep 24 16:12 fs
drwxr-xr-x  6 root  root  4096 Sep 24 15:37 gdm
drwxr-xr-x  2 root  root  4096 Sep 24 15:34 lbxproxy
-rwxr-xr-x  1 root  root  1298 Sep  4 13:23 prefdm
drwxr-xr-x  2 root  root  4096 Sep 24 15:34 proxymngr
drwxr-xr-x  4 root  root  4096 Sep 24 15:34 rstart
drwxr-xr-x  2 root  root  4096 Jul 10 2001 serverconfig
drwxr-xr-x  2 root  root  4096 Jul 10 2001 starthere
drwxr-xr-x  2 root  root  4096 Jul 10 2001 sysconfig
drwxr-xr-x  2 root  root  4096 Sep 24 15:36 twm
lrwxrwxrwx  1 root  root    27 Sep 24 16:28 X -> ../../usr/X11R6/bin/XFree86
drwxr-xr-x  3 root  root  4096 Sep 24 15:56 xdm
-rw-r--r--  1 root  root  3323 Sep 24 16:28 XF86Config
....< lines deleted >....
drwxr-xr-x  2 root  root  4096 Sep 24 15:34 xsm
```

Book II
Chapter 4

Navigating the
Red Hat Linux
File System

This listing shows considerable information about each directory entry — which can be a file or another directory. Looking at a line from the right column to the left, you see that the rightmost column shows the name of the directory entry. The date and time before the name show when the last modifications to that file were made. To the left of the date and time is the size of the file, in bytes.

The file's group and owner appear to the left of the column that shows the file size. The next number to the left indicates the number of links to the file. (A link is like a shortcut in Windows.) Finally, the leftmost column shows the file's permission settings, which determine who can read, write, or execute the file.

The first letter of the leftmost column has a special meaning, as the following list shows:

✦ If the first letter is l, the file is a symbolic link to another file.

✦ If the first letter is d, the file is a directory.

✦ If the first letter is a dash (-), the file is normal.

✦ If the first letter is b, the file represents a block device, such as a disk drive.

✦ If the first letter is c, the file represents a character device, such as a serial port or a terminal.

After that first letter, the leftmost column shows a sequence of nine characters. This appears as rwxrwxrwx when each letter is present. Each letter indicates a specific permission. A hyphen (-) in place of a letter indicates no permission for a specific operation on the file. Think of these nine letters as three groups of three letters (rwx), interpreted as follows:

✦ The leftmost group of rwx controls the read, write, and execute permission of the file's owner. In other words, if you see rwx in this position, the file's owner can read (r), write (w), and execute (x) the file. A hyphen in the place of a letter indicates no permission. Thus, the string rw- means that the owner has read and write permission but not execute permission. Typically, executable programs (including shell programs) have execute permission. However, for directories, execute permission is equivalent to use permission — a user must have execute permission on a directory to open and read the contents of the directory.

✦ The middle three rwx letters control the read, write, and execute permission of any user belonging to that file's group.

✦ The rightmost group of rwx letters controls the read, write, and execute permission of all other users (collectively referred to as the world).

Thus, a file with the permission setting rwx—— is accessible only to the file's owner, whereas the permission setting rwxr–r– makes the file readable by the world.

An interesting feature of the ls command is that it does not list any file whose name begins with a period. To see these files, you must use the ls command with the -a option, as follows:

```
ls -a
```

Try this command in your home directory, and compare the result with what you see when you don't use the -a option:

1. **Type** cd **to change to your home directory.**

2. **Type** ls -F **to see the files and directories in your home directory.**

3. **Type** ls -aF **to see everything, including the hidden files.**

Most Linux commands take single-character options, each with a minus sign (think of this sign as a hyphen) as a prefix. When you want to use several options, type a hyphen and concatenate the option letters one after another. Therefore, ls -al is equivalent to ls -a -l.

Commands for changing permissions and ownerships

You may need to change a file's permission settings to protect from others. Use the chmod command to change the permission settings of a file or a directory.

To use chmod effectively, you have to learn how to specify the permission settings. A good way is to concatenate letters from the columns of the Table 4-3 in the order shown (Who/Action/Permission):

Table 4-3	Letter Codes for File Permissions	
Who	*Action*	*Permission*
u (user)	+ (add)	r (read)
g (group)	- (remove)	w (write)
o (others)	= (assign)	x (execute)
a (all)	s (set user ID)	

Use the single character from each column — the text in parentheses is for explanation only.

For example, to give everyone read access to all files in a directory, pick a (for all) from the first column, + (for add) from the second column, and r (for read) from the third column to come up with the permission setting a+r. Then use it with chmod, like this:

```
chmod a+r *.
```

On the other hand, to permit everyone to execute a specific file, type

```
chmod a+x filename
```

Let's think of a file named mystuff that you want to protect. You can make it not accessible to anyone but you with the following commands, in this order:

```
chmod a-rwx mystuff
chmod u+rw mystuff
```

The first command turns off all permissions for everyone, and the second command turns on the read and write permissions for the owner (you). Type ls -l to verify that the change took place (you should see a permission setting of -rw-------). Here's a sample output from ls -l:

```
-rw-------    1 naba      naba       3 Jun 30 18:45 mystuff
```

Note the third and fourth fields that show naba naba. These two fields show the file's user and group ownership. In this case, the name of the user is naba and the name of the group is naba as well (because Red Hat Linux creates a group for each user).

Sometimes you have to change a file's user or group ownership for everything to work correctly. For example, suppose you are instructed (by a manual, what else) to create a directory named cups and give it the ownership of user ID lp and group ID sys. How would you do it?

Well, you can log in as root and create the directory with the command mkdir:

```
mkdir cups
```

If you check the file's details with the ls -l command, you see that the user and group ownership is root root.

To change the owner, use the chown command. For example, to change the ownership of the cups directory to user ID lp and group ID sys, type

```
chown lp.sys cups
```

Commands for working with files

To copy files from one directory to another, use the cp command. For example, to copy the file /usr/X11R6/lib/X11/xinit/Xclients to the Xclients.sample file in the current directory (such as your home directory), type the following:

```
cp /usr/X11R6/lib/X11/xinit/Xclients Xclients.sample
```

If you want to copy a file to the current directory but retain the original name, use a period (.) as the second argument of the cp command. Thus, the following command copies the XF86Config file from the /etc/X11 directory to the current directory (denoted by a single period):

```
cp /etc/X11/XF86Config .
```

The cp command makes a new copy of a file and leaves the original intact.

If you want to copy the entire contents of a directory — including all subdirectories and their contents — to another directory, use the command cp -ar *sourcedir destdir* (this copies everything under *sourcedir* directory to *destdir*). For example, to copy all files from the /etc/X11 directory to the current directory, type the following command:

```
cp -ar /etc/X11 .
```

To move a file to a new location, use the mv command. The original copy is gone, and a new copy appears at the destination. You can use mv to rename a file. If you want to change the name of the today.list to old.list, use the mv command, as follows:

```
mv today.list old.list
```

On the other hand, if you want to move the today.list file to a subdirectory named saved, use this command:

```
mv today.list saved
```

An interesting feature of mv is the fact that you can use it to move entire directories, with all their subdirectories and files, to a new location. If you have a directory named data that contains many files and subdirectories, you can move that entire directory structure to old_data by using the following command:

```
mv data old_data
```

Book II
Chapter 4

Navigating the
Red Hat Linux
File System

To delete files, use the `rm` command. For example, to delete a file named `old.list`, type the following command:

```
rm old.list
```

Be careful with the `rm` command — in particular, when you log in as `root`. It's very easy to inadvertently delete important files with `rm`.

Commands for working with directories

To organize files in your home directory, you have to create new directories. Use the `mkdir` command to create a directory. For example, to create a directory named `images` in the current directory, type the following:

```
mkdir images
```

After you create the directory, you can use the `cd images` command to change to that directory.

You can create an entire directory tree by using the `-p` option with the `mkdir` command. For example, suppose your system has a `/usr/src` directory and you want to create the directory tree `/usr/src/book/java/examples/applets`. You can create this directory hierarchy by typing the following command:

```
mkdir -p /usr/src/book/java/examples/applets
```

When you no longer need a directory, use the `rmdir` command to delete it. You can delete a directory only when the directory is empty.

To remove an empty directory tree, you can use the `-p` option, like this:

```
rmdir -p /usr/src/book/java/examples/applets
```

This command removes the empty parent directories of `applets`. The command stops when it encounters a directory that's not empty.

Commands for finding files

The `find` command is very useful for locating files (and directories) that meet your search criteria.

When I began using UNIX many years ago (Berkeley UNIX in the early 1980s), I was confounded by the `find` command. I stayed with one basic syntax of `find` for a long time before graduating to more complex forms. The basic syntax I learned first was for finding a file anywhere in the file system. Here's how it goes.

Suppose you want to find any file or directory with a name that starts with gnome. Type the following find command to find these files:

```
find / -name "gnome*" -print
```

If you're not logged in as root, you may get a bunch of error messages. If these error messages annoy you, just modify the command like this and the error messages are history (or, as UNIX aficionados say, the error messages will go to the bit bucket).

```
find / -name "gnome*" -print 2> /dev/null
```

This command tells find to start looking at the root directory (/), to look for filenames that match gnome*, and to display the full pathname of any matching file. The last part (2> /dev/null) simply sends the error messages to a special file that's equivalent of simply ignoring them.

You can use variations of this simple form of find to locate a file in any directory (as well as any subdirectories contained in the directory). If you forget where in your home directory you have stored all files named report* (names that start with report), you can search for the files by using the following command:

```
find ~ -name "report*" -print
```

When you become comfortable with this syntax of find, you can use other options of find. For example, to find only specific types of files (such as directories), use the type option. The following command displays all top-level directory names in your Linux system:

```
find / -type d -maxdepth 1 -print
```

You probably do not have to use the complex forms of find in a typical Linux system, but if you ever need to, you can look up the rest of the find options by using the following command:

```
man find
```

Commands for mounting and unmounting

Suppose you want to access the files on this book's companion CD-ROM when you are logged in at a text console (no GUI to help you). To do so, you have to first mount the CD-ROM drive's file system on a specific directory in the Red Hat Linux file system.

Log in as `root` (or type `su -` to become `root`), insert the CD-ROM in the CD-ROM drive, and then type the following command:

```
mount /dev/cdrom /mnt/cdrom
```

This command mounts the file system on the device named `/dev/cdrom` (the CD-ROM) on the `/mnt/cdrom` directory (which is also called the mount point) in the Linux file system.

After the `mount` command successfully completes its task, you can access the files in the CD-ROM by referring to the `/mnt/cdrom` directory as the top-level directory of the CD-ROM. In other words, to see the contents of the CD-ROM, type

```
ls -F /mnt/cdrom
```

When you are done using the CD-ROM and before you eject it from the drive, you have to "unmount" the CD-ROM with the following `umount` command:

```
umount /dev/cdrom
```

It is customary to mount devices on directories in the `/mnt` directory. Red Hat Linux comes with the two predefined directories: `/mnt/cdrom` for mounting the CD-ROM and `/mnt/floppy` for mounting the floppy drive.

Commands for checking disk space usage

I want to tell you about two commands — `df` and `du` — that you can use to check the disk space usage on your system. These commands are simple to use. The `df` command shows you a summary of disk space usage for all mounted devices, as shown in this example:

```
df
Filesystem      1K-blocks      Used Available Use% Mounted on
/dev/hda2        3858236    2165160   1497084  60% /
/dev/hda1         101089       9379     86491  10% /boot
none               30768          0     30768   0% /dev/shm
/dev/cdrom        659488     659488         0 100% /mnt/cdrom
```

The output is a table that shows the device, the total kilobytes of storage, how much is in use, how much is available, the percentage being used, and the mount point.

To see the output of `df` in a more human-readable format, type **df -h**. Here is the output of the `df -h` command:

```
Filesystem              Size  Used Avail Use% Mounted on
/dev/hda2               3.7G  2.1G  1.4G  60% /
/dev/hda1                99M  9.2M   84M  10% /boot
none                     30M     0   30M   0% /dev/shm
/dev/cdrom              644M  645M     0 100% /mnt/cdrom
```

If you compare this output with the output of plain df (see previous listing), you see that df -h prints the sizes with terms like M for megabytes and G for gigabytes. These are clearly easier to understand that 1K-blocks.

The other command — du — is useful for finding out how much space a directory takes up. For example, type the following command to view the contents of all the directories in the /etc/rc.d directory (this directory contains system startup files):

```
du /etc/rc.d
288     /etc/rc.d/init.d
4       /etc/rc.d/rc0.d
4       /etc/rc.d/rc1.d
4       /etc/rc.d/rc2.d
4       /etc/rc.d/rc3.d
4       /etc/rc.d/rc4.d
4       /etc/rc.d/rc5.d
4       /etc/rc.d/rc6.d
352     /etc/rc.d
```

Each directory name is preceded by a number — that number denotes the number of kilobytes of disk space used by that directory. Thus, the /etc/rc.d directory, as a whole, uses 352K disk space whereas the /etc/rc.d/init.d subdirectory uses 288K. If you simply want the total disk space used by a directory (including all the files and subdirectories contained in that directory), use the -s option, as follows:

```
du -s /etc/rc.d
352     /etc/rc.d
```

The -s option causes du to print just the summary information for the /etc/rc.d directory.

Just as df -h prints the disk space information in megabytes and gigabytes, you can use the du -h command to view the output of du in more human-readable form. For example, here's how I combine it with the -s option to see the space I am using in my home directory (/home/naba):

```
du -sh /home/naba
29M     /home/naba
```

Book II
Chapter 4

Navigating the
Red Hat Linux
File System

Chapter 5: Exploring Red Hat Linux Applications

In This Chapter

✔ Taking stock of Red Hat Linux applications

✔ Using office applications

✔ Setting up databases

✔ Playing with multimedia

✔ Working with images

Red Hat Linux comes with a whole lot of applications. All you have to do is look at the menus in GNOME or KDE and you'll see what I mean. Often, there is more than one application of each type. Both GNOME and KDE come with the OpenOffice.org office application suite with word-processor and spreadsheet software. There are also many choices for CD players and multimedia players. Not to mention the games and utility programs, as well as useful tools such as scanner and digital camera applications.

I give you an overview of some of these applications and briefly show you some interesting and useful applications. After you know about these applications, you can try them out when you need them.

If your system has both GNOME and KDE installed, remember that you can access all KDE applications through the GNOME menu as well. To get to the KDE applications, select Main Menu⇨Extras from the GNOME desktop.

Taking Stock of the Red Hat Linux Applications

Table 5-1 shows a sampling of major Red Hat Linux applications, organized by category. For the major applications, I also show a relevant Web site where you can get more information about that application. This list is by no means comprehensive. Red Hat Linux distribution comes with many more applications and utilities than the ones I show in this table.

If your system has both GNOME and KDE installed, then most of these applications should already be available from either GUI desktop.

I briefly introduce some of the applications from Table 5-1, selecting one or two from each category. I describe the Internet applications in Book IV.

Table 5-1	A Sampling of Red Hat Linux Applications
Application	*Description*
Office Applications	
OpenOffice.org Writer	A free word processing program similar to Microsoft Word (`www.openoffice.org`)
OpenOffice.org Calc	A spreadsheet program similar to Microsoft Excel (`www.openoffice.org`)
OpenOffice.org Impress	A presentation application similar to Microsoft PowerPoint (`www.openoffice.org`)
OpenOffice.org Draw	A vector graphics drawing program (`www.openoffice.org`)
OpenOffice.org Math	An equation editor for writing mathematical equations that you can then include in OpenOffice.org Writer documents (`www.openoffice.org`)
Dia	A drawing program, designed to be like the Windows application called Visio (`www.gnome.org/gnome-office/dia.shtml`)
Office Tools	
GNOME Calculator	A simple calculator
Kcalc	A calculator (part of KDE)
KOrganizer	A calendar (part of KDE)
Aspell	A text-mode spell checker (`aspell.sourceforge.net`)
Dictionary	A graphical client for the `dict.org` dictionary server so that you can look up words
Database	
PostgreSQL	A sophisticated object-relational database-management system that supports Structured Query Language (SQL) (`www.pgsql.com`)
MySQL	A popular relational database-management system that supports SQL (`www.mysql.com`)
Multimedia	
GNOME CD Player	An audio CD player (needs a working sound card)
KsCD	Audio CD player from KDE (needs a working sound card)
XMMS	X Multimedia System — a multimedia audio player that can play MP3 among other sound formats (`www.xmms.org`)

Application	Description
KonCD	A CD burner that can burn audio CDs on CD-R and CD-RW drives (`www.koncd.org`)
gtkam	A digital camera application that works with over 150 digital cameras (`www.gphoto.org/gphoto2/`)
Graphics and Imaging	
The GIMP	The GNU Image Manipulation Program, an application suitable for tasks such as photo retouching, image composition, and image authoring (`www.gimp.org`)
GQView	A powerful image viewer (`gqview.sourceforge.net`)
Kview	A simple image viewer for KDE
Kghostview	A PostScript and PDF file viewer
Xsane	A graphical frontend for accessing scanners with the SANE (Scanner Access Now Easy) library (`www.xsane.org`)
Ksnapshot	A screen-capture program
Internet	
Ximian Evolution	A personal information management application that integrates e-mail, calendar, contact management, and online task lists (`www.ximian.com/products/ximian_evolution`)
GFTP	An FTP client for downloading files from the Internet
Gaim	An AOL Instant Messenger client (`gaim.sourceforge.net`)
Mozilla	A well-known open-source Web browser that started with source code from Netscape (`www.mozilla.org`)
Kmail	An e-mail client for KDE (`kmail.kde.org`)

Office Applications and Tools

Word processor, spreadsheet, presentation software, calendar, calculator — these are some of the staples of the office. Both GNOME and KDE come with the OpenOffice.org set of office applications and tools. You can try out all of them one by one and see which one takes your fancy. Each application is fairly intuitive to use. Even though some nuances of the user interface may be new to you, you can learn it after using it a few times. I briefly introduce the following applications in this section:

✦ OpenOffice.org Writer — a Microsoft Word-like word processor

✦ OpenOffice.org Calc — a Microsoft Excel-like spreadsheet program

✦ OpenOffice.org Impress — a Microsoft PowerPoint-like presentation program

- ✦ KOrganizer — KDE calendar
- ✦ Calculators — GNOME calculator and KDE calculator
- ✦ aspell — spelling checker
- ✦ Commercially available office applications for Linux

OpenOffice.org Writer

OpenOffice.org Writer is a word-processing program. It's part of an open-source office application suite, OpenOffice.org project (`www.abisource.com`). To start OpenOffice.org Writer, select Main Menu⇨Office⇨OpenOffice.org Writer from GNOME or KDE. OpenOffice.org Writer prompts you to register and displays a blank document in its main window. Using Writer is simple — it's similar to other word processors such as Microsoft Word. For example, you can type text into the blank document, format text, and save text when done.

You can also open documents that you have prepared with Microsoft Word on a Windows machine. Figure 5-1 shows a Microsoft Word document being opened in OpenOffice.org Writer.

When you save a document, by default Writer saves it in OpenOffice.org 1.0 Text Document format in a file with the `.sxw` extension.

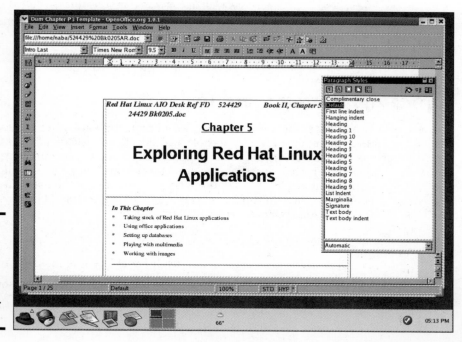

Figure 5-1:
You can prepare documents in OpenOffice. org Writer.

TIP

If you need to share OpenOffice.org Writer documents with Microsoft Word, save the documents in several formats, including Microsoft Word 97/2000/XP, Microsoft Word 95, Microsoft Word 6.0, and Rich Text Format (.rtf). Microsoft Word can open .rtf files.

I won't explain how to use Writer because it is simple and intuitive to use. If you need it, online help is available. Select Help⇨Contents from the Writer menu. This brings up the OpenOffice.org Help window (Figure 5-2) with help information on the Writer. You can then click the links to view specific help information.

Book II
Chapter 5

Exploring Red Hat
Linux Applications

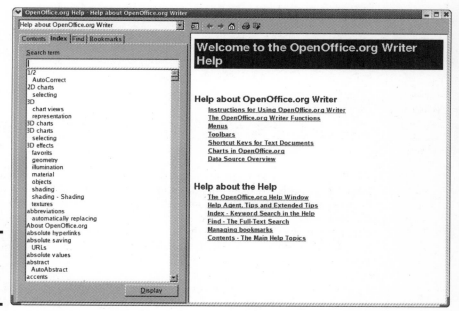

Figure 5-2:
Help from
OpenOffice.
org Writer.

OpenOffice.org Calc

Calc is the spreadsheet program in the OpenOffice.org application suite. To start Calc, select Main Menu⇨Office⇨OpenOffice.org Calc from the GNOME or KDE panel. The Calc program displays its main window, which looks similar to Windows-based spreadsheets, such as Microsoft Excel. (In fact, Calc can read and write Microsoft Excel format spreadsheet files.)

Use Gnumeric in the same way you use Microsoft Excel. You can type entries in cells, use formulas, and format the cells (such as specifying the type of value and the number of digits after the decimal point). Figure 5-3 shows a typical spreadsheet in Calc.

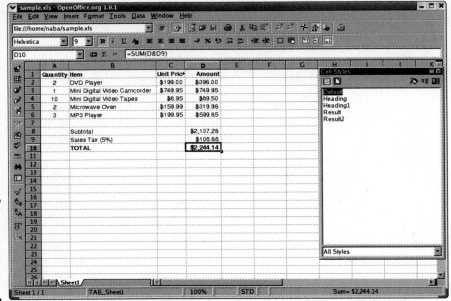

Figure 5-3:
Prepare
your spread-
sheets using
OpenOffice.
org Calc.

When preparing the spreadsheet, use formulas you normally use in Microsoft Excel. For example, use the formula SUM(D2:D6) to add up the entries from cell D2 to D6. To set cell D2 as the product of the entries A2 and C2, type **=A2*C2** in cell D2. To learn more about the functions available in OpenOffice.org Calc, select Help⇨Contents from the menu. This opens the OpenOffice.org Help window from which you can browse the functions by category and click a function to read more about it.

To save the spreadsheet, select File⇨Save As. A dialog box appears, from which you can specify the file format, the directory location, and the name of the file. OpenOffice.org Calc can save the file in a number of formats, including Microsoft Excel 97/2000/XP, Microsoft Excel 95, Microsoft Excel 5.0, and text file with comma-separated values (CSV).

TIP

If you want to exchange files with Microsoft Excel, save the spreadsheet in Microsoft Excel format (choose an appropriate version of Excel). Then you can transfer that file to a Windows system and open it in Microsoft Excel.

OpenOffice.org Impress

OpenOffice.org Impress is part of the OpenOffice.org office application suite. You can prepare briefing packages (slide presentations) using Impress. It's similar to Microsoft PowerPoint. To run Impress, select Main Menu⇨Office⇨OpenOffice.org Impress from the GNOME or KDE desktop.

To begin working, select the type of document (paper or screen presentation) and any template you want to use. The template provides a style for the presentation package you want to prepare. You can also choose to open an existing document.

Figure 5-4 shows a typical slide presentation in Impress.

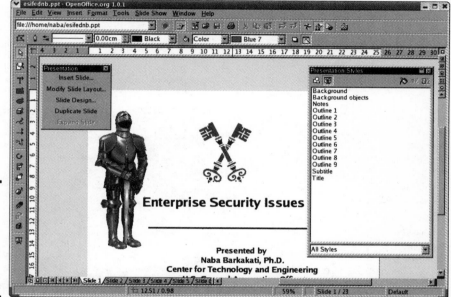

Figure 5-4:
You can prepare briefing packages in OpenOffice. org Impress.

The Impress window shows the first slide. The exact appearance depends on the document type and template you select. You can begin adding text and other graphic objects such as images, text, and lines to the slide.

To insert a new slide, select Insert Slide... from the floating menu. A gallery of slide layouts appears in a dialog box. Click the style of slide you want in the dialog box. You can then add text and graphics to that new slide.

To save a presentation, select File⇨Save from the menu. For new documents, you have to provide a file name and select the directory where to save the file.

If you want to share the slides with someone who uses Microsoft PowerPoint, save the presentation in Microsoft PowerPoint 97/2000/XP format.

Calendars

KDE comes with KOrganizer — a calendar program that you can run from either KDE or GNOME. To start KOrganizer, select Main Menu⇨Extras⇨ Accessories⇨KOrganizer from the KDE or GNOME desktop. The KOrganizer program displays a window from which you can click a date to set or view that day's schedule. Figure 5-5 shows a typical calendar.

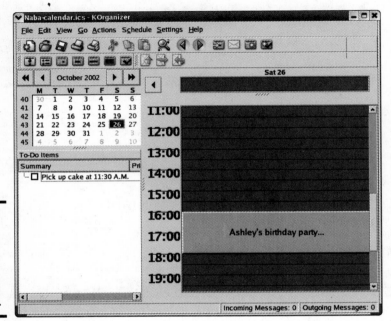

Figure 5-5: Store your appointments and view your calendar in KOrganizer.

You can go to a different month or year by clicking the arrows next to the month and the year. To add an event or to-do item for a specific date, select the date from the calendar, right-click the blank area under the calendar, and select New To-Do to type a description of the event.

To add appointments for a specific time, double-click the time, and type a brief description of the appointment in the dialog box that appears. Click OK when done. After you finish adding events and appointments, select File⇨Save to save the calendar. The first time you save the calendar, you have to provide a name for the file.

Calculators

You have a choice of the GNOME calculator or the KDE calculator. Both are scientific calculators, and you can do the typical scientific calculations such as square root and inverse, as well as trigonometric functions, such as sine, cosine, and tangent.

To run the GNOME calculator, select Main Menu⇨Accessories⇨Calculator in the GNOME panel. Figure 5-6 shows the GNOME calculator.

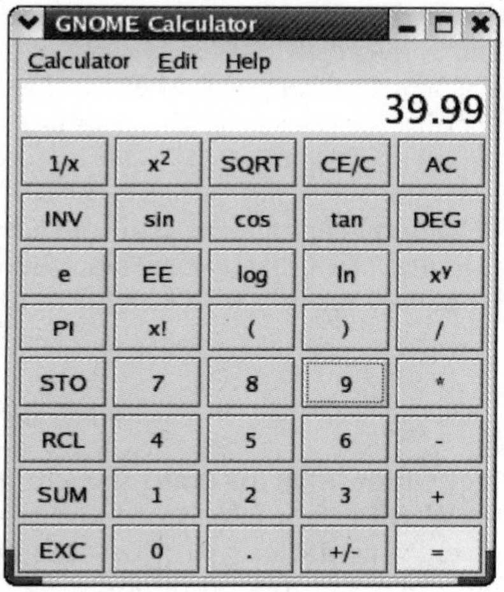

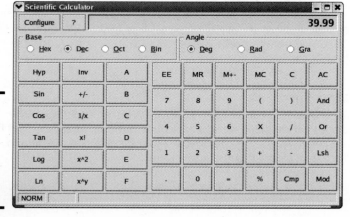

Figure 5-6:
Do your calculations in the GNOME calculator.

Book II
Chapter 5

Exploring Red Hat
Linux Applications

The KDE calculator has more features than the GNOME calculator. For example, it can perform calculations in hexadecimal, decimal, octal, and binary format. From the KDE desktop, you can start the KDE calculator by selecting Main Menu⇨Accessories⇨Scientific Calculator. Figure 5-7 shows the KDE calculator.

Figure 5-7:
Square roots anyone? Compute it in the KDE calculator.

Commercially available office applications for Linux

Because office applications are important to many businesses as well as individuals, I want to briefly mention some of the commercial office applications available for Red Hat Linux. These commercial offerings include WordPerfect Office 2000 for Linux, Anyware (formerly Applixware) Office, and StarOffice. These products do cost some money, but the cost is usually less than that for Microsoft Office — the leading office application suite for Windows. (In case you don't know, Microsoft Office is a collection of several applications: Microsoft Word for word processing; Microsoft Excel for spreadsheets; Microsoft PowerPoint for presentation graphics; and Microsoft Access for databases.)

This book's companion CD-ROMs do not include any of these commercial office applications for Red Hat Linux, but I briefly describe them in the next few sections. You can visit each vendor's Web site for more about the products.

WordPerfect Office 2000 for Linux

Corel Corporation's WordPerfect Office 2000 for Linux is a complete office applications suite that includes WordPerfect 9 for word processing, Quattro Pro 9 for spreadsheets, and Corel Presentations 9 for presentation graphics. The product comes bundled with many more components, such as Adobe Acrobat Reader (for PDF files), as well as many clip art images. Corel even bundles a copy of Corel Linux (based on the Debian distribution), but you can also install and use WordPerfect Office 2000 on Red Hat Linux.

WordPerfect Office can open, edit, and save files in a number of Microsoft Word and Microsoft Excel formats, as well as WordPerfect formats from other systems. According to Corel, you need about 140MB of hard disk space for a typical installation of WordPerfect Office 2000; the full installation requires about 450MB.

You can learn more about the latest release of WordPerfect Office 2000 for Linux by visiting Corel's Web site at `linux.corel.com/products/wpo2000_linux/index.htm`.

Anyware Office

Anyware Office, formerly known as Applixware Office, is another prominent office application suite for all Linux distributions, including Red Hat Linux. In April 2000, Applix, Inc., formed a separate group — VistaSource, Inc.— that focuses solely on Linux applications.

Like other office suites, Anyware Office includes Words (for word processing), Spreadsheets (for spreadsheets), and Graphics and Presents (for presentation graphics). In addition, it also has Mail (an e-mail interface) and Data (an interactive relational database-browsing tool). Anyware Office can also read and write documents in Microsoft Office and Corel WordPerfect formats, as well as in several other file formats. Although trial versions are not offered, the entire Anyware Office suite is currently priced at less than $100 in the U.S.

You can learn more about Applixware at VistaSource's Web site (`www.vistasource.com/products`).

StarOffice

StarOffice is another commercial office applications suite; it was created by StarDivision of Hamburg, Germany, and recently purchased by Sun Microsystems. StarOffice is a cross-platform solution — it runs on Linux, Windows 95/98/Me/NT/2000/XP, Sun Solaris SPARC, and Sun Solaris x86. Also, StarOffice is available in several languages: English, French, German, Spanish, Italian, and Swedish.

StarOffice is unique in that it combines all of its components into a common desktop from which you can open new documents, drag and drop documents from one application to another, and access the Internet. Here's what StarOffice 6.0 includes:

Book II
Chapter 5

Exploring Red Hat
Linux Applications

+ StarOffice Writer for word processing (Microsoft Word-compatible)

+ StarOffice Calc for spreadsheets (Microsoft Excel-compatible)

+ StarOffice Impress for presentations (Microsoft PowerPoint-compatible)

+ StarOffice Draw for vector graphics drawing

+ StarOffice Base for data management

You can buy a copy of StarOffice from `www.sun.com/staroffice`. You can also find the details of Sun's StarOffice licensing policy at the same URL.

In October 2000, Sun released the source code of StarOffice under open-source licenses. OpenOffice.org, an open-source project that Sun supports, released the OpenOffice.org 1.0 office productivity suite in May 2002. Red Hat Linux 8 comes with OpenOffice.org 1.0.1. To learn more about OpenOffice.org, visit `www.openoffice.org`.

aspell spelling checker

The `aspell` utility is an interactive spelling checker. You can use it to check the spelling of words in a text file. To do so, simply type the following command in a terminal window:

```
aspell check filename
```

If you want to try out `aspell`, type some notes and save them in a text file named `notes.txt` (the filename can be anything, but I use this filename in the discussions). To run the spelling checker on that file, type the following command in a terminal window:

```
aspell check notes.txt
This note describes the *concensus* reached during the August
    16 meeting.
1) consensus                    6) consensual
2) con census                   7) consciences
3) con-census                   8) incenses
4) condenses                    9) consensus's
5) concerns                     0) consensuses
i) Ignore                       I) Ignore all
r) Replace                      R) Replace all
a) Add                          x) Exit
?
```

Everything from the second line on is what `aspell` displays. When `aspell` finds a misspelled word (any word that does not appear in `aspell`'s dictionary) it displays the sentence with the misspelled word (`concensus`) and highlights that word by enclosing it in a pair of asterisks. Below that sentence, `aspell` lists possible corrections, numbering them sequentially from 1. In this case, `aspell` lists `consensus` — the right choice — as the first correction for `concensus`.

At the end of the list of options, `aspell` displays a list of 16 other options — 10 numbered 0 through 9 and 6 labeled with single letters i, r, a, I, R, and x — followed by a question mark prompt. You have to press one of the numbers or letters from the list shown in `aspell`'s output to indicate what you want `aspell` to do. The numbered options show 10 possible replacement words for the misspelled word. Here are the meanings of the letter options:

✦ Space means accept the word this time.

✦ i means ignore the misspelled word.

✦ I means ignore all occurrences of the word.

✦ r means replace this occurrence (you have to type a replacement word).

✦ R means replace all occurrences (you have to type a replacement word).

✦ a means accept the word and add it to the your private dictionary.

✦ x means save the rest of the file and exit, ignoring misspellings.

Databases

Red Hat Linux comes with two relational databases — PostgreSQL and MySQL. I briefly show you how to use MySQL.

MySQL, pronounced *My Ess Que Ell,* is a popular relational database (a relational database lets you think of the database as a collection of tables). You can use the Structured Query Language (SQL) to work with the database.

A Swedish company called MySQL AB develops MySQL (`www.mysql.com`). MySQL AB has released it as an open-source product.

Book II
Chapter 5

To check if MySQL is installed on your system, type **rpm -q mysql**. If a message informs you that the package is not installed, you can install it from the second CD using these steps:

1. **Log in as** `root` **and insert the second CD into the CD-ROM drive.**

   If you are using GNOME or KDE, the CD should mount automatically. If not, type the following command in a terminal window to mount the CD:

   ```
   mount /mnt/cdrom
   ```

2. **Type the following commands to install MySQL:**

   ```
   cd /mnt/cdrom/RedHat/RPMS
   rpm -ivh mysql*
   ```

   This installs all the packages you need to use MySQL on your system.

To use MySQL, you have to first log in as `root` and start the database server with the following command:

```
/etc/init.d/mysqld start
```

The database server `mysqld` is a daemon (a background process that runs continuously) that accepts database queries from the MySQL monitor.

Now you have to design a database, create that database in MySQL, and load it with the data. To illustrate how to create and load a database, I set up a simple book catalog database.

Reviewing the steps to build the database

Follow this basic sequence of steps to build a database:

Exploring Red Hat Linux Applications

1. **Design the database.**

   This involves defining the tables and attributes that will be used to store the information.

2. **Create an empty database.**

   Before you can add tables, database systems require you to build an empty database.

3. **Create the tables in the database.**

   In this step, you define the tables using the `CREATE TABLE` statement of SQL.

4. **Load the tables with any fixed data.**

   For example, if you have a table of manufacturer names or publisher names (in the case of books), you want to load that table with information that's already known.

5. **Back up the initial database.**

   This step is necessary to ensure that you can create the database from scratch, if necessary.

6. **Load data into tables.**

   You may either load data from an earlier dump of the database or interactively through forms.

7. **Use the database.**

   Make queries, update records, or insert new records using SQL commands.

Designing the database

In my simple example, I won't follow all the steps of database building. For the example, the database design step is going to be trivial because my book catalog database will include a single table. The attributes of the table are as follows:

+ Book's title with up to 50 characters

+ Name of first author with up to 20 characters

+ Name of second author (if any) with up to 20 characters

+ Name of publisher with up to 30 characters

+ Page count as a number

+ Year published as a number (such as 2002)

+ International Standard Book Number (ISBN), as a 10-character text (such as 0764524429)

I store the ISBN without the dashes embedded in a typical book's ISBN. I also use the ISBN as the primary key of the table because ISBN is a world-wide identification system for books. That means each book entry must have a unique ISBN, which we know to be true for books.

Creating an empty database

To create the empty database in MySQL, use the `mysqladmin` program. For example, to create an empty database named `books`, I type the following command:

```
mysqladmin create books
```

You have to log in as `root` to run the `mysqladmin` program. As the name suggests, `mysqladmin` is the database administration program for MySQL.

In addition to creating a database, you can use `mysqladmin` to remove a database and shut down the database server and check the MySQL version. For example, to see the version information, type the following command:

```
mysqladmin version
```

Using the MySQL monitor

After you create the empty database, all of your interactions with the database are through the `mysql` program — the MySQL monitor that acts as a client to the database server. You need to run `mysql` with the name of a database as argument. The `mysql` program then prompts you for input. Here is an example:

```
mysql books
Reading table information for completion of table and column names
You can turn off this feature to get a quicker startup with -A

Welcome to the MySQL monitor. Commands end with ; or \g.
Your MySQL connection id is 10 to server version: 3.23.49

Type 'help;' or '\h' for help. Type '\c' to clear the buffer.

mysql>
```

When creating tables or loading data into tables, a typical approach is to place the SQL statements (along with `mysql` commands such as `\g`) in a file and then run `mysql` with the standard input directed from that file. For example, suppose a file named `sample.sql` contains some SQL commands that you want to try out on a database named `books`. Then, you should run `mysql` with the following command:

```
mysql books < sample.sql
```

I use `mysql` in this manner to create a database table.

Defining a table

To create a table named `books`, I edited a text file named `makedb.sql` and placed the following line in that file:

```
#
# Table structure for table 'books'
#
CREATE TABLE books (
   isbn CHAR(10) NOT NULL PRIMARY KEY,
   title CHAR(50),
   author1 CHAR(20),
   author2 CHAR(20),
   pubname CHAR(30),
   pubyear INT,
   pagecount INT
) \g
```

`CREATE TABLE books` is an SQL statement to create the table named `books`. The `\g` at the end of the statement is an `mysql` command. The attributes of the table appear in the lines enclosed in parentheses.

If a table contains fixed data, you can also include other SQL statements (such as `INSERT INTO`) to load the data into the table right after the table is created.

To execute the SQL statements in the `makedb.sql` file create the `books` table, I run `mysql` as follows:

```
mysql books < makedb.sql
```

Now the `books` database should have a table named `books`. (Okay, maybe I should have named them differently, but it seemed convenient to call them by the same name.) I can now begin loading data into the table.

Inserting records into a table

One way to load data into the table is to prepare SQL statements in another file and then run `mysql` with that file as input. For example, suppose I want to add the following book information into the `books` table:

```
isbn = '156884798X'
title = 'Linux SECRETS'
author1 = 'Naba Barkakati'
author2 = NULL
pubname = 'IDG Books Worldwide'
pubyear = 1996
pagecount = 900
```

Then, the following MySQL statement loads this information into the `books` table:

```
INSERT INTO books VALUES
( '156884798X', 'Linux SECRETS', 'Naba Barkakati', NULL,
'IDG Books Worldwide', 1996, 900) \g
```

On the other hand, suppose you have the various fields available in a different order (than the order in which the table's attributes are defined by the `CREATE TABLE` statement). In that case, you can use a different form of the `INSERT INTO` command to add the row, as shown in the following example:

```
INSERT INTO books (pubyear, author1, author2, title,
    pagecount, pubname, isbn) values
(1996, 'Naba Barkakati', NULL, 'Linux SECRETS', 900, 'IDG
    Books Worldwide', '156884798X')\g
```

Essentially, you have to specify the list of attributes as well as the values and make sure that the order of the attributes matches that of the values.

If I save all the `INSERT INTO` commands in a file named `additems.sql`, then I can load the database from the `mysql` command line by using the `source` command like this (type **mysql books** to start the SQL client):

```
mysql> source additems.sql
```

Querying the database

You can query the database interactively through the `mysql` monitor. You do have to know SQL to do this. For example, to query the `books` database, I start the SQL client with the command:

```
mysql books
```

Then I would type SQL commands at the `mysql>` prompt to look up items from the database. When done, I type **quit** to exit the `mysql` program. Here's an example (I typed all of this in a terminal window):

```
mysql> select title from books where pubyear < 2000 \g
+------------------------------------+
| title                              |
+------------------------------------+
| Linux SECRETS                      |
| Red Hat Linux SECRETS, 2nd Edition |
+------------------------------------+
2 rows in set (0.00 sec)
mysql> quit
Bye
```

Multimedia Applications

Red Hat Linux includes a whole slew of multimedia applications — mostly multimedia audio players and CD players, but also applications for using digital cameras and burning CD-ROMs. I briefly describe a few typical multimedia applications:

✦ gtkam — for using digital cameras in Red Hat Linux

✦ Audio CD players

✦ XMMS — a multimedia audio player

✦ KOnCD — a CD burner application

gtkam digital camera application

gtkam is a digital camera application that you can use to download pictures from digital cameras. gtkam is a GUI front-end to the gPhoto2 command-line application that works with many different makes and models of digital cameras. Depending on the model, the cameras can connect to the serial port or the Universal Serial Bus (USB) port. Visit the gPhoto Web site (`www.gphoto.org/gphoto2`) for the latest list of supported cameras.

To use gtkam with your digital camera, follow these steps:

1. **Connect your digital camera to the serial port or USB port (whichever interface the camera supports) and turn the camera on.**

2. **Select Main Menu⇨Graphics⇨Digital Camera Tool to start gtkam.**

3. **From the gtkam menu, select Camera⇨Add Camera.**

4. **In the dialog box that appears, click Detect. Your camera should be detected. Figure 5-8 shows an example of gtkam detecting a Canon Powershot S30 camera connected to the USB port.**

5. **gtkam displays a camera icon and the camera name on the left-hand panel. Double-click the camera icon to download and view thumbnail pictures in the right-hand panel.**

6. **Click the thumbnails to select the images you want to download. After selecting, select File⇨Save or click the Save button on the toolbar.**

   gtkam then downloads the images and places each image in a separate file in your home directory. You can now edit the photos in the GIMP or your favorite photo editor.

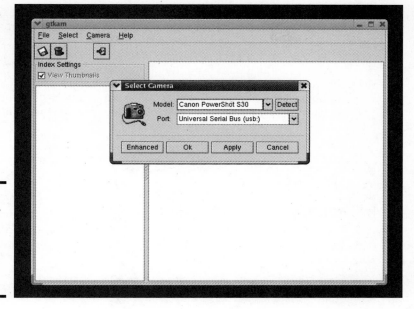

Figure 5-8:
Select your
camera
model and
detect it
from this
dialog.

Audio CD players

Both GNOME and KDE come with CD players. To play an audio CD, you need
a sound card, and that sound card must be configured to work in Red Hat
Linux.

If you are using the GNOME desktop, you can play audio CDs by using the
GNOME CD Player application. Launch the GNOME CD Player by selecting
Main Menu⇨Sound & Video⇨CD Player. Figure 5-9 shows this CD player
playing a track from an audio CD.

Figure 5-9:
Play audio
CDs with the
GNOME CD
Player.

The GNOME CD Player displays the title of the CD and the name of the current track. The GNOME CD Player gets the song titles from Compact Disc Database (CDDB) — a CD database on the Internet (www.cddb.com). This means that you need an active Internet connection for the CD Player to download song information from the CD database. After the CD Player downloads information about a particular CD, it caches that information in a local database for future use. The CD player's user interface is intuitive, and you can learn it easily. One nice feature is that you have the ability to select a track by title, as shown in Figure 5-10.

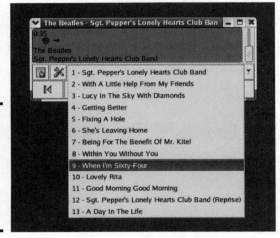

Figure 5-10:
In the GNOME CD Player, you can select a specific audio track to play.

If you use KDE as your desktop, you find a similar audio CD player in KDE. Start the KDE CD player by selecting Main Menu⇨Sound & Video⇨KsCD.

XMMS multimedia audio player

You can use the X Multimedia System (XMMS) to open and play a sound file. XMMS can play many types of sound files, including Ogg Vorbis and Windows WAV. You will find many WAV sound files — which usually have names that end with the .wav extension — in the /usr/share/sounds directory of your Red Hat Linux system.

Red Hat has removed from XMMS the code needed to play MP3 files, so you have to translate MP3s into a supported format such as WAV before you can play them. Red Hat recommends that you use the Ogg Vorbis format for compressed audio files because Ogg Vorbis is a patent- and royalty-free format.

To start XMMS from the GNOME or KDE desktop, select Main Menu⇨Sound & Video⇨Audio Player. XMMS has a simple user interface. To open a sound file, select Window Menu⇨Play File, or press L to select a .wav or .mp3 file from the Load File dialog box. Select a file and click OK. XMMS starts playing the sound file. Figure 5-11 shows a typical XMMS window when it's playing a sound file.

Figure 5-11:
You can play many different types of sound files in XMMS.

If you get an error message from XMMS, select Window Menu⇨Options⇨ Preferences, and select the OSS Driver as the Output Plugin. If you want to adjust the volume or other attributes of the sound, start the audio mixer by selecting Main Menu⇨Sound & Video⇨Volume Control. The Volume Control window appears (Figure 5-12). Drag the sliders to adjust the volume, bass, treble, and other attributes of the sound.

Figure 5-12:
You can adjust the sound's volume and other attributes from this window.

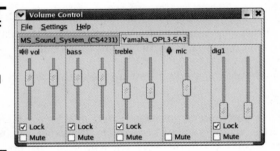

KOnCD CD burning application

Red Hat Linux includes the KOnCD, a graphical CD burner application with a lot of features. It can create both data CDs and audio CDs. You can also *rip* (copy) music from audio CDs to files on the hard drive.

Before you can burn a CD, you need a CD-R or CD-RW drive (CD burner) connected to your PC. It can be an internal or an external CD burner. Internal CD burners are usually IDE or ATAPI devices connected to the same card that supports the PC's hard disk and any other CD-ROM drive.

If you have an external CD burner, it probably connects to your PC's USB port. When you connect such a burner to the USB port and power up the burner, Red Hat Linux should automatically recognize the device and load the appropriate USB driver.

To use KOnCD, log in as `root` and then select Main Menu⇨Extras⇨System Tools⇨KOnCD from the KDE or GNOME desktop (you need to log in as `root` so that you can access the CD burner device). The main KOnCD window appears (Figure 5-13).

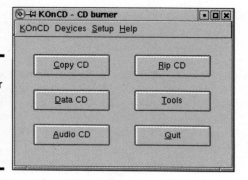

Figure 5-13: Control your CD burning needs from the main KOnCD window.

KOnCD's main window is deceptively simple, but don't let the simple interface fool you. You can do quite a lot with each of those buttons.

The first thing you should do is select Devices⇨Writer⇨Load from the KOnCD menu.

To burn an audio CD, you have to get together the tracks you want and then copy them all at once to a blank CD. You provide the tracks as audio files in one of three formats: MP3, WAV, and OGG. These formats are basically different ways to store sound in a digital format. You may have heard of MP3 and WAV already. The OGG format refers to Ogg Vorbis — a new audio compression format (if this piques your interest, stop by at `www.vorbis.com` to learn more about Ogg Vorbis).

To rip the tracks from an audio CD, follow these steps:

1. **Place the audio CD (you want to rip tracks from this CD) in the CD burner (CD burners can also read CDs). Then click the Rip CD button. The Rip CD dialog box appears.**

2. **Click the open folder icon and select a directory where you want to copy the tracks.**

You can pick the /tmp directory that's meant for temporary files. You need about 700MB of free space (less if you want fewer songs) to hold a CD full of tracks.

3. **Select the output file format from the list that appears when you click the button to the right of the folder icon. Pick one of MP3, WAV, or Ogg Vorbis.**

4. **Click Read tracks from CD. A list of tracks appears.**

5. **Select the tracks you want to rip. Hold down the Ctrl key and click the tracks you want.**

6. **Click Start to begin ripping the tracks.**

   A progress dialog box appears as the tracks are copied to the disk (Figure 5-14). For a USB 1.1 interface, this could take quite a while.

7. **Click Quit when the copying is finished.**

You can repeat these steps to rip tracks from other audio CDs until you have assembled all the tracks and you are ready to burn the audio CD.

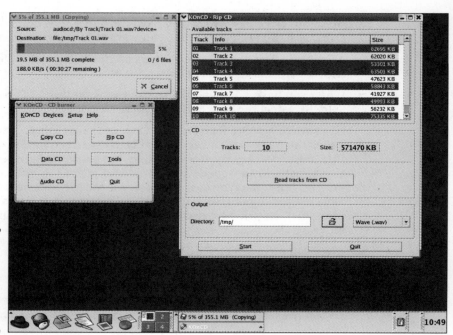

Figure 5-14: Rip selected audio tracks using KOnCD's Rip CD function.

Before you start burning audio CDs, you have to install the cdrdao package that KOnCD uses to burn audio CDs. To install that package, place the second companion CD-ROM in the CD-ROM drive. Open a terminal window. If you are not logged in as root, type **su -** to become root. Then type the following commands:

```
mount /dev/cdrom
cd /mnt/cdrom/RedHat/RPMS
rpm -ivh cdrdao*.rpm
```

To burn an audio CD with KOnCD, follow these steps (I am assuming that you still have KOnCD running; if not, select K Menu⇨Multimedia⇨KOnCD to run it):

1. **Place a blank CD-R disc into your CD burner.**

2. **Click Audio CD in the KOnCD main window.**

   The Audio CD dialog box appears.

3. **Click the button with an open folder icon.**

   The Open dialog box appears.

4. **Go to the directory where you have the audio files (MP3, WAV, or OGG) and then select the files you want to include on the CD.**

   As you add files, the CD size appears on the dialog box. Figure 5-15 shows a typical selection of tracks.

5. **When you have added all the tracks you want (for a CD size of about 660MB), select the appropriate options.**

   You have to select either Track-at-Once or Disc-at-Once. Track-at-Once writes the tracks with a two-second pause between tracks, whereas Disc-at-Once writes the tracks without the pauses in between. You can also select a writing speed appropriate for your CD burner and, for external ones, the type of connection you have. For example, even if you have a super-duper USB 2.0 CD burner, if you connect it to a USB 1.1 port, then the writing speed is limited to 4x. If you don't mind waiting a bit, leave the speed at 1x.

6. **After you have selected all the options, click Start to start burning the CD.**

   KOnCD converts the files to a format appropriate for the audio CD. After converting the files, KOnCD uses the cdrdao utility to write to the CD. If all goes well, after a long while, your new audio CD should be ready.

Unfortunately, KOnCD will fail if cdrdao cannot recognize your CD burner model and fails to select the correct driver.

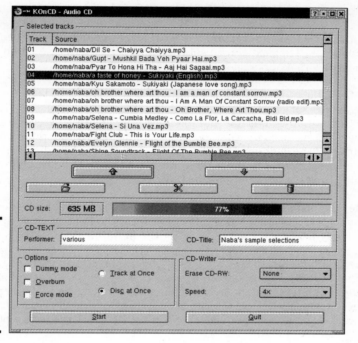

**Book II
Chapter 5**

**Exploring Red Hat
Linux Applications**

Figure 5-15:
Add the
tracks you
want in
KOnCD's
Audio CD
dialog box.

Graphics and Imaging

You can use graphics and imaging applications to work with images and
graphics (line drawings and shapes). I discuss two applications:

✦ **The GIMP** *(GNU Image Manipulation Program)* — A program for viewing
and performing image-manipulation tasks, such as photo retouching,
image composition, and image creation

✦ **KGhostview** — A KDE application capable of displaying PostScript and
PDF files

The GIMP

The GIMP (GNU Image Manipulation Program) is an image-manipulation program written by Peter Mattis and Spencer Kimball and released under the
GNU General Public License (GPL). It is installed if you select the Graphics
Manipulation package when you install Red Hat Linux from this book's companion CD-ROMs. The GIMP is comparable to other image-manipulation programs, such as Adobe Photoshop and Corel Photopaint.

To try out the GIMP, select Main Menu⇨Graphics⇨The GIMP from the GNOME or KDE desktop. The GIMP starts and displays a window with copyright and license information. Click the Continue button to proceed with the installation. The next screen shows the directories to be created when you proceed with a personal installation of the GIMP.

GIMP installation involves creating a directory called `.gimp-1.2` in your home directory and placing a number of files in that directory. This directory essentially holds information about any changes to user preferences you might make to the GIMP. Go ahead and click the Continue button at the bottom of the window. The GIMP creates the necessary directories, copies the necessary files to those directories, and guides you through a series of dialog boxes to complete the installation.

After the installation is done, click the Continue button. From now on, you won't see the installation window anymore; you have to deal with installation only when you run the GIMP for the first time.

The GIMP then loads any plug-ins — external modules that enhance its functionality. It displays a startup window that shows a message about each plug-in as it has loaded. After finishing the startup, the GIMP displays a tip of the day in a window. You can browse the tips and click the Close button to close the tip window. At the same time, the GIMP displays a number of windows (Figure 5-16).

These windows include a main toolbox window titled The GIMP, a Tool Options window, a Brush Selection window, and a Layers, Channels & Paths window. Of these, the main toolbox window is the most important — in fact, you can close the other windows and work by using the menus and buttons in the toolbox.

The toolbox has three menus on the menu bar: File, Xtns (extensions), and Help. The File menu has options to create a new image, open an existing image, save and print an image, mail an image, and quit the GIMP. The Xtns menu gives you access to numerous extensions to the GIMP. The exact content of the Xtns menu depends on which extensions are installed on your system. You can get help and view tips through the Help menu. For example, select Help⇨Help... to bring up the GIMP Help Browser with online information about the GIMP.

To open an image file in the GIMP, select File⇨Open. This brings up the Load Image dialog box from which you can select an image file. You can change directories and select the image file you want to open. GIMP can read all common image-file formats, such as GIF, JPEG, TIFF, PCX, BMP, PNG, and

PostScript. After you select the file and click the OK button, the GIMP loads the image into a new window. Figure 5-16 shows an image the GIMP has opened, along with all the other GIMP windows.

**Book II
Chapter 5**

**Exploring Red Hat
Linux Applications**

Figure 5-16:
Touch up
your photos
with the
GIMP.

The toolbox also has many buttons that represent the tools you use to edit the image and apply special effects. You can get pop-up help on each tool button by placing the mouse pointer on the button. You can select a tool by clicking the tool button, and you can apply that tool's effects on the image.

For your convenience, the GIMP displays a pop-up menu when you right-click your mouse on the image window. The pop-up menu has most of the options from the File and Xtns menus in the toolbox. You can then select specific actions from these menus.

You can do much more than just load and view images with the GIMP, but a complete discussion of all of its features is beyond the scope of this book. If you want to try the other features of the GIMP, consult the GIMP User Manual

(GUM), available online at manual.gimp.org. You can also select Xtns⇨Web Browser⇨GIMP.ORG⇨Documentation to access the online documentation for the GIMP (you'd need an Internet connection for this to work).

Some documentation about the GIMP is installed in the /usr/share/doc directory. To go to that directory, type **cd /usr/share/doc/gimp*** (the actual directory name depends on the current version of the GIMP). The README file in that directory points you to other resources on the Web where you can learn more about the GIMP. In particular, visit the GIMP home page at www.gimp.org to learn the latest news about the GIMP and to find links to other resources.

KGhostview

KGhostview is a KDE application that's ideal for viewing and printing PostScript and PDF documents. For a long document, you can view and print selected pages. You can also view the document at various levels of magnification by zooming in or out.

To run KGhostview, select Main Menu⇨Extras⇨Graphics⇨PS/PDF Viewer from the GNOME or KDE desktop. This causes the KGhostview application window to appear. In addition to the menu bar and toolbar along the top edge, the main display area of the window is divided vertically into two parts.

To load and view a PostScript document in KGhostview, select File⇨Open, or click the open folder icon on the toolbar. This action causes KGhostview to display a file-selection dialog box. Use this dialog box to navigate the file system and select a PostScript file. You can select one of the PostScript files that comes with Ghostscript. For example, open the file tiger.ps in the /usr/share/ghostscript/7.05/examples directory. (If your system has a version of Ghostscript later than 7.05, you have to use the new version number in place of 7.05.)

To open the selected file, click the Open File button in the file-selection dialog box. Ghostview opens the selected file, processes its contents, and displays the output in its window, as shown in Figure 5-17.

KGhostview is useful for viewing various kinds of documentation that come in PostScript and PDF format (these files typically have the .ps or .pdf extension in their names).

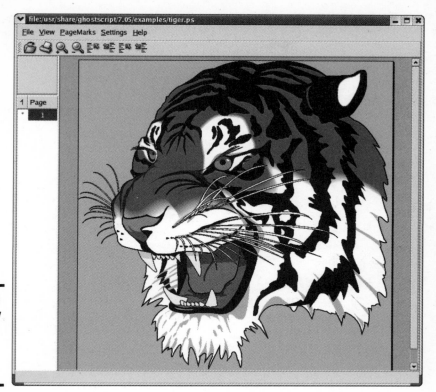

Figure 5-17:
KGhostview
can display
PostScript
and PDF
files.

Chapter 6: Using Text Editors

In This Chapter

✓ **Using GUI text editors**

✓ **Learning the** ed **text editor**

✓ **Learning the** vi **text editor**

*1*n Red Hat Linux, most system configuration files are text files. If you write any shell scripts or other computer programs, these are text files also. Sometimes you have to edit these files using text editors. For example, you may need to edit files such as /etc/hosts, /etc/modules.conf, /etc/X11/XF86Config-4, /etc/xinetd.d/telnet, and many more.

I introduce to you to a few text editors — both the GUI editors and text-mode editors.

Using GUI Text Editors

Each of the GUI desktops — GNOME and KDE — comes with GUI text editors (these are text editors that have graphical user interfaces).

To use the GNOME text editor, select Main Menu⇨Accessories⇨Text Editor from the GNOME desktop. You can open a file by clicking the Open button on the toolbar. This brings up the Open File dialog box. You can then change directories and select the file to edit by clicking the OK button.

The GNOME text editor then loads the file in its window. You can open more than one file and move among them as you edit the files. Figure 6-1 shows a typical editing session with the editor.

In this case, the editor has three files — fstab, hosts, and innittab (all from the /etc directory) — open for editing. The filenames appear as tabs below the toolbar of the editor's window. You can switch among the files by clicking the tabs.

If you open a file for which you have read permission only, the filename is preceded by the text RO- to indicate that the file "read only."

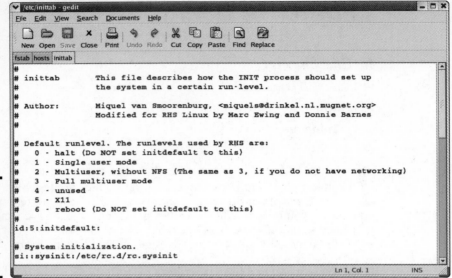

Figure 6-1:
You can use
the GNOME
text editor
to edit
text files.

The rest of the text-editing steps are intuitive. To enter new text, click to position the cursor and begin typing. You can select text, copy, cut, and paste using the buttons on the toolbar above the text-editing area.

From the KDE desktop, you can start the KDE text editor by selecting Main Menu⇨Accessories⇨Kate. To open a text file, select File⇨Open from the menu. A dialog box appears. From this dialog box, you can go to the right directory, select the file to open, and click the OK button. The KDE text editor then opens the file and displays its contents in the window. You can then edit the file.

Text Editing with ed and vi

Red Hat Linux comes with two text-mode text editors:

✦ ed, a line-oriented text editor

✦ vi, a full-screen text editor that supports the command set of an earlier editor named ex

The ed and vi editors are cryptic compared to the graphical text editors. However, you should still learn the basic editing commands of ed and vi because sometimes these two may be the only editors available.

For example, when Red Hat Linux refuses to boot from the hard disk, you may have to boot from a floppy. In this case, you have to edit system files with the ed editor because that editor is small enough to fit on the floppy. I walk you through the basic text-editing commands of ed and vi. You'll see — they're not that hard.

Using ed

Typically, you have to use ed only when you boot a minimal version of Linux (for example, from a boot floppy) and the system does not support full-screen mode. In all other situations, you can use the vi editor that works in a text mode full-screen.

When you use ed, you work in either command mode or text-input mode:

✦ **Command mode** is what you get by default. In this mode, anything that you type is interpreted as a command. The ed text editor has a simple command set where each command consists of one or more characters.

✦ **Text-input mode** is for typing text. You can enter input mode with the commands a (append), c (change), or i (insert). After entering lines of text, you can leave input mode by entering a period (.) on a line by itself.

To practice editing a file, copy the /etc/fstab file to your home directory with the following commands:

```
cd
cp /etc/fstab .
```

Now you should have a file named fstab in your home directory. Type the following command to begin editing a file in ed:

```
ed -p: fstab
696
:
```

This example uses the -p option to set the prompt to the colon character (:) and opens the fstab file (in the current directory, which should be your home directory) for editing. The ed editor opens the file, reports the number of characters in the file (696), displays the prompt (:), and waits for a command.

When editing with ed, it's helpful to always turn on a prompt character using the -p option. Without the prompt, it's difficult to tell whether ed is in input mode or command mode.

After `ed` opens a file for editing, the current line is the last line of the file. To see the current line number (the current line is the line to which `ed` applies your command), use the `.=` command:

```
:.=
9
```

This output tells you that the `fstab` file has nine lines. (Your system's `/etc/fstab` file may have a different number of lines, in which case `ed` shows a different number.)

You can use the `1,$p` command to see all lines in a file, as the following example shows:

```
:1,$p
LABEL=/         /           ext3  defaults    1 1
LABEL=/boot     /boot         ext3  defaults    1 2
none          /dev/pts      devpts gid=5,mode=620 0 0
none          /proc       proc  defaults    0 0
none          /dev/shm      tmpfs defaults    0 0
/dev/hda3       swap        swap  defaults    0 0
/dev/cdrom      /mnt/cdrom      iso9660 noauto,owner,kudzu,ro 0 0
/dev/hdd4       /mnt/zip100.0    auto  noauto,owner,kudzu 0 0
/dev/fd0       /mnt/floppy     auto  noauto,owner,kudzu 0 0
:
```

To go to a specific line, type the line number:

```
:6
/dev/hda3       swap        swap  defaults    0 0
:
```

The editor responds by displaying that line.

Suppose you want to delete the line that contains `cdrom`. To search for a string, type a slash (/) followed by the string that you want to locate:

```
:/cdrom
/dev/cdrom      /mnt/cdrom      iso9660 noauto,owner,kudzu,ro 0 0
:
```

The editor locates the line that contains the string and then displays it. That line becomes the current line.

To delete the current line, use the `d` command as follows:

```
:d
:
```

To replace a string with another, use the `s` command. To replace `cdrom` with the string `cd`, for example, use this command:

```
:s/cdrom/cd/
:
```

To insert a line in front of the current line, use the i command:

```
:i
    (type the line you want to insert)
.   (type a single period to indicate you're done)
:
```

You can enter as many lines as you want. After the last line, enter a period (.) on a line by itself. That period marks the end of text-input mode, and the editor switches to command mode. In this case, you can tell that ed switched to command mode because you see the prompt (:).

When you are happy with the changes, you can write them to the file with the w command. If you want to save the changes and exit, type **wq** to perform both steps at the same time:

```
:wq
693
```

The ed editor saves the changes in the file, displays the number of saved characters, and exits. If you want to quit the editor without saving any changes, use the Q command.

This should give you an idea of how to use ed commands to perform the basic tasks of editing a text file. Table 6-1 lists some of the commonly used ed commands.

Table 6-1	Commonly Used ed Commands
Command	*Does the Following*
!*command*	Executes a shell command (for example, !pwd shows the current directory).
$	Goes to last line in the buffer.
%	Applies a command that follows to all lines in the buffer (for example, %p prints all lines).
+	Goes to next line.
+n	Goes to nth next line (n is a number).
,	Applies a command that follows to all lines in the buffer (for example, ,p prints all lines); similar to %.
-	Goes to preceding line.
-n	Goes to nth previous line (n is a number).

(continued)

Table 6-1 *(continued)*

Command	Does the Following
.	Refers to the current line in the buffer.
/text/	Searches forward for the specified text.
;	Refers to a range of line: current through last line in the buffer.
=	Prints line number.
?text?	Searches backward for the specified text.
^	Goes to the preceding line; also see the - command.
^n	Goes to nth previous line (where n is a number); also see the -n command.
a	Appends after current line.
c	Changes specified lines.
d	Deletes specified lines.
i	Inserts text before current line.
n	Goes to line number n.
Press Enter	Displays next line and makes that line current.
q	Quits editor.
Q	Quits editor without saving changes.
r file	Reads and inserts contents of file after the current line.
s/old/new/	Replaces old string with new.
u	Undoes the last command.
W file	Appends contents of buffer to the end of the specified file.
w file	Saves buffer in the specified file (if no file is named, saves in the default file — the file whose contents ed is currently editing).

Using vi

The vi editor is a full-screen text editor, so you can view several lines at the same time. Most UNIX systems, including Red Hat Linux, come with vi. Therefore, if you learn the basic features of vi, you'll be able to edit text files on almost any UNIX system.

When vi edits a file, it reads the file into a buffer — a block of memory — so that you can change the text in the buffer. The vi editor also uses temporary files during editing, but the original file is not altered until you save the changes.

To start the editor, type **vi** followed by the name of the file you want to edit, like this:

```
vi /etc/fstab
```

The `vi` editor then loads the file into memory and displays the first few lines in a text screen and positions the cursor on the first line (Figure 6-2).

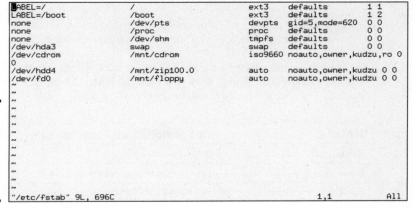

```
LABEL=/              /              ext3     defaults          1 1
LABEL=/boot          /boot          ext3     defaults          1 2
none                 /dev/pts       devpts   gid=5,mode=620    0 0
none                 /proc          proc     defaults          0 0
none                 /dev/shm       tmpfs    defaults          0 0
/dev/hda3            swap           swap     defaults          0 0
/dev/cdrom           /mnt/cdrom     iso9660  noauto,owner,kudzu,ro 0
0
/dev/hdd4            /mnt/zip100.0  auto     noauto,owner,kudzu 0 0
/dev/fd0             /mnt/floppy    auto     noauto,owner,kudzu 0 0
~
~
~
~
~
~
~
~
~
~
~
~
~
"/etc/fstab" 9L, 696C                             1,1            All
```

Figure 6-2: You can edit text files with the `vi` full-screen text editor.

Book II
Chapter 6

Using Text Editors

The last line shows the pathname of the file as well as the number of lines (9) and the number of characters (696) in the file. Later, this area functions as a command-entry area. The rest of the lines display the file. If the file contains fewer lines than the screen, `vi` displays the empty lines with a tilde (~) in the first column.

The current line is marked by the cursor, which appears as a small black rectangle. The cursor appears on top of a character.

When using `vi`, you work in one of three modes:

✦ **Visual command mode** is what you get by default. In this mode, anything that you type is interpreted as a command that applies to the line containing the cursor. The `vi` commands are similar to the `ed` commands.

✦ **Colon command mode** is for reading or writing files, setting `vi` options, and quitting `vi`. All colon commands start with a colon (:). When you enter the colon, `vi` positions the cursor on the last line and waits for you to type a command. The command takes effect when you press Enter.

✦ **Text input mode** is for typing text. You can enter input mode with the command a (insert after cursor), A (append at end of line), or i (insert after cursor). After entering lines of text, you have to press Esc to leave input mode and reenter visual command mode.

One problem with all these modes is that you cannot easily tell vi's current mode. It is frustrating to begin typing only to realize that vi is not in input mode.

If you want to make sure that vi is in command mode, just press Esc a few times. (Pressing Esc more than once doesn't hurt.)

To view online help in vi, type **:help** while in command mode. Type **:q** to exit the help screen and return to the file you are editing.

The vi editor initially positions the cursor on the first character of the first line. One of the first things that you need to learn is how to move the cursor around. Try the following commands shown in Table 6-2:

Table 6-2	Cursor Movement Commands in vi
Keypress	*Does the Following*
Down arrow	Moves the cursor one line down.
Up arrow	Moves the cursor one line up.
Left arrow	Moves the cursor one character to the left.
Right arrow	Moves the cursor one character to the right.
W	Moves the cursor one word forward.
B	Moves the cursor one word backward.
Ctrl+D	Moves down half a screen.
Ctrl+U	Scrolls up half a screen.

You can go to a specific line number at any time. This is when a colon command comes in. To go to line 6, for example, type the following and then press Enter:

```
:6
```

When you type the colon, vi displays the colon on the last line of the screen. From then on, vi uses the text that you type as a command. You have to press Enter to submit the command to vi. In colon command mode, vi accepts all the commands that the ed editor accepts and then some.

To search for a string, first type a slash (/). The vi editor displays the slash on the last line of the screen. Type the search string and then press Enter. The vi editor locates the string and positions the cursor at the beginning of that string. Thus, to locate the string cdrom in the file /etc/fstab, type

```
/cdrom
```

To delete the line that contains the cursor, type **dd** (two lowercase *d*s). The vi editor deletes that line of text and makes the next line the current one.

To begin entering text in front of the cursor, type **i** (a lowercase *i* all by itself). The vi editor switches to text input mode. Now you can enter text. When you finish entering text, press Esc to return to visual command mode.

After you finish editing the file, you can save the changes in the file with the :w command. To quit the editor without saving any changes, use the :q! command. If you want to save the changes and exit, you can type **:wq** to perform both steps at the same time. The vi editor saves the changes in the file and exits. You can also save the changes and exit the editor by pressing Shift+zz (hold the Shift key down and press *z* twice).

In addition to these commands, vi accepts a large number of commands. Table 6-3 lists some commonly used vi commands, organized by task.

Table 6-3	Commonly Used vi Commands
Command	*Does the Following*
Insert Text	
A	Inserts text after the cursor.
A	Inserts text at the end of the current line.
I	Inserts text at the beginning of the current line.
i	Inserts text before the cursor.
Delete Text	
D	Deletes up to the end of the current line.
dd	Deletes the current line.
dw	Deletes from the cursor to the end of the following word.
x	Deletes the character on which the cursor rests.
Change Text	
C	Changes up to the end of the current line.
cc	Changes the current line.
J	Joins the current line with the next one.
rx	Replaces the character under the cursor with *x* (x is any character).
Move Cursor	
h or Left arrow	Moves one character to the left.
j or Down arrow	Moves one line down.
k or Up arrow	Moves one line up.
L	Moves cursor to the end of the screen.
l or Right arrow	Moves one character to the right.
w	Moves to the beginning of the following word.

(continued)

Table 6-3 *(continued)*

Command	Does the Following
Scroll Text	
Ctrl-d	Scrolls forward by half a screen.
Ctrl-u	Scrolls backward by half a screen.
Refresh Screen	
Ctrl-L	Redraws screen.
Cut and Paste Text	
P	Puts yanked line above the current line.
p	Puts yanked line below the current line.
yy	Yanks (copies) current line into an unnamed buffer.
Colon Commands	
:!*command*	Executes shell command.
:q	Quits editor.
:q!	Quits without saving changes.
:r *filename*	Reads file and inserts after current line.
:w *filename*	Writes buffer to file.
:wq	Saves changes and exits.
Search Text	
/*string*	Searches forward for string.
?*string*	Searches backward for string.
Miscellaneous	
u	Undoes last command.
Esc	Ends input mode and enters visual command mode.
U	Undoes recent changes to current line.

Book III

Networking

The 5th Wave   By Rich Tennant

"If it works, it works. I've just never seen network cabling connected with Chinese handcuffs before."

Contents at a Glance

Chapter 1: Connecting to the Internet

In This Chapter

✔ **Understanding the Internet**

✔ **Deciding how to connect to the Internet**

✔ **Connecting to the Internet with DSL**

✔ **Connecting to the Internet with cable modem**

✔ **Setting up a dial-up PPP link**

The Internet is fast becoming a lifeline for most of us. Seems like we can't get by a day without it. I know I could not write the book without it. Sometimes I wonder how we ever managed without the Internet. You no doubt want to connect your Red Hat Linux system to the Internet. In this chapter, I show you how to connect to the Internet in several different ways — depending on whether you have DSL, cable modem, or dial-up network connection.

Two of the options for connecting to the Internet — DSL and cable modem — involve connecting a special modem to an Ethernet card on your Red Hat Linux system. In these cases, you have to set up Ethernet networking on your Red Hat Linux system. (I explain this in Book III, Chapter 2.) In this chapter I show you in detail how to set up a DSL or a cable modem connection.

I also show you the other option — dial-up networking — which involves dialing up an Internet Service Provider (ISP) from your Red Hat Linux system.

Understanding the Internet

How you view the Internet depends on your perspective. Common folks like us see the Internet in terms of the services we use. For example, as users we think of electronic mail (e-mail), the Web, and maybe even newsgroups as the Internet.

The users see the Internet as an information exchange medium with features such as

✦ **E-mail** — Send e-mail to any other user on the Internet, using addresses such as `mom@home.net`.

✦ **Web** — Download and view documents from millions of servers throughout the Internet.

✦ **Newsgroups** — Read newsgroups and post news items to newsgroups with names such as `comp.os.linux.networking` or `comp.os.linux.setup`.

✦ **Information sharing** — Download software, music files, videos, and so on. Reciprocally, you may provide files that users on other systems can download.

✦ **Remote access** — Log on to another computer on the Internet, assuming that you have access to that remote computer.

The techies among us would say the Internet is a worldwide network of networks. The term *internet* (without capitalization) is a short form of *internetworking* — the interconnection of networks. The Internet Protocol (IP) was designed with the idea of connecting many separate networks.

In terms of physical connections, the Internet is similar to a network of highways and roads. This similarity is what has prompted the popular press to dub the Internet "the Information Superhighway." Just as the network of highways and roads includes some interstate highways, many state roads, and many more residential streets, the Internet has some very high-capacity networks (for example, 10 Gbps backbone — that's 10 billion bits per second) and a large number of lower-capacity networks ranging from 56 Kbps dial-up connections to 45 Mbps T3 links (*Kbps* is thousand bits per second and *Mbps* is a million bits per second). The high-capacity network is the backbone of the Internet.

In terms of management, the Internet is not run by a single organization, nor is it managed by any central computer. You can view the physical Internet as a "network of networks" managed collectively by thousands of cooperating organizations. Yes, a collection of networks managed by thousands of organizations — sounds amazing, but it works!

Deciding How to Connect to the Internet

So you want to connect to the Internet, but don't know how? Let me count the ways. Nowadays, you have three popular options for connecting homes and small offices to the Internet (of course, huge corporations and governments have many other ways to connect to the Internet):

✦ **Digital Subscriber Line (DSL)** — This is something your local telephone company, as well as other telecommunications companies, may offer. DSL provides a way to send high-speed digital data over a regular phone line. Typically, DSL offers data transfer rates of anywhere between 128 Kbps and 1.5 Mbps. You can download from the Internet at much higher rates than when you send data from your PC to the Internet (upload). One caveat with DSL is that your home must be between 12,000 and 15,000 feet from your central office (this is a phone company facility where your phone lines end up). The distance limitation varies from provider to provider. In the U.S., you can check out the distance limits for many providers at www.dslreports.com/distance.

✦ **Cable modem** — If the cable television company in your area offers Internet access over cable, you can use that service to hook up your Red Hat Linux system to the Internet. Typically, cable modems offer higher data transfer rates than DSL for the same cost. Downloading data from the Internet is much faster than sending data from your PC to the Internet. You can expect routine download speeds of 1.5 Mbps and upload speeds of around 128 Kbps, but sometimes you may even get higher speeds than these.

✦ **Dial-up networking** — This is what most of us were using before DSL and cable modem came along. You hook up your PC to a modem that's connected to the phone lines. Then dial up an ISP to connect to the Internet. That's why we call it dial-up networking — establishing a network connection between your Red Hat Linux PC and another network (the Internet) through a dial-up modem. In this case, the maximum data-transfer rate is 56 Kbps.

As far as costs go, DSL and cable modem service connect you to the Internet and also act as your Internet Service Provider (ISP) — they provide you with an IP address and give you e-mail accounts. If you use a dial-up modem to connect to the Internet, you get the phone line from the phone company and then select a separate ISP that gives you a phone number that you dial and all the other necessary goodies like an IP address and e-mail accounts.

**Book III
Chapter 1**

Connecting to
the Internet

Table 1-1 summarizes all these options. You can consult that table and select the type of connection that's available to you and that best suits your needs.

Table 1-1	Comparison of Dial-up, DSL, and Cable		
Feature	**Dial-up**	**DSL**	**Cable**
Equipment	Modem	DSL modem, Ethernet card	Cable modem, Ethernet card
Also Requires	Phone service and an Internet Service Provider (ISP)	Phone service and location within 12,000 to 15,000 feet of central office	Cable TV connection
Connection type	Dial to connect	Always on, dedicated	Always on, shared
Typical speed	56 Kbps maximum	640 Kbps download, 128 Kbps upload (higher speeds cost more)	1.5 Mbps download, 128 Kbps upload
One-time costs (estimate)	None	Install = $100–200 Equipment = $200–300 (may require activation cost)	Install = $100–200, Equipment = $200–300
Typical monthly cost (2002)	Phone charges = $20/month, ISP charges = $15-30/month	$50/month, may require monthly modem lease	$50/month, may require monthly modem lease

Note: Costs vary by region. Costs shown are typical ones for U.S. metropolitan areas.

Connecting with DSL

DSL stands for *Digital Subscriber Line*. DSL uses your existing phone line to send digital data in addition to the normal analog voice signals (*analog* means continuously varying, whereas digital data is represented by 1s and 0). The phone line goes from your home to a central office where the line connects to the phone company's network — by the way, the connection from your home to the central office is called the *local loop*. When you sign up for DSL service, the phone company has to hook up your phone line to some special equipment at the central office. That equipment can separate the digital data from the voice. From then on, your phone line can carry digital data that can then be directly sent to an Internet connection at the central office.

How DSL works

A special box called a *DSL modem* takes care of sending digital data from your PC to the phone company's central office over your phone line. Your PC can connect to the Internet with the same phone line that you use for your normal telephone calls — you can make voice calls even as the line is being used for DSL. Figure 1-1 shows a typical DSL connection to the Internet.

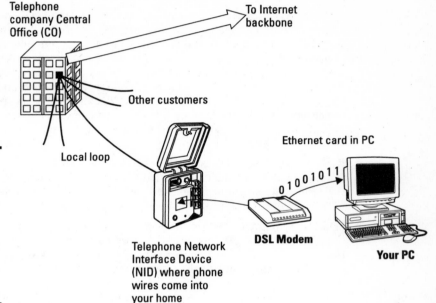

Figure 1-1: DSL provides a high-speed connection to the Internet over a regular phone line.

Your PC talks to the DSL modem through an Ethernet connection, which means that you need an Ethernet card in your Red Hat Linux system.

Your PC sends digital data over the Ethernet connection to the DSL modem. The DSL modem sends the digital data at different frequencies than those used by the analog voice signals. The voice signals occupy a small portion of all the frequencies that the phone line can carry. DSL uses the higher frequencies to transfer digital data, so both voice and data can travel on the same phone line.

The distance between your home and the central office — the loop length — is a factor in DSL's performance. Unfortunately, the phone line can reliably carry the DSL signals only over a limited distance — typically three miles or less. This means that you can get DSL service only if your home (or office) is located within about three miles of your phone's central office. Your phone company can tell you whether your location can get DSL or not. Often it has a Web site where you can type in your phone number and get a response about DSL availability. For example, try www.dslavailability.com for U.S locations.

DSL alphabet soup — ADSL, IDSL, SDSL

I have been using the term *DSL* as if there were only one kind of DSL. As you may imagine, nothing is ever that simple. There are in fact three variants of DSL, each with different features. Take a look:

✦ **ADSL** — Asymmetric DSL, the most common form of DSL, has much higher download speeds (from the Internet to your PC) than upload speeds (from your PC to the Internet). ADSL can have download speeds of up to 8 Mpbs and upload speeds of up to 1 Mbps. ADSL works best when your location is within about 2½ miles (12,000 feet) of your central office. ADSL service is priced according to the download and upload speeds you want. A popular form of ADSL, called G.lite, is specifically designed to work on the same line that you use for voice calls. G.lite has a maximum download speed of 1.5 Mbps and maximum upload speed of 512 Kbps.

✦ **IDSL** — ISDN DSL (ISDN is an older technology called *Integrated Services Digital Network*) is a special type of DSL that works at distances of up to five miles between your phone and the central office. The downside is that IDSL only offers downstream and upstream speeds of up to 144 Kbps.

✦ **SDSL** — Symmetric DSL provides the equal download and upload speed of up to 1.5 Mbps. SDSL is priced according to the speed you want, with the higher speeds costing more. The closer your location is to the phone company central office, the faster the connection you can get.

DSL speeds are typically specified by two numbers like this: 1500/384. The numbers refer to data transfer speeds in kilobits per second (Kbps or thousand bits per second). The first number is the download speed, the second the upload. Thus, 1500/384 means you can expect to download from the Internet at a maximum rate of 1,500 Kbps (or 1.5 Mbps) and upload to the Internet at 384 Kbps. If your phone line's condition is not perfect, you may not get these maximum rates — both ADSL and SDSL adjust the speeds to suit the line conditions.

The price of DSL service depends on which variant — ADSL, IDSL, or SDSL — you select. For most home users, the primary choice is ADSL or, more accurately, the G.lite form of ADSL with transfer speed ratings of 1500/128.

Typical DSL setup

To get DSL for your home or business, you have to contact a DSL provider. In addition to your phone company, there are many other DSL providers. No matter who provides the DSL service, some work has to be done at your central office — the place where your phone lines connect to the rest of the phone network. The work involves connecting your phone line to equipment that can work with the DSL modem at your home or office. The central office equipment and the DSL modem at your location can then do whatever magic is needed to send and receive digital data over your phone line.

Because of the need to set up your line at the central office, it takes some time after you place an order to get your line ready for DSL.

The first step for you is to check out the DSL providers that provide service and see if you can actually get the service. Because DSL can work only over certain distances — typically less than 2.5 miles — between your location and the central office, you have to check to see if you are within that distance limit. Contact your phone company to verify. You may be able to check this on the Web. Try typing into Google (`www.google.com`) the words **DSL**, **availability**, and your local phone company's name. You probably get a Web site where you can type in your phone number and learn if DSL is available for your number.

If DSL is available, you can look for the types of service — ADSL vs. SDSL — and the pricing. The price depends on the download and upload speeds you want. Sometimes phone companies offer a simple residential DSL that's basically the G.lite form of ADSL with a 1500/128 speed rating — meaning you can download at 1,500 Kbps and upload at 128 Kbps. Of course, these are the maximums, and your mileage may vary.

After selecting the type of DSL service and provider, you can place an order and have the provider install the necessary equipment at your home or office. Figure 1-2 shows a sample connection diagram for a typical residential DSL.

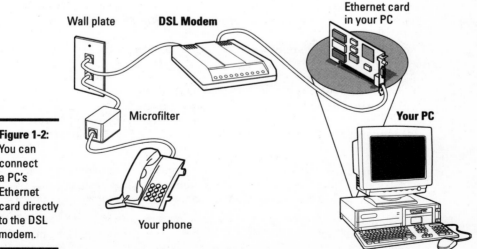

Figure 1-2:
You can connect a PC's Ethernet card directly to the DSL modem.

Here are some key points to note in Figure 1-2:

✦ Connect your DSL modem's data connection to the phone jack on a wall plate.

✦ Connect the DSL modem's Ethernet connection to the Ethernet card on your PC.

✦ When you connect other telephones or fax machines on the same phone line, install a microfilter between the wall plate and each of these devices.

Because the same phone line carries both voice signals and DSL data, you need the microfilters to protect the DSL data from possible interference. You can buy them at electronic stores or from the DSL provider.

When you connect your Red Hat Linux PC to the Internet using DSL, the connection is always on and there is more potential for outsiders to break into the PC. You should make sure that the Red Hat Linux firewall setting is set at High Security. To configure the firewall settings, select Main Menu⇨System Settings⇨Security Level from the GNOME desktop.

There is another way to protect your Red Hat Linux system from intruders and, as an added bonus, share the high-speed connection with other PCs in a local area network (LAN). To do this you need a router that can perform Network Address Translation (NAT). The NAT router translates private Internet Protocol (IP) addresses from an internal LAN into a single public IP address and makes it possible for all the internal PCs to access the Internet.

If you also want to set up a local area network, you need an Ethernet hub to connect the other PCs to the network. Figure 1-3 shows a typical setup the connects a LAN to the Internet through a NAT router and a DSL modem.

Here are the points to note when setting up a connection like the one shown in Figure 1-3:

✦ You need a NAT router with two 10 BASE-T Ethernet ports (the 10 BASE-T port looks like a large phone jack, also known as RJ-45 jack). Typically one Ethernet port is labeled Internet (or External or WAN for wide area network) and the other one is labeled Local or LAN (for local area network).

✦ You also need an Ethernet hub. For a small home network, you can buy a 4- or 8-port Ethernet hub. Basically, you want a hub with as many ports as the number of PCs you want to connect to your local area network.

✦ Connect the Ethernet port of the DSL modem to the Internet port of the NAT router using a 10 BASE-T Ethernet cable (these look like phone wires with bigger RJ-45 jacks and are often labeled Category 5 or Cat 5 wire).

✦ Connect the Local Ethernet port of the NAT router to one of the ports on the Ethernet hub using a 10 BASE-T Ethernet cable.

✦ Now connect each of the PCs to the Ethernet hub. Of course, you must have an Ethernet card installed in each PC.

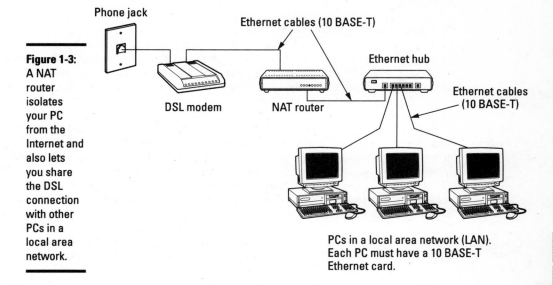

Figure 1-3: A NAT router isolates your PC from the Internet and also lets you share the DSL connection with other PCs in a local area network.

Phone jack

Ethernet cables (10 BASE-T)

Ethernet hub

DSL modem   NAT router

Ethernet cables (10 BASE-T)

PCs in a local area network (LAN). Each PC must have a 10 BASE-T Ethernet card.

Book III
Chapter 1

Connecting to the Internet

You can also buy a NAT router with built-in 4- or 8-port Ethernet hub. With a combined router-hub, you need only one box to set up a LAN and connect it to Internet with a DSL modem. These boxes are typically sold under the name Cable/DSL router because they work with both DSL and a cable modem.

Consult Book III, Chapter 2 for information on how to configure networking on the Red Hat Linux system so that the system can access the Internet.

Connecting with Cable Modem

Cable TV companies also offer high-speed Internet access over the same coaxial cable that carries television signals to your home. After the cable company installs the necessary equipment at its facility to send and receive digital data over the coaxial cables, customers can sign up for cable Internet service. You can then get high-speed Internet access over the same cable that delivers cable TV signals to your home.

How cable modem works

A box called *cable modem* is at the heart of Internet access over the cable TV network (see Figure 1-4). The cable modem takes digital data from your PC's Ethernet card and puts in an unused block of frequency (think of it as another TV channel, but instead of pictures and sound, this channel carries digital data).

The cable modem places *upstream data* — data that's being sent from your PC to the Internet — in a different channel than the downstream data that's coming from the Internet to your PC. By design, the speed of downstream data transfers is much higher than upstream transfers. The assumption is that people download far more stuff from the Internet than they upload. Probably true for most of us.

The coaxial cable that carries all those hundreds of cable TV channels to your home is a very capable signal carrier. In particular, the coaxial cable can carry signals covering a huge range of frequencies — hundreds of megahertz (MHz). Each TV channel requires 6 MHz and the coaxial cable can carry hundreds of such channels. The cable modem places the upstream data in a small frequency band and expects to receive the downstream data in another frequency band.

At the other end of your cable connection to the Internet is a *Cable Modem Termination System* (CMTS) that your cable company installs at its central facility. The CMTS connects the cable TV network to the Internet. It also extracts the digital upstream data sent by your cable modem (and by your neighbors as well) and sends them to the Internet. The CMTS also puts digital data into the upstream channels so that your cable modem can extract that data and provide it to your PC via the Ethernet card.

Cable modems can receive downstream data at the rate of about 30 Mbps and send data at around 3 Mbps upstream. However, all the cable modems in a neighborhood share the same downstream capacity. Each cable modem filters out — separates — the data it needs from the stream of data that the CMTS sends out.

In practice, with a cable modem you can get downstream transfer rates of around 1.5 Mbps and upstream rates of 128 Kbps.

If you want to check your downstream transfer speed, go to `bandwidth place.com/speedtest` and click the link to start the test. For my cable modem connection, the tests reported a downstream transfer rate of about 1.4 Mbps.

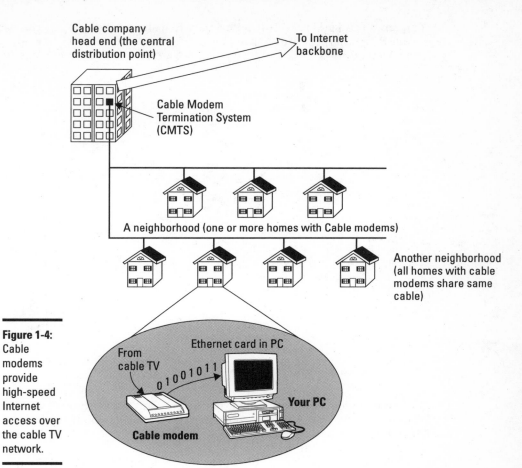

Figure 1-4:
Cable
modems
provide
high-speed
Internet
access over
the cable TV
network.

Typical cable modem setup

To set up cable modem access, your cable TV provider must offer high-speed Internet access. If the service is available, you can call to sign up. The cable companies often have promotional offers such as no installation fee or a reduced rate for three months. Look for these offers. If you are lucky, they may have a promotion going on just when you want to sign up.

The installation is typically done by a technician who splits your incoming cable into two — one side goes to the TV and the other to the cable modem. The technician provides information about the cable modem to the cable company's head end for setup at its end. When all that is done, you can plug in your PC's Ethernet card to the cable modem and you're all set to enjoy high-speed Internet access. Figure 1-5 shows a typical cable modem hookup.

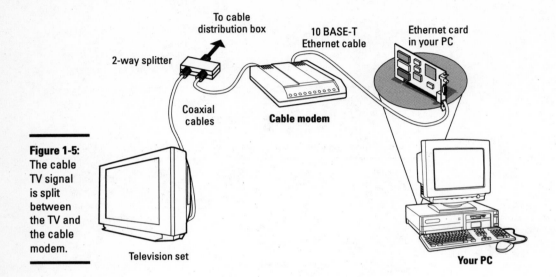

Figure 1-5: The cable TV signal is split between the TV and the cable modem.

The cable modem connects to an Ethernet card in your PC. So you need an Ethernet card in your PC. The cable company technician often provides an Ethernet card.

Here are some key points to note about the cable modem setup in Figure 1-5:

✦ Split the incoming cable TV signal into two parts by using a 2-way splitter (the cable company technician installs this). By the way, the 2-way splitter should be rated for 1 GHz; otherwise, it may not pass through the frequencies that contain the downstream data from the Internet.

✦ Connect one of the video outputs from the splitter to your cable modem's F-type video connector using a coaxial cable.

✦ Connect the cable modem's 10 BASET-T Ethernet connection to the Ethernet card on your PC.

✦ Connect your TV to the other video output from the 2-way splitter.

WARNING!

When you use cable modem to connect your Red Hat Linux PC to the Internet, the connection is always on, so there is more chance that someone may try to break into the PC. You should set the firewall setting to High Security. To configure the firewall settings, select Main Menu⇨System Settings⇨Security Level from the GNOME desktop.

TIP

You may want to add a *NAT* (Network Address Translation) router between your PC and the cable modem. As an added bonus, you can even share a cable modem connection with all the PCs in your own local area network (LAN) by adding an Ethernet hub. Better yet, buy a combination NAT router and hub so you have only box to do the job. By the way, the NAT router/hubs are typically sold under the name *Cable/DSL router* because they work with both DSL and cable modem.

The NAT router translates private Internet Protocol (IP) addresses into a public IP address. When connected through a NAT router, any PC in the internal LAN can access the Internet as if it had its own unique IP address. The end result is that a single Internet connection is shared among many PCs. An ideal solution for an entire family of Net surfers!

Figure 1-6 shows a typical setup with a cable modem connection being shared by a number of PCs in a LAN.

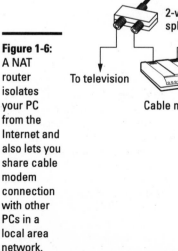

Figure 1-6:
A NAT router isolates your PC from the Internet and also lets you share cable modem connection with other PCs in a local area network.

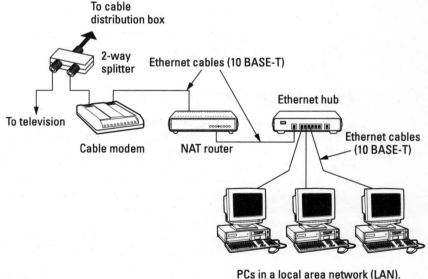

PCs in a local area network (LAN). Each PC must have a 10 BASE-T Ethernet card.

Here are the points to note when setting up a connection like the one shown in Figure 1-6:

✦ You need a Cable/DSL NAT router with two 10 BASE-T Ethernet ports (the 10 BASE-T port looks like a large phone jack — it's also known as a RJ-45 jack). Typically, one Ethernet port is labeled Internet (or External or WAN for wide area network) and the other one is labeled Local.

✦ If you plan to set up a LAN, you also need an Ethernet hub. For a small home network, you can buy a 4- or 8-port Ethernet hub. Basically, you want a hub with as many ports as the number of PCs you want to connect to your local area network.

✦ Consider buying a single box that acts as a NAT router and also a hub with a number of Ethernet ports.

✦ Connect the video cable to the video input port of the cable modem.

✦ Connect the Ethernet port of the cable modem to the Internet port of the NAT router using a 10 BASE-T Ethernet cable (these look like phone wires, except that the Ethernet cables have bigger RJ-45 jacks and are often labeled Category 5 or Cat 5 wire).

✦ Connect the Local Ethernet port of the NAT router to one of the ports on the Ethernet hub using a 10 BASE-T Ethernet cable.

✦ Now connect each of the PCs to the Ethernet hub. Of course, each PC must have an Ethernet card.

I explain in Book III, Chapter 2 how to configure the PCs in such a LAN so that they can all access the Internet.

Setting Up Dial-Up Networking

Dial-up networking refers to connecting a PC to a remote network through a dial-up modem. If you are ancient enough to remember the days of dialing up with Procomm or some serial communications software, there is a significant difference between dial-up networking and the old days of serial communication. Both approaches use a modem to dial up a remote computer and to establish a communication path, but the serial-communication software makes your computer behave like a dumb terminal connected to the remote computer. The serial-communication software exclusively uses dial-up connection. You cannot run another copy of the communication software and use the same modem connection, for example.

In dial-up networking, both your PC and the remote system run network-protocol (called TCP/IP) software. When your PC dials up and sets up a communication path, the network protocols exchange data packets over that dial-up connection. The neat part is that any number of applications can use the same dial-up connection to send and receive data packets. So your PC becomes a part of the network to which the remote computer belongs. (If the remote computer is not on a network, dial-up networking creates a network that consists of the remote computer and your PC.)

In Book III, Chapter 2, I describe TCP/IP protocol some more, but I have to use the term as well as a few concepts such as *Internet Protocol* (IP) address and *Domain Name Service* (DNS) when describing how to set up dial-up networking.

Setting up a TCP/IP network over a dial-up link involves specifying the protocol — the convention — for packaging a data packet over the communication link. *Point-to-Point Protocol* (PPP) is such a protocol for establishing a TCP/IP connection over any point-to-point link, including dial-up phone lines. Red Hat Linux supports PPP, and it comes with the configuration tools you can use to set up PPP so that your system can establish a PPP connection with your ISP.

Here's what you have to do to set up dial-up networking in Red Hat Linux:

✦ Install an internal or external modem in your PC. If your PC did not already come with an internal modem, you can buy an external modem and connect it to the PC's serial port.

✦ Connect the modem to the phone line.

✦ Get an account with an ISP. Every ISP provides you a phone number to dial, a user name, and a password. Additionally, the ISP should give you the full names of servers for e-mail and news. Typically, your system automatically gets an IP address.

✦ Test your modem and make sure it's working. You can do this testing with a serial communication package called `minicom` that comes with Red Hat Linux.

✦ Run the Internet Configuration Wizard to set up a PPP connection.

✦ Activate the PPP connection to connect to the Internet.

I briefly go over these steps in the following sections.

Connecting the modem

Modem is a contraction of modulator/demodulator — a device that converts digital signals (string of 1s and 0s) into continuously varying analog signals that can be transmitted over telephone lines and radio waves. Thus, the modem is the intermediary between the digital world of the PC and the analog world of telephones. Figure 1-7 illustrates the concept of a modem.

Figure 1-7:
A modem bridges the digital world of PCs and the analog world of telephones.

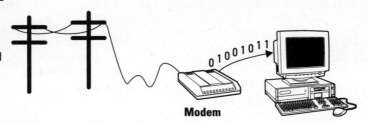

Modem

Inside the PC, 1s and 0s are represented with voltage levels, but signals carried over telephone lines are usually tones of different frequencies. The modem sits between the PC and the telephone lines and makes data communication possible over the phone lines. The modem converts information back and forth between the voltage/no voltage representation of digital circuits and different frequency tones that are appropriate for transmission over phone lines.

A quick word of caution about *winmodems* that come with many new PCs and laptops. These are software-based internal modems and totally different from the traditional hardware modems. Winmodems work only with special software, so they are often called *software modems*. These software modems come with special driver software for Microsoft Windows only and that's why they are called winmodems (for Windows modems). When it comes to winmodems and Linux, you are pretty much on your own, but there is useful guidance online at the Linux Winmodem Support homepage at `www.linmodems.org`.

Before you can dial out using the modem, you have to make sure that the modem is properly connected to one of the serial ports of your PC and that the Linux kernel has recognized the serial port.

If you have an external modem, make sure that your modem is properly connected to the power supply and that the modem is connected to the telephone line. Buy the right type of cable to connect the modem to the PC. You need a straight-through serial cable to connect the modem to the PC. The connectors at the ends of the cable depend on the type of serial connector on your PC. The modem end of the cable needs a male 25-pin connector. The PC end of the cable often is a female 9-pin connector. You can buy modem cables at most computer stores. The 9-pin female to 25-pin male modem cables are often sold under the label "AT Modem Cable."

If your PC has an internal modem (pray that it's not a winmodem), all you have to do is connect the phone line to the phone jack that's at the back of the internal-modem card.

Learning the serial-device names

The PC typically has two serial ports, called COM1 and COM2 in MS-DOS parlance. Many new PCs with *Universal Serial Bus* (USB) have only one serial port. The PC also can support two more serial ports: COM3 and COM4. Because of these port names, we often refer to the serial ports as *COM ports*.

Like other devices, the serial-port devices are represented by device files in the /dev directory. The serial ports also need interrupt-request (IRQ) numbers and I/O port addresses. Two IRQs — 3 and 4 — are shared among the four COM ports. Table 1-2 lists the serial device names corresponding to the PC's COM ports, as well as the IRQs and I/O port addresses assigned to the four serial ports.

Table 1-2	Device Names for Serial Ports		
COM port	*Device name*	*IRQ*	*I/O Address*
COM1	/dev/ttyS0	4	0x3f8
COM2	/dev/ttyS1	3	0x2f8
COM3	/dev/ttyS2	4	0x3e8
COM4	/dev/ttyS3	3	0x2e8

All of these the devices should already be in your Red Hat Linux system. In a terminal window, type **ls -l /dev/ttyS*** to see a listing of these device files.

Checking if the Linux kernel detected the serial port

To verify that the Linux kernel detected the serial port correctly, check the boot messages with the following command:

```
dmesg | grep ttyS
```

If you see a message such as the following, Linux has detected a serial port in your PC:

```
ttyS00 at 0x03f8 (irq = 4) is a 16550A
```

In this case, the message indicates that the Linux kernel has detected the first serial port (COM1). It shows the I/O address (in hexadecimal), 0x3f8 and IRQ 4. The last part of the message — 16550A — refers to the identifying number of the universal asynchronous receiver/transmitter (UART) chip, which is at the heart of all serial communications hardware (the UART converts each byte to a stream of 1s and 0s and vice versa).

You can also check for the serial ports with the `setserial` command. Type the following command to see detailed information about the serial ports:

```
setserial -g /dev/ttyS?
```

Testing the modem

After you complete the physical installation of the modem and verify that the Linux kernel detected the serial port, you can try to dial out through the modem. The best approach is to use the Minicom serial communications program that comes with Red Hat Linux.

Minicom is similar to other communications software, such as Procomm or Crosstalk, that you may have used under MS-DOS or Windows.

To run Minicom, log in as `root` and type **minicom** at the shell prompt in the terminal window or in a virtual console. Minicom runs and resets the modem. Figure 1-8 shows the result of running Minicom in an terminal window.

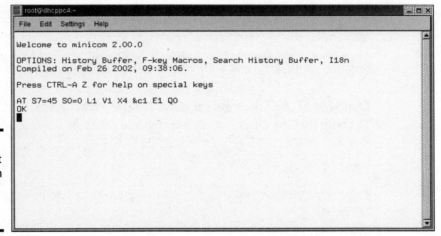

Figure 1-8:
You can test your modem manually with Minicom.

Press Ctrl+A to get the attention of the Minicom program. After you press Ctrl+A, if you press Z, a help screen appears in the form of a text window. In the help screen, you can get information about other Minicom commands. From the help screen, press Enter to go back to online mode. In online mode, you can use the modem's AT commands to dial out. In particular, you can use the ATDT command to dial the phone number of another modem (for example, dial your ISP's number). When you get the login prompt, you know that the modem is working. Figure 1-9 shows the results of a typical dial-up using Minicom. Only 24.4 Kbps with a 56 Kbps modem. No wonder I needed DSL or cable modem!

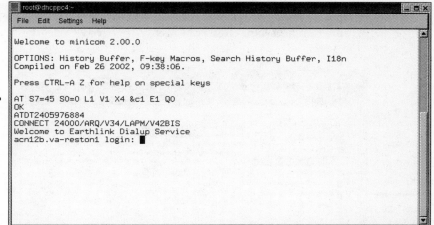

Figure 1-9:
Use the
ATDT
command to
manually
dial out
using
Minicom.

To exit Minicom, press Ctrl+A and then type **X**. Press Enter again to close Minicom.

Setting up and activating a PPP connection

Most ISPs provide PPP dial-up access to the Internet through one or more systems that the ISP maintains. If you sign up for such a service, the ISP should provide you the information that you need to make a PPP connection to the ISP's system. Typically, this information includes the following:

✦ The phone number to dial to connect to the remote system

✦ The user name and password that you must use to log into the remote system

✦ The names of the ISP's mail and news servers

✦ The IP address for your PPP connection. ISP does not provide this address if the IP address is assigned dynamically (this means the IP address may change every time your system establishes a connection).

✦ IP addresses of the ISP's *Domain Name Servers* (DNS). The ISP does not provide these addresses if it assigns the IP address dynamically.

Of this information, the first two items are what you need to set up a PPP connection.

Follow these steps to set up a PPP connection using Red Hat's Internet Configuration Wizard:

1. **Log in as** root **and select Main Menu⇨System Tools⇨Internet Configuration Wizard from the GNOME desktop (if you are not logged**

in as `root`, you'll be prompted for the `root` **password). The Select
Device Type dialog box appears (Figure 1-10). Click the Modem connection and then click Forward.**

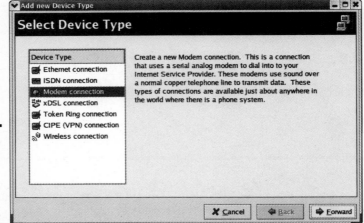

Figure 1-10:
Configure
the modem
connection
from this
dialog box.

2. **The Select Modem dialog box shows information about your modem.
Click Forward to continue.**

3. **The Select Provider dialog box appears. Fill in the connection information — the ISP's phone number, your login name, and password —
in the text boxes (Figure 1-11). Click Forward to continue.**

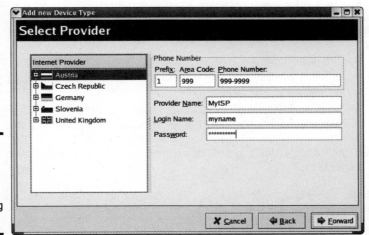

Figure 1-11:
Fill in the
connection
information
in this dialog
box.

4. Click Apply to save the dial-up configuration information and close the Internet Configuration Wizard.

5. The Network Configuration dialog box appears with the name of the new dial-up connection in a list (Figure 1-12). Click the connection name and click Activate.

Figure 1-12: Click Activate in the Network Configuration dialog box to establish the PPP connection.

6. When you're done, click Deactivate to turn the PPP connection off.

Chapter 2: Setting Up a Local Area Network

Red Hat Linux comes with built-in support for TCP/IP *(Transmission Control Protocol/Internet Protocol)* networking, as do most modern operating systems from Windows to MacOS. You can have TCP/IP networking over many different physical interfaces, such as Ethernet cards, serial ports, and parallel ports.

Typically, you use an Ethernet network for your local area network (LAN) — at your office or even your home (if you happen to have several systems at home). To connect to remote systems over a modem, you use TCP/IP networking over *Point-to-Point Protocol* (PPP).

In this chapter I describe how to set up an Ethernet network. Even if you have a single PC, you may need to set up an Ethernet network interface so that you can connect your PC to high-speed Internet access using DSL or cable modem. (I cover DSL and cable modem in Book III, Chapter 1.)

Understanding TCP/IP

You can understand TCP/IP networking best if you think in terms of a layered model with four layers. Think of these layers as being responsible for performing a particular task. The layered model describes the flow of data between the physical connection to the network and the end-user application. Figure 2-1 shows the four-layer network model for TCP/IP.

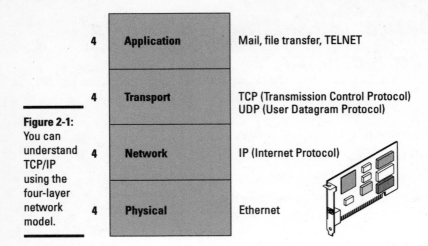

Figure 2-1:
You can understand TCP/IP using the four-layer network model.

In this four-layer model, information always moves from one layer to the next. For example, when an application sends data to another application, the data goes through the layers in this order: Application⇨Transport⇨ Network⇨Physical. At the receiving end, the data goes up from Physical⇨ Network⇨Transport⇨Application.

Each layer has its own set of protocols — conventions — for handling and formatting the data. If you think of sending data as something akin to sending letters through the postal service, then a typical protocol would be something like how to address an envelope (first the name, then the street address, and then city, state, and zip or other postal code).

Here's what each of the four layers does, top to bottom:

✦ **Application Layer** — Runs the applications that users use, such as e-mail readers, file transfers, and Web browsers. There are application-level protocols such as Simple Mail Transfer Protocol (SMTP) and Post Office Protocol (POP) for e-mail; Hyper Text Transfer Protocol (HTTP) for the Web; and File Transfer Protocol (FTP) for file transfers. Application-level protocols also have a *port number* that you can think of as an identifier for a specific application. For example, port 80 is associated with HTTP or the Web server.

✦ **Transport Layer** — Sends data from one application to another. The two key protocols in this layer are *Transmission Control Protocol* (TCP) and *User Datagram Protocol* (UDP). TCP guarantees delivery of data, whereas UDP just sends the data without ensuring if it actually reaches the destination.

✦ **Network Layer** — Is responsible for getting data packets from one network to another. If the networks are distant from one another, the data packets are routed from one network to the next until they reach the destination. The primary protocol in this layer is the Internet Protocol (IP).

✦ **Physical Layer** — Refers to the physical networking hardware such as an Ethernet card or Token Ring card that carries the data packets in a network.

The beauty of the layered model is that each layer only takes care of its specific task, leaving the rest to the other layers. The layers can mix and match, which means that you can have TCP/IP network over any type of physical network medium from Ethernet to radio waves (in a wireless network). The software is modular as well because an application can simply make use of the Transport and Internet layers that already exist as part of the operating system.

TCP/IP and the Internet

TCP/IP has become the protocol of choice on the Internet — the "network of networks" that evolved from ARPAnet. The U.S. Government's Advanced Research Projects Agency (ARPA) initiated research in the 1970s on a new way of sending information using packets sent over a network. ARPAnet evolved from this research. Subsequently, ARPA acquired a Defense prefix and became DARPA. Under the auspices of DARPA, the TCP/IP protocols emerged as a popular collection of protocols for internetworking — a term that describes communication among networks.

TCP/IP has flourished because the protocol is open. That means the technical descriptions of the protocol appear in public documents, so anyone can implement TCP/IP on specific hardware and software.

TCP/IP also made great inroads because there was stable working software available. Instead of a paper description of the network architecture and protocols, the TCP/IP protocols started out as working software, and who can argue with working software! By now, TCP/IP rules the Internet.

IP addresses

When you have many computers on a network, you need a way to identify each one uniquely. In TCP/IP networking, the address of a computer is the IP address. Because TCP/IP deals with internetworking, the address is based on the concepts of a network address and a host address. You may think of the idea of a network address and a host address as having to provide two addresses to identify a computer uniquely:

✦ **Network address** indicates the network on which the computer is located.

✦ **Host address** indicates a specific computer on that network.

**Book III
Chapter 2**

**Setting Up a Local
Area Network**

Next-generation IP (IPv6)

When the 4-byte IP address was created, the number of addresses seemed to be adequate. By now, however, the 4-byte addresses are running out. The Internet Engineering Task Force (IETF) recognized the potential for running out of IP addresses in 1991, and began work on the next-generation IP addressing scheme, named IPng, which will eventually replace the old 4-byte addressing scheme (called IPv4, for IP Version 4).

Several alternative addressing schemes for IPng were proposed and debated. The final contender, with a 128-bit (16-byte) address, was dubbed IPv6 (for IP Version 6). On September 18, 1995, the IETF declared the core set of IPv6 addressing protocols to be an IETF Proposed Standard.

IPv6 is designed to be an evolutionary step from IPv4. The proposed standard provides direct interoperability between hosts using the older IPv4 addresses and any new IPv6 hosts. The idea is that users can upgrade their systems to use IPv6 when they want and that network operators are free to upgrade their network hardware to use IPv6 without affecting current users of IPv4. Sample implementations of IPv6 are being developed for many operating systems, including Linux. For more information about IPv6 in Linux, consult the Linux IPv6 FAQ/HOWTO at www.linuxhq.com/IPv6/.

The IPv6 128-bit addressing scheme allows for 170,141,183,460,469,232,000,000,000,000,000,000,000 unique hosts! That should last us for a while!

The network and host addresses together constitute an IP address and it's a 4-byte (32-bit) value. The convention is to write each byte as a decimal value and to put a dot (.) after each number. Thus, you see network addresses such as 132.250.112.52. This way of writing IP addresses is known as *dotted-decimal* notation.

In decimal notation, a byte (it has 8 bits) can have a value between 0 and 255. This means that a valid IP addresses can have only numbers between 0 and 255 in the dotted-decimal notation.

Internet services and port numbers

The TCP/IP protocol suite has become the *lingua franca* of the Internet because many standard services are available on any system that supports TCP/IP. These services make the Internet tick by facilitating the transfer of mail, news, and Web pages. These services go by well-known names such as the following:

✦ **FTP** (File Transfer Protocol) is used to transfer files between computers on the Internet. FTP uses two ports — data is transferred on port 20, while control information is exchanged on port 21.

✦ **HTTP** (HyperText Transfer Protocol) is a protocol for sending documents from one system to another. HTTP is the underlying protocol of the Web. By default, the Web server and client communicate on port 80.

✦ **SMTP** (Simple Mail Transfer Protocol) is for exchanging e-mail messages between systems. SMTP uses port 25 for information exchange.

✦ **NNTP** (Network News Transfer Protocol) is for distribution of news articles in a store-and-forward fashion across the Internet. NNTP uses port 119.

✦ **TELNET** is used by a user on one system to log into another system on the Internet (the user must provide a valid user ID and password to log into the remote system). TELNET uses port 23 by default. However, the TELNET client can connect to any port.

✦ **SNMP** (Simple Network Management Protocol) is for managing all types of network devices on the Internet. Like FTP, SNMP uses two ports: 161 and 162.

✦ **NFS** (Network File System) is for sharing files among computers. NFS uses Sun's Remote Procedure Call (RPC) facility, which exchanges information through port 111.

A well-known port is associated with each of these services. The TCP protocol uses this port to locate a service on any system. (A server process — a computer program running on a system — provides each service.)

Setting Up an Ethernet LAN

Ethernet is a standard way to move packets of data between two or more computers connected to a single cable. (You can create larger networks by connecting multiple Ethernet segments with gateways.) To set up an Ethernet Local Area Network (LAN), you need an Ethernet card for each PC. Red Hat Linux supports a wide variety of Ethernet cards for the PC.

Ethernet is a good choice for the physical data-transport mechanism for the following reasons:

✦ Ethernet is a proven technology (it has been in use since the early 1980s).

✦ Ethernet provides good data-transfer rates: typically 10 million bits per second (10 Mbps), although there is now 100 Mbps Ethernet and Gigabit Ethernet (1,000 Mbps).

✦ Ethernet hardware is relatively low cost (PC Ethernet cards cost about $20 U.S.).

How Ethernet works

In an Ethernet network, all systems in a segment are connected to the same wire. Because a single wire is used, a protocol has to be used for sending and receiving data because only one data packet can exist on the cable at any time. An Ethernet LAN uses a data-transmission protocol known as *Carrier Sense Multiple Access/Collision Detection* (CSMA/CD) to share the single transmission cable among all the computers. Ethernet cards in the computers follow the CSMA/CD protocol to transmit and receive Ethernet packets.

The idea behind the CSMA/CD protocol is similar to the way in which you have a conversation at a party. You listen for a pause (that's carrier sense) and talk when no one else is speaking. If you and another person begin talking at the same time, both of you realize the problem (that's collision detection) and pause for a moment; then one of you starts speaking again. As you know from experience, everything works out.

In an Ethernet LAN, each Ethernet card checks the cable for signals — that's the carrier-sense part. If the signal level is low, the Ethernet card sends its packets on the cable; the packet contains information about the sender and the intended recipient. All Ethernet cards on the LAN listen to the signal, and the recipient receives the packet. If two cards send out a packet simultaneously, the signal level in the cable rises above a threshold, and the cards know a collision has occurred (two packets have been sent out at the same time). Both cards wait for a random amount of time before sending their packets again.

Ethernet was invented in the early 1970s at the Xerox Palo Alto Research Center (PARC) by Robert M. Metcalfe. In the 1980s, Ethernet was standardized by the cooperative effort of three companies: Digital Equipment Corporation (DEC), Intel, and Xerox. Using the first initials of the company names, that Ethernet standard became known as the DIX standard. Later, the DIX standard was included in the 802-series standards developed by the Institute of Electrical and Electronics Engineers (IEEE). The final Ethernet specification is formally known as IEEE 802.3 CSMA/CD, but people continue to call it Ethernet.

Ethernet sends data in *packets* (also known as frames). You don't need to know much about the innards of Ethernet packets except to note the 6-byte source and destination addresses. Each Ethernet controller has a unique 6-byte (48-bit) address. At the physical level, packets must be addressed with these 6-byte addresses.

Ethernet cables

The original Ethernet standard used a thick coaxial cable, nearly half an inch in diameter. This wiring is called *thickwire* or thick Ethernet, although the

IEEE 802.3 standard calls it 10 BASE-5. That designation means several things: The data-transmission rate is 10 megabits per second (10 Mbps); the transmission is baseband (which simply means that the cable's signal-carrying capacity is devoted to transmitting Ethernet packets only); and the total length of the cable can be no more than 500 meters. Thickwire was expensive, and the cable was rather unwieldy. Unless you're a technology history buff, you don't have to care one whit about 10 BASE-5 cables.

Nowadays, two other forms of Ethernet cabling are more popular. The first alternative to thick Ethernet cable is *thinwire,* or 10 BASE-2, which uses a thin, flexible coaxial cable. A thinwire Ethernet segment can be, at most, 185 meters long. The other, more recent, alternative is Ethernet over unshielded twisted-pair cable (UTP), known as 10 BASE-T.

To set up a 10 BASE-T Ethernet network, you need an Ethernet hub — a hardware box with RJ-45 jacks (these look like big telephone jacks). You build the network by running twisted-pair wires (usually, Category 5, or Cat5, cables) from each PC's Ethernet card to this hub. You can get a 4-port 10 BASE-T hub for about $50 U.S. Figure 2-2 shows a typical small 10 BASE-T Ethernet LAN that you might set up at a small office or your home.

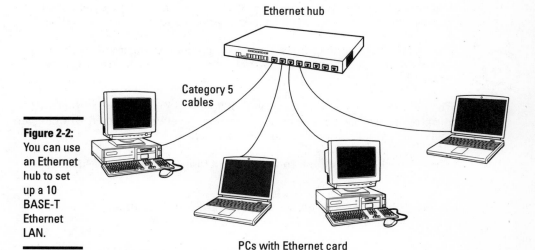

Ethernet hub

Category 5 cables

PCs with Ethernet card

Figure 2-2: You can use an Ethernet hub to set up a 10 BASE-T Ethernet LAN.

When you install Red Hat Linux from this book's companion CD-ROM on a PC connected with an Ethernet card, the Red Hat installer should automatically detect the Ethernet card and install the appropriate drivers. The installer should also let you set up TCP/IP networking.

When properly installed, the Linux kernel should load the driver for the Ethernet card every time it boots. To verify that the Ethernet driver is loaded, type the following command in a terminal window:

```
dmesg | grep eth0
```

This command searches the boot messages for any line that contains the string eth0 (that's the device name for the first Ethernet card in your Red Hat Linux system). On my PC, I have an Intel Ethernet Pro 100 card installed. I get the following output when I type dmesg | grep eth0 on my system:

```
eth0: Intel Corp. 82557 [Ethernet Pro 100], 00:A0:C9:83:D0:54, IRQ 11.
```

You should see something similar showing the name of the Ethernet card and other relevant parameters.

Configuring TCP/IP Networking

When you set up TCP/IP networking during Red Hat Linux installation, the installation program prepares all appropriate configuration files using the information you provide. However, Red Hat Linux does come with the graphical network configuration tool that you can use to add a new network interface or alter information such as name servers and host names.

Use the network configuration tool to set up networking if you are adding a new Ethernet card or if the Ethernet card was not configured during installation.

To start the network configuration tool, log in as root and from the GNOME desktop, select Main Menu⇨System Settings⇨Network. If you are not logged in as root, you're prompted for the root password.

The network configuration tool displays a tabbed dialog box, as shown in Figure 2-3.

You can configure your network through the four tabs that appear along the top of the dialog box. Here's what each of the tabs does:

✦ **Devices** — Has options to a new network interface (for example, an Ethernet card), sets the IP address of the interface, and activates the interface.

✦ **Hardware** — Lets you add a new hardware device such as an Ethernet card, modem, or an ISDN device. You can then provide information such as interrupt request (IRQ), I/O port numbers, and DMA channels for the device.

✦ **Hosts** — Shows you the local table of hosts and IP addresses and lets you add, remove, or edit entries.

✦ **DNS** — Lets you enter the host name for your system and enter the IP addresses of name servers.

Figure 2-3:
Configure the Ethernet network with the Red Hat network configuration tool.

To add and activate a new Ethernet network interface, do the following:

1. **In the Devices tab, click the Add button.**

2. **The Select Device Type dialog box appears. Select Ethernet connection and click Forward.**

3. **The Select Ethernet Device dialog box appears. Select the Other Ethernet Card and click Forward.**

4. **The Select Ethernet Adapter dialog box appears. Select your Ethernet card from the drop-down list. Then click Forward.**

5. **The Configure Network Settings dialog box appears (Figure 2-4). Select the way in which the Ethernet card gets its IP address. If it can automatically obtain an IP address (this is the case when the Ethernet card is connected to DSL or cable modem), click the radio button labeled** Automatically obtain IP address settings with dhcp. **When you do so, also click the checkbox labeled** Automatically obtain DNS information from provider. **Otherwise, click the radio button that says** Statically set IP addresses **and then enter** an IP address. For a home network use a private IP address such as 192.168.0.2 (anything that begins with 192.168. would work). After entering all the information, click Forward.

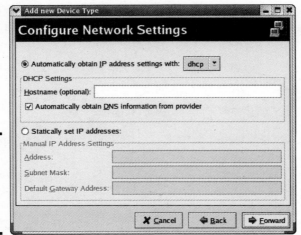

Figure 2-4:
Configure
the network
settings in
this dialog
box.

6. **Click Apply to complete the Ethernet setup.**

7. **You'll be back in the Network Configuration dialog box. Select the eth0 device and click Activate to turn the Ethernet network on.**

If you are running a private network, you may use IP addresses in the range 192.168.0.0 to 192.168.255.255. (There are other ranges of addresses reserved for private networks, but this range should suffice for most needs.)

Connecting Your LAN to the Internet

If you have a LAN with several PCs, you can connect the entire LAN to the Internet by using DSL or cable modem. Basically, you can share the high-speed DSL or cable modem connection with the all the PCs in the LAN.

In Book III, Chapter 1, I explain how to set up DSL or cable modem. In this section, I briefly explain how to connect a LAN to the Internet so that all the PCs can access the Internet.

The most convenient way to connect a LAN to the Internet via DSL or cable modem is to buy a hardware device called DSL/Cable Modem NAT Router with a 4- or 8-port Ethernet hub. NAT stands for Network Address Translation and the NAT router can translate many private IP addresses into a single externally known IP address. The Ethernet hub part appears to you as a number of RJ-45 Ethernet ports where you can connect the PCs to set up a LAN. In other words, you need only one extra box besides the DSL or cable modem.

Figure 2-5 shows how you might connect your LAN to the Internet through a NAT router with a built-in Ethernet hub. Of course, you need a DSL or cable modem hookup for this to work (and you have to sign up with the phone company for DSL service or with the cable provider for cable Internet service).

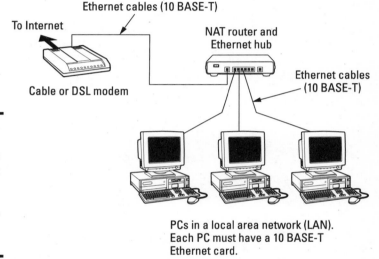

Figure 2-5:
Connect your LAN to the Internet through a NAT router with a built-in Ethernet hub.

**Book III
Chapter 2**

**Setting Up a Local
Area Network**

When you connect a LAN to the Internet like this, the NAT router acts as a gateway for your LAN. The NAT router also dynamically provides IP addresses to the PCs in your LAN. Therefore, on each PC you should set up the networking options to indicate that the IP address is to be obtained dynamically.

Your LAN can have a mix and match of all kinds of computers — some may be running Red Hat Linux and some may be running Microsoft Windows. On the Red Hat Linux PCs, you can set up Ethernet networking using the network configuration tool (select Main Menu⇨System Settings⇨Network from GNOME desktop). When configuring the network settings (see Figure 2-4), remember to click the radio button that says `Automatically obtain IP address settings with dhcp`. Also click to turn on the checkbox labeled `Automatically obtain DNS information from provider`.

Chapter 3: Managing the Network

In This Chapter

✓ Learning the TCP/IP configuration files

✓ Checking TCP/IP networks

✓ Configuring networks at boot time

*L*ike almost everything else in Red Hat Linux, TCP/IP setup is a matter of preparing numerous configuration files (text files you can edit with any text editor). Most of these configuration files are in the /etc directory. The Red Hat installer helps by hiding the details of the TCP/IP configuration files. Nevertheless, it's better if you know the names of the files and their purposes so that you can edit the files manually, if necessary.

Learning the TCP/IP Configuration Files

Running the Red Hat network configuration tool should be enough to get TCP/IP configured on your system. However, if you want to effectively manage the network, you should become familiar with the TCP/IP configuration files so that you can edit the files, if necessary. For example, if you want to check if the name servers are specified correctly, you have to know about the /etc/resolv.conf file, which stores the IP addresses of name servers.

Table 3-1 summarizes the basic TCP/IP configuration files. I describe these configuration files in the next few sections.

Table 3-1	Basic TCP/IP Network Configuration Files
This File	*Contains the Following*
/etc/hosts	IP addresses and host names for your local network as well as any other systems you access often
/etc/networks	Names and IP addresses of networks
/etc/host.conf	Instructions on how to translate host names into IP addresses
/etc/resolv.conf	IP addresses of name servers

(continued)

Table 3-1 *(continued)*

This File	Contains the Following
/etc/hosts.allow	Instructions on which systems can access Internet services on your system
/etc/hosts.deny	Instructions on which systems must be denied access to Internet services on your system
/etc/nsswitch.conf	Instructions on how to translate host names into IP addresses

/etc/hosts

The /etc/hosts text file contains a list of IP addresses and host names for your local network. In the absence of a name server, any network program on your system consults this file to determine the IP address that corresponds to a host name. Think of /etc/hosts as the local phone directory where you can look up the IP address (instead of a phone number) for a local host.

Here is the /etc/hosts file from a system, showing the IP addresses and names of other hosts on a typical LAN:

```
127.0.0.1         localhost          localhost.localdomain
# Other hosts on the LAN
192.168.0.100     lnbp933
192.168.0.50      lnbp600
192.168.0.200     lnbp200
192.168.0.233     lnbp233
192.168.0.40      lnbp400
```

As the example shows, each line in the file starts with an IP address, followed by the host name for that IP address. You can have more than one host name for a given IP address.

/etc/networks

/etc/networks is another text file that contains the names and IP addresses of networks. These network names are commonly used in the routing command (/sbin/route) to specify a network by name instead of by its IP address.

Don't be alarmed if your Linux PC does not have the /etc/networks file. Your TCP/IP network works fine without this file. In fact, the Red Hat Linux installer does not create a /etc/networks file.

/etc/host.conf

Red Hat Linux uses a special library (library refers to collection of computer code), called the *resolver library,* to obtain the IP address that corresponds to a host name. The `/etc/host.conf` file specifies how names are resolved. A typical `/etc/host.conf` file might contain the following lines:

```
order hosts, bind
multi on
```

The entries in the `/etc/host.conf` file tell the resolver library what services to use (and in which order) to resolve names.

The `order` option indicates the order of services. The sample entry tells the resolver library to first consult the `/etc/hosts` file, and then check the name server to resolve a name.

Use the `multi` option to indicate whether or not a host in the `/etc/hosts` file can have multiple IP addresses. Hosts that have more than one IP address are called *multihomed* because the presence of multiple IP addresses implies that the host has several network interfaces (the host "lives" in several networks simultaneously).

/etc/resolv.conf

The `/etc/resolv.conf` file is another text file used by the resolver — the library that determines the IP address for a host name. Here is a sample `/etc/resolv.conf` file:

```
search mtgmry1.md.home.com
nameserver 164.109.1.3
nameserver 164.109.10.23
```

**Book III
Chapter 3**

Managing the
Network

The first line tells the resolver how to search for a host name. For example, when trying to locate a host name `myhost`, the `search` directive in the example would cause the resolver to try `myhost.mtgmry1.md.home.com` first, then `myhost.md.home.com`, and finally `myhost.home.com`.

The `nameserver` line provides the IP addresses of name servers for your domain. If you have multiple name servers, you should list them on separate lines. They are queried in the order in which they appear in the file.

If you do not have a name server for your network, you can safely ignore this file. TCP/IP should still work, even though you may not be able to refer to hosts by name (other than those listed in the `/etc/hosts` file).

/etc/hosts.allow

The `/etc/hosts.allow` file specifies which hosts are allowed to use the Internet services (such as TELNET and FTP) running on your system. This file is consulted before certain Internet services start. The services start only if the entries in the `hosts.allow` file imply that the requesting host is allowed to use the services.

The entries in `/etc/hosts.allow` are in the form of a *servername:IP address* format, where *server* refers to the name of the program providing a specific Internet service, and *IP address* identifies the host allowed to use that service. For example, if you want all hosts in your local network (which has the network address 192.168.0.0) to access the FTP service (which is provided by the `vsftpd` program), add the following line in the `/etc/hosts.allow` file:

```
vsftpd:192.168.0.
```

If you want to let all local hosts have access to all Internet services, you can use the `ALL` keyword and rewrite the line as follows:

```
ALL:192.168.0.
```

Finally, to open all Internet services to all hosts, you can replace the IP address with `ALL`, as follows:

```
ALL:ALL
```

You can also use host names in place of IP addresses.

To learn the detailed syntax of the entries in the `/etc/hosts.allow` file, type **man hosts.allow** at the shell prompt in a terminal window.

/etc/hosts.deny

This file is just the opposite of `/etc/hosts.allow` — whereas `hosts.allow` specifies which hosts may access Internet services (such as TELNET and FTP) on your system, the `hosts.deny` file identifies the hosts that must be denied services. The `/etc/hosts.deny` file is consulted if there are no rules in the `/etc/hosts.allow` file that apply to the requesting host. Service is denied if the `hosts.deny` file has a rule that applies to the host.

The entries in `/etc/hosts.deny` file have the same format as those in the `/etc/hosts.allow` file — they are in the form of a *server:IP address* format, where *server* refers to the name of the program providing a specific Internet service and *IP address* identifies the host that must not be allowed to use that service.

If you have already set up entries in the `/etc/hosts.allow` file to allow access to specific hosts, you can place the following line in `/etc/hosts.deny` to deny all other hosts access to any service on your system:

```
ALL:ALL
```

To learn the detailed syntax of the entries in the `/etc/hosts.deny` file, type **man hosts.deny** at the shell prompt in a terminal window.

/etc/nsswitch.conf

This file, known as the name service switch (NSS) file, specifies how services such as the name resolver library, NIS, NIS+, and local configuration files such as /etc/hosts and /etc/shadow interact (NIS and NIS+ are network information service — another type of name lookup service). Newer versions of the Linux kernel use the /etc/nsswitch.conf file to determine what takes precedence: a local configuration file or a service such as DNS (Domain Name Service) or NIS.

As an example, the following hosts entry in the /etc/nsswitch.conf file says that the resolver library should first try the /etc/hosts file, then try NIS+, and finally try DNS:

```
hosts:        files nisplus dns
```

You can learn more about the /etc/nsswitch.conf file by typing **info libc** **"Name Service Switch"** in a terminal window.

Checking Out TCP/IP Networks

After you configure Ethernet and TCP/IP (during Red Hat Linux installation or by running the Network Configuration tool later on), you should be able to use various networking applications without any problem. If you do run into any problems, Red Hat Linux includes several tools that help you monitor and diagnose problems.

Checking the network interfaces

Use the /sbin/ifconfig command to view the currently configured network interfaces. The ifconfig command is used to configure a network interface (that is, to associate an IP address with a network device). If you run ifconfig without any command-line arguments, the command displays information about the current network interfaces. The following is a typical invocation of ifconfig and the resulting output:

```
/sbin/ifconfig
eth0    Link encap:Ethernet HWaddr 02:60:8C:8E:C6:A9
        inet addr:192.168.0.5 Bcast:192.168.0.255 Mask:255.255.255.0
        UP BROADCAST NOTRAILERS RUNNING MULTICAST MTU:1500 Metric:1
        RX packets:8104 errors:0 dropped:0 overruns:0 frame:1
        TX packets:1273 errors:0 dropped:0 overruns:0 carrier:0
        collisions:4 txqueuelen:100
        RX bytes:869342 (848.9 Kb) TX bytes:232276 (226.8 Kb)
        Interrupt:5 Base address:0x300

lo      Link encap:Local Loopback
        inet addr:127.0.0.1 Mask:255.0.0.0
        UP LOOPBACK RUNNING MTU:16436 Metric:1
        RX packets:94 errors:0 dropped:0 overruns:0 frame:0
```

Book III
Chapter 3

Managing the Network

```
TX packets:94 errors:0 dropped:0 overruns:0 carrier:0
collisions:0 txqueuelen:0
RX bytes:6184 (6.0 Kb) TX bytes:6184 (6.0 Kb)
```

This output shows that two network interfaces — the loopback interface (`lo`) and an Ethernet card (`eth0`) — are currently active on this system. For each interface, you can see the IP address, as well as statistics on packets delivered and sent. If the Red Hat Linux system had a dial-up PPP link up and running, you'd also see an item for the `ppp0` interface in the output.

Checking the IP routing table

The other network configuration command, `/sbin/route`, also provides status information when it is run without any command-line argument. If you are having trouble checking a connection to another host (that you specify with an IP address), check the IP routing table to see whether a default gateway is specified. Then check the gateway's routing table to ensure that paths to an outside network appear in that routing table.

A typical output from the `/sbin/route` command looks like the following:

```
/sbin/route
Kernel IP routing table
Destination  Gateway      Genmask      Flags Metric Ref Use Iface
192.168.0.0  *            255.255.255.0 U    0      0   0 eth0
127.0.0.0    *            255.0.0.0    U     0      0   0 lo
default      192.168.0.1  0.0.0.0      UG    0      0   0 eth0
```

As this routing table shows, the local network uses the `eth0` Ethernet interface, and the default gateway is also that Ethernet interface. The default gateway is a routing device that handles packets addressed to any network, other than the one in which the Red Hat Linux system resides. In this example, packets addressed to any network address other than ones that begin with 192.168.0 are sent to the gateway — 192.168.0.1. The gateway forwards those packets to other networks (assuming, of course, that the gateway is connected to another network, preferably the Internet).

Checking connectivity to a host

To check for a network connection to a specific host, use the `ping` command. Ping is a widely used TCP/IP tool that uses a series of Internet Control Message Protocol (ICMP, pronounced as eye-comp) messages. ICMP provides for an Echo message to which every host responds. Using the ICMP messages and replies, Ping can determine whether or not the other system is alive and can compute the round-trip delay in communicating with that system.

The following example shows how I run `ping` to see whether or not one of the systems on my network is alive:

```
ping 192.168.0.1
PING 192.168.0.1 (192.168.0.1) from 192.168.0.7 : 56(84) bytes of data.
64 bytes from 192.168.0.1: icmp_seq=1 ttl=254 time=1.36 ms
64 bytes from 192.168.0.1: icmp_seq=2 ttl=254 time=1.33 ms
64 bytes from 192.168.0.1: icmp_seq=3 ttl=254 time=1.36 ms
64 bytes from 192.168.0.1: icmp_seq=4 ttl=254 time=1.34 ms

--- 192.168.0.1 ping statistics ---
4 packets transmitted, 4 received, 0% loss, time 3026ms
rtt min/avg/max/mdev = 1.338/1.352/1.366/0.038 ms
```

In Red Hat Linux, `ping` continues to run until you press Ctrl+C to stop it; then it displays summary statistics showing the typical time it takes to send a packet between the two systems. On some systems, `ping` simply reports that a remote host is alive. However, you can still get the timing information with appropriate command-line arguments.

Checking network status

To check the status of the network, use the `netstat` command. This command displays the status of network connections of various types (such as TCP and UDP connections). You can view the status of the interfaces quickly with `netstat -i`, as follows:

```
netstat -i
Kernel Interface table
Iface  MTU Met  RX-OK RX-ERR RX-DRP RX-OVR  TX-OK TX-ERR TX-DRP TX-OVR Flg
eth0  1500 0   1678   0    0    0    651   0    0    0 BMNRU
lo   16436 0    50   0    0    0    50   0    0    0 LRU
```

In this case, the output shows the current status of the loopback and Ethernet interfaces. Table 3-2 describes the meanings of the columns.

Table 3-2	Meaning of Columns in the Kernel Interface Table
Column	*Meaning*
`Iface`	Name of the interface
`MTU`	Maximum Transfer Unit — the maximum number of bytes that a packet can contain
`RX-OK, TX-OK`	Number of error-free packets received (RX) or transmitted (TX)
`RX-ERR, TX-ERR`	Number of packets with errors
`RX-DRP, TX-DRP`	Number of dropped packets
`RX-OVR, TX-OVR`	Number of packets lost due to overflow
`Flg`	A = receive multicast; B = broadcast allowed; D = debugging turned on; L = loopback interface (notice the flag on `lo`), M = all packets received, N = trailers avoided; O = no ARP on this interface; P = point-to-point interface; R = interface is running; and U = interface is up.

Another useful form of netstat option is -t, which shows all active TCP connections. Following is a typical result of netstat -t on one Red Hat Linux PC:

```
netstat -t
Active Internet connections (w/o servers)
Proto Recv-Q Send-Q Local Address       Foreign Address       State
tcp    0      0 dhcppc4:1031        www.redhat.com:http   ESTABLISHED
tcp    0    126 dhcppc4:telnet       192.168.0.6:1238      ESTABLISHED
tcp    0      0 dhcppc4:1032        www.redhat.com:https  ESTABLISHED
tcp    0      0 dhcppc4:1033        www.redhat.com:https  ESTABLISHED
tcp    0    138 dhcppc4:telnet       192.168.0.6:1238      ESTABLISHED
tcp    0      0 dhcppc4:ftp          192.168.0.6:1548      TIME_WAIT
```

In this case, the output columns show the protocol (Proto); the number of bytes in the receive and transmit queues (Recv-Q, Send-Q); the local TCP port in hostname:service format (Local Address); the remote port (Foreign Address); and the state of the connection.

Type **netstat -ta** to see all TCP connections — both active and the ones your Red Hat Linux system is listening to (but no connection has been established yet). For example, here's a typical output from the netstat -ta command:

```
Active Internet connections (servers and established)
Proto Recv-Q Send-Q Local Address       Foreign Address       State
tcp    0      0 *:1024        *:*            LISTEN
tcp    0      0 localhost.localdom:1025 *:*            LISTEN
tcp    0      0 *:sunrpc       *:*           LISTEN
tcp    0      0 *:x11          *:*           LISTEN
tcp    0      0 *:ftp          *:*           LISTEN
tcp    0      0 *:ssh          *:*           LISTEN
tcp    0      0 *:telnet       *:*           LISTEN
tcp    0      0 localhost.localdom:smtp *:*            LISTEN
tcp    0    138 dhcppc3:telnet       dhcppc4:1037      ESTABLISHED
tcp    0      0 dhcppc3:ftp          dhcppc4:1060      ESTABLISHED
```

Sniffing network packets

Sniffing network packets — sounds like something illegal, doesn't it? Nothing like that. Sniffing simply refers to the idea of viewing the TCP/IP network data packets. The concept is to capture all the network packets so you can examine them later.

If you feel like sniffing TCP/IP packets, you can use tcpdump, a command-line utility that comes with Red Hat Linux. As the name implies, "dumps" (prints) the headers of TCP/IP network packets.

To use tcpdump, log in as root and type the tcpdump command in a terminal window. Typically, you would want to save the output in a file and examine that file later. Otherwise, tcpdump will start spewing out results that just flash by on the window. For example, to capture 1,000 packets in a file named tdout and attempt to convert the IP addresses to names, type the following command:

```
tcpdump -a -c 1000 > tdout
```

After capturing 1,000 packets, `tcpdump` quits. Then you can examine the output file, `tdout`. It's a text file, so you can simply open it in a text editor or type **more tdout** to view the captured packets.

Just to whet your curiosity, here are some lines from a typical output from `tcpdump`:

```
20:39:56.929241 dhcppc6.telnet > 192.168.0.6.4272: P 3225722544:3225722572(28)
    ack 1449612018 win 5840 (DF) [tos 0x10]
20:39:57.120308 192.168.0.6.4272 > dhcppc6.telnet: . ack 28 win 16199 (DF)
20:39:57.155930 arp who-has 192.168.0.1 tell dhcppc6
20:39:57.156915 arp reply 192.168.0.1 is-at 0:a0:c5:e1:ae:ae
20:39:57.156956 dhcppc6.1025 > 192.168.0.1.domain: 33598+ PTR? 6.0.168.192.in-
    addr.arpa. (42) (DF)
20:39:57.838984 192.168.0.1.domain > dhcppc6.1025: 33598 NXDomain* 0/1/0 (119)
    (DF)
20:39:57.840892 dhcppc6.1025 > 192.168.0.1.domain: 33599+ PTR? 1.0.168.192.in-
    addr.arpa. (42) (DF)
20:39:57.855757 192.168.0.1.domain > dhcppc6.1025: 33599 NXDomain 0/1/0 (119)
    (DF)
20:40:05.513863 192.168.0.1.router > 192.168.0.255.router: RIPv1-resp [items 2]:
    {0.0.0.0}(1) {68.49.48.0}(1) [ttl 1]
... lines deleted...
```

You can sort of understand the output — each line shows information about one network packet. Each line starts with a timestamp, followed by details of the packet, information such as where it originates and where it is going. I won't try to explain the details, but you can type **man tcpdump** to learn more about some of the details, and, more importantly, to see what other ways you can use `tcpdump`.

Configuring Networks at Boot Time

You want to start your network automatically every time you boot the system. For this to happen, various startup scripts must contain appropriate commands. You should not have to do anything special other than configure your network during installation or by using the Red Hat Network Configuration tool at a later time. However, if you need to troubleshoot why the network is not starting up, you can check the files I am going to mention in this section.

The network initialization is done through a set of text files in the `/etc/sysconfig` directory. The network activation script checks the variables defined in the `/etc/sysconfig/network` file to decide whether or not to activate the network. In `/etc/sysconfig/network`, you should see a line with the `NETWORKING` variable as follows:

```
NETWORKING=yes
```

The network is activated only if the NETWORKING variable is set to yes.

A number of scripts in the /etc/sysconfig/network-scripts directory activate specific network interfaces. For example, the configuration file for activating the Ethernet interface eth0, is the file /etc/sysconfig/network-scripts/ifcfg-eth0. Here is what a typical /etc/sysconfig/network-scripts/ifcfg-eth0 file contains:

```
DEVICE=eth0
BOOTPROTO=dhcp
ONBOOT=yes
```

The DEVICE line provides the network device name. The BOOTPROTO variable is set to dhcp to indicate that the IP address is obtained dynamically by using the Dynamic Host Configuration Protocol (DHCP), a standard way to get IP addresses dynamically. The ONBOOT variable says whether this network interface should be activated when Red Hat Linux boots. If your PC has an Ethernet card and you want to activate the eth0 interface at boot time, ONBOOT must be set to yes.

Of course, the configuration file ifcfg-eth0 in the /etc/sysconfig/network-scripts directory works only if your PC has an Ethernet card and the Linux kernel has detected and loaded the driver for that card.

Book IV

Internet

The 5th Wave   By Rich Tennant

'I like getting complaint letters by e-mail It's easier to delete than to shred."

Contents at a Glance

Chapter 1: Reading Your Mail

In This Chapter

- ✔ Understanding electronic mail
- ✔ Taking stock of mail readers and IM (Instant Messaging) clients
- ✔ Using Ximian Evolution
- ✔ Using Mozilla Mail
- ✔ Instant messaging with Gaim

*E*lectronic mail (e-mail) is a mainstay of the Internet. E-mail is great because you can exchange messages and documents with anyone on the Internet. One of the most common ways people use the Internet is to keep in touch with friends, acquaintances, loved ones, and strangers through e-mail. You can send a message to a friend thousands of miles away and get a reply within a couple of minutes. Essentially, you can send messages anywhere in the world from an Internet host, and that message typically makes its way to its destination within minutes — something you cannot do with paper mail (also known as *snail mail,* and appropriately so).

I love e-mail because I can communicate without having to play the game of "phone tag," in which two people leave telephone messages for each other without successfully making contact. When I send an e-mail message, it waits in the recipient's mailbox to be read at the recipient's convenience. I guess I like the converse even better — when people send me e-mail, I can read and reply at *my* convenience.

Red Hat Linux comes with several mail clients that can download mail from your Internet Service Provider (ISP). You can also read e-mail and send e-mail using these mail clients. In this chapter, I mention most of the mail clients available in Red Hat Linux and describe a few of them. And when you know one, you can easily use any of the mail readers.

There is yet another type of "keeping in touch" that's more in line with today's teenagers. I'm talking about *IM* — instant messaging. IM is basically one-to-one chat, and Red Hat Linux includes IM clients for AOL Instant Messenger (or AIM). I briefly describe the AIM clients in this chapter.

Understanding Electronic Mail

E-mail messages are addressed to a user name at a host (*host* is just a fancy name for a computer). That means if John Doe logs in with the user name `jdoe`, e-mail to him is addressed to `jdoe`. The only other piece of information needed to identify the recipient uniquely is the fully qualified domain name of the recipient's system. Thus, if John Doe's system is named `someplace.com`, his complete e-mail address becomes `jdoe@someplace.com`. Given that address, anyone on the Internet can send e-mail to John Doe.

How MUA and MTA work

There are two types of mail software:

+ **Mail-user agent (MUA)** is the fancy name for a mail reader — a client that you use to read your mail messages, write replies, and compose new messages. Typically, the mail-user agent retrieves messages from the mail server by using the POP3 or IMAP4 protocol. POP3 is the *Post Office Protocol Version 3,* and IMAP4 is the *Internet Message Access Protocol Version 4.* Red Hat Linux comes with mail-user agents such as Balsa, Mozilla Mail, KMail, and Ximian Evolution.

+ **Mail-transport agent (MTA)** is the fancy name for a mail server that actually sends and receives mail-message text. The exact method used for mail transport depends on the underlying network. In TCP/IP networks, the mail-transport agent delivers mail using the *Simple Mail Transfer Protocol* (SMTP). Red Hat Linux includes sendmail, a powerful and popular mail-transport agent for TCP/IP networks.

Figure 1-1 shows how the MUAs and MTAs work with one another when Alice sends an e-mail message to Bob. In case you didn't know, it's customary to use Alice and Bob to explain e-mail and cryptography (just pick up any book on cryptography and you'll see what I mean). And you may already know this, but the Internet is always a cloud — the boundaries of the Internet are so fuzzy that a cloud seems just right to represent it (or is it because no one knows where it starts and where it ends?).

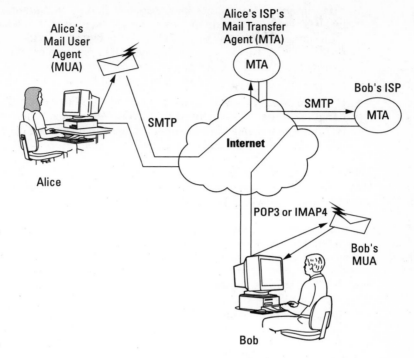

Figure 1-1:
How Alice
sends
e-mail to
Bob (or all
about MUAs
and MTAs).

The scenario in Figure 1-1 is typical of most people. Alice and Bob both connect to the Internet through an ISP and get and send their e-mail through their ISPs. When Alice types a message and sends it, her mail user agent (MUA) sends the message to her ISP's mail transfer agent (MTA) using the Simple Mail Transfer Protocol (SMTP). The sending MTA then sends that message to the receiving MTA — Bob's ISP's MTA — using SMTP. When Bob connects to the Internet, his MUA downloads the message from his ISP's MTA using the POP3 (or IMAP4) protocol. That's the way mail moves around the Internet — from sending MUA to sending MTA to receiving MTA to receiving MUA.

Mail message enhancements

Mail messages used to be plain text and most still are, but many messages today have much more than text. Two typical new features of today's mail are

✦ **Attachments** — Many messages today include attachments, which can be anything from documents to images. The recipient can save the attachment on the disk or open it directly from the mail reader. Unfortunately, this is one of the ways hackers try to get viruses and worms into your PC. If it's any consolation, most Windows-based viruses and worms do not work in Red Hat Linux.

✦ **HTML messages** — Mail messages can be in *HTML* (HyperText Markup Language), the language used to lay out Web pages. When you read an HTML message on a capable mail reader, the message appears in its full glory with nice fonts and embedded graphics.

While HTML messages are nice, they don't appear right when you use a text-based mail reader. In a text mail reader, HTML messages appear as a bunch of gobbledygook (which is just the HTML code).

If you have an ISP account, all you need is a mail client (excuse me, a mail user agent) to access your e-mail. In this case, your e-mail resides on your ISP's server and the mail reader downloads mail when you run it. You have to do some setup before you can start reading mail from your ISP's mail server. The setup essentially requires you to enter information that you get from your ISP — the mail server's name, server type (POP3, for example), your user name, and your password.

Taking Stock of Mail Readers and IM Clients in Red Hat Linux

Time was when most mail readers were text programs, but times have changed. Now mail readers are graphical applications capable of displaying HTML messages and handling attachments with ease. They are easy to use. When you have seen one, you can use any of the graphical mail readers. Red Hat Linux comes with several mail readers.

IM (instant messaging) is a more recent phenomenon, but Red Hat Linux tries to stay on top of things, so it comes with two AOL IM clients. Table 1-1 gives you an overview of the mail readers and IM clients in Red Hat Linux.

Table 1-1	Red Hat Linux Mail Readers and AIM Clients
Software	*Description*
KMail	The KDE e-mail client that supports both POP3 and IMAP
Mozilla Mail	A mail as well as a news reader that's part of the Mozilla open source Web browser (open source incarnation of Netscape Communicator)

Software	Description
Ximian Evolution	A *personal information manager* (PIM) that includes e-mail, calendar, contact management, and an online task list
Gaim	An IM client for GNOME that supports a number of instant messaging protocols such as AOL IM, ICQ, Yahoo, MSN, Gadu-Gadu, and Jabber
Kit	An AOL IM client for KDE

Using Ximian Evolution

I have heard so much about Ximian Evolution that I want to start with it. What better way than to jump right in!

Select Main Menu⇨Internet⇨Email from the GNOME or KDE desktop. If this is your first time with Evolution, the Evolution Setup Assistant starts up (Figure 1-2).

Figure 1-2: Evolution Setup Assistant guides you through the initial setup.

Click Next in the Welcome screen and the Setup Assistant guides you through the following steps:

1. **Enter your name and e-mail address in the Identity screen and click Next.**

For example, if your e-mail address is joe@someplace.com, that's what you enter. You can also specify a signature file — a text file whose contents get appended to every message you send out. Typically, you'd put your name and contact information in the signature file.

2. **Set up the options for receiving e-mail and click Next.**

   Select the type of mail download protocol — POP or IMAP. Then provide the name of the mail server (for example, `mail.comcast.net`).

3. **Provide further information about receiving e-mail — how often to check for mail and whether to leave messages on the server — and then click Next.**

   Typically, you would want to download the messages and delete them on the server; otherwise the ISP would complain after your mail piles up.

4. **Set up the options for sending e-mail. Select the server type as SMTP. Then enter the name of the server such as** `smtp.comcast.net`**. If the server requires you to log in, click the checkbox that says** `Server requires authentication`**. Then enter your username (this is the username you need to log into your ISP's mail server). Click Next.**

5. **Indicate if you want this e-mail account to be your default account. Click Next.**

6. **Set your time zone by clicking on a map. Click Next.**

7. **Click Finish to complete the Evolution setup.**

After you complete the setup, Evolution opens its main window (Figure 1-3).

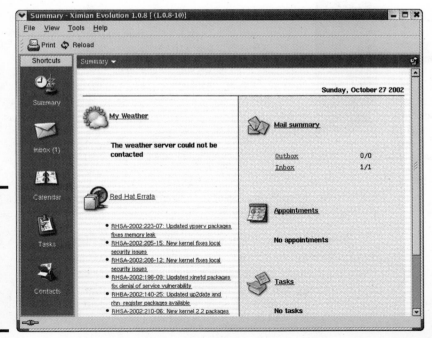

Figure 1-3: Evolution takes care of mail, calendar, contact management, and to-do lists.

The main display area is vertically divided into two windows — a narrow Shortcuts window on the left with a number of shortcut icons and a bigger window, where Evolution displays information relevant to the currently selected shortcut.

Initially, Evolution displays a summary view that shows information about your mail, appointments, and tasks, as well as other useful information such as weather. By default, Evolution initially displays the weather for Boston, Massachusetts, USA.

Some of these come from Web links. For example, the list of Red Hat Errata comes from the Red Hat Web site.

You can click the icons in the left-hand window to switch to different views. Table 1-2 describes what happens when you click each of the five shortcut icons in Evolution's Shortcuts window.

Table 1-2	Shortcut Icons in Ximian Evolution
When You Click This Icon	*It Does the Following*
	Displays a summary view of all information — mail, calendar, tasks, and some other information.
	Shows the contents of your inbox where you can read mail and send mail.
	Opens your calendar where you can look up and add appointments.
	Shows your task ("to do") list where you can add new tasks and check what's due when.
	Opens your contact list where you can add new contacts or look up someone from your current list.

As the buttons in Table 1-2 show, Ximian Evolution has all the necessary components of a PIM — e-mail, calendar, task list, and contacts.

To access your e-mail in Evolution, click the Inbox icon. Evolution opens your Inbox (Figure 1-4). If you had turned on the feature to automatically check for mail every so often, Evolution would have already prompted you for your mail password and downloaded your mail. The e-mail inbox looks very much like any other mail reader's inbox, such as the Outlook Express inbox.

**Book IV
Chapter 1**

Reading Your Mail

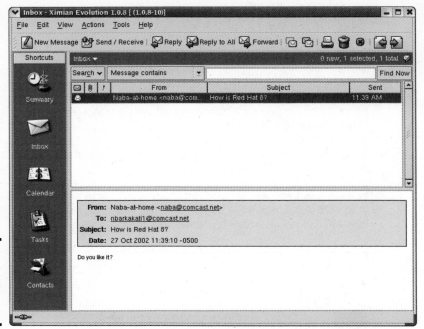

Figure 1-4:
Read your
e-mail in the
Evolution
Inbox.

To read a message, click the message in the upper window of the Inbox and the message text appears in the lower window.

To reply to the current message, click the Reply button on the toolbar. A message composition window pops up (Figure 1-5). You can write your reply and then click the Send button on the toolbar to send the reply. Simple, isn't it?

To send a new e-mail, click the New Message button on the Evolution toolbar. A new message composition window appears and you can type your message in that window; then click Send.

Ximian Evolution comes with extensive online help. Select Help⇨Table of Contents from the Evolution menu and *A User's Guide to Ximian Evolution* appears in a Nautilus window.

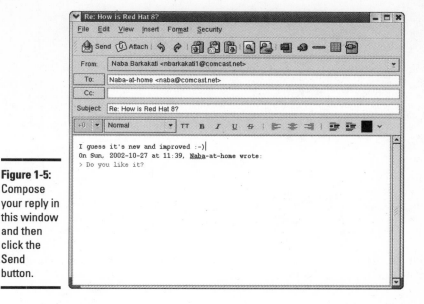

Figure 1-5:
Compose your reply in this window and then click the Send button.

Using Mozilla Mail

Mozilla Mail is the mail and news reader that comes with Mozilla — the open source successor to Netscape Communicator. Mozilla is a Web browser that also includes a mail and news reader.

To use Mozilla Mail, start by running the Mozilla Web browser. Click the Mozilla icon (the earth lassoed by the mouse cord) on the panel, and the Mozilla Web browser window appears. To access Mozilla Mail mail and news reader, select Window⇨Mail and Newsgroups from the menu. Mozilla Mail runs, starts the Account Wizard (Figure 1-6), and prompts you for information about your e-mail account.

Figure 1-6:
Provide your
e-mail
account
information
to Mozilla
Mail's
Account
Wizard.

Select the Email Account radio box and click Next. The Account Wizard then takes you through the following steps:

1. **Enter your identity information — your name and your full e-mail address such as** joe@someplace.com. **Click Next.**

2. **Provide information about your ISP's mail server — the protocol type (POP or IMAP) as well as the incoming and outgoing server names — and click Next.**

   The incoming server is the POP or IMAP server, whereas the outgoing server is the one through which you send mail out (it's the SMTP server).

3. **Enter the user name that your ISP has given you. Click Next.**

4. **Enter a name that you want to use to identify this account and click Next.**

   This is just for Mozilla Mail, so you can pick anything you want like "My home account."

5. **The Account Wizard displays a summary of the information you entered. Verify the information, and if correct, click Finish. Otherwise, click Back and go back to fix the errors.**

After you set up the e-mail account, Mozilla Mail's main window appears and shows you the contents of your inbox. Soon a dialog box pops up and asks you for your e-mail password. Mozilla Mail needs this to download your e-mail messages from your ISP. Enter your password and click OK.

Mozilla Mail downloads your messages and displays them in a familiar format. To read a message, click that message, and the full text appears in the lower window. (Figure 1-7).

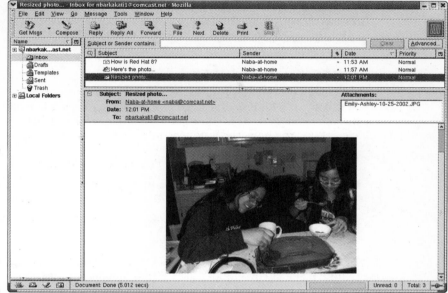

Figure 1-7:
You can
read and
send e-mail
messages
and a whole
lot more
from Mozilla
Mail.

Mozilla Mail is intuitive to use. Most of the time you can click the toolbar buttons to do most anything you want to do with the e-mail messages. Here's what each toolbar button does:

✦ **Get Msgs** — Downloads messages from your e-mail accounts (you can set up as many as you want).

✦ **Compose** — Opens a window where you can compose and send a message.

✦ **Reply** — Opens a window where you can send back a reply to the person who sent you the message you are reading now.

✦ **Reply All** — Opens a window for sending a reply to everyone who was on the addressee list of the message you are reading now.

✦ **Forward** — Brings up the current message in a window so that you can forward it to someone else.

✦ **File** — Files selected messages in folders.

✦ **Next** — Shows the next unread message.

✦ **Delete** — Deletes the selected message.

✦ **Print** — Prints the message you are reading now.

✦ **Stop** — Stops the current message transfer.

If you use any GUI mail reader from Microsoft Outlook Express to Novell Groupwise, you should find a similar set of toolbar buttons. I describe how to perform a few common e-mail-related tasks.

Managing your inbox

Mozilla Mail downloads your incoming mail and stores it in the Inbox folder. You can see the folders organized along the narrow window on the left-hand side (refer to Figure 1-7). There's a set of folders for each e-mail account you have set up. You have the following folders by default:

✦ **Inbox** — Holds all of your incoming messages for this e-mail account.

✦ **Drafts** — Contains the messages that you saved as draft (click the Save button on the message composition window).

✦ **Templates** — Contains the messages you saved as templates.

✦ **Sent** — Holds all the messages you have sent.

✦ **Trash** — Contains the messages you have deleted (to empty the Trash folder, select File⇨Empty Trash from Mozilla Mail menu).

You can create other folders to better organize your mail. To create a folder, do the following:

1. **Select File⇨New⇨Folder.**

The New Folder dialog box appears.

2. **Fill in the folder name and select where you want to put the folder (Figure 1-8). Then click OK.**

The new folder appears in the left-hand window of Mozilla Mail.

Figure 1-8: You can create new folders to organize your mail messages in Mozilla Mail.

When you select a folder from the left-hand window, Mozilla Mail displays the contents of that folder in the upper window on the right-hand side. The list is normally sorted by date, with the latest messages shown at the end of the list. If you want to sort the list any other way — say, by sender or by subject — simply click that column heading and Mozilla Mail sorts the list according to that column.

Composing and sending messages

To send a e-mail message, you either write a new message or reply to a message you are reading. The general steps for sending an e-mail message are

1. **To reply to a message, click the Reply or Reply All button on the toolbar as you are reading the message. To write a new message, click the Compose button on the toolbar. To forward a message, click the Forward button.**

A message composition window appears (Figure 1-9).

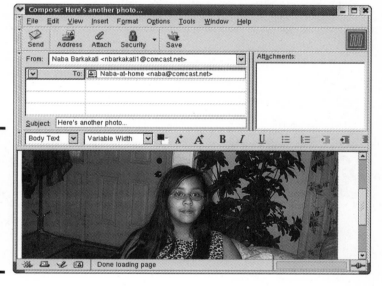

Figure 1-9: Compose your message and then enter the addresses of the recipients.

2. **In the message composition window, type your message. The message can include links to Web sites and images. To insert any of these items select Insert➪Link or Insert➪Image from the menu.**

3. **If it's a new message or a forwarded message, also type the e-mail addresses of the recipients. To select addressees from the Address Book, click the Address button on the toolbar. This opens up your Address Book, from which you can select the addressees.**

4. **After preparing and addressing the message, click the Send button.**

5. **Mozilla Mail prompts you if you want to send in HTML format or plain text or both. If you have inserted images and Web links and you know the recipient can read HTML mail, select HTML format. Then click Send to send the message.**

If you want to complete a message later on, click Save in the message composition window and then close the window. Mozilla Mail saves the message in the Drafts folder. When you are ready to work on that message again, click the Drafts folder and then double-click on the saved message.

Instant Messaging with Gaim

You can use Gaim to keep in touch with all of your buddies on AOL Instant Messenger (or *AIM,* as it's commonly known). If you use AOL's AIM, you'll be right at home with Gaim, a client for AOL's AIM.

Start Gaim by selecting Main Menu➪Internet➪Gaim from the GNOME desktop. The initial Gaim window appears (Figure 1-10).

Figure 1-10: Sign on to AIM with Gaim.

If you have used AIM before, you already have a screen name. Just type it in and enter the password, and click Signon. Gaim logs you in and opens the standard Buddy List window. The Buddy List is initially empty. To add buddies, click the Edit Buddies tab (Figure 1-11).

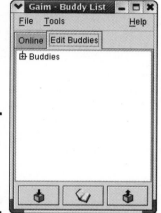

Figure 1-11:
Add your
AOL IM
buddies to
this Buddy
List window.

To add a buddy, click the leftmost button along the bottom of the Buddy List window. In the Add Buddy window that appears, enter the screen name of the buddy and click Add. To create a new group, click the middle button along the bottom of the window in Figure 1-11. Type the name of the new group in the Add Group window that appears and then click Add.

Finally, the rightmost button in Figure 1-11 is for removing a group or a buddy from your list. Just select the item and click this button to give your buddy the boot.

If any of your buddies are online, their names show up in the Online tab in the Buddy List window (Figure 1-11). To send a message to a buddy, double-click the name and a message window pops up. And should someone send you a message, a message window pops up with the message and you can begin conversing in that window.

Well, if you know AIM, you know what to do. Have fun IM'ing with Gaim!

**Book IV
Chapter 1**

Reading Your Mail

Chapter 2: Using the Web

In This Chapter

✓ Discovering the World Wide Web

✓ Understanding a URL

✓ Learning about Web servers and Web browsers

✓ Web browsing with Mozilla

✓ Creating Web pages with Mozilla Composer

I suspect you already know about the Web, but did you know that the Web, or more formally the World Wide Web, made the Internet what it is today? The Internet was around for quite a while, but it did not reach the masses until the Web came along in 1993.

Before the Web came along, you had to use arcane UNIX commands to download and use files — it was simply too complicated for most of us. With the Web, however, anyone could enjoy the benefits of the Internet using a Web browser — a graphical application that downloads and displays Web documents. A click of the mouse is all it takes to go from reading a document from your company Web site to downloading a video clip from across the country.

In this chapter, I briefly describe the Web and introduce Mozilla — the primary Web browser (and, for that matter, a mail and news reader, too) in Red Hat Linux. I also briefly discuss how you can develop your own Web pages.

Discovering the World Wide Web

If you have used a file server at work, you know the convenience of sharing files. You can use the word processor on your desktop to get to any document on the shared server.

Now imagine a word processor that enables you to open and view a document that resides on any computer on the Internet. You can view the document in its full glory, with formatted text and graphics. If the document makes a reference to another document (possibly residing on yet another computer), you can open that linked document by clicking the reference. That kind of easy access to distributed documents is essentially what the World Wide Web provides.

Of course, the documents have to be in a standard format, so that any computer (with the appropriate Web browser software) can access and interpret the document. And a standard protocol is necessary for transferring Web documents from one system to another.

The standard Web document format is *HyperText Markup Language* (HTML), and the standard protocol for exchanging Web documents is *HyperText Transfer Protocol* (HTTP). HTML documents are text files and don't depend on any specific operating system, so they work on any system from Windows and Mac to any type of UNIX and Linux.

A *Web server* is the software that provides HTML documents to any client that makes the appropriate HTTP requests. A *Web browser* is the client software that actually downloads an HTML document from a Web server and displays the contents graphically.

Like a giant spider's web

The World Wide Web is the combination of the Web servers and the HTML documents that the servers offer. When you look at it this way, the Web is like a giant book whose pages are scattered throughout the Internet. You use a Web browser running on your computer to view the pages — it's like a giant spider's web with the documents everywhere (Figure 2-1).

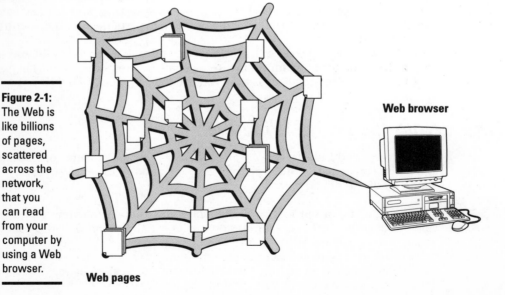

Figure 2-1: The Web is like billions of pages, scattered across the network, that you can read from your computer by using a Web browser.

Web browser

Web pages

Imagine that the Web pages — HTML documents — are linked by network connections that resemble a giant spider's web, so you can see why the Web is called "the Web." The "World Wide" part comes from the fact that the Web pages are scattered around the world.

Links and URLs

Like the pages of real books, Web pages contain text and graphics. Unlike real books, however, Web pages can include multimedia, such as video clips, sound, and links to other Web pages that can actually take you to those Web pages.

The *links* in a Web page are references to other Web pages that you can follow to go from one page to another. The Web browser typically displays these links as underlined text (in a different color) or as images. Each link is like an instruction to you — something like, "For more information, please consult Chapter 4" that you may find in a real book. In a Web page, all you have to do is click the link; the Web browser brings up the referenced page, even though that document may actually reside on a far-away computer somewhere on the Internet.

The links in a Web page are referred to as *hypertext links,* because when you click a link, the Web browser jumps to the Web page referenced by that link.

This arrangement brings up a question. In a real book, you might ask the reader to go to a specific chapter or page in the book. How does a hypertext link indicate the location of the referenced Web page? In the World Wide Web, each Web page has a special name, called a *Uniform Resource Locator* (URL). A URL uniquely specifies the location of a file on a computer. Figure 2-2 shows the parts of a URL.

Figure 2-2:
The parts of a Uniform Resource Locator (URL).

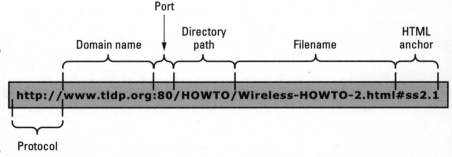

As Figure 2-2 shows, a URL has the following parts:

✦ **Protocol** — Name of the protocol that the Web browser uses to access the data from the file the URL specifies. In Figure 2-2, the protocol is `http://`, which means that the URL specifies the location of a Web page. Here are some of the common protocol types and their meanings:

- `file://` means the URL is pointing to a local file. You can use this URL to view HTML files without having to connect to the Internet. For example, `file:///var/www/html/index.html` opens the file `/var/www/html/index.html` from your Red Hat Linux system.

- `ftp://` means download a file using the File Transfer Protocol (FTP). For example, `ftp://ftp.purdue.edu/pub/uns/NASA/nasa.jpg` refers to the image file `nasa.jpg` from the `/pub/uns/NASA` directory of the FTP server `ftp.purdue.edu`.

- `http://` means that the file should be downloaded using the HyperText Transfer Protocol (HTTP). This is the well-known format of URL for all Web sites, such as `http://www.redhat.com` for Red Hat's home page. If the URL does not have a filename, the Web server sends a default HTML file named `index.html` (that's the default filename for the popular UNIX-based Apache Web servers; Microsoft Windows Web servers use a different default filename).

- `https://` specifies that the file is to be accessed through a Secure Sockets Layer (SSL) connection — a protocol designed by Netscape Communications for encrypted data transfers across the Internet. This form of URL is typically used when the Web browser sends sensitive information such as a credit card number, user name, and password to a Web server. For example, a URL such as `https://some.site.com/secure/takeorder.html` might display an HTML form that requests credit card information and other personal information such as name, address, and phone number.

- `mailto://` specifies an e-mail address you can use to send an e-mail message. For example, `mailto:webmaster@someplace.com` refers to the Webmaster at the host `someplace.com`.

- `news://` specifies a newsgroup you can read by means of the Network News Transfer Protocol (NNTP). For example, `news://news.md.comcast.giganews.com/comp.os.linux.setup` accesses the `comp.os.linux.setup` newsgroup at the news server `news.md.comcast.giganews.com`. If you have a default news server configured for the Web browser, you can omit the news server's name and use the URL `news: comp.os.linux.setup` to access the newsgroup.

✦ **Domain name** — Contains the fully qualified domain name of the computer that has the file this URL specifies. You can also provide an IP address in this field. The domain name is not case-sensitive.

✦ **Port** — Port number that is being used by the protocol listed in the first part of the URL. This part of the URL is optional; there are default ports for all protocols. The default port for HTTP, for example, is 80. If a site configures the Web server to listen to a different port, then the URL has to include the port number.

✦ **Directory path** — Directory path of the file being referred to in the URL. For Web pages, this field is the directory path of the HTML file. The directory path is case-sensitive.

✦ **Filename** — Name of the file. For Web pages, the filename typically ends with `.htm` or `.html`. If you omit the filename, the Web server returns a default file (often named `index.html`). The filename is case-sensitive.

✦ **HTML anchor** — Optional part of the URL that makes the Web browser jump to a specific location in the file. If this part starts with a question mark (?) instead of a hash mark (#), the browser takes the text following the question mark to be a query. The Web server returns information based on such queries.

Web servers and Web browsers

The Web server serves up the Web pages, and the Web browser downloads them and displays them to the user. That's pretty much the story with these two cooperating software packages that make the Web work.

In a typical scenario, the user sits in front of a computer that's connected to the Internet and runs a Web browser. When the user clicks a link or types a URL into the Web browser, the browser connects to the Web server and requests a document from the server. The Web server sends the document (usually in HTML format) and ends the connection. The Web browser interprets and displays the HTML document with text and graphics. Figure 2-3 illustrates this typical scenario of a user browsing the Web.

The Web browser's connection to the Web server ends after the server sends the document. When the user browses through the downloaded document and clicks another hypertext link, the Web browser again connects to the Web server named in the hypertext link, downloads the document, ends the connection, and displays the new document. That's how the user can move from one document to another with ease.

A Web browser can do more than simply "talk" HTTP with the Web server — in fact, Web browsers can also download documents using FTP and many have integrated mail and news readers as well.

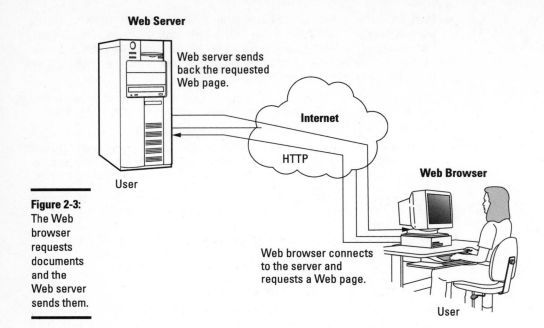

Figure 2-3: The Web browser requests documents and the Web server sends them.

Web Browsing in Red Hat Linux

Web browsing is fun because so many of today's Web pages are so full of graphics and multimedia. Then there is the element of surprise — you can click a link and end up at unexpected Web pages. Links are the most curious (and useful) aspect of the Web. You can start at a page that shows today's weather and a click later, you can be reading this week's issue of *Time* magazine.

To browse the Web, all you need is a Web browser and an Internet connection. I assume that you've already taken care of the Internet connection, so all you need to know are the Web browsers in Red Hat Linux.

Checking out the Web browsers in Red Hat Linux

Red Hat Linux comes with the Mozilla Web browser. Mozilla is an open-source version of Netscape Communicator, and it's replacing Netscape as the primary Web browser in Red Hat Linux.

Red Hat Linux includes several other Web browsers. I briefly mention the other browsers, but I focus on Mozilla in the rest of the discussions. Here are the major Web browsers that come with Red Hat Linux:

✦ **Mozilla** — The reincarnation of that old workhorse — Netscape Communicator — only better. Includes mail and a news reader. The Web browser is called the Mozilla Navigator, or simply Navigator (just as it was in Netscape Communicator).

✦ **Galeon** — The GNOME Web browser that uses parts of the Mozilla code to draw the Web pages, but has a simpler user interface than Mozilla. Galeon is not installed by default, but it should be on one of the CDs.

✦ **Konqueror** — The KDE Web browser that also doubles as a file manager and a universal viewer.

In addition to these three, many other applications are capable of downloading and displaying Web pages.

Starting Mozilla

From the GNOME desktop, you can start Mozilla in one of two ways:

✦ Click the Web Browser icon (the earth and mouse) on the GNOME or KDE panel.

✦ Select Main Menu⇨Internet⇨Web Browser from GNOME.

When Mozilla starts, it displays a browser window with a default home page (the main Web page on a Web server is known as the home page). You can configure Mozilla to use a different Web page as the default home page.

Learning Mozilla's user interface

Figure 2-4 shows a Web page from the Wiley Web site (www.wiley.com), as well as the main elements of the Mozilla's browser window.

The Mozilla Web browser has lots in its user interface, but you can master it easily. You can turn off some of the items that make it look busy. You can also start with just the basics to get going with Mozilla and then gradually expand to areas that you have not yet explored.

Mozilla toolbars

Starting from the top of the window, you see the standard menu bar, then a Navigation toolbar, followed by a thinner Personal toolbar with icons such as Home and Bookmarks. The area underneath the Personal toolbar is vertically split into two parts — a narrower, left-hand side called the Sidebar and a wider, right-hand side where the current Web page appears.

**Book IV
Chapter 2**

Using the Web

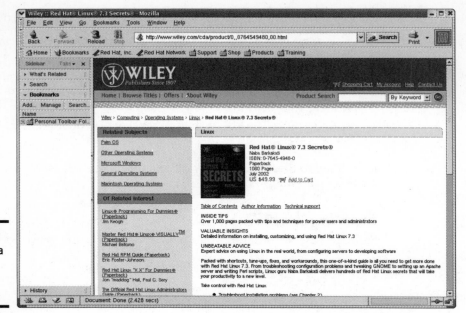

Figure 2-4:
The Mozilla
Web
browser
in action.

Notice the X button on the Sidebar. If you click there, the Sidebar goes away.
I usually like to get rid of the Sidebar, just so I can see more of the Web page.
Go ahead and click the Sidebar X button to close it.

Without the Sidebar, the Mozilla window looks cleaner and simpler (Figure 2-5). Now you can see clearly the menu bar with the standard menus
(File, Edit, and so forth), followed by the two toolbars — Navigation toolbar
and Personal toolbar.

Here's what you can do with the buttons on the Navigation toolbar that
appear just below the menu bar:

✦ **Back** — Moves to the previous Web page.

✦ **Forward** — Moves to the page from where you may have gone
backward.

✦ **Reload** — Reloads the current Web page.

✦ **Stop** — Stops loading the current page.

✦ **Location text box** — Shows the URL of the current Web page. (Type a
URL in this box to view that Web page.)

+ **Search** — Searches the Netscape search site (`search.netscape.com`) with the current Web page URL as a search string.

+ **Print** — Prints the current Web page (you can also preview how the page will appear when printed).

+ **Mozilla icon** — Takes you to the Mozilla.org Web site (`www.mozilla.org`).

Immediately below the Navigation toolbar comes the Personal toolbar with the Home and Bookmarks buttons. These two buttons serve the following purpose:

+ **Home** — Takes you to the Home page.

+ **Bookmarks** — Displays a menu from which you can bookmark the current page as well as manage your bookmarks.

There are two more links on the Personal toolbar. Clicking the Red Hat, Inc. link takes you to the Red Hat Web site (`www.redhat.com`). The Red Hat Network link takes you to the Red Hat Network site (`rhn.redhat.com`) where you can register to receive updates to Red Hat Linux.

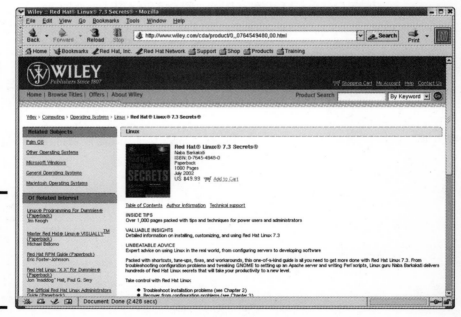

Figure 2-5:
Close the
Sidebar to
simplify
Mozilla's
user
interface.

**Book IV
Chapter 2**

Using the Web

Status bar

You can think of the bar along the bottom edge of the Mozilla window as the status bar because the middle part of that area displays status information as Mozilla loads a Web page.

The left side of the status bar includes a number of icons (Figure 2-6). If you want a hint about what any of these icons do, simply mouse over the button, and Mozilla displays a small balloon help message.

Figure 2-6:
Use these icons to open different Mozilla windows.

You can click these icons to open other Mozilla windows to perform various tasks. Table 2-1 explains what you can do with these icons.

Table 2-1	Icons on Mozilla's Status Bar
When You Click This Icon	*It Does the Following*
	Opens another Navigator (Web browser) window.
	Opens a Mozilla Mail window for reading mail and newsgroups.
	Opens an HTML composer window where you can prepare an HTML document.
	Opens the Address Book window for looking up addresses.

In the right-hand corner of Mozila's status bar, to the right of the status message, you see two icons. The icon on the left indicates that you are online. If you click it, Mozilla goes offline. The rightmost icon is a security padlock. Mozilla supports a secure version of HTTP that uses a protocol called *Secure Sockets Layer* (SSL) to transfer encrypted data between the browser and the Web server. When Mozilla connects to a Web server that supports secure HTTP, the security padlock appears locked. Otherwise the security padlock is open, signifying an insecure connection. The URL for secure HTTP transfers begins with `https://` instead of the usual `http://` (note the extra `s` in `https`).

Mozilla displays status messages in the mid portion of the status bar. You can watch the messages in this area to see what's going on. When Mozilla is done downloading a Web page, it displays a message showing the number of seconds it took to download that page.

Mozilla menus

I haven't mentioned the Mozilla menus much. That's because you can usually get by without having to go to the menus. Nevertheless, it's worthwhile to take a quick look through the Mozilla menus so that you know what each menu has. Table 2-2 gives you an overview of the Mozilla menus.

Table 2-2	Mozilla Menus
This Menu	*Enables You to Do the Following*
File	Open a file or Web location, close the browser, send a Web page or link by mail, edit a Web page, print the current page, and quit Mozilla.
Edit	Copy and paste selections, find text in the current page, and edit your preferences.
View	Show or hide various toolbars, reload the current page, make the text larger or smaller, view the HTML code for the page, and view information about the page.
Go	Go back and forward in the list of pages you have visited and also jump to other recently visited Web pages.
Bookmarks	Bookmark this page, manage the bookmarks, and add links to the Personal toolbar folder (these then appear in the Personal toolbar).
Tools	Search the Web and manage various aspects of the Web page such as image loading, cookies, and stored passwords.
Window	Open other Mozilla windows such as Mozilla Mail, Navigator, Address Book, and Composer.
Help	Get online help on Mozilla.

Changing your home page

Your home page is the page that Mozilla loads when you start it. By default, Mozilla loads a Web page from the Mozilla.org Web site. It's easy to change the home page.

First locate the page that you want to be the home page. You can get to that page any way you want. You can search on a search engine to find the page you want, you can type in the URL in the Location text box, or you may even accidentally end up on a page that you want to make your home page. It does not matter.

When you are viewing the Web page that you feel would be good as your home page, select Edit➪Preferences from the Mozilla menu. The Preferences window appears (Figure 2-7).

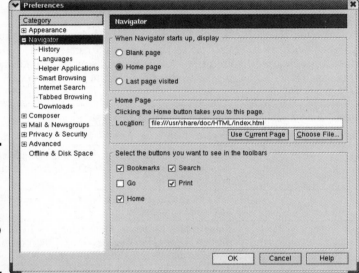

Figure 2-7: Click the Use Current Page button to make the current Web page your home page.

On the right-hand side, notice that the Home Page radio button is on. This means that when Mozilla Navigator starts up, it should display the home page. Then there is a URL for the home page, and underneath there is a button labeled Use Current Page. Click that button to make the current page your home page.

You can set a lot of other options using the Preferences window. Although I am not explaining all the options, you can click around to explore everything that you can do from this window. For example. you can click the Choose File button to select a file on your local system as the home page.

Changing Mozilla's appearance

Mozilla supports themes. A *theme* is basically the look and feel of Mozilla's user interface (which includes how the background and the buttons look).

The default theme is called the Classic theme, which gives you a look and feel that's similar to what Netscape used to have.

TIP

Mozilla comes with another theme called Modern, and you can download many other themes from the Net. Visit `themes.mozdev.org` to browse some of the available themes and download the ones you want to try. You can also get new themes by selecting View⇨Apply Theme⇨Get New Themes from the Mozilla menu.

Changing the theme is easy. If you want to see the theme you are selecting before you select it, follow these steps:

1. **Select Edit⇨Preferences from the Mozilla menu.**

The Preferences window appears.

2. **Click the plus sign next to Appearance on the left side of the window.**

The Appearance item opens up.

3. **Click the Themes item.**

The right-hand side now shows the available themes.

4. **Click a theme you want.**

You see a preview of the buttons and the color in the area underneath the list of themes (Figure 2-8).

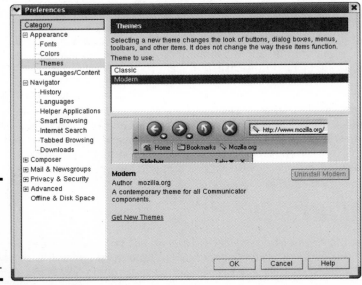

Figure 2-8:
Select a
theme to
change
Mozilla's
appearance.

**Book IV
Chapter 2**

Using the Web

5. After you select a theme you like, click OK to close the Preferences window.

A dialog box tells you that the new theme will take effect the next time you start Mozilla.

To see the full effect of a theme, go ahead and close Mozilla and then start it again.

Surfing the Net with Mozilla

Where you go from the Mozilla home page depends on you. All you have to do is click and see where you end up. Move your mouse around. You know when you are on a link because the mouse pointer changes to a hand with an extended index finger. Click the link, and Mozilla downloads the Web page referenced by that link.

How you use the Web depends on what you want to do. When you first get started, you may explore a lot — browsing through Web sites and following links without any specific goal in mind. This is what you might call Web window shopping.

The other, more purposeful, use of the Web is to find specific information from the Net. For example, you may want locate all the Web sites that contain documents with a specified keyword. For such searches, you can use one of many Web search tools that are available on the Net. For example, many people swear by Google (`www.google.com`). Mozilla's Search button takes you to the Ask Jeeves Net Search page.

A third type of use is a visit to a specific site with a known URL. For example, when reading about a specific topic in this book, you may come across a specific URL. In that case, you want to go directly to that Web page.

If you want to surf the Net with Mozilla, all you need is a starting Web page and then click whatever catches your fancy. For example, select the text in the Location text box in Mozilla's Navigation toolbar, type **search.netscape. com** and press Enter. You'll get to the Netscape search page that shows Netscape's Web directory — organized by subject. There's your starting point. All you have to do is click and you are on your way!

Creating Web Pages

If you get your Internet access from an ISP, you probably get a free Web page as well. The only catch is you have to upload an HTML file for your Web page, which means you have to somehow prepare a Web page.

One way to prepare a Web page is to simply use a text editor and type HTML code. After all, a Web page is just a text file with HTML tags. Even though I won't put anyone through the agony of typing all those HTML tags, I want to show you a very basic HTML document, just so you know the structure.

Before I get into the HTML code for a bit, I want to give you a bit of good news. Mozilla comes with something called a Composer, which you can use to prepare HTML documents — Web pages — without having to learn HTML tags. Now that you know relief is on the way, I quickly show you the innards of an HTML document.

Introducing HTML

Typically, when a client (a Web browser) connects to a Web server, the server sends back an HTML file named `index.html`. When you have your Web site, the `index.html` file is your home page. I'll introduce HTML by creating an `index.html` file and improving it through iterations. In the process, you'll see most of the important HTML features.

To begin, open any text editor and type the following lines of text:

```
<html>

<head>
<TITLE>
My Home Page
</TITLE>
</head>

<body>

<center>
<h1>
My Home Page
</h1>
</center>

<hr>
This page is under construction.
<hr>

Copyright &copy; 2002 Someone
<a href="mailto:webmaster@myplace.com">
<address>
webmaster@myplace.com
</address>
</a>

</body>
</html>
```

This is a bare-bones HTML file. Go ahead and save it with the file name `index.html`.

To see how it looks, select File⇨Open File from the Mozilla menu. Browse through the directories and pick the `index.html` file from wherever you stored it. Click Open to open the file in Mozilla. Figure 2-9 shows how the Web page looks in Mozilla. By the way, the Mozilla window in Figure 2-9 has the Modern theme. That's why it looks different from the usual Mozilla window (see, for example, Figure 2-4).

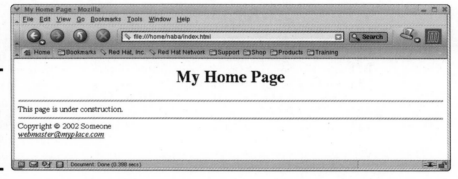

Figure 2-9:
View your
HTML file in
Mozilla to
see how
it looks.

Getting back to the Web page itself, it looks quite nice, doesn't it? No wonder we love Web pages.

At this point, you should correlate the Web page in Figure 2-9 with the HTML codes so that you can see the effect of each HTML tag. In particular, notice the following things:

✦ HTML tags are enclosed in angle brackets ⟨...⟩, and there is a pair of tags — a beginning tag and an ending tag — that goes like this ⟨/...⟩.

✦ HTML tags are not case-sensitive. Thus, you can type the title tag as ⟨title⟩ or ⟨TITLE⟩; both mean the same.

✦ The ⟨html⟩ ... ⟨/html⟩ tag pair simply indicates that the document is an HTML document; that tag does not have any visual effect.

✦ The ⟨head⟩ ... ⟨/head⟩ tags enclose the header information. In this case, the header defines the title of the page. That title appears in the title bar of the Mozilla window.

✦ The ⟨body⟩ ... ⟨/body⟩ tag pair encloses the entire HTML document.

✦ The body of the Web page shows the text `My Home Page` in header level 1 (⟨h1⟩ ... ⟨/h1⟩) and centered (⟨center⟩ ... ⟨/center⟩).

✦ The ⟨hr⟩ tag causes the browser to display a horizontal rule.

✦ The HTML keyword `&copy;` displays a copyright symbol.

✦ The `<a href= ...> ... </a>` tag adds a hyperlink. All the lines between the start tag `<a href="mailto:webmaster@myplace.com">` and the end tag `</a>` are called the *anchor* (or `<a>`) *element.* The keyword `href` that appears in the start tag of the anchor element is called an attribute.

✦ The `<address> ... </address>` tags display the enclosed text as an address (in italics).

I won't go any further with the HTML tags; this much should give you a feel for the overall structure of a typical Web page.

If you are ever curious about HTML code corresponding to any Web page, simply select View⇨Page Source from the Mozilla menu and you'll see the HTML code for the current page.

Composing Web pages with Mozilla Composer

Mozilla Composer is a graphical tool for creating Web pages without having to know much HTML. If you know HTML, you can certainly make use of that knowledge in Composer. The nice part is that you can create a nice Web page even if you don't know any HTML.

A sample editing session in Composer

If you are creating a new Web page from scratch, select Window⇨Composer from the Mozilla menu.

If you want to edit an existing Web page and you've opened it in Mozilla, select File⇨Edit Page. Mozilla opens a Composer window with the same HTML file.

You can start with the page shown in Figure 2-9 and begin editing it. In the Composer window, the Web page looks similar to that in Figure 2-9, but now it behaves like a word processor. You can start editing the text and changing the layout, just as you would in a word processor. To add text, simply click and type. To apply text formatting effects such as boldface, italic, and underline, use the text-formatting toolbar that looks very much like similar toolbars in any word processor.

You can also insert images. Here's how:

1. **Gather the image files you want to use (in formats such as JPEG or GIF). You can either prepare the images in a drawing and paint program or get the images from some other source (for example, from a**

Web site such as `thefreesite.com/Free_Graphics/Free_clipart/ index.html`). **Save the image files somewhere on your Red Hat Linux PC.**

2. **Position the cursor where you want an image; then select Insert⇨ Image from the Composer menu.**

   The Image Properties dialog box appears.

3. **Click Choose File and select the image file from the Select Image File dialog box.**

4. **Enter alternate text for the image — this is the text that would appear in text-only browsers.**

5. **After filling all the information, click OK.**

   The image should appear where you positioned the cursor (Figure 2-10).

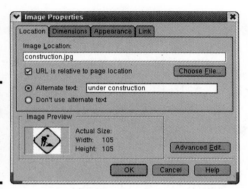

Figure 2-10: You can add an image to a Web page from this dialog box.

6. **Repeat Steps 2 through 5 for other images. After inserting all the images, select File⇨Save to save the HTML file. If you are creating a new Web page, Composer prompts you for a filename.**

Figure 2-11 shows the Web page of Figure 2-9 after I added some text and inserted an image.

With this brief example, I have barely scratched the surface as far as what Composer can do. If you begin to try out these features on sample Web pages, you'll figure out Composer's features in no time.

As you are working in Composer, if you ever wonder what any of the toolbar buttons do, simply mouse over the button and a small balloon help pops up with a helpful hint. Figure 2-12 shows an example of what happens when you mouse over the Link button.

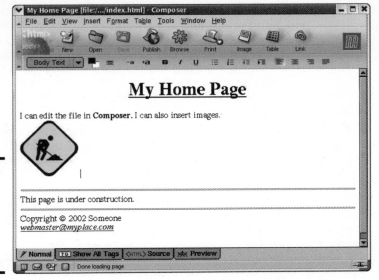

Figure 2-11:
You can create or edit your Web pages in Composer.

Figure 2-12:
Mouse over a button and Composer displays a balloon help.

Views in Composer

Notice that the Composer window has four tabs along the bottom. These tabs enable you to view the Web page in different forms. You typically edit the file in the Normal view, but you can switch to the other views; for example, you can edit HTML directly if you so desire. To change to a different view, click on the tab.

The four tabs are as follows:

✦ **Normal** — This view shows the Web page in nearly complete layout, but also lets you edit the page. You typically do most of your editing and formatting in this view.

✦ **Show All Tags** — This view shows the Web page with the HTML tags as small icons. You can quickly check what HTML tags are affecting which parts of the document and, perhaps, fix any formatting problems.

✦ **<HTML> Source** — This view shows you the HTML text in its full glory. If you used WordPerfect, this is like WordPerfect's "Reveal Codes" option. If something weird happens to the Web page layout, you can go into this window, find the offending code, and fix it. Of course, you have to know some HTML, but don't worry — you'll start picking it up if you start working with Web pages. You can also use this view to write the Web page directly in HTML and go to Normal or Preview views to check up on the layout.

✦ **Preview** — This view essentially shows you what the Web page looks like in Mozilla Navigator. It's a quick way to check the final layout without having to open the file in a Navigator window. You cannot edit in this view.

The Show All Tags view can be handy when you want to quickly spot extraneous HTML tags. Figure 2-13 shows the Show All Tags view of the Web page shown in Figure 2-11.

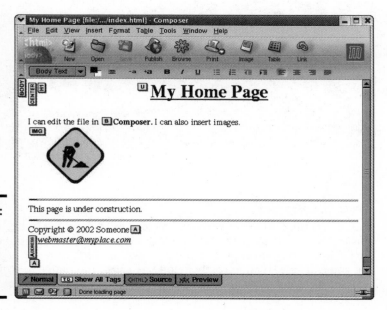

Figure 2-13: Show All Tags view shows the HTML tags as icons.

Each tag appears in yellow with the tag name such as CENTER (for centered text), BIG (for bigger font), H1 (for header level 1), IMG (for image), and so on. You can see if any extraneous tags appear in the Web page and remove them if you want (although they often don't do any harm — for example when a blank line is centered).

Chapter 3: Reading Newsgroups

*I*nternet newsgroups are like the bulletin board systems (BBS) of the pre-Web age or forums on online systems such as AOL and MSN. Essentially, newsgroups provide a distributed conferencing system that spans the globe. You can post articles — essentially e-mail messages to a whole group of people — and respond to articles others have posted.

Think of an Internet newsgroup as a gathering place — a virtual meeting place where you can ask questions and discuss various issues (and best of all, everything you discuss gets archived for posterity).

To participate in newsgroups, you need access to a news server — your Internet Service Provider (ISP) should give you this access. You also need a news reader. Luckily, Red Hat Linux comes with software such as Pan and Mozilla Mail that you can use to read newsgroups. In this chapter, I introduce you to newsgroups and show you how to read newsgroups with a few of the news readers. I also briefly explain how you can read and search newsgroups for free from a few Web sites.

Understanding Newsgroups

Newsgroups originated in Usenet — a store-and-forward messaging network that was widely used for exchanging e-mail and news items. Usenet works like a telegraph in that news and mail are relayed from one system to another. In Usenet, the systems are not on any network; they simply dial up and use the UNIX-to-UNIX Copy Protocol (UUCP) to transfer text messages.

Usenet is a very loosely connected collection of computers that has worked well and continues to be used because very little expense is involved in connecting to it. All you need is a modem and a site willing to store and forward your mail and news. You have to set up UUCP on your system, but you do not need a sustained network connection; just a few phone calls are all it takes to keep the e-mail and news flowing. The downside is that you cannot use TCP/IP services such as the Web, TELNET, or FTP.

From their Usenet origins, the newsgroups have now migrated to the Internet (even though the newsgroups are still called *Usenet newsgroups*). Instead of UUCP, the news is now transported by means of the Network News Transfer Protocol (NNTP).

Although the news transport protocol has changed from UUCP to NNTP, the store-and-forward concept of news transfer remains. Thus, if you want to get news on your Red Hat Linux system, you have to find a news server from which your system can download news. Typically, this would be your ISP's news server.

Newsgroup hierarchy

The Internet newsgroups are organized in a hierarchy for ease of maintenance as well as ease of use. The newsgroup names show the hierarchy, but they are written in Internet-speak. They are, however, easy to understand with a little bit of explanation.

A typical newsgroup name looks like this:

```
comp.os.linux.announce
```

This name says that `comp.os.linux.announce` is a newsgroup for announcements (`announce`) about the Linux operating system (`os.linux`) and that these subjects fall under the broad category of computers (`comp`).

As you can see, the format of a newsgroup name is a sequence of words separated by periods. These words denote the hierarchy of the newsgroup. Figure 3-1 illustrates the concept of hierarchical organization of newsgroups.

To understand the newsgroup hierarchy, compare the newsgroup name with the path name of a file (such as `/usr/lib/X11/xinit/Xclients`) in Linux. Just as a file's path name shows the directory hierarchy of the file, the newsgroup name shows the newsgroup hierarchy. In filenames, a slash (`/`) separates the names of directories; in a newsgroup's name, a period (`.`) separates the different levels in the newsgroup hierarchy.

In a newsgroup name, the first word represents the newsgroup category. The `comp.os.linux.announce` newsgroup, for example, is in the `comp` category, whereas `alt.books.technical` is in the `alt` category.

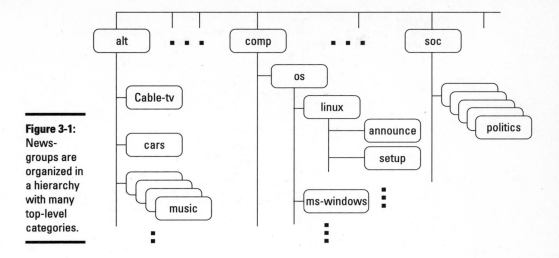

Figure 3-1: News-groups are organized in a hierarchy with many top-level categories.

Top-level newsgroup categories

Table 3-1 lists some of the major newsgroup categories. You'll find a wide variety of newsgroups covering subjects ranging from politics to computers. The Linux-related newsgroups are in the `comp.os.linux` hierarchy.

Table 3-1	Some Major Newsgroup Categories
Category	*Subject*
`alt`	"Alternative" newsgroups (not subject to any rules), which run the gamut from the mundane to the bizarre
`bionet`	Biology newsgroups
`bit`	Bitnet newsgroups
`biz`	Business newsgroups
`clari`	Clarinet news service (daily news)
`comp`	Computer hardware and software newsgroups (includes operating systems such as Linux and Microsoft Windows)

(continued)

Table 3-1 *(continued)*

Category	Subject
ieee	Newsgroups for the Institute of Electrical and Electronics Engineers (IEEE)
k12	Newsgroups devoted to elementary and secondary education
linux	Newsgroups devoted to Linux (includes a `linux.redhat` hierarchy)
misc	Miscellaneous newsgroups
news	Newsgroups about Internet news administration
rec	Recreational and art newsgroups
sci	Science and engineering newsgroups
soc	Newsgroups for discussing social issues and various cultures
talk	Discussions of current issues (such as "talk radio")

This short list of categories is deceptive because it does not really tell you about the wide-ranging variety of newsgroups available in each category. The top-level categories alone number close to a thousand, but many top-level categories are distributed only in specific regions of the world. Because each newsgroup category contains several levels of subcategories, the overall count of newsgroups can be close to 60, or 70,000! The `comp` category alone has more than 500 newsgroups.

To browse newsgroup categories and get a feel for the breadth of topics covered by the newsgroups, visit the Free Usenet Newsgroup News Web site at `newsone.net`.

Linux-related newsgroups

Typically, you have to narrow your choice of newsgroups according to your interests. If you are interested in Linux, for example, you can pick one or more of these newsgroups:

✦ `comp.os.linux.admin` — Information about Linux system administration

✦ `comp.os.linux.advocacy` — Discussions about promoting Linux

✦ `comp.os.linux.announce` — Important announcements about Linux. This newsgroup is moderated, which means you must mail the article to the moderator, who then posts it to the newsgroup if the article is appropriate for the newsgroup (this keeps the riff-raffs from clogging up the newsgroup with their own marketing pitches).

✦ `comp.os.linux.answers` — Questions and answers about Linux. All the Linux HOWTOs are posted in this moderated newsgroup.

✦ `comp.os.linux.development` — Current Linux development work

✦ `comp.os.linux.development.apps` — Linux application development

- ✦ `comp.os.linux.development.system` — Linux operating-system development

- ✦ `comp.os.linux.hardware` — Discussions about Linux and various types of hardware

- ✦ `comp.os.linux.help` — Help with various aspects of Linux

- ✦ `comp.os.linux.misc` — Miscellaneous Linux-related topics

- ✦ `comp.os.linux.networking` — Networking under Linux

- ✦ `comp.os.linux.redhat` — Red Hat Linux-related topics

- ✦ `comp.os.linux.setup` — Linux setup and installation

- ✦ `comp.os.linux.x` — Discussions about setting up and running the X Window System under Linux

- ✦ `linux.redhat` — Discussions about Red Hat Linux

You have to be selective about what newsgroups you read because it's impossible to keep up with all the news, even in a specific area such as Linux. When you first install and set up Red Hat Linux, you might read newsgroups such as `comp.os.linux.redhat`, `comp.os.linux.setup`, `comp.os.linux.hardware`, and `comp.os.linux.x` (especially if you run X). After you have Linux up and running, you may want to find out about only new things happening in Linux. For such information, read the `comp.os.linux.announce` newsgroup.

Reading Newsgroups from Your ISP

If you have signed up with an ISP for Internet access, it should provide you with access to a news server. Such Internet news servers communicate by using the Network News Transfer Protocol (NNTP). Then you can use an NNTP-capable newsreader, such as Pan, to access the news server and read selected newsgroups. You can also read news by using the news reader that comes with Mozilla (included with Red Hat Linux). This is the easiest way to access news from your Red Hat Linux Internet system.

My discussion about reading newsgroups assumes that you have obtained access to a news server from your ISP. The ISP provides you the name of the news server and any necessary user name and password. You need this information to set up your news account on the newsreader you use.

To read news, you need a *newsreader* — a program that enables you to select a newsgroup and view the items in that newsgroup. You also need to understand the newsgroup hierarchy and naming convention, which is described in the "Newsgroup hierarchy" section of this chapter. Now I show you how to read news from a news server.

REMEMBER

If you don't have access to newsgroups through your ISP, you can try to use one of the many public news servers that are out there. For a list of public news servers, visit NewzBot at www.newzbot.com. At this Web site, you can search for news servers that carry specific newsgroups.

Reading newsgroups with Mozilla Mail

You can browse newsgroups and post articles from Mozilla Mail, one of the components of Mozilla. When you are starting to read newsgroups for the first time, follow these steps to set up the news account:

1. **Click the Mozilla icon (the red lizard with sunglasses) or select Main Menu➪Internet➪Web Browser from the GNOME panel.**

This starts Mozilla.

2. **Select Windows➪Mail & Newsgroups from the Mozilla menu.**

The Mozilla Mail and News (called Mozilla Mail, for short) window appears.

3. **Select Edit➪Mail & Newsgroups Account Settings from the Mozilla Mail menu.**

A dialog box appears.

4. **Click Add Account.**

The Account Wizard appears.

5. **Click the Newsgroup Account radio button (Figure 3-2) and click Next.**

Figure 3-2:
Mozilla's
Account
Setup
wizard
guides you
through the
newsgroup
account
setup.

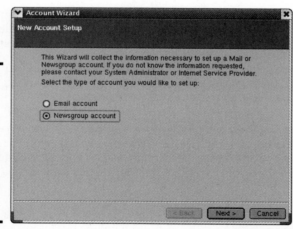

6. **Fill in your identity information — name and e-mail address — and click Next.**

7. **Enter your news server name and click Next.**

8. **Enter a descriptive name of the newsgroup account and click Next.**

9. **Click Finish to complete the newsgroup account setup.**

The new newsgroup account now appears in the list of accounts on the left-hand side of the Mozilla Mail window. Click the newsgroup account name, and the right-hand side shows the options for the newsgroup account.

Click the Subscribe to newsgroups link. Mozilla Mail starts to download the list of newsgroups from the news server.

If your ISP's news server requires a user name and password, you are prompted for that information. After that, Mozilla Mail downloads the list of newsgroups and displays them in the Subscribe dialog box. You can enter a search string in a text box to narrow the list. When you find the newsgroups you want, click the checkbox to subscribe to these newsgroups (Figure 3-3). Then click OK to close the dialog box.

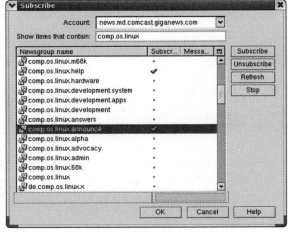

Figure 3-3: Indicate which newsgroups you want to subscribe to in this dialog box.

Book IV Chapter 3

Reading Newsgroups

After you subscribe to newsgroups, these newsgroups appear under the newsgroup account name in the left-hand side of the Mozilla Mail window. You can then read a newsgroup using these steps:

1. **Click a newsgroup name (for example, `comp.os.linux.announce`).**

This brings up a dialog box that asks you how many message headers you want to download.

2. **Specify the number of headers (for example, 500) you want and then click OK to proceed.**

Mozilla Mail downloads the headers from the newsgroup and displays a list in the upper right-hand area of the window.

3. **From the list of headers, click an item to read that article (Figure 3-4).**

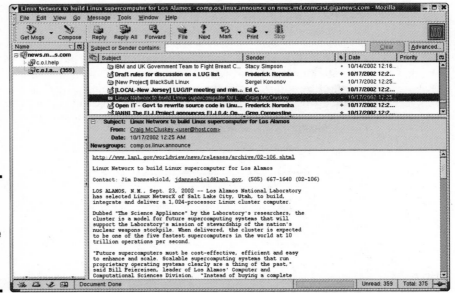

Figure 3-4: Click an article to read it in the lower right-hand window.

To select other subscribed newsgroups, simply click the newsgroup's name in the left-hand side of the window.

Newsgroup subscriptions

Unlike magazines or newspapers, newsgroups do not require that you subscribe to them; you can read any newsgroup that is available on the news server. The news server administrator may decide to exclude certain newsgroups, however; in that case, you cannot read them.

The only thing that can be called "subscribing" is when you indicate the newsgroups you routinely want to read. The news server does not receive any of this subscription information — the information is used only by the news reader to determine what to download from the news server.

How to post news

You can use any news reader to post a news article (a new item or a reply to an old posting) to one or more newsgroups. The exact command for posting a news item depends on the news reader. For example, in the Mozilla Mail newsreader, follow these steps to post an article:

1. **Click Reply on the toolbar to post a follow-up to a news item you are reading. To post a new news article, click Compose.**

2. **A window appears where you can compose the message. Type the names of the newsgroups, just as you type the addresses of recipients when sending e-mail. Then enter the subject and your message. For this test posting, type** ignore **as the subject line and enter** misc.test **as the name of the newsgroup.**

   Otherwise, any site that receives your article replies by mail to tell you the article has reached the site; that's in keeping with the purpose of the `misc.test` newsgroup. Figure 3-5 shows the message being composed in Netscape Communicator.

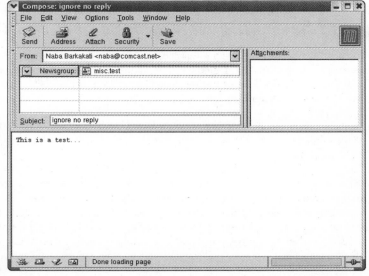

Figure 3-5: You can post follow-ups or new news articles from Mozilla Mail news reader.

3. **After you finish composing the message, click Send on the toolbar (see Figure 3-5).**

   Mozilla Mail sends the message to the news server, which in turn sends it to other news servers, and soon it's all over the world!

4. **To verify that the test message has reached the newsgroup, choose File⇨Subscribe; then subscribe to the** `misc.test` **newsgroup (that's where you've recently posted the new article). Look at the latest article (or one of the most recent ones) in** `misc.test`, **which should be the article you've recently posted.**

If you post an article and read the newsgroup immediately, you see the new article, but that does not mean the article has reached other sites on the Internet. After all, your posting shows up on your news server immediately because that's where you have posted the article. Because of the store-and-forward model of news distribution, the news article gradually propagates from your news server to others around the world.

The `misc.test` newsgroup provides a way to see whether or not your news posting is really getting around. If you post to that newsgroup and do not include the word *ignore* in the subject, news servers acknowledge receipt of the article by sending an e-mail message to the address listed in the Reply-To field of the article's header.

Reading and Searching Newsgroups at Web Sites

If you don't have access to newsgroups through your ISP, you can still read newsgroups and post articles to newsgroups at a number of Web sites. Some of them archive old news articles and provide good search capabilities, so you can search these for articles related to some question you may have.

The best part about reading newsgroups through a Web site is that you don't even need access to a news server and you can read news from your Web browser.

Table 3-2 lists Web sites that offer free access to Usenet newsgroups. There are some sites that offer Usenet newsgroup service for a fee. I don't list them here, but you can search for them in Google (`www.google.com`) — type the search words **usenet newsgroup access** and you should get a list of all Web sites that offer newsgroup access (including the ones that charge a fee).

Table 3-2	Web Sites with Free Access to Usenet Newsgroups
Web Site	*URL*
Google Groups	`groups.google.com`
NewsOne.Net	`newsone.net`
Mailgate	`www.mailgate.org`

One of the best places to read newsgroups, post articles, and search old newsgroup archives is Google Groups — Google's Usenet discussion forums — on the Web at `groups.google.com`. At that Web site, you can select a newsgroup to browse and you can post replies to articles posted on various newsgroups.

The best part of Google Groups is the search capability. You already know how good Google's Web search is; you get that same comprehensive search capability to locate newsgroup postings that relate to your search words. To search newsgroups, fill in the search form at `groups.google.com` and press Enter.

To browse newsgroups in Google Groups, ignore the search box and look at the list of high-level newsgroup categories such as `alt`, `comp`, and `soc`. Click the category and you can gradually drill down to specific newsgroups. When viewing an article in Google Groups, you can click a link that enables you to post a follow-up to that article.

Chapter 4: Transferring Files with FTP

In This Chapter

✔ **Using the GNOME FTP client**

✔ **Using the Mozilla Web browser as FTP client**

✔ **Learning to use the FTP command**

*J*ust as the name implies, *File Transfer Protocol* (FTP) is used to transfer files between computers. For example, if your Internet Service Provider (ISP) gives you space for a personal Web page, you may have already used FTP to upload the Web page. Using an FTP client on your computer, you log into your ISP account, provide your password, and then copy the files from your home system to the ISP's server.

You can also use FTP to download other files, such as open-source software from other computers on the Internet. In this case, you don't need an account on the remote system to download files. You can simply log in using the `anonymous` user name and provide your e-mail address as the password (in fact, your Web browser can do this on your behalf, so you may not even know this is happening). This type of anonymous FTP is great for distributing files to anyone who wants them. For example, a hardware vendor might use anonymous FTP to provide updated device drivers to anyone who needs them.

Red Hat Linux comes with several FTP clients, both command-line ones and GUI ones. In this chapter, I introduce you to a few GUI FTP clients and, for the command-line FTP client, describe the commands you use to work with remote directories.

Using Graphical FTP Clients

You can use one of the following GUI FTP clients in Red Hat Linux:

✦ gFTP — a graphical FTP client

✦ Mozilla Web browser for anonymous FTP downloads

For uploading files, you want to use gFTP because you typically need to provide a user name and password for such transfers. Web browsers work fine for anonymous downloads, which is how you typically download software from the Internet.

I briefly describe both GUI FTP clients in the next two sections.

Using gFTP

GNOME comes with gFTP, a graphical FTP client. To start gFTP, select from the GNOME or KDE desktop Main Menu⇨Extras⇨Internet⇨gFTP. The gFTP window appears (Figure 4-1).

The gFTP window has a menu bar with menus for performing various tasks. Just below the menu bar is a toolbar with a number of buttons and text fields. Here you can type the name or IP address of the remote host, the user name, and the password needed to log into the remote host. Figure 4-1 shows the gFTP window after you have filled in this information.

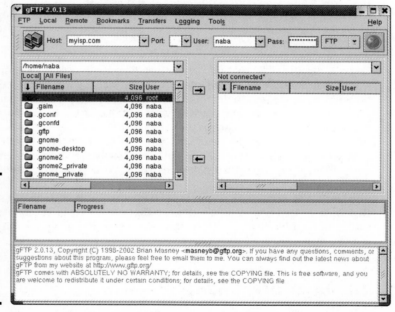

Figure 4-1: The gFTP window just before opening a connection to a remote FTP server.

To upload or download files using gFTP, follow these steps:

1. **Fill in the host name or the IP address of the remote system in the Host field.**

If you have used that host before, you can select it from the drop-down list that appears when you click the downward-pointing arrow next to the Host field.

2. **Provide the user name in the User field and the password in the Pass field.**

3. **Click the button with the icon showing two computers to the left of the Host field.**

   This causes gFTP to connect to that host and to log in with the user name and password you have provided.

4. **The lower part of the gFTP window shows the FTP protocol messages exchanged between the two systems.**

   Observe this area for any indication of error messages.

5. **The directory listing of the remote system appears in the right half of the gFTP window. The left half shows the current local directory.**

6. **To upload one or more files from the current system to the remote system, select the files in the left-hand list and then click the right arrow button.**

7. **To download files from the remote system, select the filenames in the right-hand list and then click the left arrow button.**

8. **When you are done transferring files, select FTP⇨Quit from the menu.**

As these steps show, transferring files with a GUI FTP client such as gFTP is a simple task.

Believe it or not, gFTP is not for FTP transfers alone. It can also transfer files using the HTTP protocol and secure file transfers using the Secure Shell (SSH) protocol.

Using a Web browser as an FTP client

Any Web browser can act as an FTP client, but they are best for anonymous FTP downloads, where the Web browser can log in using the anonymous user name and any password.

In Red Hat Linux, you can use the Mozilla Web browser as an FTP client. All you need to know is how to write the URL so that the Web browser can tell that you want to download a file using FTP. The syntax of the FTP URL is like this:

```
ftp://hostname/pathname
```

The first part (ftp://) indicates that you want an FTP transfer. The hostname part should be the name of the FTP server (the name often starts with an ftp — for example, ftp.netscape.com). The *pathname* is the full directory path and filename of the file you want to download.

If you simply provide the hostname for the FTP server, the Web browser displays the contents of the anonymous FTP directory. If you want to try this on your Red Hat Linux system, start Mozilla (click the Mozilla icon on the GNOME panel) and then type the following line in the location text box:

ftp://localhost

Then press Enter. Mozilla shows the contents of the anonymous FTP directory on your Red Hat Linux system. Figure 4-2 shows a typical appearance of an anonymous FTP directory in Mozilla. You can click folders to see their contents and download any files.

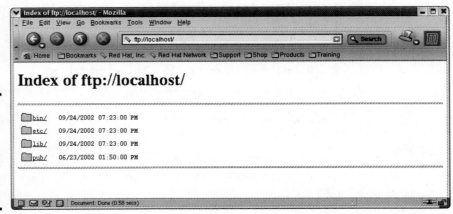

Figure 4-2:
You can use
Mozilla to
download
files from
anonymous
FTP servers.

When you use the ftp://localhost URL, you won't get a response from your system if you are not running an FTP server or if you have set up your firewall so that no FTP connections are allowed.

The same approach of accessing anonymous FTP sites would work if you were to type the hostname of some other anonymous FTP server. For example, try typing the following URL:

```
ftp://ftp.netscape.com
```

You should get the directory of the `ftp.netscape.com` **server.**

Using the Command-Line FTP Client

It's good to know how to use FTP from the command line. For example, your GUI desktop may not be working and what you need is to download some files to fix the problem. If you know how to use the command line FTP client, you can download the files and take care of the problem. It's not that hard.

The best way to learn the command-line FTP client is to try it out. The command is called `ftp` and you can try out the `ftp` commands from your Red Hat Linux system. You don't even need any Internet connection because you can use the `ftp` command to connect to your own system — I show you how.

In the following sample FTP session, I use the command-line FTP client to log in using my user name (`naba`) and browse the directories on my system. When you try this, replace the name with your user name and provide your password. Here's the listing showing the commands (my comments appear in italics):

```
ftp localhost
Connected to localhost (127.0.0.1).
220 ready, dude (vsFTPd 1.0.1: beat me, break me)
Name (localhost:naba):    (I press Enter)
331 Please specify the password.
Password:        (I type my password)
230 Login successful. Have fun.
Remote system type is UNIX.
Using binary mode to transfer files.
ftp> help        (I type help to see a list of FTP commands)
Commands may be abbreviated.  Commands are:

!            debug       mdir      sendport    site
!            debug       mdir      sendport    site
$            dir         mget      put         size
account      disconnect  mkdir     pwd         status
append       exit        mls       quit        struct
ascii        form        mode      quote       system
bell         get         modtime   recv        sunique
binary       glob        mput      reget       tenex
bye          hash        newer     rstatus     tick
case         help        nmap      rhelp       trace
```

```
cd              idle            nlist           rename          type
cdup            image           ntrans          reset           user
chmod           lcd             open            restart         umask
close           ls              prompt          rmdir           verbose
cr              macdef          passive         runique         ?
delete          mdelete         proxy           send
ftp> help mget      (I can get help on a specific command)
mget            get multiple files
ftp> cd /var/ftp (This changes directory to /var/ftp)
250 Directory successfully changed.
ftp> ls   (This command lists the contents of the directory)
227 Entering Passive Mode (127,0,0,1,43,151)
150 Here comes the directory listing.
d--x--x--x     2 0           0             4096 Jul 12 21:22 bin
d--x--x--x     2 0           0             4096 Jul 12 21:22 etc
drwxr-xr-x     2 0           0             4096 Jul 12 21:22 lib
drwxr-sr-x     2 0           50            4096 Jun 23 13:50 pub
226 Directory send OK.
ftp> bye            (This command ends the session)
221 Goodbye.
```

As the listing shows, you can start the command-line FTP client by typing the command `ftp` *hostname*, where *hostname* is the name of the system you want to access. When the FTP client establishes a connection with the FTP server at the remote system, the FTP server prompts you for a user name and password. After you've supplied the information, the FTP client displays the `ftp>` prompt, and you can begin typing commands to perform specific tasks. If you can't remember a specific FTP command, type **help** to view a list of them. You can get additional help for a specific command by typing **help *command***, where *command* is what you want help on.

Many of the FTP commands are similar to Linux commands for navigating the file system. For example, `cd` changes directory, `pwd` prints the name of the current working directory, and `ls` lists the contents of the current directory. Two other common commands are `get` and `put` — `get` downloads a file from the remote system to your system, and `put` uploads (sends) a file from your system to the remote host.

Table 4-1 describes some commonly used FTP commands. You don't have to type the entire FTP command. For a long command, you have to type the first few characters only — enough to identify the command uniquely. For example, to delete a file, you can type **dele** and to change the file transfer mode to binary, you can type **bin**.

When downloading files from the Internet, you almost always want to transfer the files in binary mode because the software is usually archived and compressed (that means they are not plain text files, they're binary). So always use the `binary` command to set the mode to binary. Then use the `get` command to download the files.

Table 4-1	Commonly Used FTP Commands
Command	*Description*
!	Executes a shell command on the local system. For example, `!ls` lists the contents of the current directory on the remote system.
?	Displays a list of commands (same as `help`).
append	Appends a local file to a remote file.
ascii	Sets the file transfer type to ASCII (or plain text). This is the default file transfer type.
binary	Sets the file transfer type to binary.
bye	Ends the FTP session with the remote FTP server and quits the FTP client.
cd	Changes the directory on the remote system. For example, `cd /pub/Linux` changes the remote directory to `/pub/Linux`.
chmod	Changes the permission settings of a remote file. For example, `chmod 644 index.html` changes the permission settings of the `index.html` file on the remote system.
close	Ends the FTP session with the FTP server and returns to the FTP client's prompt.
delete	Deletes a remote file. For example, `delete bigimage.jpg` deletes that file on the remote system.
dir	Lists the contents of the current directory on the remote system.
disconnect	Ends the FTP session and returns to the FTP client's prompt. (This is the same as `close`.)
get	Downloads a remote file. For example, `get junk.tar.gz junk.tgz` downloads the file `junk.tar.gz` from the remote system and saves it as the file `junk.tgz` on the local system.
hash	Turns on or off hash mark (#) printing showing the progress of file transfer. When turned on, a hash mark is printed for every 1,024 bytes transferred from the remote system.
help	Displays a list of commands.
image	Same as `binary`.
lcd	Changes the current directory on the local system. For example, `lcd /var/ftp/pub` changes the current local directory to `/var/ftp/pub`.
ls	Lists the contents of the current remote directory.
mdelete	Deletes multiple files on a remote system. For example, `mdelete *.jpg` deletes all remote files with names ending in `.jpg` in the current directory.

(continued)

Table 4-1 *(continued)*

Command	Description
mdir	Lists multiple remote files and saves the listing in a specified local file. For example, `mdir /usr/share/doc/w* wlist` saves the listing in the local file named `wlist`.
mget	Downloads multiple files. For example, `mget *.jpg` downloads all files with names ending in `.jpg`. If the prompt is turned on, the FTP client asks for confirmation before each file is downloaded.
mkdir	Creates a directory on the remote system. `mkdir images` creates a directory named images in the current directory on the remote system.
mls	Same as `mdir`.
mput	Uploads multiple files. For example, `mput *.jpg` sends all files with names ending in .jpg to the remote system. If the prompt is turned on, the FTP client asks for confirmation before each file is sent.
open	Opens a connection to the FTP server on the specified host. For example, an `open ftp.netscape.com` connects to the FTP server on the host `ftp.netscape.com`.
prompt	Turns the prompt on or off. When the prompt is on, the FTP client prompts you for confirmation before downloading or uploading each file during a multifile transfer.
put	Sends a file to the remote system. For example, `put index.html` sends the `index.html` file from the local system to the remote system.
pwd	Displays the full path name of the current directory on the remote system. When you log in as a user, the initial current working directory is your home directory.
quit	Same as `bye`.
recv	Same as `get`.
rename	Renames a file on the remote system. For example, `rename old.html new.html` renames the file `old.html` to `new.html` on the remote system.
rmdir	Deletes a directory on the remote system. For example, `rmdir images` deletes the `images` directory in the current directory of the remote system.
send	Same as `put`.
size	Shows the size of a remote file. For example, size `bigfile.tar.gz` shows the size of that remote file.
status	Shows the current status of the FTP client.
user	Sends new user information to the FTP server. For example, user `naba` sends the user name `naba`; the FTP server then prompts for the password for that user name.

Book V

Administration

"It's called 'Linux Poker.' Everyone gets to see everyone elses cards, everythings wild, you can play off your opponent's hands, and everyone wins except Bill Gates, whose face appears on the Jokers."

Contents at a Glance

Chapter 1: Performing Basic System Administration

In This Chapter

✔ **Becoming** root

✔ **Understanding the system startup process**

✔ **Taking stock of the system configuration files**

✔ **Viewing system information through the** /proc **file system**

✔ **Monitoring system performance**

✔ **Scheduling jobs**

*S*ystem administration refers to whatever has to be done to keep a computer system up and running, and the *system administrator* is whoever is in charge of taking care of these tasks.

If you are running Red Hat Linux at home or in a small office, you are most likely the system administrator. Or maybe you are the system administrator for a whole LAN-full of Red Hat Linux systems. No matter. In this chapter, I introduce you to the basic system administration tasks and show you how to perform some common tasks.

Red Hat Linux comes with quite a few graphical tools for performing specific system administration tasks. I describe some of these tools in this chapter and the other chapters of this minibook.

Taking Stock of System Administration Tasks

So what are some system administration tasks? My off-the-cuff reply is anything you need to do to keep the system running well. More accurately though, as a system administrator, your typical tasks include the following:

✦ **Adding and removing users.** You have to add new user accounts and remove unnecessary user accounts. If a user forgets the password, you have to change the password.

✦ **Managing the printing system.** You have to turn the print queue on or off, check the print queue status, and delete print jobs.

✦ **Installing, configuring, and upgrading the operating system and various utilities.** You have to install or upgrade parts of the Linux operating system and other software packages.

✦ **Installing new software.** You have to install software that comes in Red Hat Package Manager (RPM) files. You also have to download and unpack software that comes in source code form and then build the executable programs from the source code.

✦ **Managing hardware.** Sometimes you have to add new hardware and install drivers so that the device works properly.

✦ **Making backups.** You have to back up files either in a Zip drive or on tape (if you have a tape drive).

✦ **Mounting and unmounting file systems.** When you want to access the files on a CD-ROM, for example, you have to mount that CD-ROM's file system on one of the directories of the Linux file system. You'd also have to mount floppies, both Linux format and DOS format.

✦ **Automating tasks.** You have to schedule jobs to perform tasks automatically at specific times or periodically.

✦ **Monitoring the system's performance.** You may want to keep an eye on the system performance to see where the processor is spending most of its time and to see the amount of free and used memory in the system.

✦ **Starting and shutting down the system.** Although starting the system typically involves nothing more than powering up the PC, you do have to take some care when you want to shut down your Linux system. If your system is set up for a graphical login screen, you can perform the shutdown operation by selecting a menu item from the login screen. Otherwise, you should use the shutdown command to stop all programs before turning off your PC's power switch.

✦ **Monitoring network status.** If you have a network (either a LAN or a DSL or cable modem connection), you may want to check the status of various network interfaces and make sure that the network connection is up and running.

✦ **Setting up host and network security.** You have to make sure that system files are protected and protect your system against attacks over the network.

✦ **Monitoring security.** You have to keep an eye on any intrusions, usually by checking the log files.

That's a long list of tasks! I won't cover all of them in this chapter, but the rest of the minibook describes most of these tasks. Here I focus on some of the basics such as how to become root (the super user), learning the system configuration files, monitoring system performance, and setting up periodic jobs.

How to Become Root

You have to be logged in as `root` to perform the system administration tasks. The `root` user is the super user and the only account with all the privileges needed to do anything in the system.

The common wisdom is that you should not normally log in as `root`. That's because when you're `root`, one misstep and you could easily delete all the files — especially when typing commands. Take, for example, the command `rm *.html` that you may type to delete all files with the .html extension. What if you accidentally press the spacebar after the asterisk (*)? The shell takes the command to be `rm * .html` and, because * matches any file name, deletes everything in the current directory. Seems implausible until it happens to you!

Using the su - command

If you are logged in as a normal user, how do you do any system administration chores? Well, you become `root` for the time being. If you are working at a terminal window or console, type

```
su -
```

Then enter the root password in response to the prompt. From this point on, you're `root`. Do whatever you have to do. To return back to your usual self, type

```
exit
```

That's it! It's that easy.

Becoming root for the GUI utilities

If you use any of Red Hat's GUI utilities to perform a system administration chore, it's even easier. Typically, the utility pops up a dialog box that prompts you for the `root` password (Figure 1-1). Just type the password and press Enter. If you don't want to use the utility, click Close.

Figure 1-1:
Type the
`root` pass-
word and
press Enter
to gain root
privileges.

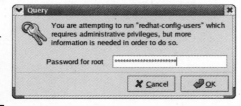

Recovering from a forgotten root password

To perform system administration tasks, you have to know the root password. What happens if you forget the root password? Not to fear. Just reboot the PC and you can reset the root password. Just follow these steps:

1. **Reboot the PC (select Reboot as you log out of the GUI screen) or power up as usual. Soon you see the graphical GRUB screen with the names of operating systems you can boot.**

2. **Press** *a* **(just the letter "a"). GRUB prompts you for commands to add to its default boot command.**

3. **Press the spacebar, type the following word, and then press Enter:**

   ```
   single
   ```

   This causes Linux to start up as usual, but run in a single-user mode that does not require you to log in. After Linux starts, you see the following command-line prompt:

   ```
   bash#
   ```

4. **Use the** passwd **command to change the** root **password as follows:**

   ```
   bash# passwd
   New UNIX password:
   ```

   Type the new root password that you want to use (it won't appear onscreen) and then press Enter. Linux asks for the password again, like this:

   ```
   Retype new UNIX password:
   ```

   Type the password again, and press Enter. If you enter the same password both times, the passwd command changes the password and displays the following message:

   ```
   passwd: all authentication tokens updated successfully
   ```

5. **Now type** reboot **to reboot the PC. After Linux starts, it displays the familiar login screen. Now you should be able to log in as** root **with the new password.**

Make sure that your Red Hat Linux PC is physically secure. As this procedure shows, anyone who can physically access your Red Hat Linux PC can simply reboot, set a new root password, and do whatever they want with the system.

Understanding How Red Hat Linux Boots

It is important to know the sequence in which Red Hat Linux starts processes as it boots. You can use this knowledge to start and stop services, such as the Web server and Network File System (NFS). The next few sections provide you with an overview of how Red Hat Linux boots and starts the initial set of processes. These sections also familiarize you with the shell scripts that start various services on a Red Hat Linux system.

Understanding the init process

When Red Hat Linux boots, it loads and runs the core operating-system program from the hard disk. The core operating system is designed to run other programs. A process named init starts the initial set of processes on your Linux system.

To see the processes currently running on the system, type

```
ps ax | more
```

You get an output listing that starts off like this:

```
PID TTY       STAT    TIME COMMAND
  1 ?         S       0:03 init
```

The first column, with the heading PID, shows a number for each process. PID stands for *process ID* (identification) — a sequential number assigned by the Linux kernel. The first entry in the process list, with a process ID (PID) of 1, is the init process. It's the first process, and it starts all other processes in your Red Hat Linux system. That's why init is sometimes referred to as the "mother of all processes."

What the init process starts depends on the following:

✦ The *run level*, an identifier that identifies a system configuration in which only a selected group of processes exists

✦ The contents of the /etc/inittab file, a text file that specifies the processes to start at different run levels

✦ A number of shell scripts (located in the /etc/rc.d directory and its subdirectories) that are executed at a specific run level

There are seven run levels — 0 through 6 — and Table 1-1 shows the meaning of these run levels.

Table 1-1	Run Levels in Red Hat Linux
Run Level	*Meaning*
0	Shut down the system
1	Run in single user stand-alone mode (no one else can log in; you work at the text console)
2	Run in multiuser mode without the network services (in multiuser mode, other users can log in)
3	Run in full multiuser mode, but with a text-mode login
4	Unused in Red Hat Linux
5	All services running and graphical logon is enabled
6	Reboot the system

The current run level, together with the contents of the /etc/inittab file, controls which processes init starts. The initial default run level is 3 for text-mode login screens and 5 for the graphical login screen. You can change the default run level by editing a line in the /etc/inittab file.

To check the current run level, type the following command in a terminal window:

```
/sbin/runlevel
```

The runlevel command should print an output like this:

```
N 5
```

The first character of the output shows the previous run level (N means there is no previous run level), and the second character shows the current run level (5). In this case, the system was started at run level 5.

Examining the /etc/inittab file

The /etc/inittab file is the key to understanding the processes that init starts at various run levels. You can look at the contents of the file by using the more command, as follows:

```
more /etc/inittab
```

To see the contents of the /etc/inittab file with the more command, you do not have to log in as root.

To interpret the contents of the /etc/inittab file, follow these steps:

1. **Look for the line that looks like this:**

```
id:5:initdefault:
```

That line shows the default run level. In this case, it's 5.

2. **Find all the lines that specify what** `init` **should run at run level 5. Look for a line that has a 5 between the first two colons (:). Here are the two relevant lines:**

```
l5:5:wait:/etc/rc.d/rc 5
x:5:respawn:/etc/X11/prefdm -nodaemon
```

The first line specifies that `init` should execute the file `/etc/rc.d/rc` with 5 as an argument. The second line causes `init` to run `/etc/X11/prefdm`, a shell script that starts the graphical display manager. The display manager, in turn, displays the graphical login dialog box that enables you to log into the system.

If you look at the file `/etc/rc.d/rc`, you find that it is a shell script. You can study this file to see how it starts various processes for run levels 1 through 5.

Each entry in the `/etc/inittab` file tells `init` what to do at one or more run levels — you simply list all the run levels at which the process should run. Each `inittab` entry has four fields — separated by colons — in the following format:

```
id:runlevels:action:process
```

Table 1-2 shows what each of these fields means.

Table 1-2	Meaning of the Fields in Each inittab Entry
Field	*Meaning*
`id`	A unique one- or two-character identifier. The `init` process uses this field internally. You can use any identifier you want, as long as you do not use the same identifier on more than one line.
`runlevels`	A sequence of zero or more characters, each denoting a run level. For example, if the `runlevels` field is 12345, that entry applies to each of the run levels 1 through 5. This field is ignored if the `action` field is set to `sysinit`, `boot`, or `bootwait`.
`action`	Tells the `init` process what to do with that entry. If this field is `initdefault`, for example, `init` interprets the `runlevels` field as the default run level. If this field is set to `wait`, `init` starts the program or script specified in the `process` field and waits until that process exits.
`process`	Name of the script or program that `init` has to start. Of course, some settings of the action field require no `process` field. For example, when action is `initdefault`, there is no need for a `process` field.

Trying out a new run level with the init command

To try a new run level, you do not have to change the default run level in the /etc/inittab file. If you log in as root, you can change the run level (and, consequently, the processes that run in Red Hat Linux) by typing **init** followed by the run level (usually 1, 3, or 5).

For example, to put the system in single-user mode, type the following:

```
init 1
```

Thus, if you want to try run level 5 (assuming your system is not set up for a graphical login screen yet) without changing the /etc/inittab file, enter the following command at the shell prompt:

```
init 5
```

The system should end all current processes and enter run level 5. By default, the init command waits 20 seconds before stopping all current processes and starting the new processes for run level 5.

To switch to run level 5 immediately, type the command **init -t0 5**. The number after the -t option indicates the number of seconds init waits before changing the run level.

You can also use the telinit command, which is simply a symbolic link to init. If you make changes to the /etc/inittab file and want init to reload its configuration file, use the command telinit q.

Understanding the Red Hat Linux startup scripts

The init process runs a number of scripts at system startup. If you look at the /etc/inittab file, you find the following line near the beginning of the file:

```
# System initialization.
si::sysinit:/etc/rc.d/rc.sysinit
```

The first one is a comment line. The second line causes init to run the /etc/rc.d/rc.sysinit script — the first Red Hat Linux startup script that init runs. The rc.sysinit script performs many initialization tasks, such as mounting the file systems, setting the clock, configuring the keyboard layout, starting the network, and loading many other driver modules. The rc.sysinit script performs these initialization tasks by calling many other scripts and reading configuration files located in the /etc/sysconfig directory.

After executing the `/etc/rc.d/rc.sysinit` script, the `init` process runs the `/etc/rc.d/rc` script with the run level as argument. For example, for run level 5, the following line in `/etc/inittab` specifies what `init` has to execute:

```
l5:5:wait:/etc/rc.d/rc 5
```

This says that `init` should execute the command `/etc/rc.d/rc 5` and wait until that command completes.

The `/etc/rc.d/rc` script is somewhat complicated. Here is how it works:

✦ It changes to the directory corresponding to the run level. For example, to change to run level 5, the script changes to the `/etc/rc.d/rc5.d` directory.

✦ In the directory that corresponds with the run level, `/etc/rc.d/rc` looks for all files that begin with a K and executes each of them with the argument stop. This kills currently running processes. Then it locates all files that begin with an S and executes each file with an argument of start. This starts the processes needed for the specified run level.

To see what gets executed at run level 5, type the following command:

```
ls -l /etc/rc.d/rc5.d
```

In the resulting listing, the K scripts — the files whose names begin with K — stop ("kill") servers, whereas the S scripts start servers. The `/etc/rc.d/rc` script executes these files exactly in the order that they appear in the directory listing.

A script with the name `/etc/rc.d/rc.local` is executed after all other scripts. So you can place in that script any command you want executed whenever your Red Hat Linux system boots.

Manually starting and stopping servers

Most of the server startup scripts reside in the `/etc/init.d` directory (the scripts are actually in `/etc/rc.d/init.d`, but `/etc/init.d` is a shortcut to `/etc/rc.d/init.d`). You can manually invoke scripts in this directory to start, stop, or restart specific processes — usually servers. For example, to stop the Web server (the server program is called `httpd`), type the following command:

```
/etc/rc.d/init.d/httpd stop
```

If httpd is already running and you want to restart it, type the following command:

```
/etc/init.d/httpd restart
```

You can enhance your system administration skills by familiarizing yourself with the scripts in the /etc/init.d directory. To see its listing, type the following command:

```
ls /etc/init.d
```

For example, here is a typical list of scripts in my system:

```
aep1000    dhcrelay    irda       network    radvd        snmptrapd   yppasswdd
anacron    firstboot   isdn       nfs        random       squid       ypserv
apmd       functions   kdcrotate  nfslock    rawdevices   sshd        ypxfrd
atd        gpm         keytable   nscd       rhnsd        syslog
autofs     halt        killall    ntpd       saslauthd    tux
bcm5820    httpd       kudzu      pcmcia     sendmail     vncserver
crond      identd      lpd        portmap    single       winbind
cups       innd        named      postfix    smb          xfs
dhcpd      iptables    netfs      postgresql snmpd        xinetd
```

The script names give you some clue about which server the script can start and stop. For example, the nfs script starts and stops the processes required for NFS (Network File System) services. At your leisure, you may want to study some of these scripts to see what each one does. You don't have to understand all the shell programming; the comments should help you learn the purpose of each script.

Use the service command as a shortcut to run the scripts in /etc/init.d that you use to start, stop, or restart servers. For example, to start the Web server, you type this command:

```
service httpd stop
```

To restart that server, type the following command:

```
service httpd restart
```

Automatically starting servers at system startup

You want some servers to start automatically every time you boot the system. For example, if you run a Web server, you want the httpd server to start whenever the system starts. You can make that happen by using the chkconfig command. For example, to set httpd to start whenever the system boots into run level 3, 4, or 5, you type the following command (while logged in as root):

```
chkconfig --level 345 httpd on
```

You can also use the `chkconfig` command to check which servers are turned on or off. For example, to see the complete list of all servers for all run levels, type the following command:

```
chkconfig --list
```

If you want to view the status of a single server, such as `httpd`, add that server's name to the `chkconfig` command, like this:

```
chkconfig --list httpd
```

You should see an output similar to the following:

```
httpd     0:off  1:off  2:off  3:on  4:on  5:on  6:off
```

Taking Stock of Red Hat Linux System Configuration Files

Red Hat Linux includes a host of configuration files. All of these files share text files that you can edit with any text editor. You have to log in as `root` to be able to edit these files. I won't discuss the files individually, but I show a selection of the configuration files in Table 1-3, along with a brief description of each. This listing gives you an idea about the types of configuration files a system administrator has to work with. In many cases, Red Hat Linux includes GUI utility programs to set up many of these configuration files.

Table 1-3	Red Hat Linux Configuration Files
Configuration File	*Description*
/boot/module-info	Module information for the Linux kernel
/boot/System.map	Map of the Linux kernel (maps kernel addresses into names of functions and variables)
/boot/vmlinuz	The Linux kernel (this is the operating system core)
/etc/X11/XF86Config	Configuration file for XFree86 version 4.x
/etc/at.allow	Usernames of users allowed to use the `at` command to schedule jobs for later execution
/etc/at.deny	Usernames of users forbidden to use the `at` command
/etc/bashrc	Systemwide functions and aliases for the BASH shell

(continued)

Table 1-3 *(continued)*

Configuration File	Description
`/etc/cups/cupsd.conf`	Configuration file for the Common UNIX Printing System (CUPS) scheduler (present only when CUPS is installed)
`/etc/cups/cupsd.conf`	Printer configuration file for the Common UNIX Printing System (CUPS) scheduler (present only when CUPS is installed)
`/etc/fstab`	Information about file systems available for mounting
`/etc/group`	Information about groups
`/etc/grub.conf`	The configuration for the Grand Unified Bootloader (GRUB) — the default boot loader in Red Hat Linux
`/etc/hosts`	List of IP numbers and corresponding hostnames
`/etc/hosts.allow`	Hosts allowed to access Internet services on this system
`/etc/hosts.deny`	Hosts forbidden to access Internet services on this system
`/etc/httpd/conf/httpd.conf`	Configuration file for the Apache Web server
`/etc/init.d`	Directory with scripts to start and stop many servers
`/etc/inittab`	Configuration file used by the `init` process that starts all the other processes
`/etc/issue`	File containing message to be printed before displaying the text-mode login prompt (usually the Red Hat Linux version number)
`/etc/lilo.conf`	The configuration for the Linux Loader (LILO) — one of the boot loaders that can load the operating system from disk
`/etc/login.defs`	Default information for creating user accounts, used by the `useradd` command
`/etc/modules.conf`	Configuration file with directives for loading kernel modules (for example, Ethernet and sound drivers)
`/etc/mtab`	Information about currently mounted file systems
`/etc/passwd`	Information about all user accounts (actual passwords are stored in `/etc/shadow`)
`/etc/profile`	Systemwide environment and startup file for the BASH shell
`/etc/rc.d`	Directory that holds system startup and shutdown scripts
`/etc/rc.d/rc.sysinit`	Red Hat Linux initialization script
`/etc/shadow`	Secure file with encrypted passwords for all user accounts (can be read by `root` only)

Configuration File	Description
/etc/shells	List of all the shells on the system that the user can use
/etc/skel	Directory that holds initial versions of files such as .bash_profile that are copied to new user's home directory
/etc/sysconfig	Red Hat Linux configuration files
/etc/termcap	Database of terminal capabilities and options
/etc/xinetd.conf	Configuration for the xinetd daemon that starts a number of Internet services on demand
/var/log/cron	Log from the cron process that runs scheduled jobs
/var/log/httpd/access_log	Web server access log
/var/log/httpd/error_log	Web server error log
/var/log/messages	System log

Monitoring System Performance

When you are the system administrator, you have to keep an eye on how well your Red Hat Linux system is performing. You can monitor the overall performance of your system by looking at information such as

✦ Central Processing Unit (CPU) usage

✦ Physical memory usage

✦ Virtual memory (swap space) usage

✦ Hard disk usage

Red Hat Linux comes with a number of utilities that you can use to monitor one or more of these performance parameters. Here I introduce a few of these utilities and show you how to understand the information presented by these utilities.

Using the top utility

To view the top CPU processes — the ones that are using most of the CPU time — you can use the top utility. To start that utility, type **top** in a terminal window (or text console). The top utility then displays a text screen listing the current processes, arranged in the order of CPU usage, along with various other information such as memory and swap space usage. Figure 1-2 shows a typical output from the top utility.

```
root@dhcppc3:~                                                    _ □ ✕
File  Edit  View  Terminal  Go  Help
  9:00pm  up 29 days, 11:45,  3 users,   load average: 0.70, 0.94, 0.83
87 processes: 83 sleeping, 4 running, 0 zombie, 0 stopped
CPU states:  3.7% user,  1.5% system,  0.0% nice, 94.7% idle
Mem:    61540K av,   59024K used,    2516K free,      0K shrd,    420K buff
Swap:  192772K av,   96624K used,   96148K free                15904K cached

  PID USER     PRI  NI  SIZE  RSS SHARE STAT %CPU %MEM    TIME COMMAND
 7141 root       5 -10 26084  13M  4236 S <   2.1 21.8  2105m X
27738 root      15   0  8372 8368  6628 R     1.5 13.5   0:02 gnome-terminal
27765 root      15   0  1092 1092   840 R     1.3  1.7   0:01 top
    1 root      15   0   476  436   424 S     0.0  0.7   0:16 init
    2 root      15   0     0    0     0 SW    0.0  0.0   0:00 keventd
    3 root      15   0     0    0     0 SW    0.0  0.0   0:07 kapmd
    4 root      34  19     0    0     0 SWN   0.0  0.0   0:00 ksoftirqd_CPU0
    5 root      15   0     0    0     0 SW    0.0  0.0   2:30 kswapd
    6 root      15   0     0    0     0 SW    0.0  0.0   0:00 bdflush
    7 root      15   0     0    0     0 SW    0.0  0.0   0:03 kupdated
    8 root      25   0     0    0     0 SW    0.0  0.0   0:00 mdrecoveryd
   12 root      15   0     0    0     0 SW    0.0  0.0   1:01 kjournald
   68 root      15   0     0    0     0 SW    0.0  0.0   0:00 khubd
  161 root      15   0     0    0     0 SW    0.0  0.0   0:00 kjournald
  461 root      15   0   748  460   456 S     0.0  0.7   0:00 dhclient
  500 root      15   0   568  500   496 S     0.0  0.8   0:02 syslogd
```

Figure 1-2:
You can see the top CPU processes by using the `top` command.

The `top` utility updates the display every 5 seconds. You can keep `top` running in a window so that you can continually monitor the status of your Red Hat Linux system. To quit `top`, press Ctrl+C or by closing the terminal window.

The first five lines of the output screen provide summary information about the system. Here is what these five lines show:

✦ The first line shows the current time, how long the system has been up, how many users are logged in, and three load averages — these are the average number of process ready to run during the last 1, 5, and 15 minutes.

✦ The second line lists the total number of processes and the status of these processes.

✦ The third line shows CPU usage — what percentage of CPU time is used by user processes, what percentage by system (kernel) processes, and what percentage of time the CPU is idle.

✦ The fourth line shows how the physical memory is being used — the total amount, how much is used, how much is free, how much is shared, and how much is allocated to buffers (for reading from disk, for example).

✦ The fifth line shows how the virtual memory (or swap space) is being used — the total amount of swap space, how much is used, how much is free, and how much is being cached.

Monitoring System Performance **345**

**Book V
Chapter 1**

**Performing
Basic System
Administration**

The table that appears below the summary information (refer to Figure 1-2) lists information about the current processes, arranged in decreasing order of CPU time usage. Table 1-4 summarizes the meanings of the column headings in the table that `top` displays.

If the RSS field is drastically smaller than the SIZE field for a process, it means that the process is using too little physical memory compared to what it needs. The result is a lot of swapping as the process runs. You can use the `vmstat` utility (which you'll try later in this section) to find out how much your system is swapping.

Table 1-4	Meaning of the Column Headings in the top's Output
Heading	*Meaning*
PID	The process ID of the process
USER	Username under which the process is running
PRI	Priority of the process
NI	Nice value of the process — the value ranges from –20 (highest priority) to 19 (lowest priority) and the default is 0
SIZE	Total size of the process in kilobytes
RSS	Total physical memory used by task (typically shown in kilobytes, but an M suffix indicates megabytes)
SHARE	Amount of shared memory used by process
STAT	State of the process (S for sleeping, D for uninterruptible sleep, R for running, Z for zombies — processes that should be dead, but are still running — or T for stopped; a trailing < means the process has negative nice value)
%CPU	Percentage of CPU time used since last screen update
%MEM	Percentage of physical memory used by the process
TIME	Total CPU time the process has used since it started
COMMAND	Shortened form of the command that started the process

Using the GNOME system monitor

Like the text mode `top` utility, the GNOME System Monitor tool also enables you to view the system load in terms of the number of processes that are currently running, their memory usage, and the free disk space on your system. To run the tool, select Main Menu⇨System Tools⇨System Monitor. The tool starts and displays its output in a window, as shown in Figure 1-3.

The output is similar to the output you see when you type **top** in a text-mode console or a terminal window, except that with the GNOME System Monitor, you can decide which columns you want to see. Figure 1-3 shows the default view with the process name, user who is running the process, memory used, percentage of CPU time, and the process ID. The GNOME System Monitor keeps updating the display to reflect the current state of the system.

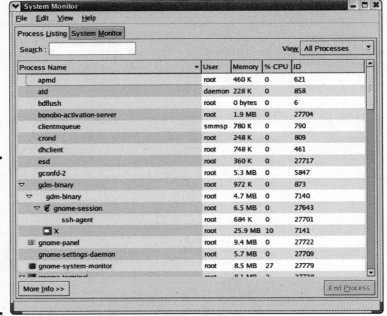

Figure 1-3:
Use the
GNOME
System
Monitor
to view
information
about the
current
processes.

The GNOME System Monitor window has another tab labeled System Monitor. Click that tab to view a summary of CPU, memory, and disk usage. Figure 1-4 shows a typical view of the System Monitor tab.

The upper plot in Figure 1-4 shows the percentage of CPU usage with time. The next plot shows the history of memory use and swap space use. The disk space use is summarized in a table at the bottom.

Using the uptime command

You can use the uptime command to get a summary of the system's state. Just type the command like this:

```
uptime
```

It displays a output similar to the following:

```
11:40am up 32 days, 57 min, 3 users, load average: 0.13, 0.23, 0.27
```

The output shows the current time, how long the system has been up, the number of users, and, finally, the three load averages — the average number of processes that were ready to run in the past 1, 5, and 15 minutes. Load averages greater than one imply that many processes are competing for the CPU time simultaneously.

The load averages give you an indication of how busy the system is.

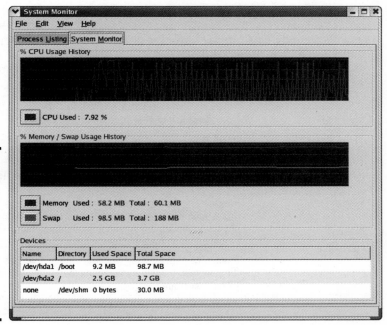

Figure 1-4:
The GNOME System Monitor displays summary CPU, memory, and disk-usage information.

Using the vmstat utility

You can get summary information about the overall system usage with the vmstat utility. To view system usage information averaged over 5-second intervals, type the following command (the second argument indicates the total number of lines of output vmstat should display):

```
vmstat 5 8
```

You should see output similar to the following listing:

```
procs                    memory  swap      io   system      cpu
r b w  swpd  free  buff cache si so  bi  bo   in  cs us sy id
0 0 0 31116  1512  1620 19216  0  0   4   2  104 138 43  6 51
1 0 0 31116  1512  1628 19216  0  0   0   6 1020 112 24  3 73
0 0 0 31116  1256  1644 19216  0  0   0  14 1008  82 26  3 70
0 0 0 31116  1316  1652 19216  0  0   0  10 1008  74 29  5 66
0 0 0 31116  1316  1660 19216  0  0   0   2 1006  65 27  5 67
0 0 0 31116  1316  1668 19216  0  0   0   2 1006  61 16  3 81
0 0 0 31116  1316  1676 19216  0  0   0   2 1006  69 27  5 68
0 0 0 31116  1316  1684 19216  0  0   0   2 1006  70 27  6 67
```

The first line of output shows the averages since the last reboot. After that, vmstat displays the 5-second average data seven more times, covering the next 35 seconds. The tabular output is grouped into six categories of information, as indicated by the fields in the first line of output. The second line shows further details for each of the six major fields. You can interpret these fields using Table 1-5.

Table 1-5	Meaning of Fields in vmstat's Output
Field Name	*Description*
procs	Number of processes and their types: r = processes waiting to run; b = processes in uninterruptible sleep; w = processes swapped out, but ready to run
memory	Information about physical memory and swap space usage (all numbers in kilobytes): swpd = virtual memory used; free = free physical memory; buff = memory used as buffers; cache = virtual memory that's cached
swap	Amount of swapping (the numbers are in kilobytes per second): si = amount of memory swapped in from disk; so = amount of memory swapped to disk
io	Information about input and output (the numbers are in blocks per second where the block size depends on the disk device): bi = rate of blocks sent to disk; bo = rate of blocks received from disk
system	Information about the system: in = number of interrupts per second (including clock interrupts); cs = number of context switches per second — the number of times the kernel changed which process was running
cpu	Percentages of CPU time used: us = percentage of CPU time used by user processes; sy = percentage CPU time used by system processes; id = percentage of time CPU is idle

In the vmstat utility's output, high values in the si and so fields indicate too much swapping (*swapping* refers to the copying of information between physical memory and the virtual memory on the hard disk). High numbers in the bi and bo fields indicate too much disk activity.

Checking disk performance and disk usage

Red Hat Linux comes with the /sbin/hdparm program that you can use to control IDE or ATAPI hard disks that are common on most PCs. One feature of the hdparm program is that you can use the -t option to determine the rate at which data can be read from the disk into a buffer in memory. For example, here's the result of the command on my system:

```
/sbin/hdparm -t /dev/hda

/dev/hda:
 Timing buffered disk reads:  64 MB in  5.68 seconds = 11.28
    MB/sec
```

The command requires the IDE drive's device name (/dev/hda) as an argument. If you have an IDE hard disk, you can try this command to see how fast data can be read from your system's disk drive.

To display the space available in the currently mounted file systems, use the df command. If you want a more human-readable output from df, type the following command:

```
df -h
```

Here's a typical output from this command:

```
Filesystem          Size  Used Avail Use% Mounted on
/dev/hda2           3.7G  2.3G  1.2G  65% /
/dev/hda1            99M  9.2M   84M  10% /boot
none                 30M     0   30M   0% /dev/shm
```

As this example shows, the -h option causes the df command to show the sizes in gigabytes (G) and megabytes (M).

To check the disk space being used by a specific directory, use the du command — you can specify the -h option to view the output in kilobytes (k) and megabytes (M), as shown in the following example:

```
du -h /var/log
```

Here's a typical output of that command:

```
4.0K    /var/log/httpd
4.0K    /var/log/news/OLD
8.0K    /var/log/news
4.0K    /var/log/cups
```

```
4.0K    /var/log/vbox
212K    /var/log/gdm
4.0K    /var/log/squid
4.0K    /var/log/samba
1.1M    /var/log
```

The du command displays the disk space used by each directory and the last line shows the total disk space used by that directory. If you want to see only the total space used by a directory, use the -s option, like this:

```
du -sh /home
25M     /home
```

Viewing System Information through the /proc File System

Your Red Hat Linux system has a special file system called the /proc file system. You can find out many things about your system from this file system. In fact, you can even change kernel parameters through the /proc file system (just by writing to a file in that file system) and thereby modify the system's behavior.

The /proc file system is not a real directory on the disk but a collection of data structures in memory, managed by the Linux kernel, that appears to you as a set of directories and files. The purpose of /proc (also called the *process file system*) is to allow you to access information about the Linux kernel as well as find out about all the processes that are currently running on your system.

You can access the /proc file system just as you access any other directory, but you have to know the meaning of various files to interpret the information. Typically, you can use the cat or more commands to view the contents of a file in /proc; the file's contents provide information about some aspect of the system.

As with any directory, start by looking at a detailed directory listing of /proc. To do so, log in as root and type **ls -l /proc** in a terminal window. In the output, the first set of directories (indicated by the letter d at the beginning of the line) represents the processes that are currently running on your system. Each directory that corresponds to a process has the process ID (a number) as its name.

You'll also notice a very large file named /proc/kcore; that file represents the entire physical memory of your system. Although /proc/kcore appears in the listing as a huge file, there is no physical file occupying that much space on your hard disk, so you should not try to remove the file to reclaim disk space.

Several files and directories in /proc contain interesting information about your Red Hat Linux PC. The /proc/cpuinfo file, for example, lists the key characteristics of your system, such as processor type and floating-point processor information. You can view the processor information by typing **cat /proc/cpuinfo.** For example, here is what I get when I type **cat /proc/cpuinfo** on my system:

```
processor       : 0
vendor_id       : GenuineIntel
cpu family      : 6
model           : 3
model name      : Pentium II (Klamath)
stepping        : 4
cpu MHz         : 233.341
cache size      : 512 KB
fdiv_bug        : no
hlt_bug         : no
f00f_bug        : no
coma_bug        : no
fpu             : yes
fpu_exception   : yes
cpuid level     : 2
wp              : yes
flags           : fpu vme de pse tsc msr pae mce cx8 sep mtrr
    pge mca cmov mmx
bogomips        : 459.77
```

This output is from an old 233 MHz Pentium II system. The listing shows many interesting characteristics of the processor. Notice the line that starts with fdiv_bug. Remember the infamous Pentium floating-point-division bug? The bug is in an instruction called fdiv (for floating-point division). Thus, the fdiv_bug line indicates whether this particular Pentium has the bug (fortunately, my PC's processor does not).

The last line in the /proc/cpuinfo file shows the BogoMips for the processor, as computed by the Linux kernel when it boots. BogoMips is something that Linux uses internally to time-delay loops.

Table 1-6 summarizes some of the files in the /proc file system, from which you can get information about your Red Hat Linux system. You can view some of these files on your system to see what they contain. Note that not all the files shown in Table 1-6 will be present on your system — the contents of the /proc file system depends on the kernel configuration and the driver modules that are loaded (which, in turn, depend on your PC's hardware configuration).

You can navigate the /proc file system just as you would work with any other directories and files in Red Hat Linux. Use the more or cat commands to view the contents of a file.

Table 1-6	Some of the Files and Directories in /proc
File Name	*Content*
/proc/apm	Information about advanced power management (APM)
/proc/bus	Directory with bus-specific information for each bus type such as PCI
/proc/cmdline	The command line used to start the Linux kernel (for example, auto BOOT_IMAGE=linux ro root=303)
/proc/cpuinfo	Information about the CPU (the microprocessor)
/proc/devices	Available block and character devices in your system
/proc/dma	Information about DMA (direct memory access) channels that are being used
/proc/driver/rtc	Information about the PC's real-time clock (RTC)
/proc/filesystems	List of supported file systems
/proc/ide	Directory containing information about IDE devices
/proc/interrupts	Information about interrupt request (IRQ) numbers and how they are being used
/proc/ioports	Information about input/output (I/O) port addresses and how they are being used
/proc/kcore	Image of the physical memory
/proc/kmsg	Kernel messages
/proc/ksyms	Kernel symbol table
/proc/loadavg	Load average (average number of processes waiting to run in the last 1, 5, and 15 minutes)
/proc/locks	Current kernel locks (used to ensure that multiple processes do not write to a file at the same time)
/proc/meminfo	Information about physical memory and swap space usage
/proc/misc	Miscellaneous information
/proc/modules	List of loaded driver modules
/proc/mounts	List of mounted file systems

File Name	Content
/proc/net	Directory with many subdirectories that contain information about networking
/proc/partitions	List of partitions known to the Linux kernel
/proc/pci	Information about PCI devices found on the system
/proc/scsi	Directory with information about SCSI devices found on the system (present only if you have a SCSI device)
/proc/stat	Overall statistics about the system
/proc/swaps	Information about the swap space and how much is used
/proc/sys	Directory with information about the system (you can change kernel parameters by writing to files in this directory — this is one way to tune the system's performance, but requires expertise to do it properly)
/proc/uptime	Information about how long the system has been up
/proc/version	Kernel version number

Scheduling Jobs in Red Hat Linux

As a system administrator, you may need to run some programs automatically at regular intervals or execute one or more commands at a specified time in the future. Your Red Hat Linux system includes the facilities to schedule jobs to run at any future date or time you want. You can set up the system to perform a task periodically or just once. Here are some typical tasks you can perform by scheduling jobs on your Linux system:

✦ Back up the files in the middle of the night.

✦ Download large files in the early morning when the system is not busy.

✦ Send yourself messages as reminders of meetings.

✦ Analyze the system logs periodically and look for any abnormal activities.

You can set up these jobs by using the at command or the crontab facility of Red Hat Linux. In the next few sections, I introduce these job-scheduling features of Red Hat Linux.

Scheduling one-time jobs

If you want to run one or more commands at a later time, you can use the at command. The atd daemon — a program designed to process jobs submitted using at — runs your commands at the specified time and mails the output to you.

Before you try out the at command, you need to know that the following configuration files control which users can schedule tasks using the at command:

✦ /etc/at.allow contains the names of the users who may submit jobs using the at command.

✦ /etc/at.deny contains the names of users not allowed to submit jobs using the at command.

If these files are not present, or if there is an empty /etc/at.deny file, any user can submit jobs using the at command. The default in Red Hat Linux is an empty /etc/at.deny file, so anyone can use the at command. If you do not want some users to use at, simply list those usernames in the /etc/at.deny file.

To use at to schedule a one-time job for execution at a later time, follow these steps:

1. **Run the at command with the date or time when you want your commands executed. When you press Enter, the at> prompt appears, as follows:**

   ```
   at 21:30
   at>
   ```

   This is the simplest way to indicate the time when you want to execute one or more commands — simply specify the time in a 24-hour format. In this case, you want to execute the commands at 9:30 p.m. tonight (or tomorrow, if it's already past 9:30 p.m.). You can, however, specify the execution time in many different ways (see Table 1-7 for examples).

2. **At the at> prompt, type the commands you want to execute as if typing at the shell prompt. After each command, press Enter and continue with the next command. When you are finished entering the commands you want to execute, press Ctrl+D to indicate the end.**

   Here is an example showing how to execute the ps command at a future time:

   ```
   at> ps
   at> <EOT>
   job 1 at 2002-07-18 21:30
   ```

   After you press Ctrl+D, the at command responds with a job number and the date and time when the job will execute.

Table 1-7   **Formats for the Time of Execution with the at Command**

Command	When the Job Will Run
at now	Immediately
at now + 15 minutes	15 minutes from the current time
at now + 4 hours	4 hours from the current time
at now + 7 days	7 days from the current time
at noon	At noontime today (or tomorrow, if already past noon)
at now next hour	Exactly 60 minutes from now
at now next day	At the same time tomorrow
at 17:00 tomorrow	At 5:00 p.m. tomorrow
at 4:45pm	At 4:45 p.m. today (or tomorrow, if already past 4:45 p.m.)
at 3:00 Aug 16, 2002	At 3:00 a.m. on August 16, 2002

After you enter one or more jobs, you can view the current list of scheduled jobs with the `atq` command:

```
atq
```

The output looks similar to the following:

```
4          2002-08-16 03:00 a root
5          2002-10-26 21:57 a root
6          2002-10-26 16:45 a root
```

The first field on each line shows the job number — the same number that the `at` command displays when you submit the job. The next field shows the year, month, day, and time of execution. The last field shows the jobs pending in the queue named `a`.

If you want to cancel a job, use the `atrm` command to remove that job from the queue. When removing a job with the `atrm` command, refer to the job by its number, as follows:

```
atrm 4
```

This deletes job 4 scheduled for 3:00 a.m. August 16, 2002.

When a job executes, the output is mailed to you. Type **mail** at a terminal window to read your mail and to view the output from your jobs.

Scheduling recurring jobs

Although at is good for running commands at a specific time, it's not useful for running a program automatically at repeated intervals. You have to use crontab to schedule such recurring jobs. You need to do this, for example, if you want to back up your files to tape at midnight every day.

You schedule recurring jobs by placing job information in a file with a specific format and submitting this file with the crontab command. The cron daemon — crond — checks the job information every minute and executes the recurring jobs at the specified times. Because the cron daemon processes recurring jobs, such jobs are also referred to as *cron jobs*.

Any output from a cron job is mailed to the user who submits the job. (In the submitted job-information file, you can specify a different recipient for the mailed output.)

Two configuration files control who can schedule cron jobs using crontab:

✦ /etc/cron.allow contains the names of the users who may submit jobs using the crontab command.

✦ /etc/cron.deny contains the names of users not allowed to submit jobs using the crontab command.

If the /etc/cron.allow file exists, only users listed in this file can schedule cron jobs. If only the /etc/cron.deny file exists, users listed in this file cannot schedule cron jobs. If neither file exists, the default Red Hat Linux setup enables any user to submit cron jobs.

To submit a cron job, follow these steps:

1. **Prepare a shell script (or an executable program in any programming language) that can perform the recurring task you want to perform.**

You can skip this step if you want to execute an existing program periodically.

2. **Prepare a text file with information about the times when you want the shell script or program (from Step 1) to execute. Submit this file using crontab.**

You can submit several recurring jobs with a single file. Each line with timing information about a job has a standard format with six fields — the first five specify when the job runs, and the sixth and subsequent fields constitute the actual command that runs. For example, here is a line that executes the myjob shell script in a user's home directory at five minutes past midnight each day:

```
5 0 * * * $HOME/myjob
```

Table 1-8 shows the meaning of the first five fields. Note that an asterisk (*) means all possible values for that field. Also, an entry in any of the first five fields can be a single number, a comma-separated list of numbers, a pair of numbers separated by a dash (indicating a range of numbers), or an asterisk.

3. **Suppose the text file** jobinfo **(in the current directory) contains the job information. Submit this information to** crontab **with the following command:**

```
crontab jobinfo
```

That's it! You should be set with the cron job. From now on, the cron job should run at regular intervals (as specified in the job information file), and you should receive mail messages with the output from the job.

To verify that the job is indeed scheduled, type the following command:

```
crontab -l
```

The output of the crontab -l command shows the cron jobs currently installed in your name. To remove your cron jobs, type **crontab -r.**

Table 1-8	Format for the Time of Execution in crontab Files	
Field Number	*Meaning of Field*	*Acceptable Range of Values**
1	Minute	0–59
2	Hour of the day	0–23
3	Day of the month	0–31
4	Month	1–12 (1 means January, 2 means February, and so on) or the names of months using the first three letters (Jan, Feb, Mar, Apr, May, Jun, Jul, Aug, Sep, Oct, Nov, Dec)
5	Day of the week	0–6 (0 means Sunday, 1 means Monday, and so on) or the three-letter abbreviations of the week (Sun, Mon, Tue, Wed, Thu, Fri, Sat)

* An asterisk in a field means all possible values for that field. For example, if an asterisk in the third field, the job is executed every day.

If you log in as `root`, you can also set up, examine, and remove cron jobs for any user. To set up cron jobs for a user, use this command:

```
crontab -u username filename
```

Here, `username` is the user for whom you install the cron jobs, and `filename` is the file that contains information about the jobs.

Use the following form of `crontab` command to view the cron jobs for a user:

```
crontab -u username -l
```

To remove a user's cron jobs, use the following command:

```
crontab -u username -r
```

Note that the cron daemon also executes the cron jobs listed in the system-wide cron-job file `/etc/crontab`. Here's the default `/etc/crontab` file in Red Hat Linux (type `cat /etc/crontab` to view the file):

```
SHELL=/bin/bash
PATH=/sbin:/bin:/usr/sbin:/usr/bin
MAILTO=root
HOME=/

# run-parts
01 * * * * root run-parts /etc/cron.hourly
02 4 * * * root run-parts /etc/cron.daily
22 4 * * 0 root run-parts /etc/cron.weekly
42 4 1 * * root run-parts /etc/cron.monthly
```

The first four lines set up several environment variables for the jobs listed in this file. The `MAILTO` environment variable specifies the user who receives the mail message with the output from the cron jobs in this file.

The line that begins with a # is a comment line. The four lines following the `run-parts` comment execute the `run-parts` shell script (located in the `/usr/bin` directory) at various times with the name of a specific directory as argument. Each of the arguments to `run-parts` — `/etc/cron.hourly`, `/etc/cron.daily`, `/etc/cron.weekly`, and `/etc/cron.monthly` — are directories. Essentially, `run-parts` executes all scripts located in the directory that you provide as an argument.

Table 1-9 lists the directories where these scripts are located and when they are executed. You have to look at the scripts in these directories to learn what gets executed at these periodic intervals.

Table 1-9	Script Directories for cron Jobs
Directory Name	*Contents*
/etc/cron.hourly	Scripts executed every hour
/etc/cron.daily	Scripts executed each day at 4:02 a.m.
/etc/cron.weekly	Scripts executed weekly on Sunday at 4:22 a.m.
/etc/cron.monthly	Scripts to be executed at 4:42 a.m. on the first day of each month

Chapter 2: Managing Users

In This Chapter

✔ Adding user accounts

✔ Understanding the password file

✔ Managing groups

✔ Exploring the user environment

✔ Changing user and group ownerships of files and directories

Red Hat Linux is a multiuser system, so it has many user accounts. Even if you are the only user on your system, many servers require a unique user name and group name. Take, for example, the Apache Web server. It runs under the user name `apache`. There are a whole host of system users that are not for people, but just for running specific programs.

Also, users can belong to one or more groups. Typically, each user name has a corresponding private group name. By default, each user belongs to that corresponding private group. However, you can define other groups for the purpose of providing access to specific files and directories based on group membership.

The user and group ownerships of files are often used as a way to make sure that only the right people (or the right process) can access the right files and directories. Managing the user and group accounts is a typical system administration job. It's not that hard to do this part of the job, given the tools that come with Red Hat Linux. I show you how.

Adding User Accounts

You get the chance to add user accounts as you install Red Hat Linux. The `root` account is the only one that must be set up during installation. If you didn't add other user accounts during installation, you can do so later on. You can use the Red Hat User Manager or the `useradd` command to add a new user account on your system.

 It's a good idea to create other user accounts besides `root`. Even if you're the only user of the system, logging in as a less-privileged user is good practice, because you can't damage any important system files inadvertently. If necessary, you can type the `su -` command to log in as `root` and perform any system administration tasks.

Using Red Hat User Manager to add user accounts

You can use the Red Hat User Manager to add user accounts. To start the Red Hat User Manager, log in as `root` at the graphical login screen and then select Main Menu➪System Settings➪Users and Groups from the GNOME Panel. If you're not logged in as `root`, the Red Hat User Manager prompts you for the `root` password. If prompted, enter the password and click OK. Then the Red Hat User Manager window appears.

The window shows two tabs: Users and Groups (Figure 2-1). The Users tab displays the current list of users from the `/etc/passwd` file. The Groups tab lists the name of groups from the `/etc/group`. Initially, the Red Hat User Manager filters out any system users and groups. However, you can turn off the filter by selecting Preferences➪Filter system users and groups. Figure 2-1 shows the Red Hat User Manager window with a listing of all user accounts, including the system ones.

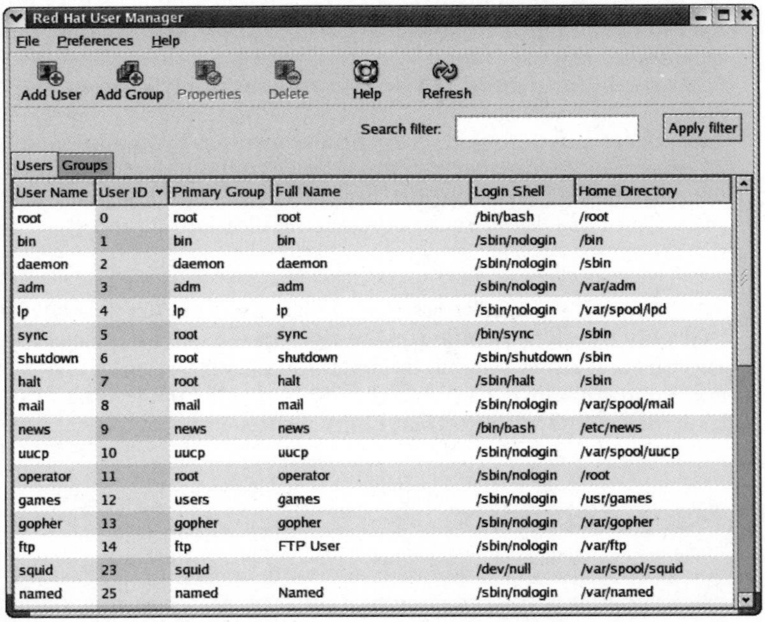

Figure 2-1:
You can manage user accounts and groups from the Red Hat User Manager window.

You can add new users and groups or edit existing users and groups from the Red Hat User Manager window.

To edit the information for an existing user, follow these steps:

1. **Click the user name in the list in the Users tab and then click the Properties button on the toolbar.**

   That user's information appears in a User Properties dialog box (Figure 2-2).

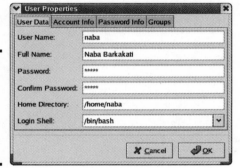

Figure 2-2:
Edit an existing user's information in this dialog box.

2. **Edit the information and click OK to make the changes.**

To add a new user, follow these steps:

1. **Click the Add User button on the toolbar.**

   This action opens the Create New User dialog box (Figure 2-3).

2. **Fill in the requested information.**

   In particular, you must enter the user name and the password. After filling in all the fields, click the OK button. The new user should now appear in the list on the Users tab in the Red Hat User Manager window.

Notice the checkbox labeled `Create a private group for the user`. It's checked by default, and that means each new user is in a separate private user group. However, sometimes you want a user to be in a specific group so that the user can access the files owned by that group. It's easy to add a user to another group. For example, suppose I want to add the user name `naba` to the group called `wheel`. I can do this simply by typing the following command in a terminal window:

```
usermod -G wheel naba
```

Create New User

User Name:	ashley
Full Name:	Ashley Barkakati
Password:	*********
Confirm Password:	*********
Login Shell:	/bin/bash

☑ Create home directory

Home Directory: /home/ashley

☑ Create a private group for the user

☐ Specify user ID manually

UID: 500

✗ Cancel   ✓ OK

Figure 2-3:
Create a new user account by filling in the information in this dialog box.

To remove a user account, click the user name in the list on the Users tab that displays all user accounts (see Figure 2-1). Then click the Delete button on the toolbar.

Using commands to manage user accounts

If you're working from a text console, you can create a new user account by using the useradd command. Follow these steps to add an account for a new user:

1. **Log in as** root.

(If you're not already logged in as root, type su - to become root.)

2. **Type the following** useradd **command with the** -c **option to create the account:**

```
/usr/sbin/useradd -c "Ashley Barkakati" ashley
```

3. **Set Ashley's password by using the** passwd **command, as follows:**

```
passwd ashley
```

You are prompted for the password twice. If you type a password that someone can easily guess, the passwd program rejects it.

The useradd command consults the following configuration files to obtain default information about various parameters for the new user account:

✦ `/etc/default/useradd` — Specifies the default shell (`/bin/bash`) and the default home directory location (`/home`).

✦ `/etc/login.defs` — Provides systemwide defaults for automatic group and user IDs, as well as password-expiration parameters.

Examine these files with the `cat` or `more` commands to see what they contain.

You can delete a user account by using the `userdel` command. Simply type **/usr/sbin/userdel** *username* at the command prompt to delete a user's account. To wipe out that user's home directory as well, type **/usr/sbin/userdel -r** *username*.

To modify any information in a user account, use the `usermod` command. For example, if I want my user name, naba, to have `root` as the primary group, I would type:

```
usermod -g root naba
```

To find out more about the `useradd`, `userdel`, and `usermod` commands, type **man useradd**, **man userdel**, or **man usermod** in a terminal window.

Understanding the /etc/passwd File

The `/etc/passwd` file is a list of all user accounts. It's a text file and any user can read it, no special privileges needed. Each line in `/etc/passwd` has seven fields, separated by colons (:).

Here is a typical entry from the `/etc/passwd` file:

```
naba:x:500:10:Naba Barkakati:/home/naba:/bin/bash
```

Figure 2-4 uses this typical entry to explain the meaning of the seven fields.

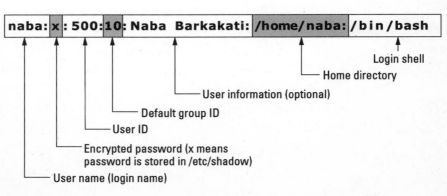

Figure 2-4:
This typical entry illustrates the meaning of the various fields.

As the example shows, the format of each line in /etc/passwd looks like this:

```
username:password:UID:GID:GECOS:homedir:shell
```

Table 2-1 explains the meaning of the seven fields in each /etc/passwd entry.

Table 2-1	Meaning of the Fields in /etc/passwd File
This Field	*Contains*
username	An alphanumeric user name, usually eight characters long and unique (Red Hat Linux allows user names to be longer than eight characters, but some other operating systems do not)
password	When present, a 13-character encrypted password (an empty field means that no password is required to access the account, an x means the password is stored in the /etc/shadow file, which is more secure)
UID	A unique number that serves as the user identifier (root has a UID of 0 and usually the UIDs between 1 to 100 are reserved for non-human users such as servers, it's best to keep the UID less than 32,767)
GID	The default group ID of the group to which the user belongs (GID 0 is for group root, other groups are defined in /etc/group and users can be and usually are in more than one group at a time)
GECOS	Optional personal information about the user (the finger command uses this field and GECOS stands for General Electric Comprehensive Operating System, a long-forgotten operating system that's immortalized by the name of this field in /etc/passwd)
homedir	The name of the user's home directory
shell	The command interpreter (shell) such as Bash (/bin/bash) that's executed when this user logs in

Managing Groups

A group is a something to which users belong. A group has a name and an identification number (ID). After a group is defined, users can belong to one or more of these groups.

You'll find all the existing groups listed in /etc/group. For example, here is the line that defines the group named wheel:

```
wheel:x:10:root,naba
```

As this example shows, each line in /etc/group has the following format with four fields separated by colons:

```
groupname:password:GID:membership
```

Table 2-2 explains the meaning of the four fields in a group definition.

Table 2-2	Meaning of Fields in /etc/group File
Field Name	*Meaning*
groupname	The name of the group (for example, wheel)
password	The group password (an x means the password is stored in the /etc/shadow- file)
GID	The numerical group ID (for example, 10)
membership	A comma-separated list of user names who belong to this group (for example, root,naba)

If you want to create a new group, you can simply click the Add Group button in the Red Hat User Manager (Figure 2-1). An even quicker way is to use the groupadd command. For example, to add a new group called class with an automatically selected group ID, just type the following command in a terminal window (you have to be logged in as root):

```
groupadd class
```

Then you can add users to this group with the usermod command. For example, to add the users naba and ashley to the group named class, I type the following commands:

```
usermod -G class naba
usermod -G class ashley
```

That's it. Now I check /etc/group to find that it contains the following definition of class:

```
class:x:502:naba,ashley
```

It's that simple!

If you want to remove a group, use the groupdel command. For example, to remove group named class, type

```
groupdel class
```

Exploring the User Environment

When you log in as a user, you get a set of environment variables that control many aspects of what you see and do on your Red Hat Linux system. If you want to see your current environment, go ahead and type the following command in a terminal window:

```
env
```

(By the way, the `printenv` command also displays the environment, but `env` is shorter.)

The `env` command should print a long list of lines. That whole collection of lines is the current environment and each line defines an environment variable. For example, here is a typical line displayed by the `env` command:

```
HOSTNAME=localhost.localdomain
```

This line defines the environment variable `HOSTNAME`, and it's defined as `localhost.localdomain`.

An environment variable is nothing more than a name associated with a string. For example, the environment variable named `PATH` is typically defined as follows:

```
PATH=/usr/local/bin:/bin:/usr/bin:/usr/X11R6/bin
```

The string to the right of the equal sign is the value of the `PATH` environment variable. By convention, the `PATH` environment variable is a sequence of directory names, each name separated from the preceding one by a colon (`:`).

Each environment variable has a specific purpose. For example, when the shell has to search for a file, it simply searches the directories listed in the `PATH` environment variable. The shell searches the directories in `PATH` in the order of their appearance. Therefore, if two programs have the same name, the shell executes the one it finds first.

In a fashion similar to the shell's use of the `PATH` environment variable, an editor such as `vi` uses the value of the `TERM` environment variable to figure out how to display the file you are editing with `vi`. To see the current setting of `TERM`, type the following command at the shell prompt:

```
echo $TERM
```

If you type this command in a terminal window, the output is as follows:

```
xterm
```

To define an environment variable in Bash, use the following syntax:

```
export NAME=Value
```

Here, *NAME* denotes the name of the environment variable, and *Value* is the string representing its value. Therefore, you set TERM to the value xterm by using the following command:

```
export TERM=xterm
```

After you define an environment variable, you can change its value by simply specifying the new value with the syntax NAME=new-value. For example, to change the definition of TERM to vt100, type **TERM=vt100** at the shell prompt.

With an environment variable such as PATH, you typically want to append a new directory name to the existing definition, rather than define the PATH from scratch. The following example shows how to accomplish this task:

```
export PATH="$PATH:/usr/games"
```

This command appends the string :/usr/games to the current definition of the PATH environment variable. The net effect is to add /usr/games to the list of directories in PATH.

Note that you also can write this export command as follows:

```
export PATH=${PATH}:/usr/games
```

After you type that command, you can access programs in the /usr/games directory such as fortune, a program that prints a terse and often witty (and sometimes confusing) saying. If you are curious, go ahead and type the following command:

```
fortune
```

What fortune prints is random, but it can be amusing. The result should be a terse, witty, and/or confusing saying.

PATH and TERM are only two of a handful of common environment variables. Table 2-3 lists some of the environment variables for a typical Red Hat Linux user.

Table 2-3	Typical Environment Variables in Red Hat Linux
Environment Variable	*Contents*
DISPLAY	The name of the display on which the X Window System displays output (typically set to :0.0)
HOME	Your home directory
HOSTNAME	The host name of your system
LOGNAME	Your login name
MAIL	The location of your mail directory
PATH	The list of directories in which the shell looks for programs
SHELL	Your shell (SHELL=/bin/bash for Bash)
TERM	The type of terminal

Changing User and Group Ownerships of Files

In Red Hat Linux, each file or directory has two types of owners — a user and a group. In other words, each file and directory is owned by a user and a group. The user and group ownerships can be used to control who can access a file or directory.

To view the owner of a file or directory, use the ls -l command to see the detailed listing of a directory. For example, here's a typical file's information:

```
-rw-rw-r--  1 naba     naba     40909 07-14 20:37 composer.txt
```

In this example, the first set of characters shows the file's permission setting — who can read, write, or execute the file. The third and fourth fields (in this sample, naba naba) indicate the user and group owner of the file. Each user has a private group that has the same name as the user name. So most files' user and group ownership appear to show the user name twice.

As a system administrator, you may decide to change the group ownership of a file to a common group. For example, suppose you want to change the group ownership of the composer.txt file to the class group. To do that, log in as root and type the following command:

```
chgrp class composer.txt
```

This chgrp command changes the group ownership of composer.txt to class. After I tried this, I typed **ls -l** again to verify the ownership, and here's what I got:

```
-rw-rw-r--  1 naba     class    40909 07-14 20:37 composer.txt
```

You can use the `chown` command to change the user owner. The command has the following format:

```
chown username filename
```

For example, to change the user ownership of a file named `sample.jpg` to `naba`, I type:

```
chown naba sample.jpg
```

In fact, `chown` can change both the user and group owner at the same time. For example, to change the user owner to `naba` and the group owner to `class`, I type:

```
chown naba.class composer.txt
```

In other words, you simply append the group name to the user name with a period in between and use that as the name of the owner.

Chapter 3: Managing the File System

The *file system* refers to the organization of files and directories. As a system administrator, you have to perform certain operations to manage the file system. For example, you have to learn how to *mount* — add a file system on a storage medium to the overall Red Hat Linux file system. You also need to back up important data and learn how to restore files from a backup. Other file system operations include sharing files with the *Network File System* (NFS) and accessing MS-DOS files. In this chapter, I show you how to perform all the file system management tasks.

Learning the Red Hat Linux File System

The files and directories in your PC store information in an organized manner just like paper filing systems. When you store information on paper, you typically put several pages in a folder and then save the folder in a file cabinet. If you have many folders, you probably have some sort of filing system. For example, you may label each folder's tab and then arrange them alphabetically in the file cabinet. You probably have several file cabinets, each with lots of drawers, which, in turn, contain folders full of pages.

Operating systems such as Red Hat Linux organize information in your computer in a manner similar to your paper filing system. Red Hat Linux uses a file system to organize all information in your computer. Of course, unlike a filing cabinet, the storage medium is not a metal cabinet and paper. Instead, Red Hat Linux stores information on devices such as hard disk drives, floppy disk drives, and CD-ROM drives.

To draw an analogy between your computer's file system and a paper filing system, think of a disk drive as the file cabinet. The drawers in the file cabinet correspond to the directories in the file system. The folders in each drawer are also directories — because a directory in a computer file system can contain other directories. You can think of the pages inside a folder as files. The file is where the actual information is stored. Figure 3-1 illustrates the analogy between a file cabinet and the Red Hat Linux file system.

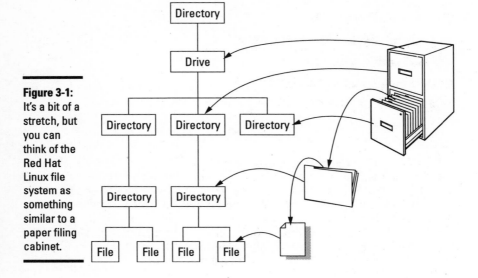

Figure 3-1:
It's a bit of a stretch, but you can think of the Red Hat Linux file system as something similar to a paper filing cabinet.

The Red Hat Linux file system has a hierarchical structure with individual files stored in directories. A directory, in turn, can contain other directories, which is why the file system is called *hierarchical*.

Everything in your Red Hat Linux system is organized in files and directories in the file system. To access and use documents and programs on your system, you have to be familiar with the file system.

Understanding the file system hierarchy

The Red Hat Linux file system is organized like a tree with a root directory that's represented by a single slash (/). Then there is a hierarchy of files and directories. Parts of the file system can be in different physical drives or different hard-disk partitions.

Red Hat Linux uses a standard directory hierarchy. Figure 3-2 shows the standard parts of the Red Hat Linux file system. Of course, you can create new directories anywhere in this structure.

Figure 3-2:
The Red Hat
Linux file
system
uses this
standard
directory
hierarchy.

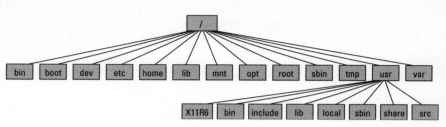

Write the name of any file or directory by concatenating the names of directories that identify where that file or directory is and using the forward slash (/) as a separator. For example, in Figure 3-2 the usr directory at the top level is written as /usr because the root directory (/) contains usr. On the other hand, the X11R6 directory is inside usr directory, which is inside the root directory (/). Therefore, the X11R6 directory is uniquely identified by the name /usr/X11R6. This type of full name is called *pathname* because the name identifies the path you take from the root directory to reach a file. Thus /usr/X11R6 is a pathname.

Each of the standard directories in the Red Hat Linux file system is meant to be used for a specific purpose. Table 3-1 summarizes these directories.

Table 3-1	Standard Directories in Red Hat Linux File System
Directory	*Used to Store*
/bin	Executable files for user commands (for use by all users)
/boot	Files needed by the boot loader to load the Linux kernel
/dev	Device files
/etc	Host-specific system configuration files
/home	User home directories
/lib	Shared libraries and kernel modules
/mnt	Mount point for a temporarily mounted file system
/opt	Add-on application software packages
/root	Home directory for the root user
/sbin	Utilities for system administration
/tmp	Temporary files
Iusr Hierarchy	
/usr/X11R6	X Window System, Version 11 Release 6
/usr/bin	Most user commands

(continued)

Table 3-1 *(continued)*

Directory	Used to Store
/usr Hierarchy	
/usr/include	Directory for standard include files used in developing Linux applications
/usr/lib	Libraries used by software packages and for programming
/usr/libexec	Libraries for applications
/usr/local	Any local software
/usr/sbin	Nonessential system administrator utilities
/usr/share	Shared data that does not depend on the system architecture (whether the system is a Intel PC or a Sun SPARC workstation)
/usr/src	Source code
The /var Hierarchy	
/var/cache	Cached data for a applications
/var/lib	Information relating to the current state of applications
/var/lock	Lock files to ensure that a resource is used by one application only
/var/log	Log files organized into subdirectories
/var/mail	User mailbox files
/var/opt	Variable data for packages stored in /opt directory
/var/run	Data describing the system since it was booted
/var/spool	Data that's waiting for some kind of processing
/var/tmp	Temporary files preserved between system reboots
/var/yp	Network Information Service (NIS) database files

Mounting a device on the file system

The storage devices that you use in Red Hat Linux contain Linux file systems. Each device has its own local file system consisting of a hierarchy of directories. Before you can access the files on a device, you have to attach the device's directory hierarchy to the tree that represents the overall Red Hat Linux file system.

Mounting is the operation that you perform to cause the file system on a physical storage device (a hard-disk partition or a CD-ROM) to appear as part of the Linux file system. Figure 3-3 illustrates the concept of mounting.

Figure 3-3 shows each device with a name that begins with /dev. For example, /dev/cdrom is the CD-ROM drive and /dev/fd0 is the floppy drive. These physical devices are mounted at specific mount points on the Red Hat Linux file system. For example, the CD-ROM drive, /dev/cdrom, is mounted on /mnt/cdrom in the file system. After mounting the CD-ROM in this way, the RedHat directory on the CD-ROM appears as /mnt/cdrom/RedHat in the Red Hat Linux file system.

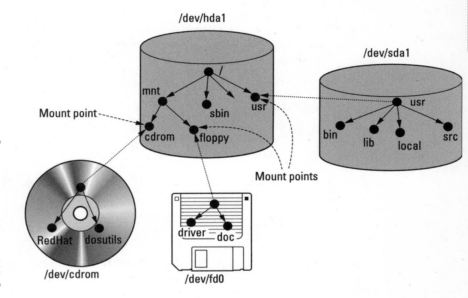

Figure 3-3:
You have to mount a device on the Red Hat Linux file system before accessing it.

You can use the mount command to manually mount a device on the Red Hat Linux file system at a specified directory. That directory is the *mount point*. For example, to mount the CD-ROM drive at /mnt/cdrom directory, you would type the following command (after logging in as root):

```
mount /dev/cdrom /mnt/cdrom
```

The mount command reports an error if the CD-ROM device is mounted already or if no CD-ROM is in the drive. Otherwise, the mount operation succeeds, and you can access the CD-ROM's contents through the /mnt/cdrom directory.

You can use any directory as the mount point. If you mount a device on a nonempty directory, however, you cannot access the files in that directory until you unmount the device by using the umount command. You should always, therefore, use an empty directory as the mount point.

Red Hat Linux comes with the /mnt/cdrom directory for mounting CD-ROMs and /mnt/floppy for mounting floppy drives.

To unmount a device when you no longer need it, use the umount command. For example, to unmount the CD-ROM device, type

```
umount /dev/cdrom
```

The umount command succeeds as long as no one is using the CD-ROM. If you get an error when trying to unmount the CD-ROM, check to see if the current working directory is on the CD-ROM. If you are currently in one of the CD-ROM's directories, that also qualifies as a use of the CD-ROM.

Examining the /etc/fstab file

The mount command has the following general format:

```
mount device-name mount-point
```

However, you can mount the CD-ROM by typing one of the following commands:

```
mount /dev/cdrom
mount /mnt/cdrom
```

You can mount by specifying only the CD-ROM device name or the mount point name because of what's in a file named /etc/fstab. There is a line in the /etc/fstab file for the /mnt/cdrom mount point. That entry specifies the CD-ROM device name and the file system type. That's why you can mount the CD-ROM with a shorter mount command.

The /etc/fstab file is a *configuration file* — a text file containing information that the mount and umount commands use. Each line in the /etc/fstab file provides information about a device and its mount point in the Red Hat Linux file system. Essentially, the /etc/fstab file associates various mount points within the file system with specific devices, which enables the mount command to work from the command line with only the mount point or the device as argument.

Here is a /etc/fstab file from a typical Red Hat Linux system:

```
LABEL=/         /           ext3      defaults          1 1
LABEL=/boot     /boot       ext3      defaults          1 2
none            /dev/pts    devpts    gid=5,mode=620    0 0
none            /proc       proc      defaults          0 0
none            /dev/shm    tmpfs     defaults          0 0
/dev/hda3       swap        swap      defaults          0 0
```

```
/dev/cdrom      /mnt/cdrom       iso9660  noauto,owner,kudzu,ro  0  0
/dev/fd0        /mnt/floppy      auto     noauto,owner,kudzu      0  0
```

The first field on each line shows a device name, such as a hard-disk partition (or it identifies a partition by a LABEL keyword). The second field is the mount point, and the third field indicates the type of file system on the device. You can ignore the last three fields for now.

This /etc/fstab file shows that the /dev/hda3 device (the third primary partition on the first IDE hard disk) functions as a swap device for virtual memory, which is why both the mount point and the file-system type are set to swap.

The Linux operating system uses the contents of the /etc/fstab file to mount various file systems automatically. During Red Hat Linux startup, the init process executes a shell script that runs the mount -a command. That command reads the /etc/fstab file and mounts all listed file systems (except those with the noauto option).

The fourth field on each line of the /etc/fstab file shows a comma-separated list of options that apply to a specific device. Typically, you find the defaults option in this field. The defaults option implies — among other things — that the device mounts at boot time; that only the root user can mount the device; and that the device mounts for reading and writing. If the options include noauto, the device doesn't mount automatically as the system boots.

Sharing Files with NFS

Sharing files through the Network File System (NFS) is simple and involves two basic steps:

✦ On the NFS server, export one or more directories by listing them in the /etc/exports file and by running the /usr/sbin/exportfs command. In addition, you must run the NFS server (you can do this by logging in as root and typing **/etc/init.d/nfs start**).

✦ On each client system, use the mount command to mount the directories the server has exported.

The only problem in using NFS is that each client system must support it. Most PCs do not come with NFS. That means you have to buy NFS software separately if you want to share files by using NFS. However, it makes sense to use NFS if all systems on your LAN run Linux (or other variants of UNIX with built-in NFS support).

Note that NFS has security vulnerabilities. Therefore, you should not set up NFS on systems directly connected to the Internet.

I walk you through an NFS setup, using an example of two Linux PCs on a LAN.

Exporting a file system with NFS

Start with the server system that *exports* — makes available to the client systems — the contents of a directory. On the server, you must run the NFS service and also designate one or more file systems that are to be exported, or made available to the client systems.

To export a file system, you have to add an appropriate entry to the /etc/exports file. For example, suppose you want to export the /home directory and you want to enable the host named LNBP75 to mount this file system for read-and-write operations. You can do this by adding the following entry to the /etc/exports file:

```
/home LNBP75(rw)
```

After adding the entry in the /etc/exports file, manually export the file system by typing **/usr/sbin/exportfs -a** in a terminal window. This command exports all file systems defined in the /etc/exports file.

Now you need to start the NFS server. To do this, log in as root and type the following command in a terminal window:

```
/etc/init.d/nfs start
```

To restart the NFS service, type **/etc/init.d/nfs restart**.

When the NFS service is up, the server side of NFS is ready. Now you can try to mount the exported file system from a client system and access the exported file system.

If you ever make any changes to the exported file systems listed in the /etc/exports file, remember to restart the NFS service. To do this, type **/etc/init.d/nfs restart** in a terminal window.

Mounting an NFS file system

To access an exported NFS file system on a client system, you have to mount that file system on a mount point. The mount point is nothing more than a local directory. For example, suppose you want to access the /home directory exported from the server named LNBP200 at the local directory /mnt/lnbp200 on the client system. To do this, follow these steps:

1. **Log in as** root, **and create the directory with the following command:**

   ```
   mkdir /mnt/lnbp200
   ```

2. **Type the following command to perform the** mount **operation:**

   ```
   mount lnbp200:/home/public /mnt/lnbp200
   ```

3. **Change the directory to** /mnt/lnbp200 **with the command** cd /mnt/lnbp200. **Now you can view and access exported files from this directory.**

To confirm that the NFS file system is indeed mounted, log in as root on the client system and type **mount** in a terminal window. You should see a line similar to the following one about the NFS file system:

```
lnbp200:/home/public on /mnt/lnbp200 type nfs (rw,addr=192.168.1.200)
```

Backing Up and Restoring Files

Backing up and restoring files is a crucial system administration task. If something happens to your system's hard disk, you have to rely on the backups to recover important files. Here I present some backup strategies, describe several backup media, and explain how to back up and restore files by using the tape archiver (tar) program that comes with Red Hat Linux. Also, you learn how to perform incremental and automatic backups on tapes.

Selecting a backup strategy and media

Your Red Hat Linux system's hard disk contains everything needed to keep the system running, as well as other files, such as documents and databases, that you need to keep your business running. You need to back up these files so that you can recover quickly and bring the system back to normal in case the hard disk crashes. Typically, you have to follow a strict regimen of regular backups because you can never tell when the hard disk may fail or the file system may get corrupted. To implement such a regimen, you need to decide which files you want to back up, how often, and what backup storage media to use. This is what I mean by selecting a backup strategy and backup media.

Your choice of backup strategy and backup media depends on your assessment of the risk of business disruption due to hard disk failure. Depending on how you use your Red Hat Linux system, a disk failure may or may not have much impact on you.

For example, if you use your Red Hat Linux system as a learning tool (to learn about Linux or programming), all you may need are backup copies of some system files required to configure Linux. In this case, your backup strategy can be to save important system-configuration files on one or more floppies every time you change any system configuration.

On the other hand, if you use your Red Hat Linux system as an office server that provides shared file storage for many users, the risk of business disruption due to disk failure is much higher. In this case, you have to back up all the files every week and back up any new or changed files every day. You should perform these backups in an automated manner (this is where you can use the job-scheduling features I describe in Book V, Chapter 1). Also, you probably need a backup storage medium that can store large amounts (multiple gigabytes) of data on a single tape. In other words, for high-risk situations, your backup strategy is more elaborate and requires additional equipment (such as a tape drive).

Your choice of backup media depends on the amount of data you have to back up. For a small amount of data, such as system-configuration files, you can use floppy disks as the backup media. If your PC has a Zip drive, you can use Zip disks as backup media; these are good for backing up a single-user directory. To back up servers, use a tape drive, typically a 4mm or 8mm tape drive that connects to a SCSI controller. Such tape drives can store several gigabytes of data per tape, and you can use them to back up an entire file system on a single tape.

When backing up files to these backup media, you have to refer to the backup device by name. Table 3-2 lists device names for some common backup devices.

Table 3-2	Device Names for Common Backup Devices
Backup Device	**Linux Device Name**
Floppy disk	`/dev/fd0`
IDE Zip drive	`/dev/hdc4` or `/dev/hdd4`
SCSI Zip drive	`/dev/sda` (assuming it's the first SCSI drive; otherwise, the device name depends on the SCSI ID)
SCSI tape drive	`/dev/st0` or `/dev/nst0` (the n prefix means that the tape is not rewound after files are copied to the tape)

Commercial backup utilities for Linux

I explain how to back up and restore files using the tape archiver (tar) program that comes with Red Hat Linux. Although you can manage backups with tar, a number of commercial backup utilities come with graphical user interfaces and other features to simplify backups. Here are some well-known commercial backup utilities for Red Hat Linux:

✦ **BRU** — Backup and Restore Utility from The TOLIS Group, Inc. (www.tolisgroup.com)

✦ **LONE-TAR** — Tape-backup software package from Lone Star Software Corporation (www.cactus.com)

✦ **Arkeia** — Backup and recovery software for heterogeneous networks from Knox Software (www.knox-software.com)

✦ **CTAR** — Backup and recovery software for UNIX systems from UniTrends Software Corporation (www.unitrends.com)

✦ **BrightStor ARCserve Backup for Linux** — Data-protection technology for Linux systems from Computer Associates (www3.ca.com/Solutions/Product.asp?ID=3370)

Using the tape archiver — tar

You can use the tar command to archive files to a device such as a floppy disk or tape. The tar program creates an archive file that can contain other directories and files and (optionally) compress the archive for efficient storage. The archive is then written to a specified device or another file. In fact, many software packages are distributed in the form of a compressed tar file.

The command syntax of the tar program is as follows:

```
tar options destination source
```

Here, *options* are usually specified by a sequence of single letters, with each letter specifying what tar should do. The *destination* is the device name of the backup device. And *source* is a list of file or directory names denoting the files to back up.

Backing up and restoring a single-volume archive

For example, suppose you want to back up the contents of the /etc/X11 directory on a floppy disk. Log in as root, place a disk in the floppy drive, and type the following command:

```
tar zcvf /dev/fd0 /etc/X11
```

The `tar` program displays a list of filenames as each file is copied to the compressed `tar` archive on the floppy disk. In this case, the options are `zcvf`, the destination is `/dev/fd0` (the floppy disk), and the source is the `/etc/X11` directory (which implies all its subdirectories and their contents). You can use a similar `tar` command to back up files to a tape — simply replace `/dev/fd0` with the tape device — such as `/dev/st0` for a SCSI tape drive.

Table 3-3 defines a few common `tar` options.

Table 3-3	Common tar Options
Option	*Does the Following*
c	Creates a new archive.
f	Specifies the name of the archive file or device on the next field in the command line.
M	Specifies a multivolume archive (the next section describes multivolume archives).
t	Lists the contents of the archive.
v	Displays verbose messages.
x	Extracts files from the archive.
z	Compresses the tar archive using gzip.

To view the contents of the `tar` archive you create on the floppy disk, type the following command:

```
tar ztf /dev/fd0
```

You should see a list of the filenames (each begins with `/etc/X11`) indicating what's in the backup. In this `tar` command, the t option lists the contents of the `tar` archive.

To extract the files from a `tar` backup, follow these steps while logged in as `root`:

1. **Change the directory to** `/tmp` **by typing this command:**

   ```
   cd /tmp
   ```

   This is where you can practice extracting the files from the `tar` backup. For a real backup, change the directory to an appropriate location (typically, you would type `cd /`).

2. **Type the following command:**

```
tar zxvf /dev/fd0
```

This `tar` command uses the `x` option to extract the files from the archive stored on `/dev/fd0` (the floppy disk).

Now if you check the contents of the `/tmp` directory, you notice that the `tar` command creates an `etc/X11` directory tree in `/tmp` and restores all the files from the `tar` archive into that directory. The `tar` command strips off the leading `/` from the filenames in the archive and restores the files in the current directory. If you want to restore the `/etc/X11` directory from the archive on the floppy, use this command:

```
tar zxvf /dev/fd0 -C /
```

The `/` at the end of the command denotes the directory where you want to restore the backup files.

You can use the `tar` command to create, view, and restore an archive. You can store the archive in a file or in any device you specify with a device name.

Backing up and restoring a multivolume archive

Sometimes the capacity of a single storage medium is less than the total storage space needed to store the archive. In this case, you can use the `M` option for a multivolume archive — meaning the archive can span multiple tapes or floppies. Note, however, that you cannot create a compressed, multivolume archive. That means you have to drop the `z` option. To see how multivolume archives work, log in as `root`, place one disk in the floppy drive, and type the following `tar` command:

```
tar cvfM /dev/fd0 /usr/share/doc/ghostscript*
```

Note the `M` option in the option letters; it tells `tar` to create a multivolume archive. The `tar` command prompts you for a second floppy when the first one is filled. Take out the first floppy, and insert another floppy when you see the following prompt:

```
Prepare volume #2 for `/dev/fd0' and hit return:
```

When you press Enter, the `tar` program continues with the second floppy. In this example, you need only two floppies to store the archive; for larger archives, the `tar` program continues to prompt for floppies in case more floppies are needed.

To restore from this multivolume archive, type **cd /tmp** to change the directory to /tmp. Then type

```
tar xvfM /dev/fd0
```

The tar program prompts you to feed the floppies as necessary.

Use the du -s command to determine the amount of storage you need to archive a directory. For example, here's how you can get the total size of the /etc directory in kilobytes:

```
du -s /etc
11632   /etc
```

The resulting output shows that the /etc directory requires at least 11,632K of storage space to back up. If you plan to back up on multiple high-density floppies, you need about 11,632/1,400 = 9 floppies.

Backing up on tapes

Although backing up on tapes is as simple as using the right device name in the tar command, you do need to know some nuances of the tape device to use it well. When you use tar to back up to the device named /dev/st0 (the first SCSI tape drive), the tape device automatically rewinds the tape after the tar program finishes copying the archive to the tape. The /dev/st0 device is called a rewinding tape device because it rewinds tapes by default.

If your tape can hold several gigabytes of data, you may want to write several tar archives — one after another — to the same tape (otherwise, much of the tape may be empty). To do this, you do not want the tape device to rewind the tape after the tar program finishes. To help you with this, several Linux tape devices are nonrewinding. The nonrewinding SCSI tape device is called /dev/nst0. Use this device name if you want to write one archive after another on a tape.

After each archive, the nonrewinding tape device writes an *end-of-file* (EOF) marker to separate one archive from the next. Use the mt command to control the tape — you can move from one marker to the next or rewind the tape. For example, after you finish writing several archives to a tape using the /dev/nst0 device name, you can rewind the tape with the following command:

```
mt -f /dev/nst0 rewind
```

After rewinding the tape, you can use the following command to extract files from the first archive to the current disk directory:

```
tar xvf /dev/nst0
```

After that, you must move past the EOF marker to the next archive. To do this, use the following `mt` command:

```
mt -f /dev/nst0 fsf 1
```

This positions the tape at the beginning of the next archive. Now use the `tar xvf` command again to read this archive.

If you save multiple archives on a tape, you have to keep track of the archives yourself. This can be hard to remember, so you may be better off simply saving one archive per tape.

Performing incremental backups

Suppose you back up your system's hard disk on a tape by using `tar`. Because such a full backup can take quite some time, you do not want to repeat this task every night. (Besides, only a small number of files may have changed during the day.) You can use the `find` command to list those files that have changed in the past 24 hours:

```
find / -mtime -1 -type f -print
```

This command prints a list of files that have changed within the last day. The `-mtime -1` option means you want the files that were last modified less than one day ago. You can now combine this `find` command with the `tar` command to back up only those files that have changed within the last day:

```
tar cvf /dev/st0 `find / -mtime -1 -type f -print`
```

When you place a command between single back quotes, the shell executes that command and places the output at that point in the command line. The net result is that the `tar` program saves only the changed files in the archive. Thus, you get an incremental backup that includes files that have changed since the previous day.

Performing automated backups

In Book V, Chapter 1, you learn to use `crontab` to set up recurring jobs (called *cron jobs*). The Linux system performs these tasks at regular intervals. Backing up your system is a good use of the `crontab` facility. Suppose your backup strategy is as follows:

✦ Every Sunday at 1:15 a.m., your system backs up the entire disk on the tape.

✦ Monday through Saturday, your system performs an incremental backup at 3:10 a.m. by saving only those files that have changed during the past 24 hours.

To set up this automated backup schedule, log in as `root` and type the following lines in a file named `backups` (this example assumes that you use a SCSI tape drive):

```
15 1 * * 0 tar zcvf /dev/st0 /
10 3 * * 1-6 tar zcvf /dev/st0 `find / -mtime -1 -type f -print`
```

Next, submit this job schedule by using the following `crontab` command:

```
crontab backups
```

Now you should be set for an automated backup. All you need to do is place a new tape in the tape drive everyday. You should also give each tape an appropriate label.

Accessing a DOS File System

If you have Microsoft Windows 95/98/Me installed on your hard disk, you've probably already mounted the DOS partition under Red Hat Linux. If not, you can easily mount DOS partitions in Red Hat Linux. Mounting makes the DOS directory hierarchy appear as part of the Linux file system. To identify the DOS partitions easily, you may want to mount the first DOS partition as `/dosc`, the second one as `/dosd`, and so on.

To determine whether your DOS hard disk partitions are set up to mount automatically, type the following `grep` command to look for the string `vfat` in the file `/etc/fstab.`:

```
grep vfat /etc/fstab
```

If the output shows one or more lines that contain `vfat`, your Red Hat Linux system mounts DOS/Windows hard-disk partitions automatically.

If the `grep` command doesn't show any lines that contain the string `vfat` in `/etc/fstab`, your system doesn't mount any DOS/Windows hard-disk partitions automatically. Of course, a very good reason may be that your hard disk doesn't have any DOS partitions.

Even if you don't have any DOS partitions on your hard disk, you should learn how to access a DOS file system from Red Hat Linux because you may need to access a DOS floppy disk on your Red Hat Linux system.

Mounting a DOS disk partition

To mount a DOS hard disk partition or floppy, use the `mount` command
but include the option `-t vfat` to indicate the file system type as DOS. For
example, if your DOS partition happens to be the first partition on your *IDE*
(Integrated Drive Electronics) drive and you want to mount it on `/dosc`, use
the following `mount` command:

```
mount -t vfat /dev/hda1 /dosc
```

The `-t vfat` part of the `mount` command specifies that the device you
mount — `/dev/hda1` — has an MS-DOS file system. Figure 3-4 illustrates the
effect of this `mount` command.

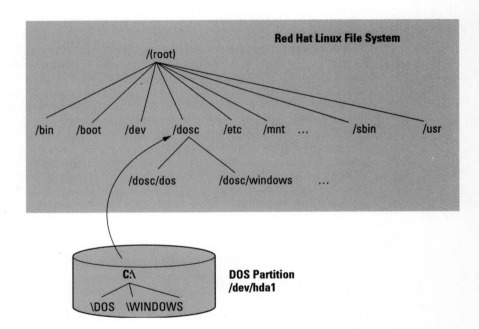

Figure 3-4:
Here's how
you mount
a DOS
partition on
the `/dosc`
directory.

Figure 3-4 shows how directories in your DOS partition map to the Linux file
system. What was the `C:\DOS` directory under DOS becomes `/dosc/dos`
under Red Hat Linux. Similarly, `C:\WINDOWS` now is `/dosc/windows`. You
probably can see the pattern. To convert a DOS filename to Linux (when you
`mount` the DOS partition on `/dosc`), perform the following steps:

1. **Change the DOS names to lowercase.**

2. **Change** `C:\` **to** `/dosc/`.

3. **Change all backslashes (\) to slashes (/).**

Mounting DOS floppy disks

Just as you mount a DOS hard disk partition on the Red Hat Linux file system, you can also mount a DOS floppy disk. You must log in as `root` to mount a floppy, but you can follow the steps shown in the latter part of this section to set up your system so that any user can mount a DOS floppy disk. You also need to know the device name for the floppy drive. By default, Linux defines the following two generic floppy-device names:

✦ `/dev/fd0` is the A drive (the first floppy drive)

✦ `/dev/fd1` is the B drive (the second floppy drive, if you have one)

As for the mount point, you can use any empty directory in the file system as the mount point, but the Red Hat Linux system comes with a directory, `/mnt/floppy`, specifically mounting a floppy disk.

To mount a DOS floppy disk on the `/mnt/floppy` directory, put the floppy in the drive and type the following command:

```
mount -t vfat /dev/fd0 /mnt/floppy
```

After you mount the floppy, you can copy files to and from the floppy by using Linux's copy command (`cp`). To copy the file `gnome1.pcx` from the current directory to the floppy, type the following:

```
cp gnome1.pcx /mnt/floppy
```

Similarly, to see the contents of the floppy disk, type the following:

```
ls /mnt/floppy
```

If you want to remove the floppy disk from the drive, first unmount the floppy drive. Unmounting removes the association between the floppy disk's file system and the mount point on the Red Hat Linux file system. Use the `umount` command to unmount the floppy disk like this:

```
umount /dev/fd0
```

You can set up your Red Hat Linux system so that any user can mount a DOS floppy. To enable any user to mount a DOS floppy in the A drive on the /a directory, for example, perform the following steps:

1. **Log in as** root.

2. **Create the** /a **directory (the mount point) by typing the following command in a terminal window:**

    mkdir /a

3. **Edit the** /etc/fstab **file in a text editor (such as vi or Emacs), insert the following line and then save the file and quit the editor:**

    /dev/fd0   /a   vfat   noauto,user   0 0

The first field in that line is the device name of the floppy drive (/dev/fd0); the second field is the mount directory (/a); and the third field shows the type of file system (vfat). The user option (which appears next to noauto) is what enables all users to mount DOS floppy disks.

4. **Log out and log in as a normal user.**

5. **To confirm that you can mount a DOS floppy as a normal user and not just as** root, **insert a DOS floppy in the A drive and type the following command:**

    mount /a

The mount operation should succeed, and you should see a listing of the DOS floppy when you type the command **ls /a**.

6. **To unmount the DOS floppy, type** umount /a.

Using mtools

One way to access the MS-DOS file systems is to mount the DOS hard disk or floppy disk by using the mount command and then use regular Linux commands, such as ls and cp, to work with the mounted DOS file system. This approach of mounting a DOS file system is fine for hard disks. Linux can mount the DOS partition automatically at startup, and you can access the DOS directories on the hard disk at any time.

If you want a quick directory listing of a DOS floppy disk, however, mounting can soon become quite tedious. First, you must mount the floppy drive. Then you must use the ls command. Finally, you must use the umount command before ejecting the floppy out of the drive.

This is where the mtools package comes to the rescue. The mtools package implements most common DOS commands; the commands use the same names as in DOS except that you add an m prefix to each command. Thus the command for getting a directory listing is mdir, and mcopy copies files. The best part of mtools is the fact that you don't need to mount the floppy disk to use the mtools commands.

Because the mtools commands write to and read from the physical device (floppy disk), you must log in as root to perform these commands. If you want any user to access the mtools commands, you must alter the permission settings for the floppy drive devices. Use the following command to permit anyone to read from and write to the first floppy drive:

```
chmod o+rw /dev/fd0
```

Trying mtools

To try out mtools, follow these steps:

1. **Log in as** root **or type** su - **and then enter the** root **password.**

2. **Place an MS-DOS floppy disk in your system's A drive.**

3. **Type** mdir.

You should see the directory of the floppy disk (in the standard DOS directory-listing format).

Typically, you would use the mtools utilities to access the floppy disks. The default configuration file, /etc/mtools.conf, is set up to access the floppy drive as the A drive. Although you can edit that file to define C and D drives for your DOS hard-disk partitions, you can as well access the hard disk partitions by using the Linux mount command to mount them. Because you can mount the hard-disk partitions automatically at startup, accessing them through the Linux commands is normally just as easy.

You also can access Iomega Zip drives through mtools. Simply specify a drive letter and the appropriate device's file name. For built-in IDE (ATAPI) Zip drives, try /dev/hdd4 as the device file and add the following line in the /etc/mtools.conf file:

```
drive e: file="/dev/hdd4"
```

After that you should be able to use mtools commands to access the Zip drive (refer to it as the E drive). For example, to see the directory listing, place Zip disk in the Zip drive and type:

```
mdir e:
```

Learning the mtools commands

The mtools package is a collection of utilities. So far, I have been using mdir — the mtools counterpart of the DIR command in DOS. The other mtools commands are fairly easy to use.

If you know the MS-DOS commands, you find that using the mtools commands is very easy. Type the DOS command in lowercase letters, and remember to add m in front of each command. Because the Linux commands and filenames are case-sensitive, you must use all lowercase letters as you type mtools commands.

Table 3-4 summarizes the commands available in mtools.

Table 3-4	The mtools Commands	
mtools Utility	*MS-DOS Command (If Any)*	*The mtools Utility Does the Following*
mattrib	ATTRIB	Changes MS-DOS file-attribute flags.
mbadblocks		Tests a floppy disk and marks the bad blocks in the file allocation table (FAT).
mcd	CD	Changes an MS-DOS directory.
mcopy	COPY	Copies files between MS-DOS and Linux.
mdel	DEL or ERASE	Deletes an MS-DOS file.
mdeltree	DELTREE	Recursively deletes an MS-DOS directory.
mdir	DIR	Displays an MS-DOS directory listing.
mdu		Lists space that a directory and its contents occupy.
mformat	FORMAT	Places an MS-DOS file system on a low-level-formatted floppy disk (Use fdformat to low-level-format a floppy in Red Hat Linux).
minfo		Gets information about an MS-DOS file system.
mkmanifest		Makes a list of short name equivalents.
mlabel	LABEL	Initializes an MS-DOS volume label.

(continued)

Table 3-4 *(continued)*

mtools Utility	MS-DOS Command (If Any)	The mtools Utility Does the Following
mmd	MD or MKDIR	Creates an MS-DOS directory.
mmove		Moves or renames an MS-DOS file or subdirectory.
mmount		Mounts an MS-DOS disk.
mpartition		Creates an MS-DOS file system as a partition.
mrd	RD or RMDIR	Deletes an MS-DOS directory.
mren	REN or RENAME	Renames an existing MS-DOS file.
mshowfat		Shows FAT entries for an MS-DOS file.
mtoolstest		Tests and displays the current mtools configuration.
mtype	TYPE	Displays the contents of an MS-DOS file.
mwrite	COPY	Copies a Linux file to MS-DOS.
mzip		Performs certain operations on SCSI Zip disks.

You can use the mtools commands just as you use the corresponding DOS commands. The mdir command, for example, works the same as the DIR command in DOS. The same goes for all the other mtools commands shown in Table 3-4.

You can use wildcard characters (such as *) with mtools commands, but you must remember that the Linux shell is the first program to see your command. If you don't want the shell to expand the wildcard character, use quotation marks around filenames that contain any wildcard characters. For example, to copy all *.txt files from the A drive to your current Red Hat Linux directory, use the following command:

```
mcopy "a:*.txt".
```

If you omit the quotation marks, the shell tries to expand the string a:*.txt with filenames from the current Linux directory. It also tries to copy those files (if any) from the DOS floppy disk.

On the other hand, if you want to copy files from the Linux directory to the DOS floppy disk, you do want the shell to expand any wildcard characters.

To copy all `*.jpg` files from the current Linux directory to the DOS floppy disk, for example, use `mcopy` like this:

```
mcopy *.jpg a:
```

With the `mtools` utilities you can use the backslash character (\) as the directory separator, just as you would in DOS. However, when you type a filename that contains the backslash character, you must enclose the name in double quotation marks. For example, here's a command that copies a file from a subdirectory on the A drive to the current Linux directory:

```
mcopy "a:\test\sample.dat".
```

Formatting a DOS floppy

Suppose that you run Red Hat Linux on your home PC and MS-DOS is no longer on your system, but you need to copy some files onto an MS-DOS floppy disk and take the disk to your office. If you already have a formatted MS-DOS floppy, you can simply mount that floppy and copy the file to the floppy by using the Linux `cp` command. But what if you don't have a formatted DOS floppy? The `mtools` package again comes to the rescue.

The `mtools` package provides the `mformat` utility, which can format a floppy disk for use in MS-DOS. Unlike the DOS format command that formats a floppy in a single step, the `mformat` command requires you to follow a two-step process:

1. **Use the `fdformat` command to low-level-format a floppy disk.**

The `fdformat` command uses the floppy device name as the argument; the device name includes all the parameters necessary for formatting the floppy disk.

Figure 3-5 illustrates the device-naming convention for the floppy-drive device. Based on the information shown in Figure 3-5, you use the following command to format a 3.5-inch, high-density floppy disk in your system's A drive:

```
fdformat /dev/fd0H1440
```

2. **Use the `mformat` command to put an MS-DOS file system on the low-level-formatted floppy disk. If the floppy is in drive A, type the following command to create a formatted DOS floppy:**

```
mformat a:
```

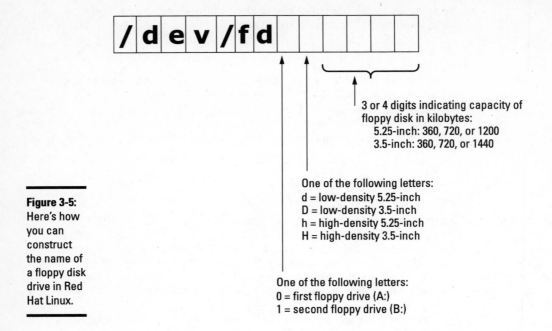

3 or 4 digits indicating capacity of
floppy disk in kilobytes:
5.25-inch: 360, 720, or 1200
3.5-inch: 360, 720, or 1440

One of the following letters:
d = low-density 5.25-inch
D = low-density 3.5-inch
h = high-density 5.25-inch
H = high-density 3.5-inch

Figure 3-5:
Here's how
you can
construct
the name of
a floppy disk
drive in Red
Hat Linux.

One of the following letters:
0 = first floppy drive (A:)
1 = second floppy drive (B:)

Chapter 4: Managing Applications

In This Chapter

✔ **Learning RPMs**

✔ **Installing and removing software RPMs**

✔ **Building applications from source files**

✔ **Updating Red Hat Linux applications with Red Hat Network**

Most software packages for Red Hat Linux are distributed in special files called *Red Hat Package Manager* (RPM) files, which is why you should know how to install or remove software packages that come in the form of RPM files. In this chapter, I show you how to work with RPM files.

Many other open-source software packages come in source-code form, usually in compressed archives. You have to build and install the software to use it. I describe the steps you typically follow when downloading, building, and installing source-based software packages.

Finally, I briefly describe the Red Hat Network and how, after registering with it, you can use Red Hat's Update agent to update Red Hat Linux applications.

Working with the Red Hat Package Manager

Red Hat Package Manager (RPM) is a system for packaging all the necessary files for a software product in a single file — called an *RPM file* or simply an *RPM*. In fact, the entire Red Hat Linux distribution is a whole lot of RPMs. The best way to work with RPMs is through the RPM commands. You have to type these commands at the shell prompt in a terminal window or a text console.

Using the RPM commands

When you install Red Hat Linux from the companion CD-ROMs, the Red Hat installer uses the rpm command to unpack the packages (RPM files) and to copy the contents to your hard disk.

You don't need to understand the internal structure of an RPM file, but you should know how to use the rpm command to work with RPM files. Here are some of the things you can do with the rpm command:

✦ Find out the version numbers and other information about the RPMs installed on your system.

✦ Install a new software package from an RPM. For example, you may install a package you have skipped during the initial installation. For example, you have to install the source files for the Linux kernel before you can rebuild the kernel. You can do that with the `rpm` command.

✦ Remove (uninstall) unneeded software you have previously installed from an RPM. You may uninstall a package to reclaim the disk space, if you find that you rarely (or never) use the package.

✦ Upgrade an older version of an RPM with a new one. You may upgrade after you download a new version of a package from Red Hat's FTP server. Often, you must upgrade an RPM to benefit from the fixes in the new version.

✦ Verify that an RPM is in working order. You can verify a package to check that all necessary files are in the correct locations.

As you can see, the `rpm` command is versatile — it can do a lot of different things depending on the options you use.

If you ever forget the `rpm` options, type the following command to see a list:

```
rpm --help | more
```

The number of `rpm` options will amaze you!

Understanding RPM filenames

An RPM contains a number of files, but it appears as a single file on your Red Hat Linux system. By convention, the RPM filenames have a specific format. To see the names of some of the RPM files on the companion CD-ROMs, follow these steps:

1. **Place the first CD-ROM in the CD-ROM drive. The CD-ROM should be automatically mounted if you are using GNOME or KDE graphical desktops. Otherwise, mount it with the following command (you must be logged in as `root`):**

```
mount /dev/cdrom
```

2. **Type the following command to go to the directory in which the RPMs are located:**

```
cd /mnt/cdrom/RedHat/RPMS
```

3. **View the listing using the `ls` command. For example to see RPMs with names that start with `cups`, type**

```
ls cups*
```

You should see a listing that looks like this:

```
cups-devel-1.1.15-10.i386.rpm
cups-libs-1.1.15-10.i386.rpm
... lines deleted ...
```

As you may guess from the listing, the names of RPM files end with an `.rpm` extension. To understand the various parts of the filename, consider the following RPM:

```
cups-devel-1.1.15-10.i386.rpm
```

This filename has the following parts, separated by dashes (-):

- ✦ Package name — `cups-devel`
- ✦ Version number — `1.1.15`
- ✦ Release number — `10` (this is a Red Hat-assigned release number)
- ✦ Architecture — `i386` (this package is for Intel 80386-compatible processors)

Usually, the package name is descriptive enough for you to guess what the RPM may contain. The version number is the same as that of the software package's current version number (even when it is distributed in some other form, such as a `tar` file). Red Hat assigns the release number to keep track of changes. The architecture should be `i386` or `noarch` for the RPMs you want to install on a PC with an Intel x86-compatible processor.

Finding out about RPMs

As it installs packages, the `rpm` command builds a database of installed RPMs. You can use the `rpm -q` command to query this database to find out information about packages installed on your system.

For example, to find out the version number of the Linux kernel installed on your system, type the following `rpm -q` command:

```
rpm -q kernel
```

You should see a response similar to the following:

```
kernel-2.4.18-14
```

The response is the name of the RPM for the kernel (this is the executable version of the kernel, not the source files). The name is the same as the RPM filename, except that the last part — `.i386.rpm` — is not shown. In this case, the version part of the RPM tells you that the kernel is 2.4.18.

You can see a list of all installed RPMs by using the following command:

```
rpm -qa
```

You see a long list of RPMs scroll by your screen. To view the list one screen at a time, type

```
rpm -qa | more
```

If you want to search for a specific package, feed the output of `rpm -qa` to the `grep` command. For example, to see all packages with `kernel` in their names, type

```
rpm -qa | grep kernel
```

The result depends on what parts of the kernel RPMs are installed on a system. For example, on my system this command shows the following:

```
kernel-source-2.4.18-14
kernel-2.4.18-14
kernel-pcmcia-cs-3.1.31-9
```

You can query much more than a package's version number with the `rpm -q` command. By adding single-letter options, you can find out other useful information. For example, try the following command to see the files in the kernel package:

```
rpm -ql kernel
```

Here are a few lines from the output of this command:

```
/boot/System.map-2.4.18-14
/boot/config-2.4.18-14
/boot/module-info-2.4.18-14
/boot/vmlinux-2.4.18-14
/boot/vmlinuz-2.4.18-14
/dev/shm
/lib/modules
/lib/modules/2.4.18-14
/lib/modules/2.4.18-14/build
/lib/modules/2.4.18-14/kernel
/lib/modules/2.4.18-14/kernel/abi
/lib/modules/2.4.18-14/kernel/abi/cxenix
/lib/modules/2.4.18-14/kernel/abi/cxenix/abi-cxenix.o
/lib/modules/2.4.18-14/kernel/abi/ibcs
/lib/modules/2.4.18-14/kernel/abi/ibcs/abi-ibcs.o
 (rest of the listing deleted)
```

Here are few more useful forms of the `rpm -q` commands to query information about a package (to use any of these `rpm -q` commands, type the command, followed by the package name):

✦ `rpm -qc` — Lists all configuration files in a package.

✦ `rpm -qd` — Lists all documentation files in a package. These are usually the online manual pages (also known as *man pages*).

✦ `rpm -qf` — Displays the name of the package (if any) to which a specified file belongs.

✦ `rpm -qi` — Displays detailed information about a package, including version number, size, installation date, and a brief description.

✦ `rpm -ql` — Lists all the files in a package. For some packages, this can be a very long list.

✦ `rpm -qs` — Lists the state of all files in a package.

These `rpm` commands provide information about installed packages only. If you want to find information about an uninstalled RPM file, add the letter *p* to the command-line option of each command. For example, to view the list of files in the RPM file named `rdist-6.1.5-24.i386.rpm`, use the following command:

```
rpm -qpl rdist-*.rpm
```

Of course, this works only if the current directory contains that RPM file.

Installing an RPM

To install an RPM, use the `rpm -i` command. You have to provide the name of the RPM file as the argument. A typical example is installing an RPM from this book's companion CD-ROMs containing the Red Hat Linux RPMs. As usual, you have to mount the CD-ROM and change to the directory in which the RPMs are located. Then use the `rpm -i` command to install the RPM. If you want to view the progress of the RPM installation, use `rpm -ivh`. A series of hash marks (#) is displayed as the package is unpacked.

For example, to install the `kernel-source` RPM (which contains the source files for the Linux operating system) from the companion CD-ROMs, I insert the CD and after it's mounted, type the following commands:

```
cd /mnt/cdrom/RedHat/RPMS
rpm -ivh kernel-source*
```

You do not have to type the full RPM filename — you can use a few characters from the beginning of the name followed by an asterisk (*). Make sure you type enough of the name to identify the RPM file uniquely.

If you try to install an RPM that's already installed, the rpm -i command displays an error message. For example, here is what happens when I type the following command to install the man package on my system:

```
rpm -i man-1*
```

I get the following error message from the rpm -i command:

```
package man-1.5j-8 is already installed
```

To force the rpm command to install a package even if errors are present, just add —force to the rpm -i command, like this:

```
rpm -i --force man-1*
```

Removing an RPM

You may want to remove — uninstall — a package if you realize you don't really need the software. For example, if you have installed the X Window System development package but discover you are not interested in writing X applications, you can easily remove the package by using the rpm -e command.

You need to know the name of the package before you can remove it. One good way to find the name is to use rpm -qa in conjunction with grep to search for the appropriate RPM file. For example, to locate the X Window System development RPM, try the following command:

```
rpm -qa | grep XFree86
```

XFree86-devel happens to be the package name of the X Window System development RPM. To remove that package, type

```
rpm -e XFree86-devel
```

To remove an RPM, you do not need the full RPM filename; all you need is the package name — the first part of the filename up to the dash (-) before the version number.

The rpm -e command does not remove a package other packages need. For example, to remove the vim-common package, I type the following command:

```
rpm -e vim-common
```

Then I get the following error message:

```
error: removing these packages would break dependencies:
        vim-common is needed by vim-minimal-6.1-6
        vim-common is needed by vim-enhanced-6.1-6
```

Upgrading an RPM

Use the `rpm -U` command to upgrade an RPM. You must provide the name of the RPM file that contains the new software. For example, if I have version 2.0.36 of Apache `httpd` (Web server) installed on my system but I want to upgrade to version 2.0.39, I download the RPM file `httpd-2.0.39-1.i386.rpm` from one of Red Hat update sites listed at `www.redhat.com/mirrors.html` and use the following command:

```
rpm -U httpd-2.0.39-1.i386.rpm
```

The `rpm` command performs the upgrade by removing the old version of the `httpd` package and installing the new RPM.

Whenever possible, you should upgrade rather than remove the old package and install a new one. Upgrading automatically saves the old configuration files, which saves you the hassle of configuring the software after a fresh installation.

When you are upgrading the `kernel` packages that contain a ready-to-run Linux kernel, install it by using the `rpm -i` command (instead of the `rpm -U` command). That way you won't overwrite the current kernel.

Verifying an RPM

You may not do this often, but if you suspect that a software package is not properly installed, use the `rpm -V` command to verify it. For example, to verify the kernel package, type the following:

```
rpm -V kernel
```

This causes `rpm` to compare the size and other attributes of each file in the package against those of the original files. If everything verifies correctly, the `rpm -V` command does not print anything. If there are any discrepancies, you see a report of them. For example, I have modified the configuration files for the Apache `httpd` Web server. Here is what I type to verify the `httpd` package:

```
rpm -V httpd
```

Here's the result I get:

```
S.5....T c /etc/httpd/conf/httpd.conf
```

In this case, the output from rpm -V tells me that a configuration file has changed. Each line of this command's output has three parts:

✦ The line starts with eight characters: each character indicates the type of discrepancy found. For example, S means the size is different, and T means the time of last modification is different. Table 4-1 shows each character and its meaning. A period means that that specific attribute matches the original.

✦ For configuration files, a c appears next; otherwise, this field is blank. That's how you can tell whether or not a file is a configuration file. Typically, you shouldn't worry if a configuration file has changed; you have probably made the changes yourself.

✦ The last part of the line is the full pathname of the file. From this part, you can tell exactly where the file is located.

Table 4-1	Characters Used in RPM Verification Reports
Character	*Meaning*
S	Size has changed.
M	Permissions and file type are different.
5	Checksum computed with the MD5 algorithm is different.
D	Device type is different.
L	Symbolic link is different.
U	File's user is different.
G	File's group is different.
T	File's modification time is different.

Building Software Packages from Source Files

Many open-source software packages are distributed in source-code form, without executable binaries. Before you can use such software, you have to build the executable binary files by compiling, and you have to follow some instructions to install the package. In this section, I show you how to build software packages from source files.

Downloading and unpacking the software

Open-source software source files are typically distributed in compressed tar archives. These archives are created by the tar program and compressed with the `gzip` program. The distribution is in the form of a single large file with the `.tar.gz` or `.tar.Z` extension — often referred to as a *compressed tarball.* If you want the software, you have to download the compressed tarball and unpack it.

Download the compressed `tar` file by using anonymous FTP or through your Web browser. Typically, this involves no effort on your part beyond clicking a link and saving the file in an appropriate directory on your system.

To try your hand at downloading and building a software package, you can practice on the X Multimedia System (XMMS) — a graphical X application for playing MP3 and other multimedia files. XMMS is bundled with Red Hat Linux and should already be installed on your system. However, there is no harm in downloading and rebuilding the XMMS package again.

Download the source files for XMMS from `www.xmms.org/download.html`. The files are packed in the form of a compressed `tar` archive. Click the `ftp` link for the source files and then save them in the `/usr/local/src` directory in your Red Hat Linux system (be sure to log in as `root`; otherwise, you cannot save in the `/usr/local/src` directory).

After downloading the compressed `tar` file, examine the contents with the following `tar` command:

```
tar ztf xmms*.gz | more
```

You should see a listing similar to the following:

```
xmms-1.2.7/
xmms-1.2.7/Makefile.in
xmms-1.2.7/README
xmms-1.2.7/stamp-h1.in
xmms-1.2.7/ABOUT-NLS
xmms-1.2.7/AUTHORS
xmms-1.2.7/COPYING
xmms-1.2.7/ChangeLog
xmms-1.2.7/INSTALL
xmms-1.2.7/Makefile.am
xmms-1.2.7/NEWS
xmms-1.2.7/TODO
xmms-1.2.7/acconfig.h
xmms-1.2.7/acinclude.m4
xmms-1.2.7/aclocal.m4
xmms-1.2.7/config.guess
xmms-1.2.7/config.h.in
xmms-1.2.7/config.sub
xmms-1.2.7/configure
... rest of the output not shown ...
```

The output of this `tar` command shows you what's in the archive and gives you an idea of the directories that will be created after you unpack the archive. In this case, a directory named `xmms-1.2.7` will be created in the current directory, which, in my case, is `/usr/local/src`. From the listing, you'll also learn the programming language used to write the package. If you see `.c` and `.h` files, that means the source files are in the C programming language, which is used to write many open-source software packages.

To extract the contents of the compressed `tar` archive, type the following `tar` command:

```
tar zxvf xmms*.gz
```

You'll again see the long list of files as they are extracted from the archive and copied to the appropriate directories on your hard disk.

Now you are ready to build the software.

Building the software from source files

After you unpack the compressed `tar` archive, all source files will be in a directory whose name is usually that of the software package with a version-number suffix. For example, the XMMS version 1.2.7 source files are extracted to the `xmms-1.2.7` directory. To start building the software, change directories with the following command:

```
cd xmms*
```

You don't have to type the entire name — the shell can expand the directory name and change to the `xmms-1.2.7` directory.

Nearly all software packages come with some sort of `README` or `INSTALL` file — a text file that tells you how to build and install the package. XMMS is no exception; it comes with a `README` file you can peruse by typing **more README**. There is also an `INSTALL` file that contains instructions for building and installing XMMS.

Most open-source software packages, including XMMS, also come with a file named `COPYING`. This file contains the full text of the *GNU General Public License* (GPL), which spells out the conditions under which you can use and redistribute the software. If you are not familiar with the GNU GPL, read this file and show the license to your legal counsel for a full interpretation and an assessment of applicability to your business.

To build the software package, follow the instructions in the `README` or `INSTALL` file. For the XMMS package, the `README` file lists some of the prerequisites (such as libraries) and tells you what commands to type to build and install the package. In the case of XMMS, the instructions tell you to use the following steps:

1. **Type** ./configure **to run a shell script that checks your system configuration and creates a file named** Makefile — **a file the** make **command uses to build and install the package. (You can type** ./configure —help **to see a list of options that configure accepts.)**

2. **Type** make **to build the software.**

   This step compiles the source files in all the subdirectories (compiling source code converts each source file into an object file — a file containing binary instructions that your PC's processor can understand).

3. **Type** make install **to install the software.**

   This step copies libraries and executable binary files to appropriate directories on your system.

Although these steps are specific to XMMS, most other packages follow these steps — configure, make, and install. The configure shell script guesses system-dependent variables and creates a Makefile with commands needed to build and install the software.

Usually, you do not have to do anything but type the commands to build the software, but you must install the software-development tools on your system. This means you must install the Software Development package when you install Red Hat Linux. To build and run XMMS, you must also install the X Software Development package because it's an X application.

To begin building XMMS, type the following command to run the configure script (you must be in the xmms-1.2.7 directory when you type this command):

```
./configure
```

The configure script starts running and prints lots of messages as it checks various features of your system — from the existence of the C compiler to various libraries needed to build XMMS. Finally, the configure script creates a Makefile you can use to build the software.

If the configure script displays error messages and fails, review the INSTALL and README files to find any clues to solving the problem. You may be able to circumvent it by providing some information to the configure script through command-line arguments.

After the configure script finishes, build the software by typing **make**. This command runs the GNU make utility, which reads the Makefile and starts compiling the source files according to information specified in the `Makefile`. The `make` command goes through all the source directories, compiles the source files, and creates the executable files and libraries needed to run XMMS. You'll see a lot of messages scroll by as each file is compiled. These messages show the commands used to compile and link the files.

The `make` command can take 10 to 15 minutes to complete. After `make` is done, you can install the XMMS software with the following command:

```
make install
```

This command also runs GNU `make`, but the `install` argument instructs GNU make to perform a specific set of commands from the `Makefile`. These instructions essentially go through all the subdirectories and copy various files to their final locations. For example, the binary executable files `xmms`, `gnomexmms`, `wmxmms`, and `xmms-config` are copied to the `/usr/bin` directory.

Now that you have installed XMMS, try running it from the GNOME or KDE desktop by typing **xmms** in a terminal window. From the XMMS window, you can open an MP3 file and try playing it. Your PC must have a sound card, and the sound card must be configured correctly for XMMS to work. Figure 4-1 shows a typical view of XMMS playing an MP3 music clip.

Figure 4-1:
You can play
MP3 music
with XMMS.

Here's an overview of the steps you follow to download, unpack, build, and install a typical software package:

1. **Use a Web browser to download the source code, usually in the form of a** `.tar.gz` **file, from the anonymous FTP site or Web site.**

2. **Unpack the file with a** `tar zxvf filename` **command.**

3. **Change the directory to the new subdirectory where the software is unpacked, with a command such as** `cd software_dir`.

4. **Read any** `README` **or** `INSTALL` **files to learn any specific instructions you must follow to build and install the software.**

5. **The details of building the software may differ slightly from one soft-ware package to another, but typically you type the following commands to build and install the software:**

```
./configure
make
make install
```

6. **Read any other documentation that comes with the software to learn how to use the software and whether you must configure the software further before using it.**

Updating Red Hat Linux Applications with the Update Agent

Red Hat Linux comes with a service called Red Hat Network. The idea behind Red Hat Network is to enable registered users to keep their Red Hat Linux system and applications current. The idea is that you register with the Red Hat Network and provide information about your system's hardware and the RPMs currently installed on your system. After you've done this, an Update Agent can download any new RPM files your system requires and install those files for you.

I briefly provide an overview of how to update your system by using the Update Agent and the Red Hat Network.

Registering with Red Hat Network

To take full advantage of the Red Hat Network's facilities, you must register with the Red Hat Network and provide information about your Red Hat Linux system. To register, follow these steps:

1. **Make sure your Internet connection is up; then select Main Menu⇨ System Tools⇨Red Hat Network.**

   If this is the first time, a configuration dialog box appears from which you can configure some options such as what to do with downloaded packages, what packages to skip, and whether to verify authenticity of packages. You can typically click OK to proceed. You also get a prompt that asks you if you want to install Red Hat's GPG key (used to verify that packages are securely signed by Red Hat). Click Yes to install the key.

2. **The Red Hat Update Agent runs and displays a message explaining the purpose of the program. Click Forward to continue.**

3. When you run the Red Hat Update Agent for the first time, it registers you with the Red Hat Network. It starts by displaying a privacy statement explaining the information to be collected and sent to Red Hat's server during registration. The information includes an inventory of RPM files on your system and an inventory of your system hardware. Read the privacy policy; if you want to continue, click the Forward button.

4. You are prompted for a username and password to establish a new user account with Red Hat. Fill in the requested information and click Forward to continue.

5. The next screen asks you to enter more information about yourself, including your name, address, and phone number. Fill in the information, and click the Forward button.

6. The Red Hat Update Agent shows some information about your system and asks you to provide a name for the system profile (the collection of information about your system). Enter a descriptive name and then click Forward.

7. The Red Hat Update Agent displays a list of RPMs (names of software packages) to be included in the profile information. When the Update Agent checks for updated software, it uses this list. If you don't care about updating some of the packages, uncheck these names. Then click Forward.

8. The Red Hat Update Agent informs you that it's about to send your system information to the Red Hat Network. Click Forward to continue.

9. The Red Hat Update Agent sends your information (the information mentioned in the privacy statement) to the Red Hat Network. If all goes well, the upload begins and a progress bar shows the percentage sent so far. Otherwise, you may get a message from the server that due to high load access to the Red Hat Network is limited to subscription customers only. If this happens, you have to try to register after waiting for some time.

10. After the Red Hat Update Agent successfully uploads your system profile to the Red Hat Network, the final window displays a message telling you to visit rhn.redhat.com to log in and to access Red Hat Network. That Web site is where you can also buy subscriptions to the Red Hat Network. Click the Finish button to complete the registration process.

Updating Red Hat Linux packages

After you're registered with Red Hat Network, you can use the Red Hat Update Agent to update Red Hat Linux. Red Hat gives you a free subscription to Red Hat Network for one PC, but you have to pay for anything beyond that. If you want to buy a subscription, visit `rhn.redhat.com`, log in, and follow the directions.

To update software packages, follow these steps:

1. **Log in as** `root`, **and select Main Menu⇨System Tools⇨Red Hat Network.**

The Red Hat Update Agent starts, and a dialog box prompts you to install Red Hat's public key in your GPG key ring. (*GPG* refers to GNU Privacy Guard or GnuPG, a program for encrypting, decrypting, and signing e-mail and other data using the OpenPGP Internet standard.) Red Hat's public GPG key is used to verify that Red Hat has securely signed the packages the Update Agent has downloaded.

2. **Click the Yes button to install Red Hat's key.**

3. **The Red Hat Update Agent displays a window with a welcome message. Click the Forward button to proceed.**

The Update Agent retrieves a list of all available packages from the Red Hat Network. (This may take a few minutes.) Then the Update Agent downloads the headers for all available packages. For each download, a progress bar shows the percentage of data downloaded so far. The header download takes quite a bit of time over a slow connection to the Internet.

4. **After the Red Hat Update Agent downloads the headers, it displays a list of packages to be skipped. You can accept the list and click the Forward button to continue.**

5. **The Update Agent displays a list of all the packages available for update from Red Hat Network. Scroll through the list and pick the package updates you want to download. Click the box to the left of a package's name to select it.**

As you select packages, the Update Agent displays the total size of the packages you have selected so far.

6. **After selecting the packages, click the Forward button to proceed with the download.**

7. The Update Agent then checks for any package dependencies and begins downloading the packages. Progress bars show the status of the download. After the download is finished, click the Forward button to proceed with the installation.

8. The Update Agent displays progress bars as it installs each package update. Click the Forward button when the installation is complete.

9. The Update Agent displays a message about the package or packages it has installed successfully. Click the Finish button to exit the Red Hat Update Agent.

After you have registered with the Red Hat Network, you can use the Red Hat Update Agent to keep Red Hat Linux up to date.

Chapter 5: Managing Devices and Printers

In This Chapter

✔ Understanding device drivers

✔ Managing loadable driver modules

✔ Managing print queues

*E*verything you use to work with your computer is a device. The keyboard and mouse you use to type and click around, the hard disk where you store everything, and the printer where you get your hard copies — these are all devices. And guess what, you have to manage them. It's not as hard as it sounds. All you have to do is load the device driver and perhaps configure the device a bit. To do this managing, it helps if you understand device drivers a bit and learn to use the tools Red Hat Linux includes to help you manage devices. In this chapter, I provide a brief overview of device drivers and explain how to manage driver modules. Because printers are a common type of device you have to manage, I also show you how to manage print queues.

Understanding Device Drivers

The Linux kernel treats all devices as files and uses a device just as it would use a file — opens it, writes data to it, reads data from it, and closes it when done. This ability to treat every device as a file comes through the use of device drivers. A *device driver* is a special program that controls a particular type of hardware. When the kernel writes data to the device, the device driver does whatever is appropriate for that device. For example, when the kernel writes data to the floppy drive, the floppy device driver puts that data onto the physical medium of the floppy disk. On the other hand, if the kernel writes data to the parallel port device, the parallel port driver sends the data to the printer connected to the parallel port.

Thus, the device driver isolates the device-specific code from the rest of the kernel and makes a device look like a file. Any application can access a device by opening the file specific to that device. Figure 5-1 illustrates this concept of a Linux device driver.

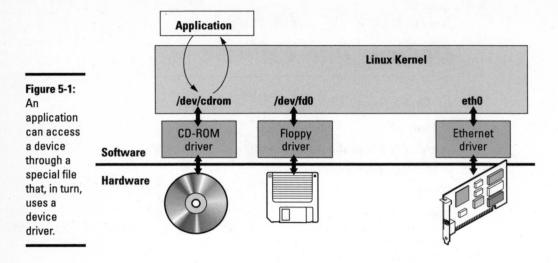

Figure 5-1:
An application can access a device through a special file that, in turn, uses a device driver.

Device files

As Figure 5-1 shows, applications can access a device as if it were a file. These files are special files called *device files,* and they appear in the /dev directory in the Red Hat Linux file system.

If you use the ls command to look at the list of files in the /dev directory, you'll see several thousand files. This does not mean that your system has several thousand devices. The /dev directory has files for all possible types of devices — that's why the number of device files is so large.

So how does the kernel know which device driver to use when an application opens a specific device file? The answer is in two numbers called the *major* and *minor device numbers*. Each device file is mapped to a specific device driver through these numbers.

To see an example of the major and minor device numbers, type the following command in a terminal window:

```
ls -l /dev/hda
```

You should see a line of output similar to the following:

```
brw-rw----  1 root   disk   3,  0 Jul 23 14:50 /dev/hda
```

In this line, the major and minor device numbers appear just before the date. In this case, the major device number is 3 and the minor device number is 0. The kernel selects the device driver for this device file by using the major device number.

You don't really need to know much about the device files and the device numbers, except to be aware of their existence.

Block devices

The first letter in the listing of a device file also provides an important clue. For the /dev/hda device, the first letter is a b, which indicates that /dev/hda is a block device — one that can accept or provide data in chunks (typically 512 bytes or 1KB). By the way, /dev/hda refers to the first IDE hard disk on your system (the C drive in Windows). Hard drives, floppy drives, and CD-ROM drives are all examples of block devices.

Character devices

If the first letter in the listing of a device file is a c, then the device is a character device — one that can receive and send data one character (one byte) at a time. For example, the serial port and parallel ports are character devices. To see the listing of a character device, type the following command in a terminal window:

```
ls -l /dev/ttyS0
```

The listing of this device should be similar to the following:

```
crw-rw----   1 root    uucp     4, 64 Jul 23 14:50 /dev/ttyS0
```

Notice that the very first letter is a c because /dev/ttyS0 — the first serial port — is a character device.

Network devices

The network devices such as Ethernet and dial-up *point-to-point protocol* (PPP) connections are somewhat special in that they do not have a file corresponding to the device; instead the kernel uses a special name for the device. For example, the Ethernet devices are named eth0 for the first Ethernet card, eth1 for the second one, and so on. The PPP connections are named ppp0, ppp1, and so on.

Because the network devices are not mapped to device files, there are no files corresponding to these devices in the /dev directory.

Managing Loadable Driver Modules

To use any device, the Linux kernel must contain the driver. If the driver code is linked into the kernel as a *monolithic* program (a program that's in the form of a single large file), then adding a new driver means rebuilding the kernel with the new driver code. Rebuilding the kernel means you have to reboot the PC with the new kernel before you can use the new device driver. Luckily, the Linux kernel uses a modular design that does away with all the rebooting hassles. Linux device drivers can be created in the form of modules that the kernel can load and unload without having to restart the PC.

Driver modules are one type of a broader category of software modules called Loadable Kernel Modules. Other types of kernel modules include code that can support new types of file systems, modules for network protocols, and modules that interpret different formats of executable files.

Loading and unloading modules

You can manage the loadable device driver modules by using a set of commands. Table 5-1 summarizes these commands. You have to log in as `root` to use some of these commands. I explain a few of the commonly used module commands.

Table 5-1	Commands to Manage Kernel Modules
This Command	*Does the Following*
`insmod`	Inserts a module into the kernel.
`rmmod`	Removes a module from the kernel.
`depmod`	Determines interdependencies between modules.
`ksyms`	Displays a list of symbols along with the name of the module that defined the symbol.
`lsmod`	Lists all currently loaded modules.
`modinfo`	Displays information about a kernel module.
`modprobe`	Inserts or removes a module or a set of modules intelligently. For example, if module A requires B, then `modprobe` will automatically load B when asked to load B.

If you need to use any of these commands, log in as `root` or type **su -** in a terminal window to become `root`.

To see what modules are currently loaded, type

```
lsmod
```

You should see a list of modules. For example, here is a list on one of my PCs:

```
Module                  Size  Used by    Not tainted
opl3sa2                10320  0
mpu401                 23908  0 [opl3sa2]
```

```
ad1848           28492    0   [opl3sa2]
sound            73780    0   [opl3sa2 mpu401 ad1848]
soundcore         6500    6   [sound]
autofs           13308    0   (autoclean) (unused)
eepro100         23896    1
iptable_filter    2412    0   (autoclean) (unused)
ip_tables        14744    1   [iptable_filter]
ide-cd           33316    0   (autoclean)
cdrom            32992    0   (autoclean) [ide-cd]
mousedev          5492    1
keybdev           2976    0   (unused)
hid              22052    0   (unused)
input             5888    0   [mousedev keybdev hid]
usb-uhci         25996    0   (unused)
usbcore          76640    1   [hid usb-uhci]
ext3             87208    2
jbd              52148    2   [ext3]
mbcache           6608    1   [ext3]
```

As you may expect, the list of modules depends on the types of devices installed on your system.

The first column lists the names of the modules in the last-to-first order. Thus, the first module in the list is the last one to be loaded. The Size column shows the number of bytes that the module occupies in your PC's memory. The remaining columns show other information about each module such as how many applications are currently using the module and the names of the modules that require the module.

The list displayed by lsmod includes all types of Linux kernel modules, not just device drivers. For example, the last three modules — mbcache, jbd, and ext3 — are all part of the EXT3 file system (the latest file system for Linux).

Besides lsmod, one commonly used module command is modprobe. Use modprobe whenever you need to manually load or remove one or more modules. The best thing about modprobe is that you don't need to worry if a module requires other modules to work. The modprobe command automatically loads any other module that is needed by a module. For example, on my system I can manually load the sound driver with the command

```
modprobe sound-slot-0
```

This command causes modprobe to load everything needed to make sound work. On my system, the modprobe sound-slot-0 command loads soundcore, sound, ad1848, mpu401, and opl3sa2 — in that order.

You can use modprobe with the -r option to remove modules. For example, to remove the sound modules, I use the following command:

```
modprobe -r sound-slot-0
```

This command gets rid of all the modules that the modprobe sound-slot-0 command had loaded.

The /etc/modules.conf file

How does the modprobe command know that it should load the opl3sa2 driver module when I use a module name sound-slot-0? The answer is in the /etc/modules.conf configuration file. That file contains a line that tells modprobe what it should load when it sees the module name sound-slot-0.

To view the contents of /etc/modules.conf, type

```
cat /etc/modules.conf
```

On my Red Hat Linux PC, the file contains the following lines:

```
alias parport_lowlevel parport_pc
alias eth0 eepro100
alias usb-controller usb-uhci
alias sound-slot-0 opl3sa2
```

Each line that begins with the keyword alias defines a standard name for an actual driver module. For example, the second line defines eepro100 as the actual driver name for the alias eth0, which stands for the first Ethernet card. Similarly, the fourth line defines opl3sa2 as the module to load when I use the name sound-slot-0.

The modprobe command consults the /etc/modules.conf file to convert an alias to the real name of a driver module as well as for other tasks such as obtaining parameters for driver modules. For example, you can insert lines that begin with the options keyword to provide values of parameters that a driver may need.

For example, to set the interrupt request (IRQ) parameter for the sound card to 5, I would add the following line to the /etc/modules.conf file:

```
options opl3sa2 irq=5
```

This line specifies 5 as the value of the parameter named irq in the opl3sa2 module.

If you want to know the names of the parameters that a module accepts, use the `modinfo` command. For example, to view information about the `opl3sa2` driver module, I type

```
modinfo opl3sa2
```

From the resulting output I can tell that `irq` is the name of the parameter for the Interrupt Request parameter.

Unfortunately, the information shown by the `modinfo` command can be somewhat cryptic. The only saving grace is that you may not need to do much more than use a graphical utility to configure the device, and the utility will take care of adding whatever is needed to configuration files such as `/etc/modules.conf`.

Managing Print Queues in Red Hat Linux

PCs typically come with one parallel port, and you typically connect the printer to the PC's parallel port. You can set up a printer fairly easily by using Red Hat's graphical printer configuration utility, but you also have to learn how to manage the print queue.

Spooling and print jobs

Spooling refers to the capability to print in the background. When you print from a word processor in Windows, for example, the output first goes to a file on the disk. Then, while you continue working with the word processor, a background process sends that output to the printer. The Red Hat Linux printing environment also supports spooling.

Print job refers to what you print with a single print command. The printing environment queues print jobs by storing them in the spool directory. A background process periodically sends the print jobs from the spool directory to the printer.

Red Hat Linux comes with two printing environments — LPRng and the Common UNIX Printing System (CUPS). LPRng is similar to a classic UNIX print spooler that was part of the Berkeley Software Distribution (BSD) UNIX. CUPS is a newer print spooler based on the Internet Printing Protocol. In the future, Red Hat Linux will use CUPS as its default printing environment, but for now, it supports LPRng. I cover the LPRng print spooler because it's currently the default print spooler in Red Hat Linux.

In the LPRng printing environment, you use a client program — `lpr` — to send the files to be printed to a server called `lpd` over a TCP/IP network connection. The lpd server then queues the files and sends them to the printer one by one.

Although you typically have only one printer connected to your PC, one advantage of the LPRng printing system is the capability to print on a printer connected to another system on a network. Printing to a remote printer is handled in the same fashion as printing to a local printer; the local lpr program simply sends the files to the remote system's lpd server.

A good way to understand the LPRng print spooling system is to trace a print request from the lpr program all the way to the actual output at the printer. As Figure 5-2 shows, the programs lpr and lpd and an optional filter program make up the printing process.

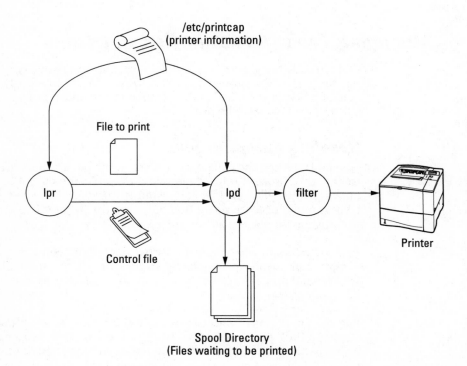

Figure 5-2:
The LPRng print spooler can queue up print jobs and send them to a printer.

As you can see from Figure 5-2, the steps of the LPRng print spooling process are:

1. The lpr program takes the file to be printed, prepares a control file with information about the print job, and sends both files to the lpd server over a TCP/IP connection.

2. The lpd server stores the files for the print job temporarily in a spool directory. lpd also sorts the queue and determines the print order.

3. For each print job, lpd sends the file through a filter program to convert the file into a format suitable for the printer and sends the filter's output to the printer. If there is no filter (this is specified in the /etc/printcap file), lpd sends the file directly to the printer.

Both the lpr and lpd programs consult the /etc/printcap file for information about the printer. That, in a nutshell, is how a print spooling system works.

Printing with the lpr command

You can print a file by using the lpr command. For example, to print the file /etc/inittab, type the following in a terminal window:

```
lpr /etc/inittab
```

The lpr command queues a print job by sending the file and appropriate control information to lpd, the print spooler. By default, the lpd print spooler accepts files to be printed, holds them in the print queue, and forwards them to the printer (or to another system if the printer is attached to a remote system on the network).

Checking the print queue using lpq

When lpr queues a print job, it does not print any messages. If you mistakenly print a large file and want to stop the print job before you waste too much paper, you have to use the lpq command to look at the current print jobs. Following is a typical listing of print jobs you get when you type lpq:

```
Printer: epson@localhost
 Queue: 1 printable job
 Server: pid 3073 active
 Unspooler: pid 3074 active
 Status: IF filter 'mf_wrapper' filter msg - 'foomatic-gswrapper: gs '-dBATCH' '
-dSAFER' '-dQUIET' '-dNOPAUSE' '-sDEVICE=stcolor' '-r360x360' '-dnoWeave' '-sDit
hering=gscmyk' '-sOutputCode=runlength' '-sOutputFile=/dev/fd/3' '/dev/fd/0' 3>&
1 1>&2' at 21:41:29.713
 Rank   Owner/ID          Class Job Files          Size Time
active root@localhost+72     A  72 /etc/inittab     1756 21:41:28
```

In this case, the last row shows information about the single job currently queued for printing. The rest of the rows (if any) show jobs in the order in which they'll be printed. If you do not see your print job listed, it has finished printing. The Job column shows the job number of each print job; in this case, the job number is 72.

Canceling the print job using lprm

To remove a job from the print queue, use the `lprm` command. For example, to remove print job 72, I type the following command:

```
lprm 72
```

The `lprm` utility then displays a message about the deleted print job:

```
Printer epson@localhost:
  checking perms 'root@localhost+72'
  dequeued 'root@localhost+72'
```

If you are in a hurry and want to cancel all print jobs you have submitted so far, use `lprm` with `-a` as the argument, as follows:

```
lprm -a
```

Checking the printer status using lpstat

To see the status of print jobs, use the `lpstat` command. Here is a typical output from the `lpstat` command:

```
Printer: epson@localhost
 Queue: no printable jobs in queue
 Server: no server active
 Status: job 'root@localhost+118' saved at 21:53:17.866
 Rank  Owner/ID          Class Job Files        Size Time
done  root@localhost+118      A  118 /etc/inittab    1756 21:52:12
```

This sample output shows the status of a printer named `epson@localhost` — the printer named `epson` followed by an @ sign and the host name (`localhost`).

Controlling the printer using lpc

If you log in as `root`, you can use `lpc` to control the printer, such as starting and stopping spooling, enabling and disabling printers, and rearranging the order of print jobs. You can use the second argument to `lpc` to perform a specific task or run `lpc` in interactive mode.

To run `lpc` in interactive mode, type **lpc** in a terminal window. At the `lpc>` prompt, type **help** to see a list of commands that `lpc` understands. To get more help about a command, type **help** *command-name* (*command-name* is one of the `lpc` commands). For example, here is what you get when you type `lpc help`:

```
usage: lpc [-a][-Ddebuglevel][-Pprinter][-Shost][-Uusername][-V]
    [command]
 with no command, reads from STDIN
 -a      - alias for -Pall
```

```
-Ddebuglevel - debug level
-Pprinter  - printer or printer@host
-Shost     - connect to lpd server on host
-Uuser     - identify command as coming from user
-V         - increase information verbosity
commands:
active  (printer[@host])    - check for active server
abort   (printer[@host] | all) - stop server
class   printer[@host] (class | off)   - show/set class printing
disable (printer[@host] | all) - disable queueing
debug   (printer[@host] | all) debugparms - set debug level for printer
down    (printer[@host] | all) - disable printing and queueing
enable  (printer[@host] | all) - enable queueing
flush   (printer[@host] | all) - flush cached status
hold    (printer[@host] | all) (name[@host] | job | all)* - hold job
holdall (printer[@host] | all) - hold all jobs on
kill    (printer[@host] | all) - stop and restart server
lpd     (printer[@host]) - get LPD PID
lpq     (printer[@host] | all) (name[@host] | job | all)* - invoke LPQ
lprm    (printer[@host] | all) (name[@host]|host|job| all)* - invoke LPRM
msg printer message text - set status message
move printer (user|jobid)* target - move jobs to new queue
noholdall (printer[@host] | all) - hold all jobs off
printcap (printer[@host] | all) - report printcap values
quit                - exit LPC
redirect (printer[@host] | all) (printer@host | off )*    - redirect jobs
redo    (printer[@host] | all) (name[@host] | job | all)* - release job
release (printer[@host] | all) (name[@host] | job | all)* - release job
reread  (printer[@host])    - LPD reread database information
start   (printer[@host] | all) - start printing
status  (printer[@host] | all) - status of printers
stop    (printer[@host] | all) - stop printing
topq    (printer[@host] | all) (name[@host] | job | all)* - reorder job
up      (printer[@host] | all) - enable printing and queueing
 diagnostic:
  defaultq        - show default queue for LPD server
  defaults        - show default configuration values
  lang          - show current i18n (iNTERNATIONALIZATIONn) support
  client (printer | all) - client config and printcap information
  server (printer | all) - server config and printcap
```

If you are using lpc in the interactive mode, type **quit** at the lpc> prompt to exit lpc.

To perform a single operation, you can type lpc followed by one of the lpc commands and any necessary arguments. For example, to stop the print-spooling on the default printer, move print job 72 to the top of the queue, and start spooling again, type the following commands while you are logged in as root:

```
lpc stop
lpc topq 72
lpc start
```

Table 5-2 lists the lpc commands anyone can use. If you are logged in as a normal user, type **/usr/sbin/lpc** instead of just plain **lpc**.

Table 5-2	lpc Commands Anyone Can Use
This Command	*Does the Following*
status *printer-name*	Displays the status of the specified printer. If you do not provide a printer name, this command shows the status of the default printer.
exit	Exits lpc (use in interactive mode only).
quit	Exits lpc (use in interactive mode only).

Table 5-3 lists the lpc commands that only root can use.

Table 5-3	lpc Commands Only root Can Use
This Command	*Does the Following*
abort *printer-name*	Behaves like stop but does not allow the current job to complete. When printing is restarted, the current job prints again.
disable *printer-name*	Disables spooling of print jobs to a specified printer. When spooling is disabled, users can no longer use lpr to print.
down *printer-name*	Disables spooling and stops the printer daemon from printing the spooled print jobs (combines the actions of disable and stop).
enable *printer-name*	Enables spooling of print jobs to a specified printer.
reread *printer-name*	Sends a request to the lpd server to reread the configuration file (/etc/lpd.conf) and the /etc/printcap file. You might try this command if the printer appears to be fine but nothing is printed, even though lpq shows jobs waiting in the spool area.
start *printer-name*	Enables the lpd server so that it can begin printing any jobs in that printer's spool directory.
stop *printer-name*	Waits for the current print job to complete and disables the lpd server so that it stops printing the jobs in that printer's spool directory.
topq *printer-name job-id*	Moves the specified print job to the beginning of the printer's queue. If you use a user name in place of *job-id*, all jobs that belong to that user are moved to the beginning of the queue.
up *printer-name*	Reverses the action of the down command, enables spooling, and starts the lpd server (combines the actions of enable and start).

Chapter 6: Upgrading and Customizing the Kernel

In This Chapter

✔ Upgrading with a Red Hat kernel RPM

✔ Configuring the kernel

✔ Building a new kernel

✔ Building and installing the modules

✔ Installing the kernel and setting up GRUB

*O*ne reason Linux is so exciting is that many programmers are constantly improving it. Some programmers, for example, write drivers that add support for new hardware, such as a new sound card or a new networking card. All these innovations come to you in the form of new versions of the Linux kernel.

Although you do not have to upgrade or modify the Linux operating system — the kernel — every time a new version is available, sometimes you need to upgrade simply because the new version corrects some problems or supports your hardware better. On the other hand, if an earlier kernel version has everything you need, there is no need to rush out and upgrade.

Sometimes you may want to rebuild the kernel even when there are no fixes or enhancements. The Linux kernel on the companion CD-ROM is generic and uses modules to support all types of hardware. You may want to build a new kernel that links in the drivers for only the devices installed on your system. In particular, if you have a SCSI hard disk, you may want to create a kernel that supports your SCSI adapter. Depending on your needs, you may also want to change some of the kernel-configuration options, such as creating a kernel that's specific for your processor (instead of a generic Intel 386 processor).

In this chapter, I explain how to upgrade a kernel using a kernel RPM as well as how to rebuild and install a new Linux kernel.

Upgrading with a Red Hat Kernel RPM

Red Hat distributes all software updates, including new versions of kernels, in the form of RPM files. To download and install the kernel RPMs, follow these steps:

1. **Use a Web server to download the kernel RPM files from Red Hat's FTP server (I explain the details in the next section). If you want to rebuild the kernel, you have to download the** `kernel-source` **RPM corresponding to the new version of the kernel.**

2. **Install the RPMs by using the** `rpm -i` **command.**

3. **Create a new, initial RAM disk by running the** `/sbin/mkinitrd` **command.**

4. **Reconfigure GRUB to boot the new kernel.**

5. **Try out the new kernel by rebooting the system.**

I further describe these steps in the next few sections.

Downloading new kernel RPMs

Red Hat makes software updates available in the form of RPMs — packages — at its FTP server or one of the mirror sites listed at `www.redhat.com/download/mirror.html`. The updates are organized in directories according to Red Hat Linux version numbers. For example, any updates for Red Hat Linux 8.0 for Intel x86 systems reside in the `8.0/en/os/i386` directory. Use a Web browser (for example, Mozilla) to visit the FTP site and download any kernel RPMs available at that site.

Installing the kernel RPMs

To install the kernel and the modules, follow these steps:

1. **Log in as** `root`.

2. **Use the** `cd` **command to change the directory to where the RPM files (the ones you have downloaded from Red Hat's FTP server) are located.**

3. **Type the following command to install the kernel RPM:**

   ```
   rpm -ivh kernel*.rpm
   ```

You need to install the `kernel-source` RPM only if you want to build a new kernel.

Making a new, initial RAM disk

Next, you have to make a new, initial RAM disk image — a file that the kernel can copy into a block of memory and use as a memory-resident disk.

Usually, the initial RAM disk image is stored in a file whose name begins with initrd. initrd is shorthand for *initial RAM disk;* the mkinitrd command is so named because it makes an initrd file.

Log in as root and type a command line of the following form to create the initrd file:

```
mkinitrd /boot/initrd-filename.img   module-dir-name
```

The initrd file has to be in the /boot directory where the kernel is located. You can use any filename for initrd-filename. The module-dir-name is the name of the directory in /lib/modules where the module files are located. By convention, the module directory name is the same as the kernel version number. For example, if your kernel version (type the uname -r command to see the version number) is 2.4.18-14, the module directory name is 2.4.18-14. Another common practice is to use an initrd filename created by appending the version number to the initrd- prefix. Thus, for kernel version 2.4.18-14, the initrd file is initrd- 2.4.18-14.img.

To create the initial RAM disk image for kernel version 2.4.18-14, type the following command:

```
/sbin/mkinitrd /boot/initrd-2.4.18-14.img 2.4.18-14
```

This creates the file initrd- 2.4.18-14.img in the /boot directory. You refer to this initrd file in the GRUB configuration file (/etc/grub.conf).

Reconfiguring GRUB

After you install the kernel RPMs and create the initial RAM disk image, you have to reconfigure GRUB so that it can boot the new kernel.

Use a text editor such as vi or Emacs to edit the /etc/grub.conf file. Add the following lines near the beginning of that file right after the splashimage line:

```
title Red Hat Linux (NEW)
        root (hd0,0)
        kernel /vmlinuz- 2.4.18-14 ro root=/dev/hda2
        initrd /initrd- 2.4.18-14.img
```

In the kernel line where it says `root=/dev/hda2`, change `/dev/hda2` to the correct device name for the disk partition where your Linux system's root file system (`/`) is located. Also, make sure that the correct names are used for the kernel and `initrd` file names — these names depend on the version number of the kernel you have downloaded.

After editing and saving the `/etc/grub.conf` file, you can reboot the system and try out the new version of the kernel.

Trying out the new kernel

After installing the new kernel RPM, creating the initial RAM disk file, and reconfiguring GRUB, it's time to try the new kernel. To restart the system, log in as `root` and type the following command from the Linux prompt:

```
reboot
```

You may also reboot the system from the graphical login screen. Select Reboot from the Options menu on the login dialog box.

When the system reboots and you see the GRUB screen, press the arrow key to select the new kernel's name. If you have added the new kernel description before all other operating systems in the GRUB configuration file, that kernel should boot even if you don't do anything at the boot screen.

After Red Hat Linux starts, you should see the usual graphical login screen. Log in as a user, open a terminal window, and type the `uname -sr` command to see the version number. The response should show that your system is running the new version of the kernel.

Rebuilding the Kernel

Rebuilding the kernel refers to creating a new binary file for the core Linux operating system. This binary file is the one that runs when Red Hat Linux boots. You may wonder why you would ever want to rebuild the kernel. Well, here are a few reasons:

✦ After you initially install Linux, you may want to create a new kernel that includes support for only the hardware installed on your system. In particular, if you have a SCSI adapter, you may want to create a kernel that links in the SCSI driver. The kernel in the companion CD-ROM includes the SCSI driver as an external module you load at startup.

✦ If you have a system with hardware for which only experimental support is available, you have to rebuild the kernel to include that support into the operating system.

✦ You may want to recompile the kernel and generate code that works
well on your specific Pentium processor (instead of the generic 386
processor code that comes in the standard Red Hat Linux distribution).

Never rebuild and install a new kernel without first making sure you have an
emergency boot floppy. If you do have an emergency boot floppy, use the
mkbootdisk command to create the boot floppy. Type **man mkbootdisk** to
learn the syntax of that command. The exact command line to build the
emergency boot floppy depends on the kernel version number. For example,
to create a boot floppy for version 2.4.18-14, log in as root and type the following command in a terminal window (you have to insert a blank floppy
disk when prompted):

```
mkbootdisk -device /dev/fd0 2.4.18-14
```

Replace 2.4.18-14 with the version number of your Linux kernel (type the
uname -r command to see the version number).

To rebuild the Linux kernel, you need the kernel source files. The kernel
source files are not normally installed. Use the following steps to install the
kernel source files on your system:

1. **Log in as** root **and insert the second Red Hat Linux CD-ROM into the
CD drive.**

2. **If the CD-ROM drive does not mount automatically, type the following
command to mount the CD-ROM drive:**

```
mount /mnt/cdrom
```

If you are using GNOME or KDE, the CD-ROM is automatically mounted,
and you should not have to perform this step manually.

3. **Change the directory to the** RedHat/RPMS **directory on the CD-ROM,
and use the** rpm **command to install the kernel source files. Type the
following commands:**

```
cd /mnt/cdrom/RedHat/RPMS
rpm -ivh kernel-source*
```

After the rpm command finishes installing the kernel source package,
the source files appear in the /usr/src/linux-2.4 directory.

Building the kernel involves the following phases:

✦ Configuring the kernel

✦ Building the kernel

✦ Building and installing the modules (if any)

✦ Installing the kernel and setting up GRUB

I explain these phases in the next few sections, but first you should know the difference between linking in a driver vs. building a driver as a loadable module.

Creating a monolithic vs. a modular kernel

You have two options for the device drivers needed to support various hardware devices in Linux:

✦ **Link in support** — You can link the drivers for all hardware on your system into the kernel. The size of the kernel grows as device-driver code is incorporated into the kernel. A kernel that links in all necessary code is called a *monolithic kernel* because it's one big file.

✦ **Use modules** — You can create the device drivers in the form of loadable modules. A *module* is a block of code the kernel can load after it starts running. A typical use of modules is to add support for a device without having to rebuild the kernel for each new device. Modules do not have to be device drivers; they can also add new functionality to the kernel. A kernel that uses modules is called a *modular kernel.*

You do not have to create a fully monolithic or fully modular kernel. In fact, it is common practice to link some support directly into the kernel but build infrequently used device drivers in the form of modules. For a company such as Red Hat, it makes sense to distribute a modular kernel. Red Hat provides a generic kernel, along with a large number of modules that can support many different types of hardware. Then the Red Hat installer configures the system to load only modules that are needed to support the hardware installed in a user's system.

When you create a custom kernel for your hardware configuration, you may want to link all required device drivers into the kernel. You can keep the size of such a monolithic kernel under control because you link in device drivers only for the hardware installed on your system.

Configuring the kernel

The first phase in rebuilding a kernel is to configure it. To configure the kernel, log in as `root`. Then change the kernel source directory by using the `cd` command as follows:

```
cd /usr/src/linux*
```

To configure the kernel, you have to indicate which features and device drivers you want to include in your Linux kernel. In essence, you build your very own version of the Linux kernel with the just the features you want.

Red Hat Linux provides several ways for you to configure the kernel:

✦ Type **make menuconfig** to enter the kernel-configuration parameters through a text-based interface similar to the one the Red Hat installation program uses.

✦ Type **make xconfig** to use an X Window System-based configuration program to configure the kernel. You have to run X to use this configuration program with a graphical interface.

✦ Type **make config** to use a shell script that prompts you for each configuration option one by one. You can use this configuration program from the Linux command prompt. When you use this option, you undergo a long question-and-answer process to specify the configuration parameters. For each question, respond with a *y* to link support into the kernel, *m* to build a module, and *n* to skip the support for that specific device.

The make menuconfig, make xconfig, and make config commands achieve the same end result — each stores your choices in a text file named .config located in the /usr/src/linux* directory. Because the filename starts with a period, you don't see it when you use the ls command alone to list the directory. Instead, type **ls -a** to see the .config file in the directory listing.

The kernel-configuration step merely captures your choices in the .config file. (In fact, the .config file does not exist until you configure the kernel once.) The kernel file does not change until you compile the kernel with the make command. That means you can go through the kernel-configuration option as many times as you want. If you want to start over with default settings, type the following command before you start configuring the kernel:

```
make mrproper
```

Running the kernel configuration tool

You can use any of the configuration tools — make xconfig, make menuconfig, or make config — to configure the kernel, but the easiest way is to log in as root and type the following command in a terminal window:

```
make xconfig
```

This command builds an X Window System-based configuration tool and runs it. The initial Linux Kernel Configuration window displays a set of buttons, each representing a category of kernel configuration options, as shown in Figure 6-1.

Linux Kernel Configuration

Code maturity level options	ATA/IDE/MFM/RLL support	Crypto Hardware support
Loadable module support	SCSI support	File systems
Processor type and features	Fusion MPT device support	Console drivers
General setup	IEEE 1394 (FireWire) support (EXPERIMENTAL)	Sound
Binary emulation of other systems	I2O device support	USB support
Memory Technology Devices (MTD)	Network device support	Bluetooth support
Parallel port support	Amateur Radio support	Kernel hacking
Plug and Play configuration	IrDA (infrared) support	Library routines
Block devices	ISDN subsystem	
Multi-device support (RAID and LVM)	Old CD-ROM drivers (not SCSI, not IDE)	Save and Exit
Cryptography support (CryptoAPI)	Input core support	Quit Without Saving
Networking options	Character devices	Load Configuration from File
Telephony Support	Multimedia devices	Store Configuration to File

Figure 6-1:
You can configure groups of kernel options through the buttons in this window.

Through the four buttons, grouped together in the lower-right corner of the window, you can perform tasks such as save the configurations and exit.

To change a category of configuration options, click the relevant button. For example, if you click on the button labeled *Processor type and features* on the upper-left corner, the configuration program displays another window with all the options you can set. From the new window you can then set specific options. For example, Figure 6-2 shows a drop-down menu from which you can pick the specific processor type (in this case, Pentium III).

Notice the Help buttons along the right edge of the window. Whenever you have a question about a configuration option, click the corresponding Help button to view help information for that option. Figure 6-3 shows the result of clicking the Help button next to the Processor type option. Click OK to close the Help window after you finish reading the information.

You can follow these steps to specify options for each category of options:

1. **In the main window (refer to Figure 6-1), click the option category.**

   The configuration program displays another window with the options for that category (refer to Figure 6-2).

2. **Set the options you want. Click the appropriate radio box (*y* for yes and *n* for no) to indicate your choice. If you need help on an option, click the Help button next to that option.**

3. **After completing that category of options, click Main Menu to return to the window of Figure 6-1 or click Next to move on to the next category of options.**

Rebuilding the Kernel **433**

**Book V
Chapter 6**

**Upgrading and
Customizing
the Kernel**

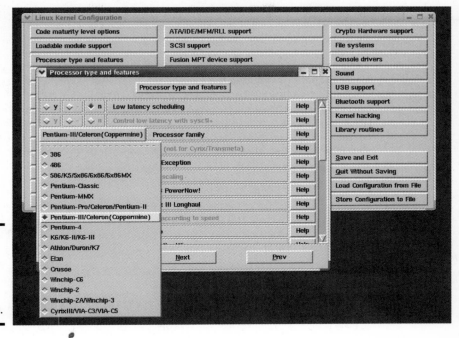

Figure 6-2:
Select a
processor
type from
the drop-
down menu.

Figure 6-3:
Context-
sensitive
help is
available
in the
xconfig
kernel
configura-
tion tool.

I describe some of the important and interesting categories of options. The section headings match the labels on the buttons in Figure 6-1, so you can easily locate a section that interests you.

A final word of caution before you start configuring the kernel options. Many kernel options depend on one another. For example, if the parallel port option is not set to Yes, then the configuration program grays out all options related to parallel port devices. The best way to logically proceed through the configuration steps is to start with the button at the upper-left corner — *Code maturity level options* — and then click Next on each successive window. That way, you always set the options in the correct order.

Code maturity level options

The very first group of options has only one item — you are asked if you want to use experimental device drivers or not. If you want to try some experimental drivers such as the ones that support IEEE 1394 (FireWire), then set this option to Yes.

Loadable module support

This group of options (see Figure 6-4) asks you about support for loadable modules. You want to include support for modules, so set the first option to Yes. The next option is about including version information in each module. If modules have version information, the module is checked for compatibility with the current kernel version. Because it is easy to unload a module that does not work, I tend to set this option to No. However, you may safely accept the default and press Enter. The third question asks whether or not you want the kernel to be capable of loading required modules. You should set this option to Yes.

Figure 6-4:
Enable
loadable
module
support
from this
configura-
tion
window.

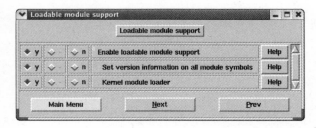

Processor type and features

This set of options (Figure 6-5) is for setting the processor type and support for specific processor-related features. The first option of this set queries you about your system's processor type. If you answer 386, the compiled kernel can run on any other processor (such as a 486 or any type of Pentium). However, if you are creating a kernel specifically for your system, select your processor type from the drop-down list that appears when you click on the processor family. You can also enable symmetric multiprocessing (SMP) support from this window, but you should do so only if your system's motherboard has two or more processors.

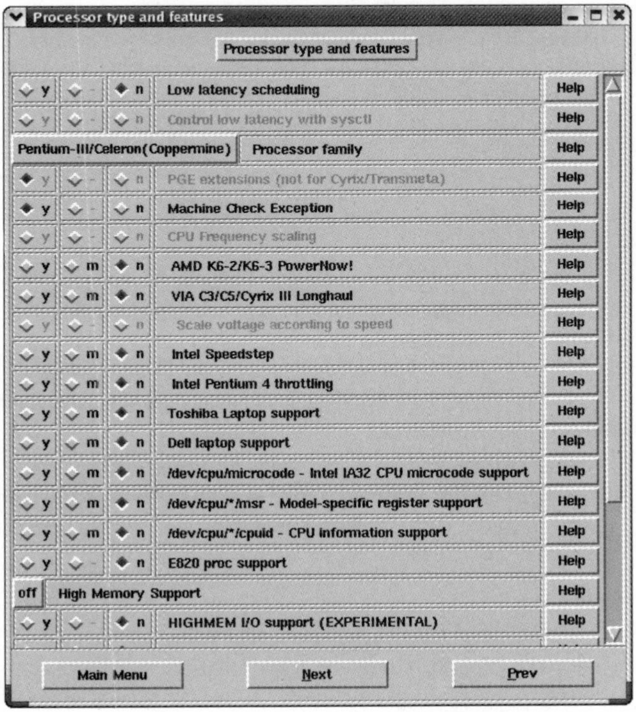

Figure 6-5:
Set the processor type and other processor-related features in this configuration window.

General setup

This is a set of general options (Figure 6-6) that deals with networking, PCI bus, MCA bus, parallel port, and advanced power management (APM) BIOS support. You can simply accept the default settings for these options. If you don't understand what an option means, click the Help button next to an option to get help on that option.

Parallel port support

These options (Figure 6-7) are important if you use any devices such as printers or parallel-port Zip drives connected to the parallel port of your PC. Set the *Parallel port support* and *PC-style hardware* options to Module so that the drivers are built as modules.

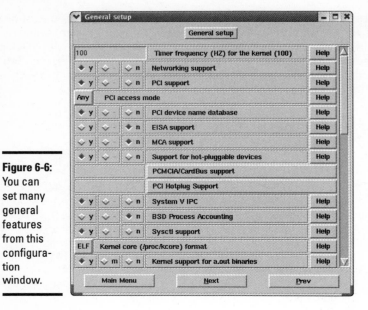

Figure 6-6:
You can set many general features from this configuration window.

Plug-and-Play configuration

These options (Figure 6-8) ask if you want to enable Plug-and-Play (PnP) support in the kernel. If you enable PnP support, the kernel automatically configures PnP devices (just as Windows does). Accept the default settings of Yes for these two options.

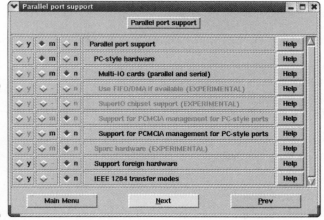

Figure 6-7:
Specify options for the parallel port support from this configuration window.

Rebuilding the Kernel **437**

**Book V
Chapter 6**

**Upgrading and
Customizing
the Kernel**

Figure 6-8:
Turn on
Plug-and-
Play support
through
these
options.

Block devices

Block devices refers to devices such as a disk drive that transfer data in chunks (as opposed to a keyboard that transfers data one character at a time). This set of options (Figure 6-9) involves the floppy and IDE (Integrated Drive Electronics) devices connected to the PC's parallel port as well as other block devices.

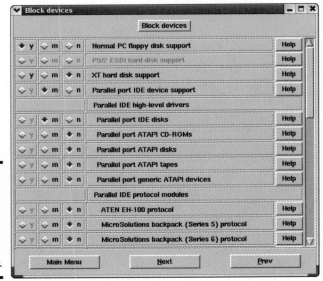

Figure 6-9:
Set options
for block
devices
from this
configura-
tion window.

The first option asks if you want floppy-drive support. Because most PCs do have a floppy drive, your answer generally is Yes. Select Module for the *Parallel port IDE device support* if you have external CD-ROM or disk devices that connect through your PC's parallel port.

If you scroll down the list of options in Figure 6-9, you find more options for block devices. Setting the *Loopback device support* option to Yes or Module lets the Linux kernel manipulate an entire file system inside a single large file. This is useful if you want to check a CD image before burning the CD.

The *RAM disk support* option allows the kernel to use a portion of your system's memory as a disk capable of storing a file system. Typically, a RAM disk functions only during system startup when the hard disk may not be available yet. The RAM disk is essential if you are booting a SCSI disk and you haven't compiled the SCSI drivers into the kernel.

Networking options

This set of options (Figure 6-10) deals with networking. How you set these options depends on how you want to use your Red Hat Linux system in a network. Always enable the *TCP/IP networking* option because the X Window System uses TCP/IP networking (even if your PC is not on any network).

Set the *Network packet filtering (replaces ipchains)* option to Yes if you want to use your Red Hat Linux system as a firewall — an intermediary system that controls information flowing between a local area network (LAN) and the Internet.

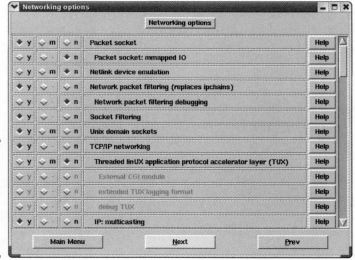

Figure 6-10: Configure the networking options from this configuration window.

Telephony support

With the right hardware and software, the telephony support options enable you to use the Red Hat Linux system for making phone calls over the Internet (also known as *voiceover IP* or *VoIP*). You can choose to build driver modules for telephony support if you have a telephony card, such as the Internet PhoneJACK or Internet LineJACK manufactured by Quicknet Technologies, Inc. If you do not have any Quicknet telephony cards, you can safely set these options to No.

ATA/IDE/MFM/RLL support

When you're configuring an operating system, you have to expect a fair share of acronyms — this one has four acronyms: ATA, IDE, MFM, and RLL. All of these relate to hard disks or the interface of disk drives to the PC. Here's what they mean:

✦ **ATA** stands for *AT Attachment* and refers to the PC-AT style interface used to connect hard disks and CD-ROM drives to the PC's motherboard.

✦ **IDE** stands for *Integrated Drive Electronics* and refers to the original PC hard disks that integrate the disk controller onto the hard disk itself. The IDE interface is more accurately described as *AT Attachment Packet Interface* or ATAPI. You typically see the terms IDE, ATA, and ATAPI used interchangeably.

✦ **MFM** stands for *Modified Frequency Modulation* and refers to the way data was encoded on older hard drives. These hard drives can work over an IDE interface.

✦ **RLL** stands for *Run Length Limited* and is also a technique for storing data on hard disk. RLL disks can work over an IDE interface.

You should leave the *ATA/IDE/MFM/RLL support* set to Yes. When you press Next from this window, you get another configuration window (Figure 6-11) with many more options involving IDE devices, such as hard disks and ATAPI CD-ROM drives.

The first option is for enhanced IDE support, which refers to full-featured IDE controllers that can control up to 10 IDE interfaces. Because each IDE interface can have a master and a slave device, this enables Linux to access a total of up to 20 IDE devices, such as disks or CD-ROM drives. You should leave this option set to Yes.

The second button in Figure 6-11 is a comment that refers you to the file `Documentation/ide.txt` for help with IDE devices. To read these help files (these are all text files), type the following command to change the directory:

```
cd /usr/src/linux*/Documentation
```

Now you can browse the directory for text files relating to specific devices. You can also use GNOME or KDE file managers to browse the documentation.

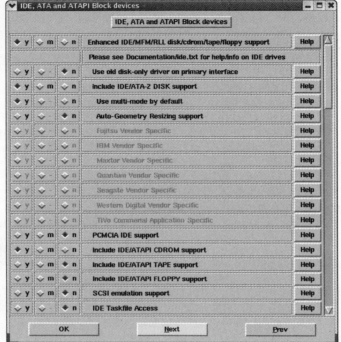

Figure 6-11:
Set options
for IDE
devices
from this
configura-
tion window.

Note that IDE/ATAPI FLOPPY refers to IDE floppy drives, such as Iomega Zip drive or Imation Superdisk LS-120 drive. If you have a IDE ZIP drive, set this option to Module or Yes.

SCSI support

SCSI stands for *Small Computer Systems Interface* and refers to a type of interface through which you can connect multiple devices such as hard disks and scanners to the PC. This set of options (Figure 6-12) has to do with SCSI devices. If your system has a SCSI adapter, start by setting the *SCSI support* option to Yes. After that, you can set the options relating to the types of devices (disk, tape, CD-ROM) connected to the SCSI adapter. Finally, you must enable support for the specific SCSI adapter model on your system.

If your system has a SCSI adapter, always select *y* for all the needed SCSI options. In particular, select *y* for the SCSI low-level driver for your specific brand of SCSI adapter.

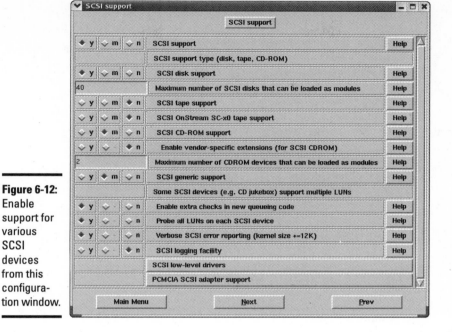

Figure 6-12:
Enable
support for
various
SCSI
devices
from this
configura-
tion window.

IEEE 1394 (FireWire) support (Experimental)

IEEE 1394 is a high-speed serial bus for connecting peripherals to PCs. Apple calls this bus FireWire; Sony calls it i.Link. IEEE 1394 is similar to USB, but it can transfer data at rates up to 400Mbps, which is more than 30 times the data rate of the older USB version 1.1 (note that USB 2.0 is much faster; it can transfer data at rates of up to 480Mbps). Because of its high data-transfer rates, IEEE 1394 is ideal for connecting high-speed peripherals such as digital audio and video devices and external hard drives to the PC.

The Linux kernel includes experimental support for the IEEE 1394 bus. Currently, Linux supports IEEE 1394 chipsets that are compatible with Texas Instruments PCILynx/PCILynx2 and OHCI chipsets. If your PC has an IEEE 1394 adapter, you can build the necessary drivers through these options (Figure 6-13).

Because the IEEE 1394 drivers are experimental, you can set these options only if you have said Yes to experimental drivers in the code maturity level options.

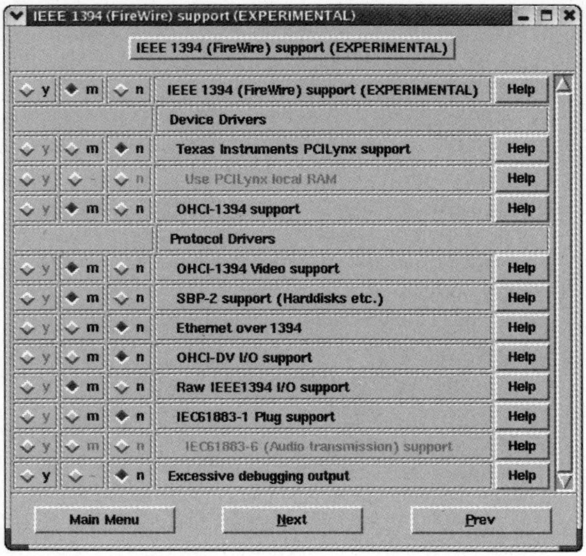

Figure 6-13:
Configure support for IEEE 1394 (FireWire) devices from this configuration window.

To learn more about using IEEE 1394 peripherals in Linux, visit the Web site of the IEEE 1394 for Linux project at `www.linux1394.org`.

I2O device support

Pronounced *eye-two-oh,* I2O refers to Intelligent Input/Output — a new device driver architecture independent of the operating system and the controlled device. The basic concept of I2O is to separate the part responsible for managing the device from the part that contains operating system-specific details (it's called the I2O Split Driver model). The two parts of an I2O driver are the OS Services Module (OSM), which works with the operating system, and the Hardware Device Module (HDM) that interfaces with the particular device the driver manages. The OSM and HDM communicate by passing messages to each other. To learn more about I2O, visit the Intelligent-IO.com Web site at `www.intelligent-io.com`. Linux comes with some I2O drivers for SCSI and PCI devices. You can configure these drivers from this category of options.

Network device support

This category of options involves the drivers for network interface cards. It includes the configuration of network devices such as Ethernet, Token Ring, ARCnet, and AppleTalk network adapters. If you have an Ethernet card installed on your PC, remember to build the driver for your Ethernet card by selecting Yes or Module for that card.

You can also enable dial-up and wide area network (WAN) support by using SLIP and PPP through options in this category.

ISDN subsystem

This set of options enables you to include support for *ISDN* (Integrated Services Digital Network) — a digital telephone line you can use to connect the Linux system to the Internet. These ISDN-related options include the configuration of specific ISDN adapters.

You should build the ISDN driver only if your PC has an ISDN card. If you anticipate adding an ISDN card and purchase ISDN service from the phone company, you can build the driver as a module. Read the file `/usr/src/linux*/Documentation/isdn/README` for more information on how to set up and use the ISDN driver in Linux.

Character devices

These options deal with configuring character devices, which include devices connected to the serial and parallel ports. These options also include configuration of multiport serial interface cards that enable you to connect multiple terminals or other devices to your Red Hat Linux system. Answer No if you do not have any such devices on your system.

This list of options includes the *Parallel printer support option*. If you plan to connect a printer to the parallel port, set this option to Yes.

A subcategory of the character device options refers to I2C support. I2C — pronounced *eye-squared-see* — is a protocol Philips has developed for communication over a pair of wires at rates between 10 and 100kHz. System Management Bus (SMBus) is a subset of the I2C protocol. Many modern motherboards have an SMBus meant for connecting devices such as EEPROM (electrically erasable programmable read-only memory) and chips for hardware monitoring. Linux supports the I2C and SMBus protocols. You need this support for Video for Linux. If you have any hardware sensors or video equipment that needs I2C support, set the I2C support option to *m* (for module) and answer *m* to the specific driver for your hardware. To learn more about the I2C, read the documentation in the `/usr/src/linux*/Documentation/i2c` directory. In particular, the `summary` file briefly describes the I2C and SMBus protocols.

Other subcategories of character devices include

✦ **Mice** — You can specify the type of mouse on your PC (what's important is how the mouse is connected to the PC, not the make and model of the mouse). You have choices such as bus mouse, PS/2 mouse, and specialized devices such as digitizer pad and touch screen.

✦ **Joysticks** — You can set the options for any joysticks or special game controllers (steering wheel, game pad, and so on) on your PC.

✦ **Watchdog cards** — You can enable support for special watchdog cards that can monitor the PC's status (including the temperature, for instance) and reboots the PC when necessary. This can be helpful if you want to have a networked PC automatically reboot after it hangs up for whatever reason.

✦ **Ftape or the floppy tape device driver** — If you have a tape drive connected to your floppy controller, you can configure it through this category of options.

✦ **PCMCIA character devices** — These options are for configuring PC card modems and serial ports that are meant for laptop or notebook PCs.

Multimedia devices

This category of options configures support for multimedia devices such as video cameras, television tuners, and FM radio cards. For more information on these devices, consult the documentation in the `/usr/src/linux*/Documentation/video4linux` directory.

File systems

Through this category of options (Figure 6-14) you can turn on support for specific types of file systems. You'd be amazed by the many different file systems that the Linux kernel can support. Table 6-1 lists some of the file systems that Linux can support. You would typically build a kernel with support for the core Linux file systems (ext2 and ext3), CD-ROM file system (ISO 9660 and Joliet), and DOS/Windows file systems (MSDOS, FAT, and VFAT).

Table 6-1	Some File Systems Supported by Linux Kernel
File System	*Description*
Apple Macintosh	The Macintosh HFS file system (Linux can read and write Macintosh-formatted floppy disks and hard disks)
Coda	An advanced network file system that is similar to NFS but that better supports disconnected operation (for example, laptops) and is a better security model
Ext2	The second extended file system — the current standard file system for Linux
Ext3	Ext2 file system with support for journalling — a facility that allows quick recovery of the disk after a crash

File System	Description
FAT	Refers to any File Allocation Table (FAT)-based file system (including MS-DOS and Windows 95 VFAT file systems)
HPFS	The OS/2 HPFS file system (Linux can only read HPFS files)
ISO 9660	The standard ISO 9660 file system used on CD-ROMs (this is also known as the High Sierra File System and is referred to as hsfs on some UNIX workstations)
Joliet	Microsoft's Joliet extension for the ISO 9660 CD-ROM file system, which allows for long filenames in Unicode format (Unicode is the new 16-bit character code that can encode the characters of almost all languages of the world.)
MSDOS	The MS-DOS file system
NFS	Network File System for sharing files and directories from other systems on a network
NTFS	NT file system (NTFS) — the file system used by Microsoft Windows NT (Linux can only read NTFS disks)
/proc	A virtual file system through which you can get information about the kernel. The /proc file system does not exist on the disk; files are created when you access them
ROM	A very small, read-only, memory-resident file system used in the initial RAM disk (initrd) during Red Hat Linux installation
SMB	File system that uses Server Message Block (SMB) protocol to access shared directories from networked PCs running Windows 95/98/NT/2000
System V	File system used by SCO, Xenix, and Coherent variants of UNIX for Intel PCs
UFS	File system used by the BSD (Berkeley Software Distribution) variants of UNIX (such as SunOS, FreeBSD, NetBSD, and NeXTstep)
VFAT	Windows 95/98/NT/2000 file systems with long file names

Sound

Use this set of options to configure sound-card support. If you have a sound card installed, start by answering *y* or *m* to the *Sound card support* option. After that, you have to enable a number of options for the sound card installed in your PC. You can always select *m* to build the sound support in the form of modules that you can load when needed.

USB support

Use this category of options (Figure 6-15) to configure support for the Universal Serial Bus (USB) — a serial bus that comes built into most new

PCs. USB version 1.1 supports data-transfer rates as high as 12Mbps — 12 million bits per second or 1.5 megabytes per second — compared with 115Kbps or the 0.115Mbps transfer rate of a standard serial port (such as COM1). You can daisy-chain up to 127 devices on a USB bus. The bus also provides power to the devices, and you can attach or remove devices while the PC is running — a capability commonly referred to as hot swapping. USB version 2.0 (or USB 2.0 or USB2, for short) ups the ante by raising the data transfer rates to a whopping 480Mbps, slightly faster than the competing IEEE 1394 (FireWire) bus.

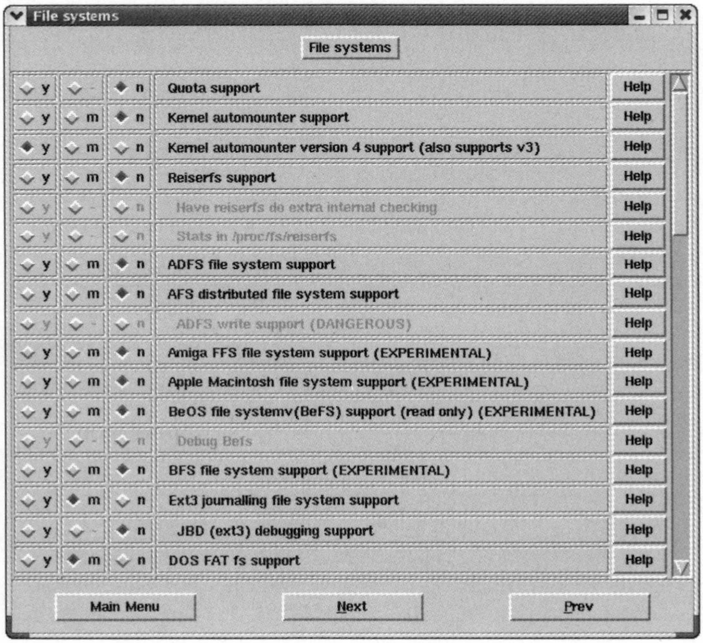

Figure 6-14:
Turn on support for specific file systems from this configuration window.

USB can replace the functionality of the PC's serial and parallel ports, as well as the keyboard and mouse ports. Nowadays, many PC peripherals — such as mouse, keyboard, printer, scanner, modem, digital camera, and so on — are designed to connect to the PC through a USB port.

If your PC has a USB port, set the *USB support* option to *y* or *m*. Then you have to answer *m* to the UHCI or OHCI option, depending on the type of USB interface — UHCI (Intel) or OHCI (Compaq and others) — your PC has. To determine the type of USB interface, type **lspci** and look for the USB controller's make and model in the output. If the controller is by Intel, use the UHCI driver.

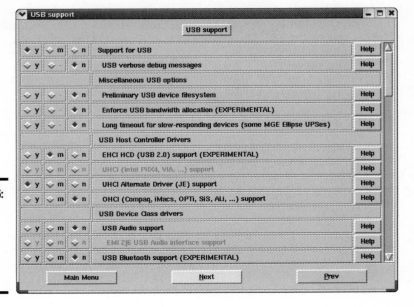

Figure 6-15:
Configure
USB
support
through
these
options.

For USB 2.0 support, you can set the EHCI HCD (that's host controller
device) option to *y* or *m*.

After you select the UHCI or OHCI interface support, you have to build the
driver modules for specific USB devices on your system. For more information on USB devices, consult the documentation in the /usr/src/linux*/
Documentation/usb directory — especially the links in the usb-help.txt
file.

Kernel hacking

This set of options enables you to use the SysRq key (equivalent to pressing
Alt+PrintScreen on your keyboard) to get important status information right
after a system crash. This information is useful if you are a Linux developer
who expects to debug the kernel. Most users set these options to No (because
most users run a stable version of the kernel and do not expect to fix kernel
errors).

Building the Kernel

After configuring the kernel options, click the Save and Exit button in the
main configuration window (Figure 6-1). Now you have to build the kernel.
This involves typing three commands to perform three tasks.

Initiate the next three tasks by using a single command line (you can enter multiple semicolon-separated commands on the same line) so that you can type the line; then press Enter, and take a break. This part takes a while. Depending on your system, making a new kernel can take anywhere from a few minutes to over an hour.

Type the following on a single line to initiate the process:

```
make dep; make clean; make zImage
```

The make dep command determines which files have changed and what needs to be compiled again. The make clean command deletes old, unneeded files (such as old copies of the kernel). Finally, make zImage creates the new kernel in a compressed file named zImage and places it in a certain directory.

If you link too many features into the kernel (by answering Yes to many configuration options), the kernel file size may be too big to fit in the 640K of memory a PC can use as it boots up. This 640K limit exists because Intel x86 processors start in real mode and can only access 1MB of memory, of which 640K is available for programs. This limit is a leftover from the old MS-DOS days, and it applies only as the Linux kernel is initially loaded as the PC starts. In this case, the make command displays an error message such as the following:

```
System is too big. Try using bzImage or modules.
```

If you get a "System too big" error, type **make bzImage** to use a different type of compressed kernel that may fit within the memory limits. Otherwise, go through the make config step again and eliminate unnecessary features by selecting No for those configuration questions. For other features you really need or may want to try out, select *m* to create modules. Although the kernel size is limited at startup, the kernel can load as many modules as it needs once the boot process is complete.

As the kernel is built, you see a lot of messages on the screen. When it's all over, there is a new kernel in the form of a compressed file named zImage in the /usr/src/linux*/arch/i386/boot directory.

To use the new kernel, you have to copy the kernel to the /boot directory under a specific name and edit the /etc/grub.conf file to set up GRUB — the boot loader. Before you proceed with the kernel installation, however, you have to build and install the modules.

Building and Installing the Modules

If you select any modules during the kernel configuration, you have to build the modules and install them. Perform these tasks with the following steps:

1. **Type the following commands to build the modules:**

   ```
   cd /usr/src/linux*
   make modules
   ```

   The current set of modules in a directory is named after the version of the Linux kernel your system is running. For example, if your system runs kernel version 2.4.18-14, the modules are in the following directory:

   ```
   /lib/modules/2.4.18-14
   ```

2. **Move the module directory to a new location as follows:**

   ```
   mv /lib/modules/2.4.18-14 /lib/modules/2.4.18-14-old
   ```

3. **Install the new modules with the following command:**

   ```
   make modules_install
   ```

Now you can install the kernel and make it available for GRUB to boot.

Installing the New Kernel and Setting Up GRUB

Red Hat Linux uses GRUB to load the Linux kernel from the disk. The configuration file `/etc/grub.conf` lists the kernel binary file that GRUB runs. You can examine the contents of the GRUB configuration file by typing the following command:

```
cat /etc/grub.conf
```

Here is what I see when I try this command on one of my systems:

```
# grub.conf generated by anaconda
#
# Note that you do not have to rerun grub after making changes to this file
# NOTICE: You have a /boot partition. This means that
#    all kernel and initrd paths are relative to /boot/, eg.
#    root (hd0,0)
#    kernel /vmlinuz-version ro root=/dev/hda2
#    initrd /initrd-version.img
#boot=/dev/hda
default=0
timeout=10
splashimage=(hd0,0)/grub/splash.xpm.gz
title Red Hat Linux (2.4.18-14)
    root (hd0,0)
    kernel /vmlinuz-2.4.18-14 ro root=LABEL=/
    initrd /initrd-2.4.18-14.img
```

Here's what the lines in `/etc/grub.conf` file mean (the lines that begin with `#` are comments):

✦ `default=0` — Specifies the first boot entry as the default one that GRUB should boot.

✦ `timeout=10` — Causes GRUB to boot the default entry automatically after waiting for 10 seconds. If other boot entries are in the file, the user may select another one from a boot menu GRUB displays.

✦ The four lines starting with `title Red Hat Linux (2.4.18-14)` define a specific kernel file GRUB can boot. You can make GRUB boot another kernel by adding a similar section to the configuration file.

✦ `root (hd0,0)` — Sets the root device to the first partition of the first hard disk.

✦ `kernel /vmlinuz-2.4.18-14 ro root=LABEL=/` — Identifies the kernel GRUB loads. In this case, the kernel file is `vmlinuz-2.4.18-14`, which is located in the root device. In my system, that partition is mounted on the `/boot` directory. In other words, GRUB loads the kernel file `/boot/vmlinuz-2.4.18-14`.

✦ `initrd /initrd-2.4.18-14.img` line specifies a file that contains an initial RAM disk (`initrd` stands for initial RAM disk) image that serves as a file system before the disks are available. The Linux kernel uses the RAM disk — a block of memory used as a disk — to get started; then it loads other driver modules and begins using the hard disk.

On systems that have an MS-DOS partition, the GRUB configuration file may include another section with details for the operating system (perhaps Windows 95/98) on that partition.

To configure GRUB to boot the new Linux kernel (the one you just built), follow these steps:

1. **Copy the new kernel binary to the `/boot` directory.**

The new, compressed kernel file is in the `/usr/src/linux*/arch/i386/boot` directory. If you have typed the command `make zImage`, the kernel filename is `zImage`; if you have built the kernel with the `make bzImage` command, the filename is `bzImage`. I simply copy that file to the `/boot` directory with the same name:

```
cp /usr/src/linux*/arch/i386/boot/zImage /boot
```

If the kernel filename is `bzImage`, make sure you use `bzImage` instead of `zImage`. You can use any other filename you want, as long as you use the same filename when referring to the kernel in the `/etc/grub.conf` file in Step 3.

2. **Save the old** `System.map` **file in the** `/boot` **directory, and copy the
new map file.**

   (I assume you have rebuilt kernel version 2.4.18-14 after changing some
   configuration options):

   ```
   mv /boot/System.map-2.4.18-14 /boot/System.map-2.4.18-14-old
   cp /usr/src/linux*/System.map /boot/System.map-2.4.18-14
   cd /boot
   ln -s System.map-2.4.18-14 System.map
   ```

3. **Use your favorite text editor to edit the** `/etc/grub.conf` **file to add
   the following lines just after the timeout line in the file:**

   ```
   title Red Hat Linux (2.4.18-14 NEW)
           root (hd0,0)
           kernel /zImage ro root=/dev/hda2
   ```

   On your system, you should make sure the root line is correct —
   instead of `/dev/hda2`, you should list the correct disk partition where
   the Linux root directory (/) is located. Also, use the correct filename for
   the kernel image file (for example, `/boot/bzImage` if the kernel file is so
   named).

   Note that I do not show the `initrd` line anymore because I assume you
   are no longer using a modular SCSI driver even if your system has a SCSI
   adapter.

4. **Save the** `grub.conf` **file, and exit the editor.**

   Now you are ready to reboot the system and try out the new kernel.

Rebooting the System

After you finish configuring GRUB, you can restart the system. While you are
still logged in as `root`, type the following command to reboot the system:

```
reboot
```

When you see the GRUB screen, select the name you have assigned to the
new kernel in the `/etc/grub.conf` file.

After the system reboots, you should see the familiar graphical login screen.
To see proof that you are indeed running the new kernel, log in as a user,
open a terminal window, and type **uname -srv**. This command shows you
the kernel version, as well as the date and time when this kernel was built.
If you have upgraded the kernel source, you should see the version number
for the new kernel. If you have simply rebuilt the kernel for the same old

kernel version, the date and time should match the time when you rebuilt the kernel. That's your proof that the system is running the new kernel.

If the system hangs (nothing seems to happen — there is no output on the screen and no disk activity), you may have skipped a step during the kernel rebuild. You can power the PC off and on to reboot. This time, select the name of the old working kernel at the GRUB screen.

If you cannot boot the older version of Red Hat Linux either, use the emergency boot disk (containing an earlier, but working, version of Linux) to start the system. Then you can repeat the kernel rebuild and installation process, making sure you follow all the steps correctly.

Book VI

Security

The 5th Wave   By Rich Tennant

"We take network security very seriously here."

Contents at a Glance

Chapter 1: Understanding Network and Host Security

In This Chapter

✔ **Establishing a security policy and framework**

✔ **Understanding host security issues**

✔ **Understanding network security issues**

✔ **Learning computer security terminology**

✔ **Keeping up with security news and updates**

*I*n this chapter, I explain why you should worry about security and then give you a high-level view of how to get a handle on security. I explain the idea of an overall security framework and explain the two key aspects of security — host security and network security. I end this chapter by introducing you to the terminology used in discussing computer security.

Why Worry about Security?

In today's networked world, you have to worry about your Red Hat Linux system's security. For a stand-alone system, or a system used in an isolated local area network (LAN), you have to focus on protecting the system from the users and the users from one another. In other words, you do not want a user to modify or delete system files, whether intentionally or unintentionally. Also, you do not want a user destroying another user's files.

If your Red Hat Linux system is connected to the Internet, you have to secure the system from unwanted accesses over the Internet. These intruders or *crackers,* as they are commonly known, typically impersonate a user, steal or destroy information, and even deny you access to your own system (this is known as a *Denial of Service* or *DoS* attack).

By its very nature, an Internet connection makes your system accessible to any other system on the Internet. After all, the Internet connects a huge number of networks across the globe. In fact, the client/server architecture of Internet services, such as HTTP (Web) and FTP, rely on the wide-open network access the Internet provides. Unfortunately, the easy accessibility to Internet services running on your system also means anyone on the Net can easily access your system.

If you operate an Internet host that provides information to others, you certainly want everyone to access your system's Internet services, such as FTP and Web servers. However, these servers often have vulnerabilities that crackers may exploit in order to cause harm to your system. You need to know about the potential security risks of Internet services and the precautions you can take to minimize the risk of someone exploiting the weaknesses of your FTP or Web server.

You also want to protect your company's internal network from outsiders, even though your goal is to provide information to the outside world through a Web or FTP server. You can protect your internal network by setting up an Internet *firewall* — a controlled access point to the internal network — and placing the Web and FTP servers on a host outside the firewall.

Establishing a Security Framework

The first step in securing your Red Hat Linux system is to set up a security policy. The security policy is your guide to what you enable users (as well as visitors over the Internet) to do on the Red Hat Linux system. The level of security you establish depends on how you use the Red Hat Linux system and how much is at risk if someone gains unauthorized access to your system.

If you are a system administrator for one or more Red Hat Linux systems at an organization, you probably want to involve the management, as well as the users, in setting up the security policy. Obviously, you cannot create a draconian policy that prevents anyone from effectively working on the system. On the other hand, if the users are creating or using data valuable to the organization, you have to set up a policy that protects the data from disclosure to outsiders. In other words, the security policy should strike a balance between the users' needs and the need to protect the system.

For a stand-alone Red Hat Linux system, or a home system that you occasionally connect to the Internet, the security policy can be just a listing of the Internet services you want to run on the system and the user accounts you plan to set up on the system. For any larger organization, you probably have one or more Red Hat Linux systems on a LAN connected to the Internet — preferably through a firewall (to reiterate, a firewall is a device that controls the flow of Internet Protocol — IP — packets between the LAN and the Internet). In such cases, it is best to think of computer security across the entire organization systematically. Figure 1-1 shows the key elements of an organizationwide framework for computer security.

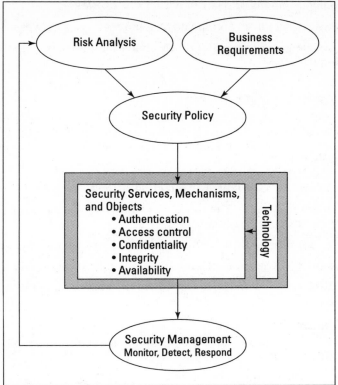

Figure 1-1:
Start with an organizationwide framework for computer security.

The security framework outlined in Figure 1-1 starts with the development of a security policy based on business requirements and risk analysis.

Determine business requirements for security

The business requirements identify the security needs of the business — the computer resources and information you have to protect (including any requirements imposed by applicable laws, such as the requirement to protect the privacy of some types of data). Typical security requirements may include items such as the following:

✦ Enable access to information by authorized users

✦ Implement business rules that specify who has access to what information

✦ Employ a strong user-authentication system

✦ Deny malicious or destructive actions on data

✦ Protect data from end to end as it moves across networks

✦ Implement all security and privacy requirements that applicable laws impose

Perform risk analysis

Risk analysis is all about identifying and assessing risks — potential events that can harm your Red Hat Linux system. The analysis involves determining the following and performing some analysis to determine the priority of handling the risks:

✦ **Threats** — What you are protecting against

✦ **Vulnerabilities** — The weaknesses that may be exploited (these are the risks)

✦ **Probability** — The likelihood that a vulnerability will be exploited

✦ **Impact** — The effect of exploiting a specific vulnerability

✦ **Mitigation** — What to do to reduce the vulnerabilities

Typical threats

Before I describe risk analysis some more, here are some typical threats to your Red Hat Linux system:

✦ **Denial of Service** — The computer and network are tied up so that legitimate users cannot make use of the systems. For businesses, Denial of Service can mean loss of revenue.

✦ **Unauthorized access** — Use of the computer and network by someone who is not an authorized user. The unauthorized user can steal information or maliciously corrupt or destroy data. Some businesses may be hurt by the negative publicity from the mere act of an unauthorized user gaining access to the system, even if there is no explicit damage to any data.

✦ **Disclosure of information to the public** — The unauthorized release of information to the public. For example, the disclosure of a password file enables potential attackers to figure out username and password combinations for accessing a system. Exposure of other sensitive information, such as financial and medical data, may be a potential liability for a business.

Typical vulnerabilities

The threats to your system and network come from exploitation of vulnerabilities in your organization's computer and people resources. Some common vulnerabilities are the following:

+ People (divulging passwords, losing security cards, and so on)

+ Internal network connections (routers, switches)

+ Interconnection points (gateways — routers and firewalls — between the Internet and the internal network)

+ Third-party network providers (ISPs, long-distance carriers)

+ Operating-system security holes (potential holes in Internet servers, such as sendmail, named, bind, and so on)

+ Application security holes (known security holes in specific applications)

The 1-2-3 of risk analysis (probability and impact)

To perform risk analysis, assign a numeric value to the probability and impact of each potential vulnerability. A workable risk analysis approach is to do the following for each vulnerability or risk:

1. Assign subjective ratings of Low, Medium, and High for the probability. As the ratings suggest, Low probability means a lesser chance that the vulnerability will be exploited; High probability means a greater chance.

2. Assign similar ratings to impact. What you consider impact is up to you. If the exploitation of a vulnerability will affect your business greatly, assign it a High impact.

3. Assign a numeric value to the three levels — Low = 1, Medium = 2, and High = 3 — for both probability and impact.

4. Compute the product of the probability and impact — you can think of this as the risk level. Then make a decision to develop protections for vulnerabilities that exceed a specific threshold for the product of probability and impact. For example, you may choose to handle all vulnerabilities with a probability times impact greater than 6.

If you want to characterize the probability and impact with a finer level of granularity, pick a scale of 1 through 5, for example, and follow the same steps as before.

Establish security policy

Based on the risk analysis and any business requirements you may need to address regardless of risk level, you can craft a security policy for the organization. The security policy typically addresses the following areas:

✦ **Authentication** — What method will be used to ensure that a user is the real user? Who gets access to the system? What is the minimum length and complexity of passwords? How often do users change passwords? How long can a user be idle before that user is logged out automatically?

✦ **Authorization** — What can different classes of users do on the system? Who can have the `root` password?

✦ **Data protection** — What data must be protected? Who has access to the data? Is encryption necessary for some data?

✦ **Internet access** — What are the restrictions on users (from the LAN) accessing the Internet? What Internet services (such as Web, Internet Relay Chat, and so on) can users access? Are incoming e-mails and attachments scanned for viruses? Is there a network firewall? Are virtual private networks (VPNs) used to connect private networks across the Internet?

✦ **Internet services** — What Internet services are allowed on each Linux system? Are there any file servers? Mail servers? Web servers? What services run on each type of server? What services, if any, run on Linux systems used as desktop workstations?

✦ **Security audits** — Who tests whether the security is adequate? How often is the security tested? How are problems found during security testing handled?

✦ **Incident handling** — What are the procedures for handling any computer security incidents? Who must be informed? What information must be gathered to help with the investigation of incidents?

✦ **Responsibilities** — Who is responsible for maintaining security? Who monitors log files and audit trails for signs of unauthorized access? Who maintains the database of security policy?

Implement security solutions (mitigation)

After you analyze the risks — vulnerabilities — and develop a security policy, you have to select the mitigation approach: how to protect against specific vulnerabilities. This is where you develop an overall security solution based on security policy, business requirements, and available technology — a solution that consists of the following:

✦ Services (authentication, access control, encryption)

✦ Mechanisms (username/password, firewalls)

✦ Objects (hardware, software)

Manage security

In addition to implementing security solutions, you have to install security management that continually monitors, detects, and responds to any security incidents.

The combination of the risk analysis, security policy, security solutions, and security management provides the overall security framework. Such a framework helps establish a common level of understanding of security and a common basis for the design and implementation of security solutions.

Securing Red Hat Linux

After you have defined a security policy, you can proceed to secure the system according to the policy. The exact steps depend on what you want to do with the system — whether it is a server or a workstation and how many users must access the system.

To secure the Red Hat Linux system, you have to handle two broad categories of security issues:

✦ **Host security issues** that relate to securing the operating system and the files and directories on the system

✦ **Network security issues** that refer to the threat of attacks over the network connection

Understanding the host security issues

Here are some high-level guidelines to address host security (I cover some of these topics in detail in Book VI, Chapter 2):

✦ When installing Red Hat Linux, select only those package groups you need for your system. Do not install unnecessary software. For example, if your system is used as a workstation, you do not need to install most of the servers (Web server, news server, and so on).

✦ Create initial user accounts and make sure all passwords are strong ones that password-cracking programs can't "guess." Red Hat Linux includes tools to enforce strong passwords.

✦ Set file ownerships and permissions to protect important files and directories. Use the new access control lists (ACLs) to manage who gets to use which files and directories.

✦ Use the GNU Privacy Guard (GnuPG) to encrypt or decrypt files with sensitive information and to authenticate files that you download from Red Hat. GnuPG comes with Red Hat Linux and you can use the `gpg` command to perform the tasks such as encrypt or decrypt a file and digitally sign a file.

✦ Use file-integrity checking tools, such as Tripwire, to monitor any changes to crucial system files and directories.

✦ Periodically check various log files for signs of any break-ins or attempted break-ins. These log files are in the `/var/log` directory of your system.

✦ Install security updates from Red Hat, as soon as they become available. These security updates fix known vulnerabilities in Red Hat Linux.

Understanding network security issues

The issue of security comes up as soon as you connect your organization's internal network to the Internet. This is true even if you connect a single computer to the Internet, but security concerns are more pressing when an entire internal network is opened to the world.

If you are an experienced system administrator, you already know that it's not the cost of managing an Internet presence that worries corporate management; their main concern is security. To get your management's backing for the Web site, you need to lay out a plan to keep the corporate network secure from intruders.

You may think that you can avoid jeopardizing the internal network by connecting only the external servers, such as Web and FTP servers, to the Internet. However, this simplistic approach is not wise. It is like deciding not to drive because you may have an accident. Not having a network connection between your Web server and your internal network also has the following drawbacks:

✦ You cannot use network file transfers, such as FTP, to copy documents and data from your internal network to the Web server.

✦ Users on the internal network cannot access the corporate Web server.

✦ Users on the internal network do not have access to Web servers on the Internet. Such a restriction makes a valuable resource — the Web — inaccessible to the users in your organization.

A practical solution to this problem is to set up an Internet firewall and to put the Web server on a highly secured host outside the firewall.

In addition to using a firewall, here are some of the other steps you should take to address network security (I explain these further in Book VI, Chapter 3):

✦ Enable only those Internet services you need on a system. In particular, do not enable services that are not properly configured.

✦ Use Secure Shell (ssh) for remote logins. Do not use the "r" commands, such as rlogin and rsh.

✦ Secure any Internet services such as FTP or TELNET that you want to run on your system. You can use the TCP wrapper access control files — /etc/hosts.allow and /etc/hosts.deny — to secure some of these services.

✦ Promptly fix any known vulnerabilities of Internet services that you choose to run. Typically you do this by downloading and installing the latest server RPM file from Red Hat.

Learning Computer Security Terminology

Computer books, magazine articles, and experts on computer security use a number of terms with unique meanings. You need to know these terms to understand discussions about computer security (and to communicate effectively with security vendors). Table 1-1 describes some of the commonly used computer security terms.

Table 1-1	Commonly Used Computer Security Terminology
Term	*Description*
Application gateway	A proxy service that acts as a gateway for application-level protocols, such as FTP, TELNET, and HTTP
Authentication	The process of confirming that a user is indeed who he or she claims to be. The typical authentication method is a challenge-response method wherein the user enters a username and secret password to confirm his or her identity.
Backdoor	A security weakness a cracker places on a host in order to bypass security features

(continued)

Table 1-1 *(continued)*

Term	Description
Bastion host	A highly secured computer that serves as an organization's main point of presence on the Internet. A bastion host typically resides on the perimeter network, but a dual-homed host (with one network interface connected to the Internet and the other to the internal network) is also a bastion host.
Buffer overflow	A security flaw in a program that enables a cracker to send an excessive amount of data to that program and to overwrite parts of the running program with code in the data being sent. The result is that the cracker can execute arbitrary code on the system and possibly gain access to the system as a privileged user.
Certificate	An electronic document that identifies an entity (such as an individual, an organization, or a computer) and associates a public key with that identity. A certificate contains the certificate holder's name, a serial number, expiration date, a copy of the certificate holder's public key, and the digital signature of the Certificate Authority so that a recipient can verify that the certificate is real.
Certificate Authority (CA)	An organization that validates identities and issues certificates
Cracker	A person who breaks into (or attempts to break into) a host, often with malicious intent
Confidentiality	Of data, a state of being accessible by no one but you (usually achieved by encryption)
Decryption	The process of transforming encrypted information into its original, intelligible form
Denial of Service (DoS)	An attack that uses so many of the resources on your computer and network that legitimate users cannot access and use the system
Digital signature	A one-way MD5 or SHA-1 hash of a message encrypted with the private key of the message originator, used to verify the integrity of a message and assure nonrepudiation
DMZ	Another name for the perimeter network. (DMZ stands for demilitarized zone, the buffer zone separating North and South Korea.)
Dual-homed host	A computer with two network interfaces (think of each network as a home)
Encryption	The process of transforming information so it is unintelligible to anyone but the intended recipient. The transformation is done by a mathematical operation between a key and the information.

Term	Description
Firewall	A controlled-access gateway between an organization's internal network and the Internet. A dual-homed host can be configured as a firewall.
Hash	A mathematical function converts a message into a fixed-size numeric value known as a message digest or hash. The MD5 algorithm produces a 128-bit message digest, whereas the Secure Hash Algorithm-1 (SHA-1) generates a 160-bit message digest. The hash of a message is encrypted with the private key of the sender to produce the digital signature.
Host	A computer on any network (so called because it offers many services)
Integrity	Of received data, a state of being the same data that were sent (unaltered in transit).
IPSec (IP Security Protocol)	A security protocol for the network layer that is designed to provide cryptographic security services for IP packets. IPSec provides encryption-based authentication, integrity, access control, and confidentiality (visit `www.ietf.org/html.charters/ipsec-charter.html` for the list of RFCs related to IPSec).
IP spoofing	An attack in which a cracker figures out the IP address of a trusted host and then sends packets that appear to come from the trusted host. The attacker can only send packets, but cannot see any responses. However, the attacker can predict the sequence of packets and essentially send commands that will set up a backdoor for future break-ins.
Nonrepudiation	A security feature that prevents the sender of data from being able to deny ever having sent the data
Packet	A collection of bytes that serves as the basic unit of communication on a network. On TCP/IP networks, the packet may be referred to as an IP packet or a TCP/IP packet.
Packet filtering	Selective blocking of packets based on the type of packet (as specified by the source and destination IP address or port).
Perimeter network	A network between the Internet and the protected internal network. The bastion host resides on the perimeter network (also known as DMZ).
Port scanning	A method for discovering which ports are open (in other words, which Internet services are enabled) on a system. Performed by sending connection requests to the ports, one by one. This is usually a precursor to further attacks.

(continued)

Table 1-1 *(continued)*

Term	Description
Proxy server	A server on the bastion host that enables internal clients to access external servers (and enables external clients to access servers inside the protected network). There are proxy servers for various Internet services, such as FTP and HTTP.
Public-key cryptography	An encryption method that uses a pair of keys — a private key and a public key — to encrypt and decrypt the information. Anything encrypted with the public key can be decrypted with the corresponding private key, and vice versa.
Public Key Infrastructure (PKI)	A set of standards and services that enables the use of public-key cryptography and certificates in a networked environment. PKI facilitates tasks, such as issuing, renewing, and revoking certificates, and generating and distributing public-private key pairs.
Screening router	An Internet router that filters packets
Setuid program	A program that runs with the permissions of the owner regardless of who runs the program. For example, if a setuid program is owned by `root`, that program has `root` privileges regardless of who has started the program. Crackers often exploit vulnerabilities in setuid programs to gain privileged access to a system.
Symmetric-key encryption	An encryption method wherein the same key is used to encrypt and decrypt the information
Threat	An event or activity, deliberate or unintentional, with the potential for causing harm to a system or network
Trojan Horse	A program that masquerades as a benign program, but, in fact is a backdoor used for attacking a system. Attackers often install a collection of Trojan Horse programs that enable the attacker to freely access the system with `root` privileges, yet hide that fact from the system administrator. Such collection of Trojan Horse programs are called *rootkits*.
Virus	A self-replicating program that spreads from one computer to another by attaching itself to other programs
Vulnerability	A flaw or weakness that may cause harm to a system or network
Worm	A self-replicating program that copies itself from one computer to another over a network

Keeping Up with Security News and Updates

To keep up with the latest security alerts, you may want to visit one or more of the following sites on a daily basis:

✦ CERT Coordination Center at `www.cert.org`

✦ Computer Incident Advisory Capability (CIAC) at `www.ciac.org/ciac/`

✦ National Infrastructure Protection Center at `www.nipc.gov`

If you have access to Internet newsgroups, you can periodically browse the following:

✦ `comp.security.announce` — A moderated newsgroup that includes announcements from CERT about security.

✦ `comp.security.unix` — A newsgroup that includes discussions of UNIX security issues, including items related to Red Hat Linux.

If you prefer to receive regular security updates through e-mail, you can also sign up for, or subscribe to, various mailing lists:

✦ `redhat-watch-list` — Follow the directions in `www.redhat.com/mailing-lists/` to subscribe to this mailing list.

✦ `linux-security` — Follow the directions in `www.redhat.com/mailing-lists/` to subscribe to this mailing list.

✦ FOCUS-LINUX — Fill out the form in `www.securityfocus.com/cgi-bin/subscribe.pl` to subscribe to this mailing list focused on Linux security issues.

✦ Cert Advisory mailing list — Follow the directions in `www.cert.org/contact_cert/certmaillist.html` to subscribe to this mailing list.

Finally, you should check Red Hat's Web site at `www.redhat.com/apps/support/errata/index.html` for updates that may fix any known security problems with Red Hat Linux.

Chapter 2: Securing the Host

In This Chapter

✓ Securing passwords

✓ Protecting files and directories

✓ Encrypting and signing files with GnuPG

✓ Using Tripwire to monitor the integrity of your system files

✓ Examining log files

*H*ost is the techie term for your Red Hat Linux system. It makes sense when you think of the computer as the host for everything — the operating system and all the applications — that run on it. A key aspect of computer security is to secure the host.

In this chapter, I take you through a few key steps you should follow in securing your Red Hat Linux host. These steps include installing operating system updates, protecting passwords, protecting the files and directories, using encryption if necessary, and monitoring the security of the system. You can monitor host security by examining log files for any suspicious activities and by using the Tripwire tool to see if anyone has messed with important files on your system.

Installing Operating System Updates

Red Hat Linux and related application updates come in RPM files. To manually download and install the updates, follow these steps:

1. **Log in as** root **and create a directory for the updates:**

   ```
   mkdir /usr/local/updates
   cd /usr/local/updates
   ```

2. **Use the** wget **command to download the updates from Red Hat's FTP site.**

   For example, to download the updates for the i386 version of Red Hat Linux version 8.0, type

   ```
   wget ftp://updates.redhat.com/8.0/en/os/i386/\*.rpm
   wget ftp://updates.redhat.com/8.0/en/os/noarch/\*.rpm
   ```

3. **Install all updates with the following command:**

   ```
   rpm -F *
   ```

4. **Delete the update files with the command:**

   ```
   rm -fr /usr/local/updates
   ```

Securing Passwords

Historically, UNIX passwords are stored in the `/etc/passwd` file, which any user can read. For example, a typical old-style `/etc/passwd` file entry for the `root` user looks like this:

```
root:t6Z7NWDK1K8sU:0:0:root:/root:/bin/bash
```

The fields are separated by colons (`:`), and the second field contains the password in encrypted form. To check if a password is valid, the login program encrypts the plain-text password the user enters and compares the password with the contents of the `/etc/passwd` file. If there is a match, the user is allowed to log in.

Password-cracking programs work just like the login program, except that these programs pick one word at a time from a dictionary, encrypt the word, and compare the encrypted word with the encrypted passwords in the `/etc/passwd` file for a match. To crack the passwords, the intruder needs the `/etc/passwd` file. Often, crackers use weaknesses of various Internet servers (such as mail and FTP) to get a copy of the `/etc/passwd` file.

Recently, several improvements have made passwords more secure in Red Hat Linux. These include shadow passwords and pluggable authentication modules, and you can install these easily as you install Red Hat Linux. During Red Hat Linux installation, one step involves making selections in an Authentication Configuration screen. If you accept the default selections — Enable MD5 passwords and Enable shadow passwords — you automatically enable more secure passwords in Red Hat Linux.

Shadow passwords

Instead of storing them in the `/etc/passwd` file, which any user can read, passwords are now stored in a shadow password file. On Red Hat Linux, the shadow passwords are in `/etc/shadow` file. Only the super user (`root`) can read this file. For example, here is the entry for `root` in the new-style `/etc/passwd` file:

```
root:x:0:0:root:/root:/bin/bash
```

In this case, the second field contains an x, instead of an encrypted password. The encrypted password is now stored in the /etc/shadow file where the entry for root is like this:

```
root:$1$AAAni/yN$uESHbzUpy9Cgfoo1Bf0tSO:11077:0:99999:7:-1:-1:134540356
```

The format of the /etc/shadow entries with colon-separated fields resembles the entries in the /etc/passwd file, but the meanings of most fields differ. The first field is still the username, and the second one is the encrypted password.

The remaining fields in each /etc/shadow entry control when the password expires. You do not need to interpret or change these entries in the /etc/shadow file. Instead, use the chage command to change the password-expiration information. For starters, you can check a user's password-expiration information by using the chage command with the -l option, as follows (in this case, you have to be logged in as root):

```
chage -l root
```

This command displays various expiration information, including how long the password lasts and how often you can change the password.

If you want to ensure that the user is forced to change a password every 90 days, you can use the -M option to set the maximum number of days the password stays valid. For example, to make sure that user naba is prompted to change the password in 90 days, I log in as root and type the following command:

```
chage -M 90 naba
```

You can do this for each user account to ensure that all passwords expire when appropriate and that all users must pick new passwords.

Pluggable Authentication Modules (PAMs)

In addition to improving the password file's security by using the shadow passwords, Red Hat Linux also improves the actual encryption of the passwords stored in the /etc/shadow file. Password encryption is now done using the MD5 message-digest algorithm to convert the plain-text password into a 128-bit fingerprint or digest. The MD5 algorithm, described in RFC 1321 (www.faqs.org/rfcs/rfc1321.html or www.cis.ohio-state.edu/cgi-bin/rfc/rfc1321.html), reduces a message of any length to a 128-bit message digest. MD5 is used to create message digests for documents so that you can digitally sign them through encryption with your private key. MD5 works quite well for password encryption, too.

Another advantage of MD5 over the older-style password encryption is that the older passwords were limited to a maximum of eight characters; new passwords (encrypted with MD5) can be much longer. Longer passwords are harder to guess, even if the /etc/shadow file falls into the wrong hands.

A clue to the use of MD5 encryption in the /etc/shadow file is the increased length of the encrypted password and the 1 prefix, as in the second field of the following sample entry:

```
root:$1$AAAni/yN$uESHbzUpy9Cgfoo1Bf0tS0:11077:0:99999:7:-1:-1:134540356
```

A Pluggable Authentication Module (PAM) performs the actual MD5 encryption. PAM provides a flexible method for authenticating users on Red Hat Linux systems. Through settings in configuration files, you can change the authentication method on the fly, without having to actually modify programs, such as login and passwd, that verify a user's identity.

Red Hat Linux uses PAM extensively, and the configuration files are in the /etc/pam.d directory of your system. Check out the contents of this directory on your system by typing the following command:

```
ls /etc/pam.d
```

Each configuration file in this directory specifies how users are authenticated for a specific utility. For example, there is a file for login, passwd, and su. Here's what I see when I type **cat /etc/pam.d/passwd** file on my system:

```
#%PAM-1.0
auth       required   /lib/security/pam_stack.so service=system-auth
account   required   /lib/security/pam_stack.so service=system-auth
password required   /lib/security/pam_stack.so service=system-auth
```

These lines indicate that authentication, account management, and password-checking should all be done by using the pam_stack module (/lib/security/pam_stack.so) with the argument service=system-auth. Essentially, the pam_stack module refers to another configuration file in the /etc/pam.d directory. In this case, the configuration file is /etc/pam.d/system-auth. Here's the content of the /etc/pam.d/system-auth file on my Red Hat Linux PC:

```
#%PAM-1.0
# This file is auto-generated.
# User changes will be destroyed the next time authconfig is run.
auth      required  /lib/security/pFFFFam_env.so
auth      sufficient /lib/security/pam_unix.so likeauth nullok
auth      required  /lib/security/pam_deny.so
account  required  /lib/security/pam_unix.so
password required  /lib/security/pam_cracklib.so retry=3 type=
```

```
password  sufficient /lib/security/pam_unix.so nullok use_authtok md5 shadow
password  required   /lib/security/pam_deny.so
session   required   /lib/security/pam_limits.so
session   required   /lib/security/pam_unix.so
```

Although I won't go over all the details, here's a brief explanation of some of these lines. The first `auth` line loads the PAM module `/lib/security/pam_env.so.` that can set or unset environment variables. The second `auth` line specifies an authentication module that checks the user's identity by using the PAM module `/lib/security/pam_unix.so` with the argument string `likeauth nullok`. The options in the argument string have the following meanings:

✦ `likeauth` — Returns the same value whether the module is used to set new credentials or authenticate an existing username.

✦ `nullok` — Allows a blank password.

The third `auth` line in the `/etc/pam.d/system-auth` file denies access to the system if the `pam_unix.so` module's authentication is unsuccessful.

The `account` line in the `/etc/pam.d/system-auth` file checks to make sure that the user account has not expired, that the user is allowed to log in at a given time of day, and so on.

The next two `password` lines in the `/etc/pam.d/system-auth` file specify how passwords are set. The first password line uses the `/lib/security/pam_cracklib.so` module to try to crack the new password (that's what the `cracklib` in the module's name indicates). The `retry=3` part indicates that the user can try to enter a new password three times at most. The second `password` line indicates that the MD5 encryption is used to store the password in the `/etc/shadow` file.

The `/etc/pam.d/passwd` configuration file applies when you use the `passwd` command to change passwords. Here's an example where I am trying to change my password (the text in italic is my comment):

```
passwd
Changing password for naba
(current) UNIX password:  I type my current password
New UNIX password: I type "xyzz"
BAD PASSWORD: it is too short
New UNIX password:  I type "transport" as password
BAD PASSWORD: it is based on a dictionary word
New UNIX password:  I type "naba12" as the new password
BAD PASSWORD: it is based on your username
passwd: Authentication token manipulation error
```

In this case, the passwd program is using the PAM module to check my identity (when I first type my current password) and make sure that each of the new passwords I try are strong. Finally, the PAM modules abort the passwd program after I fail to select a good password in three tries.

Protecting Files and Directories

One important aspect of securing the host is to protect important system files and the directories that contain these files. You can protect the files through the file ownership and through the permission settings that control who can read, write, or execute (in case of executable programs) the file.

Setting file ownership and permissions

The default Red Hat Linux file security is controlled through the following settings for each file or directory:

+ User ownership
+ Group ownership
+ Read, Write, Execute permissions for owner
+ Read, Write, Execute permissions for group
+ Read, Write, Execute permissions for others (everyone else)

Viewing ownerships and permissions

You can see these settings for a file when you look at the detailed listing with the ls -l command. For example, type the following command to see the detailed listing of the /etc/inittab file:

```
ls -l /etc/inittab
```

The resulting listing should look something like this:

```
-rw-r--r--  1 root    root     1756 Aug 1 17:00 /etc/inittab
```

The first set of characters describes the file permissions for user, group, and others. The third and fourth fields show the user and group that own this file. In this case, both user and group names are the same: root.

Changing file ownerships

You can set the user and group ownerships with the chown command. For example if the file /dev/hda should be owned by the user root and the group disk, then you would type the following command as root to set up this ownership:

```
chown root.disk /dev/hda
```

To change the group ownership alone, use the `chgrp` command. For example, here's how you can change the group ownership of a file to the group named `accounting`:

```
chgrp accounting ledger.out
```

Changing file permissions

Use the `chmod` command to set the file permissions. To use `chmod` effectively, you have to learn how to specify the permission settings. One way is to concatenate one or more letters from each of the following tables in the order shown (Who/Action/Permission), as shown in Table 2-1:

Table 2-1	File Permission Codes	
Who	*Action*	*Permission*
u user	+ add	r read
g group	− remove	w write
o others	= assign	x execute
a all	s set user ID	

To give everyone read and write access to all files in a directory, type **chmod a+rw ***. On the other hand, to permit everyone to execute a specific file, type **chmod a+x *filename*.**

Another way to specify a permission setting is to use a three-digit sequence of numbers. In a detailed listing, the read, write, and execute permission settings for the user, group, and others appear as the sequence

```
rwxrwxrwx
```

with dashes in place of letters for disallowed operations. Think of `rwxrwxrwx` as three occurrences of the string `rwx`. Now assign the values r=4, w=2, and x=1. To get the value of the sequence `rwx`, simply add the values of r, w, and x. Thus, `rwx` = 7. Using this formula, you can assign a three-digit value to any permission setting. For example, if the user can read and write the file but everyone else can only read the file, the permission setting is `rw-r--r--` (that's how it appears in the listing), and the value is 644. Thus, if you want all files in a directory to be readable by everyone but writeable by only the user, use the command:

```
chmod 644 *
```

Setting default permission

What permission setting does a file get when you (or a program) creates a new file? The answer is in what is known as the user file-creation mask that you can see and set using the umask command.

Type **umask**, and it prints out a number showing the current file-creation mask. The default setting is different for the root user and other normal users. For the root user the mask is set to 022, whereas the mask for normal users is 002. To see the effect of this file-creation mask and to interpret the meaning of the mask, follow these steps:

1. **Log in as** root **and type the following command:**

```
touch junkfile
```

This creates a file named junkfile with nothing in it.

2. **Type ls -l junkfile to that file's permissions.**

You should see a line similar to the following:

```
-rw-r--r--  1 root    root      0 Aug 24 10:56 junkfile
```

Interpret the numerical value of the permission setting by converting each three-letter permission in the first field (excluding the very first letter) into a number between 0 and 7. For each letter that's present, the first letter gets a value of 4, second letter is 2, and the third is 1. For example, rw- translates to 4+2+0 (because the third letter is missing) or 6. Similarly, r-- is 4+0+0 = 4. Thus the permission string -rw-r--r-- becomes 644.

3. **Subtract the numerical permission setting from 666 and what you get is the** umask **setting.**

In this case, 666 - 644 gives us a umask of 022.

So, a umask of 022 results in a default permission setting of 666-022 = 644. When you rewrite 644 in terms of a permission string, it becomes rw-r--r--.

To set a new umask, type **umask** followed by the numerical value of the mask. Here is how you should go about it:

1. **Figure out what permission settings you want for new files.**

For example, if you want new files that can be read and written by the owner only and nobody else, then the permission setting would look like

```
rw-------
```

2. Convert the permissions into a numerical value by using the conversion method that assigns 4 to the first field, 2 to the second, and 1 to the third.

Thus, for files that are readable and writable by owner only, the permission setting is 600.

3. Subtract the desired permission setting from 666 to get the value of the mask.

For a permission setting of 600, the mask then becomes 666-600 = 066.

4. Use the umask **command to set the file-creation mask:**

    umask 066

Book VI
Chapter 2

Securing the Host

A default umask of 022 is good for system security because it translates to files that have read and write permission for the owner and read permissions for everyone else. The bottom line is that you don't want a default umask that results in files that are writable by the whole wide world.

Checking for set user ID permission

There is another permission setting that can be a security hazard. This permission setting, called the set user ID (or setuid for short), applies to executable files. When the setuid permission is enabled, the file is executed under the user ID of the file's owner. In other words, if an executable program is owned by root and the setuid permission is set, then no matter who executes that program, it runs as if being executed by root. This means that that program can do a lot more (for example, read all files, create new files, and delete files) than what a normal user program could do. Another risk is that if a setuid program file has some security hole, crackers can do a lot more damage through such programs than through other vulnerabilities.

You can find all setuid programs with a simple find command:

```
find / -type f -perm +4000 -print
```

You should see a list of files such as the following:

```
/usr/bin/chage
/usr/bin/gpasswd
/usr/bin/at
/usr/bin/passwd
/usr/bin/chfn
/usr/bin/chsh
/usr/bin/newgrp
/usr/bin/crontab
/usr/bin/lppasswd
/usr/bin/ssh
... lines deleted ...
```

Many of the programs have the `setuid` permission because they need it, but check the complete list and make sure that there are no strange `setuid` programs (for example, `setuid` programs in a user's home directory).

If you want to see how these permissions are listed by the `ls` command, type **ls -l /usr/bin/passwd** and you should see the permission settings:

```
-r-s--x--x  1 root    root    15104 Mar 13 20:44 /usr/bin/passwd
```

The `s` in the owner's permission setting (`r-s`) tells you that the `setuid` permission is set.

Using access control lists

A new way to control access to files and directories is through access control lists (ACLs). As you probably guessed from the name, an *access control list* is basically a list of names of users who can access a file or a directory. There are two commands — `setfacl` and `getfacl` — to set and view the access control lists of a file. For example, to see the access control list of the file `/etc/inittab`, type the following command:

```
getfacl /etc/inittab
```

The output from this command should be similar to the following (and it shows the usual file permissions in a different format):

```
getfacl: Removing leading '/' from absolute path names
# file: etc/inittab
# owner: root
# group: root
user::rw-
group::r--
other::r--
```

With access control lists, you can add as many users as you want to the list and provide each user specific types of access. For example, suppose I want the user `naba` to have read access to the log file `/var/log/messages`. Here's how I can accomplish that with the following `setfacl` command:

```
setfacl -m u:naba:r /var/log/messages
```

To learn more about the `setfacl` command, type **man setfacl** in a terminal window.

Encrypting and Signing Files with GnuPG

Red Hat Linux comes with the *GNU Privacy Guard* (GnuPG or, simply GPG) encryption and authentication utility. With GPG, you can create your public and private key pair, encrypt files using your key, and also digitally sign a message to authenticate that it's really from you. If you send a digitally signed message to someone who has your public key, the recipient can verify that it was you who signed the message.

Understanding public key encryption

The basic idea behind public key encryption is to use a pair of keys — one private and the other public — that are related but one cannot be guessed from the other. Anything encrypted with the private key can be decrypted with the corresponding public key and vice versa. The public key is for distribution to other people while you keep the private key in a safe place.

You can use public key encryption for securely communicating with others. Figure 2-1 illustrates the basic idea. Suppose Alice wants to send secure messages to Bob. Each of them would generate public-private key pairs and exchange their public keys. When Alice wants to send a message to Bob, she simply encrypts the message using Bob's public key and sends the encrypted message to him. Now the message is secure from any eavesdropping because only Bob's private key can decrypt the message, and only Bob has that key. When Bob receives the message, he uses his private key to decrypt the message and read it.

**Book VI
Chapter 2**

Securing the Host

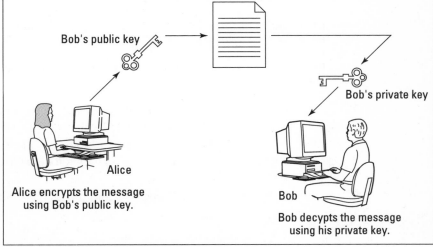

Figure 2-1:
Bob and Alice can communicate securely with public key encryption.

Bob's public key

Bob's private key

Alice

Alice encrypts the message using Bob's public key.

Bob

Bob decypts the message using his private key.

At this point, you should stop and think and say "Wait a minute!" How does Bob know the message really came from Alice? What if someone else uses Bob's public key and sends a message as if it came from Alice? This is where digital signature comes in.

Understanding digital signatures

The purpose of digital or electronic signatures is the same as pen-and-ink signatures, but how you sign digitally is completely different. Unlike pen-and-ink signatures, your digital signature depends on the message you are signing. The first step is to apply a mathematical function on the message and reduce it to a fixed-size message digest (also called *hash*). No matter how big your message is, the message digest is always around 128 or 160 bits, depending on the hashing function.

The next step is to apply public key encryption. Simply encrypt the message digest with your private key, and you get the digital signature for the message. Typically, the digital signature is appended to the end of the message and you got a electronically signed message.

What good does the digital signature do? Well, anyone who wants to verify that the message is indeed signed by you takes your public key and decrypts the digital signature. What they get is the message digest of the message. Then they apply the same hash function to the message and compare the computed hash with the decrypted value. If the two match, no one has tampered with the message. Because your public key was used to verify the signature, the message must have been signed with the private key known only to you. So the message must be from you!

In the theoretical scenario of Alice sending private messages to Bob, Alice can digitally sign her message to make sure that Bob can tell that the message is really from her. Figure 2-2 illustrates the use of digital signature along with normal public key encryption.

Here's how Alice sends her private message to Bob with the assurance that Bob can really tell it's from her:

1. Alice uses some software to compute the message digest of the message and then encrypts the digest using her private key. This is her digital signature for the message.

2. Alice encrypts (again, using some convenient software) the message using Bob's public key.

3. She sends both the encrypted message and the digital signature to Bob.

4. Bob decrypts the message using his private key.

5. Bob decrypts the digital signature using Alice's public key. This gives him the message digest.

6. Bob computes the message digest of the message and compares with what he got by decrypting the digital signature.

7. If the two message digests match, Bob can be sure that the message really came from Alice.

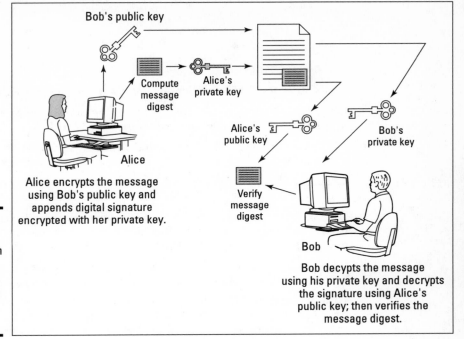

Figure 2-2:
Alice can
digitally sign
her mess-
age so that
Bob can tell
it's really
from her.

Using GPG

GPG includes the tools you need to use public key encryption and digital
signatures. What you use is the gpg command. You can learn to use GPG
gradually as you begin using encryption. I show you some of the typical
tasks you may perform with GPG.

Generating the key pair

The first thing you have to do is generate your own private-public key pair.
Type the following command in a terminal window to generate the key pair:

```
gpg --gen-key
```

If this is your first time with gpg, it creates a .gnupg directory in your home
directory and a file named options in that directory. Then gpg exits with a
message that asks you to run gpg again. Now you can rerun the command.
The steps for generating the key pairs go like this:

1. **Type the** gpg --gen-key **command again.**

You should see a message like this:

```
Please select what kind of key you want:
   (1) DSA and ElGamal (default)
   (2) DSA (sign only)
   (4) ElGamal (sign and encrypt)
   (5) RSA (sign only)
Your selection?
```

2. **Press Enter for the default choice because it's good enough.**

3. **GPG then prompts you for the key size (the number of bits). Again, press enter to accept the default value of 1024 bits.**

4. **GPG asks you when the keys should expire. The default is to never expire. If that's what you want (and why not?), press Enter.**

5. **GPG asks if you really want the keys to never expire. Press y to confirm.**

6. **GPG prompts you for your name, then your e-mail address, and finally a comment so that the key pair can be associated with your name. Type each requested information and press Enter.**

7. **GPG gives you a chance to change the information or confirm it as is. To confirm, type o and then press Enter.**

8. **GPG prompts you for a passphrase that will be used to protect your private key. Type a long phrase that includes lower- and upper-case letters, numbers, and punctuation marks — the longer the better. Careful though; pick a passphrase that you can easily remember as well. Type the passphrase and press Enter.**

9. **GPG generates the keys. It may ask you to perform some work on the PC so that the random number generator can generate enough random numbers for the key-generation process.**

Exchanging keys

To communicate with others, you have to give them your public key. You also have to get public keys from those who may send you a message (or someone who might sign a file and you want to verify the signature). GPG keeps the public keys in your key ring. To list the keys in your key ring, type

```
gpg --list-keys
```

To send your public key to someone or place it on a Web site, you have to export the key to a file. The best way is to put the key in what GPG documentation calls a ASCII-armored format with a command like this:

```
gpg --armor --export naba@comcast.net > nabakey.asc
```

This command saves my public key in an ASCII-armored format (it basically looks like garbled text) in the file named nabakey.asc. Of course, you should replace the e-mail address with your e-mail address (the one you used when you created the key) and the output file name to something different.

After you export the public key to a file, you can mail that file to others or place it in a Web site for use by others.

When you import a key from someone else, you typically get it in an ASCII-armored format as well. For example, if I have Red Hat's GPG public key in a file named `redhatkey.asc`, I would import it into my key ring with the following command:

```
gpg --import redhatkey.asc
```

**Book VI
Chapter 2**

Securing the Host

Use the `gpg --list-keys` to verify that the key is in your key ring. For example, here's what I see when I type `gpg --list-keys` on my system:

```
gpg: please see http://www.gnupg.org/faq.html for more information
/home/naba/.gnupg/pubring.gpg
----------------------------
pub  1024D/CF492215 2002-08-23 Naba Barkakati (Author) <naba@comcast.net>
sub  1024g/47FED643 2002-08-23

pub  1024D/DB42A60E 1999-09-23 Red Hat, Inc <security@redhat.com>
sub  2048g/961630A2 1999-09-23
```

The next step is to check the fingerprint of the new key. I type the following command to get the fingerprint of the Red Hat key:

```
gpg --fingerprint security@redhat.com
```

This causes GPG to print the fingerprint:

```
pub  1024D/DB42A60E 1999-09-23 Red Hat, Inc <security@redhat.com>
    Key fingerprint = CA20 8686 2BD6 9DFC 65F6  ECC4 2191 80CD DB42 A60E
sub  2048g/961630A2 1999-09-23
```

At this point, you should verify the key fingerprint with someone at Red Hat. For a company like Red Hat, you can verify the fingerprint from a Web page (`www.redhat.com/solutions/security/news/publickey.html`). If you think the key fingerprint is good, you can sign the key and validate it. Here's the command you use to sign the key:

```
gpg --sign-key security@redhat.com
```

GPG displays a message and prompts you on the level of key verification you have performed:

```
gpg: Warning: using insecure memory!
gpg: please see http://www.gnupg.org/faq.html for more information
```

```
gpg: checking the trustdb
gpg: checking at depth 0 signed=0 ot(-/q/n/m/f/u)=0/0/0/0/0/1
pub 1024D/DB42A60E created: 1999-09-23 expires: never   trust: -/-
sub 2048g/961630A2 created: 1999-09-23 expires: never
(1). Red Hat, Inc <security@redhat.com>


pub 1024D/DB42A60E created: 1999-09-23 expires: never   trust: -/-
        Fingerprint: CA20 8686 2BD6 9DFC 65F6 ECC4 2191 80CD DB42 A60E

   Red Hat, Inc <security@redhat.com>

How carefully have you verified the key you are about to sign actually belongs
to the person named above? If you don't know what to answer, enter "0".

   (0) I will not answer. (default)
   (1) I have not checked at all.
   (2) I have done casual checking.
   (3) I have done very careful checking.

Your selection?
```

After you answer and press Enter, GPG asks for confirmation and then prompts you for your passphrase. After that GPG signs the key.

Because the key verification and signing is a potential weak link in GPG, be careful about what keys you sign. By signing a key, you basically say that you trust the key to be from that person or organization.

Signing a file

You find it useful to sign files if you send out a file to someone and want to assure the recipient that no one has tampered with the file and that it was you who sent the file. GPG makes it very easy to sign a file. You can compress and sign a file named `message` with the following command:

```
gpg -o message.sig -s message
```

To verify the signature, type

```
gpg --verify message.sig
```

To get back the original document, simply type

```
gpg -o message --decrypt message.sig
```

Sometimes you don't care about keeping a message secret, but simply want to sign it to indicate that the message is from you. In this case, you can generate and append a clear text signature with the following command:

```
gpg -o message.asc --clearsign message
```

This command basically appends a clear text signature to the text message. Here's a typical clear text signature block:

```
-----BEGIN PGP SIGNATURE-----
Version: GnuPG v1.0.7 (GNU/Linux)

iD8DBQE9ZYUtjre6e89JIhURAmUzAKDAK8tdQMRrA2qSpaG8rKpYO5dZuACeI9kT
26EaLE5s/zHDiapiW+geXdo=
=U26+
-----END PGP SIGNATURE-----
```

When a message has a clear text signature appended, you can use GPG to verify the signature with the command like this:

```
gpg --verify message.asc
```

The last line of the output should say that it's good signature.

Encrypting and decrypting documents

To encrypt a message meant for a recipient, you can use the `--encrypt` (or `-e`) GPG command. Here's how you might encrypt a message for me if you had my public GPG key:

```
gpg -o message.gpg -e -r naba@comcast.net message
```

The message would be encrypted using my public key (without any signature, but you can add the signature with an `-s` command).

When I receive the `message.gpg` file, I have to decrypt it using my private key. Here's the command I would use:

```
gpg -o message --decrypt message.gpg
```

GPG then prompts me for the passphrase to unlock my private key and then decrypts the message and saves the output in the file named `message`.

If you simply want to encrypt a file and no one else has to decrypt the file, you can use GPG to perform what is called *symmetric encryption*. In this case, you provide a passphrase to encrypt the file with the following GPG command:

```
gpg -o secret.gpg -c somefile
```

GPG prompts you for the passphrase and asks you to repeat the passphrase (to make sure that you didn't mistype anything). Then GPG encrypts the file using a key generated from the passphrase.

To decrypt a file encrypted with a symmetric key, type

```
gpg -o myfile --decrypt secret.gpg
```

GPG prompts you for the passphrase. If you enter the correct passphrase, GPG decrypts the file and saves the output (in this example) in the file named `myfile`.

Monitoring System Security

Even if you have secured your system, you have to monitor the log files periodically for signs of intrusion. You should also install the Tripwire software to monitor the integrity of critical system files and directories.

I briefly describe how to use Tripwire and what log files to check periodically.

Using Tripwire to monitor the integrity of system files

The worst security breaches are the ones that go undetected. A savvy cracker may manage to get access to a system, replace critical system programs with Trojan Horses, and hide his or her tracks by modifying the log files (the Trojan Horse programs are often called *root kits* because they allow the cracker to get `root` access to your system). Later on, the cracker may use the Trojan Horse programs to access the system at will. The problem is that the system administrator may never even suspect that anything is out of the ordinary. Using software such as Tripwire to monitor file integrity can help avoid this type of problem.

Red Hat Linux comes with the Tripwire package. It is not installed by default, but you can easily install it and configure it to monitor any changes to specified system files and directories.

Installing Tripwire

To install the Tripwire package, place the second CD-ROM in the CD-ROM drive and mount it with the mount `/mnt/cdrom` command (or, if you are running the GNOME desktop, wait until the `magicdev` device automatically mounts the CD-ROM). Then type the following commands to install the Tripwire package:

```
cd /mnt/cdrom/RedHat/RPMS
rpm -ivh tripwire*
```

The Tripwire installation does the following:

+ Installs the programs `siggen`, `tripwire`, `twadmin`, and `twprint` in the `/usr/sbin` directory.

+ Creates the `/etc/tripwire` directory and places some files in it, including the shell script `/etc/tripwire/twinstall.sh`, which you have to run after installing the package.

+ Installs the `tripwire-check` script in the `/etc/cron.daily` directory. This causes the `tripwire-check` script to be executed daily.

+ Installs the man pages for `twconfig`, `twpolicy`, `twfiles`, `siggen`, `tripwire`, `twadmin`, `twintro`, and `twprint`. You can read these man pages with commands, such as `man tripwire`.

+ Installs some Tripwire documentation in the `/usr/share/doc` directory. To change to the Tripwire documentation directory, type **cd /usr/share/doc/tripwire***.

+ Creates the `/var/lib/tripwire/report` directory in which to store Tripwire reports.

**Book VI
Chapter 2**

Securing the Host

After installing the Tripwire package, you have to run the `/etc/tripwire/twinstall.sh` script to generate cryptographic keys. Type the following command:

```
/etc/tripwire/twinstall.sh
```

You have to enter a site passphrase and a local passphrase. The necessary keys are then generated, the policy file is signed, and the Tripwire installation ends with the following message:

```
A clear-text version of the Tripwire policy file
/etc/tripwire/twpol.txt
has been preserved for your inspection.  This implements
a minimal policy, intended only to test essential
Tripwire functionality.  You should edit the policy file
to describe your system, and then use twadmin to generate
a new signed copy of the Tripwire policy.
```

You can examine the `/etc/tripwire/twpol.txt` file to see how Tripwire policy is specified. The policy file identifies the program and configuration files that are critical to system security. Tripwire then periodically checks the integrity of these files.

Initializing the Tripwire database

After installing Tripwire, you have to initialize the Tripwire database with the following command:

```
/usr/sbin/tripwire --init
```

Tripwire prompts you for the local passphrase and then works for a while as it creates a database file.

You may get a few error messages for files that are not in your system but are referred to in the Tripwire policy file /etc/tripwire/twpol.txt. At the end of all the processing, Tripwire writes a database file named after your system's hostname and saves that file in the /var/lib/tripwire directory. The database file is digitally signed with the key generated during the step when you ran the /etc/tripwire/twinstall.sh script (a digital signature is a hash of a file's contents, encrypted with the local private key — the hash is a fixed-length binary number computed with a mathematical function such as the MD5 or SHA-1).

Checking file integrity

After the Tripwire database is initialized, you should periodically run Tripwire in integrity-checking mode with the command /usr/sbin/tripwire --check. In this mode, Tripwire uses the policy file, /etc/tripwire/tw.pol, and compares the state of the current files against what's stored in the initial database. Tripwire prints a report on the standard output and saves the report in the /var/lib/tripwire/report directory.

For example, when I log in as root and type the following command

```
/usr/sbin/tripwire --check
```

Tripwire displays some error messages about missing files (the same ones I get when I initialize the Tripwire database with the /usr/sbin/tripwire --init command). After that, Tripwire prints the report to the standard output and writes it to a file.

The name of the Tripwire report file depends on your system's host name and the date and time when you run the /usr/sbin/tripwire --check command. You can see the report files in the /var/lib/tripwire/report directory.

Each report file's name is created by appending the date and time to the host name, with dashes as separators, and then appending a .twr as file extension. The report is in binary format. To print the report, follow these steps:

1. **Change the directory to the Tripwire report directory by typing**

   ```
   cd /var/lib/tripwire/report
   ```

2. **Use the ls command to look at the list of report files in that directory.**

3. **Print the report using the** `/usr/sbin/twprint` **command with the following syntax:**

   `/usr/sbin/twprint --print-report -r reportfilename.twr`

   Replace `reportfilename.twr` with the report that you want to view. If it's scrolling by too fast, simply pipe the output through the `more` command (append | `more` to the command).

The Tripwire report file lists any violations of the Tripwire policy — basically any files that have changed since the last time the Tripwire database was generated. You should always verify that the changes are expected and not suspicious.

Book VI
Chapter 2

Securing the Host

When you install Tripwire, your system is already set up to run the `/etc/cron.daily/tripwire-check` script every day. The `/etc/cron.daily/tripwire-check` script executes the `/usr/sbin/tripwire --check` command to generate a report. All you need to do is log in as `root` and use the `/usr/sbin/twprint` command to review the latest report each day.

Examining log files

Many Red Hat Linux applications, including some servers, write log information using the logging capabilities of `syslogd`. On Red Hat Linux systems, the log files written by `syslogd` reside in the `/var/log` directory. Make sure that only the `root` user can read and write these files.

The `syslogd` configuration file is `/etc/syslog.conf`. The default configuration of `syslogd` should generate the necessary log files; however, if you want to examine and understand the configuration file, type **man syslog.conf** for more information.

You should routinely monitor the following log files:

✦ `/var/log/messages` contains a wide variety of logging messages, from user logins to messages from services started by the TCP wrapper.

✦ `/var/log/secure` contains reports from services, such as `in.telnetd` and `in.ftpd`, which `xinetd` starts through the TCP wrapper.

✦ `/var/log/maillog` contains reports from sendmail.

✦ `/var/log/xferlog` contains a log of all FTP file transfers.

Red Hat Linux comes with a graphical log file viewer utility. To use this tool, select Main Menu⇨System Tools⇨System Logs from the GNOME panel. Figure 2-3 shows the System Logs utility.

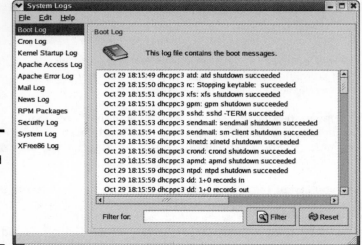

Figure 2-3:
Use the Red
Hat System
Log Files
utility to
view log
files.

The System Logs utility is simple to use. Click the log file name on the
left-hand window and view the contents in the scrolling text window to
the right.

Because many potential intruders use port-scanning tools in an attempt
to establish TCP/IP connections to well-known ports on your system,
you should look for messages that indicate attempted connections from
unknown hosts (indicated by names or IP addresses). To do this, click
Security Log on the left window and then browse the log messages that
appear in the right-hand window. You'll see lines such as the following:

```
Aug 24 15:35:36 dhcppc5 xinetd[11348]: START: telnet pid=11557 from=192.168.0.4
Aug 24 16:31:11 dhcppc5 xinetd[11348]: START: ftp pid=11689 from=192.168.0.4
```

These lines show you the type of connection (telnet, ftp, etc.) and the IP
addresses from where the connections originated. If you want to browse
through these messages using a text editor, they are in the
/var/log/secure file.

Chapter 3: Securing the Network

In This Chapter

✔ Securing Internet services

✔ Using Secure Shell (SSH) for secure remote logins

✔ Setting up simple firewalls

✔ Enabling packet filtering on your Red Hat Linux system

To secure your Red Hat Linux system, you have to pay attention to both host security and network security. The distinction between the two types of security is somewhat arbitrary because securing the network involves fixing up things on the host that relate to what Internet services your system offers. In this chapter, I explain how you can secure the Internet services (mostly by not offering unnecessary services), how you can use a firewall to stop unwanted network packets from reaching your network, and how to use Secure Shell for secure remote logins.

Securing Internet Services

For an Internet-connected Red Hat Linux system (or even one on a TCP/IP LAN that's not connected to the Internet), a significant threat is the possibility that someone will use one of many Internet services to gain access to your system. Each service — such as mail, Web, or FTP — requires running a server program that responds to client requests arriving over the TCP/IP network. Some of these server programs have weaknesses that can allow an outsider to log in to your system — maybe with `root` privileges. Luckily, Red Hat Linux comes with some facilities that you can use to make the Internet services more secure.

Potential intruders can employ a port-scanning tool — a program that attempts to establish a TCP/IP connection at a port and to look for a response — to check which Internet servers are running on your system. Then, to gain access to your system, the intruders can potentially exploit any known weaknesses of one or more services.

Using the chkconfig command to disable stand-alone services

To provide Internet services such as Web, mail, and FTP, your Red Hat Linux system has to run server programs that listen to incoming TCP/IP network requests. Some of these servers are started when your system boots, and they run all the time. We call such servers *stand-alone servers.* The Web server and mail server are examples of stand-alone servers. The other servers are started on demand by another server called xinetd.

You can turn the stand-alone servers on or off using the chkconfig command. Here's how you should use chkconfig to stop unneeded services:

✦ Log in as root and type **chkconfig --list** to view all the services set to start automatically at run levels 0 through 6.

✦ The services for run levels 3 and 5 matter most because your Red Hat Linux system is usually at run level 3 (text mode) or 5 (graphical login). Type **runlevel** to see the current run level.

✦ Decide which services you don't need. What you need or don't need depends on how you use your Red Hat Linux system. For example, if it's just a personal workstation, you don't need to run most services.

✦ To stop a service, use the following form of the chkconfig command:

```
chkconfig --level 345 service_name off
```

where *service_name*, is the name of the service you want to turn off. For example, to prevent the ypserv service from automatically starting at run levels 3, 4, and 5, type the following command:

```
chkconfig --level 345 ypserv off
```

Using this approach you can stop all unneeded services from starting at boot time by using chkconfig.

To immediately stop a service, use the service command like this:

```
service service_name stop
```

where *service_name* is the name of the service to stop. For example, if the mail server (sendmail) is already running, you can stop it with the command:

```
service sendmail stop
```

Configuring the xinetd server to disable services

In addition to the stand-alone servers such as Web server (httpd), mail (sendmail), and domain name server (named), you have to configure another server separately. That other server, xinetd (the Internet super server), starts a host of other Internet services, such as FTP, TELNET, and so on whenever a client makes a request over the network. The xinetd server includes some security features that you can use to disable the services that it can start on demand.

The xinetd server reads a configuration file named /etc/xinetd.conf at startup. This file, in turn, refers to configuration files stored in the /etc/xinetd.d directory. The configuration files in /etc/xinetd.d tell xinetd which ports to listen to and which server to start for each port. Type **ls /etc/xinetd.d** to see a list of the files in /etc/xinetd.d directory on your system. On my system, here's what the ls /etc/xinetd.d command lists:

```
chargen    echo    imaps pop3s  rsync    talk    vsftpd

chargen-udp echo-udp ipop2 rexec   servers   telnet

daytime    finger  ipop3 rlogin services time

daytime-udp imap    ntalk rsh   sgi_fam  time-udp
```

**Book VI
Chapter 3**

**Securing
the Network**

This list shows all the services xinetd can start. However, the configuration file for a service can also turn off a service simply by having a disable = yes line in the file. For example, here's the telnet file's content:

```
# default: on
# description: The telnet server serves telnet sessions;
#      it uses unencrypted username/password pairs for
#      authentication.
service telnet
{
        flags           = REUSE
        socket_type     = stream
        wait            = no
        user            = root
        server          = /usr/sbin/in.telnetd
        log_on_failure  += USERID
        disable         = yes
}
```

Notice the last line in the configuration file — that line disables the TELNET service.

I won't explain the format of the xinetd configuration files, except to reiterate that you can turn off a service simply by adding the following line in the configuration file somewhere between the two curly braces { ... }:

```
        disable         = yes
```

Depending on how you use your system, you may be able to disable many of the services. If you do not want anyone to log in remotely or download files from your system, simply disable the TELNET and FTP services.

After you make any changes to the `xinetd` configuration files, you must restart the `xinetd` server; otherwise the changes won't take effect. To restart the `xinetd` server, type the following command:

```
service xinetd restart
```

This stops the `xinetd` server and then starts it again. When it restarts, it'll read the configuration files, and the changes will take effect.

Another security feature of `xinetd` is its use of the TCP wrapper to start various services. The TCP wrapper provides an access-control facility for Internet services. The TCP wrapper can start other services, such as FTP and TELNET; but before starting a service, it consults the `/etc/hosts.allow` file to see if the host requesting service is allowed that service. If nothing appears in `/etc/hosts.allow` about that host, TCP wrapper checks the `/etc/hosts.deny` file to see if it should deny the service. If both files are empty, TCP wrapper provides access to the requested service.

Here are the steps to follow to tighten the access to the services that `xinetd` is configured to start:

1. **Use a text editor to edit the** `/etc/hosts.deny` **file, adding the following line into that file:**

   ```
   ALL:ALL
   ```

   This denies all hosts access to any Internet services on your system.

2. **Edit the** `/etc/hosts.allow` **file and add to it the names of hosts that can access services on your system.**

   For example, to enable only hosts from the 192.168.1.0 network and the `localhost` (IP address 127.0.0.1) access the services on your system, and place the following line in the `/etc/hosts.allow` file:

   ```
   ALL: 192.168.1.0/255.255.255.0 127.0.0.1
   ```

3. **If you want to permit access to a specific Internet service to a specific remote host, you can do so using the following syntax for a line in** `/etc/hosts.allow`**:**

   ```
   server_program_name: hosts
   ```

   Here, *server_program_name* is the name of the server program (for example, `in.telnetd` for TELNET and `vsftpd` for FTP), and *hosts* is a comma-separated list of hosts that can access the service. You may also

write *hosts* as a network address or an entire domain name, such as
`.mycompany.com`. For example, here's how you can give TELNET access
to all systems in the `mycompany.com` domain:

```
in.telnetd: .mycompany.com
```

Edit configuration files in `/etc/xinetd.d` directory to turn off unneeded
services and use the `/etc/hosts.deny` and `/etc/hosts.allow` files to
control access to the services that are allowed to run on your system. After
you edit the files in the `/etc/xinetd.d` directory, remember to type **service xinetd restart** to restart the `xinetd` server.

Using Secure Shell (SSH) for Remote Logins

Red Hat Linux comes with the *Open Secure Shell* (OpenSSH) software, a suite
of programs that provides a secure replacement for the Berkeley `r` commands: `rlogin` (remote login), `rsh` (remote shell), and `rcp` (remote copy).
OpenSSH uses public-key cryptography to authenticate users and to
encrypt the communication between two hosts, so users can securely log in
from remote systems and copy files securely.

In this section, I briefly describe how to use the OpenSSH software in Red
Hat Linux. To learn more about OpenSSH and read the latest news about it,
visit `www.openssh.com` or `www.openssh.org`.

The OpenSSH software is installed during Red Hat Linux installation. Table
3-1 lists the main components of the OpenSSH software.

Table 3-1	Components of the OpenSSH Software
Component	*Description*
`/usr/sbin/sshd`	The Secure Shell daemon that must run on a host if you want users on remote systems to use the `ssh` client to log in securely. When a connection from an `ssh` client arrives, `sshd` performs authentication using public-key cryptography and establishes an encrypted communication link with the `ssh` client.
`/usr/bin/ssh`	The Secure Shell client that users can run to log in to a host that is running `sshd`. Users can also use `ssh` to execute a command on another host.
`/usr/bin/slogin`	A symbolic link to `/usr/bin/ssh`.
`/usr/bin/scp`	The secure copy program that works like `rcp`, but securely. The `scp` program uses `ssh` for data transfer and provides the same authentication and security as `ssh`.

(continued)

Table 3-1 (continued)

Component	Description
/usr/bin/ssh-keygen	The program you use to generate the public and private key pairs you need for the public-key cryptography used in OpenSSH. The ssh-keygen program can generate key pairs for both RSA and DSA (Digital Signature Algorithm) authentication.
/etc/ssh/sshd_config	The configuration file for the sshd server. This file specifies many parameters for sshd, including the port to listen to, the protocol to use (there are two versions of SSH protocols, SSH1 and SSH2, both supported by OpenSSH), and the location of other files.
/etc/ssh/ssh_config	The configuration file for the ssh client. Each user can also have a ssh configuration file named config in the .ssh subdirectory of the user's home directory.

OpenSSH uses public-key encryption where the sender and receiver both have a pair of keys — a public key and a private key. The public keys are freely distributed, and each party knows the other's public key. The sender encrypts data by using the recipient's public key. Only the recipient's private key can then decrypt those data.

To use OpenSSH, do the following:

✦ If you want to support SSH-based remote logins on a host, start the sshd server on your system. Type **ps ax | grep sshd** to see if the server is already running. If not, log in as root, and type the following command at the shell prompt to ensure that the sshd server starts at system reboot:

```
chkconfig --add sshd
```

To start the sshd server immediately, type the following command:

```
service sshd start
```

✦ Generate the host keys with the following command:

```
ssh-keygen -d -f /etc/ssh/ssh_host_key -N ''
```

The -d flag causes the ssh-keygen program to generate DSA keys, which the SSH2 protocol uses. If you see a message saying that the file /etc/ssh/ssh_host_key already exists, that means that the key pairs were generated during Red Hat Linux installation. You can then use the existing file without having to regenerate the keys.

A user who wants to log in using ssh has to generate the public-private key pair also. For example, here is what I do so that I can log in from another system on my Red Hat Linux system using SSH:

1. I type the following command to generate the DSA keys for use with SSH2:

```
ssh-keygen -d
```

I am prompted for a passphrase and the last message informs me that my public key is saved in `/home/naba/.ssh/id_dsa.pub`.

2. I copy my public key — the `/home/naba/.ssh/id_dsa.pub` file — to the remote system and save it as the `~/.ssh/authorized_keys2` file (this refers to the `authorized_keys2` file in the `.ssh` subdirectory of the other system, assuming that the remote system is also another Red Hat Linux system). Note that the *2* in the name of the `authorized_keys2` file refers to the SSH2 protocol.

3. To log into my account on my Red Hat Linux system (with hostname `lnbp200`), I type the following command on the remote system:

```
ssh lnbp200 -l naba
```

I can also login to this account with the following equivalent command:

```
ssh naba@lnbp200
```

If I simply want to copy a file securely from the `lnbp200` system, I can use `scp` like this:

```
scp lnbp200:/etc/ssh/ssh_config .
```

This command securely copies the `/etc/ssh/ssh_config` file from the `lnbp200` host to the system from which I type the command.

Setting Up Simple Firewalls

An Internet *firewall* is an intermediary between your internal network and the Internet. The firewall controls access to and from the protected internal network.

If you connect an internal network directly to the Internet, you have to make sure that every system on the internal network is properly secured — which can be nearly impossible, because it takes only one careless user to render the entire internal network vulnerable. A firewall is a single point of connection to the Internet: You can direct all of your efforts toward making that firewall system a daunting barrier to unauthorized external users.

To be useful, a firewall should have the following general characteristics:

✦ It must control the flow of packets between the Internet and the internal network.

✦ It must not provide dynamic routing, because dynamic routing tables are subject to route *spoofing* — use of fake routes by intruders. Instead, the firewall should use static routing tables (which you can set up with the `route` command on Red Hat Linux systems).

✦ It must not allow any external user to log in as `root`. That way, even if the firewall system is compromised, the intruder may not be able to become `root` from a remote login.

✦ It must be kept in a physically secure location.

✦ It must distinguish between packets that come from the Internet and packets that come from the internal protected network. This feature allows the firewall to reject packets that come from the Internet, but have the IP address of a trusted system on the internal network (an attack wherein packets use fake IP addresses is known as *IP spoofing*).

✦ It should act as the SMTP mail gateway for the internal network. The sendmail software should be set up so that all outgoing mail appears to come from the firewall system.

✦ It should not have any user accounts. However, the firewall system may need to have a few user accounts for those internal users who need access to external systems. External users who need access to the internal network should use SSH for remote login (see discussion of SSH earlier in this chapter).

✦ It should keep a log of all system activities, such as successful and unsuccessful login attempts.

✦ It should provide DNS name-lookup service to the outside world to resolve any host names that should be known to the outside world.

✦ It should provide good performance so that it does not hinder the internal users' access to specific Internet services (such as HTTP and FTP).

A firewall can take many different forms. Here are three common forms of a firewall:

✦ **Screening router with packet filtering:** This simple firewall uses a router capable of filtering (blocking) packets based on IP addresses.

✦ **Dual-homed host with proxy services:** In this case, a host with two network interfaces — one on the Internet and the other on the internal network — runs proxy services that act as a gateway for services, such as FTP and HTTP.

✦ **Perimeter network with bastion host:** This firewall configuration includes a perimeter network between the Internet and the protected internal network. A secure bastion host resides on the perimeter network and provides various services.

In a large organization, you may also need to isolate smaller internal networks from the corporate network. You can set up such internal firewalls the same way you set up Internet firewalls.

In the next few sections, I describe the common forms of a firewall: screening router with packet filtering, dual-homed host, perimeter network with bastion host, and application gateway.

Screening the router with packet filtering

If you were to directly connect your organization's internal network to the Internet, you would have to use a router to ensure proper exchange of packets between the internal network and the Internet. Most routers can block a packet based on its source or its destination IP address (as well as port number). The router's packet-filtering capability can serve as a simple firewall. Figure 3-1 illustrates the basic concept of packet filtering.

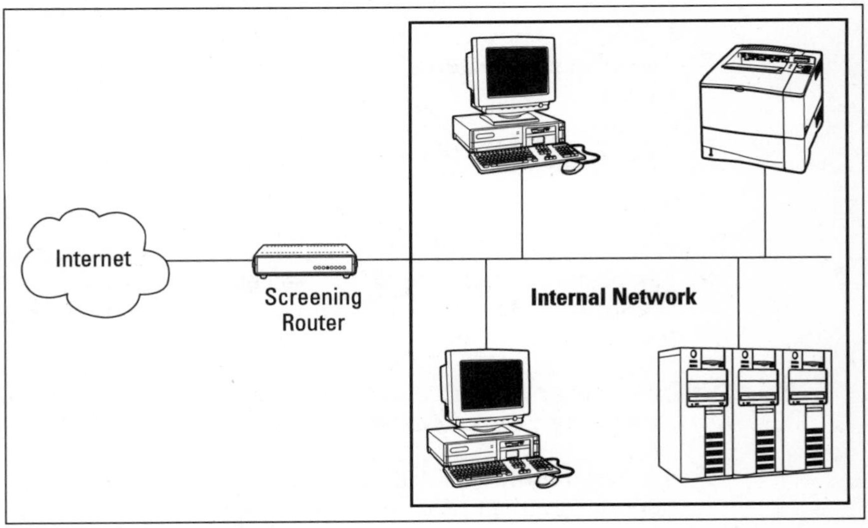

Figure 3-1:
Packet
filtering with
a screening
router
provides a
simple
firewall.

Internet

Screening
Router

Internal Network

Many router vendors, such as Cisco and 3Com, offer routers that can be programmed to perform packet filtering. The exact details of filtering depend on the router vendor, but all routers operate according to rules that refer to the basic attributes of an Internet packet:

✦ Source IP address

✦ Destination IP address

+ Protocol (TCP, UDP, or ICMP)

+ Source port number (if protocol is TCP or UDP)

+ Destination port number (if protocol is TCP or UDP)

+ ICMP message type

In addition, the router knows the physical interface on which the packet arrived and the interface on which the packet will go out (if it is not blocked by the filtering rules).

Most packet filters operate in the following sequence:

1. You define the rules for allowing or blocking specific types of packets based on IP addresses and port numbers. These packet-filtering rules are stored in the router.

2. The screening router examines the header of each packet that arrives for the information (such as IP addresses and port numbers) to which your rules apply.

3. The screening router applies the rules in the order in which they are stored.

4. If a rule allows the packet to be forwarded, the router sends the packet to its destination.

5. If a rule blocks the packet, the router drops the packet (stops processing it).

6. If none of the rules applies, the packet is blocked. This rule epitomizes the security philosophy that one should "deny unless expressly permitted."

Although packet filtering with a screening router is better than no security, packet filtering suffers from the following drawbacks:

+ It is easy for the network administrator to introduce errors inadvertently into the filtering rules.

+ Packets are filtered on the basis of IP addresses, which represent specific hosts. Essentially, packet filtering either blocks or routes all packets from a specific host. That means that anyone who breaks into a trusted host can immediately gain access to your protected network.

+ Because it is based on IP addresses, packet filtering can be defeated by a technique known as *IP spoofing,* whereby a cracker sends packets with the IP address of a trusted host (by appropriating the IP address of a trusted host and setting up an appropriate route).

✦ Packet filtering is susceptible to routing-attack programs that can create a bogus route that allows an intruder to receive all packets meant for the protected internal network.

✦ Screening routers that implement packet filtering do not keep logs of activities. That makes it hard for you to determine if anyone is attempting to break into the protected network. As you see in the next section, a dual-homed host can provide logging.

✦ A screening router does not hide the host names and IP addresses of the internal network. Outsiders can access and use this information to mount attacks against the protected network.

A more sophisticated approach is to use an application gateway that controls network traffic, based on specific applications instead of on a per-packet basis. You can implement an application gateway with a dual-homed host, known also as a *bastion host*.

Dual-homed host

A *dual-homed host* is a system with two network interfaces — one connected to the Internet and the other on an internal network that needs protection. The term "dual-homed" refers to the fact that the host "lives" in two networks.

In fact, if your operating system supports IP routing — the ability to forward network packets from one interface to another — the dual-homed host can serve as a router. However, you must turn off the IP forwarding feature to use the dual-homed host as a firewall system.

The Linux kernel supports the IP forwarding feature. If you plan to use a dual-homed host as a firewall, you have to use the `sysctl` command to disable IP forwarding.

With IP forwarding turned off, systems on both networks — the internal network as well as the Internet — can reach the dual-homed host, but no one from the Internet can access the internal network (nor can anyone from the internal network access the Internet). In this configuration, the dual-homed host completely isolates the two networks. Figure 3-2 shows the basic architecture of a dual-homed host.

The dual-homed host is turned into a firewall by running application gateways — proxy services — on the dual-homed host. These proxy services allow specific applications, such as FTP and HTTP, to work across the dual-homed host. That means that you can configure the firewall so that internal clients (on the internal network) are able to access Web and FTP servers on the Internet.

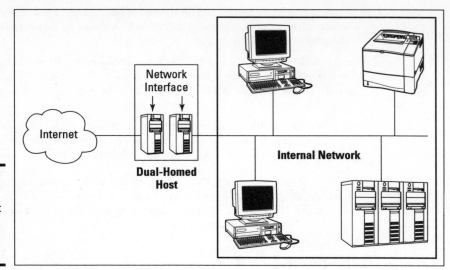

Figure 3-2:
A dual-homed host can act as an Internet firewall.

Your public Web site can also run on the dual-homed host and be accessible to everyone on the Internet.

Don't allow user logins on the dual-homed host. Anyone logged into the host can have access to both the internal network as well as the Internet. Because the dual-homed host is your only barrier between the Internet and the internal network, it's best not to increase the chances of a break-in by allowing users to login to the firewall system. By having user accounts, you increase the chances of an intruder gaining access to the firewall by cracking a user's password.

Perimeter network with bastion host

An Internet firewall is often more complicated than a single dual-homed host that connects to both the Internet and the protected internal network. In particular, if you provide a number of Internet services, you may need more than one system to host them. Imagine that you have two systems: one to run the Web and FTP servers and the other to provide mail (SMTP) and domain name system (DNS) lookups. In this case, you place these two systems on a network that sits between the Internet and the internal network. Figure 3-3 illustrates this concept of an Internet firewall.

In this case, the firewall includes a perimeter network that connects to the Internet through an exterior router. The perimeter network, in turn, connects to the internal network through an interior router. The perimeter network has one or more hosts that run Internet services, including proxy services that allow internal hosts to access Web servers on the Internet.

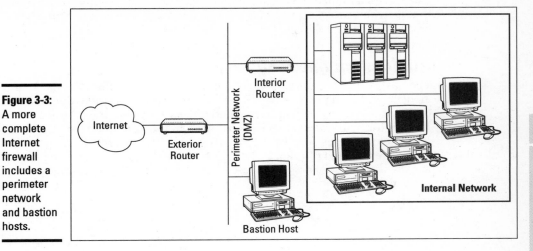

Figure 3-3: A more complete Internet firewall includes a perimeter network and bastion hosts.

The term *bastion host* refers to any system on the perimeter network, because such a system is on the Internet and has to be well fortified. The dual-homed host is also a bastion host because the dual-homed host is also accessible from the Internet and has to be protected.

In the firewall configuration shown in Figure 3-3, the perimeter network is known as a DMZ (demilitarized zone) network because that network acts as a buffer between the Internet and the internal network (just as the real-life DMZ is a buffer between North and South Korea).

Usually, you would combine a packet-filtering router with a bastion host. Your Internet Service Provider typically provides the external router, which means you do not have much control over that router's configuration. But you provide the internal router, which means you can choose a screening router and employ some packet-filtering rules. For example, you might employ the following packet-filtering rules:

✦ From the internal network, allow only packets addressed to the bastion host.

✦ From the DMZ, allow only packets originating from the bastion host.

✦ Block all other packets.

This ensures that the internal network communicates only with the bastion host (or hosts).

Like the dual-homed host, the bastion host also runs an application gateway that provides proxy services for various Internet services, such as TELNET, FTP, SMTP, and HTTP.

Application gateway

The bastion host or the dual-homed host is the system that acts as the intermediary between the Internet and the protected internal network. As such, that system serves as the internal network's gateway to the Internet. Toward this end, the system runs software to forward and filter TCP/IP packets for various services, such as TELNET, FTP, and HTTP. The software for forwarding and filtering TCP/IP packets for specific applications are known as *proxy services*. Figure 3-4 illustrates a proxy server's role in a firewall.

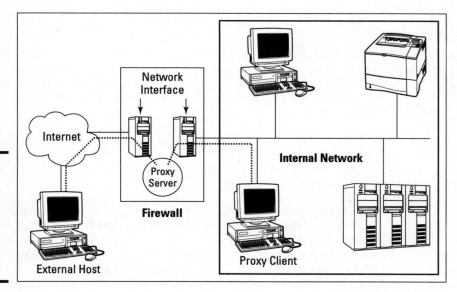

Figure 3-4: A proxy server lets internal hosts access Internet servers.

A proxy server accepts a connection for a specific protocol, such as FTP, and forwards the request to another server. In other words, the proxy server acts as a proxy for an actual server. Because it acts as a gateway for a specific application (such as HTTP or FTP), a proxy server is also known as an *application gateway*.

Unlike a screening router, which blocks packets only on the basis of information in the packet header (such as source and destination IP addresses), a proxy server uses the packet's data to decide what to do. For example, a proxy server does not blindly forward packets to an Internet service. The proxy server can enforce a site's security policy and disallow certain operations, depending on the specific application. For example, an FTP proxy server may prevent users from internal networks from using the FTP put command to send files to the Internet.

Accessing an Internet service through a proxy server can be a bit more involved than accessing that service directly. For example, a user on the internal network establishes a TELNET session with an Internet host with the following steps:

1. The user establishes a TELNET session with the firewall host — the system that runs the TELNET proxy. To do this, the user has to enter a username and password so that the firewall host can verify that the user has permission to connect to the Internet.

2. The user enters a command (which the TELNET proxy accepts) to connect to the Internet host. The TELNET proxy, in turn, establishes a TELNET connection between itself and the Internet host.

3. The TELNET proxy on the firewall begins passing packets back and forth between the Internet host and the user's system (until the user ends the TELNET session with the Internet host).

Besides acting as a gateway, the TELNET proxy also logs the user's session with the Internet host. The logging is part of an application gateway's security feature because the log file keeps track of all firewall accesses (as well as attempted accesses that may fail because of a wrong username or password).

Although the TELNET session involves two steps — first TELNET to the firewall host and then connect to the Internet host — the process of accessing services through a proxy need not be too cumbersome. The exact steps you take to access services through a firewall depend on the proxy software and the client program you use to access a service. With the right client program, proxies can be transparent to the user. For example, many Web browsers make it easy to access a Web site through an HTTP proxy. All you need to do is indicate through a menu choice the HTTP proxy you want to use.

Enabling Packet Filtering on Your Red Hat Linux System

Your Red Hat Linux system comes with built-in packet-filtering software in the form of something called netfilter that's in the Linux kernel. All you have to do is use the `iptables` command to set up the rules for what happens to the packets based on the IP addresses in their header and the network connection type.

The built-in packet-filtering capability is handy when you do not have a dedicated firewall between your Red Hat Linux system and the Internet. This is the case, for example, when you connect your Red Hat system to the Internet through a DSL or cable modem. You can essentially have a packet-filtering firewall inside your Red Hat Linux system, sitting between the kernel and the applications.

Using the security level configuration tool

You can turn on different levels of packet filtering through the graphical Security Level Configuration tool. To run the tool, log in as `root` and select Main Menu⇨System Settings⇨Security Level. The Security Level Configuration window appears (Figure 3-5).

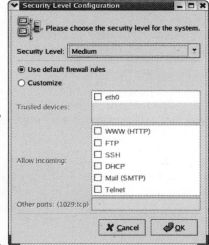

Figure 3-5: You can set up predefined levels of packet filtering with this tool.

You can select three predefined levels of simple firewalling (more precisely, packet filtering) with the Security Level Configuration tool:

✦ **High** — Rejects all connection requests except DNS (for querying IP addresses corresponding to names) and DHCP (for obtaining an IP address for a network interface).

✦ **Medium** — Rejects connection requests to ports lower than 1023 (these are the standard reserved ports used by Internet services such as FTP,

SSH, TELNET, and HTTP). Some other ports used by NFS, the X Window System, and the X Font Server are also blocked.

✦ **No firewall** — Does not perform any filtering, and all connections are allowed (you can still turn off Internet services by not running the servers or disabling them in the xinetd configuration files). This security level is fine if your Red Hat Linux system is inside a protected local area network.

With High and Medium settings, you can also click the Customize radio button and then select one or more trusted devices (network interfaces) or allow incoming packets meant for specific Internet services such as SSH, TELNET, and FTP. If you select a network interface such as eth0 (the first Ethernet card) as trusted, then all network traffic over that interface will be allowed without any filtering.

Using iptables command

It is somewhat complex to use the iptables command. iptables uses the concept of a chain, which is a sequence of rules. Each rule says what to do with a packet if the header contains certain information (such as the source or destination IP address). If a rule does not apply, iptables consults the next rule in the chain. By default, there are three chains:

✦ **INPUT** chain — The first set of rules against which packets are tested. The packets continue to the next chain only if the input chain does not specify DROP or REJECT.

✦ **FORWARD** chain — Contains the rules that apply to packets attempting to pass through this system to another system (for example, when you use as Red Hat Linux system as a router between your LAN and the Internet).

✦ **OUTPUT** chain — Includes the rules applied to packets before they are sent out (either to another network or to an application).

You can add rules to these chains or create new chains of rules by using the iptables command. You can also view the current chains and save them to a file. For example, if you have done nothing else, the iptables -L command should show the following:

```
Chain INPUT (policy ACCEPT)
target     prot opt source              destination

Chain FORWARD (policy ACCEPT)
target     prot opt source              destination

Chain OUTPUT (policy ACCEPT)
target     prot opt source              destination
```

In this case, all three chains — INPUT, FORWARD, and OUTPUT — show the same ACCEPT policy, which means everything is wide open.

If you are setting up a packet filter, the first thing you do is specify the packets that you want to accept. For example, to accept packets from the 192.168.0.0 network, add the following rule to the input chain:

```
iptables -A INPUT -s 192.168.0.0/24 -j ACCEPT
```

Now add a rule to drop everything except local loopback (the lo network interface) traffic and stop all forwarding with the following commands:

```
iptables -A INPUT -i ! lo -j REJECT
iptables -A forward -j REJECT
```

The first iptables command, for example, appends to the input chain (-A INPUT) the rule that if the packet does not come from the lo interface (-i ! lo), iptables should reject the packet (-j REJECT).

Before rejecting all other packets, you may also add more rules to each of the INPUT chain to allow specific packets in. You can select packets to accept or reject based on many different parameters such as IP addresses, protocol types (TCP, UDP), network interface, port numbers.

Don't type iptables commands from a remote login session. A rule that begins denying packets from all addresses can also stop what you type from reaching the system; once that happens, you may have no way of accessing the system over the network. To avoid unpleasant surprises, always type iptables rules at the console — the keyboard and monitor that are connected directly to your Red Hat Linux PC that is running the packet filter.

I won't provide all the details of the iptables commands in this section. Type **man iptables** to read a summary of the commands. You can also read about netfilter and iptables at www.iptables.org.

After you define the rules by using the iptables command, they are in the memory and will be gone when you reboot the system. To save them, use the iptables-save command to store the rules in a file. For example, you can save the rules in a file named iptables.rules by using the following commands:

```
iptables-save > iptables.rules
```

Here's a listing of the iptables.rules file, generated on a Red Hat Linux system:

```
# Generated by iptables-save v1.2.6a on Sun Aug 25 10:43:54 2002
*nat
:PREROUTING ACCEPT [31:3150]
:POSTROUTING ACCEPT [13:2434]
:OUTPUT ACCEPT [13:2434]
COMMIT
# Completed on Sun Aug 25 10:43:54 2002
# Generated by iptables-save v1.2.6a on Sun Aug 25 10:43:54 2002
*filter
:INPUT ACCEPT [24:2828]
:FORWARD ACCEPT [0:0]
:OUTPUT ACCEPT [127:19047]
-A INPUT -s 192.168.0.0/255.255.255.0 -j ACCEPT
-A INPUT -i ! lo -j DROP
-A FORWARD -j DROP
COMMIT
# Completed on Sun Aug 25 10:43:54 2002
```

If you want to load these saved rules into `iptables`, use the following command:

```
iptables-restore < iptables.rules
```

On a Red Hat Linux system, the process of saving and restoring firewall rules is automated by saving the `iptables` rules in the file `/etc/sysconfig/iptables` and by enabling `iptables` with the following command:

```
chkconfig iptables on
```

That should ensure that the `/etc/init.d/iptables start` command is executed at system startup. The `/etc/init.d/iptables` script then runs the `/sbin/iptables-restore` command to restore the `iptables` rules from the `/etc/sysconfig/iptables` file.

Chapter 4: Performing Security Audits

In This Chapter

✔ **Understanding computer security audits**

✔ **Learning a security test methodology**

✔ **Reviewing host and network security**

✔ **Exploring security testing tools**

You see the term "audit" and you think tax audit, right? Well, there are many different types of audits, and one of them is computer security audit. The purpose of a computer security audit is to basically test your system and network security. For larger organizations, the security audit may be done by an independent auditor (much like the auditing of financial statements). If you have only a few Red Hat Linux systems or a small network, you can do the security audit as a self-assessment, just to figure out if you are doing everything okay or not.

In this chapter, I explain how to perform computer security audits and show you a number of free tools and resources to help you test your system's security.

Understanding Security Audits

An *audit* is simply an independent assessment of whatever it is you are auditing. So a computer security audit is an independent assessment of computer security. If someone is conducting a computer security audit of your organization, he or she focuses typically on two areas:

✦ Independent verification of whether your organization is complying with its existing policies and procedures for computer security. This is the nontechnical part of the security audit.

✦ Independent testing of how effective your security controls (any hardware and software mechanisms you use to secure the system) are. This is the technical part of the security audit.

Why do we need security audits? We need them for the same reason we need financial audits — mainly to verify that everything is being done the way it is supposed to be done. For public as well as private organizations, management may want independent security audits to assure themselves that their security is A-OK. Irrespective of your organization's size, you can always perform security audits on your own, either to prepare for independent security audits or simply to know that you're doing everything right.

No matter whether you have independent security audits or a self-assessment, here are some of the benefits you get from security audits:

+ Periodic risk assessments that consider internal and external threats to systems and data.

+ Periodic testing of the effectiveness of security policies, security controls, and techniques.

+ Identification of any significant deficiencies in your system's security (so you know what to fix).

+ In case of self-assessments, preparation for any annual independent security testing that your organization might have to face.

Nontechnical aspects

The nontechnical side of computer security audits focuses on your organizationwide security framework. The audit examines how well the organization has set up and implemented the policies, plans, and procedures for computer security. Some of the items to be verified include

+ Risks are periodically assessed.

+ There is an entitywide security program plan.

+ A security program-management structure is put in place.

+ Computer security responsibilities are clearly assigned.

+ Effective security-related personnel policies are in place.

+ The security program's effectiveness is monitored and changes are made when needed.

As you may expect, the nontechnical aspects of the security audit involve reviewing documents and interviewing appropriate individuals to learn how the organization manages computer security. Of course, for a small organization or a home PC, it's ridiculous to expect plans and procedures in documents. In those cases, all you need to make sure is that you have some technical controls in place to secure your system and your network connection.

Technical aspects

The technical side of computer security audits focuses on testing the technical controls that secure your hosts and network. The testing involves determining

+ **How well the host is secured.** Are all operating system patches applied? Are the file permissions set correctly? Are user accounts protected? Are file changes monitored? Are log files monitored? And so on.

+ **How well the network is secured.** Are unnecessary Internet services turned off? Is a firewall installed? Are remote logins secured with tools such as SSH? Are TCP wrapper access controls used? And so on.

Typically, security experts use automated tools to perform these two security reviews — host and network.

Learning a Security Test Methodology

A key element of computer security audit is the security test that checks the technical mechanisms used to secure a host and the network. The security test methodology follows these high-level steps:

1. Take stock of the organization's networks, hosts, network devices (routers, switches, firewalls, and so on), and how the network is connected to the Internet.

2. If there are many hosts and network connections, determine what are the important hosts and network devices that should be tested. The importance of a host depends on the kind of applications it runs.

3. Test the hosts individually. Typically, this involves logging in as a system administrator and then checking various aspects of host security, from passwords to system log files.

4. Test the network. This is usually done by attempting to break through the network defenses from another system on the Internet. If there is a firewall, the testing checks that the firewall is indeed configured correctly.

5. Analyze the test results of both host and network tests to determine the vulnerabilities and risks.

Each of the two types of testing — host and network — focuses on three areas that comprise overall computer security:

+ **Prevention** — Includes the mechanisms (nontechnical and technical) that help prevent attacks on the system and the network.

✦ **Detection** — Refers to techniques such as monitoring log files, checking file integrity, and intrusion detection systems that can detect when someone is about to or has already broken into your system.

✦ **Response** — Includes the steps such as reporting an incident to authorities and restoring important files from backup that you perform when a computer security incident has occurred.

For host and network security, each of these areas has some overlaps. For example, prevention mechanisms for host security such as good passwords or file permissions can also provide network security. Nevertheless, it helps to think in terms of the three areas — prevention, detection, and response.

Before you can think of prevention, however, you need to know the types of problems you are trying to prevent. In other words, what are the common security vulnerabilities? The prevention and detection steps typically depend on what these vulnerabilities are.

Some common computer vulnerabilities

The specific tests of the host and network security depend on the common vulnerabilities. Basically, the idea is to check if a host or a network has the vulnerabilities that crackers are most likely to exploit.

Online resources on computer vulnerabilities

There are several online resources that identify and categorize computer security vulnerabilities:

✦ **SANS Institute** publishes a list of the Top 20 most critical Internet security vulnerabilities at `www.sans.org/top20.htm`.

✦ **CVE** (Common Vulnerabilities and Exposures) is a list of standardized names of vulnerabilities. For more information on CVE, see `cve.mitre.org` (the list has over 2,200 names of vulnerabilities). It's common practice to use the CVE name to describe vulnerabilities.

✦ **ICAT Metabase** is a searchable index of information on computer vulnerabilities, published by National Institute of Standards and Technology (NIST), a United States government agency. The ICAT vulnerability index is online at `icat.nist.gov`. ICAT has nearly 4,800 vulnerabilities and it provides links to vulnerability advisory and patch information for each vulnerability. ICAT also a Top 10 List that lists the vulnerabilities that were most queried during the past year.

Typical Top 20 computer vulnerabilities

The SANS Top 20 vulnerabilities list includes three types of vulnerabilities — general ones that affect all systems, Windows, and UNIX. Of these, the general and UNIX vulnerabilities are relevant to Red Hat Linux. Table 4-1 summarizes the general and UNIX vulnerabilities that apply to Red Hat Linux. You can read the complete details about these vulnerabilities at `www.sans.org/top20.htm`.

Table 4-1	Some Common Computer Vulnerability Types
Vulnerability Type	*Description*
General Vulnerabilities	
Default install options	These are the vulnerabilities introduced due to default install options that often install unneeded software or configure software less securely.
Weak or no password	Many user accounts have weak passwords that can be easily cracked by password-cracking programs. Also, some software packages may add user accounts with no password or a standard password that everyone knows.
Incomplete or no backups	If a security incident occurs, the files may have to be restored from backups. However, it's a common mistake to either not do backups regularly or not test the backups for completeness.
Large number of open ports	The open ports refer to Internet services that are enabled on a system. Sometimes there are many unnecessary Internet services running on a system.
Incorrect or no filtering of packets	An IP address-based packet filter can cut back on attacks, but many systems do not have any packet filtering enabled. With `iptables`, it's easy to turn on packet filtering in Red Hat Linux.
Incomplete or no logging	The system logs are the only way to figure out the sequence of events that led to someone breaking into your system. Unfortunately, sometimes the logging is not set up correctly.
Vulnerable CGI programs	This vulnerability refers to the common gateway interface (CGI) that's used on Web servers to process interactive Web pages (for example, forms that request input from users). A CGI program with vulnerability (such as buffer flow) can provide attackers a way to do bad things to your system.
UNIX Vulnerabilities	
RPC buffer overflows (NFS, NIS)	Services such as Network File System (NFS) and Network Information System (NIS) use remote procedure calls (RPC) and there are some known vulnerabilities in RPC.

(continued)

**Book VI
Chapter 4**

**Performing
Security Audits**

Table 4-1 *(continued)*

Vulnerability Type	Description
Sendmail vulnerabilities	Sendmail is a complex program used to transport mail messages from one system to another and some versions of Sendmail have vulnerabilities.
BIND (DNS) weaknesses	Berkeley Internet Name Domain (BIND) is a package that implements Domain Name System (DNS), the Internet's name service that translates a name to an IP address. Some versions of BIND have vulnerabilities.
R command (`rlogin`, `rsh`, `rcp`) vulnerabilities	The so-called R commands allow an attacker to easily access any system that has an implicit trust relationship with others (the R commands assume a trust relationship).
LPD (remote printing) vulnerabilities	LPD is the print server process and it listens on port 515 for remote printing requests. Unfortunately, the remote printing capability has a buffer overflow vulnerability.
Default SNMP strings	Simple Network Management Protocol (SNMP) is used to remotely monitor and administer various network-connected systems ranging from routers to computers. SNMP lacks good access control, so, if SNMP is running on your system, an attacker may be able to reconfigure or shut down your system.

Host security review

When reviewing host security, focus on assessing the security mechanisms in each of the following areas:

+ **Prevention:** Install operating system updates, secure passwords, improve file permissions, set up a password for a boot loader, and use encryption.

+ **Detection:** Capture log messages and check file integrity with Tripwire.

+ **Response:** Make routine backups and develop incident response procedures.

I describe how to review a few of these host security mechanisms.

Operating system updates

Red Hat issues Red Hat Linux updates as soon it learns of any security vulnerabilities, but it's up to you or a system administrator to download and install the updates. One way to keep up with the Red Hat Linux security patches is to sign up for the Red Hat Network service (it's free for a single machine, but costs a subscription for other machines).

You can install them using the `rpm` command. If you place all current updates in a single directory, you can use the following command to install them:

```
rpm -F *.rpm
```

For larger organizations, an authorized system administrator should install the operating system updates.

To assess whether the operating system updates are current, an auditor gets a current list of updates for key Red Hat Linux components and then uses the `rpm` command to check if they are installed. For example, if a list shows that `glibc` version 2.2.5 is what the system should have, the auditor types the following command to view the current `glibc` version number

```
rpm -q glibc
```

If the version number is less than 2.2.5, the conclusion is that operating system updates are not being installed.

File permissions

Key system files should be protected with appropriate file ownerships and file permissions. The key steps in assigning file system ownerships and permissions are to

✦ Figure out which files contain sensitive information and why. Some files may contain sensitive data related to your work or business, whereas many other files are sensitive because they control the Red Hat Linux system configuration.

✦ Maintain a current list of authorized users and what they are authorized to do on the system.

✦ Set up passwords, groups, file ownerships, and file permissions to allow only authorized users to access the files.

Table 4-2 lists some of the important system files in Red Hat Linux. The table also shows the numeric permission setting for each file.

Table 4-2		Important System Files and Their Permissions
File Pathname	*Permission*	*Description*
`/boot/grub/grub.conf`	600	GRUB bootloader configuration file
`/etc/cron.allow`	400	List of users permitted to use `cron` to submit periodic jobs
`/etc/cron.deny`	400	List of users who cannot use `cron` to submit periodic jobs
`/etc/crontab`	644	Systemwide periodic jobs
`/etc/hosts.allow`	644	List of hosts allowed to use Internet services that are started using TCP wrappers
`/etc/hosts.deny`	644	List of hosts denied access to Internet services that are started using TCP wrappers
`/etc/logrotate.conf`	644	File that controls how log files are rotated
`/etc/pam.d`	755	Directory with configuration files for pluggable authentication modules (PAM)
`/etc/passwd`	644	Old-style password file with user account information but not the passwords
`/etc/rc.d`	755	Directory with system startup scripts
`/etc/securetty`	600	TTY interfaces (terminals) from which root can login
`/etc/security`	755	Policy files that control system access
`/etc/shadow`	400	File with encrypted passwords and password expiry information
`/etc/shutdown.allow`	400	Users who can shut down or reboot by pressing Ctrl+Alt+Delete
`/etc/ssh`	755	Directory with configuration files for the Secure Shell (SSH)
`/etc/sysconfig`	755	System configuration files
`/etc/sysctl.conf`	644	Kernel configuration parameters
`/etc/syslog.conf`	644	Configuration file for `syslogd` server that logs messages
`/etc/vsftpd`	600	Configuration file for the very secure FTP server
`/etc/vsftpd.ftpusers`	600	List of users who cannot use FTP to transfer files

File Pathname	Permission	Description
/etc/xinetd.conf	644	Configuration file for the xinetd server
/etc/xinetd.d	755	Directory containing configuration files for specific services that the xinetd server can start
/var/log	755	Directory with all log files
/var/log/lastlog	644	Information about all previous logins
/var/log/messages	644	Main system message log file
/var/log/secure	400	Security-related log file
/var/log/wtmp	664	Information about current logins

Another important check is to look for executable program files that have the setuid permission. If a program has setuid permission and it's owned by root, then the program runs with root privileges, no matter who runs the program. You can find all setuid programs with the following find command:

```
find / -perm +4000 -print
```

You may want to save the output in a file (just append > *filename* to the command) and then examine the file for any unusual setuid programs. For example, a setuid program in a user's home directory would be unusual.

Password security

Verify that the password, group, and shadow password files are protected. In particular, the shadow password file should be write-protected and readable only by root. The filenames and their recommended permissions are shown in Table 4-3:

Table 4-3	Ownership and Permission of Password Files	
File Pathname	**Ownership**	**Permission**
/etc/group	root.root	644
/etc/passwd	root.root	644
/etc/shadow	root.root	400

Incident response

Incident response is the answer to the question of what to do if something does happen. In other words, if someone has broken into your system, what you need to do.

Your response to an incident depends on how you use your system and how important it is to you or your business. For a comprehensive incident response, here are some key points to remember:

✦ Figure out how critical and important your computer and network are and identify who or what resources can help you protect your system.

✦ Take steps to prevent and minimize potential damage and interruption.

✦ Develop and document a comprehensive contingency plan.

✦ Periodically test the contingency plan and revise the procedures as appropriate.

Network security review

Network security review focuses on assessing the security mechanisms in each of the following areas:

✦ **Prevention:** Set up a firewall, enable packet filtering, disable unnecessary `xinetd` services, turn off unneeded Internet services, use TCP wrappers access control, and use SSH for secure remote logins.

✦ **Detection:** Use network intrusion detection and capture system logs.

✦ **Response:** Develop incident-response procedures.

I briefly describe some key steps in assessing the network security.

Services started by xinetd

Many Internet services such as TELNET and FTP are started by the `xinetd` server. The decision to turn on some of these services depends on factors such as how the system is connected to the Internet and how the system is being used. You can usually turn off most `xinetd` services.

Check which `xinetd` services are turned on by using one of the following ways:

✦ Check the configuration files in the `/etc/xinetd.d` directory for all the services that `xinetd` can start. If a service is turned off, the configuration file has a line like this:

```
disable = yes
```

Remember that the `disable = yes` line doesn't count if it's commented out by placing a # at the beginning of the line.

✦ Type the following command:

```
chkconfig --list | more
```

In the output, look for the lines that follow:

```
xinetd based services:
```

These lines list all the services that `xinetd` can start and whether they are on or off. For example, here are a few lines showing the status of `xinetd` services on a system:

```
chargen-udp:      off
chargen:          off
daytime-udp:      off
daytime:          off
echo-udp:         off
echo:     off
services:         off
servers:          off
time-udp:         off
time:     off
sgi_fam:          on
rsync:    off
vsftpd:   on
imap:     off
... lines deleted ...
```

In this case, the `sgi_fam` (a server that reports changes to any file) and `vsftpd` (FTP) services are on, but everything else is off.

Also check the following files for any access controls used with the `xinetd` services:

✦ `/etc/hosts.allow` lists hosts allowed to access specific services.

✦ `/etc/hosts.deny` lists hosts that should be denied access to services.

Stand-alone services

Many services such as the `httpd` (Web server) and `sendmail` (mail server) start automatically at boot time, assuming they are configured to start that way. You can use the `chkconfig` command to check which stand-alone servers are set to start at various run levels. Typically, your Red Hat Linux system starts up at run level 3 (for text login) or 5 (for graphical login). Therefore, what matters is the setting for the servers in levels 3 and 5. To view the list of servers, type the following command:

```
chkconfig --list | more
```

Here's a partial listing of what you might see:

```
ntpd        0:off  1:off  2:on   3:on   4:on   5:on   6:off
syslog      0:off  1:off  2:on   3:on   4:on   5:on   6:off
httpd       0:off  1:off  2:off  3:off  4:off  5:off  6:off
netfs       0:off  1:off  2:off  3:on   4:on   5:on   6:off
network     0:off  1:off  2:on   3:on   4:on   5:on   6:off
random      0:off  1:off  2:on   3:on   4:on   5:on   6:off
rawdevices  0:off  1:off  2:off  3:on   4:on   5:on   6:off
saslauthd   0:off  1:off  2:off  3:off  4:off  5:off  6:off
xinetd      0:off  1:off  2:off  3:on   4:on   5:on   6:off
portmap     0:off  1:off  2:off  3:on   4:on   5:on   6:off
apmd        0:off  1:off  2:on   3:on   4:on   5:on   6:off
atd         0:off  1:off  2:off  3:on   4:on   5:on   6:off
gpm         0:off  1:off  2:on   3:on   4:on   5:on   6:off
autofs      0:off  1:off  2:off  3:on   4:on   5:on   6:off
irda        0:off  1:off  2:off  3:off  4:off  5:off  6:off
isdn        0:off  1:off  2:on   3:on   4:on   5:on   6:off
keytable    0:off  1:on   2:on   3:on   4:on   5:on   6:off
kudzu       0:off  1:off  2:off  3:on   4:on   5:on   6:off
snmpd       0:off  1:off  2:off  3:off  4:off  5:off  6:off
...lines deleted...
```

The first column shows the names of the servers. Look at the column of entries that begin with 3: and the ones that begin with 5:. These are the ones that show the status of the server for run levels 3 and 5. The ones that appear as on are automatically started when your Red Hat Linux system starts.

If you are doing a self-assessment of your network security and you find that some servers should not be running, you can turn them off for run levels 3 and 5 with the chkconfig command like this:

```
chkconfig --level 35 servicename off
```

Replace *servicename* with the name of the server you want to turn off.

If you are auditing network security, make a note of all the servers that are turned on and then try to determine if they should really be on, based on what you know about the system. The decision to turn on services depends on how a system is used (as a Web server or a desktop system) and how it is connected to the Internet (through a firewall or directly).

Penetration test

A penetration test is the best way to tell what services are really running on a Red Hat Linux system. *Penetration testing* involves trying to get access to your system from an attacker's perspective. Typically, you perform this test from a system on the Internet and try to see if you can break in or, at a minimum, get access to services running on your Red Hat Linux system.

One aspect of penetration testing is to see what ports are open on your Red Hat Linux system. The port number is simply a number that identifies specific TCP/IP network connections to the system. The attempt to connect to a port succeeds only if a server is running on that port (or put another way, if a server is "listening on that port"). A port is considered to be open if a server responds when a connection request for that port arrives.

The first step in penetration testing is to perform a port scan. The term *port scan* is used to describe the automated process of trying to connect to each port number to see if a valid response comes back. There are many automated tools available to perform port scanning — Red Hat Linux comes with a popular port-scanning tool called nmap (I describe it later in this chapter).

After performing a port scan, you know the potential vulnerabilities that could be exploited. Not all servers have security problems, but many servers have well-known vulnerabilities, and an open port provides a cracker a way to attack your system through one of the servers. In fact, you can use automated tools called *vulnerability scanners* to identify vulnerabilities that exist in your system. (I describe some vulnerability scanners next.) Whether your Red Hat Linux system is connected to the Internet directly (through DSL or cable modem) or through a firewall, use the port-scanning and vulnerability-scanning tools to figure out if you have any holes in your defenses. Better you than them!

Exploring Security Testing Tools

There are many automated tools available to perform security testing. Some tools are meant for finding the open ports on every system in a range of IP addresses. Others are meant to find the vulnerabilities associated with the open ports. Yet other tools can capture (or *sniff*) them and help you analyze them so you can glean useful information about what's going on in your network.

You can browse a list of the top 50 security tools (based on informal poll of nmap users) at www.insecure.org/tools.html. Table 4-4 lists a number of tools by category. I describe a few of the freely available vulnerability scanners in the next few sections.

Table 4-4	Some Popular Computer Security Tools
Type	*Names of Tools*
Port scanners	nmap, Strobe
Vulnerability scanners	Nessus Security Scanner, SAINT, SARA, Whisker (CGI scanner), ISS Internet Scanner, CyberCop Scanner, Vetescan, Retina Network Security Scanner

(continued)

Table 4-4 *(continued)*

Type	*Names of Tools*
Network utilities	Netcat, hping2, Firewalk, Cheops, ntop, ping
Host security tools	Tripwire, lsof
Packet sniffers	tcpdump, Ethereal, dsniff, sniffit
Intrusion detection system (IDS)	Snort, Abacus portsentry, scanlogd, NFR, LIDS
Password-checking tools	John the Ripper, LC4
Log analysis and monitoring tools	logcolorise, tcpdstats, nlog, logcheck, Swatch

Nmap

Nmap (short for Network Mapper) is a port-scanning tool. It can rapidly scan large networks and determine what hosts are available on the network, what services they are offering, what operating system (and the operating system version) they are running, what type of packet filters or firewalls are in use, and dozens of other characteristics. Red Hat Linux comes with nmap. You can read more about nmap at www.insecure.org/nmap.

If you want to try out nmap to scan your local area network, just type a command similar to the following (replace the IP address range with addresses appropriate for your network):

```
nmap -O -sS 192.168.0.2-10
```

Here's a typical output listing from that command:

```
Starting nmap V. 2.54BETA22 ( www.insecure.org/nmap/ )
Interesting ports on (192.168.0.2):
(The 1541 ports scanned but not shown below are in state: closed)
Port     State   Service
139/tcp  open    netbios-ssn

Remote operating system guess: Windows NT4 / Win95 / Win98
Interesting ports on (192.168.0.3):
(The 1541 ports scanned but not shown below are in state: closed)
Port     State   Service
139/tcp  open    netbios-ssn

Remote operating system guess: Windows NT4 / Win95 / Win98
Insufficient responses for TCP sequencing (3), OS detection may be less accurate
Interesting ports on dhcppc3 (192.168.0.4):
(The 1536 ports scanned but not shown below are in state: closed)
Port     State   Service
21/tcp    open    ftp
22/tcp    open    ssh
23/tcp    open    telnet
111/tcp   open    sunrpc
1024/tcp  open    kdm
1241/tcp  open    msg
6000/tcp  open    X11
```

```
Remote operating system guess: Linux Kernel 2.4.0 - 2.4.17 (X86)
<<Lines deleted...>
Nmap run completed -- 9 IP addresses (4 hosts up) scanned in 45 seconds
```

As you can see, nmap displays the names of the open ports and hazards a guess at the operating system name and version number.

Nessus

The Nessus Security Scanner is a modular security auditing tool that uses plugins written in Nessus scripting language to test for a wide variety of network vulnerabilities. Nessus uses a client-server software architecture with a server called nessusd and a client called nessus.

**Book VI
Chapter 4**

**Performing
Security Audits**

To download and install Nessus, follow these steps:

1. **Read the instructions on www.nessus.org/posix.html. Then click a link to an appropriate FTP site and download the files nessus-installer.sh and MD5.**

2. **Type the following command to install Nessus (you must have the development tools, including the GIMP Toolkit, installed):**

```
sh nessus-installer.sh
```

After the installation is complete, here are the steps to use Nessus:

1. **Log in as root and type the following command to create the Nessus SSL certificate used for secure communication between the Nessus client and the Nessus server:**

```
nessus-mkcert
```

2. **Provide the requested information to complete the certificate-generation process.**

3. **Create a nessusd account with the following command:**

```
nessus-adduser
```

4. **When prompted, enter user name, password, and any rules (press Ctrl+D if you don't know what rules to enter).**

5. **If you want to, you can configure nessusd by editing the configuration file /usr/local/etc/nessus/nessusd.conf. If you want to try out Nessus, you can proceed with the default configuration file.**

6. **Start the Nessus server with this command:**

```
nessusd -D
```

7. **Run the Nessus client by typing the following command in a terminal window:**

```
nessus
```

The Nessus Setup window appears.

8. **Type a** `nessusd` **user name and password and then click Log In. Nessus displays the certificate used to establish the secure connection and asks if you accept it. Click Yes. After the client connects to the server, the Log in button changes to Log out, and a Connected label appears at its left. (Figure 4-1).**

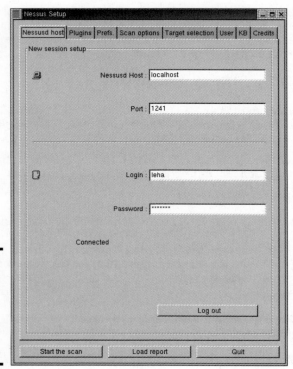

Figure 4-1: The Nessus client screen looks like this after a user logs in.

9. **Click the Target selection tab. Enter a range of IP addresses to scan all hosts in a network.**

For example, to scan the first eight hosts in a private network 192.168.0.0, I enter the address as:

```
192.168.0.0/29
```

10. **Click Start the Scan.**

Nessus starts scanning the IP addresses and checks for many different vulnerabilities. Progress bars show the status of the scan (Figure 4-2).

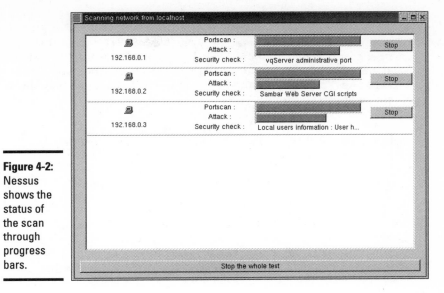

Figure 4-2:
Nessus shows the status of the scan through progress bars.

After Nessus completes the vulnerability scan of the hosts, it displays the result in a nice combination of graphical and text formats (Figure 4-3). The report is interactive — you can click a host address to view the report on that host, and you can drill down on a specific vulnerability (including the CVE number that identifies the vulnerability).

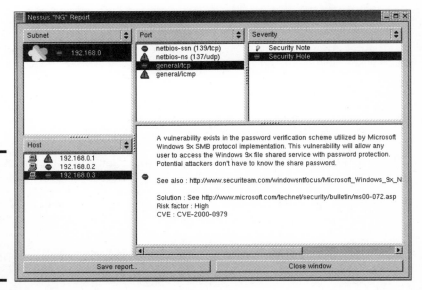

Figure 4-3:
Nessus displays results of scanning in an interactive report.

SAINT

Security Administrator's Integrated Network Tool (SAINT) scans hosts for a variety of security vulnerabilities. For the vulnerabilities it finds, SAINT shows the Common Vulnerabilities and Exposures (CVE) identifier. Older versions of SAINT are free, but the latest version is available to only those who purchase SAINTWriter or SAINTexpress.

You can download an older version of SAINT from `www.wwdsi.com/products/download.html` and try it out. After downloading the file, install it using these steps:

1. **Unpack the downloaded file with the following command:**

   ```
   tar zxvf saint*
   ```

2. **Use a text editor to edit the file named** `reconfig`. **Locate the line containing** `netscape` **and change** `netscape` **to** `mozilla` **(because** `mozilla` **is the name of the Web browser binary in the current version of Red Hat Linux and SAINT uses the Web browser as the user interface). Save the** `reconfig` **file.**

3. **Configure the software with the following commands:**

   ```
   cd saint*
   ./configure
   ```

4. **To build the software, type**

   ```
   make
   ```

5. **To install SAINT, type**

   ```
   make install
   ```

After completing these steps, run SAINT by typing the command:

```
./saint
```

SAINT starts the Mozilla Web browser and displays its initial window (Figure 4-4). You can perform all SAINT tasks through the links on the left side of the Web browser window.

To perform a vulnerability scan, click the Target Selection link. A form appears from which you can select one or more hosts or a whole network to scan. You can also select the level of scan. After making the selections, click the Start Scan button at the bottom of the form. SAINT performs the vulnerability scan, collects the data, and shows the progress in a Web page.

After SAINT completes the data collection, click the Continue with Report and Analysis link at the bottom of the page. You can then view the vulnerabilities in many different ways (for example, by danger level, by type, by host name, etc.). For example, Figure 4-5 shows a report of the vulnerabilities by danger level.

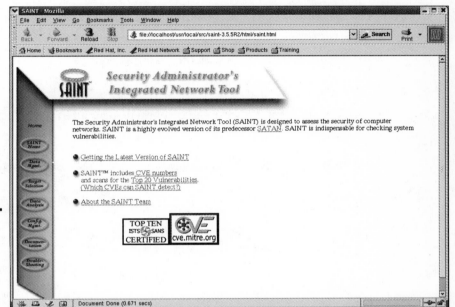

Figure 4-4:
SAINT uses
the Web
browser as
its user
interface.

You can click the vulnerability links to get more information about that vulnerability. The detailed information also shows the CVE number for that vulnerability.

SARA

Security Auditor's Research Assistant (SARA) is a vulnerability-scanning tool based on SAINT. SARA scans for known vulnerabilities, including those in the CVE list and the SANS Top 20 List (www.sans.org/top20.htm).

To try out SARA, download the latest version of SARA from www-arc. com/sara/downloads/. After downloading the compressed tar file, build and install the software using these steps:

1. **Unpack `tar` file with the command**

   ```
   tar zxvf sara*
   ```

2. **To configure SARA, type the following commands:**

   ```
   cd sara*
   ./configure
   ```

3. **To build the software, type**

   ```
   make
   ```

After SARA is built, run it with the following command:

```
./sara
```

SARA starts a Web browser and displays its user interface in the Web browser (Figure 4-6).

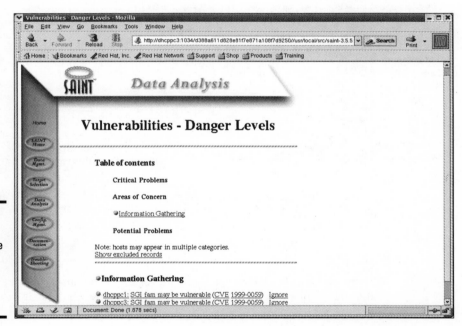

Figure 4-5:
SAINT displays the vulnerabilities by danger level.

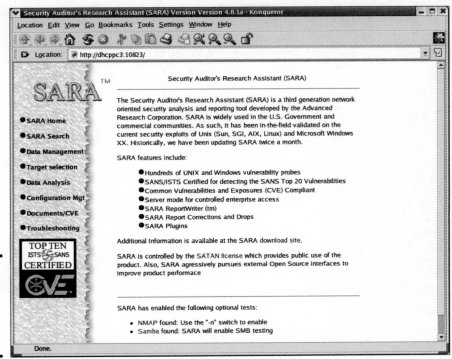

Figure 4-6: SARA starts its user interface in a Web browser.

You can perform various tasks by clicking the links along the left-hand side of the Web browser. For example, to perform a vulnerability scan, click the Target Selection link. SARA brings up a form (Figure 4-7) where you can provide information about hosts and networks to scan. You can also specify the scanning level — anywhere from light to extreme.

After filling in the information, click the Start the Scan button at the bottom of the form. SARA starts to perform the vulnerability scan. During the scan, SARA displays a data-collection page that indicates progress of the scan.

After the scan is compete, you can proceed to data analysis and view the vulnerability information.

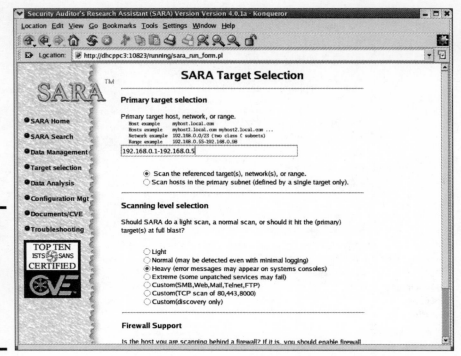

Figure 4-7:
In this form
you can
specify the
host or
network
addresses
for SARA
to scan.

Book VII

Internet Servers

The 5th Wave   By Rich Tennant

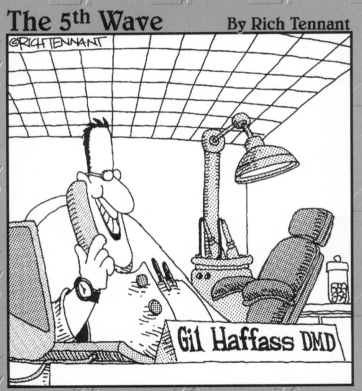

Gil Haffass DMD

"Good news, honey! No one's registered our last name as a domain name yet! Hellooo Haffassoralsurgery.com!"

Contents at a Glance

Chapter 1: Managing the Servers

In This Chapter

- ✓ **Understanding Internet services**
- ✓ **Controlling servers through xinetd**
- ✓ **Using** `chkconfig` **to manage servers**
- ✓ **Using the service configuration utility**

The Internet is a world of clients and servers. Clients make requests to servers, and servers respond to the requests. For example, your Web browser is a client that downloads information from Web servers and displays it to you. Of course, the clients and servers are computer programs that run on a wide variety of computers. A Red Hat Linux system is an ideal system to run a wide variety of servers from a Web server to a Windows file and print server. In this chapter, I provide an overview of typical Internet service, its client/server architecture, and how to manage the servers in Red Hat Linux. You can use the information in this chapter to manage any server running on your Red Hat Linux system.

Understanding Internet Services

Internet services are network applications that are designed to deliver information from one system to another. By design, each Internet service is implemented in two parts — a server that provides information, and one or more clients that request information.

Such client/server architecture is the most common way to build distributed information systems. The clients and servers are computer programs that run on these computers and communicate through the network. The neat part is that you can be running a client at your desktop computer and access information from a server running on a computer anywhere in the world (as long as it's on the Internet).

Web, e-mail, and FTP (File Transfer Protocol) are examples of Internet services that use the client/server model. For example, when you use the Web, you use the Web browser client to download and view Web pages from the Web server.

Client/server architecture requires clients to communicate with the servers. That's where the *Transmission Control Protocol/Internet Protocol* — TCP/IP — comes in. TCP/IP provides a standard way for clients and servers to exchange packets of data. In the next few sections, I explain how TCP/IP-based services communicate.

TCP/IP and sockets

Client/server applications such as Web and FTP use TCP/IP for the data transfers between the client and the server. These Internet applications typically use TCP/IP communications using the Berkeley Sockets interface (so named because the socket interface was introduced in Berkeley UNIX around 1982). The sockets interface is nothing physical — it's simply some computer code that a computer programmer can use to create applications that can communicate with other applications on the Internet.

Even if you do not write network applications using sockets, you may have to use or set up many network applications. Knowledge of sockets can help you understand how network-based applications work, which in turn helps you find and correct any problems with these applications.

Socket definition

Network applications use sockets to communicate over a TCP/IP network. A socket represents one end-point of a connection. Because a socket is bidirectional, data can be sent as well as received through it. A socket has three attributes:

✦ The network address (the IP address) of the system

✦ The port number identifying the process (a process is a computer program running on a computer) that exchanges data through the socket

✦ The type of socket identifying the protocol for data exchange

Essentially, the IP address identifies a computer (host) on the network; the port number identifies a process (server) on the node; and the socket type determines the manner in which data is exchanged — through a connection-oriented (stream) or connectionless (datagram) protocol.

Connection-oriented protocols

The socket type indicates the protocol being used to communicate through the socket. A connection-oriented protocol works like a normal phone conversation. When you want to talk to your friend, you have to dial your friend's phone number and establish a connection before you can have a conversation. In the same way, connection-oriented data exchange requires both the sending and receiving processes to establish a connection before data exchange can begin.

In the TCP/IP protocol suite, TCP — *Transmission Control Protocol* — supports a connection-oriented data transfer between two processes running on two computers on the Internet. TCP provides reliable two-way data exchange between processes.

As the name TCP/IP suggests, TCP relies on IP — *Internet Protocol* — for delivery of packets. IP does not guarantee delivery of packets; nor does it deliver packets in any particular sequence. IP does, however, efficiently move packets from one network to another. TCP is responsible for arranging the packets in the proper sequence, detecting whether or not errors have occurred, and requesting retransmission of packets in case of an error.

TCP is useful for applications that plan to exchange large amounts of data at a time. In addition, applications that need reliable data exchange use TCP. For example, FTP uses TCP to transfer files.

In the sockets model, a socket that uses TCP is referred to as a *stream socket*.

Connectionless protocols

A connectionless data-exchange protocol does not require the sender and receiver to explicitly establish a connection. It's like shouting to your friend in a crowded room — you can't be sure if your friend hears you.

In the TCP/IP protocol suite, the *User Datagram Protocol* (UDP) provides connectionless service for sending and receiving packets known as *datagrams*. Unlike TCP, UDP does not guarantee that datagrams ever reach their intended destination. Nor does UDP ensure that datagrams are delivered in the order they have been sent.

UDP is used by applications that exchange small amounts of data at a time or by applications that do not need the reliability and sequencing of data delivery. For example, SNMP *(Simple Network Management Protocol)* uses UDP to transfer data.

In the sockets model, a socket that uses UDP is referred to as a *datagram socket*.

Sockets and the client/server model

It takes two sockets to complete a communication path. When two processes communicate, they use the client/server model to establish the connection. Figure 1-1 illustrates the concept. The server application listens on a specific port on the system — the server is completely identified by the IP address of the system where it runs and the port number where it listens for connections. The client initiates connection from any available port and tries to connect to the server (identified by the IP address and port number). When the connection is established, the client and the server can exchange data according to their own protocol.

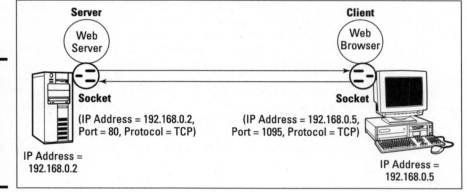

Figure 1-1: Client and server processes use two sockets to communicate.

The sequence of events in sockets-based data exchanges depends on whether the transfer is connection oriented (TCP) or connectionless (UDP).

For a connection-oriented data transfer using sockets, the server "listens" on a specific port, waiting for clients to request connection. Data transfer begins only after a connection is established.

For connectionless data transfers, the server waits for a datagram to arrive at a specified port. The client does not wait to establish a connection; it simply sends a datagram to the server.

Regardless of whether it's a server or a client, each application first creates a socket. Then it associates (binds) the socket with the local computer's IP address and a port number. The IP address identifies the machine (where the application is running), and the port number identifies the application using the socket.

Servers typically listen to a well-known port number so that clients can connect to that port to access the server. For a client application, the process of binding a socket to the IP address and port is the same as that for a server, but the client can use 0 as the port number — the sockets library automatically uses an unused port number for the client.

For a connection-oriented stream socket, the communicating client and server applications have to establish a connection. The exact steps for establishing a connection depend on whether the application is a server or a client.

In the client/server model, the server has to be up and running before the client can run. After creating a socket and binding the socket to a port, the server application sets up a queue of connections, which determines how many clients can connect to the server. Typically, a server listens to any-where from one to five connections. However, the size of the listen queue is one of the parameters you can adjust (especially for a Web server) to ensure that the server responds to as many clients as possible. After setting up the listen queue, the server waits for a connection from a client.

Establishing the connection from the client side is somewhat simpler. After creating a socket and binding the socket to an IP address, the client estab-lishes connection with the server. To make the connection, the client needs to know the host name or IP address of the server, as well as the port on which the server accepts connection. All Internet services have well-known standard port numbers.

After a client establishes connection to a server using a connection-oriented stream socket, the client and server can exchange data by calling appropriate sockets API functions. Like a conversation between two persons, the server and client alternately send and receive data — the meaning of the data depends on the message protocol the server and clients use. Usually, a server is designed for a specific task; inherent in that design is a message protocol that the server and clients use to exchange necessary data. For example, the Web server and the Web browser (client) communicate using the HTTP (HyperText Transfer Protocol).

**Book VII
Chapter 1**

**Managing
the Servers**

Internet services and port numbers

The TCP/IP protocol suite is the *lingua franca* of the Internet because the Internet services "speak" TCP/IP. These services make the Internet tick by making possible the transfer of mail, news, and Web pages. Each Internet service has its own protocol that relies on TCP/IP for the actual transfer of the information. Each service also has one or more assigned port numbers that it uses to do whatever it's designed to do. Here are some of the well-known Internet services and their associated protocols:

✦ **FTP (File Transfer Protocol)** is used to transfer files between computers on the Internet. FTP uses two ports — data is transferred on port 20, while control information is exchanged on port 21.

✦ **HTTP (HyperText Transfer Protocol)** is for sending documents from one system to another. HTTP is the underlying protocol of the Web. By default, the Web server and client communicate on port 80.

✦ **SMTP (Simple Mail Transfer Protocol)** is for exchanging e-mail messages between systems. SMTP uses port 25 for information exchange.

✦ **NNTP (Network News Transfer Protocol)** is for distribution of news articles in a store-and-forward fashion across the Internet. NNTP uses port 119.

✦ **TELNET** enables a user on one system to log into another system on the Internet (the user must provide a valid user ID and password to log into the remote system). TELNET uses port 23 by default. However, the TELNET client can connect to any specified port.

✦ **NFS (Network File System)** is for sharing files among computers. NFS uses Sun's Remote Procedure Call (RPC) facility, which exchanges information through port 111.

✦ **NTP (Network Time Protocol)** is used by client computers to synchronize the system time with that on a server (one with a more accurate clock). NTP uses port 123.

✦ **SNMP (Simple Network Management Protocol)** is for managing all types of network devices on the Internet. Like FTP, SNMP uses two ports: 161 and 162.

✦ **TFTP (Trivial File Transfer Protocol)** is for transferring files from one system to another (typically used by X terminals and diskless workstations to download boot files from another host on the network). TFTP data transfer takes place on port 69.

Each service is provided by a server process — a computer program running on a system. That process expects client requests to arrive at the well-known port that is associated with its service. Thus, the Web server expects client requests at port 80, the standard port for HTTP service.

The `/etc/services` text file on your Red Hat Linux system stores the association between a service name and a port number (as well as a protocol). Here is a small subset of entries in the `/etc/services` file from a Red Hat Linux system:

```
ftp-data    20/tcp
ftp         21/tcp
ssh         22/tcp              # SSH Remote Login Protocol
ssh         22/udp              # SSH Remote Login Protocol
telnet      23/tcp
smtp        25/tcp      mail
time        37/tcp      timserver
time        37/udp      timserver
rlp         39/udp      resource    # resource location
nameserver  42/udp      name        # IEN 116
whois       43/tcp      nicname
```

A quick look through the entries in the /etc/services file can be instructive because they show the breadth of networking services available under TCP/IP.

Note that port number 80 is designated for Web service. In other words, if you set up a Web server on your system, that server listens to port 80. By the way, IANA — the Internet Assigned Numbers Authority (www.iana.org) — is responsible for coordinating the assignment of port numbers below 1,024.

Using the xinetd Super Server

The client/server architecture of Internet services requires that the server be up and running before a client makes a request for service. A simplistic idea would be to run all the servers all the time. However, this idea is not practical because each server process would use up system resources in the form of memory and processor time. Besides, you don't really need all the services up and ready at all times. A smart solution to this problem is to run a single server, xinetd, that listens to all the ports and then starts the appropriate server when a client request comes in. (The xinetd server is a replacement for an older server named inetd but with improved access control and logging. The name xinetd stands for *extended inetd*.)

For example, when a client tries to connect to the FTP port, xinetd starts the FTP server and lets it communicate directly with the client (and the FTP server exits when the client disconnects).

Because it starts various servers on demand, xinetd is known as the Internet super server. Typically, a UNIX system starts xinetd when the system boots. The xinetd server reads a configuration file named /etc/xinetd.conf at startup. This file tells xinetd which ports to listen to and what server to start for each port. The file can contain instructions that include other configuration files. In Red Hat Linux, the /etc/xinetd.conf file looks like the following:

```
# Simple configuration file for xinetd
#
# Some defaults, and include /etc/xinetd.d/

defaults
{
        instances               = 60
        log_type                = SYSLOG authpriv
        log_on_success          = HOST PID
```

```
        log_on_failure          = HOST
        cps                     = 25 30
}
includedir /etc/xinetd.d
```

Comment lines begin with the pound sign (#). The `defaults` block of attributes, enclosed in curly braces ({...}), specifies default values for some attributes. These default values apply to all other services in the configuration file. The `instances` attribute is set to 60, which means there can be, at most, 60 servers simultaneously active for any service.

The last line in the `/etc/xinetd.conf` file uses the `includedir` directive to include all files inside the `/etc/xinetd.d` directory, excluding files that begin with a period (.). The idea is that the `/etc/xinetd.d` directory would contain all service configuration files — one file for each type of service the `xinetd` server is expected to manage.

Here is the listing of files that appears when I type the `ls /etc/xinetd.d` command on a typical Red Hat Linux system:

```
chargen    echo    imaps pop3s  rsync    talk    vsftpd
chargen-udp echo-udp ipop2 rexec  servers telnet
daytime    finger  ipop3 rlogin services time
daytime-udp imap    ntalk rsh    sgi_fam time-udp
```

Each of these files specifies the attributes for one service. For example, the following listing shows the contents of the `/etc/xinetd.d/vsftpd` file, which specifies the `xinetd` configuration for the FTP service:

```
# default: off
# description: The vsftpd FTP server serves FTP connections. It uses \
#    normal, unencrypted usernames and passwords for authentication.
service ftp
{
    disable = yes
    socket_type        = stream
    wait         = no
    user         = root
    server        = /usr/sbin/vsftpd
    nice         = 10
}
```

The filename (in this case, `vsftpd`) can be anything; what matters is the service name that appears next to the `service` keyword in the file. In this case, the line `service ftp` tells `xinetd` the name of the service. `xinetd` uses this name to look up the port number from the `/etc/services` file. To look for `ftp` in the `/etc/services` file, type the following command:

```
grep "^ftp" /etc/services
```

The command displays the following lines:

```
ftp-data        20/tcp
ftp-data        20/udp
ftp             21/tcp
ftp             21/udp              fsp fspd
```

This listing shows that the port number of the FTP service is 21. This tells `xinetd` that any connection requests arriving at port 21 are meant for FTP service. The configuration file `/etc/xinetd.d/vsftpd` then tells `xinetd` what to do to take care of these service requests.

The attributes in `/etc/xinetd.d/vsftpd`, enclosed in curly braces, have the following meanings:

◆ The `disable` attribute turns off the service if it's set to `yes`. By default the `disable` attribute is set to `yes` and FTP is turned off.

◆ The `socket_type` attribute is set to `stream`, which tells `xinetd` that the FTP service uses a connection-oriented TCP socket to communicate with the client. For services that use the connectionless UDP sockets, this attribute would be set to `dgram`.

◆ The `wait` attribute is set to `no`, which tells `xinetd` to start a new server for each request. If this attribute is set to `yes`, `xinetd` waits until the server exits before starting the server again.

◆ The `user` attribute provides the user ID that `xinetd` uses to run the server. In this case, the server runs the FTP server as `root`.

◆ The `server` attribute specifies the program to run for this service. In this case, `xinetd` runs the `/usr/sbin/vsftpd` program to provide FTP service.

◆ The `nice` attribute determines the priority that `xinetd` assigns to the server (−20 is the highest priority; 19 is the lowest priority). Only privileged processes can set the priority to a negative value, which means higher priority.

Browse through the files in the `/etc/xinetd.d` directory on your Red Hat Linux system to find out the kinds of services `xinetd` is set up to start. Some of these services, such as `finger`, provide information that intruders may use to break into your system. If they are not already disabled, you may want to turn off these services by placing the following line inside the curly braces that enclose all attributes:

```
disable         = yes
```

On the other hand, if you find that you cannot seem to connect to your Red Hat Linux system by using `telnet` or `ftp`, check the appropriate files in the `/etc/xinetd.d` directory and make sure the `disable` attribute is set to `no` or that line is commented out (by placing # at the beginning of the line).

When you make such a change to the `xinetd` configuration files, you must restart the `xinetd` server by typing the following command:

```
/etc/init.d/xinetd restart
```

If you want to type a little less, use the following command that does the exact same thing:

```
service xinetd restart
```

Running Stand-Alone Servers

Starting servers through `xinetd` is a smart approach, but it's not efficient if a service has to be started very often. If the Web server were controlled by `xinetd`, you'd have a situation where that server is started often because every time a user clicks a link on a Web page, a request arrives for the Web service. For such high-demand services, it's best to start the server in a stand-alone manner. Such stand-alone servers are designed to run as *daemons* — processes that run continuously and never die. That means the server listens on the assigned port and whenever a request arrives, the server handles it by making a copy of itself. In this way, the server keeps running forever. A more-efficient strategy, used for Web servers, is to run multiple copies of the server and let each copy handle some of the incoming requests.

You can easily configure your Red Hat Linux system to start various stand-alone servers automatically. I show you how.

Starting and stopping servers manually

To start a service that's not running, use the server command. For example, if the Web server (`httpd`) is not running, you can start it by running a special shell script with the following command:

```
/etc/init.d/httpd start
```

That command runs the `/etc/init.d/httpd` script with `start` as the argument. If the `httpd` server is already running and you want to stop it, run the same command with `stop` as the argument, like this:

```
/etc/init.d/httpd stop
```

To stop and start a server again, just use `restart` as the argument:

`/etc/init.d/httpd restart`

Red Hat Linux includes another script called `service` that does the same job, but is a bit easier to remember. Basically, you can strip off the `/etc/init.d` and replace it with `service` followed by a space. Thus, to start `httpd`, you would type

`service httpd start`

What are all the services that you can start and stop? Well, the answer is in the files in `/etc/init.d` directory. Type the following command:

`ls /etc/init.d`

All the files you see listed in response to this command are the services that are installed on your Red Hat Linux system, and these are the services you can start and stop. For example, here's a typical list of services on a Red Hat Linux system:

```
aep1000   functions kdcrotate nfs     random   snmptrapd ypbind
anacron   gpm       keytable  nfslock rawdevices squid    yppasswdd
apmd      halt      killall   nscd    rhnsd    sshd       ypserv
atd       httpd     kudzu     ntpd    saslauthd syslog    ypxfrd
autofs    innd      lpd       pcmcia  sendmail tux
bcm5820   iptables  named     portmap single   winbind
crond     irda      netfs     postfix smb      xfs
firstboot isdn      network   pxe     snmpd    xinetd
```

That's over 50 services!

Starting servers automatically at boot time

You can start, stop, and restart servers manually by using the scripts in the `/etc/init.d` directory, but you would want some of the services to start as soon as you boot the Red Hat Linux system. You can configure servers to start automatically at boot time by using the `chkconfig` command or a graphical server configuration utility.

Using chkconfig command

The `chkconfig` program is a command-line utility for checking and updating the current setting of servers in Red Hat Linux. Various combinations of servers are set up to start automatically at different run levels. Each run level represents a system configuration in which a selected set of processes runs. You are usually concerned about run levels 3 and 5 because run level 3 is for text mode login and run level 5 is for graphical login.

**Book VII
Chapter 1**

**Managing
the Servers**

The chkconfig command is simple to use. For example, suppose you want to automatically start the named server at run levels 3 and 5. All you need to do is log in as root and type the following command at the shell prompt:

```
chkconfig --level 35 named on
```

To see the status of the named server, type the following command:

```
chkconfig --list named
```

You should see a line of output similar to the following:

```
named   0:off  1:off  2:off  3:on   4:off  5:on   6:off
```

The output shows you the status of the named server at run levels 0 through 6. As you can see, named is set to run as run levels 3 and 5.

If you want to turn named off, you can do so with this command:

```
chkconfig --level 35 named off
```

You can use chkconfig to see the status of all services, including the ones started through xinetd. For example, you can view the status of all services by typing the following command:

```
chkconfig --list | more
```

Here's a typical output:

```
ntpd       0:off  1:off  2:on   3:on   4:on   5:on   6:off
syslog     0:off  1:off  2:on   3:on   4:on   5:on   6:off
httpd      0:off  1:off  2:off  3:off  4:off  5:off  6:off
netfs      0:off  1:off  2:off  3:on   4:on   5:on   6:off
network    0:off  1:off  2:on   3:on   4:on   5:on   6:off
random     0:off  1:off  2:on   3:on   4:on   5:on   6:off
rawdevices 0:off  1:off  2:off  3:on   4:on   5:on   6:off
saslauthd  0:off  1:off  2:off  3:off  4:off  5:off  6:off
xinetd     0:off  1:off  2:off  3:on   4:on   5:on   6:off
portmap    0:off  1:off  2:off  3:on   4:on   5:on   6:off
apmd       0:off  1:off  2:on   3:on   4:on   5:on   6:off
atd        0:off  1:off  2:off  3:on   4:on   5:on   6:off
... many lines of output deleted ...
```

The output shows the status of each service for each of the run levels from 0 through 6. For each run level, the service is either on or off. At the very end of the listing, chkconfig displays a list of the services that xinetd controls. Each xinetd-based service is also marked on or off, depending on whether or not xinetd is configured to start the service.

Using the Red Hat service configuration utility

If you don't like typing the `chkconfig` commands, you can use a graphical service configuration utility program to configure the services. To run the service configuration utility, log in as `root` and select Main Menu⇨Server Settings⇨Services from the GNOME desktop. You can then turn services on or off from the service configuration window (Figure 1-2).

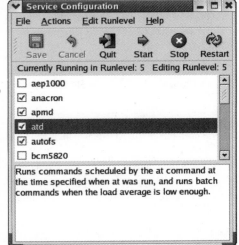

Figure 1-2: From the service configuration window you can set services to start automatically at boot time.

The service configuration utility shows the names of services in a scrolling list. Each line in the list shows the name of a service with a box in front of the name. A check mark in the box indicates that the service is already selected to start at boot time for the current run level. When the dialog box first appears, many services are already selected.

You can scroll up and down the list and click the box to select or deselect a service. If you click the box, the check mark alternately turns on and off. To learn more about a service, click the service name and a brief description appears in the lower part of the window. For example, Figure 1-2 shows the help text for the `atd` service.

After you select all the servers you want to start when the system boots, click Save on the toolbar to save the changes. Then press Quit to exit.

By default, the service configuration utility configures the selected services for the current run level. That means if you are doing this from the graphical desktop, the system is in run level 5 and the services you configure are set to start at run level 5. If you want to set up the services for a different level, select that run level from the Edit Runlevel menu.

Table 1-1 shows a list of the services, along with a brief description of each one. The first column shows the name of the service, which is the same as the name of the program that has to run to provide the service. You may not see all of these services listed when you run the service configuration utility on your system because the exact list of services depends on what is installed on your Red Hat Linux system.

Table 1-1	Some Common Services in Red Hat Linux
Service Name	*Description*
aep1000	Loads and unloads the driver for the Accelerated Encryption Processing card called the AEP1000, which can do encryption fast (use this only if you have the card installed in your system).
anacron	Executes commands that are scheduled to run periodically.
apmd	Monitors the Advanced Power Management (APM) BIOS and logs the status of electric power (AC or battery backup).
atd	Runs commands scheduled by the at and cron commands.
autofs	Automatically mounts file systems (for example, when you insert a CD-ROM in the CD-ROM drive).
bcm5820	Loads and unloads the driver for Broadcom's BCM5820 Cryptonet SSL (secure sockets layer) accelerator chip (use this service only if you have the hardware installed).
crond	Runs user-specified programs according to a periodic schedule the crontab command has set.
finger	Answers finger protocol requests (for user information, such as login name and last login time). You have to enable xinetd for this service to run.
gpm	Enables use of mouse in text-mode screens.
httpd	This is the Apache World Wide Web (WWW) server.
imap	Allows remote IMAP (Internet Message Access Protocol) clients to download mail messages. You have to enable xinetd for this service to run.
imaps	Allows remote IMAP (Internet Message Access Protocol) clients with secure sockets layer (SSL) support to securely download mail messages. You have to enable xinetd for this service to run.
innd	This is the InterNetNews daemon — the Internet news server you can use to support local newsgroups on your system.

Service Name	Description
ipop3	Allows remote POP3 (Post Office Protocol version 3) clients to download mail messages. You have to enable xinetd for this service to run.
iptables	Automates a packet-filtering firewall with iptables.
irda	Supports communications with IrDA-compliant infrared devices in Linux (IrDA is a standard for infrared wireless communication at speeds ranging from 2400bps to 4Mbps.).
isdn	Starts and stops ISDN (Integrated Services Digital Network) services — a digital communication service over regular phone lines (enable only if you have ISDN service).
keytable	Loads the selected keyboard map as specified in the file /etc/sysconfig/keyboard. You should leave this service running on your system.
kudzu	Probes for new hardware and configures changed hardware.
lpd	Server that manages the queue of print jobs and sends the print jobs to the printer. You need this server if you want to do any printing from the Red Hat Linux system.
named	This is a server for the Domain Name System (DNS) that translates host names into IP addresses. You can run a copy on your system if you want.
netfs	Enables you to mount and unmount all network file systems (NFS, Samba, and Netware).
network	Enables you to activate or deactivate all network interfaces configured to start at system boot time.
nfs	Enables sharing of file systems specified in the /etc/exports file using the Network File System (NFS) protocol.
nfslock	Provides file-locking capability for file systems exported using the Network File System (NFS) protocol, so that other systems (running NFS) can share files from your system.
ntalk	Provides support for chatting with users on different systems.
ntpd	This is the server for Network Time Protocol version 4 (NTPv4) that is used for synchronizing clocks on computers in a network.
pcmcia	Provides support for PCMCIA devices.
pop3s	Allows remote POP3 (Post Office Protocol version 3) clients that support SSL to securely download mail messages. You have to enable xinetd for this service to run.
portmap	Server used by any software that relies on Remote Procedure Calls (RPC). For example, NFS requires the portmap service.
postgresql	Starts or stops the PostgreSQL server that handles database requests. (PostgreSQL is a free database that comes with Red Hat Linux.)

**Book VII
Chapter 1**

**Managing
the Servers**

(continued)

Table 1-1 *(continued)*

Service Name	Description
pxe	Server for preboot execution environment (PXE) that's used to boot other systems over the network.
random	Server needed to generate high-quality random numbers on the Red Hat Linux system.
rawdevices	Assigns raw devices to block devices (needed for applications such as Oracle).
rexec	Supports remote execution with authentication based on username and password. You have to enable xinetd for this service to run.
rhnsd	Periodically connects to the Red Hat Network Services servers to check for updates and notifications.
rlogin	Server that supports remote login. You have to enable xinetd for this service to run.
rsh	Server that supports remote execution of commands. You have to enable xinetd for this service to run.
rsync	Server that supports remote copying of files. You have to enable xinetd for this service to run.
saslauthd	Supports authentication using the Cyrus-SASL (Simple Authentication and Security Layer) software.
sendmail	Moves mail messages from one machine to another. Start this service if you want to send mail from your Red Hat Linux system. If you do not plan to use your Red Hat Linux system as a mail server, do not start the sendmail server because it can slow down the booting process and consume unnecessary resources.
sgi_fam	Implements a file alternation monitor (FAM) that can be used to get reports when files change.
smb	Starts and stops the Samba smbd and nmbd services that support LAN Manager services on a Red Hat Linux system.
snmpd	Simple Network Management Protocol (SNMP) service used for network-management functions.
squid	A caching server for Internet objects — anything that can be accessed through HTTP and FTP.
sshd	Server for the OpenSSH (Secure Shell) secure remote login facility.
swat	Server for the Samba Web Administration Tool (SWAT) used to configure Samba through a Web browser.
syslog	Service used by many other programs (including other services) to log various error and status messages in a log file (usually the /var/log/messages file). You should always run this service.
talk	Server that supports chatting with users on other systems. You have to enable xinetd for this service to run.

Service Name	Description
telnet	Server that supports TELNET remote login sessions. You have to enable xinetd for this service to run.
tux	This is the kernel-based HTTP server.
vsftpd	Washington University FTP daemon for file transfers using the File Transfer Protocol (FTP).
winbind	Starts and stops the Samba winbindd server that provides a name-switch capability similar to that provided by the /etc/nsswitch:conf file.
xfs	Server that starts and stops the X Font Server.
xinetd	This is the Internet super server, a replacement for the older inetd. It starts other Internet services, such as TELNET and FTP, whenever they are needed.
yppasswdd	Service needed for password changes in Network Information System (NIS). You do not need to start yppasswdd unless you are using NIS.
ypserv	The server for Network Information System (NIS). You do not need to start ypserv unless you are using NIS.
ypxfrd	A server that helps ypserv. Start this service only if you are using Network Information System (NIS).

Chapter 2: Running the Apache Web Server

In This Chapter

✔ Exploring HTTP

✔ Installing the Apache Web server

✔ Configuring the Apache Web server

✔ Supporting virtual hosts with the Apache Web server

The World Wide Web (*WWW* or the *Web*) has catapulted the Internet into the mainstream because Web browsers make it easy for users to browse documents stored on various Internet hosts. Whether you run a small business or manage computer systems and networks for a large company, chances are good that you have to set up and maintain a Web server. Because of its built-in networking support, a Red Hat Linux PC makes an affordable Web server. This chapter describes how to configure the Apache Web server on a Red Hat Linux PC.

Exploring HTTP

Web servers provide information using HTTP. Web servers are also known as *HTTP daemons* (because continuously running server processes are called daemons in UNIX) or *HTTPD* for short. The Web server program (such as the Apache Web server that comes with Red Hat Linux) is usually named httpd.

HTTP stands for *HyperText Transfer Protocol.* The *HyperText* part refers to the fact that Web pages include hypertext links. The *Transfer Protocol* part refers to the standard conventions for transferring a Web page across the network from one computer to another. Although you really do not have to understand HTTP to set up a Web server or use a Web browser, it does help you understand how the Web works.

You can get a firsthand experience with HTTP by using the TELNET program to connect to the port where a Web server listens. On most systems, the Web server listens to port 80 and responds to any HTTP requests sent to that port. Therefore, you can use the TELNET program to connect to port 80 of a system (if it has a Web server) and try some HTTP commands.

Is HTTP an Internet standard?

Despite its widespread use in the Web since 1990, HTTP was not an Internet standard until recently. All Internet standards are distributed as a *Request for Comment* (RFC). The first HTTP-related RFC was RFC 1945, "HyperText Transfer Protocol — HTTP/1.0" (T. Berners-Lee, R. Fielding, and H. Frystyk, May 1996). However, RFC 1945 is considered an informational document, not a standard.

RFC 2616, "HyperText Transfer Protocol — HTTP/1.1" (R. Fielding, J. Gettys, J. Mogul, H. Frystyk, L. Masinter, P. Leach, T. Berners-Lee, June 1999) is the Draft Internet standard for HTTP.

To read these RFCs, point your Web browser to either `www.rfc-editor.org/rfc.html` or `www.cis.ohio-state.edu/htbin/rfc/rfc-index.html`.

To learn more about HTTP/1.1 and other Web-related standards, use a Web browser to access `www.w3.org/pub/WWW/Protocols/`.

To see an example of HTTP at work, follow these steps:

1. **Make sure your Linux PC's connection to the Internet is up and running. (If you use SLIP or PPP, for example, make sure you have established a connection.)**

2. **Type the following command:**

   ```
   telnet www.gao.gov 80
   ```

3. **After you see the** `Connected...` **message, type the following HTTP command and then press Enter twice:**

   ```
   GET / HTTP/1.0
   ```

   In response to this HTTP command, the Web server returns some useful information, followed by the contents of the default HTML file (usually called `index.html`).

The following is what I get when I try the `GET` command on the U. S. General Accounting Office's Web site:

```
Trying 161.203.16.2...
Connected to www.gao.gov.
Escape character is '^]'.
HTTP/1.1 200 OK
Date: Fri, 04 Oct 2002 23:48:15 GMT
Server: Apache/1.3.26 (Unix) PHP/4.1.2 mod_ssl/2.8.10
    OpenSSL/0.9.6g
X-Powered-By: PHP/4.1.2
Connection: close
Content-Type: text/html
```

```
<!DOCTYPE HTML PUBLIC "-//W3C//DTD HTML 4.0 Transitional//EN"
    "http://www.w3.org
/TR/REC-html40/loose.dtd">

<HTML>
<HEAD>
<TITLE>The United States General Accounting Office</TITLE>
...... (lines deleted)
</HEAD>

...... (lines deleted)

</BODY>
</html>
Connection closed by foreign host.
```

When you try this example with TELNET, you see exactly what the
Web server sends back to the Web browser. The first few lines are
administrative information for the browser. The server returns this
information:

+ A line that shows that the server uses HTTP protocol version 1.1 and a
  status code of 200 indicating success:

  ```
  HTTP/1.1 200 OK
  ```

+ The current date and time. A sample date and time string looks
  like this:

  ```
  Date: Fri, 04 Oct 2002 23:48:15 GMT
  ```

+ The name and version of the Web-server software. For example, for a
  site running the Apache Web server version 1.3.26 with the PHP hypertext processor version 4.1.2 along with a number of Apache modules,
  the server returns the following string:

  ```
  Server: Apache/1.3.26 (Unix) PHP/4.1.2 mod_ssl/2.8.10
  OpenSSL/0.9.6g
  ```

+ The type of document the Web server returns. For HTML documents,
  the content type is reported as follows:

  ```
  Content-type: text/html
  ```

The document itself follows the administrative information. An HTML document has the following general layout:

```
<title>Document's title goes here</title>
<html>
<body optional attributes go here >
... The rest of the document goes here
</body>
</html>
```

You can identify this layout by looking through the listing that shows what the Web server returns in response to the GET command. Because the example uses a telnet command to get the document, you see the HTML content as lines of text. If you were to access the same Web site (www.gao.gov) with a Web browser (such as Mozilla), you would see the page in its graphical form (Figure 2-1).

The example of HTTP commands shows the result of the GET command. GET is the most common HTTP command; it causes the server to return a specified HTML document.

The other two HTTP commands are HEAD and POST. The HEAD command is almost like GET: it causes the server to return everything in the document except the body. The POST command sends information to the server; it's up to the server to decide how to act on the information.

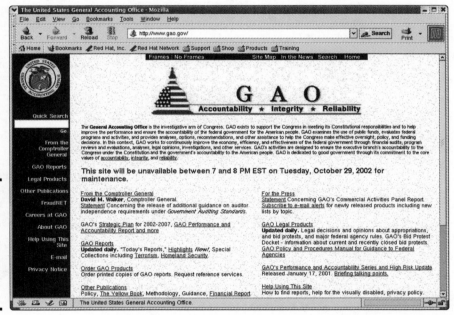

Figure 2-1: The www. gao.gov Web site viewed with the Mozilla Web browser.

Exploring the Apache Web Server

You probably already know how it feels to use the Web, but you may not know how to set up a Web server so that you, too, can provide information to the world through Web pages. To become an information provider on the Web, you have to run a Web server on your Red Hat Linux PC on the Internet. You also have to prepare the Web pages for your Web site — a task that may be more demanding than the Web server setup.

Among the available Web servers, the Apache Web server is the most popular, and it comes with Red Hat Linux. The Apache Web server started out as an improved version of the NCSA HTTPD server but soon grew into a separate development effort. Like NCSA HTTPD, the Apache server is developed and maintained by a team of collaborators. Apache is freely available over the Internet.

Installing the Apache Web server

Depending on the Red Hat Linux installation options, the Apache Web server may be already installed in your system. To check if it's installed, type the following command:

```
rpm -q httpd
```

If the Web server is installed, you should see an output like this:

```
httpd-2.0.40-8
```

If you get a message that `httpd` is not installed, then you can install it easily from this book's companion CD-ROMs using these steps:

1. **Log in as** `root` **and insert the first CD-ROM into the CD drive. If you are in GNOME or KDE graphical desktop, the CD should be automatically mounted. If not, type the command** `mount /dev/cdrom` **to mount the CD-ROM.**

2. **Type the following commands to install the Apache Web server:**

```
cd /mnt/cdrom/RedHat/RPMS
rpm -ivh httpd*
```

That's it! You can now run the Apache Web server.

Starting the Apache Web server

Even if the Apache Web server is installed, it may not be set up to start at boot time. If you want to try it out, you have to start the server. To do so, log in as `root` and type the following command:

```
service httpd start
```

Why is it called Apache?

According to the information about the Apache Web server project on `www.apache.org/foundation/faq.html`, the Apache group was formed in March 1995 by a number of people who provided patch files that had been written to fix bugs in NCSA HTTPD 1.3. The result after applying the patches to NCSA HTTPD was what they called a *patchy server* (that's how the name Apache came about). The Apache Group has now evolved into The Apache Software Foundation (ASF), a nonprofit corporation that was incorporated in Delaware, USA, in June 1999. ASF has a number of other ongoing projects. You can read about these projects at `www.apache.org`. In particular, visit `httpd.apache.org` for more information about the Apache Web server project.

According to the August 2002 Netcraft Web Server Survey at `www.netcraft.co.uk/Survey/`, the Apache Web server is the most popular — 63.51 percent of 35,991,815 sites reported using the Apache server. Microsoft Internet Information Server (IIS) is a distant second, with 25.39 percent of the sites.

To see whether or not the `httpd` process (`httpd` is the name of the Apache Web server program) is running, type the following command:

```
ps ax | grep httpd
```

The output should show a number of `httpd` processes. It is a common approach to run several Web server processes — one parent and several child processes — so that several HTTP requests can be handled efficiently by assigning each request to an `httpd` process.

If there is no `httpd` process, there may be errors in the Apache configuration file. If this is the case, there should be some error messages that give you a clue about the cause of the error. You have to fix the problem in the configuration file and start the server again.

If the httpd processes are up and running, you can use the TELNET program to see if it works, but first you need to add a default home page in the /var/www/html directory. If you don't have time to prepare one, copy the Web page that's supposed to be sent out in case of errors. Here's the command you type (while logged in as root):

```
cp /var/www/error/noindex.html /var/www/html/index.html
```

Now you have a default home page and you can type the following command in a terminal window to check out if the Web server is working or not:

```
telnet localhost 80
```

After you get the `Connected` message, type

```
HEAD / HTTP/1.0
```

Then press Enter twice. You should get a response that looks similar to the following (of course with different dates and numbers):

```
HTTP/1.1 200 OK
Date: Sun, 01 Sep 2002 19:20:16 GMT
Server: Apache/2.0.40 (Red Hat Linux)
Last-Modified: Sun, 01 Sep 2002 19:19:53 GMT
ETag: "64a0f-b52-f8b80840"
Accept-Ranges: bytes
Content-Length: 2898
Connection: close
Content-Type: text/html; charset=ISO-8859-1

Connection closed by foreign host.
```

The response shows some information about the Web server and the default home page. You can also check out the Web server by using a Web browser such as Mozilla running on your Red Hat Linux system. For example, if your system's IP address is 192.168.0.5, use the URL `http://192/168.0.5/` and see what happens. You should see a Web page with the title "Test Page for the Apache Web Server on Red Hat Linux."

If you want to start the Apache Web server automatically at boot time, type the following command to set it up:

```
chkconfig --levels 35 httpd on
```

Configuring the Apache Web Server

Red Hat Linux configures the Apache Web server software to use these directories:

✦ The Web server program — `httpd` — is installed in the `/usr/sbin` directory.

✦ The Apache Web server configuration file — `httpd.conf` — is located in the `/etc/httpd/conf` directory. The configuration file is a text file with directives that specify various aspects of the Web server. The `/etc/httpd/conf` directory also contains information about the Secure Sockets Layer (SSL) implementation needs. (The SSL implementation comes as part of the Apache Web server.)

✦ The Apache Web server is set up to serve the HTML documents from the `/var/www/html` directory. Therefore, you should place your Web pages in this directory.

✦ If you have any Common Gateway Interface (CGI) programs — programs the Web server can invoke to access other files and databases — you should place these in the `/var/www/cgi-bin/` directory.

✦ The `/var/log/httpd` directory is meant for Web server log files (access logs and error logs).

✦ The `/etc/init.d/httpd` script starts the `httpd` process as your Red Hat Linux system boots, provided you have enabled it by using the `chkconfig` command.

Using Apache configuration tools

Red Hat Linux comes with a graphical configuration tool that you can use to configure the Apache Web server. To run this configuration tool, log in as `root` and select Main Menu⇨Server Settings⇨HTTP Server from the GNOME desktop. The Apache Configuration window appears (Figure 2-2).

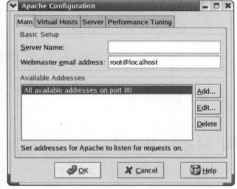

Figure 2-2: You can configure the Apache HTTP server from this configuration window.

The Apache Configuration window is organized into four tabs. You can set various options from each of these tabs:

✦ **Main** — From this tab you can specify the IP addresses and port number where Apache should expect requests for Web service. You can also set the e-mail address of the Webmaster.

✦ **Virtual Hosts** — Here you can set up virtual hosts. I discuss the options for virtual hosts later in this chapter. You can also edit the default settings that apply to all virtual hosts. Clicking the Edit Default Settings button in the Virtual Hosts tab brings up another window (Figure 2-3) from which you can set a number of different options.

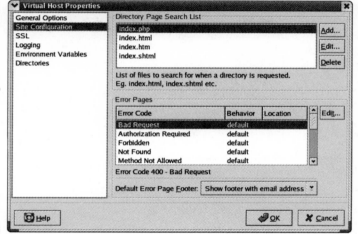

Figure 2-3:
You can
configure
the virtual
host
properties
from this
configura-
tion window.

**Book VII
Chapter 2**

**Running the Apache
Web Server**

✦ **Server** — This tab has settings for the server such as the user and group names under which the HTTP server should run and the locations of the file where the process ID is stored.

✦ **Performance Tuning** — On this tab you can set some parameters that control the overall performance. You can set the maximum number of connections allowed, the timeout period for connections, and maximum number of requests per connection.

Initially the configuration window displays the default values from the configuration file /etc/httpd/conf/httpd.conf. After you make any changes, click the OK button. The configuration tool prompts you if you really want to save the changes and exit. If you do, click Yes and you should be done.

When you configure the Apache HTTP server from this configuration tool, all you are doing is changing options and attributes stored in the /etc/ httpd/conf/httpd.conf file. You can just as easily make the changes by editing the configuration file, which is a plain text file. In the next sections, I introduce you to some common configuration directives in the Apache configuration file.

Apache configuration files

The Apache server's operation is controlled by the httpd.conf configuration file located in the /etc/httpd/conf directory. This file controls how the server runs, what documents it serves, and who can access these documents.

In the next few sections, I summarize the key information about the `httpd.conf` configuration file. Typically, you do not have to change anything in the configuration files to run the Apache Web server. However, it is useful to know the format of the configuration files and the meaning of the various keywords used in them.

As you study the configuration files in the `/etc/httpd/conf` directory, keep these syntax rules in mind:

- ✦ Each configuration file is a text file that you can edit with your favorite text editor and view with the `more` command.
- ✦ All comment lines begin with a #.
- ✦ Each line can have only one directive.
- ✦ Extra spaces and blank lines are ignored.
- ✦ All entries, except pathnames and URLs, are case insensitive.

The httpd.conf configuration file

The `/etc/httpd/conf/httpd.conf` file is the main HTTP daemon configuration file — it includes directives that control how the Apache Web server runs. For example, the `httpd.conf` file specifies the port number the server uses, the name of the Web site, and the e-mail address to which mail is sent in case of any problems with the server. In addition, `httpd.conf` also includes information on where the Web pages are located and who can access what directories.

In the following sections, I present the Apache directives grouped into three separate categories: general HTTPD directives, resource configuration directives, and access-control directives. Finally, I explain how virtual hosts can be set up in Apache Web server so that a single Web server can handle Web requests sent to several IP addresses or host names.

General HTTPD directives

Some interesting items from the `httpd.conf` file are

- ✦ `ServerName` specifies the host name of your Web site (of the form `www.your.domain`) and the port number where the Web server accepts connections. `ServerName` is used only when redirecting a Web page to another Web page. The name should be a registered domain name other users can locate through their name servers. Here is an example:

    ```
    ServerName  www.myhost.com:80
    ```

    If you do not have registered domain name, use the IP address of your Red Hat Linux system.

✦ ServerAdmin is the e-mail address that the Web server provides to clients in case any errors occur. The default value for ServerAdmin is root@localhost. You should set this to a valid e-mail address that anyone on the Internet can use to report errors your Web site contains.

Many more directives control the way that the Apache Web server works. The following list summarizes some of the directives you can use in the httpd.conf file. You can leave most of these directives in their default settings, but it's important to know about them if you are maintaining a Web server.

✦ Listen *IP-Address:Port* — Forces the Web server to listen to a specific IP address and port number. By default, the Web server responds to all IP addresses associated with the host.

✦ User *name* [#*id*] — Specifies the user name (or ID) the HTTP daemon uses. You can leave this directive at the default setting (apache). If you specify a user ID, use a hash (#) prefix for the numeric ID.

✦ Group *name* [#*id*] — Specifies the group name (or ID) of the HTTP daemon when running in stand-alone mode. The default group name is apache.

✦ ServerRoot *pathname* — Specifies the directory where the Web server is located. By default, the configuration and log files are expected to reside in subdirectories of this directory. In Red Hat Linux, ServerRoot is set to /etc/httpd.

✦ ServerName *www.company.com*:80 — Sets the server's host name to *www.company.com* and the port number to 80. ServerName is used only when redirecting a Web page to another.

✦ StartServers *num* — Sets the number of child processes that start as soon as the Apache Web server runs. The default value is 8.

✦ MaxSpareServers *num* — Sets the desired maximum number of idle child-server processes (a child process is considered idle if it is not handling an HTTP request). The default value is 20.

✦ MinSpareServers *num* — Sets the desired minimum number of idle child server processes (a child process is considered idle if it is not handling an HTTP request). A new spare process is created every second if the number falls below this threshold. The default value is 5.

✦ Timeout *numsec* — Sets the number of seconds that the server waits for a client to send a query after the client establishes connection. The default Timeout is 300 seconds (five minutes).

✦ ErrorLog *filename* — Sets the file where httpd logs the errors it encounters. If the filename does not begin with a slash (/), the name is

**Book VII
Chapter 2**

**Running the Apache
Web Server**

taken to be relative to `ServerRoot`. The default `ErrorLog` is `/etc/httpd`
`/logs/error_log`, but `/etc/httpd/logs` is a symbolic link to the
`/var/log/httpd` directory. Therefore, the log files are in `/var/`
`log/.httpd` directory. Typical error-log entries include events such
as server restarts and any warning messages, such as the following:

```
[Sun Sep 01 11:42:50 2002] [notice] Apache/2.0.40 (Red Hat Linux)
    configured -- resuming normal operations
[Sun Sep 01 11:42:59 2002] [error] [client 127.0.0.1] Directory index
    forbidden by rule: /var/www/html/
```

✦ `TransferLog` *filename* — Sets the file where `httpd` records all client
accesses (including failed accesses). The default `TransferLog` is `/var/`
`log/httpd/access_log`. The following example shows how a typical
access is recorded in this log file:

```
192.168.0.5 - - [01/Sep/2002:15:26:15 -0400] "GET / HTTP/1.1" 200 2898
    "-" "Mozilla/4.0 (compatible; MSIE 6.0; Windows NT 5.1)"
192.168.0.5 - - [01/Sep/2002:15:26:15 -0400] "GET /icons/apache_pb.gif
    HTTP/1.1" 304 0 "http://192.168.0.4/" "Mozilla/4.0 (compatible; MSIE
    6.0; Windows NT 5.1)"
192.168.0.5 - - [01/Sep/2002:15:26:15 -0400] "GET /icons/powered_by.gif
    HTTP/1.1" 304 0 "http://192.168.0.4/" "Mozilla/4.0 (compatible; MSIE
    6.0; Windows NT 5.1)"
```

✦ `LogFormat` *formatstring formatname* — Specifies the format of
log-file entries for the `TransferLog`. This format is also used by the
`CustomLog` directive to produce logs in a specific format.

✦ `CustomLog` *filename formatname* — Sets the name of the custom log
file where `httpd` records all client accesses (including failed accesses)
in a format specified by *formatname* (which you define using a
`LogFormat` directive).

✦ `PidFile` *filename* — Sets the file where HTTPD stores its process ID.
The default `PidFile` is `/var/run/httpd.pid`. You can use this
information to kill or restart the HTTP daemon. The following example
shows how to restart `httpd`:

```
kill -HUP `cat /var/run/httpd.pid`
```

✦ `MaxClients` *num* — Sets the limit on the number of clients that can
simultaneously connect to the server. The default value is 150. The
value of `MaxClients` cannot be more than 256.

✦ `LoadModule` *module* `modules/modfile.so` — Loads a module that
was built as a Dynamic Shared Object (DSO). You have to specify the
module name and the module's object file. Because the order in which
modules are loaded is important, you should leave these directives as
they appear in the default configuration file.

Resource configuration directives

The resource configuration directives specify the location of the Web pages, as well as how to specify the data types of various files. To get started, you can leave the directives at their default settings. These are some of the resource configuration directives for the Apache Web server:

✦ `DocumentRoot` *pathname* — Specifies the directory where the HTTP server finds the Web pages. In Red Hat Linux, the default `DocumentRoot` is `/var/www/html`. If you place your HTML documents in another directory, set `DocumentRoot` to that directory.

✦ `UserDir` *dirname* — Specifies the directory below a user's home directory where the HTTP server looks for the Web pages when a user-name appears in the URL (in an URL such as `http://www.psn.net/~naba`, for example, which includes a username with a tilde prefix). By default the `UserDir` feature is turned off by setting *dirname* to `disable`. If you want it enabled, you can set it to `public_html`, which means that a user's Web pages are in the `public_html` subdirectory of that user's home directory.

✦ `DirectoryIndex` *filename1 filename2 ...* — Indicates the default file or files to be returned by the server when the client does not specify a document. The default `DirectoryIndex` is `index.html`. If httpd does not find this file, it returns an index (basically, a nice-looking listing of the files) of that directory provided indexing is allowed for that directory.

✦ `AccessFileName` *filename* — Specifies the name of the file that may appear in each directory that contains documents and that indicates who has permission to access the contents of that directory. The default `AccessFileName` is `.htaccess`. The syntax of this file is the same as that of Apache access-control directives, which I discuss in the next section.

✦ `AddType` *type/subtype extension* — Associates a file extension with a MIME data type (of the form *type/subtype*, such as `text/plain` or `image/gif`). Thus, to have the server treat files with the `.lst` extension as plain-text files, specify the following:

```
AddType text/plain .lst
```

The default MIME types and extensions are listed in the `/etc/mime.types` file.

✦ `AddEncoding` *type extension* — Associates an encoding type with a file extension. To have the server mark files ending with `.gz` or `.tgz` as encoded with the `x-gzip` encoding method (the standard name for the GZIP encoding), specify the following:

```
AddEncoding x-gzip gz tgz
```

✦ DefaultType `type/subtype` — Specifies the MIME type that the server should use if it cannot determine the type from the file extension. If you do not specify `DefaultType`, HTTPD assumes the MIME type to be `text/html`. In the default `httpd.conf` file, `DefaultType` is specified as `text/plain`.

✦ Redirect `requested-file actual-URL` — Specifies that any requests for `requested-file` are to be redirected to `actual-URL`.

✦ Alias `requested-dir actual-dir` — Specifies that the server use `actual-dir` to locate files in the `requested-dir` directory (in other words, `requested-dir` is an alias for `actual-dir`). To have requests for the `/icons` directory go to `/var/www/icons`, specify the following:

```
Alias /icons/ /var/www/icons/
```

✦ ScriptAlias `requested-dir actual-dir` — Specifies the real name of the directory where scripts for the Common Gateway Interface (CGI) are located. The default configuration file contains this directive:

```
ScriptAlias /cgi-bin/ "/var/www/cgi-bin/"
```

This directive means that when a Web browser requests a script, such as `/cgi-bin/test-cgi`, the HTTP server runs the script `/var/www/cgi-bin/test-cgi`.

✦ DefaultIcon `iconfile` — Specifies the location of the default icon that the server should use for files that have no icon information. By default, `DefaultIcon` is `/icons/unknown.gif`.

✦ ReadmeName `filename` — Specifies the name of a `README` file whose contents are added to the end of an automatically generated directory listing. The default `ReadmeName` is `README`.

✦ HeaderName `filename` — Specifies the name a header file whose contents are prepended to an automatically generated directory listing. The default `HeaderName` is `HEADER`.

✦ AddDescription `"file description" filename` — Specifies that the `file description` string be displayed next to the specified filename in the directory listing. You can use a wildcard, such as `*.html`, as the filename. For example, the following directive describes files ending with `.tgz` as GZIP compressed `tar` archives:

```
AddDescription "GZIP compressed tar archive" .tgz
```

✦ AddIcon `iconfile extension1 extension2 ...` — Associates an icon with one or more file extensions. The following directive associates the icon file `/icons/text.gif` with the file extension `.txt`:

```
AddIcon /icons/text.gif .txt
```

✦ AddIconByType *iconfile MIME-types* — Associates an icon with a group of file types specified as a wildcard form of MIME types (such as text/* or image/*). To associate an icon file of /icons/text.gif with all text types, specify the following:

```
AddIconByType (TXT,/icons/text.gif) text/*
```

This directive also tells the server to use TXT in place of the icon for clients that cannot accept images. (Browsers tell the server what types of data they can accept.)

✦ AddIconByEncoding *iconfile encoding1 encoding2 ...* — Specifies an icon to be displayed for one or more encoding types (such as x-compress or x-gzip).

✦ IndexIgnore *filename1 filename2 ...* — Instructs the server to ignore the specified filenames (they typically contain wildcards) when preparing a directory listing. To leave out README, HEADER, and all files with names that begin with a period (.), a trailing tilde (~), or a trailing hash mark (#), specify the following:

```
IndexIgnore .??* *~ *# HEADER* README* RCS CVS *,v *,t
```

✦ IndexOptions *option1 option2 ...* — Indicates the options you want in the directory listing prepared by the server. Options can include one or more of the following:

- FancyIndexing turns on the fancy directory listing that includes filenames and icons representing the files' types, sizes, and last-modified dates.

- IconHeight=N specifies that icons are N pixels tall.

- IconWidth=N specifies that icons are N pixels wide.

- NameWidth=N makes the filename column N characters wide.

- IconsAreLinks makes the icons act like links.

- ScanHTMLTitles shows a description of HTML files.

- SuppressHTMLPreamble does not add a standard HTML preamble to the header file (specified by the HeaderName directive).

- SuppressLastModified stops display of the last date of modification.

- SuppressSize stops display of the file size.

- SuppressDescription stops display of any file description.

- SuppressColumnSorting stops the column headings from being links that enable sorting the columns.

✦ ErrorDocument *errortype filename* — Specifies a file the server should send when an error of a specific type occurs. You can also provide a text message for an error. Here are some examples:

Book VII
Chapter 2

Running the Apache Web Server

```
ErrorDocument 403 "Sorry, no access to this directory"
ErrorDocument 403 /error/noindex.html
ErrorDocument 404 /cgi-bin/bad_link.pl
ErrorDocument 401 /new_subscriber.html
```

If you do not have the `ErrorDocument` directive, the server sends a built-in error message. The *errortype* can be one of the following `HTTP/1.1` error conditions (see RFC 2616 at `www.ietf.org/rfc/rfc2616.txt` or `www.cis.ohio-state.edu/htbin/rfc/rfc2616.html` for more information):

- 400 — Bad Request
- 401 — Unauthorized
- 402 — Payment Required
- 403 — Forbidden
- 404 — Not Found
- 405 — Method Not Allowed
- 406 — Not Acceptable
- 407 — Proxy Authentication Required
- 408 — Request Timeout
- 409 — Conflict
- 410 — Gone
- 411 — Length Required
- 412 — Precondition Failed
- 413 — Request Entity Too Large
- 414 — Request-URI Too Long
- 415 — Unsupported Media Type
- 416 — Requested Range Not Satisfiable
- 417 — Expectation Failed
- 500 — Internal Server Error
- 501 — Not Implemented
- 502 — Bad Gateway
- 503 — Service Unavailable
- 504 — Gateway Timeout
- 505 — HTTP Version Not Supported

♦ TypesConfig *filename* — Specifies the file that contains the mapping of file extensions to MIME data types. (MIME stands for Multipurpose Internet Mail Extensions, which defines a way to package attachments in a single message file.) The server reports these MIME types to clients. If you do not specify a TypesConfig directive, HTTPD assumes that the TypesConfig **file is** /etc/mime.types. The following are a few selected lines from the default /etc/mime.types file:

```
application/msword              doc
application/pdf                 pdf
application/postscript          ai eps ps
application/x-tcl               tcl
audio/mpeg                      mpga mp2 mp3
audio/x-pn-realaudio            ram rm
audio/x-wav                     wav
image/gif                       gif
image/jpeg                      jpeg jpg jpe
image/png                       png
text/html                       html htm
text/plain                      asc txt
video/mpeg                      mpeg mpg mpe
```

Each line shows the MIME type (such as text/html), followed by the file extensions for that type (html or htm).

Access-control directives

Access-control directives enable you to control who can access different directories in the system. These are the global access-configuration directives. You can also have another access-configuration file with the name specified by the AccessFileName directive in each directory from which the Apache Web server can serve documents. (That per-directory access-configuration file is named .htaccess by default.)

Stripped of most of the comment lines, the access-control directive has this format:

```
# First, we configure the "default" to be a
# very restrictive set of permissions.
<Directory />
    Options FollowSymLinks
    AllowOverride None
</Directory>

# The following directory name should
# match DocumentRoot in httpd.conf
<Directory /var/www/html>
    Options Indexes FollowSymLinks
    AllowOverride None
    order allow,deny
```

```
        allow from all
</Directory>

# The directory name should match the
# location of the cgi-bin directory
<Directory "/var/www/cgi-bin">
    AllowOverride None
    Options None
    Order allow,deny
    Allow from all
</Directory>
```

Access-control directives use a different syntax from the other Apache directives. The syntax is like that of HTML. Various access-control directives are enclosed within pairs of tags, such as `<Directory>` ... `</Directory>`.

The following list describes some of the access-control directives. In particular, notice the `AuthUserFile` directive; you can have password-based access control for specific directories.

✦ `Options opt1 opt2 ...` — Specifies the access-control options for the directory section in which this directive appears. The options can be one or more of the following:

  • `None` disables all access-control features.

  • `All` turns on all features for the directory.

  • `FollowSymLinks` enables the server to follow symbolic links.

  • `SymLinksIfOwnerMatch` follows symbolic links, only if the same user of the directory owns the linked directory.

  • `ExecCGI` enables execution of CGI scripts in the directory.

  • `Includes` enables server-side include files in this directory (the term *server-side include* refers to directives, placed in an HTML file, that the Web server processes before returning the results to the Web browser).

  • `Indexes` enables clients to request indexes (directory listings) for the directory.

  • `IncludesNOEXEC` disables the #exec command in server-side includes.

✦ `AllowOverride directive1 directive2 ...` — Specifies which access-control directives can be overridden on a per-directory basis. The directive list can contain one or more of the following:

  • `None` stops any directive from being overridden.

  • `All` enables overriding of any directive on a per-directory basis.

- ◆ `Options` **enables the use of the** `Options` **directive in the directory-level file.**
- ◆ `FileInfo` **enables the use of directives controlling document type, such as** `AddType` **and** `AddEncoding`.
- ◆ `AuthConfig` **enables the use of authorization directives, such as** `AuthName`, `AuthType`, `AuthUserFile`, **and** `AuthGroupFile`.
- ◆ `Limit` **enables the use of** `Limit` **directives (**`allow`, `deny`, **and** `order`**) in a directory's access-configuration file.**

◆ `AuthName` *name* — **Specifies the authorization name for a directory.**

◆ `AuthType` *type* — **Specifies the type of authorization to be used. The only supported authorization type is Basic.**

◆ `AuthUserFile` *filename* — **Specifies the file in which usernames and passwords are stored for authorization. For example, the following directive sets the authorization file to** `/etc/httpd/conf/passwd`:

```
AuthUserFile /etc/httpd/conf/passwd
```

You have to create the authorization file with the `/usr/bin/htpasswd` **support program. To create the authorization file and add the password for a user named** `jdoe`, **specify the following:**

```
/usr/bin/htpasswd -c /etc/httpd/conf/passwd jdoe
```

When prompted for the password, enter the password and then confirm it by typing it again.

◆ `AuthGroupFile` *filename* — **Specifies the file to consult for a list of user groups for authentication.**

◆ `order` *ord* — **Specifies the order in which two other directives —** `allow` **and** `deny` — **are evaluated. The order is one of the following:**

- ◆ `deny,allow` **causes the Web server to evaluate the** `deny` **directive before** `allow`.
- ◆ `allow,deny` **causes the Web server to evaluate the** `allow` **directive before** `deny`.
- ◆ `mutual-failure` **enables only hosts in the** `allow` **list.**

◆ `deny from` *host1 host2...* — **Specifies the hosts denied access.**

◆ `allow from host1 host2...` — **Specifies the hosts allowed access. To enable all hosts in a specific domain to access the Web documents in a directory, specify the following:**

```
order deny,allow
allow from .nws.noaa.gov
```

◆ `require` *entity en1 en2...* — **This directive specifies which users can access a directory. entity is one of the following:**

- `user` enables only a list of named users.

- `group` enables only a list of named groups.

- `valid-user` enables all users listed in the `AuthUserFile` access to the directory (provided that they enter the correct password).

Virtual host setup

A useful feature of the Apache HTTP server is its ability to handle virtual Web servers. *Virtual hosting* simply means that a single Web server can respond to many different IP addresses and serve Web pages from different directories, depending on the IP address. That means you can set up a single Web server to respond to both `www.big.org` and `www.tiny.com` and serve a unique home page for each host name. A server with this capability is known as multi-homed Web server, a virtual Web server, or a server with virtual host support.

As you might guess, Internet Service Providers (ISPs) use the virtual host feature of Apache Web server to offer virtual Web sites to their customers. You need the following to support virtual hosts:

✦ The Web server must be able to respond to multiple IP addresses (each with a unique domain name) and must enable you to specify document directories, log files, and other configuration items for each IP address.

✦ The host system must be able to associate multiple IP addresses with a single physical network interface. Red Hat Linux can do this.

✦ Each domain name associated with the IP address must be a unique registered domain name with proper DNS entries.

For the latest information on how to set up virtual hosts in an Apache HTTP server, consult the following URL:

```
http://httpd.apache.org/docs-2.0/vhosts
```

The Apache HTTP server can respond to different host names with different home pages. You have two options when supporting virtual hosts:

✦ **Run multiple copies of the** `httpd` **program, one for each IP address** — In this case, you create a separate copy of the `httpd.conf` configuration file for each host and use the `Listen` directive to make the server respond to a specific IP address.

✦ **Run a single copy of the** `httpd` **program with a single** `httpd.conf` **file** — In the configuration file, set `Listen` to a port number only (so that the server responds to any IP address associated with the host), and use the `VirtualHost` directive to configure the server for each virtual host.

Run multiple HTTP daemons only if you do not expect heavy traffic on your system; the system may not able to respond well because of the overhead associated with running multiple daemons. However, you may need multiple HTTP daemons if each virtual host has a unique configuration need for the following directives:

+ `UserId` and `GroupId` (the user and group ID for the HTTP daemon)
+ `ServerRoot` (the `root` directory of the server)
+ `TypesConfig` (the MIME type configuration file)

For a site with heavy traffic, configure the Web server so that a single HTTP daemon can serve multiple virtual hosts. Of course, this recommendation implies that there is only one configuration file. In that configuration file, use the `VirtualHost` directive to configure each virtual host.

Most ISPs use the `VirtualHost` capability of Apache HTTP server to provide virtual Web sites to their customers. Unless you pay for a dedicated Web host, you typically get a virtual site where you have your own domain name, but share the server and the actual host with many other customers.

The syntax of the `VirtualHost` directive is as follows:

```
<VirtualHost hostaddr>
    ... directives that apply to this host
    ...
</VirtualHost>
```

With this syntax, you use `<VirtualHost>` and `</VirtualHost>` to enclose a group of directives that applies only to the particular virtual host identified by the *hostaddr* parameter. The *hostaddr* can be an IP address or the fully qualified domain name of the virtual host.

You can place almost any Apache directives within the `<VirtualHost>` block. At a minimum, Webmasters include the following directives in the `<VirtualHost>` block:

+ `DocumentRoot`, which specifies where this virtual host's documents reside
+ `Servername`, which identifies the server to the outside world (this should be a registered domain name DNS supports)
+ `ServerAdmin`, the e-mail address of this virtual host's Webmaster
+ `Redirect`, which specifies any URLs to be redirected to other URLs
+ `ErrorLog`, which specifies the file where errors related to this virtual host are to be logged.

✦ `CustomLog`, which specifies the file where accesses to this virtual host are logged

When the server receives a request for a document in a particular virtual host's `DocumentRoot` directory, it uses the configuration parameters within that server's `<VirtualHost>` block to handle that request.

Here is a typical example of a `<VirtualHost>` directive that sets up the virtual host `www.lnbsoft.com`:

```
<VirtualHost www.lnbsoft.com>
    DocumentRoot    /home/naba/httpd/htdocs
    ServerName   www.lnbsoft.com
    ServerAdmin   webmaster@lnbsoft.com
    ScriptAlias   /cgi-bin/   /home/naba/httpd/cgi-bin/
    ErrorLog /home/naba/httpd/logs/error_log
    CustomLog   /home/naba/httpd/logs/access_log common
</VirtualHost>
```

Here the name `common` in the `CustomLog` directive refers to the name of a format defined earlier in the `httpd.conf` file by the `LogFormat` directive, as follows:

```
LogFormat "%h %l %u %t \"%r\" %>s %b" common
```

This format string for the log produces lines in the log file looks like this:

```
dial236.dc.psn.net - - [29/Aug/2002:18:09:00 -0500] "GET /
    HTTP/1.0" 200 1243
```

The format string contains two letter tokens that start with a percent sign (%). The meaning of these tokens is shown in Table 2-1.

Table 2-1	LogFormat Tokens
Token	*Meaning*
`%b`	The number of bytes sent to the client, excluding header information
`%h`	The host name of the client machine
`%l`	The identity of the user, if available
`%r`	The HTTP request from the client (for example, `GET / HTTP/1.0`)
`%s`	The server response code from the Web server
`%t`	The current local date and time
`%u`	The user name the user supplies (only when access-control rules require user name/password authentication)

Chapter 3: Setting Up the FTP Server

In This Chapter

✔ **Installing the FTP server**

✔ **Configuring the FTP server**

✔ **Setting up anonymous FTP**

*F*ile Transfer Protocol (FTP) is a popular Internet service for transferring files from one system to another. *Anonymous FTP* is another popular Internet service for distributing files. The neat thing about anonymous FTP is that if a remote system supports anonymous FTP, anyone can use FTP with the `anonymous` user ID and can download files from that system. Although anonymous FTP is useful for distributing data, it poses a security risk if it is not set up properly.

Red Hat Linux comes with several FTP clients and the "very secure" FTP daemon (`vsftpd`), written by Chris Evans. Red Hat Linux also includes an RPM called `anonftp` that sets up the files you need to support anonymous FTP. In this chapter, I show you how to configure the FTP server through text configuration files and how to control access to the FTP server. I also describe anonymous FTP — how it's set up and how to ensure that it's secure.

Installing the FTP Server

During Red Hat Linux installation, you have the option to install the FTP Server software. To check if the FTP server is already installed, type the following command:

```
rpm -q vsftpd
```

If the software is indeed installed, you should see an output similar to the following:

```
vsftpd-1.1.0-1
```

If you get a message saying that the package is not installed, you can easily install it from the companion CD-ROMs. To install the RPM files for FTP, log in as `root` and place the first CD-ROM in the CD-ROM drive. If you are using the GNOME or KDE desktop, the CD-ROM should mount automatically. If not, type the following command to mount the CD-ROM:

```
mount /mnt/cdrom
```

Then type the following command to change the directory:

```
cd /mnt/cdrom/RedHat/RPMS
```

This is where you find the RPM files for FTP. You can install both the FTP server and the anonymous FTP package with the following RPM commands:

```
rpm -ivh vsftpd*
rpm -ivh anonftp*
```

Configuring the FTP Server

Red Hat Linux comes with the very secure FTP daemon (`vsftpd`), written by Chris Evans. The executable file for `vsftpd` is `/usr/sbin/vsftpd`, and it uses a number of configuration files in the `/etc` directory. By default, the `vsftpd` server is disabled. This means that if you want to use the FTP server, you have to first enable it. I show you how to enable it.

After you enable the `vsftpd` server, the default settings should be adequate to begin using the server. However, you should learn about the configuration files in case you need to customize them. You also need to know how the FTP server starts, so that you can control who can access it.

xinetd configuration for vsftpd

If you type **ps ax** and look at the list of processes, you won't find a `vsftpd` process. That's because the FTP server is started automatically by another server called `xinetd` — the Internet services daemon. The `xinetd` server listens on all the ports and starts the appropriate server when a client request comes in. For example, clients connect to TCP port 21 when attempting to establish an FTP connection. The following line in the `/etc/services` file associates TCP port 21 with the ftp service:

```
ftp             21/tcp
```

This tells `xinetd` to do whatever its configuration files tell it to do for the `ftp` service. The `/etc/xinetd.d/vsftpd` file contains the information the `xinetd` server uses to handle the request for `ftp` service:

```
# default: off
```

```
# description: The vsftpd FTP server serves FTP connections. It uses \
#   normal, unencrypted usernames and passwords for authentication.
service ftp
{
    disable         = yes
    socket_type       = stream
    wait        = no
    user        = root
    server         = /usr/sbin/vsftpd
    nice        = 10
}
```

I explain the attributes within curly braces in Book VII, Chapter 1. For this section, note that the `server` attribute specifies that the `/usr/sbin/vsftpd` program be run to handle the FTP service connections.

A key attribute is the `disable = yes` setting. As you may have guessed, that directive disables the FTP service. In other words, `xinetd` would not start the `vsftpd` server in response to a request for `ftp` service because of `disable = yes` setting.

To enable `vsftpd`, just edit the `/etc/xinetd.d/vsftpd` file and make sure that the `disable` attribute is set to `no` or comment out that line by placing a # in the first column. After you do that, type the following command to restart the `xinetd` server:

```
service xinetd restart
```

Now the `vsftpd` server should be enabled.

The `xinetd` server does not directly execute the FTP server program (`/usr/sbin/vsftpd`). Instead, it uses the TCP wrapper library to start the server. The TCP wrapper checks two files (`/etc/hosts.allow` and `/etc/hosts.deny`) to determine if the requested service should be allowed or denied. In the default setup, both `/etc/hosts.allow` and `/etc/hosts.deny` are empty. This has the effect of allowing all hosts access to all services.

If you want to limit access to FTP to specific hosts, add the following line to the `/etc/hosts.deny` file:

```
ALL: ALL
```

This denies all hosts access to any Internet service on your host. Now you can permit specific services to specific hosts (specified by name or IP address) by listing them in the `/etc/hosts.allow` file. For example, to allow only hosts from the 192.168.0.0 network access to the FTP service on your system, place the following line in the `/etc/hosts.allow` file:

```
vsftpd: 192.168.1.0/255.255.255.0
```

You must identify the service by its program name (in this case, vsftpd for the FTP server).

Before starting any xinetd-controlled service, the TCP wrapper consults the /etc/hosts.allow file to see if the host requesting service is allowed that service. If there is nothing in /etc/hosts.allow about that host, the TCP wrapper checks the /etc/hosts.deny file to see if the service should be denied. If both files are empty, the TCP wrapper allows the host access to the requested service. You can place the line ALL:ALL in the /etc/hosts.deny file to deny all hosts access to any Internet services.

vsftpd configuration files

The vsftpd server uses the following configuration files:

✦ /etc/vsftpd.conf controls how the vsftpd server works (for example, should it allow anonymous logins, should it allow file uploads, and so on).

✦ /etc/vsftpd.ftpusers lists names of users who cannot access the FTP server.

✦ /etc/vsftpd.user_list lists names of users who are denied access (not even prompted for password). However, if the userlist_deny option is set to NO in /etc/vsftpd.conf, then these users are allowed to access the FTP server.

You can usually leave most of these configuration files with their default settings. However, just in case you need to change something to make vsftpd suit your needs, I explain the configuration files briefly in the next few sections.

/etc/vsftpd.conf file

To find out what you can have in the /etc/vsftpd.conf file and how these lines affect the vsftpd server's operation, start by looking at the /etc/vsftpd.conf file that's installed by default in Red Hat Linux. The comments in this file tell you what each option does.

By default, vsftpd allows almost nothing. The options in /etc/vsftpd.conf loosen the restrictions so that users can use FTP. It's up to you to decide how loose the settings should be. Note that most options are set to YES. That's because most of the default settings are NO. To reverse the intent of an option, just comment out that option by placing a # at the beginning of that line.

Here are the options you can set in /etc/vsftpd.conf:

✦ `anon_mkdir_write_enable=YES` enables anonymous FTP users to create new directories. This is another risky option and you may want to set this to `NO`, even if you allow anonymous users to upload files.

✦ `anon_upload_enable=YES` means anonymous FTP users can upload files. This option takes effect only if `write_enable` is already set to `YES` and the directory has write permissions for everyone. Remember that allowing anonymous users to write on your system can be very risky because someone could fill up the disk or use your disk for their personal storage.

✦ `anonymous_enable=YES` enables anonymous FTP (so users can log in with the user name anonymous and provide their e-mail address as password). Comment out this line if you do not want anonymous FTP.

✦ `ascii_download_enable=YES` enables file downloads in ASCII mode. Unfortunately, a malicious remote user can issue the `SIZE` command with the name of a huge file and essentially cause the FTP server to waste huge amounts of resources opening that file and determining its size. This can be used by malicious users as a Denial of Service attack.

✦ `ascii_upload_enable=YES` enables file uploads in ASCII mode (for text files).

✦ `async_abor_enable=YES` causes `vsftpd` to recognize `ABOR` (abort) requests that arrive at any time. You may need to enable it to allow older FTP clients to work with `vsftpd`.

✦ `banned_email_file=/etc/vsftpd.banned_emails` specifies the file with the list of banned e-mail addresses (used only if `deny_email_enable` is set to `YES`).

✦ `chown_uploads=YES` causes uploaded anonymous files to be owned by a different user specified by the `chown_username` option. Don't enable this, unless absolutely necessary and don't make the `chown_username` to be `root`.

✦ `chown_username=name` specifies the user name that would own files uploaded by anonymous FTP users.

✦ `chroot_list_enable=YES` causes `vsftpd` to confine all users except those on a list specified by the `chroot_list_file` to their home directories when they log in for FTP service. This prevents these users from getting to any other files besides what's in their home directories.

✦ `chroot_list_file=/etc/vsftpd.chroot_list` is the list of users who are either confined to their home directories or not, depending on the setting of `chroot_local_user`.

✦ `connect_from_port_20=YES` causes `vsftpd` to make sure that data transfers occur through port 20 (the FTP data port).

◆ `data_connection_timeout=120` is the time in seconds after which an inactive data connection is timed out.

◆ `deny_email_enable=YES` causes `vsftpd` to check a list of banned e-mail addresses and denies access to anyone who tries to log in anonymously with a banned e-mail address as password.

◆ `dirmessage_enable=YES` causes `vsftpd` to display messages when FTP users change to certain directories.

◆ `ftpd_banner=Welcome to my FTP service.` sets the banner that `vsftpd` displays when a user logs in. You can change the message to anything you want.

◆ `idle_session_timeout=600` is the time (in seconds) after which an idle session (refers to the situation where someone connects and does not do anything) times out and `vsftpd` logs the user out.

◆ `local_enable=YES` causes `vsftpd` to grant local users access to FTP.

◆ `local_umask=022` means whatever files FTP writes will have a permission of 644 (read access for everyone, but write access for owner only). You can set it to any file permission mask setting you want. For example, if you want no permissions for anyone but the owner, change this to 077.

◆ `ls_recurse_enable=YES` enables FTP users to recursively traverse directories using the `ls -R` command.

◆ `nopriv_user=ftp` identifies a unprivileged user that the FTP server can use.

◆ `pam_service_name=vsftpd` is the name of the Pluggable Authentication Module (PAM) configuration file that is used when `vsftpd` needs to authenticate a user. By default the PAM configuration files are in `/etc/pam.d` directory. That means `vsftpd`'s PAM configuration file is `/etc/pam.d/vsftpd`.

◆ `userlist_deny=YES` causes `vsftpd` to deny access to the users listed in the `/etc/vsftpd.user_list` file. These users are not even prompted for a password.

◆ `write_enable=YES` causes `vsftpd` to allow file uploads to the host.

◆ `xferlog_enable=YES` turns on the logging of file downloads and uploads (always a good idea, but takes disk space).

◆ `xferlog_file=/var/log/vsftpd.log` specifies the full pathname of the `vsftpd` log file. The default is `/var/log/vsftpd.log`.

◆ `xferlog_std_format=YES` causes `vsftpd` to generate log files in a standard format used by other FTP daemons.

/etc/vsftpd.ftpusers file

The `vsftpd` server uses the *Pluggable Authentication Module* (PAM) to authenticate users when they try to log in (just as the normal login process uses PAM to do the job). The PAM configuration file for `vsftpd` is `/etc/pam.d/vsftpd`. That PAM configuration file refers to `/etc/vsftpd.ftpusers` like this:

```
auth    required   /lib/security/pam_listfile.so item=user sense=deny
        file=/etc/vsftpd.ftpusers onerr=succeed
```

This basically says that anyone listed in the `/etc/vsftpd.ftpusers` should be denied login. The default `/etc/vsftpd.ftpusers` file contains the following list of users:

```
root
bin
daemon
adm
lp
sync
shutdown
halt
mail
news
uucp
operator
games
nobody
```

/etc/vsftpd.user_list file

If the `userlist_deny` option is set to `YES`, `vsftpd` does not allow users listed in the `/etc/vsftpd.user_list` file any access to FTP services. It does not even prompt them for a password. However, if `userlist_deny` is `NO`, the meaning is reversed and these users are the only ones allowed access (but the PAM configuration still denies anyone on the `/etc/vsftpd.ftpusers list`).

Setting Up Secure Anonymous FTP

Anonymous FTP refers to the use of the user name `anonymous`, which anyone can use with FTP to transfer files from a system. Anonymous FTP is a common way to share files on the Internet.

If you have used anonymous FTP to download files from Internet sites, you already know the convenience of that service. Anonymous FTP makes information available to anyone on the Internet. If you have a new Red Hat Linux application that you want to share with the world, set up anonymous FTP on your Linux PC and place the software in an appropriate directory. After that, all you need to do is announce to the world (probably through a posting in the comp.os.linux.announce newsgroup) that you have a new program available. Now anyone can get the software from your system at his or her convenience.

Even if you run a for-profit business, you can use anonymous FTP to support your customers. If you sell a hardware or software product, you may want to provide technical information or software "fixes" through anonymous FTP.

Unfortunately, the convenience of anonymous FTP comes at a price. If you do not configure the anonymous FTP service properly, intruders and pranksters may gain access to your system. Some intruders may simply use your system's disk as a temporary holding place for various files; others may fill your disk with junk files, effectively making your system inoperable (this sort of attack is called a *Denial of Service* attack). At the other extreme, an intruder may gain user-level (or, worse, root-level) access to your system and do much more damage. The default anonymous FTP setup in Red Hat Linux employs the necessary security precautions.

Trying anonymous FTP

To see anonymous FTP in action, try accessing your system by using an FTP client. For example, in the following sample session, I have accessed the FTP server from a terminal window on the same system (my input appears in boldface):

```
ftp localhost
Connected to localhost (127.0.0.1).
220 ready, dude (vsFTPd 1.0.1: beat me, break me)
Name (localhost:naba): anonymous
331 Please specify the password.
Password:          <-- I can type anything as password
230 Login successful. Have fun.
Remote system type is UNIX.
Using binary mode to transfer files.
ftp> ls -l
227 Entering Passive Mode (127,0,0,1,212,216)
150 Here comes the directory listing.
d--x--x--x    2 0        0            4096 Aug 28 20:50 bin
d--x--x--x    2 0        0            4096 Aug 28 20:50 etc
drwxr-xr-x    2 0        0            4096 Aug 28 20:50 lib
drwxr-sr-x    2 0        50           4096 Jun 23 13:50 pub
226 Directory send OK.
ftp> bye
221 Goodbye.
```

When you successfully log in for anonymous FTP, you access the home directory of the user named ftp (the default directory is /var/ftp). Place the publicly accessible files — the ones you want to enable others to download from your system — in the /var/ftp/pub directory.

Key features of anonymous FTP

The key features of an anonymous FTP setup are as follows:

✦ There is a user named ftp whose home directory is /var/ftp. The user does not have a shell assigned. Here is what you get when you search for ftp in the /etc/passwd file:

```
grep ftp /etc/passwd
```

The output should be something like this:

```
ftp:x:14:50:FTP User:/var/ftp:/sbin/nologin
```

The x in the second field means that no one can log in with the user name ftp.

✦ Here is the full permission setting and owner information for the /var/ftp directory:

```
drwxr-xr-x  6 root    root      4096 Aug 28 16:50 ftp
```

As this line shows, the /var/ftp directory is owned by root, and the permission is set to 755 (only root can read, write and execute; everyone else can only read and execute).

✦ You can view the contents of the /var/ftp directory with the ls -la command. The result is as follows:

```
total 24
drwxr-xr-x   6 root    root      4096 Aug 28 16:50 .
drwxr-xr-x  21 root    root      4096 Aug 28 17:30 ..
d--x--x--x   2 root    root      4096 Aug 28 16:50 bin
d--x--x--x   2 root    root      4096 Aug 28 16:50 etc
drwxr-xr-x   2 root    root      4096 Aug 28 16:50 lib
drwxr-sr-x   2 root    ftp       4096 Jun 23 09:50 pub
```

The permission settings of the bin and etc directories are 111 (execute only). All files inside the bin directory are also execute-only (permission setting 111). All files in the etc directory are read-only (permission setting 444).

✦ The pub directory is where you place any files you want to enable others to download from your system through anonymous FTP.

Chapter 4: Serving Up Mail and News

In This Chapter

- ✔ **Installing and using** `sendmail`
- ✔ **Testing mail delivery manually**
- ✔ **Configuring** `sendmail`
- ✔ **Installing the InterNetNews (INN) server**
- ✔ **Configuring and starting INN**
- ✔ **Setting up local newsgroups**

*E*lectronic mail (e-mail) is one of the popular services available on Internet hosts. E-mail software comes in two parts: a mail-transport agent (MTA), which physically sends and receives mail messages; and a mail-user agent (MUA), which reads messages and prepares new messages. In this chapter, I describe the e-mail service and show you how to configure the `sendmail` server on a Red Hat Linux PC.

Internet newsgroups provide another convenient way, besides e-mail, to discuss various topics and to share your knowledge with others. Red Hat Linux comes with the software you need to read newsgroups and to set up your own system as a news server. In this chapter, I describe how to configure and run the InterNetNews server, a popular news server. I also show you how to set up local newsgroups for your corporate intranet (or even your home network).

Installing the Mail Server

If you install the mail server software during Red Hat Linux installation, you do not have to do much more to begin using the mail service. To check if the mail server is already installed, type the following command:

```
rpm -q sendmail
```

You're all set if the response looks like this:

```
sendmail-8.12.5-7
```

This output says that `sendmail` version 8.12.5 is installed on the system.

If the output message tells you that `sendmail` is not installed, you can use the Red Hat Package Manager (RPM) to install the individual packages needed for running and configuring `sendmail`. To install the RPM files for `sendmail`, log in as `root` and insert the second CD-ROM in the CD-ROM drive. If you are using GNOME or KDE, the CD-ROM should be automatically mounted. Otherwise, type the following command to mount the CD-ROM:

```
mount /mnt/cdrom
```

Then type the following commands to install the `sendmail` files:

```
cd /mnt/cdrom/RedHat/RPMS
rpm -ivh sendmail*
```

This should install two packages:

✦ `sendmail` — A complex mail transport agent (MTA)

✦ `sendmail-cf` — Configuration files for `sendmail`

Using sendmail

To set up your system as a mail server, you must configure the `sendmail` mail-transport agent properly. `sendmail` has the reputation of being a complex but complete mail-delivery system. Just one look at `sendmail`'s configuration file, `/etc/mail/sendmail.cf`, should convince you that `sendmail` is indeed complex. Luckily, you do not have to be an expert on the `sendmail` configuration file. All you need is one of the predefined configuration files — like the one that's installed on your system — to use `sendmail`.

Your system should already have a working `sendmail` configuration file — `/etc/mail/sendmail.cf`. The default file assumes you have an Internet connection and a name server. Provided you have an Internet connection, you should be able to send and receive e-mail from your Red Hat Linux PC.

To ensure that mail delivery works correctly, your system's name must match the system name your ISP has assigned to you. Although you can give your system any host name you want, other systems can successfully deliver mail to your system only if your system's name is in the ISP's name server.

A mail-delivery test

To try out the `sendmail` mail-transfer agent, you can use the `mail` command to compose and send a mail message to yourself at a different address. For example, here's how I send myself a message using the `mail` command:

```
mail naba@comcast.net
Subject: Testing e-mail
This is from my Red Hat Linux system.
.
Cc: Press Ctrl+D
```

The `mail` command is a simple mail-user agent. In the preceding example, I specify the addressee — `naba@comcast.net` — in the command line. The `mail` program prompts for a subject line. Following the subject, I enter my message and end it with a line that contains only a period. When prompted for a Cc:, I press Ctrl+D. After I end the message, the mail-user agent passes the message to `sendmail` — the mail-transport agent — for delivery to the specified address. Because my system is already connected to the Internet, `sendmail` delivers the mail message immediately.

To verify the delivery of mail, I check my mail from my ISP and see that the message has arrived (Figure 4-1). I can also send a reply back, provided that my system has an official DNS host name and is in the ISP's DNS database.

Figure 4-1: Test `sendmail` by sending mail from your Red Hat Linux system to your ISP account.

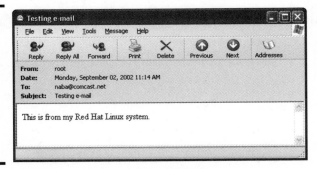

Thus, the initial `sendmail` configuration file that comes with Red Hat Linux should be adequate for sending and receiving e-mail, provided that your Red Hat Linux system has an Internet connection and a registered domain name.

The mail-delivery mechanism

On an Internet host, the `sendmail` mail-transport agent delivers mail using the *Simple Mail Transfer Protocol* (SMTP). SMTP-based mail-transport agents listen to the TCP port 25 and use a small set of text commands to exchange information with other mail-transport agents. In fact, the commands are simple enough that you can use them manually from a terminal to send a mail message. The following example shows how I use SMTP commands to send a mail message to my account on the Red Hat Linux PC from a `telnet` session running on the same system:

```
telnet localhost 25
Trying 127.0.0.1...
Connected to localhost.
Escape character is '^]'.
220 dhcppc3 ESMTP Sendmail 8.12.5/8.12.5; Mon, 2 Sep 2002 11:40:30 -0400
help
214-2.0.0 This is sendmail version 8.12.5
214-2.0.0 Topics:
214-2.0.0      HELO    EHLO    MAIL    RCPT    DATA
214-2.0.0      RSET    NOOP    QUIT    HELP    VRFY
214-2.0.0      EXPN    VERB    ETRN    DSN     AUTH
214-2.0.0      STARTTLS
214-2.0.0 For more info use "HELP <topic>".
214-2.0.0 To report bugs in the implementation send email to
214-2.0.0      sendmail-bugs@sendmail.org.
214-2.0.0 For local information send email to Postmaster at your site.
214 2.0.0 End of HELP info
HELP DATA
214-2.0.0 DATA
214-2.0.0      Following text is collected as the message.
214-2.0.0      End with a single dot.
214 2.0.0 End of HELP info
HELLO localhost
250 dhcppc3 Hello localhost.localdomain [127.0.0.1], pleased to meet you
MAIL FROM: naba
553 5.5.4 naba... Domain name required for sender address naba
MAIL FROM: naba@localhost
250 2.1.0 naba@localhost... Sender ok
RCPT TO: naba
250 2.1.5 naba... Recipient ok
DATA
354 Enter mail, end with "." on a line by itself
Testing... 1 2 3
Sending mail by telnet to port 25
.
250 2.0.0 g82FeUVn022872 Message accepted for delivery
quit
221 2.0.0 dhcppc3 closing connection
Connection closed by foreign host.
```

The `telnet` command opens a TELNET session to port 25 — the port on which `sendmail` expects SMTP commands. The `sendmail` process on the Red Hat Linux system immediately replies with an announcement.

I type `HELP` to view a list of SMTP commands. To get help on a specific command, I can type `HELP` *commandname*. The listing shows the help information `sendmail` prints when I type `HELP DATA`.

I type `HELO localhost` to initiate a session with the host. The `sendmail` process replies with a greeting. To send the mail message, I start with the `MAIL FROM:` command that specifies the sender of the message (I enter the user name on the system from which I am sending the message). `sendmail` requires a domain name along with the user name.

Next, I use the `RCPT TO:` command to specify the recipient of the message. If I want to send the message to several recipients, all I have to do is provide each recipient's address with the `RCPT TO:` command.

To enter the mail message, I use the `DATA` command. In response to the `DATA` command, `sendmail` displays an instruction that I should end the message with a period on a line by itself. I enter the message and end it with a single period on a separate line. The `sendmail` process displays a message indicating that the message has been accepted for delivery. Finally, I quit the `sendmail` session with the `QUIT` command.

Afterward, I log in to my Red Hat Linux system and check mail with the `mail` command. The following is the session with the `mail` command when I display the mail message I have sent through the sample SMTP session with `sendmail`:

```
mail
Mail version 8.1 6/6/93.  Type ? for help.
"/var/spool/mail/naba": 1 message 1 new
>N  1 naba@dhcppc3.naba      Mon Sep  2 11:43  12/412
& 1
Message 1:
From naba@dhcppc3  Mon Sep  2 11:43:23 2002
Date: Mon, 2 Sep 2002 11:40:30 -0400
From: Naba Barkakati <naba@dhcppc3.naba>

Testing... 1 2 3
Sending mail by telnet to port 25

& q
Saved 1 message in mbox
```

As this example shows, the SMTP commands are simple enough to understand. This example should help you understand how a mail-transfer agent uses SMTP to transfer mail on the Internet. Of course, this whole process is automated by e-mail programs and the `sendmail` program (through settings in the `sendmail` configuration file `/etc/mail/sendmail.cf`).

The sendmail configuration file

You don't need to understand everything in the `sendmail` configuration file, `/etc/mail/sendmail.cf`, but you should know how that file is created. That way, you can make minor changes if necessary and regenerate the `/etc/mail/sendmail.cf` file.

To be able to regenerate the `sendmail.cf` file, you have to install the `sendmail-cf` package. To check whether the `sendmail-cf` package is installed, type

```
rpm -q sendmail-cf
```

If the command does not print the name of the `sendmail-cf` package, you have to install the package. This RPM file is in the second CD-ROM bundled with this book. To install that package, log in as `root` and insert the second CD-ROM into the CD-ROM drive. In GNOME or KDE, the CD-ROM should mount automatically. Otherwise, you can mount the CD-ROM with the following command:

```
mount /mnt/cdrom
```

Then install the package by typing the following commands:

```
cd /mnt/cdrom/RedHat/RPMS
rpm -ivh sendmail-cf*
```

The `sendmail-cf` package installs in the `/usr/share/sendmail-cf` directory all the files needed to generate a new `sendmail.cf` configuration file. As I explain in the next few sections, the `sendmail.cf` file is generated from a number of m4 macro files (macro files are text files where each line eventually expands to multiple lines that mean something to some program). These macro files are organized into a number of subdirectories under `/usr/share/sendmail-cf`. You can read the README file in `/usr/share/sendmail-cf` to learn more about the creation of `sendmail` configuration files.

Now that you have taken care of the prerequisites, you can learn how to regenerate the `sendmail.cf` file.

m4 macro processor

The m4 macro processor is used to generate the `sendmail.cf` configuration file, which comes with the `sendmail` package in Red Hat Linux. The main macro file, `sendmail.mc`, is included with the `sendmail` package, but that file needs other m4 macro files that are in the `sendmail-cf` package.

So what's a macro? A *macro* is basically a symbolic name for some action or a shorthand for a long string of characters. A macro processor such as m4 usually reads its input file and copies it to the output, processing the macros along the way. The processing of a macro generally involves performing some action and generating some output. Because a macro generates a lot more text in the output than merely the macro's name, the processing of macros is referred to as *macro expansion*.

The m4 macro processor is stream-based. That means it copies the input characters to the output while expanding any macros. The m4 macro processor does not have any concept of lines, so it copies newline characters (that mark the end of a line) to the output. That's why you see the word dnl in most m4 macro files; dnl is an m4 macro that stands for "delete through newline." The dnl macro deletes all characters starting at the dnl up to and including the next newline character. The newline characters in the output don't cause any harm; they merely create unnecessary blank lines. The sendmail macro package uses dnl to avoid such blank lines in the output configuration file. Because dnl basically means delete everything up to the end of the line, m4 macro files also use dnl as the prefix for comment lines.

To see a very simple use of m4, consider the following m4 macro file that defines two macros — hello and bye — and uses them in a form letter:

```
dnl  ##############################################
dnl  #  File: ex.m4
dnl  #  A simple exmapls of m4 macros
dnl  ##############################################
define(`hello', `Dear Sir/Madam')dnl
define(`bye',
`Sincerely,


Customer Service')dnl
dnl Now type the letter and use the macros
hello,

This is to inform you that we received your recent inquiry.
We will respond to your question soon.

bye
```

Type this text by using your favorite text editor, and save it in a file named ex.m4. You can name a macro file anything you like, but it is customary to use the .m4 extension for m4 macro files.

Before you process the macro file by using m4, note the following key points about the example:

✦ Use the dnl macro to start all the comment lines (for example, the first four lines in the example).

✦ End each macro definition with the dnl macro. Otherwise, when m4 processes the macro file, it produces a blank line for each macro definition.

✦ Use the built-in m4 command define to define a new macro. The macro name and the value are both enclosed between a pair of left and right quotes (`` ` ...' ``). Note that you cannot use the plain single quote to enclose the macro name and definition.

Now process the macro file `ex.m4` by typing the following command:

```
m4 ex.m4
```

m4 processes the macros and displays the following output:

```
Dear Sir/Madam,

This is to inform you that we received your recent inquiry.
We will respond to your question soon.

Sincerely,


Customer Service
```

Sounds just like a typical customer service form letter, doesn't it?

If you compare the output with the `ex.m4` file, you'd see that m4 prints the form letter on standard output, expanding the macros `hello` and `bye` into their defined values. If you want to save the form letter in a file called `letter`, use the shell's output redirection feature, like this:

```
m4 ex.m4 > letter
```

What if you want to use the word `hello` or `bye` in the letter without expanding them? You can do so by enclosing these macros in a pair of quotes (`` ` ...' ``). You have to do this for other predefined m4 macros, such as `define`. To use define as a plain word, not as a macro to expand, type **`` `define' ``**.

sendmail.mc file

The simple example in the preceding section should give you an idea of how m4 macros are defined and used to create configuration files such as the `sendmail.cf` file. You find many complex macros stored in files in the `/usr/share/sendmail-cf` directory. A top-level macro file, `sendmail.mc`, described later in this section, brings in these macro files with the `include` macro (used to copy a file into the input stream).

By defining its own set of high-level macros in files located in the `/usr/share/sendmail-cf` directory, `sendmail` essentially creates its own macro language. The `sendmail` macro files use the `.mc` extension. The primary `sendmail` macro file you should configure is `sendmail.mc`, located in the `/etc/mail` directory.

Unlike the `/etc/mail/sendmail.cf` file, the `/etc/mail/sendmail.mc` file is short and should be easier to work with. Here is the full listing of the `/etc/mail/sendmail.mc` file that comes with Red Hat Linux:

```
divert(-1)
dnl This is the sendmail macro config file. If you make changes to this file,
dnl you need the sendmail-cf rpm installed and then have to generate a
dnl new /etc/mail/sendmail.cf by running the following command:
dnl
dnl    m4 /etc/mail/sendmail.mc > /etc/mail/sendmail.cf
dnl
include(`/usr/share/sendmail-cf/m4/cf.m4')
VERSIONID(`linux setup for Red Hat Linux')dnl
OSTYPE(`linux')
dnl Uncomment and edit the following line if your mail needs to be sent out
dnl through an external mail server:
dnl define(`SMART_HOST',`smtp.your.provider')
define(`confDEF_USER_ID',``8:12'')dnl
undefine(`UUCP_RELAY')dnl
undefine(`BITNET_RELAY')dnl
dnl define(`confAUTO_REBUILD')dnl
define(`confTO_CONNECT', `1m')dnl
define(`confTRY_NULL_MX_LIST',true)dnl
define(`confDONT_PROBE_INTERFACES',true)dnl
define(`PROCMAIL_MAILER_PATH',`/usr/bin/procmail')dnl
define(`ALIAS_FILE', `/etc/aliases')dnl
dnl define(`STATUS_FILE', `/etc/mail/statistics')dnl
define(`UUCP_MAILER_MAX', `2000000')dnl
define(`confUSERDB_SPEC', `/etc/mail/userdb.db')dnl
define(`confPRIVACY_FLAGS', `authwarnings,novrfy,noexpn,restrictqrun')dnl
define(`confAUTH_OPTIONS', `A')dnl
dnl TRUST_AUTH_MECH(`EXTERNAL DIGEST-MD5 CRAM-MD5 LOGIN PLAIN')dnl
dnl define(`confAUTH_MECHANISMS', `EXTERNAL GSSAPI DIGEST-MD5 CRAM-MD5 LOGIN PLA
IN')dnl
dnl define(`confCACERT_PATH',`/usr/share/ssl/certs')
dnl define(`confCACERT',`/usr/share/ssl/certs/ca-bundle.crt')
dnl define(`confSERVER_CERT',`/usr/share/ssl/certs/sendmail.pem')
dnl define(`confSERVER_KEY',`/usr/share/ssl/certs/sendmail.pem')
dnl define(`confTO_QUEUEWARN', `4h')dnl
dnl define(`confTO_QUEUERETURN', `5d')dnl
dnl define(`confQUEUE_LA', `12')dnl
dnl define(`confREFUSE_LA', `18')dnl
define(`confTO_IDENT', `0')dnl
dnl FEATURE(delay_checks)dnl
FEATURE(`no_default_msa',`dnl')dnl
FEATURE(`smrsh',`/usr/sbin/smrsh')dnl
FEATURE(`mailertable',`hash -o /etc/mail/mailertable.db')dnl
FEATURE(`virtusertable',`hash -o /etc/mail/virtusertable.db')dnl
FEATURE(redirect)dnl
FEATURE(always_add_domain)dnl
FEATURE(use_cw_file)dnl
FEATURE(use_ct_file)dnl
dnl The '-t' option will retry delivery if e.g. the user runs over his quota.
FEATURE(local_procmail,`',`procmail -t -Y -a $h -d $u')dnl
FEATURE(`access_db',`hash -T<TMPF> -o /etc/mail/access.db')dnl
FEATURE(`blacklist_recipients')dnl
EXPOSED_USER(`root')dnl
dnl This changes sendmail to only listen on the loopback device 127.0.0.1
dnl and not on any other network devices. Comment this out if you want
dnl to accept email over the network.
```

**Book VII
Chapter 4**

**Serving Up
Mail and News**

```
DAEMON_OPTIONS(`Port=smtp,Addr=127.0.0.1, Name=MTA')
dnl NOTE: binding both IPv4 and IPv6 daemon to the same port requires
dnl    a kernel patch
dnl DAEMON_OPTIONS(`port=smtp,Addr=::1, Name=MTA-v6, Family=inet6')
dnl We strongly recommend to comment this one out if you want to protect
dnl yourself from spam. However, the laptop and users on computers that do
dnl not have 24x7 DNS do need this.
FEATURE(`accept_unresolvable_domains')dnl
dnl FEATURE(`relay_based_on_MX')dnl
MAILER(smtp)dnl
MAILER(procmail)dnl
Cwlocalhost.localdomain
```

If you make changes to the /etc/mail/sendmail.mc file, you must generate the /etc/mail/sendmail.cf file by running the sendmail.mc file through the m4 macro processor with the following command (you have to log in as root):

```
m4 /etc/mail/sendmail.mc > /etc/mail/sendmail.cf
```

The comments also tell you that you need the sendmail-cf package to process this file.

From the previous section's description of m4 macros, you can see that the sendmail.mc file uses define to create new macros. You can also see the liberal use of dnl to avoid inserting too many blank lines into the output.

The other uppercase words such as OSTYPE, FEATURE, and MAILER are sendmail macros. These are defined in the .m4 files located in the subdirectories of the /usr/share/sendmail-cf directory and are incorporated into the sendmail.mc file with the following include macro:

```
include(`/usr/share/sendmail-cf/m4/cf.m4')
```

The /usr/share/sendmail-cf/m4/cf.m4 file, in turn, includes the cfhead.m4 file, which includes other m4 files, and so on. The net effect is that, as the m4 macro processor processes the sendmail.mc file, the macro processor incorporates many m4 files from various subdirectories of /usr/share/sendmail-cf.

Here are some key points to note about the /etc/mail/sendmail.mc file:

✦ VERSIONID(`linux setup for Red Hat Linux') macro inserts the version information enclosed in quotes into the output.

✦ OSTYPE(`linux') specifies Linux as the operating system. You have to specify this early to ensure proper configuration. It is customary to place this macro right after the VERSIONID macro.

✦ MAILER(smtp) describes the mailer. According to instructions in the /usr/share/sendmail-cf/README file, MAILER declarations should always be placed at the end of the `sendmail.mc` file, and `MAILER(`smtp')` should always precede `MAILER(`procmail')`. The mailer `smtp` refers to the SMTP mailer.

✦ `FEATURE` macros request various special features. For example, `FEATURE(`blacklist_recipients')` turns on the capability to block incoming mail for certain user names, hosts, or addresses. The specification for what mail to allow or refuse is placed in the access database (`/etc/mail/access.db` file). You also need the `FEATURE(`access_db')` macro to turn on the access database.

The `sendmail` macros such as `FEATURE` and `MAILER` are described in the `/usr/share/sendmail-cf/README` file. Consult that file to learn more about the `sendmail` macros before you make changes to the `sendmail.mc` file.

Typically, you have to add your system's host name in the last line of the `/etc/mail/sendmail.mc` file. Follow these steps to add the host name:

1. **If the host name is** `mycompany.com`, **edit the** `Cw` **line in** `/etc/mail/sendmail.mc` **as follows:**

    Cwlocalhost.localdomain mycompany.com mycompany

2. **Rebuild the** `/etc/mail/sendmail.cf` **file with the command:**

    m4 /etc/mail/sendmail.mc > /etc/mail/sendmail.cf

3. **Restart** `sendmail` **with the following command:**

    service sendmail restart

sendmail.cf file syntax

The `sendmail.cf` file's syntax is designed to be easy to parse by the `sendmail` program because `sendmail` reads this file whenever it starts. Human readability was not a primary consideration when the file's syntax was designed. Still, with a little explanation, you can understand the meaning of the control lines in `sendmail.cf`.

Each `sendmail` control line begins with a single-letter operator that defines the meaning of the rest of the line. A line that begins with a space or a tab is considered a continuation of the previous line. Blank lines and lines beginning with a pound sign (#) are comments.

Often, there is no space between the single-letter operator and the arguments that follow the operator. This makes the lines even harder to understand. For example, `sendmail.cf` uses the concept of a *class* — essentially a collection of phrases. You can define a class named `P` and add the phrase `REDIRECT` to that class with the following control line:

CPREDIRECT

Because everything is jumbled together, it's hard to decipher. On the other hand, to define a class named `Accept` and set it to the values `OK` and `RELAY`, write the following:

C{Accept}OK RELAY

This may be slightly easier to understand because the delimiters (such as the class name, `Accept`) are enclosed in curly braces.

Other more recent control lines are even easier to understand. For example, the line

O HelpFile=/etc/mail/helpfile

defines the option `HelpFile` as the filename `/etc/mail/helpfile`. That file contains help information `sendmail` uses when it receives a `HELP` command.

Table 4-1 summarizes the one-letter control operators used in `sendmail.cf`. Each entry also shows an example of that operator. This table should help you understand some of the lines in `sendmail.cf`.

Table 4-1	Control Operators Used in sendmail.cf
Operator	*Description*
C	Defines a class; a variable (think of it as a set) that can contain several values. For example, `Cwlocalhost` adds the name `localhost` to the class w.
D	Defines a macro, a name associated with a single value. For example, `DnMAILER-DAEMON` defines the macro n as `MAILER-DAEMON`.
F	Defines a class read from a file. For example, `Fw/etc/mail/local-host-names` reads the names of hosts from the file `/etc/mail/local-host-names` and adds them to the class w.
H	Defines the format of header lines that `sendmail` inserts into a message. For example, `H?P?Return-Path: <$g>` defines the `Return-Path:` field of the header.
K	Defines a map (a key-value pair database). For example, `Karith arith` defines the map named `arith` as the compiled-in map of the same name.
M	Specifies a mailer. The following lines define the `procmail` mailer: `Mprocmail,P=/usr/bin/procmail,F=DFMSPhnu9,S=EnvFromSMTP/HdrFromSMTP,R=EnvToSMTP/HdrFromSMTP,T=DNS/RFC822/X-Unix,A=procmail -Y -m $h $f $u`

Operator	Description
O	Assigns a value to an option. For example, O AliasFile=/etc/aliases defines the AliasFile option to /etc/aliases, which is the name of the sendmail alias file.
P	Defines values for the precedence field. For example, Pjunk=-100 sets to -100 the precedence of messages marked with the header field Precedence: junk.
R	Defines a rule (a rule has a left-hand side and a right-hand side; if input matches the left-hand side, it's replaced with the right-hand side — this is called rewriting). For example, the rewriting rule R$* ; $1 strips trailing semicolons.
S	Labels a ruleset you can start defining with subsequent R control lines. For example, Scanonify=3 labels the next ruleset as canonify or ruleset 3.
T	Adds a user name to the trusted class (class t). For example, Troot adds root to the class of trusted users.
V	Defines the major version number of the configuration file. For example, V10/Berkeley defines the version number as 10.

Other sendmail files

The /etc/mail directory contains other files that sendmail uses.
These files are referenced in the sendmail configuration file,
/etc/mail/sendmail.cf. For example, here's how you can search for the
/etc/mail string in the /etc/mail/sendmail.cf file:

```
grep "\/etc\/mail" /etc/mail/sendmail.cf
```

Here's what the grep command displays as a result of the search on my Red
Hat Linux system:

```
Fw/etc/mail/local-host-names
FR-o /etc/mail/relay-domains
Kmailertable hash -o /etc/mail/mailertable.db
Kvirtuser hash -o /etc/mail/virtusertable.db
Kaccess hash -T<TMPF> -o /etc/mail/access.db
#O ErrorHeader=/etc/mail/error-header
O HelpFile=/etc/mail/helpfile
O StatusFile=/etc/mail/statistics
O UserDatabaseSpec=/etc/mail/userdb.db
#O ServiceSwitchFile=/etc/mail/service.switch
#O DefaultAuthInfo=/etc/mail/default-auth-info
Ft/etc/mail/trusted-users
```

You can ignore the lines that begin with a hash mark or number sign (#)
because sendmail treats those lines as comments. The other lines are
sendmail control lines that refer to other files in the /etc/mail directory.

**Book VII
Chapter 4**

**Serving Up
Mail and News**

Here's what some of these `sendmail` files are supposed to contain (note that not all of these files need to be present in your `/etc/mail` directory and even when present, some files may be empty):

✦ `/etc/mail/access` — Names and/or IP addresses of hosts allowed to send mail (useful in stopping *spam* — unwanted mail)

✦ `/etc/mail/access.db` — Access database generated from `/etc/mail/access` file

✦ `/etc/mail/helpfile` — Help information for SMTP commands

✦ `/etc/mail/local-host-names` — Names by which this host is known

✦ `/etc/mail/mailertable` — Mailer table used to override how mail is routed

✦ `/etc/mail/relay-domains` — Hosts that permit relaying

✦ `/etc/mail/trusted-users` — List of users that are allowed to send mail as others without a warning

✦ `/etc/mail/userdb.db` — User database file with information about user's login name and real name

✦ `/etc/mail/virtusertable` — Database of users with virtual domain addresses hosted on this system

The .forward file

Users can redirect their own mail by placing a `.forward` file in their home directory. The `.forward` file is a plain text file with a comma-separated list of mail addresses. Any mail sent to the user is then forwarded to these addresses. If the `.forward` file contains a single address, all e-mail for that user is redirected to that single e-mail address. For example, suppose a `.forward` file containing the following line is placed in the home directory of a user named `emily`:

```
ashley
```

This causes `sendmail` to automatically send all e-mail addressed to `emily` to the user name `ashley` on the same system. User `emily` does not receive mail at all.

You can also forward mail to a user name on another system by listing a complete e-mail address. For example, I have added a `.forward` file with the following line to send my messages (addressed to my user name, `naba`) to the mail address `naba@comcast.net`:

```
naba@comcast.net
```

Now suppose I want to keep a copy of the message on this system, in addition to forwarding to the address `naba@comcast.net`. I can do so by adding the following line to the `.forward` file:

```
naba@comcast.net, naba\
```

I simply append my user name and end the line with a backslash. The backslash (\) at the end of the line stops `sendmail` from repeatedly forwarding the message (because when a copy is sent to my user name on the system, `sendmail` processes my `.forward` file again — the backslash tells `sendmail` not to forward the message repeatedly).

Invoking procmail in .forward file

An interesting use of the `.forward` file is to run `procmail` to handle some mail messages automatically. For example, suppose you want to delete any e-mail message that comes from an address containing the string `mailing_list`. Here's what you do to achieve that:

1. **Create a** `.forward` **file in your home directory and place the following line in it:**

```
"| /usr/bin/procmail"
```

This line causes `sendmail` to run the external program `/usr/bin/procmail` and to send the e-mail messages to the input stream of that program.

2. **Create a text file named** `.procmailrc` **in your home directory and place the following lines in that file:**

```
# Delete mail from an address that contains
mailing_list
:0
* ^From:.*mailing_list
/dev/null
```

3. **Log in as** `root` **and set up a symbolic link in** `/etc/smrsh` **to the** `/usr/bin/procmail` **program with the following command:**

```
ln -s /usr/bin/procmail /etc/smrsh/procmail
```

This step is necessary because `sendmail` uses the SendMail Restricted Shell — `smrsh` — to run external programs. Instead of running `/usr/bin/procmail`, `smrsh` runs `/etc/smrsh/procmail`. That's why you need the symbolic link. This is a security feature of `sendmail` that controls what external programs it can run.

That's it! Now if you receive any messages from an address containing `mailing_list`, the message will be deleted.

**Book VII
Chapter 4**

**Serving Up
Mail and News**

With `procmail`, you can perform other chores, such as automatically storing messages in a file or forwarding messages to others. All you have to do is create an appropriate `.procmailrc` file in your home directory. To learn more about `procmail`, type **man procmail**. To see examples of `.procmailrc`, type **man procmailex**.

The sendmail alias file

In addition to the `sendmail.cf` file, `sendmail` also consults an alias file named `/etc/aliases` to convert a name into an address. The location of the alias file appears in the `sendmail` configuration file.

Each alias is typically a shorter name for an e-mail address. The system administrator uses the `sendmail` alias file to forward mail, to create mailing lists (a single alias that identifies several users), or to refer to a user by several different names. For example, here are some typical aliases:

```
barkakati: naba
naba: naba@lnbsoft
all: naba, leha, ivy, emily, ashley
```

The first line says that mail addressed to `barkakati` should be delivered to the user named `naba` on the local system. The second line indicates that mail for `naba` should really be sent to the user name `naba` on the `lnbsoft` system. The last line defines `all` as the alias for the five users `naba`, `leha`, `ivy`, `emily`, and `ashley`. That means mail sent to `all` would go to these five users.

After defining any new aliases in the `/etc/aliases` file, you must log in as `root` and make the new alias active by typing the following command:

```
sendmail -bi
```

Installing the News Server

If you install the news server during Red Hat Linux installation, you do not have to do much more to begin using the news services. Otherwise, you can use the Red Hat Package Manager (RPM) to install the InterNetNews (INN) — a TCP/IP-based news server.

To check if INN is already installed, type the following command:

```
rpm -q inn
```

If INN is installed, you should see a line similar to this:

```
inn-2.3.3-5
```

If you get a message saying the package is not installed, you can install it manually from the companion CD-ROM. Log in as `root` and insert the first CD-ROM into the CD-ROM drive. If you are using GNOME or KDE desktop, the CD-ROM should mount automatically. Otherwise, type the following command to mount it:

```
mount /mnt/cdrom
```

Then type the following commands to install INN:

```
cd /mnt/cdrom/RedHat/RPMS
rpm -ivh inn-*
```

Configuring and Starting the INN Server

Much of the *InterNetNews* (INN) software, bundled with Red Hat Linux, is ready to go as soon as you install the RPM. All you need is to learn a bit about the various components of INN, edit the configuration files, and start `innd` — the INN server. By the way, sometimes I refer to the INN server as the *news server*.

If you want to support a selection of Internet newsgroups, you also have to arrange for a *news feed* — this is the source from which your news server gets the newsgroup articles. Typically, you can get a news feed from an ISP, but the ISP charges an additional monthly fee to cover the cost of resources required to provide the feed. You need the name of the upstream server that provides the news feed, and you have to provide that server with your server's name and the newsgroups you want to receive.

Based on the newsgroups you want to receive and the number of days you want to retain articles, you have to set aside disk space for the articles. The newsgroups are stored in a directory hierarchy (based on the newsgroup names) in the `/var/spool/news` directory of your system. If you are setting up a news server, you may want to devote a large disk partition to the `/var/spool/news` directory.

In your news server's configuration files, enter the name of the server providing the news feed. At the same time, add to the configuration files the names of any downstream news servers, if any, that receive news feeds from your server. Then you can start the news server and wait for news to arrive. Monitor the log files to ensure that the news articles are being sorted and stored properly in the `/var/spool/news` directory on your system.

When you have news up and running, you must run news maintenance and cleanup scripts. These are run using the cron jobs. On Red Hat Linux, a `cron` job is already set up to run the `/usr/bin/news.daily` script to perform the news maintenance tasks.

**Book VII
Chapter 4**

**Serving Up
Mail and News**

In the following sections, I introduce you to INN setup, but you can learn more about INN from the Internet Software Consortium (ISC), a nonprofit corporation dedicated to developing and maintaining open source Internet software, such as BIND (an implementation of Domain Name System), DHCP (Dynamic Host Configuration Protocol), and INN. Rich Salz originally wrote INN; ISC took over the development of INN in 1996. You can learn more about INN and can access other resources at ISC's INN Web page at `www.isc.org/products/INN`.

InterNetNews components

INN includes several programs that deliver and manage newsgroups. It also includes a number of files that control how the INN programs work. The most important INN programs are the following:

✦ `innd` — The news server. It runs as a *daemon* — a background process that keeps itself running to provide a specific service — and listens on the NNTP port (TCP port 119). The `innd` server accepts connections from other feed sites, as well as from local newsreader clients, but it hands off local connections to the `nnrpd`.

✦ `nnrpd` — A special server invoked by `innd` to handle requests from local news-reader clients

✦ `expire` — Removes old articles based on the specifications in the text file `/etc/news/expire.ctl`.

✦ `nntpsend` — Invokes the `innxmit` program to send news articles to a remote site by using NNTP. The configuration file `/etc/news/nntpsend.ctl` controls the `nntpsend` program.

✦ `ctlinnd` — Enables you to control the `innd` server interactively. The `ctlinnd` program can send messages to the control channel of the `innd` server.

The other important components of INN are the control files. Most of these files are in the `/etc/news` directory of your Red Hat Linux system, but a few are in the `/var/lib/news` directory also. Between the two directories, there are over 30 INN control files. Some of the important files include the following:

✦ `/etc/news/inn.conf` — Specifies configuration data for the innd server. (To view online help for this file, type **man inn.conf**.)

✦ `/etc/news/newsfeeds` — Specifies what articles to feed downstream to other news servers. (The file is complicated, but you can get help by typing **man newsfeeds**.)

✦ `/etc/news/incoming.conf` — Lists the names and addresses of hosts that provide news feeds to this server. (To view online help for this file, type **man incoming.conf**.)

✦ `/etc/news/storage.conf` — Specifies the storage methods to be used when storing news articles. (To view online help for this file, type **man storage.conf**.)

✦ `/etc/news/expire.ctl` — Controls expiration of articles, on a per-newsgroup level, if desired. (To view online help for this file, type **man expire.ctl**.)

✦ `/var/lib/news/active` — Lists all active newsgroups, showing the oldest and newest article number for each, and each newsgroup's posting status. (To view online help for this file, type **man active**.)

✦ `/var/lib/news/newsgroups` — Lists newsgroups, with a brief description of each.

✦ `/etc/news/readers.conf` — Specifies hosts and users that are permitted to read news from this news server and post news to newsgroups. The default file allows only the `localhost` to read news; you have to edit it if you want to allow other hosts in your local area network to read news. (To view online help for this file, type **man readers.conf**.)

In the next few sections, I describe how to set up some of the important control files.

inn.conf

This file holds configuration data for all INN programs and, as such, is the most important file. Each line of the file has the value of a parameter in the following format:

```
parameter:     value
```

Depending on the parameter, the value is a string, a number, or true or false. As in many other configuration files, comment lines begin with a number or pound sign (#).

Most of the parameters in the default `inn.conf` file in the `/etc/news` directory should not require changes. You may want to edit one or more of the parameters shown in Table 4-2.

**Book VII
Chapter 4**

**Serving Up
Mail and News**

Table 4-2	Configuration Parameters in /etc/news/inn.conf
Parameter Name	*Description*
Organization	Set this to the name of your organization in the way you want it to appear in the Organization: header of all news articles posted from your system. Users may override this by defining the ORGANIZATION environment variable.
Pathhost	Set this to the name of your news server as you want it to appear in the Path header of all postings that go through your server. If pathhost is not defined, the fully qualified domain name of your system is used.
Domain	Set this to the domain name for your server.
Allownewnews	Set this to true if you want INN to support the NEWNEWS command from news readers. Because this command can drastically reduce your server's performance, INN documentation recommends that you set this to false.
Storageapi	Set this to true if you want articles to be stored using the Storage Manager API. The default setting of false causes INN to use the traditional article-storage method of storing one article per file. If you set this to true, you have to choose between the storage methods timehash and cnfs, and you have to create new spool and database files (type **man storage.conf** to read more about cnfs and timehash storage methods). For a small number of newsgroups, you can leave this option at its default value of false.
Hiscachesize	Set this to the size in kilobytes that you want INN to use for caching recently used history file entries. The default setting of 0 disables history caching. Because history caching can greatly increase the number of articles your server can process per second, you may want to set a value of 16384 (for 16MB).
Innflags	Set this to any flags you want to pass to the INN server process when it starts up.

newsfeeds

The newsfeeds file specifies how incoming news articles are redistributed to other servers and to INN processes. If you provide news feeds to other servers, you have to list these news feeds in this file. (You also must have an entry labeled ME, which serves a special purpose that I explain later in this section.)

The newsfeeds file contains a series of entries, one for each feed. Each feed entry has the following format:

```
site[/exclude,exclude...]\
    :pattern,pattern...[/distrib,distrib...]\
    :flag,flag...\
    :param
```

Each entry has four fields separated by colons (:). Usually, the entries span multiple lines and a backslash (\) at the end of the line is used to continue a line to the next. Here's what the four fields mean:

✦ The first field, *site*, is the name of the feed. Each name must be unique, and for feeds to other news servers, the name is set to the host name of the remote server. Following the name is an optional slash and an exclude list (*/exclude,exclude...*) consisting of a list of names. If any of the names in this list appear in the Path line of an article, that article will not be forwarded to the feed. You can use an exclude list if you don't want to receive articles from a specific source.

✦ The second field consists of a comma-separated list of newsgroup patterns, such as *,@alt.binaries.warez.*,!control*,!local*, followed by an optional distribution list. The distribution list is a list of comma-separated keywords, with each keyword specifying a specific set of sites to which the articles are distributed. The newsgroup patterns essentially define a subscription list of sites that receive this news feed. An asterisk matches all newsgroups. A pattern beginning with an @ causes newsgroups matching that pattern to be dropped. A pattern that begins with an exclamation mark (!) means the matching newsgroups are not sent. By the way, the simple pattern-matching syntax used in INN configuration files is referred to as a *wildmat* pattern.

✦ The third field is a comma-separated list of flags. These flags determine the feed-entry type and set certain parameters for the entry. There are numerous flags; type **man newsfeeds** and read the man page for more information about the flags.

✦ The fourth field is for parameters whose values depend on the settings in the third field. Typically, this field contains names of files or external programs that the INN server uses. You can learn more about this field from the newsfeeds man page.

Now that you know the layout of the /etc/news/newsfeeds file, you can study that file as an example. The default file contains many sample feed entries, but only two are commented out:

✦ ME is a special feed entry that's always required. It serves two purposes. First, the newsgroup patterns listed in this entry are prepended to all newsgroup patterns in all other entries. Second, the ME entry's distribution list determines what distributions your server accepts from remote sites.

✦ The controlchan feed entry is used to set up INN so that an external program is used to handle control messages (these messages are used to create new newsgroups and remove groups). For example, the following controlchan entry specifies the external program

`/usr/lib/news/bin/controlchan` to handle all control messages, except `cancel` messages (meant for canceling an article):

```
controlchan!\
        :!*,control,control.*,!control.cancel\
        :Tc,Wnsm:/usr/lib/news/bin/controlchan
```

In addition to these feed entries, you add entries for any actual sites to which your news server provides news feed. Such entries have the format

```
feedme.domain.com\
              :!junk,!control/!foo\
              :Tm:innfeed!
```

where *feedme.domain.com* is the fully qualified domain name of the site to which your system sends news articles.

incoming.conf

The `incoming.conf` file describes which hosts are allowed to connect to your host to feed articles. For a single feed, you can add an entry like

```
peer mybuddy {
    hostname: a-feed-site.domain.com
}
```

where *mybuddy* is a label for the peer and *a-feed-site.domain. com* identifies the site that feeds your site.

Keep in mind that simply adding a site's name in the `incoming.conf` file does not cause that remote site to start feeding your site news — it simply enables your server to accept news articles from the remote site. At the remote site, your buddy has to configure his or her server to send articles to your site.

readers.conf

This file specifies the host names or IP addresses from which newsreader clients (such as Mozilla) can retrieve newsgroups from your server. For example, the following `readers.conf` file allows read access and post access (meaning you can submit articles) from `localhost` and any from host in the network 192.168.0.0:

```
auth "localhost" {
    hosts: "localhost, 127.0.0.1, stdin"
    default: "<localhost>"
```

```
}
access "localhost" {
    users: "<localhost>"
    newsgroups: "*"
    access: RPA
}
auth "localnet" {
    hosts: 192.168.0.0/24
    default: "<localnet>"
}
access "localnet" {
    users: "<localnet>"
    newsgroups: "*"
    access: RPA
}
```

InterNetNews startup

In addition to the configuration files, you also need to initiate cron jobs that perform periodic maintenance of the news server. In Red Hat Linux, these cron jobs are already set up. Therefore, you are now ready to start the INN server — innd.

Before you start innd, you must run makehistory and makedbz to initialize and rebuild the INN history database. Type **man makehistory** and **man makedbz** to learn more about these commands. Type the following commands to create an initial history database, associated indexes, and set the ownerships and permissions of some files:

```
/usr/lib/news/bin/makehistory -b -f history -O -l 30000 -I
cd /var/lib/news
/usr/lib/news/bin/makedbz -s `wc -l < history` -f history
chown news.news *
chown news.news /var/spool/news/overview/group.index
chmod 664 /var/spool/news/overview/group.index
```

As with any other servers in Red Hat Linux, to start innd, log in as root and type the following command:

```
service innd start
```

If you change any configuration file (such as inn.conf or newsfeeds), restart the innd server with the following command:

```
service innd restart
```

Type **ps ax** to see if the `innd` process is up and running. If all goes well, you should see two processes such as the following listed in the output of the `ps ax` command:

```
23789 ?    S    0:00 /usr/lib/news/bin/innd -p4
23794 ?    S    0:00 /usr/bin/perl /usr/lib/news/bin/controlchan
```

The `/var/log/spooler` file contains all status and error messages from `innd`. Type the following command to see the last few messages in that file:

```
tail /var/log/spooler
```

Setting Up Local Newsgroups

If you want to use newsgroups as a way to share information within your company, you can set up a hierarchy of local newsgroups. Then you can use these newsgroups to create virtual communities within your company, where people with shared interests can informally discuss issues and exchange knowledge.

Defining a newsgroup hierarchy

The first task is to define a hierarchy of newsgroups and decide what each newsgroup will discuss. For example, if your company name is XYZ Corporation, here's a partial hierarchy of newsgroups you might define:

✦ `xyz.general` — General items about XYZ Corporation

✦ `xyz.weekly.news` — Weekly news

✦ `xyz.weekly.menu` — The weekly cafeteria menu and any discussions about it

✦ `xyz.forsale` — A listing of items offered for sale by employees

✦ `xyz.jobs` — Job openings at XYZ Corporation

✦ `xyz.wanted` — Wanted (help, items to buy, and so on) postings by employees

✦ `xyz.technical.hardware` — Technical discussions about hardware

✦ `xyz.technical.software` — Technical discussions about software

Updating configuration files

Here are the steps you follow to update the configuration files for your local newsgroups and then restart the news server:

1. **Add descriptive entries for each of these newsgroups to the /var/lib/news/newsgroups file.**

   Here are the entries from the default /var/lib/news/newsgroups file:

   ```
   control           Various control messages (no posting).
   control.cancel    Cancel messages (no posting).
   control.checkgroups  Hierarchy check control messages (no posting).
   control.newgroup  Newsgroup creation control messages (no posting).
   control.rmgroup   Newsgroup removal control messages (no posting).
   junk              Unfiled articles (no posting).
   ```

   Add to this file a line for each local newsgroup — type its name, followed by a brief description. For example, here's what you might add for the xyz.general newsgroup:

   ```
   xyz.general       General items about XYZ Corporation
   ```

2. **Edit the ME entry in the /etc/news/newsfeeds file and add the phrase !xyz.* to the comma-separated list of newsgroup patterns.**

   This ensures that your local newsgroups are not distributed outside your site.

3. **Add a storage method to be used for the local newsgroups.**

   For example, you can add the following lines in /etc/news/storage.conf to define the storage method for the new xyz hierarchy of newsgroups (change xyz to whatever you name your local newsgroups):

   ```
   method tradspool {
       class: 1
       newsgroups: xyz.*
   }
   ```

4. **To make these changes effective, restart the news server with the command:**

   ```
   service innd restart.
   ```

Adding the newsgroups

The final step is to add the newsgroups. After you have configuration files updated and innd running, it's very easy to add a local newsgroup. Log in as root and use ctlinnd to perform this task. For example, here's how you add a newsgroup named xyz.general:

```
/usr/lib/news/bin/ctlinnd newgroup xyz.general
```

That's it! That command adds the xyz.general newsgroup to your site. If you use the traditional storage method, the innd server creates the directory `/var/spool/news/articles/xyz/general` and stores articles for that newsgroup in that directory (this happens the first time someone posts a news article to that newsgroup).

After you have created all the local newsgroups, users from your intranet should be able to post news articles and read articles in the local newsgroups. If they have problems accessing the newsgroups, make sure that the `/etc/news/readers.conf` file contains the IP addresses or names of the hosts that should be able to access the `innd` server.

Testing your newsgroups

For example, I have added a newsgroup named `local.news` on an INN server running on my Red Hat Linux system by using the instructions explained in the previous sections. Then I start Mozilla on another Red Hat Linux system on the LAN and set up a new news account with the news server set to my INN server. Next, I subscribe to the `local.news` newsgroup. Figure 4-2 shows the newsgroup with the test message I have posted to it. Try it! I bet you like it.

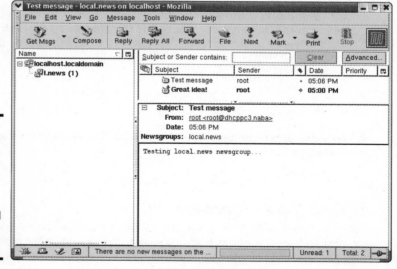

Figure 4-2:
You can read the local newsgroups by using the Mozilla Mail and News reader.

Chapter 5: Setting Up DNS and NIS

In This Chapter

✔ **Understanding DNS**

✔ **Learning about BIND**

✔ **Configuring DNS**

✔ **Setting up a caching name server**

✔ **Understanding NIS**

✔ **Configuring NIS servers and clients**

✔ **Trying out NIS**

omain Name System (DNS) is an Internet service that converts a fully qualified domain name, such as www.redhat.com, into its corresponding IP address such as 216.148.218.195. You can think of DNS as the directory of Internet hosts — DNS is the reason why you can use easy-to-remember host names even though TCP/IP requires numeric IP addresses for data transfers. DNS is basically a hierarchy of distributed DNS servers. In this chapter, I provide an overview of DNS and show you how to set up a caching DNS server on your Red Hat Linux system.

Network Information System (NIS) is another client/server service designed to manage information shared among several host computers on a network. Typically, NIS is used on UNIX (and Linux) systems to maintain a common set of user accounts and other system files for a group of hosts on a local area network (LAN). This, among other things, enables a user to log in on all hosts with the same user name and password. I briefly describe the NIS client and server software and show you how to use them on a Red Hat Linux system.

Understanding Domain Name System (DNS)

In TCP/IP networks, each network interface (for example, an Ethernet card or a dial-up modem connection) is identified by an IP address. Because IP addresses are hard to remember, an easy-to-remember name is assigned to the IP address — much like the way a name goes with a telephone number. For example, instead of having to remember that the IP address of Red Hat's

Web server is 216.148.218.195, you can simply refer to that host by its name, `www.redhat.com`. When you type `www.redhat.com` as the URL in a Web browser, the name `www.redhat.com` has to be translated into its corresponding IP address. This is where the concept of DNS comes in.

What is DNS?

DNS is a distributed, hierarchical database that holds information about computers on the Internet. The information includes the host name, the IP address, and mail-routing information. This information resides in many DNS hosts on the Internet; that's why the DNS database is called a distributed database. The primary job of DNS is to associate host names to IP addresses and vice versa.

In ARPANET — the precursor to today's Internet, the list of host names and corresponding IP addresses was maintained in a text file named `HOSTS.TXT`, which was managed centrally and periodically distributed to each host. As the number of hosts grew, it became clear that a static host table was unreasonable. DNS was proposed by Paul Mockapetris to alleviate the problems of a static host table. As formally documented in REquest for Comment (RFC) 882 and 883 (published in November 1983, see `www.faqs.org/rfcs/rfc882.html` and `www.faqs.org/rfcs/rfc883.html`), DNS introduced two key concepts:

✦ Use of hierarchical domain names, such as `www.ee.umd.edu` and `www.redhat.com`

✦ Distributed responsibility for managing the host database by using DNS servers throughout the Internet

DNS, as we know it today, is an Internet standard documented in RFCs 1034 and 1035. The standard has been updated and extended by several other RFCs — 1101, 1183, 1348, 1876, 1982, 1996, 2065, 2181, 2136, 2137, 2308, 2535, 2845, and 2931. The earlier updates define data encoding, whereas later ones focus on improving DNS security. To read these and other RFCs online, visit Ohio State University's Internet RFC page at `www.cis.ohio-state.edu/hypertext/information/rfc.html`.

DNS defines the following:

✦ A hierarchical domain-naming system for hosts

✦ A distributed database that associates a name with an IP address

✦ Library routines that network applications can use to query the distributed DNS database (this library is called the resolver library)

✦ A protocol for DNS clients and servers to exchange information about names and IP addresses

Nowadays, all hosts on the Internet rely on DNS to access various Internet services on remote hosts. As you may know from personal experience, when you obtain Internet access from an Internet Service Provider (ISP), the ISP provides you with the IP addresses of name servers. These are the DNS servers your system accesses whenever host names have to be mapped to IP addresses.

If you have a small LAN, you may decide to run a DNS server on one of the hosts or to use the name servers provided by the ISP. For medium-sized networks with several subnets, you can run a DNS server on each subnet to provide efficient DNS lookups. On a large corporate network, the corporate domain (such as `microsoft.com`) is further subdivided into a hierarchy of subdomains, and several DNS servers may be used in each subdomain.

In the following sections, I provide an overview of the hierarchical domain-naming convention and describe BIND — the DNS software used on most UNIX systems, including Red Hat Linux.

Learning hierarchical domain names

DNS uses a hierarchical tree of domains to organize the *namespace* — the entire set of names. Each higher-level domain has authority over its lower-level subdomains. Each domain represents a distinct block of the namespace and is managed by a single administrative authority. Figure 5-1 illustrates the hierarchical organization of the DNS namespace.

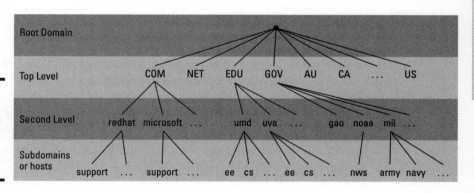

Figure 5-1:
The DNS namespace is organized in a hierarchy.

The root of the tree is called the *root domain* and is represented by a single dot (`.`). The top-level, or root-level, domains come next. The top-level domains are further divided into second-level domains, which, in turn, can be broken into further subdomains.

The top-level domains are relatively fixed and include well-known domains such as `COM`, `NET`, `ORG`, `EDU`, `GOV`, and `MIL`. These are the commonly used top-level domains in the United States. These top-level domains came about as the Internet came to widespread use in the early the 1990s.

There is another set of top-level domain names for the countries. These domain names use the two-letter country codes assigned by the International Organization for Standardization (abbreviated as ISO, see www. iso.ch). For example, the top-level country code domain for the United States is US. In the United States, many local governments and organizations use the US domain. For example, mcps.k12.md.us is the domain name of the Montgomery County Public Schools in the state of Maryland, USA.

The fully qualified domain name (FQDN) is constructed by stringing together the subdomain names, from lower to higher level, using dots (.) as separators. For example, REDHAT.COM is a fully qualified domain name; so is EE. UMD.EDU. Note that each of these may also refer to a specific host computer. Figure 5-2 illustrates the components of a fully qualified domain name.

Figure 5-2:
A fully qualified domain name has a hierarchy of components.

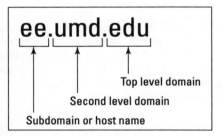

Domain names are case-insensitive. Therefore, as far as DNS is concerned, the domains UMD.EDU and umd.edu both represent University of Maryland's domain. The norm, however, is to type domain names in all lowercase.

Exploring Berkeley Internet Domain Name (BIND)

Most UNIX systems, including Red Hat Linux, come with the BIND system — a well-known implementation of DNS. The BIND software is installed during Red Hat Linux installation, as long as you select the DNS Name Server package group when selecting the packages for installation.

To see which version of BIND is installed on your Red Hat Linux system, type the following command:

```
rpm -q bind
```

If BIND is installed, this command should display a line similar to the following with the version number of the RPM file:

```
bind-9.2.1-9
```

As this output shows, BIND Version 9.2.1 is installed on my system.

BIND includes three major components:

✦ The `named` daemon — the name server — that responds to queries about host names and IP addresses

✦ A resolver library that applications can use to resolve host names into IP addresses and vice versa

✦ Command-line DNS utility programs (DNS clients), such as `dig` (Domain Internet Groper) and `host` that users can use to query DNS

I describe these components of BIND in the next few sections. In later sections I explain how to configure the resolver and the name server.

named — the BIND Name Server

The `named` daemon is the name server that responds to queries about host names and IP addresses. Based on the configuration files and the local DNS database, `named` either provides answers to queries or asks other servers and caches their responses. The `named` server also performs a function referred to as *zone transfer*, which involves copying data among the name servers in a domain.

The name server operates in one of three modes:

✦ **Primary** — In this case, the name server keeps the master copy of the domain's data on disk. There is one primary server for each domain or subdomain.

✦ **Secondary** — A secondary name server copies its domain's data from the primary server using a zone transfer operation. You can have one or more secondary name servers for a domain.

✦ **Caching** — A caching name server loads the addresses of a few authoritative servers for the root domain and gets all domain data by caching responses to queries resolved by contacting other name servers. Primary and secondary servers also cache responses.

A name server can be authoritative or not, depending on what information it is providing. As the term implies, the response from an authoritative name server is supposed to be accurate. The primary and secondary name servers are authoritative for their own domains, but they are not authoritative for responses provided from cached information. Caching name servers are never authoritative because all of their responses come from cached information.

To run a name server on your Red Hat Linux system, you have to run `named` with the appropriate configuration files. Later in this chapter, you learn about the configuration files and data files that control how the name server operates.

Resolver library

Finding an IP address for a host name is referred to as *resolving the host name*. Network-aware applications, such as a Web browser or an FTP client, use a resolver library to perform the conversion from the name to an IP address. Depending on the settings in the /etc/host.conf file, the resolver library consults the /etc/hosts file or makes a DNS query to resolve a host name to its IP address. The resolver library queries the name servers listed in the /etc/resolv.conf file.

You do not need to learn much about the resolver library unless you are writing network-aware applications. To run Internet services properly, all you need to know is how to configure the resolver. Later in this chapter, I show you how to configure this and other aspects of DNS.

DNS utility programs

You can use the DNS utility programs — dig and host — to try out DNS from the shell prompt interactively. These utility programs are DNS clients. You can use them to query the DNS database and debug any name server you may set up on your system. By default, these programs query the name server listed in your system's /etc/resolv.conf file.

You can use dig, the Domain Internet Groper program, to look up IP addresses for a domain name or vice versa. For example, to look up the IP address of addlab.nws.noaa.gov, type

dig addlab.nws.noaa.gov

dig prints the results of the DNS query with a great amount of detail. Look in the part of the output labeled ANSWER SECTION: for the result. For example, here's what that section looks like for this sample query:

```
;; ANSWER SECTION:
addlab.nws.noaa.gov.   86400   IN   A    140.90.141.131
```

Reverse lookups (finding host names for IP addresses) are also easy with dig. For example, to find the host name corresponding to the IP address 140.90.141.131, type the following:

dig -x 140.90.141.131

Again, the answer appears in the ANSWER SECTION of the output, which, for this example, looks like this:

```
;; ANSWER SECTION:
131.141.90.140.in-addr.arpa. 86400 IN  PTR   addlab.nws.noaa.gov.
```

In this case, the host name corresponding to the IP address 140.90.141.131 happens to be addlab.nws.noaa.gov.

You can also query DNS by using the host program. The host program produces output in a compact format. For example, here's a typical use of host to look up IP address for a host name:

```
host www.gao.gov
```

This generates the following one-liner:

```
www.gao.gov has address 161.203.16.2
```

By default, host prints the IP address and any MX record (these records list the names of mail handlers for the host).

For a reverse lookup, use the -t ptr option, along with the IP address as an argument, like this:

```
host -t ptr 161.203.16.2
```

Here's the relay from host:

```
2.16.203.161.in-addr.arpa. domain name pointer www.gao.gov.
```

In this case, host prints the PTR record (from the DNS database) that shows the host name corresponding to the IP address.

You can also try other types of records, such as CNAME (for canonical name), as follows:

```
host -t cname www.ee.umd.edu
```

The response from host says

```
www.ee.umd.edu is an alias for edison.eng.umd.edu.
```

This indicates that the canonical name (or alias) for www.ee.umd.edu is edison.eng.umd.edu.

Another interesting type of record is HINFO (for host information). For example, you can query the HINFO record of prep.ai.mit.edu with the following command line:

```
host -t hinfo prep.ai.mit.edu
```

In this case, the output from host says

```
prep.ai.mit.edu host information "i686" "debian-gnu/linux"
```

Although most hosts do not have HINFO records, some old hosts do include this information, which tells you some details about the host. In this case, the prep.ai.mit.edu host seems to be a Pentium PC running Debian Linux.

Configuring DNS

You configure DNS by using a number of configuration files. The exact set of files depends on whether or not you are running a name server and, if so, the type of name server — caching or primary. Some configuration files are needed whether you run a name server or not.

Configuring the resolver

You do not need a name server running on your system to use the DNS clients — dig and host. You can use them to query your domain's name server. Typically, your ISP provides you with this information. You have to list the IP addresses of these name servers in the /etc/resolv.conf file — the resolver library reads this file to determine how to resolve host names. The format of this file is

```
domain your-domain.com
search your-domain.com
nameserver A.B.C.D
nameserver X.Y.Z.W
```

where A.B.C.D and X.Y.Z.W are the IP addresses (dot-separated numeric addresses, such as 192.168.0.1) of the primary and secondary name servers your ISP provides you.

The domain line lists the local domain name. The search line specifies the domains on which a host name is searched first (usually, you put your own domain in the search line). The domain listed on the search line is appended to any host name before the resolver library tries to resolve it. For example, if you look for a host named mailhost, the resolver library first tries mailhost.your-domain.com; if that fails, it tries mailhost. The search line applies to any host name you try to access. For example, if you are trying to access www.redhat.com, the resolver first tries www.redhat.com. your-domain.com and then www.redhat.com.

Another important configuration file is /etc/host.conf — this file tells the resolver what to do when attempting to resolve a host name. A typical /etc/host/conf file contains the following line:

```
order hosts,bind
```

This tells the resolver to consult the /etc/hosts file first and, if that fails, to query the name server listed in the /etc/resolv.conf file. The /etc/ hosts file usually lists any local host names and their IP addresses. Here's a typical line from the /etc/hosts file:

```
127.0.0.1    lnbp200  localhost.localdomain  localhost
```

This line says that the IP address 127.0.0.1 is assigned to the host names lnbp200, localhost.localdomain, and localhost.

In the latest version of Linux kernel that uses GNU C Library version 2 (glibc 2) or later, the name service switch (NSS) file, /etc/nsswitch.conf, controls how services such as the resolver library, NIS, NIS+, and local files such as /etc/hosts and /etc/shadow interact. For example, the following hosts entry in the /etc/nsswitch.conf file specifies that the resolver library should first try the /etc/hosts file, then try NIS+, and finally try DNS:

```
hosts:      files nisplus dns
```

To learn more about the /etc/nsswitch.conf file and what it does, type **info libc "Name Service Switch"** in a terminal window.

Configuring a caching name server

A simple, but useful, name server is one that finds answers to host-name queries by using other name servers and then remembers the answer (by saving it in a cache) the next time you need it. This can shorten the time it takes to access hosts you have accessed recently because the answer is already in the cache.

When you install the DNS Name Server package group during Red Hat Linux installation, the configuration files for a caching name server are also installed. That means you can start running the caching name server without much work on your part. This section describes the configuration files and what you have to do to start the caching name server.

/etc/named.conf file

The first configuration file you need is /etc/named.conf. The named **server** reads this configuration file when it starts. You already have this file if you have installed the DNS Name Server during Red Hat Linux installation. Here's what the default /etc/named/conf file contains:

```
// generated by named-bootconf.pl

options {
    directory "/var/named";
    /*
     * If there is a firewall between you and nameservers you want
     * to talk to, you might need to uncomment the query-source
     * directive below. Previous versions of BIND always asked
     * questions using port 53, but BIND 8.1 uses an unprivileged
     * port by default.
     */
    // query-source address * port 53;
};

//
// a caching only nameserver config
//
controls {
    inet 127.0.0.1 allow { localhost; } keys { rndckey; };
};
zone "." IN {
    type hint;
    file "named.ca";
};

zone "localhost" IN {
    type master;
    file "localhost.zone";
    allow-update { none; };
};

zone "0.0.127.in-addr.arpa" IN {
    type master;
    file "named.local";
    allow-update { none; };
};

include "/etc/rndc.key";
```

Comments are C-style (/* ... */) or C++-style (starts with //). The file contains block statements enclosed in curly braces ({...}) and terminated by a semicolon (;). A block statement, in turn, contains other statements, each ending with a semicolon.

This /etc/named.conf file begins with an options block statement with a number of option statements. The directory option statement tells named where to look for all other files that appear on file lines in the configuration file. In this case, named looks for the files in the /var/named directory.

After the options statement, the /etc/named.conf file contains several zone statements, each enclosed in curly braces and terminated by a semicolon. Each zone statement defines a zone. The first zone is named "." (root zone); it's a hint zone that specifies the root name servers.

The next two `zone` statements in `/etc/named.conf` are master zones. The syntax for a master zone statement for an Internet class zone (indicated by the IN keyword) is as follows:

```
zone "zone-name" IN {
        type master;
        file "zone-file";
        [...other optional statements...]
};
```

The `zone-name` is the name of the zone, and `zone-file` is the zone file that contains the resource records (RR) — the database entries — for that zone. I describe zone file formats and resource record formats in the next two sections.

Zone file format

The zone file typically starts with a number of directives, each of which begins with a dollar sign ($) followed by a keyword. Two commonly used directives are `$TTL` and `$ORIGIN`.

For example, the line

```
$TTL    86400
```

**Book VII
Chapter 5**

uses the `$TTL` directive to set the default Time To Live (TTL) for subsequent records with undefined TTLs. The value is in seconds, and the valid TTLs are in the range 0 to 2147483647 seconds. In this case, the directive sets the default TTL as 86400 seconds (or one day).

The `$ORIGIN` directive sets the domain name that will be appended to any unqualified records. For example, the following `$ORIGIN` directive sets the domain name to `localhost`:

**Setting Up
DNS and NIS**

```
$ORIGIN localhost.
```

If there is no `$ORIGIN` directive, the initial `$ORIGIN` is the same as the zone name that comes after the `zone` keyword in the `/etc/named.conf` file.

After the directives, the zone file contains one or more resource records. These records follow a specific format, which is outlined in the next section.

Resource Record (RR) format

You have to understand the format of the resource records before you can understand and intelligently work with zone files. Each resource record has the following format (the optional fields are shown in square brackets):

```
[domain] [ttl] [class] type data [;comment]
```

The fields are separated by tabs or spaces and may contain some special characters, such as an @ symbol for the domain and a semicolon (;) to indicate the start of a comment.

The first field, which must begin at the first character of the line, identifies the domain. You can use the @ symbol to use the current $ORIGIN for the domain name for this record. If you have multiple records for the same domain name, leave the first field blank.

The optional ttl field specifies the Time To Live — the duration for which the data can be cached and considered valid. You can specify the duration in one of the following formats:

+ *N*, where *N* is a number meaning *N* seconds

+ *N*W, where *N* is a number meaning *N* weeks

+ *N*D, where *N* is a number meaning *N* days

+ *N*H, where *N* is a number meaning *N* hours

+ *N*M, where *N* is a number meaning *N* minutes

+ *N*S, where *N* is a number meaning *N* seconds

The letters W, D, H, M, and S can also be in lowercase. Thus, you can write 86400 or 1D (or 1d) to indicate a duration of one day. You can also combine these to specify more precise durations, such as 5w6d16h to indicate 5 weeks, 6 days, and 16 hours.

The class field specifies the network type. The most commonly used value for this field is IN for Internet.

Next in the resource record is the type field, which denotes the type of record (such as SOA, NS, A, or PTR). Table 5-1 lists the DNS resource record types. The data field comes next, and it depends on the type field.

Table 5-1		DNS Resource Record Types
Type	**Name**	**Description**
SOA	Start of Authority	Indicates that all subsequent records are authoritative for this zone.
NS	Name Server	Identifies authoritative name servers for a zone.
A	Address	Specifies the host address corresponding to a name.

Type	Name	Description
PTR	Pointer	Specifies the name corresponding to an address (used for reverse mapping — converting an IP address to a host name).
MX	Mail Exchanger	Identifies the host that accepts mail meant for a domain (used to route e-mail).
CNAME	Canonical Name	Defines the nickname or alias for a host name.
HINFO	Host Info	Identifies the hardware and operating system for a host.
RP	Responsible Person	Provides the name of a technical contact for a domain.
WKS	Well Known Services	Lists services provided by a host (this has been deprecated and is no longer used).
TXT	Text	Used to include comments and other information in the DNS database.

You should learn to read the resource records, at least the ones of type SOA, NS, A, PTR, and MX, which are some of the most commonly used. Next, I briefly describe these records, illustrating each record type through an example.

A typical SOA record has the following format:

```
@       1D IN SOA       @ root (
                        42              ; serial
                        3H              ; refresh -- 3 hours
                        15M             ; retry -- 15 minutes
                        1W              ; expiry -- 1 week
                        1D )            ; minimum -- 1 day
```

The first field specifies the domain as an @, which means the current domain (by default, the zone name, as shown in the /etc/named.conf file). The next field specifies a TTL of one day for this record. The class field is set to IN, which means the record is for Internet. The type field specifies the record type as SOA. The rest of the fields constitute the data for the SOA record. The data includes the name of the primary name server (in this case, @, or the current domain), the e-mail address of the technical contact, and five different times enclosed in parentheses.

The NS record specifies the authoritative name servers for a zone. A typical NS record looks like the following:

```
.       3600000  IN  NS   A.ROOT-SERVERS.NET.
```

Book VII Chapter 5

Setting Up DNS and NIS

In this case, the NS record lists the authoritative name server for the root zone (notice that the name of the first field is a single dot). The Time-To-Live field specifies the record to be valid for 1,000 hours (3600000 seconds). The class is IN, for Internet; and the record type is NS. The final field lists the name of the name server (A.ROOT-SERVERS.NET.), which ends with a dot.

An A record specifies the address corresponding to a name. For example, the following A record shows the address of A.ROOT-SERVERS.NET. as 198.41.0.4:

```
A.ROOT-SERVERS.NET.        3600000        A        198.41.0.4
```

In this case, the network class is not specified because the field is optional, and the default is IN.

PTR records are used for reverse mapping — converting an address to a name. Consider the following example:

```
1        IN        PTR        localhost.
```

This record comes from a file for a zone named 0.0.127.in-addr.arpa. Therefore, this record says that the name associated with the address 127.0.0.1 is localhost.

An MX record specifies the name of a host that accepts mail on behalf of a specific domain. For example, here's a typical MX record:

```
naba        IN        MX        10        mailhub.lnbsoft.com.
```

This says that mail addressed to the host named naba in the current domain should be sent to mailhub.lnbsoft.com (this host is called a mail exchanger). The number 10 is the preference value. For a list of multiple MX records with different preference values, the ones with lower preference values are tried first.

Now that you know a bit about resource records, you can go through the zone files for the caching name server.

/var/named/named.ca file

Information about the root name servers is in the file /var/named/named.ca, as specified in the zone statement for the root zone in the /etc/named.conf file. The following listing shows the /var/named/named.ca file from a Red Hat Linux system:

```
;     This file holds the information on root name servers needed to
;     initialize cache of Internet domain name servers
;     (e.g. reference this file in the "cache . <file>"
;     configuration file of BIND domain name servers).
;
;     This file is made available by InterNIC registration services
;     under anonymous FTP as
;        file         /domain/named.root
;        on server    FTP.RS.INTERNIC.NET
;     -OR- under Gopher at   RS.INTERNIC.NET
;        under menu       InterNIC Registration Services (NSI)
;         submenu         InterNIC Registration Archives
;        file             named.root
;
;     last update:  Aug 22, 1997
;     related version of root zone:  1997082200
;
;
; formerly NS.INTERNIC.NET
;
.                    3600000 IN NS   A.ROOT-SERVERS.NET.
A.ROOT-SERVERS.NET.  3600000    A   198.41.0.4
;
; formerly NS1.ISI.EDU
;
.                    3600000    NS   B.ROOT-SERVERS.NET.
B.ROOT-SERVERS.NET.  3600000    A   128.9.0.107
;
; formerly C.PSI.NET
;
.                    3600000    NS   C.ROOT-SERVERS.NET.
C.ROOT-SERVERS.NET.  3600000    A   192.33.4.12
;
; formerly TERP.UMD.EDU
;
.                    3600000    NS   D.ROOT-SERVERS.NET.
D.ROOT-SERVERS.NET.  3600000    A   128.8.10.90
;
; formerly NS.NASA.GOV
;
.                    3600000    NS   E.ROOT-SERVERS.NET.
E.ROOT-SERVERS.NET.  3600000    A   192.203.230.10
;
; formerly NS.ISC.ORG
;
.                    3600000    NS   F.ROOT-SERVERS.NET.
F.ROOT-SERVERS.NET.  3600000    A   192.5.5.241
;
; formerly NS.NIC.DDN.MIL
;
.                    3600000    NS   G.ROOT-SERVERS.NET.
G.ROOT-SERVERS.NET.  3600000    A   192.112.36.4
;
; formerly AOS.ARL.ARMY.MIL
;
.                    3600000    NS   H.ROOT-SERVERS.NET.
H.ROOT-SERVERS.NET.  3600000    A   128.63.2.53
;
; formerly NIC.NORDU.NET
;
```

**Book VII
Chapter 5**

**Setting Up
DNS and NIS**

```
.          3600000    NS  I.ROOT-SERVERS.NET.
I.ROOT-SERVERS.NET.  3600000   A   192.36.148.17
;
; temporarily housed at NSI (InterNIC)
;
.          3600000    NS  J.ROOT-SERVERS.NET.
;
; housed in LINX, operated by RIPE NCC
;
.          3600000    NS  K.ROOT-SERVERS.NET.
K.ROOT-SERVERS.NET.  3600000   A   193.0.14.129
;
; temporarily housed at ISI (IANA)
;
.          3600000    NS  L.ROOT-SERVERS.NET.
L.ROOT-SERVERS.NET.  3600000   A   198.32.64.12
;
; housed in Japan, operated by WIDE
;
.          3600000    NS  M.ROOT-SERVERS.NET.
M.ROOT-SERVERS.NET.  3600000   A   202.12.27.33
; End of File
```

This file contains NS and A resource records that specify the names of
authoritative name servers and their addresses for the root zone (indicated
by the "." in the first field of each NS record).

The comment lines in the file begin with a semicolon. These comments give
you hints about the location of the root name servers. There are 13 root
name servers for the Internet, most of the root servers are located in the
United States. This file is a necessity for any name server because the name
server has to be able to reach at least one root name server.

/var/named/localhost.zone File

The /etc/named.conf file includes a zone statement for the localhost
zone that specifies the zone file as localhost.zone. That file is located in
the /var/named directory of your Red Hat Linux system. Here's a listing of
what the /var/named/localhost.zone file contains:

```
$TTL    86400
$ORIGIN localhost.
@           1D IN SOA       @ root (
                            42                  ; serial (d.
    adams)
                            3H                  ; refresh
                            15M                 ; retry
                            1W                  ; expiry
                            1D )                ; minimum

            1D IN NS        @
            1D IN A         127.0.0.1
```

This zone file starts with a $TTL directive that sets the default TTL to one day (86400 seconds) for subsequent records with undefined TTLs. Next, a $ORIGIN directive sets the domain name to localhost.

After these two directives, the /var/named/localhost.zone file contains three resource records (RRs): an SOA record, an NS record, and an A record. The SOA and the NS record specify the localhost as the primary authoritative name server for the zone. The A record specifies the address of localhost as 127.0.0.1.

/var/named/named.local file

The third zone statement in the /etc/named.conf file specifies a reverse-mapping zone named 0.0.127.in-addr.arpa. For this zone, the zone file is /var/named/named.local, which contains the following:

```
$TTL      86400
@         IN      SOA       localhost. root.localhost. (
                                      1997022700 ; Serial
                                      28800      ; Refresh
                                      14400      ; Retry
                                      3600000    ; Expire
                                      86400 )    ; Minimum
          IN      NS        localhost.

1         IN      PTR       localhost.
```

The SOA and NS records specify localhost as the primary name server.

The SOA record also shows root.localhost. as the e-mail address of the technical contact for the domain. Note that the DNS zone files use a user. host. (notice the ending period) format for the e-mail address. When sending any e-mail to the contact, you have to replace the first dot with an @ and remove the final dot.

Caching name server startup and test

Now that you have studied the configuration files for the caching name server, you can start the name server and see it in operation. To start the name server, log in as root and type the following command in a terminal window:

```
service named start
```

This starts named — the name server daemon.

To ensure that the `named` server starts every time you reboot the system, type the following command while logged in as `root`:

```
chkconfig --level 35 named on
```

The `named` server writes diagnostic log messages in the `/var/log/messages` file. After you start `named`, you can check the log messages by opening `/var/log/messages` in a text editor. If there are no error messages from `named`, you can proceed to test the name server.

Before you try the caching name server, you have to specify that name server as your primary one. To do this, make sure that the first line in the `/etc/resolv.conf` file is the following:

```
nameserver 127.0.0.1
```

Now you can use `host` to test the name server. For example, to look up the IP address of `www.gao.gov` by using the caching name server on `localhost`, type the following command:

```
host www.gao.gov localhost
```

Here's the resulting output from the `host` command:

```
Using domain server:
Name: localhost
Address: 127.0.0.1#53
Aliases:

www.gao.gov. has address 161.203.16.2
```

As the output shows, the `host` command uses `localhost` as the DNS server and returns the IP address of `www.gao.gov`. If you get an output similar to this, the caching name server is up and running.

Understanding Network Information Service (NIS)

Network Information Service (NIS) was developed by Sun Microsystems as a way to share information among all computers in a local area network. The types of information NIS most commonly uses include the following:

✦ User names and passwords from files such as `/etc/passwd` and `/etc/shadow`

✦ Group information from the `/etc/group` file

Normally, each system has its own copy of information in respective files, and any changes require updating the files on each system individually. Using NIS, you can maintain a single set of configuration files for a collection of computers in an NIS server. All other computers running NIS clients can then access the files. For example, if your user name and password are in the NIS password database, you will be able to log in on all computers on the network running NIS client programs.

NIS was originally called Sun Yellow Pages (YP), but the name Yellow Pages is a registered trademark of British Telecom in the United Kingdom, so Sun Microsystems had to change the name. However, many NIS commands, and the NIS package names, begin with the letters yp.

How NIS works

If you want to use NIS in a network, you must set up at least one computer as an NIS server. You can have multiple NIS servers in a network, each serving a different collection of computers. You can also have a master NIS server and one or more slave NIS servers that receive a copy of the master's database. The group of computers a master NIS server supports is called an NIS domain or YP domain.

The master NIS server runs the ypserv daemon (this is the NIS server daemon) that maintains the shared information in DBM databases. (DBM refers to Data Base Management, a library of functions that maintains key-value pairs in a database.) The NIS databases are called *maps*. You can create these NIS maps directly from the text-configuration files — such as /etc/passwd and /etc/group — by using the /usr/lib/yp/makedbm program that comes with the NIS server software. More accurately, the ypserv daemon uses the Makefile in the /var/yp directory to create the maps for all shared configuration files.

The master NIS server provides the maps to all NIS client computers. The clients run the ypbind daemon through which various client programs access the master NIS server. In addition to a master server, one or more NIS slave servers may be set up to provide the NIS maps in case the master is unavailable or down. The NIS slave servers periodically copy the NIS maps from the master server (using the /usr/lib/yp/ypxfr command) and are able to provide these maps to clients when the master is down.

You can think of NIS as a way of distributing the same set of configuration files among all computers in an NIS domain. You get the benefits of sharing the same files (such as the same user name and password for all machines), yet you can still edit and maintain just one set of files — the files on the master NIS server.

In the next few sections, I explain how to set up your Red Hat Linux system as an NIS client and as an NIS server.

Setting up NIS client

If your network uses NIS centrally to administer users and passwords, you can set up your Red Hat Linux PC as an NIS client. In fact, when you install Red Hat Linux from this book's companion CD-ROMs, you can enable NIS from the Authentication Configuration screen in the GUI installer.

During Red Hat Linux installation, the Authentication Configuration screen shows you a number of different options for authenticating users — the default being shadow passwords and the MD5 password. One of these options is a button labeled Enable NIS. You can click this button to set up your Red Hat Linux PC as an NIS client. Of course, you should do this only if your network is set up with an NIS server.

If you do select the Enable NIS option, you have to provide the following information:

✦ Specify the NIS domain name. The domain name refers to the group of computers the NIS server serves.

✦ Specify the name of the NIS server.

✦ Indicate whether or not you want your PC to use IP broadcast to find NIS servers in the local network.

If you did not configure your system as an NIS client during Red Hat Linux installation, you can do so by performing these steps:

✦ Define your NIS domain name.

✦ Set up the NIS configuration file (`/etc/yp.conf`). In this file, you specify the master NIS and slave servers that provide NIS maps to your Red Hat Linux PC.

✦ Configure the NIS client daemon — `ypbind` — to start when your system boots.

I will show you how do perform these steps in the next three sections.

NIS domain-name setup

The NIS domain name identifies the group of computers that a particular NIS server supports. You can set the NIS domain name of your system by using the `domainname` command. For example, to set your NIS domain name to `admin`, log in as `root` and type the following command in a terminal window:

```
domainname admin
```

If you type `domainname` without any arguments, the command prints the current NIS domain name.

To ensure that the NIS domain name is set as soon as your system boots, the command should be run from one of the startup scripts. You can do this by adding the following line to the `/etc/sysconfig/network` file on your Red Hat Linux system:

```
NISDOMAIN="admin"
```

Of course, you should use the NIS domain name appropriate to your network.

The NIS domain is different from the DNS domain names discussed earlier in this chapter. Pick an NIS domain name that's not related to the DNS domain name. Doing so makes it harder for crackers to guess your NIS domain name (if they know the NIS domain name, there is a risk that they can get the NIS password database).

NIS configuration file setup

The `ypbind` daemon, described in the next section, needs information about the NIS domains and NIS servers to do its job. It finds this information in the `/etc/yp.conf` configuration file. The `ypbind` daemon reads the `/etc/yp.conf` file when it starts up or when it receives the `SIGHUP` signal (for example, when you restart `ypbind` with the `kill -HUP` command).

To specify one or more NIS servers for the local domain (which you have already set with the `domainname` command), all you need in `/etc/yp.conf` are lines such as the following:

```
ypserver nisadmin
ypserver 192.168.0.4
```

You can use a name such as `nisadmin` if that name is listed in the `/etc/hosts` file (that way, `ypbind` can resolve the name into an IP address without having to use NIS). Otherwise, you should specify the NIS server's IP address.

In `/etc/yp.conf`, you can also specify specific NIS servers for specific NIS domains, like this:

```
domain sales server nissales
domain admin server nisadmin
```

A third type of entry in the `/etc/yp.conf` file specifies that `ypbind` should use IP broadcast in the local network to find an NIS server for a specified domain. To do this, add a line such as the following to `/etc/yp.conf`:

```
domain admin broadcast
```

NIS client daemon setup

Every computer in an NIS domain, including the server, runs the `ypbind` daemon. Various NIS client applications, such as `ypwhich`, `ypcat`, and `yppoll`, need the `ypbind` daemon to obtain information from the master NIS server. More precisely, the C library contacts the `ypbind` daemon to locate the NIS server for the domain. Then the C library contacts the server directly to obtain administrative information. The client applications get the information through functions in the C library.

To interactively start `ypbind`, log in as `root` and type the following command:

```
service ypbind start
```

If you want `ypbind` to start when the system boots, type the following commands:

```
chkconfig --add ypbind
chkconfig --level 35 ypbind on
```

Setting up NIS server

To set up your Red Hat Linux system as an NIS server, first set it up as an NIS client — set the NIS domain name, configure the `/etc/yp.conf` file, and configure the `ypbind` daemon. (Note that the `ypbind` daemon won't work until you have an NIS server up and running). After the client configuration, you can configure the NIS server. This requires that you perform the following tasks:

✦ Create the NIS maps using `ypinit`.

✦ Configure the master NIS server — `ypserv`.

✦ Optionally, configure one or more slave NIS servers.

I explain these steps in the next two sections.

NIS map creation

Creating NIS maps involves converting the text files, such as `/etc/passwd` and `/etc/group` into DBM files using `makedbm`. The map creation is

controlled by /var/yp/Makefile, a file that can be used by the make command to perform specific tasks.

You can configure what you want the NIS server to share with the clients
in the NIS domain. You do so by editing the Makefile in the /var/yp
directory. Open /var/yp/Makefile in a text editor, and locate the line
that begins with all:. Here is a typical excerpt from the Makefile showing
the comments before the all: line:

```
# If you don't want some of these maps built, feel free to comment
# them out from this list.

all: passwd group hosts rpc services netid protocols mail \
    # netgrp shadow publickey networks ethers bootparams printcap \
    # amd.home auto.master auto.home auto.local passwd.adjunct \
    # timezone locale netmasks
```

As the comment lines (the ones that begin with #) indicate, you can comment out any maps you do not want to build. In the preceding example, the
maps listed in the last three lines will not be built.

Next, edit the /var/yp/securenets file (or create a new file if it does not
exist) to specify the IP addresses of client computers that can access the
NIS maps. For example, to allow connections from the localhost and hosts
in the 192.168.0.0 network, use the following as the content of the /var/
yp/securenets file:

```
# Always allow access for localhost
host       127.0.0.1
# allow connections from any host
# on the 192.168.0.0 network
255.255.255.0    192.168.0.0
```

The last line allows only those computers on the local network with IP
addresses in the range 192.168.0.1 through 192.168.0.254 access to the NIS
maps.

Next, you should generate the NIS map database by running the /usr/lib/
yp/ypinit program with the -m option. Here is a sample session with that
program:

```
/usr/lib/yp/ypinit -m
```

The program asks you for names of hosts that will run NIS servers. It automatically selects your host as an NIS server and prompts for the names of
any other NIS servers. You can add the server names one at a time and
press Ctrl+D when you are done. Then you have to verify that the list of NIS

servers is correct (type y). After that, the program generates the NIS maps as specified by the `all:` line in the `Makefile`. The map files are stored in a subdirectory of `/var/yp` that has the same name as the NIS domain name you have previously set for your system. For example, for the NIS domain `admin`, the map files are in the `/var/yp/admin` directory.

Master NIS server configuration

To configure the NIS server daemon, `ypserv`, you have to prepare the configuration file `/etc/ypserv.conf`. You can learn about the syntax of this file by typing the command **man ypserv.conf.**

You can add lines in `/etc/ypserv.conf` that specify access rules — which hosts can access which maps. The format of the access rules is as follows:

```
Host : Map : Security : mangle [: field_to_mangle]
```

The `field_to_mangle` is optional; it indicates which field in the map file should be mangled (the default is the second field because the password is in the second field of most files, such as `/etc/passwd`). To *mangle a field* is to replace it with an x if the request comes from an unprivileged host. The rest of the fields have the following meanings:

✦ `Host` — IP address or a wildcard (*) indicating to whom the rule applies

✦ `Map` — Name of the map to which the rule applies (the names of the maps are the same as those of the map files in the `/var/yp/domainname` directory, where `domainname` is your NIS domain name)

✦ `Security` — One of the following: `none` (to allow access always); `port` (to access from a port less than 1024); `deny` (to deny access to the map); or `des` (to require DES authentication)

✦ `mangle` — One of the following: `yes` (the field specified by `field_to_mangle` should be replaced by an x if the request is from unauthorized host) or `no` (do not mangle)

For example, the following lines in the `/etc/ypserv.conf` file restrict access to the password map to systems in the 192.168.0 network:

```
192.168.0    :    passwd.byname    : port    : yes
192.168.0    :    passwd.byuid     : port    : yes
```

If you do not specify any access rules, `ypserv` allows all computers to access all maps.

After you have set up the `/etc/ypserv.conf` file, you can start the NIS server with the following command:

```
service ypserv start
```

To ensure that `ypserv` starts whenever you reboot the system, type the following command to enable it:

```
chkconfig --level 35 ypserv on
```

To handle password changes from clients, you must also run the `rpc.yppasswdd` server on the master NIS server for the domain. The `rpc.yppasswdd` server enables users on client systems to type the `yppasswd` command and change their password in the NIS database. If you do not have the `rpc.yppasswdd` server running on the master NIS server, users will get the following error message when they type the `yppasswd` command:

```
yppasswd: yppasswdd not running on NIS master host
```

To correct this problem, log in as `root`, and type

```
service yppasswdd start
```

To start `rpc.yppasswdd` automatically at system startup, type

```
chkconfig --level 35 yppasswdd on
```

After you have the master NIS server up and running, you can test it by using various NIS client programs, such as `ypwhich`, `yppoll`, `ypcat`, and `ypmatch`.

Configuring a slave NIS server

To set up a system as a slave NIS server, first set it up as an NIS client and verify that the client works. In particular, type **ypwhich -m** and look for a list of NIS maps and the name of the master NIS server for each map. (In the next section I show you how the `ypwhich -m` command works.)

After you confirm that the system is configured as an NIS client, type the following command to set up the system as a slave NIS server:

```
/usr/lib/yp/ypinit -s nismaster
```

where `nismaster` is the name of the master NIS server for the domain.

Trying out NIS

After you have a master NIS server in your network and you have the `ypbind` client running, you can try out various NIS client programs and other utilities to see if everything is working correctly.

**Book VII
Chapter 5**

**Setting Up
DNS and NIS**

NIS servers and clients use Remote Procedure Call (RPC) to exchange information. RPC requires the `portmap` service, which maps RPC services to TCP and UDP ports. When a server that supports RPC starts up, it registers itself with `portmap` and lists both the services it supports and the ports it uses. Your Red Hat Linux system should already have `portmap` up and running. You can check for it with the following command:

```
ps ax | grep portmap
```

In the output you should see a line showing the `portmap` process. For example, here's a output of this command on a Red Hat Linux system:

```
  525 ?         S       0:00 portmap
26222 pts/2     S       0:00 grep portmap
```

To see if the `ypserv` and `ypbind` processes are running on the master NIS server, type the following command:

```
rpcinfo -p
```

The output should show `ypserv` and `ypbind` in the last column.

To figure out which NIS server your system is using, try the `ypwhich` command. Here is a typical example:

```
ypwhich
```

The output should be the name of the host that runs the NIS master server.

You can also use the `ypwhich` command to view the master NIS server for all available maps, by typing this command:

```
ypwhich -m
```

The output shows a list of the available NIS maps and, for each map, the name of the master NIS server.

To view the name of the master NIS server and information about a specific NIS map, use the `yppoll` command. For example, here is a `yppoll` query for the `passwd.byname` map:

```
yppoll passwd.byname
```

The output shows the NIS domain name and the name of the master server.

Use the `ypcat` command to print the values of the keys in an NIS map. For example, here is a `ypcat` query for the NIS map `group.byname`:

```
ypcat group.byname
```

The output is a list of group names and group IDs. Here's a typical output:

```
ivy:!:503:
ashley:!:502:
emily:!:501:
naba:!:500:
```

You can use `ypmatch` to look at the entries in an NIS map that match a specific key. For example, here is a `ypmatch` command line that looks for entries that match the key `naba` in the `group.byname` map:

```
ypmatch naba group.byname
```

Here's the output that matches the key `naba`:

```
naba:!:500:
```

If you compare this with the output from `ypcat` showing all the group names, you can see that `ypmatch` shows the line corresponding to the group name `naba`.

Chapter 6: Running Samba and NFS

In This Chapter

✔ **Sharing files with NFS**

✔ **Using the Red Hat NFS Server Configuration tool**

✔ **Installing and configuring Samba**

✔ **Setting up a Windows server using Samba**

Red Hat Linux includes two prominent file-sharing services: *Network File System* (NFS) for sharing files with other UNIX systems (or PCs with NFS client software) and Samba for file sharing and print sharing with Windows systems. In this chapter, I describe both NFS and Samba.

Sharing Files with NFS

Sharing files through NFS is simple and involves two basic steps:

✦ On the Red Hat Linux system that runs the NFS server, export (share) one or more directories by listing them in the /etc/exports file and by running the exportfs command. In addition, you must run the NFS server by logging in as root and typing the command **service nfs start**.

✦ On each client system, use the mount command to mount the directories the server has exported.

The only problem in using NFS is that each client system must support it. Microsoft Windows does not come with NFS. That means you have to buy NFS software separately if you want to share files by using NFS. However, it makes sense to use NFS if all systems on your LAN run Linux (or other variants of UNIX with built-in NFS support).

Note that NFS has security vulnerabilities. Therefore, you should not set up NFS on systems directly connected to the Internet.

In the next few sections, I walk you through NFS setup, using an example of two Red Hat Linux PCs on a LAN.

Exporting a file system with NFS

Start with the server system that exports — makes available to the client systems — the contents of a directory. On the server, you must run the NFS service and also designate one or more file systems that are to be exported — made available to the client systems.

To export a file system, you have to add an appropriate entry to the /etc/ exports file. For example, suppose you want to export the /home directory and you want to enable the host named LNBP75 to mount this file system for read and write operations. You can do this by adding the following entry to the /etc/exports file:

```
/home LNBP75(rw,sync)
```

If you want to give access to all hosts on a LAN such as 192.168.0.0, you could change this line to:

```
/home 192.168.0.0/24(rw,sync)
```

Every line in the /etc/exports file has this general format:

```
directory     host1(options)  host2(options)  ...
```

The first field is the directory being shared via NFS, followed by one or more fields that specify which hosts can mount that directory remotely and a number of options within parentheses. You can specify the hosts with names or IP addresses, including ranges of addresses.

The options within parentheses denote the kind of access each host is granted and how user and group IDs from the server are mapped to ID the client (for example, if a file is owned by root on the server, what owner should that be on the client?). Within the parentheses, the options are separated by commas. For example, if a host is allowed both read and write access and all IDs are to be mapped to the anonymous user (by default this is the user named nobody), then the options would look like this:

```
(rw,all_squash)
```

Table 6-1 shows the options you can use in the /etc/exports file. There are two types of options — general options and user ID mapping options.

Table 6-1	Options in /etc/exports
This Option	*Does the Following*
General Options	
Secure	Allows connections only from ports 1024 or lower (default).
Insecure	Allows connections from 1024 or higher.
Ro	Allows read-only access (default).
Rw	Allows both read and write access.
Sync	Performs write operations (this means writing information to the disk) when requested (default).
Async	Performs write operations when the server is ready.
no_wdelay	Performs write operations immediately.
Wdelay	Waits a bit to see if related write requests arrive and then performs them together (default).
Hide	Hides an exported directory that's a subdirectory of another exported directory (default).
no_hide	Behaves exactly the opposite of hide.
subtree_check	Performs subtree checking, which involves checking parent directories of an exported subdirectory whenever a file is accessed (default).
no_subtree_check	Turns off subtree checking (opposite of subtree_check).
insecure_locks	Allows insecure file locking.
User ID Mapping Options	
all_squash	Maps all user IDs and group IDs to the anonymous user on the client.
no_all_squash	Maps remote user and group IDs to similar IDs on the client (default).
root_squash	Maps remote root user to the anonymous user on the client (default).
no_root_squash	Maps remote root user to the local root user.
anonuid=UID	Sets the user ID of anonymous user to be used for the all_squash and root_squash options.
anongid=GID	Sets the group ID of anonymous user to be used for the all_squash and root_squash options.

**Book VII
Chapter 6**

Running Samba and NFS

After adding the entry in the /etc/exports file, manually export the file system by typing the following command in a terminal window:

```
exportfs -a
```

This command exports all file systems defined in the /etc/exports file.

Now you can start the NFS server processes. To do this, log in as root and type the following command in a terminal window:

```
service nfs start
```

If you want the NFS server to start when the system boots, type the following command to turn it on:

```
chkconfig --level 35 nfs on
```

When the NFS service is up, the server side of NFS is ready. Now you can try to mount the exported file system from a client system and access the exported file system.

If you ever make any changes to the exported file systems listed in the /etc/exports file, remember to restart the NFS service. To do this, log in as root and type the following command in a terminal window:

```
service nfs restart
```

Mounting an NFS file system

To access an exported NFS file system on a client system, you have to mount that file system on a mount point. The mount point is nothing more than a local directory. For example, suppose you want to access the /home directory exported from the server named LNBP200 at the local directory /mnt/lnbp200 on the client system. To do this, follow these steps:

1. **Log in as** root, **and create the directory with the command**

```
mkdir /mnt/lnbp200
```

2. **Type the following command to mount the directory from the remote system (**LNBP200**) on the local directory** /mnt/lnbp200**:**

```
mount lnbp200:/home /mnt/lnbp200
```

After these steps, you can view and access exported files from the local directory /mnt/lnbp200.

To confirm that the NFS file system is indeed mounted, log in as root on the client system and type **mount** in a terminal window. You should see a line similar to the following about the NFS file system:

```
lnbp200:/home/public on /mnt/lnbp200 type nfs (rw,addr=192.168.0.4)
```

Using the Red Hat NFS server configuration tool

Red Hat Linux comes with a graphical NFS server configuration tool that makes it easy to configure and start the NFS server. To configure the NFS server using this tool, follow these steps:

1. **Log in as** `root` **and select Main Menu⇨Server Settings⇨NFS Server from the GNOME desktop.**

   The NFS Server Configuration window appears.

2. **Click Add on the toolbar.**

   The Add NFS Share dialog box appears from which you can add directories you want to share via NFS. Start by specifying the directory, who has access to it (the hosts or IP addresses), and what type of access (read-only or read-write). Figure 6-1 shows the settings for `/home` directory being shared read-write with all hosts in the 192.168.0.0 network.

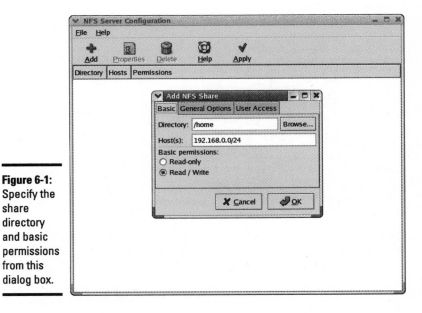

Figure 6-1:
Specify the share directory and basic permissions from this dialog box.

3. **Click the General Options tab in the Add NFS Share dialog box and set the options you want (Figure 6-2).**

   These options map to the options listed in the General Options section of Table 6-1.

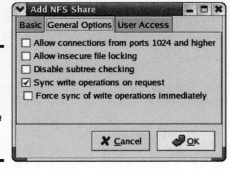

Figure 6-2:
Specify the general options for a NFS share from this dialog box.

4. **Click the User Access tab in the Add NFS Share dialog box and set the options you want (Figure 6-3).**

   These options map to the options listed in the User ID Mapping Options section of Table 6-1.

Figure 6-3:
Specify the user access options for a NFS share from this dialog box.

5. **Click OK in the Add NFS Share dialog box. Then click Apply on the toolbar. The NFS Server Configuration tool then asks if you want to start the NFS service (Figure 6-4). Click Yes to start the NFS server.**

   After completing these steps, you can mount the NFS shares on other hosts in your network.

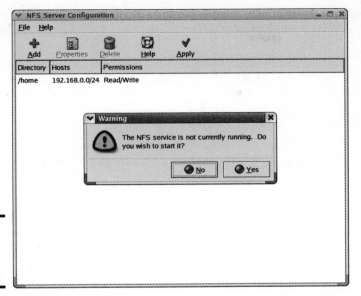

Figure 6-4:
Click Yes to
start the
NFS server.

Setting Up a Windows Server Using Samba

If you rely on Windows for file-sharing and print-sharing, you probably use Windows in your servers and clients. You can move to a Red Hat Linux PC as your server without losing the Windows file and printer sharing because Red Hat Linux can be set up as a Windows server. When you install Red Hat Linux from this book's companion CD-ROMs, you also get a chance to install the Samba software package, which performs that setup. All you have to do is select the Windows File Server package group during installation.

After you install and configure Samba on your Linux PC, client PCs (running Windows for Workgroups or Windows 95/98/NT/2000/XP) can access shared disks and printers on the Red Hat Linux PC by using the Server Message Block (SMB) protocol, the underlying protocol in Windows file and print sharing.

With the Samba package installed, you can make your Red Hat Linux PC a Windows client, which means that the Red Hat Linux PC can access disks and printers a Windows server manages.

The Samba software package has these major components:

✦ `/etc/samba/smb.conf` — The Samba configuration file the SMB server uses

✦ `/etc/samba/smbusers` — A Samba configuration file that shows the Samba user names corresponding to user names on the local Red Hat Linux PC

✦ `nmbd` — The NetBIOS name server, which clients use to look up servers. (NetBIOS stands for Network Basic Input/Output System — an interface that applications use to communicate with network transports, such as TCP/IP.)

✦ `nmblookup` — A command that returns the IP address of a Windows PC identified by its NetBIOS name

✦ `smbadduser` — A program that adds users to the SMB password file

✦ `smbcacls` — A program that manipulates Windows NT access control lists (ACLs) on shared files

✦ `smbclient` — The Windows client, which runs on Linux and allows Linux to access the files and printer on any Windows server

✦ `smbcontrol` — A program that sends messages to the `smbd`, `nmbd`, or `winbindd` processes

✦ `smbd` — The SMB server, which accepts connections from Windows clients and provides file- and print-sharing services

✦ `smbmount` — A program that mounts a Samba share directory on a Red Hat Linux PC

✦ `smbpasswd` — A program that changes the password for an SMB user

✦ `smbprint` — A script that enables printing on a printer on a SMB server

✦ `smbstatus` — A command that lists the current SMB connections for the local host

✦ `smbtar` — A program that backs up SMB shares directly to tape drives on the Red Hat Linux system

✦ `smbumount` — A program that unmounts a currently mounted Samba share directory

✦ `testparm` — A program that ensures that the Samba configuration file is correct

✦ `winbindd` — A server for resolving names from Windows NT servers

In the following sections, I describe how to install Samba from the companion CD-ROM and how to print from the Red Hat Linux PC to a shared printer on a Windows PC.

Checking whether Samba is installed

Check whether Samba is installed by typing the following command in a terminal window:

```
rpm -q samba
```

If you see an output similar to the following, Samba is already installed on your system:

```
samba-2.2.5-10
```

If you get a message saying that the package is not installed, follow these steps to install Samba from this book's companion CD-ROM:

1. **Log in as** `root` **and insert the first CD-ROM into the drive. If you are using GNOME or KDE, the CD-ROM should automatically be mounted. If not, type the following command to mount the CD-ROM:**

    ```
    mount /mnt/cdrom
    ```

2. **Change the directory to the CD-ROM — specifically to the directory where the Red Hat Package Manager (RPM) packages are located — with the following command:**

    ```
    cd /mnt/cdrom/RedHat/RPMS
    ```

3. **Use the following** `rpm` **command to install Samba:**

    ```
    rpm -ivh samba*
    ```

    If Samba is already installed, this command returns an error message. Otherwise, the `rpm` command installs Samba on your system by copying various files to their appropriate locations.

After installing the Samba software you have to configure Samba before you can use it.

Configuring Samba

To set up the Windows file-sharing and print-sharing services, you have to edit the configuration file `/etc/samba/smb.conf`. The configuration file is a text file that looks like a Microsoft Windows 3.1 INI file.

Like the old Windows INI files, the `/etc/samba/smb.conf` file has many sections, with a list of parameters in each section. Each section of the `smb.conf` file begins with the name of the section in square brackets (`[...]`). The section continues until the next section begins or until the file ends.

Each line in a section specifies the value of a parameter, using the following syntax:

```
name = value
```

Comment lines begin with a semicolon (;) or a hash mark (#).

The Samba software comes with a configuration file you can edit to get started. To prepare the configuration file, log in as root and use your favorite text editor to edit the file /etc/samba/smb.conf. Here's a sample configuration file without any comments:

```
[global]
    netbios name = LNBP200
    workgroup = LNB SOFTWARE
    server string = LNB Software-Red Hat Linux-Samba Server
    hosts allow = 192.168.0.  127.
    guest account = naba
    log file = /var/log/samba/l%m.log

# Log files can be at most 50KB
    max log size = 50

    security = user
    smb passwd file = /etc/samba/smbpasswd

# Leave the next option as is - they're for performance
    socket options = TCP_NODELAY SO_RCVBUF=8192
    SO_SNDBUF=8192

    remote browse sync = 192.168.0.255
    remote announce = 192.168.0.255/LNB SOFTWARE
    local master = yes
    os level = 33

    name resolve order = lmhosts bcast

    dns proxy = no
    unix password sync = no

[homes]
    comment = Home Directories
    browseable = no
    writable = yes

[printers]
    comment = All Printers
    path = /var/spool/samba
    browseable = no
```

```
    guest ok = no
    writable = no
    printable = yes

[tmp]
    comment = Temporary file space
    path = /tmp
    read only = no
    public = yes

[public]
    comment = Public Stuff
    path = /home/samba
    browseable = yes
    public = yes
    guest ok = yes
    writable = yes
    printable = no
    available = yes
    guest only = no
    user = naba
    only user = yes
```

Change the username from naba to your username and the IP addresses to values used for your LAN. Also make sure that all directories mentioned in the configuration file actually exist. For example, create the /home/samba directory with the command

```
mkdir /home/samba
```

After editing the Samba configuration file, add two users to the Samba password file. First add your username. Here's how I add myself:

```
smbadduser naba:naba
```

You have to enter the password for the user and repeat it again to confirm.

After making the changes to the /etc/samba/smb.conf file, type the following command to verify that the file is okay:

```
testparm
```

If the command says that it loaded the files okay, you're all set to go.

Start the SMB services with the following command:

```
service smb start
```

To start the SMB services automatically when the system reboots, type the following command:

```
chkconfig --level 35 smb on
```

Trying out Samba

You can now try to access the Samba server on the Red Hat Linux system from one of the Windows systems on the LAN. Double-click the Network Neighborhood icon on the Windows 95/98/ME desktop. On Windows XP, select Start➪My Network Places and then click View workgroup computers (Figure 6-5). This should show all the computers on the same workgroup. As you can see from the label (Figure 6-5), Lnbp200 is actually a Red Hat Linux system running Samba.

Figure 6-5: You can view a Red Hat Linux Samba server from Windows XP.

When you see the Red Hat Linux Samba server, you can open it by double-clicking the icon. This should show folders for each shared directory in the Red Hat Linux Samba server (for the sample /etc/samba/smb.conf file, you'd see two directories: tmp and public). You can then open these folders to explore the contents of the directories further.

Accessing Windows resources with smbclient

You can use the smbclient program to access shared directories and printers on Windows systems on the LAN and to ensure that your Linux

Samba server is working. One quick way to check is to use the `smbclient -L` command to view the list of services on the Red Hat Linux Samba server itself. For example, here's what I type to view information about my Samba server (with the name LNBP200):

```
smbclient -L LNBP200
```

When prompted for a password, simply press Enter. Then the `smbclient` command displays information about the shares on your system. For example, here's what I see as output in response to that `smbclient` command:

```
added interface ip=192.168.0.4 bcast=192.168.0.255 nmask=255.255.255.0
Got a positive name query response from 192.168.0.4 ( 192.168.0.4 )
Password:
Anonymous login successful
Domain=[LNB SOFTWARE] OS=[Unix] Server=[Samba 2.2.5]

    Sharename    Type    Comment
    ---------    ----    -------
    tmp       Disk    Temporary file space
    public    Disk    Public Stuff
    IPC$      IPC     IPC Service (LNB Software-Red Hat Linux-Samba Server)
    ADMIN$    Disk    IPC Service (LNB Software-Red Hat Linux-Samba Server)

    Server          Comment
    ---------       -------
    LNBP200         LNB Software-Red Hat Linux-Samba Server

    Workgroup       Master
    ---------       -------
    LNB SOFTWARE
```

 Samba comes with documentation on configuring it for SSL support. To read this documentation, change the directory with the command `cd /usr/share/doc/samba*/docs/textdocs`, and type the following command to read information on SSLeay — a free implementation of the SSL protocol:

```
more Samba-OpenSSL.txt
```

If you have other Windows servers around, you can look at their services with the `smbclient` program.

You can do much more than simply look at resources with the `smbclient` program — you can also use it to access a disk on a Windows server or to send a file to a Windows printer. The `smbclient` program is like `ftp` — you connect to a Windows server and use commands to get or put files and to send files to the printer.

The following example shows how I use `smbclient` to access a disk on a Windows XP system and view its directory:

```
smbclient //ashley-pc/SharedDocs naba mypassword
```

Here's the rest of session with `smbclient` (I type commands at the `smb: \>` prompt):

```
added interface ip=192.168.0.7 bcast=192.168.0.255 nmask=255.255.255.0
Got a positive name query response from 192.168.0.5 ( 192.168.0.5 )
Domain=[LNB SOFTWARE] OS=[Windows 5.1] Server=[Windows 2000 LAN Manager]
smb: \> dir a*
  Ashley              DA      0 Thu Aug 1 19:00:40 2002

        38154 blocks of size 2097152. 34281 blocks available
smb: \> quit
```

You can type many different `smbclient` commands at the `smb: \>` prompt. To see a list of `smbclient` commands, type `help` at the prompt. Table 6-2 is a brief summary of commonly used `smbclient` commands.

Table 6-2	Common smbclient Commands
Command	*Description*
`!`	Executes a shell command (remember that you run `smbclient` on Red Hat Linux and there is a shell available).
`? cmd`	Displays a list of commands or help on a specific command.
`cancel id`	Cancels a print job identified by its ID.
`cd dir`	Changes the remote directory.
`del file`	Deletes the specified file.
`dir file`	Displays the directory listing.
`Exit`	Logs off the Windows server.
`get rfile lfile`	Copies a remote file (`rfile`) to a local file (`lfile`).
`help cmd`	Provides help on a command (or displays a list of commands).
`lcd newdir`	Changes the local directory (on the Red Hat Linux PC).
`Lowercase`	Toggles automatic lowercase conversion of filenames when executing the `get` command.
`ls files`	Lists files on the server.
`mask name`	Applies a mask (such as `*.c`) to all file operations.
`md dirname`	Makes a directory on the server.
`mget name`	Gets all files with matching names (such as `*.doc`).
`mkdir dirname`	Makes a directory.

Command	Description
mput name	Copies files from the Red Hat Linux PC to the server.
newer file	Gets only the files that are newer than the specified file.
print name	Prints the named file.
printmode mode	Sets the print mode (the mode must be text or graphics).
Prompt	Toggles prompt mode off (similar to the command in ftp).
put lfile rfile	Copies a local file (lfile) to a remote file (rfile).
Queue	Displays the print queue.
Quit	Logs off the Windows server.
rd dir	Deletes the specified directory on the server.
Recurse	Toggles directory recursion during file get and put operations.
rm name	Deletes all files with the specified name.
rmdir name	Deletes the specified directory.
Translate	Toggles text translation (converts a line feed to a carriage return–line-feed pair).

Book VIII

Programming

Contents at a Glance

Chapter 1: Red Hat Linux Programming Essentials

In This Chapter

✔ **Learning programming**

✔ **Exploring the software development tools in Red Hat Linux**

✔ **Compiling and linking programs with GCC**

✔ **Learning to use** `make`

✔ **Debugging programs with** `gdb`

✔ **Understanding the implications of GNU GPL and LGPL**

Your Red Hat Linux system comes loaded with all the tools you need to develop software. In particular, it has all the GNU software-development tools, such as GCC (C and C++ compiler), GNU `make` and the GNU debugger. In this chapter, I start by introducing you to programming and then I describe these software-development tools and show you how to use them. Although I use examples in C and C++ programming languages, the focus is not on showing how to program in these languages, but to show how to use various software-development tools, such as compilers, `make`, and debugger.

I also briefly explain the implications of Free Software Foundation's GNU Public License (GPL) on any plans you might have to develop Linux software. You need to know this because you use GNU tools and GNU libraries to develop software in Linux.

Learning Programming

If you have written computer programs in any programming language, you can start writing programs on your Red Hat Linux system very quickly. However, if you have never written a computer program, you do need to understand the basics of programming. You also need some familiarity with computers and the major parts that make up a computer. In this section, I give you an overview of computer programming — just enough to get you going.

A simplified view of a computer

Before you get a feel for computer programming, you need to understand where computer programs fit into the rest of your computer. Figure 1-1 shows a simplified view of a computer that highlights the major parts that are important to you as a programmer.

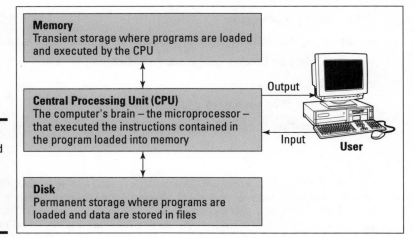

Figure 1-1:
A simplified view of a computer and how it runs programs.

At the heart of a computer is the *central processing unit* (*CPU*) that performs the instructions contained in a computer program. In a Pentium PC, the Pentium microprocessor is the CPU. In a Sun SPARC workstation, the CPU is a SPARC microprocessor. In an HP UNIX workstation, the CPU is a PA-RISC microprocessor.

Random Access Memory (RAM), or just *memory,* serves as the storage for computer programs while they are being executed by the CPU. If a program works on any data, that data is also stored in the memory. The contents of the memory are not permanent; they go away when the computer is shut down or when a program is no longer running.

The *hard disk,* or *disk,* serves as the permanent storage space for computer programs and data. The disk is organized into files, which are in turn organized in a hierarchical fashion into directories and subdirectories (somewhat like organizing paper folders into the drawers in a file cabinet). Each file is essentially a block of storage capable of holding a variety of information. For example, a file may be a human-readable text file or it may be a collection of computer instructions that make sense only to the CPU. When you create computer programs, you work a lot with files.

For a programmer, the other two important items are the *input* and *output* — the way a program gets input from the user and displays output to the user. The user provides input through the keyboard and output appears on the monitor. However, a program may accept input from a file and send output to a file.

Role of the operating system

The operating system is a special collection of computer programs whose primary purpose is to load and run other programs. All operating systems include one or more command processors (called *shells* in Red Hat Linux) that allow users to type commands and perform tasks such as running a program or printing a file. Most operating systems also include a graphical user interface (such as GNOME and KDE in Red Hat Linux) that allows the user to perform most tasks by clicking graphical icons. Red Hat Linux, Windows 95/98, Windows NT, Windows XP, and various versions of UNIX are examples of operating systems.

It's the operating system that gives a computer its personality. For example, you can run Windows 98 or Windows XP on a PC. On that same PC, you can also install and run Red Hat Linux. That means, depending on the operating system installed on it, a PC could be a Windows 98, Windows XP, or a Red Hat Linux system.

Computer programs are built on top of the operating systems. That means a computer program makes use of capabilities that the operating system includes. For example, computer programs read and write files by using built-in capabilities of the operating system.

Although the details vary, most operating systems support a number of similar concepts. As a programmer, you need to be familiar with the following handful of concepts:

✦ A *process* is a computer program that is currently running in the computer. Most operating systems allow multiple processes to run simultaneously.

✦ A *command processor,* or *shell,* is a special program that allows the user to type commands and perform various tasks such as run any program, look at a host of files, or print a file. In Windows 98 or Windows XP, you can type commands in a Command Prompt window.

✦ The term *command-line* refers to the commands that a user types to the command processor. Usually, command lines contain a command and one or more options — the command is the first word in the line and the rest are the options.

✦ *Environment variables* are essentially text strings with a name. For example, the PATH environment variable refers to a string that contains the names of directories. Operating systems use environment variables to provide useful information to processes. To see a list of environment variables in a Windows 98 or Windows XP system, type **SET** in the Command Prompt window. In Red Hat Linux, you can type the printenv command to see the environment variables.

Basics of computer programming

A *computer program* is a sequence of instructions for performing a specific task like adding two numbers or searching for some text in a file. Consequently, computer programming involves creating that list of instructions to complete a specific task. The exact instructions depend on the programming language that you use. For most programming languages, you have to go through the following steps to create a computer program:

1. Use a text editor to type in the sequence of commands from the programming language.

This is the sequence of commands that accomplishes your task. This human-readable version of the program is called the *source file* or *source code*. You can create the source file using any application (such as a word processor) that can save a document in plain text form.

2. Use a compiler to convert that text file — the source code — from human-readable form into machine-readable *object code*.

Typically, this step also combines several object code files into a single machine-readable computer program, something that the computer can actually run.

3. Use a special program called *debugger* to track down any errors and find which lines in the source file might have caused the errors.

These three steps are referred to as the Edit-Compile-Debug cycle of programming because most programmers have to repeat this sequence several times before a program works correctly.

In addition to learning the basic programming steps, you also need to be familiar with the following terms and concepts:

✦ *Variables* are used to store different types of data. You can think of each variable as being a placeholder for data — kind of like a mailbox, with a name and room to store data. The content of the variable is its value.

✦ *Expressions* combine variables by using operators. An expression may add several variables; another may extract a part of a string.

✦ *Statements* perform some action, such as assigning a value to a variable or printing a string.

✦ *Flow-control statements* allow statements to be executed in various orders, depending on the value of some expression. Typically, flow-control statements include `for`, `do-while`, `while`, and `if-then-else` statements.

✦ *Functions* (also called *subroutines* or *routines*) allow you to group several statements and give them a name. This feature allows you to execute the same set of statements by invoking the function that represents those statements. Typically, a programming language provides many predefined functions to perform tasks such as opening a file and reading from it.

Exploring the Software Development Tools in Red Hat Linux

Red Hat Linux includes these traditional UNIX software-development tools:

✦ Text editors such as `vi` and `emacs` for editing the source code

✦ A C compiler for compiling and linking programs written in C — the programming language of choice for writing UNIX applications (although nowadays, many programmers are turning to C++ and Java). Red Hat Linux includes the GNU C and C++ compilers. Originally, the GNU C Compiler was known as GCC. The acronym *GCC* now stands for GNU Compiler Collection (see description in `gcc.gnu.org`).

✦ The GNU `make` utility for automating the software *build process* — the process of combining object modules into an executable or a library

✦ A debugger for debugging programs. Red Hat Linux includes the GNU debugger `gdb`.

✦ A version-control system to keep track of various revisions of a source file. Linux comes with RCS (Revision Control System) and CVS (Concurrent Versions System). Nowadays, most open-source projects use CVS as the version-control system.

These tools are installed automatically if you select the Development Tools when you install Red Hat Linux from this book's companion CD-ROMs. In the next few sections, I briefly describe how to use these software development tools to write applications for Red Hat Linux.

GNU C and C++ compilers

The most important software-development tool in Red Hat Linux is GCC — the GNU C and C++ compiler. In fact, GCC can compile three languages: C, C++, and Objective-C (a language that adds object-oriented extensions to C). You use the same `gcc` command to compile and link both C and C++ source files. The GCC compiler supports ANSI standard C, making it easy to port any ANSI C program to Linux. In addition, if you've ever used a C compiler on other UNIX systems, you're right at home with GCC.

Using GCC

Use the gcc command to invoke GCC. By default, when you use the gcc command on a source file, GCC preprocesses, compiles, and links to create an executable file. However, you can use GCC options to stop this process at an intermediate stage. For example, you might invoke gcc by using the -c option to compile a source file and to generate an object file, but not to perform the link step.

Using GCC to compile and link a few C source files is very simple. Suppose you want to compile and link a simple program made up of two source files. I use the following program source, stored in the file area.c (this is the main program that computes the area of a circle whose radius is specified through the command line):

```c
#include <stdio.h>
#include <stdlib.h>

/* Function prototype */
double area_of_circle(double r);

int main(int argc, char **argv)
{
  if(argc < 2)
  {
    printf("Usage: %s radius\n", argv[0]);
    exit(1);
  }
  else
  {
    double radius = atof(argv[1]);
    double area = area_of_circle(radius);
    printf("Area of circle with radius %f = %f\n",
        radius, area);
  }
  return 0;
}
```

We need another file that actually computes the area of a circle. Here's the listing for the file circle.c, where I define a function that computes the area of a circle:

```c
#include <math.h>

#define SQUARE(x) ((x)*(x))
```

```
double area_of_circle(double r)
{
  return 4.0 * M_PI * SQUARE(r);
}
```

For such a simple program, of course, I could have placed everything in a single file, but I needed this contrived example to show you how to handle multiple files.

To compile these two files and to create an executable file named `area`, you use this command:

```
gcc -o area area.c circle.c
```

This invocation of GCC uses the `-o` option to specify the name of the executable file. (If you do not specify the name of an output file with the `-o` option, GCC saves the executable code in a file named `a.out`.)

If there are too many source files to compile and link, you can compile the files individually, and generate object files (that have the `.o` extension). That way, when you change a source file, you need to compile only that file and to link all the object files. The following commands show how to separate the compile and link steps for the sample program:

```
gcc -c area.c
gcc -c circle.c
gcc -o area area.o circle.o
```

The first two commands run `gcc` with the `-c` option compiling the source files. The third `gcc` command links the object files into an executable named `area`.

In case you are curious, here's how you run the `area` program (to compute the area of a circle with a radius of 1):

```
./area 1
```

The program generates the following output:

```
Area of circle with radius 1.000000 = 12.566371
```

Incidentally, you have to add the `./` prefix to the program's name (`area`) only if the current directory is not in the `PATH` environment variable. There is no harm in adding the prefix, even if your `PATH` contains the current directory.

Compiling C++ programs

GNU CC is a combined C and C++ compiler, so the `gcc` command also can compile C++ source files. GCC uses the file extension to determine whether a file is C or C++. C files have a lowercase .c extension, whereas C++ files end with .C or .cpp.

Although the gcc command can compile a C++ file, that command does not automatically link with various class libraries that C++ programs typically require. That's why it's easier to compile and link a C++ program by using the g++ command, which, in turn, runs gcc with appropriate options.

Suppose you want to compile the following simple C++ program stored in a file named hello.C (it's customary to use an uppercase C extension for C++ source files):

```
#include <iostream>

int main()
{
  using namespace std;
  cout << "Hello from Red Hat Linux!" << endl;
}
```

To compile and link this program into an executable program named hello, use this command:

```
g++ -o hello hello.C
```

This command creates the hello executable, which you can run as follows:

```
./hello
```

The program displays the following output:

```
Hello from Red Hat Linux!
```

A host of GCC options controls various aspects of compiling C and C++ programs.

Exploring GCC options

Here is the basic syntax of the gcc command:

```
gcc options filenames
```

Each option starts with a hyphen (-) and usually has a long name, such as -funsigned-char or -finline-functions. Many commonly used options are short, however, such as -c, to compile only, and -g, to generate debugging information (needed to debug the program by using the GNU debugger, gbd).

You can view a summary of all GCC options by typing the following command in a terminal window:

```
man gcc
```

Then you can browse through the commonly used GCC options. Usually, you do not have to provide GCC options explicitly because the default settings are fine for most applications. Table 1-1 lists some of the GCC options you may use.

Table 1-1	Commonly Used GCC Options
Option	*Meaning*
-ansi	Support ANSI standard C (ISO C89) syntax only. (This option disables some GNU C-specific features, such as the asm and typeof keywords.)
-c	Compile and generate object file only.
-DMACRO	Define the macro with the string "1" as its value.
-DMACRO=DEFN	Define the macro as DEFN where DEFN is some text string.
-E	Run only the C preprocessor.
-fallow-single-precision	Perform all math operations in single precision.
-fpcc-struct-return	Return all struct and union values in memory, rather than in registers. (Returning values this way is less efficient, but is compatible with other compilers.)
-fPIC	Generate position-independent code (PIC) suitable for use in a shared library.
-freg-struct-return	When possible, return struct and union values in registers.
-g	Generate debugging information. (The GNU debugger can use this information.)
-I DIRECTORY	Search the specified directory for files you include by using the #include preprocessor directive.
-L DIRECTORY	Search the specified directory for libraries.
-l LIBRARY	Search the specified library when linking.
-mcpu=cputype	Optimize code for a specific processor (cputype can take many different values — some common ones are i386, i486, i586, and i686).
-o FILE	Generate the specified output file (used to designate the name of an executable file).
-O0	Do not optimize.
-O or -O1	Optimize the generated code.

(continued)

Table 1-1 *(continued)*

Option	Meaning
-O2	Optimize even more.
-O3	Perform optimizations beyond those done for -O2.
-Os	Optimize for size (to reduce the total amount of code).
-pedantic	Generate errors if any non-ANSI standard extensions are used.
-pg	Add extra code to the program so that, when run, it generates information the gprof program can use to display timing details for various parts of the program.
-shared	Generate a shared object file (typically used to create a shared library).
-UMACRO	Undefine the specified macro.
-v	Display the version number of GCC.
-w	Don't generate any warning messages.
-Wl,OPTION	Pass the OPTION string (containing multiple comma-separated options) to the linker. To create a shared library named libXXX.so.1, for example, use the following flag: -Wl, -soname,libXXX.so.1

The GNU make utility

When an application is made up of more than a few source files, compiling and linking the files by manually typing the gcc command can get very tiresome. Also, you do not want to compile every file whenever you change something in a single source file. This is where the GNU make utility comes to your rescue.

The make utility works by reading and interpreting a *makefile* — a text file that describes which files are required to build a program and how to compile and link the files to build the program. Whenever you change one or more files, make determines which files should be recompiled and issues the appropriate commands for compiling those files and rebuilding the program.

Makefile names

By default, GNU make looks for a makefile that has one of the following names, in the order shown:

- ◆ GNUmakefile
- ◆ makefile
- ◆ Makefile

In UNIX systems, using `Makefile` as the name of the makefile is customary because it appears near the beginning of directory listings where the upper-case names appear before the lowercase names.

When you download software from the Internet, you usually find a `Makefile`, together with the source files. To build the software, you have only to type `make` at the shell prompt and `make` takes care of all the steps necessary to build the software.

If your makefile does not have a standard name, such as `Makefile`, you have to use the `-f` option with `make` to specify the makefile's name. If your makefile is called `myprogram.mak`, for example, you have to run `make` using the following command line:

```
make -f myprogram.mak
```

The makefile

For a program that's made up of several source and header files, the makefile specifies the following:

✦ The items that `make` will create — usually the object files and the executable. It's common to use the term *target* to refer to an item that `make` has to create.

✦ The files or other actions required to create the target

✦ Which commands should be executed to create each target

Suppose you have a C++ source file named `form.C` that contains the following preprocessor directive:

```
#include "form.h"  // Include header file
```

The object file `form.o` clearly depends on the source file `form.C` and the header file `form.h`. In addition to these dependencies, you must specify how `make` should convert the `form.C` file to the object file `form.o`. Suppose you want `make` to invoke `g++` (because the source file is in C++) with these options:

✦ `-c` (compile only)

✦ `-g` (generate debugging information)

✦ `-O2` (optimize some)

In the makefile, you can express this with the following rule:

```
# This a comment in the makefile
# The following lines indicate how form.o depends
# form.C and form.h and how to create form.o.

form.o: form.C form.h
        g++ -c -g -O2 form.C
```

In this example, the first noncomment line shows `form.o` as the target and `form.C` and `form.h` as the dependent files.

The line following the dependency indicates how to build the target from its dependents. This line must start with a tab.

The benefit of using `make` is that it prevents unnecessary compilations. After all, you can run `g++` (or `gcc`) from a shell script to compile and link all the files that make up your application, but the shell script compiles everything, even if the compilations are unnecessary. GNU `make`, on the other hand, builds a target, only if one or more of its dependents have changed since the last time the target was built. `make` verifies this change by examining the time of the last modification of the target and the dependents.

`make` treats the target as the name of a goal to be achieved; the target does not have to be a file. You can have a rule such as this:

```
clean:
        rm -f *.o
```

This rule specifies an abstract target named `clean` that does not depend on anything. This dependency statement says that to create the target `clean`, GNU `make` should invoke the command `rm -f *.o`, which deletes all files that have the `.o` extension (these are the object files). Thus, the net effect of creating the target named `clean` is to delete the object files.

Variables (or macros)
In addition to the basic capability of building targets from dependents, GNU `make` includes many nice features that make it easy for you to express the dependencies and rules for building a target from its dependents. If you need to compile a large number of C++ files by using GCC with the same options, for example, typing the options for each file is tedious. You can avoid this task by defining a variable or macro in `make` as follows:

```
# Define macros for name of compiler
CXX= g++

# Define a macro for the GCC flags
```

```
CXXFLAGS= -O2 -g -mcpu=i686

# A rule for building an object file
form.o: form.C form.h
        $(CXX) -c $(CXXFLAGS) form.C
```

In this example, CXX and CXXFLAGS are make variables. GNU make prefers to call them variables, but most UNIX make utilities call them macros.

To use a variable anywhere in the makefile, start with a dollar sign ($) followed by the variable within parentheses. GNU make replaces all occurrences of a variable with its definition; thus, it replaces all occurrences of $(CXXFLAGS) with the string -O2 -g -mcpu=i686.

GNU make has several predefined variables that have special meanings. Table 1-2 lists these variables. In addition to the variables listed in Table 1-2, GNU make considers all environment variables such as PATH and HOME to be predefined variables as well.

Table 1-2	Some Predefined Variables in GNU make
Variable	*Meaning*
$%	Member name for targets that are archives. If the target is libDisp.a(image.o), for example, $% is image.o, and $@ is libDisp.a.
$*	Name of the target file without the extension
$+	Names of all dependent files with duplicate dependencies, listed in their order of occurrence
$<	The name of the first dependent file
$?	Names of all dependent files (with spaces between the names) that are newer than the target
$@	Complete name of the target
$^	Names of all dependent files, with spaces between the names. Duplicates are removed from the dependent filenames.
AR	Name of the archive-maintaining program (Default value: ar)
ARFLAGS	Flags for the archive-maintaining program (Default value: rv)
AS	Name of the assembler program that converts the assembly language to object code (Default value: as)
ASFLAGS	Flags for the assembler
CC	Name of the C compiler. (Default value: cc)
CFLAGS	Flags to be passed to the C compiler
CO	Name of the program that extracts a file from RCS (Default value: co)
COFLAGS	Flags for the RCS co program

(continued)

Table 1-2 *(continued)*

Variable	Meaning
CPP	Name of the C preprocessor (Default value: $(CC) -E)
CPPFLAGS	Flags for the C preprocessor
CXX	Name of the C++ compiler (Default value: g++)
CXXFLAGS	Flags to be passed to the C++ compiler
FC	Name of the FORTRAN compiler (Default value: f77)
FFLAGS	Flags for the FORTRAN compiler
LDFLAGS	Flags for the compiler when it is supposed to invoke the linker ld
RM	Name of the command to delete a file (Default value: rm -f)

A sample makefile

You can write a makefile easily if you use GNU make's predefined variables and its built-in rules. Consider, for example, a makefile that creates the executable xdraw from three C source files (xdraw.c, xviewobj.c, and shapes.c) and two header files (xdraw.h and shapes.h). Assume that each source file includes one of the header files. Given these facts, here is what a sample makefile may look like:

```
#############################################################
# Sample makefile
# Comments start with '#'
#
#############################################################

# Use standard variables to define compile and link flags

CFLAGS= -g -O2
# Define the target "all"
all: xdraw

OBJS=xdraw.o xviewobj.o shapes.o

xdraw: $(OBJS)

# Object files
xdraw.o: Makefile xdraw.c xdraw.h

xviewobj.o: Makefile xviewobj.c xdraw.h

shapes.o: Makefile shapes.c shapes.h
```

This makefile relies on GNU make's implicit rules. The conversion of .c files to .o files uses the built-in rule. Defining the variable CFLAGS passes the flags to the C compiler.

The target named `all` is defined as the first target for a reason — if you run GNU `make` without specifying any targets in the command line (see the `make` syntax described in the following section), it builds the first target it finds in the makefile. By defining the first target `all` as `xdraw`, you can ensure that `make` builds this executable file, even if you do not explicitly specify it as a target. UNIX programmers traditionally use `all` as the name of the first target, but the target's name is immaterial; what matters is that it is the first target in the makefile.

How to run make

Typically, you run `make` by simply typing the following command at the shell prompt:

```
make
```

When ran this way, GNU `make` looks for a file named `GNUmakefile`, `makefile`, or `Makefile` — in that order. If `make` finds one of these makefiles, it builds the first target specified in that `makefile`. However, if `make` does not find an appropriate makefile, it displays the following error message and exits:

```
make: *** No targets specified and no makefile found.  Stop.
```

If your makefile happens to have a different name from the default names, you have to use the `-f` option to specify the makefile. The syntax of the `make` command with this option looks like this:

```
make -f filename
```

where `filename` is the name of the makefile.

Even when you have a makefile with a default name such as `Makefile`, you may want to build a specific target out of several targets defined in the makefile. In that case, you have to run `make` by using this syntax:

```
make target
```

For example, if the makefile contains the target named `clean`, you can build that target with this command:

```
make clean
```

Another special syntax overrides the value of a `make` variable. For example, GNU `make` uses the `CFLAGS` variable to hold the flags used when compiling C files. You can override the value of this variable when you invoke `make`. Here is an example of how you can define `CFLAGS` to be the option `-g -O2`:

```
make CFLAGS="-g -O2"
```

**Book VIII
Chapter 1**

**Red Hat Linux
Programming
Essentials**

In addition to these options, GNU `make` accepts several other command-line options. Table 1-3 lists the GNU `make` options.

Table 1-3	Options for GNU make
Option	*Meaning*
-b	Ignore but accept for compatibility with other versions of `make`.
-C *DIR*	Change to the specified directory before reading the makefile.
-d	Print debugging information.
-e	Allow environment variables to override definitions of similarly named variables in the makefile.
-f *FILE*	Read *FILE* as the makefile.
-h	Display the list of `make` options.
-i	Ignore all errors in commands executed when building a target.
-I *DIR*	Search specified directory for included makefiles (the capability to include a file in a makefile is unique to GNU `make`).
-j *NUM*	Specify the number of commands that `make` can run simultaneously.
-k	Continue to build unrelated targets, even if an error occurs when building one of the targets.
-l *LOAD*	Don't start a new job if load average is at least *LOAD* (a floating-point number).
-m	Ignore but accept for compatibility with other versions of `make`.
-n	Print the commands to be executed, but do not execute them.
-o *FILE*	Do not rebuild the file named *FILE*, even if it is older than its dependents.
-p	Display the `make` database of variables and implicit rules.
-q	Do not run anything, but return zero if all targets are up to date; return 1 if anything needs updating and 2 if an error occurs.
-r	Get rid of all built-in rules.
-R	Get rid of all built-in variables and rules.
-s	Work silently (without displaying the commands as they are executed).
-t	Change the timestamp of the files.
-v	Display the version number of `make` and a copyright notice.
-w	Display the name of the working directory before and after processing the makefile.
-W *FILE*	Assume that the specified file has been modified (used with -n to see what happens if you modify that file).

The GNU debugger

Although `make` automates the process of building a program, that part of programming is the least of your worries when a program does not work correctly or when a program suddenly quits with an error message. You need a debugger to find the cause of program errors. Red Hat Linux includes `gdb` — the versatile GNU debugger with a command-line interface.

Like any debugger, `gdb` lets you perform typical debugging tasks, such as the following:

✦ Set the breakpoint so that the program stops at a specified line.

✦ Watch the values of variables in the program.

✦ Step through the program one line at a time.

✦ Change variables in an attempt to fix errors.

The `gdb` debugger can debug C and C++ programs.

Preparing to debug a program

If you want to debug a program by using `gdb`, you have to ensure that the compiler generates and places debugging information in the executable. The debugging information contains the names of variables in your program and the mapping of addresses in the executable file to lines of code in the source file. `gdb` needs this information to perform its functions, such as stopping after executing a specified line of source code.

To ensure that the executable is properly prepared for debugging, use the -g option with GCC. You can do this by defining the variable `CFLAGS` in the makefile as

```
CFLAGS= -g
```

Running gdb

The most common way to debug a program is to run `gdb` by using the following command:

```
gdb progname
```

`progname` is the name of the program's executable file. After it runs, `gdb` displays the following message and prompts you for a command:

```
GNU gdb Red Hat Linux (5.2.1-4)
Copyright 2002 Free Software Foundation, Inc.
GDB is free software, covered by the GNU General Public License, and you are
welcome to change it and/or distribute copies of it under certain conditions.
Type "show copying" to see the conditions.
There is absolutely no warranty for GDB. Type "show warranty" for details.
This GDB was configured as "i386-redhat-linux".
(gdb)
```

You can type gdb commands at the (gdb) prompt. One useful command is help — it displays a list of commands as the next listing shows:

```
(gdb) help
List of classes of commands:

aliases -- Aliases of other commands
breakpoints -- Making program stop at certain points
data -- Examining data
files -- Specifying and examining files
internals -- Maintenance commands
obscure -- Obscure features
running -- Running the program
stack -- Examining the stack
status -- Status inquiries
support -- Support facilities
tracepoints -- Tracing of program execution without stopping the program
user-defined -- User-defined commands

Type "help" followed by a class name for a list of commands in that class.
Type "help" followed by command name for full documentation.
Command name abbreviations are allowed if unambiguous.
(gdb)
```

To quit gdb, type **q** and press Enter.

gdb has a large number of commands, but you need only a few to find the cause of an error quickly. Table 1-4 lists the commonly used gdb commands.

Table 1-4	Commonly Used gdb Commands
This Command	*Does the Following*
break *NUM*	Sets a breakpoint at the specified line number (the debugger stops at breakpoints).
Bt	Displays a trace of all stack frames. (This command shows you the sequence of function calls so far.)
clear *FILENAME:NUM*	Deletes the breakpoint at a specific line in a source file. For example, clear xdraw.c:8 clears the breakpoint at line 8 of file xdraw.c.
Continue	Continues running the program being debugged. (Use this command after the program has stopped due to a signal or breakpoint.)
display *EXPR*	Displays the value of expression (consisting of variables defined in the program) each time the program stops.

This Command	Does the Following
file *FILE*	Loads a specified executable file for debugging.
help *NAME*	Displays help on the command named *NAME*.
info break	Displays a list of current breakpoints, including information on how many times each breakpoint has been reached.
info files	Displays detailed information about the file being debugged.
info func	Displays all function names.
info local	Displays information about local variables of the current function.
info prog	Displays the execution status of the program being debugged.
info var	Displays all global and static variable names.
Kill	Ends the program you are debugging.
List	Lists a section of the source code.
Make	Runs the make utility to rebuild the executable without leaving gdb.
Next	Advances one line of source code in the current function without stepping into other functions.
print *EXPR*	Shows the value of the expression *EXPR*.
Quit	Quits gdb.
Run	Starts running the currently loaded executable.
set variable *VAR=VALUE*	Sets the value of the variable *VAR* to *VALUE*.
shell *CMD*	Executes a UNIX command *CMD*, without leaving gdb.
Step	Advances one line in the current function, stepping into other functions, if any.
watch *VAR*	Shows the value of the variable named *VAR* whenever the value changes.
Where	Displays the call sequence. Use this command to locate where your program died.
x/*F ADDR*	Examines the contents of the memory location at address *ADDR* in the format specified by the letter *F*, which can be o (octal); x (hex); d (decimal); u (unsigned decimal); t (binary); f (float); a (address); i (instruction); c (char); or s (string). You can append a letter indicating the size of data type to the format letter. Size letters are b (byte); h (halfword, 2 bytes); w (word, 4 bytes); and g (giant, 8 bytes). Typically, *ADDR* is the name of a variable or pointer.

**Book VIII
Chapter 1**

**Red Hat Linux
Programming
Essentials**

Finding bugs by using gdb

To understand how you can find bugs by using gdb, you need to see an example. The procedure is easiest to show with a simple example, so I start with a rather contrived program that contains a typical bug.

This is the contrived program, which I store in the file dbgtst.c:

```
#include <stdio.h>

static char buf[256];
void read_input(char *s);

int main(void)
{
  char *input = NULL; /* Just a pointer, no storage for
    string */

  read_input(input);
/* Process command. */
  printf("You typed: %s\n", input);

/* ... */
  return 0;
}

void read_input(char *s)
{
  printf("Command: ");
  gets(s);
}
```

This program's main function calls the read_input function to get a line of input from the user. The read_input function expects a character array in which it returns what the user types. In this example, however, main calls read_input with an uninitialized pointer — that's the bug in this simple program.

Build the program by using gcc with the -g option:

```
gcc -g -o dbgtst dbgtst.c
```

Ignore the warning message about the gets function being dangerous; we are trying to use the shortcoming of that function to show how gdb can be used to track down errors.

To see the problem with this program, run it and type **test** at the Command prompt:

```
./dbgtst
Command: test
Segmentation fault
```

The program dies after displaying the `Segmentation fault` message. For such as small program as this, you can probably find the cause by examining the source code. In a real-world application, however, you may not immediately know what causes the error. That's when you have to use `gdb` to find the cause of the problem.

To use `gdb` to locate a bug, follow these steps:

1. **Load the program under** `gdb`. **To load a program named** `dbgtst` **in** `gdb`, **type the following:**

```
gdb dbgtst
```

2. **Start executing the program under** `gdb` **by typing the** `run` **command. When the program prompts for input, type some input text.**

The program should fail as it did previously. Here's what happens with the `dbgtst` program:

```
(gdb) run
Starting program: /home/naba/rhls4e/dbgtst
Command: test

Program received signal SIGSEGV, Segmentation fault.
0x4205f1b6 in gets () from /lib/i686/libc.so.6
(gdb)
```

3. **Use the** `where` **command to determine where the program died.**

For the `dbgtst` program, this command yields this output:

```
(gdb) where
#0  0x4205f1b6 in gets () from /lib/i686/libc.so.6
#1  0x080483bd in read_input (s=0x0) at dbgtst.c:22
#2  0x0804837e in main () at dbgtst.c:10
#3  0x420157f4 in __libc_start_main () from
/lib/i686/libc.so.6
(gdb)
```

The output shows the sequence of function calls. Function call #0 — the most recent one — is to a C library function, `gets`. The `gets` call originates in the `read_input` function (at line 22 of the file `dbgtst.c`), which in turn is called from the `main` function at line 10 of the `dbgtst.c` file.

4. **Use the** `list` **command to inspect the lines of suspect source code.**

In `dbgtst`, you may start with line 22 of `dbgtst.c` file, as follows:

Book VIII
Chapter 1

```
(gdb) list dbgtst.c:22
17        }
18
19        void read_input(char *s)
20        {
21          printf("Command: ");
22          gets(s);
23        }
24
(gdb)
```

After looking at this listing, you should be able to tell that the problem might be the way read_input is called. Then you list the lines around line 10 in dbgtst.c (where the read_input call originates):

```
(gdb) list dbgtst.c:10
5
6        int main(void)
7        {
8          char *input = NULL; /* Just a pointer, no
storage for string */
9
10          read_input(input);
11
12        /* Process command. */
13          printf("You typed: %s\n", input);
14
(gdb)
```

At this point, you should be able to narrow the problem to the variable named input. That variable should be an array, not a NULL (which means zero) pointer.

Fixing bugs in gdb

Sometimes you can fix a bug directly in gdb. For the example program in the preceding section, you can try this fix immediately after the program dies after displaying an error message. Because the example is contrived, I have an extra buffer named buf defined in the dbgtst program, as follows:

```
static char buf[256];
```

I can fix the problem of the uninitialized pointer by setting the variable input to buf. The following session with gdb corrects the problem of the uninitialized pointer (this example picks up immediately after the program has run and died, due to the segmentation fault):

```
 (gdb) file dbgtst
A program is being debugged already.  Kill it? (y or n) y

Load new symbol table from "dbgtst"? (y or n) y
```

```
Reading symbols from dbgtst...
done.
(gdb) list
1       #include <stdio.h>
2
3       static char buf[256];
4       void read_input(char *s);
5
6       int main(void)
7       {
8          char *input = NULL; /* Just a pointer, no storage
   for string
*/
9
10          read_input(input);
(gdb) break 9
Breakpoint 1 at 0x8048373: file dbgtst.c, line 9.
(gdb) run
Starting program: /home/naba/rhls4e/dbgtst

Breakpoint 1, main () at dbgtst.c:10
10          read_input(input);
(gdb) set var input=buf
(gdb) cont
Continuing.
Command: test
You typed: test

Program exited normally.
(gdb)q
```

As the previous listing shows, if I stop the program just before `read_input` is called and set the variable named `input` to `buf` (which is a valid array of characters), the rest of the program runs fine.

After trying in `gdb` a fix that works, you can make the necessary changes to the source files and make the fix permanent.

Understanding the Implications of GNU Licenses

You have to pay a price for the bounty of Linux — to protect its developers and users, Linux is distributed under the GNU GPL (General Public License), which stipulates the distribution of the source code.

This does not mean, however, that you cannot write commercial software for Linux that you want to distribute (either for free or for a price) in binary form only. You can follow all the rules and still sell your Linux applications in binary form.

When writing applications for Linux, be aware of two licenses:

✦ The GNU General Public License (GPL), which governs many Linux programs, including the Linux kernel and GCC

✦ The GNU Library General Public License (LGPL), which covers many Linux libraries

The following sections provide an overview of these licenses and some suggestions on how to meet their requirements. Because I am not a lawyer, however, don't take anything in this book as legal advice. The full text for these licenses is in text files on your Red Hat Linux system; show these licenses to your legal counsel for a full interpretation and an assessment of applicability to your business.

The GNU General Public License

The text of the GNU General Public License (GPL) is in a file named COPYING in various directories in your Red Hat Linux system. For example, type the following commands to read the GPL:

```
cd /usr/share/doc/gdb*
more COPYING
```

The GPL has nothing to do with whether you charge for the software or distribute it for free; its thrust is to keep the software free for all users. GPL does this by requiring that the software is distributed in source-code form and by stipulating that any user can copy and distribute the software in source-code form to anyone else. In addition, everyone is reminded that the software comes with absolutely no warranty.

The software that GPL covers is not in the public domain. Software covered by GPL is always copyrighted and the GPL spells out the restrictions on the software's copying and distribution. From a user's point of view, of course, GPL's restrictions are not really restrictions, but benefits because the user is guaranteed access to the source code.

If your application uses parts of any software the GPL covers, your application is considered a derived work. This means that your application is also covered by GPL and you must distribute the source code to your application.

Although the GPL covers the Linux kernel, the GPL does not cover your applications that use the kernel services through system calls. Those applications are considered normal use of the kernel.

If you plan to distribute your application in binary form (as most commercial software is distributed), you must make sure your application does not use any parts of any software the GPL covers. Your application may end up using parts of other software when it calls functions in a library. Most libraries, however, are covered by a different GNU license, which I describe in the next section.

You have to watch out for only a few library and utility programs the GPL covers. The GNU dbm (gdbm) database library is one of the prominent libraries GPL covers. The GNU bison parser-generator tool is another utility the GPL covers. If you allow bison to generate code, the GPL covers that code.

Other alternatives for the GNU dbm and GNU bison are not covered by GPL. For a database library, you can use the Berkeley database library db in place of gdbm. For a parser-generator, you may use yacc instead of bison.

The GNU Library General Public License

The text of the GNU Library General Public License (LGPL) is in a file named COPYING.LIB. If you have the kernel source installed, a copy of COPYING.LIB file is in one of the source directories. To locate a copy of the COPYING.LIB file on your Red Hat Linux system, type the following command in a terminal window:

```
find /usr/share/doc -name "COPYING*" -print
```

This command lists all occurrences of COPYING and COPYING.LIB in your system. The COPYING file contains the GPL, whereas COPYING.LIB has the LGPL.

The LGPL is intended to allow use of libraries in your applications, even if you do not distribute source code for your application. The LGPL stipulates, however, that users must have access to the source code of the library you use and that users can make use of modified versions of those libraries.

The LGPL covers most Linux libraries, including the C library (libc.a). Thus, when you build your application on Red Hat Linux by using the GCC compiler, your application links with code from one or more libraries the LGPL covers. If you want to distribute your application in binary form only, you need to pay attention to LGPL.

One way to meet the intent of the LGPL is to provide the object code for your application and a makefile that relinks your object files with any updated Linux libraries the LGPL covers.

A better way to satisfy the LGPL is to use dynamic linking, in which your application and the library are separate entities, even though your application calls functions in the library when it runs. With dynamic linking, users immediately get the benefit of any updates to the libraries without ever having to relink the application.

Chapter 2: Programming in C

In This Chapter

✔ **Learning the basics of C programming**

✔ **Learning the features of C programming language**

✔ **Taking stock of the standard C library**

✔ **Using shared libraries in Red Hat Linux applications**

The composition of the C programming language — a sparse core with a large support library — makes it an ideal language for developing software. The core offers a good selection of data types and control structures while all additional tasks, including input and output (I/O), math computations, and access to peripheral devices are relegated to a library of functions. Basically, C allows you get to anything you want in a system. That means you can write anything from device drivers to graphical applications in C. In this chapter, I introduce you to C programming. I also briefly explain the importance of shared libraries and how to create one in Red Hat Linux using the C programming language.

The Structure of a C Program

A typical C program is organized into one or more source files, or modules (Figure 2-1). Each file has a similar structure with comments, preprocessor directives, declarations of variables and functions, and their definitions. You'd usually place each group of related variables and functions in a single source file.

Some files are simply a set of declarations that are used in other files through the #include directive of the C preprocessor. These files are usually referred to as *header files* and have names ending with the .h extension. In Figure 2-1, the file shapes.h is a header file that declares common data structures and functions for the program. Another file, shapes.c, defines the functions. A third file, shapetst.c, implements the main function — this is the function in which the execution of a C program begins. These files with names ending in .c are the source files where you define the functions needed by your program. Although Figure 2-1 shows only one function in each source file, in typical programs there are many functions in a source file.

```
shapes.h
/* File: shapes.h
 * Header file for data structures
 */
#ifndef _SHAPES_H
#define _SHAPES_H

enum shape_type {T_CIRCLE, T_RECTANGLE};
typedef struct RECTANGLE
{
  double x1, y1, x2, y2;
} RECTANGLE;
typedef struct CIRCLE
{
  double xc, yc, radius;
} CIRCLE;
typedef struct SHAPE
{
  enum shape_type type;
  union
  {
    RECTANGLE r;
    CIRCLE C;
  } u;
} SHAPE;

/* Function protypes */
double compute_area (SHAPE *p_s);
#endif
```

```
shapes.c
/* File: shapes.c
 * Function that computes area of shapes
 */
#include <math.h>
#include "shapes.h"

double compute_area (SHAPE *p_s)
{
  switch(p_s->type)
  {
    case T_CIRCLE;
    {
        CIRCLE *p_c = &(p_c->u.c)
        return M_PI* p_c->radius * p_c -> radius;
    }
    case T_RECTANGLE;
    {
        RECTANGLE *p_r = r(p_s->u.r);
        return fabs   (p_r->x2 - p_r->x1)*
                      (p_r->y2 - p_r->y1)*
    }
  }
}
```

```
shapetest.c
/* File: shapes.c
 * Main program to test shapes.c
 */
#include <stdio.h>
#include "shapes.h"

int main(void)
{
  SHAPE s;
  CIRCLE c;
  s_type = T_CIRCLE;
  p_c->radius = 50.0;
  p_c->xc = p_c->yc = 100.0;
  printf("Area of circle = #f\n",
compute_area(rs));
  return 0;
}
```

Figure 2-1:
Typically,
several
source files
make up a
C program.

You must compile and link the source files to create an executable program.
The exact steps for building programs from C source files depend on the
compiler and the operating system. For example, in Red Hat Linux, you can
compile and link the files shown in Figure 2-1 with the following command:

```
gcc -o shapetest shapetest.c shapes.c
```

This command creates an executable file named `shapetest`, You can then
run that file with the command

```
./shapetest
```

Here is the output the program displays:

```
Area of circle = 7853.981634
```

Declaration vs. definition

A declaration determines how the program interprets a symbol. A definition, on the other hand, actually creates a variable or a function. Definitions cause the compiler to set aside storage for data or code, but declarations do not. For example,

```
int x, y, z;
```

is a definition of three integer variables, but

```
extern int x, y, z;
```

is a declaration indicating that the three integer variables are defined in another source file.

Within each source file, the components of the program are laid out in a standard manner. As the files illustrated in Figure 2-1 show, the typical components of a C source file are the following:

1. The file starts with some comments that describe the purpose of the module and that provide some other pertinent information, such as the name of the author and revision dates. In C, comments start with /* and end with */.

2. Commands for the preprocessor, known as *preprocessor directives,* follow the comments. The first few directives typically are for including header files and defining constants.

3. Declarations of variables and functions that are visible throughout the file come next. In other words, the names of these variables and functions may be used in any of the functions in this file. Here, you also define variables needed within the file.

4. The rest of the file includes definitions of functions. Inside a function's body, you can define variables that are local to the function and that exist only while the function's code is being executed.

Preprocessor Directives

Preprocessing refers to the first step in translating or compiling a C file into machine instructions. The preprocessor processes the source file and acts on the commands, called *preprocessor directives,* embedded in the program. These directives begin with the hash mark (#) followed by a keyword. Usually, the compiler automatically invokes the preprocessor before beginning compilation, but most compilers give you the option of invoking the preprocessor alone. You can utilize three major capabilities of the preprocessor to make your programs modular, more readable, and easier to customize:

Book VIII Chapter 2

Programming in C

1. You can use the #include directive to insert the contents of a file into your program. With this, you can place common declarations in one location and use them in all source files through file inclusion. The result is a reduced risk of mismatches between declarations of variables and functions in separate program modules.

2. Through the #define directive, you can define macros that enable you to replace one string with another. You can use the #define directive to give meaningful names to numeric constants, thus improving the readability of your source files.

3. With directives such as #if, #ifdef, #else, and #endif, you can compile only selected portions of your program. You can use this feature to write source files with code for two or more systems, but compile only those parts that apply to the computer system on which you compile the program. With this strategy you can maintain multiple versions of a program using a single set of source files.

Including files

You can write modular programs by exploiting the #include directive. This is possible because the C preprocessor enables you to keep commonly used declarations in a single file that you can insert in other source files as needed. ANSI C supports three forms of the #include directive. As a C programmer, you should be familiar with the first two forms:

```
#include <stdio.h>
#include "shapes.h"
```

You use the first form of #include to read the contents of a file — in this case, the standard C header file stdio.h from the default location where all the header files reside. Put the filename within double quotes when the file (for example, shapes.h) is in the current directory. The exact conventions for locating the included files depend on the compiler.

Defining macros

A *macro* is essentially a short name for a block of C code. The code can be as simple as a numerical constant or as complicated as many lines of detailed C code. The idea is that after you define a macro, you can use that macro wherever you want to use that code in your program. When the source file is preprocessed, every occurrence of a macro's name is replaced with its definition.

A common use of macros is to define a symbolic name for a numerical constant and then use the symbol instead of the numbers in your program. This improves the readability of the source code because with a descriptive name you are not left guessing why a particular number is being used in the program. You can define such macros in a straightforward manner using the #define directive. Here are some examples:

```
#define PI          3.14159
#define GRAV_ACC    9.80665
#define BUFSIZE     512
```

After these symbols are defined, you can use PI, GRAV_ACC, and BUFSIZE instead of the numerical constants throughout the source file.

Macros, however, can do much more than simply replace a symbol for a constant or some block of code. A macro can accept a parameter and replace each occurrence of that parameter with the provided value when the macro is used in a program. Thus, the code that results from the expansion of a macro can change depending on the parameter you use when running the macro. For example, here is a macro that accepts a parameter and expands to an expression designed to calculate the square of the parameter:

```
#define square(x) ((x)*(x))
```

If you use square(z) in your program, it becomes ((z)*(z)) after the source file is preprocessed. This macro is essentially equivalent to a function that computes the square of its arguments, except that you don't call a function — the expression generated by the macro is placed directly in the source file.

Conditional directives

You can use the conditional directives, such as #if, #ifdef, #ifndef, #else, #elif, and #endif, to control which parts of a source file are compiled and under what conditions. With this feature, you maintain a single set of source files that can be selectively compiled with different compilers and in different environments. Another common use is to insert printf statements for debugging that are compiled only if a symbol named DEBUG is defined. Conditional directives start with either #if, #ifdef, or #ifndef and may be followed by any number of #elif directives (or none at all). Next comes an optional #else, followed by an #endif directive that marks the end of that conditional block. Here are some common ways of using conditional directives.

To include a header file only once, you can use the following:

```
#ifndef _ _PROJECT_H
#define _ _PROJECT_H
/*  Declarations to be included once */
/* ... */

#endif
```

The following prints a diagnostic message during debugging (when the symbol DEBUG is defined):

```
#ifdef DEBUG
    printf("In read_file: bytes_read = %d\n", bytes_read);
#endif
```

The following example shows how you can include a different header file depending on the type of system for which the program is being compiled. To selectively include a header file, you can use the following:

```
#if CPU_TYPE == I386
    #include <i386\sysdef.h>
#elif CPU_TYPE == M68K
    #include <m68k\sysdef.h>
#else
    #error Unknown CPU type.
#endif
```

The #error directive is used to display error messages during preprocessing.

Other directives

Several other preprocessor directives perform miscellaneous tasks. For example, you can use the #undef directive to remove the current definition of a symbol. The #pragma directive is another special purpose directive that you can use to convey information to the C compiler. You can use pragma to access special features of a compiler, and as such, they vary from one compiler to another.

C compilers provide several predefined macros (see Table 2-1). Of these, the macros _ _FILE_ _ and _ _LINE_ _ respectively refer to the current source filename and the current line number being processed. You can use the #line directive to change these. For example, to set _ _FILE_ _ to "file_io.c" and _ _LINE_ _ to 100, you say:

```
#line 100 "file_io.c"
```

Table 2-1	Predefined Macros in C
Macro	*Definition*
_ _DATE_ _	This is a string containing the date when you invoke the C compiler. It is of the form MMM DD YYYY (for example, Oct 26 2002).
_ _FILE_ _	This expands to a string containing the name of the source file.
_ _LINE_ _	This is a decimal integer with a value that is the line number within the current source file.
_ _STDC_ _	This macro expands to the decimal constant 1 to indicate that the C compiler conforms to the ANSI standard.
_ _TIME_ _	This string displays the time when you started compiling the source file. It is of the form HH:MM:SS (for example, 21:59:45).

Declaration and Definition of Variables

In C, you must either define or declare all variables and functions before you use them. The definition of a variable specifies three things:

✦ Its *visibility,* which indicates exactly where the variable can be used (is it defined for all files in a program, the current file, or only in a function)

✦ Its *lifetime,* which determines whether the variable exists temporarily (for example, a local variable in a function) or permanently (as long as the program is running)

✦ Its *type* and, in some cases, its *initial value.* For example, an integer variable x initialized to 1 is defined as:

```
int   x = 1;
```

If a variable that you are using is defined in another source file, you declare the variable with an extern keyword like this:

```
extern int message_count;
```

You must define this variable without the `extern` qualifier in at least one source file. When the program is built, the linker resolves all references to the `message_count` variable and ensures that they all use the same variable.

Basic data types

C has four basic data types: `char` and `int` are for storing characters and integers, and `float` and `double` are for floating-point numbers. You can define variables for these basic data types in a straightforward manner:

```
char    c;
int     i, j, bufsize;
float   volts;
double  mean, variance;
```

You can expand the basic data types into a much larger set by using the long, short, and unsigned qualifiers as prefixes. The long and short qualifiers are size modifiers. For example, a long int is at least 4 bytes long, whereas a short int has a minimum size of only 2 bytes. The size of an int is system dependent, but it will definitely be at least as large as a short.

The unsigned qualifier is reserved for int and char types only. Normally, each of these types hold negative as well as positive values. This is the default signed form of these data types. You can use the unsigned qualifier when you want the variable to hold positive values only. Here are some examples of using the short, long, and unsigned qualifiers:

**Book VIII
Chapter 2**

Programming in C

```
unsigned char mode_select, printer_status;
short     record_number; /* Same as "short int"    */
long      offset;    /* Same as "long int"       */
unsigned   i, j, msg_id; /* Same as "unsigned int"   */
unsigned short width, height; /* Same as "unsigned short int" */
unsigned long file_pos;    /* Same as "unsigned long int" */
long double  result;
```

When the short, long, and unsigned qualifiers are used with int types, you can drop the int from the declaration. You can also extend the double data type with a long prefix.

The exact sizes of the various data types and the ranges of values are defined in the header files limits .h and float .h. You can examine these files in the /usr/include directory of your Red Hat Linux system to determine the sizes of the basic data types that the GCC compiler supports.

Enumerations

You can use the enum data type to define your own enumerated list — a fixed set of named integer constants. For example, you can declare a Boolean data type named BOOLEAN using enum as follows:

```
/* Declare an enumerated type named BOOLEAN */
    enum BOOLEAN {false = 0, true = 1, stop = 0, go = 1,
                  off = 0, on = 1};

/* Define a BOOLEAN called "status" and initialize it */
    enum BOOLEAN status = stop;
```

This example first declares BOOLEAN to be an enumerated type. The list within the braces shows the enumeration constants that are valid values of an enum BOOLEAN variable. You can initialize each constant to a value of your choice, and several constants can use the same value. In this example, the constants false, stop, and off are set to 0, while true, go, and on are initialized to 1. The example then defines an enumerated BOOLEAN variable named status, which is initially set to the constant stop.

Structures, Unions, and Bit Fields

Use struct to group related data items together, and refer to that group by a name. For example, the declaration of a structure to hold variables of a queue may look like this:

```
/* Declare a structure */
struct QUEUE
```

```
{
    int   count;      /* Number of items in queue    */
    int   front;      /* Index of first item in queue */
    int   rear;       /* Index of last item in queue  */
    int   elemsize;   /* Size of each element of data */
    int   maxsize;    /* Maximum capacity of queue    */
    char  *data;      /* Pointer to queued data       */
};

/* Define two queues */
struct QUEUE rcv_q, xmit_q;
```

The elements inside the `QUEUE` structure are called its *members*. You can access these members by using the member selection operator (`.`). For instance, `rcv_q.count` refers to the `count` member of the `rcv_q` structure.

A `union` is like a `struct`, but instead of grouping related data items together as `struct` does, a `union` allocates storage for several data items starting at the same location. Thus, all members of a `union` share the same storage location. You can use unions to view the same data item in different ways. Suppose you are using a compiler that supports 4-byte `long`s, and you want to access the 4 individual bytes of a long integer. Here is a `union` that lets you accomplish this:

```
union
{
    long  file_type;
    char  bytes[4];
} header_id;
```

With this definition, `header_id.file_type` refers to the long integer, while `header_id.bytes[0]` is the first byte of that long integer.

Arrays

An *array* is a collection of one or more identical data items. You can declare arrays of any type of data, including structures and types defined by `type-def`. For example, to define an array of 80 characters, you would write the following:

```
char    string[80];
```

The characters in the string array occupy successive storage locations, beginning with location 0. Thus in this example, `string[0]` refers to the first character in this array, while `string[79]` refers to the last one. You can define arrays of other data types and structures similarly:

Book VIII
Chapter 2

Programming in C

```
struct Customer          /* Declare a structure    */
{
  int id;
  char first_name[40];
  char last_name[40];
};

struct Customer customers[100]; /* Define array of structures */
int        index[64];   /* An array of 64 integers  */
```

You can also define multidimensional arrays. For example, to represent an 80-column by 25-line text display screen, you can use a two-dimensional array as follows:

```
unsigned char text_screen[25][80];
```

Each item of `text_screen` is an array of 80 unsigned chars, and `text_screen` contains 25 such arrays. In other words, the two-dimensional array is stored by laying out one row after another in memory. You can use expressions such as `text_screen[0][0]` to refer to the first character in the first row and `text_screen[24][79]` to refer to the last character of the last row of the display screen. Higher-dimensional arrays are defined similarly:

```
float coords[3][2][5];
```

This example defines `coords` as a three-dimensional array of three data items: each item is an array of two arrays, each of which, in turn, is an array of five float variables. Thus, you interpret a multidimensional array as an "array of arrays."

Pointers

A *pointer* is a variable that can hold the address of any type of data except a bit field. For example, if p_i is a pointer to an integer variable, you can define and use it as follows:

```
/* Define an int pointer and an integer */
   int *p_i, count;

/* Set pointer to the address of the integer "count" */
   p_i = &count;
```

In this case, the compiler will allocate storage for an `int` variable count and a pointer to an integer p_i. The number of bytes necessary to represent a pointer depends on the underlying system's addressing scheme. Don't use a pointer until it contains the address of a valid object. The example shows p_i being initialized to the address of the integer variable count using the & operator, which provides the address of a variable. After p_i is initialized, you can refer to the value of `count` with the expression *p_i, which is read as "the contents of the object with its address in p_i."

Pointers are useful in many situations; an important one is the dynamic allocation of memory. The standard C libraries include functions such as malloc and calloc, which you can call to allocate storage for arrays of objects. After allocating memory, these functions return the starting address of the block of memory. Because this address is the only way to reach that memory, you must store it in a variable capable of holding an address — a pointer.

Suppose you allocated memory for an array of 50 integers and saved the returned address in p_i. Now you can treat this block of memory as an array of 50 integers with the name p_i. Thus, you can refer to the last element in the array as p_i[49], which is equivalent to *(p_i+49). Similarly, C treats the name of an array as a pointer to the first element of the array. The difference between the name of an array and a pointer variable is that the name of the array is a constant without any explicit storage necessary to hold the address of the array's first element, whereas the pointer is an actual storage location capable of holding the address of any data.

In addition to storing the address of dynamically allocated memory, pointers are also commonly used as arguments to functions. When a C function is called, all of its arguments are passed by value — that is, the function gets a copy of each argument, not the original variables appearing in the argument list of the function call. Thus, a C function cannot alter the value of its arguments. Pointers provide a way out. To change the value of a variable in a function, you can pass it a pointer to the variable and the function can alter the value through the pointer.

Type definitions

Through the typedef keyword, C provides you with a convenient way of assigning a new name to an existing data type. You can use the typedef facility to give meaningful names to data types used in a particular application. For example, a graphics application might declare a data type named Point as follows:

```
/* Declare a Point data type */
    typedef struct Point
    {
        short x;
        short y;
    } Point;

/* Declare PointPtr to be pointer to Point types */
    typedef Point *P_PointPtr;

/* Define some instances of these types
 * and initialize them */
    Point      a = {0, 0};
    PointPtr  p_a = &a;
```

As shown by the `Point` and `PointPtr` types, you can use `typedef` to declare complex data types conveniently.

Type qualifiers: const and volatile

You can use `const` and `volatile` as qualifiers in a declaration:

✦ The `const` qualifier in a declaration tells the compiler that the particular data object must not be modified by the program. This means that the compiler must not generate code that might alter the contents of the location where that data item is stored.

✦ The `volatile` qualifier specifies that the value of a variable may be changed by factors beyond the program's control.

You can use both `const` and `volatile` keywords on a single data item to mean that, while the item must not be modified by your program, it may be altered by some other process. The `const` and `volatile` keywords always qualify the item that immediately follows (to the right). The information provided by the `const` and the `volatile` qualifiers is supposed to help the compiler optimize the code it generates. For example, suppose the variable `block_size` is declared and initialized as follows:

```
const int block_size = 512;
```

In this case, the compiler does not need to generate code to load the value of `block_size` from memory. Instead, it can use the value 512 wherever your program uses `block_size`. Now suppose you added `volatile` to the declaration and changed the declaration to:

```
volatile const int block_size = 512;
```

This says that the contents of `block_size` may be changed by some external process. Therefore, the compiler cannot optimize away any reference to `block_size`. You may need to use such declarations when referring to an I/O port or video memory because these locations can be changed by factors beyond your program's control.

Expressions

An *expression* is a combination of variables, function calls, and operators that results in a single value. For example, here is an expression with a value that is the number of bytes needed to store the null-terminated string `str` (that simply means an array of `char` data types with a zero byte at the end):

```
(strlen(str) * sizeof(char) + 1)
```

This expression involves a function call, `strlen(str)`, and the multiplication (*), addition (+), and `sizeof` operators.

C has a large number of operators that are an important part of expressions. Table 2-2 provides a summary of the operators in C.

Table 2-2	Summary of C Operators	
Name of Operator	*Syntax*	*Result*
Arithmetic Operators		
Addition	x+y	Adds x and y.
Subtraction	x-y	Subtracts y from x.
Multiplication	x*y	Multiplies x and y.
Division	x/y	Divides x by y.
Remainder	x%y	Computes the remainder that results from dividing x by y.
Preincrement	++x	Increments x before use.
Postincrement	x++	Increments x after use.
Predecrement	--x	Decrements x before use.
Postdecrement	x--	Decrements x after use.
Minus	-x	Negates the value of x.
Plus	+x	Maintains the value of x unchanged.
Relational and Logical Operators		
Greater than	x>y	Value is 1 if x exceeds y; otherwise, value is 0.
Greater than or equal to	x>=y	Value is 1 if x exceeds or equals y; otherwise, value is 0.
Less than	x<y	Value is 1 if y exceeds x; otherwise, value is 0.
Less than or equal to	x<=y	Value is 1 if y exceeds or equals x; otherwise, value is 0.
Equal to	x==y	Value is 1 if x equals y; otherwise, value is 0.
Not equal to	x!=y	Value is 1 if x and y are unequal; otherwise, value is 0.
Logical NOT	!x	Value is 1 if x is 0; otherwise, value is 0.
Logical AND	x&&y	Value is 0 if either x or y is 0.
Logical OR	x||y	Value is 0 if both x and y are 0.

(continued)

Table 2-2 *(continued)*

Name of Operator	Syntax	Result
Assignment Operators		
Assignment	`x=y`	Places the value of y into x.
Compound Assignment	`x O=y`	Equivalent to x = x O y, where O is one of the following operators: +, -, *, /, %, <<, >, &, ^, or |
Data Access and Size Operators		
Subscript	`x[y]`	Selects the yth element of array x.
Member selection	`x.y`	Selects member y of structure (or union) x.
Member selection	`x->y`	Selects the member named y from a structure or union with x as its address.
Indirection	`*x`	Contents of the location with x as its address
Address of	`&x`	Address of the data object named x
Size of	`sizeof(x)`	Size (in bytes) of the data object named x
Bitwise Operators		
Bitwise NOT	`~x`	Changes all 1s to 0s and 0s to 1s.
Bitwise AND	`x&y`	Result is the bitwise AND of x and y.
Bitwise OR	`x|y`	Result is the bitwise OR of x and y.
Bitwise exclusive OR	`x^y`	Result contains 1s where corresponding bits of x and y differ.
Left shift	`x<<y`	Shifts the bits of x to the left by y bit positions. Fills 0s in the vacated bit positions.
Right shift	`x>y`	Shifts the bits of x to the right by y bit positions. Fills 0s in the vacated bit positions.
Miscellaneous Operators		
Function call	`x(y)`	Result is the value returned (if any) by function x, which is called with argument y.
Type cast	`(type)x`	Converts the value of x to the type named in parentheses.
Conditional	`z?x:y`	If z is not 0, evaluates x; otherwise, evaluates y.
Comma	`x,y`	Evaluates x first and then y.

Operator precedence

Typical C expressions consist of several operands and operators. When writing complicated expressions, you must be aware of the order in which the compiler evaluates the operators. For example, a program uses an array of pointers to integers defined as follows:

```
typedef int *IntPtr;/* Use typedef to simplify declarations*/
IntPtr  iptr[10];   /* An array of 10 pointers to int      */
```

Now, suppose that you encounter the expression `*iptr[4]`. Does this refer to the value of the `int` with the address in `iptr[4]`, or is this the fifth element from the location with the address in `iptr`? In other words, is the compiler going to evaluate the subscript operator (`[]`) before the indirection operator (`*`), or is it the other way around? To answer questions such as these, you need to know the precedence or order in which the program applies the operators.

Table 2-3 summarizes C's precedence rules. The table shows the operators in order of decreasing precedence. The operators with highest precedence — those that are applied first — are shown first. The table also shows the associativity of the operators — this is the order in which operators at the same level are evaluated.

Table 2-3	**Precedence and Associativity of C Operators**		
Operator Group	*Operator Name*	*Notation*	*Associativity*
Postfix	Subscript	x[y]	Left to right
	Function call	x(y)	
	Member selection	x.y	
	Member selection	x->y	
Unary	Postincrement	x++	Right to left
	Postdecrement	x--	
	Preincrement	++x	
	Predecrement	--x	
	Address of	&x	
	Indirection	*x	
	Plus	+x	
	Minus	-x	
	Bitwise NOT	~x	
	Logical NOT	!x	
	Sizeof	sizeof x	

(continued)

Table 2-3 *(continued)*

Operator Group	Operator Name	Notation	Associativity
	Type cast	`(type)x`	
Multiplicative	Multiply	`x*y`	Left to right
	Divide	`x/y`	
	Remainder	`x%y`	
Additive	Add	`x+y`	Left to right
	Subtract	`x-y`	
Shift	Left shift	`x<<y`	Left to right
	Right shift	`x>y`	
Relational	Greater than	`x>y`	Left to right
	Greater than or equal to	`x>=y`	
	Less than	`x<y`	
	Less than or equal to	`x<=y`	
Equality	Equal to	`x==y`	Left to right
	Not equal to	`x!=y`	
Bitwise	Bitwise AND	`x&y`	Left to right
	Bitwise exclusive OR	`x^y`	
	Bitwise OR	`x|y`	
Logical	Logical AND	`x&&y`	Left to right
	Logical OR	`x||y`	
Conditional	Conditional	`z?x:y`	Right to left
Assignment	Assignment	`x=y`	Right to left
	Multiply assign	`x *= y`	
	Divide assign	`x /= y`	
	Remainder assign	`x %= y`	
	Add assign	`x += y`	
	Subtract assign	`x -= y`	
	Left shift assign	`x <<= y`	
	Right shift assign	`x >= y`	
	Bitwise AND assign	`x &= y`	
	Bitwise XOR assign	`x ^= y`	
	Bitwise OR assign	`x |= y`	
Comma	Comma	`x,y`	Left to right

Getting back to the question of interpreting `*iptr[4]`, a quick look at Table 2-3 tells you that the `[]` operator has precedence over the `*` operator. Thus, when the compiler processes the expression `*iptr[4]`, it evaluates `iptr[4]` first, and then it applies the indirection operator, resulting in the value of the `int` with the address in `iptr[4]`.

Statements

You use statements to represent the actions C functions will perform and to control the flow of execution in the C program. A *statement* consists of keywords, expressions, and other statements. Each statement ends with a semicolon (`;`).

A special type of statement — the *compound statement* — is a group of statements enclosed in a pair of braces (`{...}`). The body of a function is a compound statement. Also known as *blocks,* such compound statements can contain local variables.

In the following alphabetically arranged sections I briefly describe the types of statements available in C.

The break statement

You use the `break` statement to jump to the statement following the innermost `do`, `for`, `switch`, or `while` statement. It is also used to exit from a switch statement. Here is an example that uses `break` to exit a `for` loop:

```
for(i = 0; i < ncommands; i++)
{
    if(strcmp(input, commands[i]) == 0) break;
}
```

The case statement

The `case` statement marks labels in a `switch` statement. Here is an example (here `interrupt_id` is an integer variable):

```
switch (interrupt_id)
{
    case XMIT_RDY:
        transmit();
        break;

    case RCV_RDY:
        receive();
        break;
}
```

A compound statement or block

A *compound statement* or block is a group of declarations followed by statements, all enclosed in a pair of braces ({ . . . }). The body of a function and the block of code following an if statement are some examples of compound statements. In the following example, the declarations and statements within the braces constitute a compound statement:

```
if(theEvent.xexpose.count == 0)
{
    int i;
/* Clear the window and draw the figures
 * in the "figures" array
 */
    XClearWindow(theDisplay, dWin);
    if(numfigures > 0)
        for(i=0; i<numfigures; i++)
            draw_figure(theDisplay, dWin, theGC, i);
}
```

The continue statement

The continue statement begins the next iteration of the innermost do, for, or while statement in which it appears. You can use continue when you want to skip the execution of the loop. For example, to add the numbers from 1 to 10, excluding 5, you can use a for loop that skips the body when the loop index (i) is 5:

```
for(i=0, sum=0; i <= 10, i++)
{
    if(i == 5) continue;    /* Exclude 5 */
    sum += i;
}
```

The default label

You use default as the label in a switch statement to mark code that will execute when none of the case labels match the switch expression.

The do statement

The do statement, together with while, forms iterative loops of the following kind:

```
do
  statement
  while(expression);
```

where the statement (usually a compound statement) executes until the expression in the `while` statement evaluates to 0. The expression is evaluated after each execution of the statement. Thus, a `do-while` block always executes at least once. For example, to add the numbers from 1 to 10, you can use the following `do` statement:

```
sum = 0;
do
{
    sum += i;
    i++;
}
while(i <= 10);
```

Expression statements

Expression statements are evaluated for their side effects. Some typical uses of expression statements include calling a function, incrementing a variable, and assigning a value to a variable. Here are some examples:

```
printf("Hello, World!\n");
i++;
num_bytes = length * sizeof(char);
```

The for statement

Use the `for` statement to execute a statement any number of times based on the value of an expression. The syntax is as follows:

```
for (expr_1; expr_2; expr_3) statement
```

where the *expr_1* is evaluated once at the beginning of the loop, and the statement is executed until the expression *expr_2* evaluates to 0. The third expression, *expr_3*, is evaluated after each execution of the statement. All three expressions are optional and the value of *expr_2* is assumed to be 1 if it is omitted. Here is an example that uses a for loop to add the numbers from 1 to 10:

```
for(i=0, sum=0; i <= 10; sum += i, i++);
```

In this example, the actual work of adding the numbers is done in the third expression, and the statement controlled by the for loop is a `null` statement (a lone ;).

The goto statement

The `goto` statement transfers control to a statement label. Here is an example that prompts the user for a value and repeats the request if the value is not acceptable:

```
ReEnter:
    printf("Enter offset: ");
    scanf(" %d", &offset);
    if(offset < 0 || offset > MAX_OFFSET)
    {
        printf("Bad offset: %d Please reenter:\n",
            offset);
        goto ReEnter;
    }
```

The *if* statement

You can use the if statement to test an expression and execute a statement only when the expression is not zero. An if statement takes the following form:

```
if ( expression )  statement
```

The statement following the if is executed only if the expression in parentheses evaluates to a non-zero value. That statement is usually a compound statement. Here is an example:

```
if(mem_left < threshold)
{
    Message("Low on memory! Close some windows.\n");
}
```

The *if-else* statement

The if-else statement is a form of the if statement together with an else clause. The statement has the syntax

```
if ( expression )
    statement_1
else
    statement_2
```

where *statement_1* is executed if the *expression* within the parentheses is not zero. Otherwise, *statement_2* is executed. Here is an example that uses if and else to pick the smaller of two variables.

```
if ( a <= b)
    smaller = a;
else
    smaller = b;
```

The null statement

The `null` statement, represented by a solitary semicolon, does nothing. You use `null` statements in loops when all processing is done in the loop expressions rather than in the body of the loop. For example, to locate the zero byte marking the end of a string, you may use the following:

```
char str[80] = "Test";
int i;

for (i=0; str[i] != '\0'; i++)
                        ;  /* Null statement */
```

The return statement

The `return` statement stops executing the current function and returns control to the calling function. The syntax is

```
return expression;
```

where the value of the *expression* is returned as the value of the function. For a function that does not return a value, use the `return` statement without the expression as follows:

```
return;
```

The switch statement

The `switch` statement performs a multiple branch, depending on the value of an expression. It has the following syntax:

```
switch (expression)
{
     case value1:
         statement_1
         break;
     case value2:
         statement_2
         break;
             .
             .
             .
     default:
         statement_default
}
```

If the *expression* being tested by switch evaluates to *value1*, *statement_1* is executed. If the expression is equal to *value2*, *statement_2* is executed.

The value is compared with each case label and the statement following the matching label is executed. If the value does not match any of the case labels, the block *statement_default* following the default label is executed. Each statement ends with a `break` statement that separates the code of one case label from another. Here is a `switch` statement that calls different routines depending on the value of an integer variable named `command`:

```
switch (command)
{
    case 'q':
        quit_app(0);

        case 'c':
        connect();
        break;

    case 's':
        set_params();
        break;

    case '?':
    case 'H':
        print_help();
        break;

    default:
        printf("Unknown command!\n");
}
```

The while statement

The `while` statement is used in the form

```
while (expression) statement
```

where the *statement* is executed until the *expression* evaluates to 0. A `while` statement evaluates the expression before each execution of the statement. Thus, a `while` loop executes the statement zero or more times. Here is a `while` statement for copying one array to another:

```
i = length;
while (i >= 0)  /* Copy one array to another */
{
    array2[i] = array1[i];
    i--;
}
```

Functions

Functions are the building blocks of C programs. A *function* is a collection of declarations and statements. Each C program has at least one function: the main function. This is the function where the execution of a C program begins. The C library contains mostly functions, although it contains quite a few macros as well.

Function prototypes

In C, you must declare a function before using it. The function declaration tells the compiler the type of value that the function returns and the number and type of arguments it takes. Declare a function as a complete *function prototype,* showing the return type as well as a list of arguments. The `calloc` function in the C library returns a void pointer and accepts two arguments, each of type `size_t`, which is an unsigned integer type of sufficient size to hold the value of the `sizeof` operator. Thus, the function prototype for `calloc` is the following:

```
void *calloc(size_t, size_t);
```

This shows the type of each argument in the argument list. You can also include an identifier for each argument and write the prototype as follows:

```
void *calloc(size_t num_elements, size_t elem_size);
```

In this case, the prototype looks exactly like the first line in the definition of the function, except that you stop short of defining the function and end the line with a semicolon. With well-chosen names for arguments, this form of prototype can provide a lot of information about the function's use. For example, one look at the prototype of `calloc` should tell you that its first argument is the number of elements to allocate, and the second one is the size of each element.

Prototypes also help the compiler check function arguments and generate code that may use a faster mechanism for passing arguments. From the prototype, the compiler can determine the exact number and type of arguments to expect. Therefore, the prototype enables the compiler to catch any mistakes you might make when calling a function, such as passing the wrong number of arguments (when the function takes a fixed number of arguments) or passing a wrong type of argument to a function.

The void type

What do you do when a function doesn't return anything nor accept any parameters? To handle these cases, C provides the `void` type, which is useful for declaring functions that return nothing and for describing pointers that can point to any type of data. For example, you can use the `void` return type to declare a function such as `exit` that does not return anything:

```
void exit(int status);
```

On the other hand, if a function doesn't accept any formal parameters, its list of arguments is represented by a `void`:

```
FILE *tmpfile(void);
```

The `void` pointer is useful for functions that work with blocks of memory. For example, when you request a certain number of bytes from the memory allocation routine `malloc`, you can use these locations to store any data that fits the space. In this case, the address of the first location of the allocated block of memory is returned as a `void` pointer. Thus, the prototype of `malloc` is written as follows:

```
void *malloc(size_t numbytes);
```

Functions with a variable number of arguments

If a function accepts a variable number of arguments, you can indicate this by using an ellipsis (. . .) in place of the argument list; however, you must provide at least one argument before the ellipsis. A good example of such functions is the `printf` family of functions defined in the header file `stdio.h`. The prototypes of these functions are as follows:

```
int fprintf(FILE *stream, const char *format, ...);
int printf(const char *format, ...);
int sprintf(char *buffer, const char *format, ...);
```

The C Library

The ANSI and ISO standards for C define all aspects of C — the language, the preprocessor, and the library. The prototypes of the functions in the library, as well as all necessary data structures and preprocessor constants, are defined in a set of standard header files. Table 2-4 lists the standard header files, including a summary of their contents.

If you are going to write applications in C, you have to become familiar with many of the standard libraries because that's where much of C's programming prowess lies. If you are writing graphical applications, you also must learn other libraries such as the GIMP toolkit.

Table 2-4	Standard Header Files in C
Header File	*Purpose*
`<assert.h>`	Defines the `assert` macro. Used for program diagnostics.
`<ctype.h>`	Declares functions for classifying and converting characters.
`<errno.h>`	Defines macros for error conditions, `EDOM` and `ERANGE`, and the integer variable `errno` where library functions return an error code.
`<float.h>`	Defines a range of values that can be stored in floating-point types.
`<iso646.h>`	Defines a number of macros that are helpful when writing C programs in non-English languages that may use character combinations such as & and ~ for other purposes.
`<limits.h>`	Defines the limiting values of all integer data types.
`<locale.h>`	Declares the `lconv` structure and the functions necessary for customizing a C program to a particular locale.
`<math.h>`	Declares common mathematical functions and the `HUGE_VAL` macro.
`<setjmp.h>`	Defines the `setjmp` and `longjmp` functions that can transfer control from one function to another without relying on normal function calls and returns. Also defines the `jmp_buf` data type used by `setjmp` and `longjmp`.
`<signal.h>`	Defines symbols and routines necessary for handling exceptional conditions.
`<stdarg.h>`	Defines macros that provide access to the unnamed arguments in a function that accepts a varying number of arguments.
`<stddef.h>`	Defines the standard data types `ptrdiff_t`, `size_t`, `wchar_t`; the symbol `NULL`; and the macro `offsetof`.
`<stdio.h>`	Declares the functions and data types necessary for input and output operations. Defines macros such as `BUFSIZ`, `EOF`, `SEEK_CUR`, `SEEK_END`, and `SEEK_SET`.
`<stdlib.h>`	Declares many utility functions, such as the string conversion routines, random number generator, memory allocation routines, and process control routines (such as `abort`, `exit`, and `system`).
`<string.h>`	Declares the string manipulation routines such as `strcmp` and `strcpy`.
`<time.h>`	Defines data types and declares functions that manipulate time. Defines the types `clock_t` and `time_t` and the `tm` data structure.
`<wchar.h>`	Defines data types and declares functions for working with wide character data types (`wchar_t`).
`<wctype.h>`	Defines data types and declares functions for classifying and converting wide character data types (`wchar_t`).

**Book VIII
Chapter 2**

Programming in C

Shared Libraries in Red Hat Linux Applications

Most Red Hat Linux programs use shared libraries. At minimum, most C programs use the C shared library `libc.so.X`, wherein *X* is a version number. Using shared libraries is desirable because many executable programs can share the same shared library — you need only one copy of the shared library loaded into memory. Also, the dynamic linking (wherein a program loads code modules and links with them at runtime) is becoming increasingly popular because it enables an application to load blocks of code only when needed, thus reducing the memory requirement of the application.

When a program uses one or more shared libraries, you need the program's executable file, as well as all the shared libraries, to run the program. In other words, your program won't run if all shared libraries are not available on a system.

If you sell an application that uses shared libraries, you need to make sure all necessary shared libraries are distributed with your software.

The subject of shared libraries is of interest to Red Hat Linux programmers because use of shared libraries reduces the size of executables. In this section I briefly describe how to create and use a shared library in a sample program.

Examining shared libraries that a program uses

Use the `ldd` utility to determine which shared libraries an executable program needs. Type the following `ldd` command to see the shared libraries used by a program (that was stored by GCC in the default file named `a.out`):

```
ldd a.out
```

Here is what `ldd` reports for a typical C program:

```
libc.so.6 => /lib/i686/libc.so.6 (0x42000000)
/lib/ld-linux.so.2 => /lib/ld-linux.so.2 (0x40000000)
```

A more complex program, such as the GIMP (a Adobe Photoshop-like program) uses many more shared libraries. To view its shared library needs, type the following command:

```
ldd /usr/bin/gimp
```

Here's the list displayed on my Red Hat Linux system:

```
libgtk-1.2.so.0 => /usr/lib/libgtk-1.2.so.0 (0x40021000)
libgdk-1.2.so.0 => /usr/lib/libgdk-1.2.so.0 (0x4017c000)
libgmodule-1.2.so.0 => /usr/lib/libgmodule-1.2.so.0 (0x401b5000)
```

```
libglib-1.2.so.0 => /usr/lib/libglib-1.2.so.0 (0x401b8000)
libdl.so.2 => /lib/libdl.so.2 (0x401de000)
libXi.so.6 => /usr/X11R6/lib/libXi.so.6 (0x401e1000)
libXext.so.6 => /usr/X11R6/lib/libXext.so.6 (0x401e9000)
libX11.so.6 => /usr/X11R6/lib/libX11.so.6 (0x401f8000)
libm.so.6 => /lib/i686/libm.so.6 (0x402d5000)
libc.so.6 => /lib/i686/libc.so.6 (0x42000000)
/lib/ld-linux.so.2 => /lib/ld-linux.so.2 (0x40000000)
```

In this case, the program uses quite a few shared libraries, including the X11 library (libX11.so.6), the GIMP toolkit (libgtk-1.2.so.0), the General Drawing Kit (GDK) library (libgdk-1.2.so.0), the Math library (libm.so.6), and the C library (libc.so.6).

Almost any Red Hat Linux application requires shared libraries to run.

Creating a shared library

Creating a shared library for your own application is fairly simple. Suppose you want to implement an object in the form of a shared library (think of an object as a bunch of code and data). A set of functions in the shared library represents the object's interfaces. To use the object, you would load its shared library, and invoke its interface functions (I show you how to do this in the following section).

Here is the C source code for this simple object, implemented as a shared library (you might also call it a *dynamically linked library*) — save this in a file named dynobj.c:

```c
/*------------------------------------------------------*/
/* File: dynobj.c
 *
 * Demonstrate use of dynamic linking.
 * Pretend this is an object that can be created by calling
 * init and destroyed by calling destroy.
 */
#include <stdio.h>
#include <stdlib.h>
#include <string.h>

/* Data structure for this object */
typedef struct OBJDATA
{
  char *name;
  int version;
} OBJDATA;


/*------------------------------------------------------*/
/* i n i t
 *
 * Initialize object (allocate storage).
```

```
 *
 */
void* init(char *name)
{
  OBJDATA *data = (OBJDATA*)calloc(1, sizeof(OBJDATA));
  if(name)
    data->name = malloc(strlen(name)+1);
  strcpy(data->name, name);

  printf("Created: %s\n", name);

  return data;
}
/*------------------------------------------------------------*/
/* s h o w
 *
 * Show the object.
 *
 */
void show(void *data)
{
  OBJDATA *d = (OBJDATA*)data;
  printf("show: %s\n", d->name);
}
/*------------------------------------------------------------*/
/* d e s t r o y
 *
 * Destroy the object (free all storage).
 *
 */
void destroy(void *data)
{
  OBJDATA *d = (OBJDATA*)data;
  if(d)
  {
    if(d->name)
    {
      printf("Destroying: %s\n", d->name);
      free(d->name);
    }
    free(d);
  }
}
```

The object offers three interface functions:

◆ init to allocate any necessary storage and initialize the object

◆ show to display the object (here, it simply prints a message)

◆ destroy to free any storage

To build the shared library named `libdobj.so`, follow these steps:

1. **Compile all source files with the** `-fPIC` **flag. In this case, compile the** `dynobj.c` **file by using this command:**

```
gcc -fPIC -c dynobj.c
```

2. **Link the objects into a shared library with the** `-shared` **flag, and provide appropriate flags for the linker. To create the shared library named** `libdobj.so.1`, **use the following:**

```
gcc -shared -Wl,-soname,libdobj.so.1 -o libdobj.so.1.0
dynobj.o
```

3. **Set up a sequence of symbolic links so that programs that use the shared library can refer to it with a standard name.**

For the sample library, the standard name is `libdobj.so`, and the symbolic links are set up by using these commands:

```
ln -sf libdobj.so.1.0 libdobj.so.1
ln -sf libdobj.so.1 libdobj.so
```

4. **When you test the shared library, define and export the** `LD_LIBRARY_PATH` **environment variable by using the following command:**

```
export LD_LIBRARY_PATH=`pwd`:$LD_LIBRARY_PATH
```

After you test the shared library and are satisfied that the library works, copy it to a standard location, such as `/usr/local/lib`, and run the `ldconfig` utility to update the link between `libdobj.so.1` and `libdobj.so.1.0`. These are the commands you use to install your shared library for everyone's use (you have to be `root` to perform these steps):

```
cp libdobj.so.1.0 /usr/local/lib
/sbin/ldconfig
cd /usr/local/lib
ln -s libdobj.so.1 libdobj.so
```

Dynamically loading a shared library

It's simple to load a shared library in your program and use the functions within the shared library. This section demonstrates the way you do this. The header file `<dlfcn.h>` (that's a standard header file in Red Hat Linux) declares the functions for loading and using a shared library. Four functions are declared in the file `dlfcn.h` for dynamic loading:

✦ `void *dlopen(const char *filename, int flag);` — Loads the shared library specified by the filename and returns a handle for the library. The flag can be `RTD_LAZY` (resolve undefined symbols as the library's code is executed); or RTD_NOW (resolve all undefined symbols before dlopen returns and fail if all symbols are not defined). If dlopen fails, it returns NULL.

✦ const char *dlerror (void); — If dlopen fails, call dlerror to get a string that contains a description of the error.

✦ void *dlsym (void *handle, char *symbol); — Returns the address of the specified symbol (function name) from the shared library identified by the handle (that was returned by dlopen).

✦ int dlclose (void *handle); — Unloads the shared library if no one else is using it.

When you use any of these functions, include the header file dlfcn.h with this preprocessor directive:

```
#include <dlfcn.h>
```

Finally, here is a simple test program — dltest.c — that shows how to load and use the object defined in the shared library libdobj.so, which you create in the preceding section:

```
/*--------------------------------------------------------------*/
/* File: dltest.c
 *
 * Test dynamic linking.
 *
 */
#include <dlfcn.h>   /* For the dynamic loading functions */
#include <stdio.h>

int main(void)
{
  void *dlobj;
  void * (*init_call)(char *name);
  void (*show_call)(void *data);
  void (*destroy_call)(void *data);

/* Open the shared library and set up the function pointers
   */
  if(dlobj = dlopen("libdobj.so.1",RTLD_LAZY))
  {
    void *data;

    init_call=dlsym(dlobj,"init");
    show_call=dlsym(dlobj,"show");
    destroy_call=dlsym(dlobj,"destroy");

/* Call the object interfaces */
    data = (*init_call)("Test Object");
```

```
    (*show_call)(data);
    (*destroy_call)(data);
  }
  return 0;
}
```

The program is straightforward: It loads the shared library, gets the pointers to the functions in the library, and calls the functions through the pointers.

You can compile and link this program in the usual way, but you must link with the -ldl option so you can use the functions declared in dlfcn.h. Here is how you build the program dltest:

```
gcc -o dltest dltest.c -ldl
```

To see the program in action, run dltest by typing the following command:

```
./dltest
```

It should display the following lines of output:

```
Created: Test Object
show: Test Object
Destroying: Test Object
```

Although this sample program is not exciting, you now have a sample program that uses a shared library.

To see the benefit of using a shared library, return to the preceding section and make some changes in the shared library source file — dynobj.c. For example, you could print some other message in a function so you can easily tell that you have made some change. Rebuild the shared library alone. Then run dltest again. The resulting output should show the effect of the changes you make in the shared library, which means you can update the shared library independently of the application.

Note that a change in a shared library can affect many applications installed on your system. Therefore, be careful when making changes to any shared library. By the same token, shared libraries can be a security risk if someone is able to replace one of the shared libraries with something else that has some malicious code.

Chapter 3: Writing Shell Scripts

In This Chapter

✔ Trying out simple shell scripts

✔ Learning the basics of shell scripting

✔ Exploring Bash's built-in commands

Red Hat Linux gives you many small and specialized commands, along with the plumbing necessary to connect these commands. By *plumbing,* I mean the way in which one command's output can be used as a second command's input. Bash (Bourne Again shell) the default shell in Linux, provides this plumbing in the form of I/O redirection and pipes. Bash also includes features such as the `if` statement that you can use to run commands only when a specific condition is true and the `for` statement that repeats commands a specified number of times. You can use these features of Bash when writing programs called *shell scripts*.

In this chapter, I show you how to write simple shell scripts — a collection of shell commands stored in a file. Shell scripts are used to automate various tasks. For example, when your Red Hat Linux boots, many shell scripts stored in various subdirectories in the `/etc` directory (for example, `/etc/init.d`) perform many initialization tasks.

Trying Out Simple Shell Scripts

If you are not a programmer, you may feel apprehensive about programming. But shell scripting (or programming) can be as simple as storing a few commands in a file. In fact, you can have a useful shell program that has a single command.

While writing this book, for example, I captured screens from the X Window System and used the screen shots in figures. I used the X screen-capture program, `xwd`, to store the screen images in the X Window Dump (XWD) format. The book's production team, however, wanted the screen shots in TIFF format. Therefore, I have used the Portable Bitmap (PBM) toolkit to convert the XWD images to TIFF format. To convert each file, I have run two programs and have deleted a temporary file, as follows:

```
xwdtopnm < file.xwd > file.pnm
pnmtotiff < file.pnm > file.tif
rm file.pnm
```

These commands assume that the xwdtopnm and pnmtotiff programs are in the /usr/bin directory — one of the directories listed in the PATH environment variable. By the way, xwdtopnm and pnmtotiff are two programs in the PBM toolkit.

After converting a few XWD files to TIFF format, I get tired of typing the same sequence of commands for each file, so I prepare a file named totif and save the following lines in it:

```
#!/bin/sh
xwdtopnm < $1.xwd > $1.pnm
pnmtotiff < $1.pnm > $1.tif
rm $1.pnm
```

Then I make the file executable by using this command:

```
chmod +x totif
```

The chmod command enables you to change the permission settings of a file. One of those settings determines whether the file is executable or not. The +x option means you want to mark the file as executable. You need to do this because Bash runs only executable files.

Now when I want to convert the file figure1.xwd to figure1.tif, I can do so by typing the following command:

```
./totif figure1
```

The ./ prefix indicates that the totif file is in the current directory — you don't need the ./ prefix if the PATH environment variable includes the current directory. The totif file is called a shell script or shell program. When you run this shell program with the command totif figure1, the shell substitutes figure1 for each occurrence of $1.

Shell scripts are popular among system administrators. If you are a system administrator, you can build a collection of custom shell scripts that help you automate tasks you perform often. If a disk seems to be getting full, for example, you may want to find all files that exceed some size (say, 1MB) and that have not been accessed in the past 30 days. In addition, you may want to send an e-mail message to all users who have large files, requesting that they archive and clean up those files. You can perform all these tasks with a shell script. You might start with the following find command to identify large files:

```
find / -type f -atime +30 -size +1000k -exec ls -l {} \; > /tmp/largefiles
```

This command creates a file named /tmp/largefiles, which contains detailed information about the old files taking up too much space. After you get a list of the files, you can use a few other Linux commands — such as sort, cut, and sed — to prepare and send mail messages to users who have large files that they should clean up. Instead of typing all these commands manually, place them in a file, and create a shell script. That, in a nutshell, is the essence of shell scripts — to gather shell commands in a file so that you can easily perform repetitive system-administration tasks.

Just as most Linux commands accept command-line options, a Bash script also accepts command-line options. Inside the script, you can refer to the options as $1, $2, and so on. The special name $0 refers to the name of the script itself.

Here's a typical Bash script that accepts arguments:

```
#!/bin/sh
echo "This script's name is: $0"
echo Argument 1: $1
echo Argument 2: $2
```

The first line runs the /bin/sh program, which subsequently processes the rest of the lines in the script. The name /bin/sh traditionally refers to the Bourne shell — the first UNIX shell. In Red Hat Linux, /bin/sh is a symbolic link to /bin/bash, which is the executable program for Bash.

Save this simple script in a file named simple, and make that file executable with the following command:

```
chmod +x simple
```

Now run the script as follows:

```
./simple
```

It displays the following output:

```
This script's name is: ./simple
Argument 1:
Argument 2:
```

The first line shows the script's name. Because you have run the script without arguments, the script displays no values for the arguments.

Now, try running the script with a few arguments, like this:

```
./simple "This is one argument" second-argument third
```

This time the script displays more output:

```
This script's name is: ./simple
Argument 1: This is one argument
Argument 2: second-argument
```

As the output shows, the shell treats the entire string within double quotation marks as a single argument. Otherwise, the shell uses spaces as separators between arguments on the command line.

This sample script ignores the third argument because the script is designed to print only the first two arguments. The script ignores all arguments after the first two.

Learning the Basics of Shell Scripting

Like any programming language, the Bash shell supports the following features:

✦ Variables that store values, including special built-in variables for accessing command-line arguments passed to a shell script and other special values

✦ The capability to evaluate expressions

✦ Control structures that enable you to loop over several shell commands or to execute some commands conditionally

✦ The capability to define functions that can be called in many places within a script. Bash also includes many built-in commands that you can use in any script.

In the next few sections, I illustrate some of these programming features through simple examples. Because you are already running Bash, you can try the examples by typing them at the shell prompt in a terminal window.

Storing stuff

You define variables in Bash just as you define environment variables. Thus, you may define a variable as follows:

```
count=12   # note no embedded spaces allowed
```

To use a variable's value, prefix the variable's name with a dollar sign ($). $PATH, for example, is the value of the variable PATH (this is the famous PATH environment variable that lists the directories that Bash searches when trying to locate an executable file). To display the value of the variable count, use the following command:

```
echo $count
```

Bash has some special variables for accessing command-line arguments. In a shell script, $0 refers to the name of the shell script. The variables $1, $2, and so on refer to the command-line arguments. The variable $* stores all the command-line arguments as a single variable, and $? contains the exit status of the last command the shell executes.

From a Bash script you can prompt the user for input and use the read command to read the input into a variable. Here is an example:

```
echo -n "Enter value: "
read value
echo "You entered: $value"
```

When this script runs, the `read value` command causes Bash to read whatever you type at the keyboard.

Note that the -n option prevents the echo command from automatically adding a new line at the end of the string that it displays.

Calling shell functions

You can group a number of shell commands into a function and assign it a name. Later, you can execute that group of commands by using the single name assigned to the function. Here is a simple script that illustrates the syntax of shell functions:

```
#!/bin/sh

hello() {
        echo -n "Hello, "
        echo $1 $2
}

hello Jane Doe
```

When you run this script, it displays the following output:

```
Hello, Jane Doe
```

This script defines a shell function named hello. The function expects two arguments. In the body of the function, these arguments are referenced by $1 and $2. The function definition begins with hello() — the name of the function, followed by parentheses. The body of the function is enclosed in curly braces — {...}. In this case, the body uses the echo command to display a line of text.

The last line of the example shows how a shell function is called with arguments. In this case, the hello function is being called with two arguments:

Jane and Doe. The `hello` function takes these two arguments and prints out a line that says `Hello, Jane Doe`.

Controlling the flow

In Bash scripts, you can control the flow of execution — the order in which the commands are executed — by using special commands such as `if`, `case`, `for`, and `while`. These control statements use the exit status of a command to decide what to do next. When any command executes, it returns an exit status — a numeric value that indicates whether or not the command has succeeded. By convention, an exit status of zero means the command has succeeded. (Yes, you read it right: Zero indicates success.) A nonzero exit status indicates that something has gone wrong with the command.

For example, suppose you want to make a backup copy of a file before editing it with the `vi` editor. More importantly, you want to avoid editing the file if a backup can't be made. Here's a Bash script that takes care of this task:

```
#!/bin/sh
if cp "$1" "#$1"
then
    vi "$1"
else
    echo "Failed to create backup copy"
fi
```

This script illustrates the syntax of the `if-then-else` structure and shows how the exit status of the `cp` command is used by the `if` command to determine the next action. If `cp` returns zero, the script uses `vi` to edit the file; otherwise, the script displays an error message and exits. By the way, the script saves the backup in a file whose name is the same as that of the original, except for a hash mark (#) added at the beginning of the file name.

Don't forget the final `fi` that terminates the `if` command. Forgetting `fi` is a common source of errors in Bash scripts.

You can use the `test` command to evaluate any expression and to use the expression's value as the exit status of the command. Suppose you want a script that edits a file only if it already exists. Using `test`, you can write such a script as follows:

```
#!/bin/sh
if test -f "$1"
then
    vi "$1"
else
    echo "No such file"
fi
```

A shorter form of the test command is to place the expression in square brackets ([...]). Using this shorthand notation, you can rewrite the preceding script like this:

```
#!/bin/sh
if [ -f "$1" ]
then
    vi "$1"
else
    echo "No such file"
fi
```

Note: You must have spaces around the two square brackets.

Another common control structure is the for loop. The following script adds the numbers 1 through 10:

```
#!/bin/sh
sum=0
for i in 1 2 3 4 5 6 7 8 9 10
do
    sum=`expr $sum + $i`
done
echo "Sum = $sum"
```

This example also illustrates the use of the expr command to evaluate an expression.

The case statement is used to execute a group of commands based on the value of a variable. For example, consider the following script, based on the confirm() function in the /etc/init.d/functions file in your Red Hat Linux system:

```
#!/bin/sh
echo -n "What should I do -- (Y)es/(N)o/(C)ontinue? [Y] "
read answer
case $answer in
    y|Y|"")
      echo "YES"
    ;;
    c|C)
      echo "CONTINUE"
    ;;
    n|N)
      echo "NO"
    ;;
    *)
      echo "UNKNOWN"
    ;;
esac
```

Book VIII
Chapter 3

Writing Shell
Scripts

Save this in a file named `confirm` and type **chmod +x confirm** to make it executable. Then try it out like this:

```
./confirm
```

When the script prompts you, type one of the characters **y**, **n**, or **c** and press Enter. The script should display `YES`, `NO`, or `CONTINUE`. For example, here's what happens when I type **c** (and press Enter):

```
What should I do -- (Y)es/(N)o/(C)ontinue? [Y] c
CONTINUE
```

The script displays a prompt and reads the input you type. Your input is stored in a variable named `answer`. Then the `case` statement executes a block of code based on the value of the answer variable. For example, when I type **c**, the following block of commands is executed:

```
c|C)
   echo "CONTINUE"
;;
```

The `echo` command causes the script to display `CONTINUE`.

From this example, you can see that the general syntax of the `case` command is as follows:

```
case $variable in
    value1 | value2)
    command1
    command2
    ...other commands...
    ;;

    value3)
    command3
    command4
    ...other commands...
    ;;
esac
```

Essentially, the `case` command begins with the word `case` and ends with `esac`. Separate blocks of code are enclosed between the values of the variable, followed by a right parenthesis and terminated by a pair of semicolons (; ;).

Exploring Bash's built-in commands

Bash has more than 50 built-in commands, including common commands such as cd and pwd, as well as many others that are used infrequently. You can use these built-in commands in any Bash script or at the shell prompt. Table 3-1 describes most of the Bask built-in commands and their arguments. After looking through this information, type **help *cmd*** to read more about a specific built-in command. For example, to learn more about the built-in command test, type the following:

```
help test
```

This displays the following information on my Red Hat Linux system:

```
test: test [expr]
    Exits with a status of 0 (true) or 1 (false) depending on
    the evaluation of EXPR. Expressions may be unary or binary. Unary
    expressions are often used to examine the status of a file. There
    are string operators as well, and numeric comparison operators.

    File operators:

      -a FILE      True if file exists.
      -b FILE      True if file is block special.
      -c FILE      True if file is character special.
      -d FILE      True if file is a directory.
      -e FILE      True if file exists.
      -f FILE      True if file exists and is a regular file.
      -g FILE      True if file is set-group-id.
      -h FILE      True if file is a symbolic link.
      -L FILE      True if file is a symbolic link.
      -k FILE      True if file has its `sticky' bit set.
      -p FILE      True if file is a named pipe.
      -r FILE      True if file is readable by you.
      -s FILE      True if file exists and is not empty.
      -S FILE      True if file is a socket.
      -t FD      True if FD is opened on a terminal.
      -u FILE      True if the file is set-user-id.
      -w FILE      True if the file is writable by you.
      -x FILE      True if the file is executable by you.
      -O FILE      True if the file is effectively owned by you.
      -G FILE      True if the file is effectively owned by your group.
    (... Lines deleted ...)
```

Where necessary, the online help from the help command includes a considerable amount of detail.

Some external programs may have the same name as Bash built-in commands. If you want to run any such external program, you have to specify explicitly the full pathname of that program. Otherwise, Bash executes the built-in command of the same name.

**Book VIII
Chapter 3**

**Writing Shell
Scripts**

Table 3-1   **Summary of Built-in Commands in Bash Shell**

This Function	*Does the Following*
`. filename [arguments]`	Reads and executes commands from the specified file using the optional arguments (works the same way as the `source` command).
`: [arguments]`	Expands the arguments but does not process them.
`[ expr ]`	Evaluates the expression `expr` and returns zero status if `expr` is true.
`alias [name[=value] ...]`	Defines an alias.
`bg [job]`	Puts the specified job in the background. If no job is specified, it puts the currently executing command in the background.
`bind [-m keymap] [-lvd] [-q name]`	Binds a key sequence to a macro.
`break [n]`	Exits from a `for`, `while`, or `until` loop. If *n* is specified, the *n*-th enclosing loop is exited.
`builtin builtin_command [arguments]`	Executes a shell built-in command.
`cd [dir]`	Changes the current directory to `dir`.
`command [-pVv] cmd [arg ...]`	Runs the command `cmd` with the specified arguments (ignoring any shell function named `cmd`).
`continue [n]`	Starts the next iteration of the `for`, `while`, or `until` loop. If *n* is specified, the next iteration of the *n*-th enclosing loop is started.
`declare [-frxi] [name[=value]]`	Declares a variable with the specified name and, optionally, assigns it a value.
`dirs [-l] [+/-n]`	Displays the list of currently remembered directories.
`echo [-neE] [arg ...]`	Displays the arguments on standard output.
`enable [-n] [-all] [name ...]`	Enables or disables the specified built-in commands.
`eval [arg ...]`	Concatenates the arguments and executes them as a command.
`exec [command [arguments]]`	Replaces the current instance of the shell with a new process that runs the specified command.
`exit [n]`	Exits the shell with the status code *n*.
`export [-nf] [name[=word]] ...`	Defines a specified environment variable and exports it to future processes.
`fc -s [pat=rep] [cmd]`	Re-executes the command after replacing the pattern `pat` with `rep`.

This Function	Does the Following
fg [*jobspec*]	Puts the specified job in the foreground. If no job is specified, it puts the most recent job in the foreground.
getopts *optstring name* [*args*]	Gets optional parameters (called in shell scripts to extract arguments from the command line).
hash [-r] [*name*]	Remembers the full pathname of a specified command.
help [*cmd* ...]	Displays help information for specified built-in commands.
history [*n*]	Displays past commands or past *n* commands, if you specify a number *n*.
jobs [-lnp] [*jobspec* ...]	Lists currently active jobs.
kill [-s *sigspec* | -*sigspec*] [*pid* | *jobspec*] ...let *arg* [*arg* ...]	Evaluates each argument and returns 1 if the last *arg* is 0.
local [*name*[=*value*] ...]	Creates a local variable with the specified name and value (used in shell functions).
logout	Exits a login shell.
popd [+/-*n*]	Removes entries from the directory stack.
pushd [*dir*]	Adds a specified directory to the top of the directory stack.
pwd	Prints the full pathname of the current working directory.
read [-r] [*name* ...]	Reads a line from standard input and parses it.
readonly [-f] [*name* ...]	Marks the specified variables as read-only, so that the variables cannot be changed later.
return [*n*]	Exits the shell function with the return value *n*.
set [—abefhkmnptuvxldCHP] [-o *option*] [*arg* ...]	Sets various flags.
shift [*n*]	Makes the *n*+1 argument $1, the *n*+2 argument $2, and so on.
source *filename* [*arguments*]	Reads and executes commands from a file.
suspend [-f]	Stops execution until a SIGCONT signal is received.
test expr	Evaluates the expression expr and returns zero if expr is true.
times	Prints the accumulated user and system times for processes run from the shell.
trap [-l] [*cmd*] [*sigspec*]	Executes cmd when the signal sigspec is received.

(continued)

**Book VIII
Chapter 3**

**Writing Shell
Scripts**

Table 3-1 *(continued)*

This Function	Does the Following
`type [-all] [-type	-path] name [name ...]`	Indicates how the shell interprets each name.
`ulimit [-SHacdfmstpnuv [limit]]`	Controls resources available to the shell.
`umask [-S] [mode]`	Sets the file creation mask — the default permission for files.
`unalias [-a] [name ...]`	Undefines a specified alias.
`unset [-fv] [name ...]`	Removes the definition of specified variables.
`wait [n]`	Waits for a specified process to terminate.

Chapter 4: Programming in Perl

In This Chapter

- ✔ Writing your first Perl program
- ✔ Getting an overview of Perl
- ✔ Understanding Perl packages and modules
- ✔ Using objects in Perl

*W*hen it comes to writing scripts, the Perl language is very popular among system administrators, especially on UNIX and Linux systems. System administrators use Perl to automate routine system administration tasks such as looking for old files that could be archived and deleted to free up disk space.

Perl is a scripting language, which means you do not have to compile and link a Perl script — a text file containing Perl commands. Instead, an interpreter executes the Perl script. This makes it easy to write and test Perl scripts, because you do not have to go through the typical edit-compile-link cycles to write Perl programs.

Besides ease of programming, another reason for Perl's popularity is that Perl is distributed freely and is available for a wide variety of computer systems, including Red Hat Linux and many others such as UNIX, Windows 95/98/NT/2000/XP, and Apple Macintosh.

In this chapter, I introduce you to Perl scripting.

Understanding Perl

Officially Perl stands for *Practical Extraction Report Language*, but Larry Wall, the creator of Perl, says people often refer to Perl as *Pathologically Eclectic Rubbish Lister*. As these names suggest, Perl was originally designed to extract information from text files and generate reports.

Perl began life in 1986 as a system administration tool created by Larry Wall. Over time Perl grew by accretion of many new features and functions. The latest version of Perl — Perl 5.8 — supports object-oriented programming and allows anyone to extend Perl by adding new modules in a specified format.

True to its origin as a system administration tool, Perl has been popular with UNIX system administrators for many years. More recently, when the World Wide Web (or Web for short) became popular and the need for Common Gateway Interface (CGI) programs arose, Perl became the natural choice for those already familiar with the language. The recent surge in Perl's popularity is primarily due to the use of Perl in writing CGI programs for the Web. Of course, as people pay more attention to Perl, they discover that Perl is useful for much more than CGI programming. That, in turn, has made Perl even more popular among users.

Perl is available on a wide variety of computer systems because, like the Linux operating system, Perl can be distributed freely.

If you are familiar with shell programming or the C programming language, you can pick up Perl quickly. If you have never programmed, becoming proficient in Perl may take a while. I encourage you to start with a small subset of Perl's features and to ignore anything you do not understand. Then, slowly add Perl features to your repertoire.

Determining Whether You Have Perl

Before you proceed with the Perl tutorial, check whether you have the perl program installed on your Red Hat Linux system. Type the following command:

```
which perl
```

The which command tells you whether it finds a specified program in the directories listed in the PATH environment variable. If perl is installed, you should see the following output:

```
/usr/bin/perl
```

If the which command complains that no such program exists in the current PATH, this does not necessarily mean you do not have perl installed; it may mean that you do not have the /usr/bin directory in PATH. Ensure that /usr/bin is in PATH; check by typing the following command:

```
echo $PATH
```

See if the output lists the /usr/bin directory. If /usr/bin is not in PATH, use the following command to redefine PATH:

```
export PATH=$PATH:/usr/bin
```

Now, try the `which perl` command again. If you still get an error, you may not have installed Perl. You can install Perl from the companion CD-ROMs by performing the following steps:

1. **Log in as** `root`.

2. **Insert the first companion CD-ROM in the CD-ROM drive. If you are working in GNOME or KDE graphical environment, the CD-ROM should mount automatically. Otherwise, mount the CD-ROM by typing the following command:**

   ```
   mount /mnt/cdrom
   ```

3. **Type the following command to change the directory to the location of the Red Hat packages:**

   ```
   cd /mnt/cdrom/RedHat/RPMS
   ```

4. **Type the following** `rpm` **(Red Hat Package Manager) command to install Perl:**

   ```
   rpm -ivh perl*
   ```

After you have installed Perl on your system, type the following command to see its version number:

```
perl -v
```

Here is typical output from that command:

```
This is perl, v5.8.0 built for i386-linux-thread-multi

Copyright 1987-2002, Larry Wall

Perl may be copied only under the terms of either the Artistic License or the
GNU General Public License, which may be found in the Perl 5 source kit.

Complete documentation for Perl, including FAQ lists, should be found on
this system using `man perl' or `perldoc perl'. If you have access to the
Internet, point your browser at http://www.perl.com/, the Perl Home Page.
```

This output tells you that you have Perl Version 5.8, patch Level 0, and that Larry Wall, the originator of Perl, holds the copyright. Perl is distributed freely under the GNU General Public License, however.

You can get the latest version of Perl by pointing your World Wide Web browser to the Comprehensive Perl Archive Network (CPAN). The following address connects you to the CPAN site nearest to you:

```
http://www.perl.com/CPAN/
```

**Book VIII
Chapter 4**

**Programming
in Perl**

Writing Your First Perl Script

Perl has many features of C, and, as you may know, most books on C start with an example program that displays `Hello, World!` on your terminal. Because Perl is an interpreted language, you can accomplish this task directly from the command line. If you enter

```
perl -e 'print "Hello, World!\n";'
```

Perl responds with the following:

```
Hello, World!
```

This command uses the `-e` option of the `perl` program to pass the Perl program as a command-line argument to the Perl interpreter. In this case, the following line constitutes the Perl program:

```
print "Hello, World!\n";
```

To convert this line to a Perl script, simply place the line in a file, and start the file with a directive to run the `perl` program (as you do in shell scripts, when you place a line such as `#!/bin/sh` to run the shell to process the script).

To try out this Perl script, follow these steps:

1. **Use a text editor to type and save the following lines in the file named** `hello.pl`:

   ```
   #!/usr/bin/perl
   # This is a comment.
   print "Hello, World!\n";
   ```

2. **Make the** `hello.pl` **file executable by using the following command:**

   ```
   chmod +x hello.pl
   ```

3. **Run the Perl script by typing the following at the shell prompt:**

   ```
   ./hello.pl
   ```

   It should display the following output:

   ```
   Hello, World!
   ```

That's it! You have written and tried your first Perl script.

Notice that the first line of a Perl script starts with #!, followed by the full pathname of the `perl` program. If the first line of a script starts with #!, the shell simply strips off the #!, appends the script file's name to the end, and runs the script. Thus, if the script file is named `hello.pl` and the first line is #!/usr/bin/perl, the shell executes the following command:

```
/usr/bin/perl hello.pl
```

Getting an Overview of Perl

Most programming languages, including Perl, have some common features:

✦ **Variables** to store different types of data. You can think of each variable as a placeholder for data — kind of like a mailbox, with a name and room to store data. The content of the variable is its value.

✦ **Expressions** that combine variables by using operators. One expression may add several variables; another might extract a part of a string.

✦ **Statements** that perform some action, such as assigning a value to a variable or printing a string.

✦ **Flow-control statements** that enable statements to be executed in various orders, depending on the value of some expression. Typically, flow-control statements include `for`, `do-while`, `while`, and `if-then-else` statements.

✦ **Functions** (also called *subroutines* or *routines*) that enable you to group several statements and give them a name. This feature enables you to execute the same set of statements by invoking the function that represents those statements. Typically, a programming language provides some predefined functions.

✦ **Packages** and **modules** that enable you to organize a set of related Perl subroutines that are designed to be reusable. (Modules were introduced in Perl 5).

In the next few sections, I provide an overview of these major features of Perl and illustrate the features through simple examples.

Basic Perl syntax

Perl is free-form, like C. There are no constraints on the exact placement of any keyword. Often, Perl programs are stored in files with names that end in `.pl`, but there is no restriction on the filenames you use.

As in C, each Perl statement ends with a semicolon (;). A hash mark or pound sign (#) marks the start of a comment; the `perl` program disregards the rest of the line beginning with the hash mark.

Groups of Perl statements are enclosed in braces ({ . . . }). This feature also is similar in C.

Variables

You don't have to declare Perl variables before using them, as you do in the C programming language. You can recognize a variable in a Perl script easily, because each variable name begins with a special character: an at symbol (@), a dollar sign ($), or a percent sign (%). These special characters denote the variable's type. The three variable types are as follows:

+ **Scalar variables** represent the basic data types: integer, floating-point number, and string. A dollar sign ($) precedes a scalar variable. Following are some examples:

```
$maxlines = 256;
$title = "Red Hat Linux All-in-One Desk Reference";
```

+ **Array variables** are collections of scalar variables. An array variable has an at symbol (@) as a prefix. Thus, the following are arrays:

```
@pages = (62, 26, 22, 24);
@commands = ("start", "stop", "draw", "exit");
```

+ **Associative arrays** are collections of key-value pairs, in which each key is a string and the value is any scalar variable. A percent-sign (%) prefix indicates an associative array. You can use associative arrays to associate a name with a value. You may store the amount of disk space each user occupies in an associative array, such as the following:

```
%disk_usage = ("root", 147178, "naba", 28547,
               "emily", 55, "ashley", 40);
```

Because each variable type has a special character prefix, you can use the same name for different variable types. Thus, `%disk_usage`, `@disk_usage`, and `$disk_usage` can appear within the same Perl program.

Scalars

A *scalar variable* can store a single value, such as a number, or a text string. Scalar variables are the basic data type in Perl. Each scalar's name begins with a dollar sign ($). Typically, you start using a scalar with an assignment statement that initializes it. You even can use a variable without initializing it; the default value for numbers is zero, and the default value of a string is an empty string. If you want to see whether a scalar is defined, use the `defined` function as follows:

```
print "Name undefined!\n" if !(defined $name);
```

The expression (defined $name) is 1 if $name is defined. You can "undefine" a variable by using the undef function. You can undefine $name, for example, as follows:

```
undef $name;
```

Variables are evaluated according to context. Following is a script that initializes and prints a few variables:

```
#!/usr/bin/perl
$title = "Red Hat Linux All-in-One Desk Reference";
$count1 = 650;
$count2 = 238;

$total = $count1 + $count2;

print "Title: $title -- $total pages\n";
```

When you run the preceding Perl program, it produces the following output:

```
Title: Red Hat Linux All-in-One Desk Reference -- 888 pages
```

As the Perl statements show, when the two numeric variables are added, their numeric values are used; but when the $total variable is printed, its string representation is displayed.

Another interesting aspect of Perl is that it evaluates all variables in a string within double quotation marks (" . . . "). However, if you write a string inside single quotation marks (' . . . '), Perl leaves that string untouched. If you write

```
 print 'Title: $title -- $total pages\n';
```

with single quotes instead of double quotes, Perl displays

```
Title: $title -- $total pages\n
```

and does not generate a new line.

A useful Perl variable is $_ (the dollar sign followed by the underscore character). This special variable is known as the default argument. The Perl interpreter determines the value of $_ depending on the context. When the Perl interpreter reads input from the standard input, $_ holds the current input line; when the interpreter is searching for a specific pattern of text, $_ holds the default search pattern.

Arrays

An *array* is a collection of scalars. The array name begins with an at symbol (@). As in C, array subscripts start at zero. You can access the elements of an array with an index. Perl allocates space for arrays dynamically.

Consider the following simple script:

```
#!/usr/bin/perl
@commands = ("start", "stop", "draw" , "exit");

$numcmd = @commands;
print "There are $numcmd commands.\n";
print "The first command is: $commands[0]\n";
```

When you run the script, it produces the following output:

```
There are 4 commands.
The first command is: start
```

As you can see, equating a scalar to the array sets the scalar to the number of elements in the array. The first element of the @commands array is referenced as $commands[0] because the index starts at zero. Thus, the fourth element in the @commands array is $commands[3].

Two special scalars are related to an array. The $[variable is the current base index (the starting index), which is zero by default. The scalar $#*arrayname* (in which *arrayname* is the name of an array variable) has the last array index as the value. Thus, for the @commands array, $#commands is 3.

You can print an entire array with a simple print statement like this:

```
print "@commands\n";
```

When Perl executes this statement, it displays the following output:

```
start stop draw exit
```

Associative arrays

Associative array variables, which are declared with a percent-sign (%) prefix, are unique features of Perl. Using associative arrays, you can index an array with a string, such as a name. A good example of an associative array is the %ENV array that Perl automatically defines for you. In Perl, %ENV is the array of environment variables you can access by using the environment-variable name as an index. The following Perl statement prints the current PATH environment variable:

```
print "PATH = $ENV{PATH}\n";
```

When Perl executes this statement, it prints the current setting of PATH. In contrast to indexing regular arrays, you have to use braces to index an associative array.

Perl has many built-in functions — such as delete, each, keys, and values — that enable you to access and manipulate associative arrays.

Predefined variables in Perl

Perl has several predefined variables that contain useful information you may need in a Perl script. Following are a few important predefined variables:

✦ @ARGV is an array of strings that contains the command-line options to the script. The first option is $ARGV[0], the second one is $ARGV[1], and so on.

✦ %ENV is an associative array that contains the environment variables. You can access this array by using the environment-variable name as a key. Thus, $ENV{HOME} is the home directory, and $ENV{PATH} is the current search path that the shell uses to locate commands.

✦ $_ is the default argument for many functions. If you see a Perl function used without any argument, the function probably is expecting its argument in the $_ variable.

✦ @_ is the list of arguments passed to a subroutine.

✦ $0 is the name of the file containing the Perl program.

✦ $^V is the version number of Perl you are using (for example, if you use Perl Version 5.8.0, $^V will be v5.8.0).

✦ $< is the user ID (an identifying number) of the user running the script.

✦ $$ is the script's process ID.

✦ $? is the status the last system call has returned.

Operators and expressions

Operators are used to combine and compare Perl variables. Typical mathematical operators are addition (+), subtraction (–), multiplication (*), and division (/). Perl and C provide nearly the same set of operators. When you use operators to combine variables, you end up with expressions. Each expression has a value.

Here are some typical Perl expressions:

```
error < 0
$count == 10
$count + $i
$users[$i]
```

These expressions are examples of the comparison operator (the first two lines), the arithmetic operator, and the array-index operator.

In Perl, don't use the == operator to determine whether two strings match; the == operator works only with numbers. To test the equality of strings, Perl includes the FORTRAN-style eq operator. Use eq to see whether two strings are identical, as follows:

```
if ($input eq "stop") { exit; }
```

Other FORTRAN-style, string-comparison operators include ne (inequality), lt (less than), gt (greater than), le (less than or equal), and ge (greater than or equal). Also, you can use the cmp operator to compare two strings. The return value is –1, 0, or 1, depending on whether the first string is less than, equal to, or greater than the second string.

Perl also provides the following unique operators. C lacks an exponentiation operator, which FORTRAN includes; Perl uses ** as the exponentiation operator. Thus, you can write the following code in Perl:

```
$x = 2;
$y = 3;
$z = $x**$y;   # z should be 8 (2 raised to the power 3)
$y **= 2; # y is now 9 (3 raised to the power 2)
```

You can initialize an array to null by using ( ) — the null-list operator — as follows:

```
@commands = ();
```

The dot operator (.) enables you to concatenate two strings, as follows:

```
$part1 = "Hello, ";
$part2 = "World!";
$message = $part1.$part2;  # Now $message = "Hello, World!"
```

The repetition operator, denoted by x=, is interesting and quite useful. You can use the x= operator to repeat a string a specified number of times. Suppose you want to initialize a string to 65 asterisks (*). The following example shows how you can initialize the string with the x= operator:

```
$marker = "*";
$marker x= 65;   # Now $marker is a string of 65 asterisks
```

Another powerful operator in Perl is range, which is represented by two periods (. .). You can initialize an array easily by using the range operator. Following are some examples:

```
@numerals = (0..9); # @numerals = 0, 1, 2, 3, 4, 5, 6, 7, 8 , 9
@alphabet = ('A'..'Z'); # @alphabet = capital letters A through Z
```

Regular expressions

If you have used any UNIX or Linux system for a while, you probably know about the `grep` command, which enables you to search files for a pattern of strings. Following is a typical use of `grep` to locate all files that have any occurrences of the string `blaster` or `Blaster` — on any line of all files with names that end in `.c`:

```
cd /usr/src/linux*/drivers/cdrom
grep "[bB]laster"  *.c
```

The preceding `grep` command finds all occurrences of `blaster` and `Blaster` in the files with names ending in `.c`.

The `grep` command's `"[bB]laster"` argument is known as a *regular expression,* a pattern that matches a set of strings. You construct a regular expression with a small set of operators and rules that resemble the ones for writing arithmetic expressions. A list of characters inside brackets (`[...]`), for example, matches any single character in the list. Thus, the regular expression `"[bB]laster"` is a set of two strings, as follows:

```
blaster    Blaster
```

Perl supports regular expressions, just as the `grep` command does. Many other Red Hat Linux programs, such as the `vi` editor and `sed` (the stream editor), also support regular expressions. The purpose of a regular expression is to search for a pattern of strings in a file. That's why editors support regular expressions.

You can construct and use complex regular expressions in Perl. The rules for these regular expressions are fairly simple. Essentially, the regular expression is a sequence of characters in which some characters have special meaning. Table 4-1 summarizes the basic rules for interpreting the characters used to construct a regular expression.

Table 4-1	Rules for Interpreting Regular Expression Characters
Expression	*Meaning*
.	Matches any single character except a newline.
x*	Matches zero or more occurrences of the character *x*.
x+	Matches one or more occurrences of the character *x*.
x?	Matches zero or one occurrence of the character *x*.

(continued)

Table 4-1 *(continued)*

Expression	Meaning
[...]	Matches any of the characters inside the brackets.
x{n}	Matches exactly *n* occurrences of the character *x*.
x{n,}	Matches *n* or more occurrences of the character *x*.
x{,m}	Matches zero or, at most, m occurrences of the character *x*.
x{n,m}	Matches at least *n* occurrences, but no more than *m* occurrences of the character *x*.
$	Matches the end of a line.
\0	Matches a null character.
\b	Matches a backspace.
\B	Matches any character not at the beginning or end of a word.
\b	Matches the beginning or end of a word — when not inside brackets.
\cX	Matches Ctrl-*X* (where *X* is any alphabetic character).
\d	Matches a single digit.
\D	Matches a nondigit character.
\f	Matches a form feed.
\n	Matches a newline (line-feed) character.
\ooo	Matches the octal value specified by the digits *ooo* (where each *o* is a digit between 0 and 7).
\r	Matches a carriage return.
\S	Matches a nonwhite space character.
\s	Matches a white space character (space, tab, or newline).
\t	Matches a tab.
\W	Matches a nonalphanumeric character.
\w	Matches an alphanumeric character.
\xhh	Matches the hexadecimal value specified by the digits *hh* (where each *h* is a digit between 0 and f).
^	Matches the beginning of a line.

If you want to match one of the characters $, |, *, ^, [,], \, and /, you have to place a backslash before them. Thus, you type these characters as \$, \|, *, \^, \[, \], \\, and \/. Regular expressions often look confusing because of the preponderance of strange character sequences and the generous sprinkling of backslashes. As with anything else, however, you can start slowly and use only a few of the features in the beginning.

So far, I have summarized the syntax of regular expressions. But I have not yet shown how to use regular expressions in Perl. Typically, you place a regular expression within a pair of slashes and use the match (=~) or not-match (!~) operators to test a string. You can write a Perl script that performs the same search as the one done with `grep` earlier in this section. Follow these steps to complete this task:

1. **Use a text editor to type and save the following script in a file named** `lookup`:

```
#!/usr/bin/perl

while (<STDIN>)
{
    if ( $_ =~ /[bB]laster/ ) { print $_; }
}
```

2. **Make the lookup file executable by using the following command:**

```
chmod +x lookup
```

3. **Try the script by using the following command:**

```
cat /usr/src/linux*/drivers/cdrom/sbpcd.c | ./lookup
```

In this case, the `cat` command feeds the contents of a specific file (which, as you know from the `grep` example, contains some lines with the regular expression) to the `lookup` script. The script simply applies Perl's regular expression-match operator (=~) and prints any matching line. The output should be similar to what the `grep` command displays with the following command:

```
grep "[bB]laster"
/usr/src/linux*/drivers/cdrom/sbpcd.c
```

The $_ variable in the `lookout` script needs some explanation. The <STDIN> expression gets a line from the standard input and, by default, stores that line in the $_ variable. Inside the `while` loop, the regular expression is matched against the $_ string. The following single Perl statement completes the lookup script's work:

```
if ( $_ =~ /[bB]laster/ ) { print $_; }
```

This example illustrates how you might use a regular expression to search for occurrences of strings in a file.

After you use regular expressions for a while, you can better appreciate their power. The trick is to find the regular expression that performs the task you want. For example, here is a search that looks for all lines that begin with exactly seven spaces and end with a right parenthesis:

**Book VIII
Chapter 4**

**Programming
in Perl**

```
while (<STDIN>)
{
    if ( $_ =~ /\)\n/ && $_ =~ /^ {7}\S/ )  { print $_; }
}
```

Flow-control statements

So far, you have seen Perl statements intended to execute in a serial fashion, one after another. Perl also includes statements that enable you to control the flow of execution of the statements. You already have seen the if statement and a while loop. Perl includes a complete set of flow-control statements just like those in C, but with a few extra features.

In Perl, all conditional statements take the following form:

```
conditional-statement
{ Perl code to execute if conditional is true }
```

Notice that you must enclose within braces ({ . . . }) the code that follows the conditional statement. The conditional statement checks the value of an expression to determine whether to execute the code within the braces. In Perl, as in C, any non-zero value is considered true, whereas a zero value is false.

Next I briefly describe the syntax of the major conditional statements in Perl.

if and unless

The Perl if statement resembles the C if statement. For example, an if statement may check a count to see whether the count exceeds a threshold, as follows:

```
if ( $count > 25 ) { print "Too many errors!\n"; }
```

You can add an else clause to the if statement, like this:

```
if ($user eq "root")
{
    print "Starting simulation...\n";
}
else
{
    print "Sorry $user, you must be \"root\" to run this pro-
    gram.\n";
    exit;
}
```

If you know C, you can see that Perl's syntax looks quite a bit like that in C. Conditionals with the `if` statement can have zero or more `elsif` clauses to account for more alternatives, such as the following:

```
print "Enter version number:"; # prompt user for version number

$os_version = <STDIN>;      # read from standard input
chop $os_version; # get rid of the newline at the end of the line
# Check version number
if ($os_version >= 10 ) { print "No upgrade necessary\n";}
elsif ($os_version >= 6 && $os_version < 9)
                { print "Standard upgrade\n";}
elsif ($os_version > 3 && $os_version < 6) { print "Reinstall\n";}
else { print "Sorry, cannot upgrade\n";}
```

The `unless` statement is unique to Perl. This statement has the same form as `if`, including the use of `elsif` and `else` clauses. The difference is that `unless` executes its statement block only if the condition is false. You can, for example, use `unless` in the following code:

```
unless ($user eq "root")
{
    print "You must be \"root\" to run this program.\n";
    exit;
}
```

In this case, unless the string `user` is `"root"`, the script exits.

while

Use Perl's `while` statement for looping — the repetition of some processing until a condition becomes false. To read a line at a time from standard input and to process that line, you may use the following `while` loop:

```
while ($in = <STDIN>)
{
# Code to process the line
    print $in;
}
```

If you read from the standard input without any argument, Perl assigns the current line of standard input to the `$_` variable. Thus, you can write the preceding `while` loop as follows:

```
while (<STDIN>)
{
# Code to process the line
    print $_;
}
```

**Book VIII
Chapter 4**

**Programming
in Perl**

Perl's while statements are more versatile than those of C because you can use almost anything as the condition to be tested. If you use an array as the condition, for example, the while loop executes until the array has no elements left, as in the following example:

```
# Assume ⌘arg has the current set of command arguments
while (⌘arg)
{
    $arg = shift ⌘arg;  # this extracts one argument
# Code to process the current argument
    print $arg;
}
```

The shift function removes the first element of an array and returns that element.

You can skip to the end of a loop with the next keyword; the last keyword exits the loop. For example, the following while loop adds the numbers from 1 to 10, skipping 5:

```
while (1)
{
  $i++;
  if($i == 5) { next;} # Jump to the next iteration if $i is 5
  if($i > 10) { last;} # When $i exceeds 10, end the loop
  $sum += $i;      # Add the numbers
}
# At this point $sum should be 50
```

for and foreach

Perl and C's for statements have similar syntax. Use the for statement to execute a statement any number of times, based on the value of an expression. The syntax is as follows:

```
for (expr_1; expr_2; expr_3) { statement block }
```

expr_1 is evaluated one time, at the beginning of the loop; the statement block is executed until expression expr_2 evaluates to zero. The third expression, expr_3, is evaluated after each execution of the statement block. You can omit any of the expressions, but you must include the semicolons. In addition, the braces around the statement block are required. Following is an example that uses a for loop to add the numbers from 1 to 10:

```
for($i=0, $sum=0; $i <= 10; $sum += $i, $i++) {}
```

In this example, the actual work of adding the numbers is done in the third expression, and the statement the for loop controls is an empty block ({ }).

The `foreach` statement is most appropriate for arrays. Following is the syntax:

```
foreach Variable (Array) { statement block }
```

The `foreach` statement assigns to *Variable* an element from the *Array* and executes the statement block. The `foreach` statement repeats this procedure until no array elements remain. The following `foreach` statement adds the numbers from 1 to 10:

```
foreach $i (1..10) { $sum += $i;}
```

Notice that I declare the array with the range operator (..). You also can use a list of comma-separated items as the array.

If you omit the *Variable* in a `foreach` statement, Perl implicitly uses the $_ variable to hold the current array element. Thus, you can use the following:

```
foreach (1..10) { $sum += $_;}
```

goto

The `goto` statement causes Perl to jump to a statement identified by a label. Here is an example that prompts the user for a value and repeats the request, if the value is not acceptable:

```
ReEnter:
print "Enter offset: ";
$offset = <STDIN>;
chop $offset;
unless ($offset > 0 && $offset < 512)
{
    print "Bad offset: $offset\n";
    goto ReEnter;
}
```

Accessing Linux commands

You can execute any Linux command from Perl in several ways:

✦ Call the `system` function with a string that contains the Linux command you want to execute.

✦ Enclose a Linux command within backquotes (`` ` ``), which also are known as grave accents. You can run a Linux command this way and capture its output.

✦ Call the `fork` function to copy the current script and process new commands in the child process. (If a process starts another process, the new one is known as a *child process*.)

✦ Call the `exec` function to overlay the current script with a new script or Linux command.

✦ Use `fork` and `exec` to provide shell-like behavior. (Monitor user input, and process each user-entered command through a child process.) In this section I present a simple example of how to accomplish this task.

The simplest way to execute a Linux command in your script is to use the `system` function with the command in a string. After the system function returns, the exit code from the command is in the `$?` variable. You can easily write a simple Perl script that reads a string from the standard input and processes that string with the system function. Follow these steps:

1. **Use a text editor to enter and save the following script in a file named** `rcmd.pl`**:**

```perl
#!/usr/bin/perl
# Read user input and process command

$prompt = "Command (\"exit\" to quit): ";
print $prompt;

while (<STDIN>)
{
    chop;
    if ($_ eq "exit") { exit 0;}

# Execute command by calling system
    system $_;
    unless ($? == 0) {print "Error executing: $_\n";}
    print $prompt;
}
```

2. **Make the** `rcmd.pl` **file executable by using the following command:**

```
chmod +x rcmd.pl
```

3. **Run the script by typing** `./rcmd.pl` **at the shell prompt.**

Here's a sample output from the `rcmd.pl` script (the output depends on what commands you enter):

```
Command ("exit" to quit): ps
  PID TTY          TIME CMD
  767 pts/0    00:00:00 bash
  940 pts/0    00:00:00 rcmd.pl
  945 pts/0    00:00:00 ps
Command ("exit" to quit): exit
```

You can also run Linux commands by using `fork` and `exec` in your Perl script. Following is an example script — `psh.pl` — that uses `fork` and `exec` to execute commands the user enters:

```
#!/usr/bin/perl

# This is a simple script that uses "fork" and "exec" to
# run a command entered by the user

$prompt = "Command (\"exit\" to quit): ";
print $prompt;

while (<STDIN>)
{
    chop;     # remove trailing newline
    if($_ eq "exit") { exit 0;}

    $status = fork;
    if($status)
    {
# In parent... wait for child process to finish...
        wait;
        print $prompt;
        next;
    }
    else
    {
        exec $_;
    }
}
```

The following sample output shows how the psh.pl script executes the
ps command:

```
Command ("exit" to quit): ps
  PID TTY          TIME CMD
  767 pts/0    00:00:00 bash
  949 pts/0    00:00:00 psh.pl
  950 pts/0    00:00:00 ps
Command ("exit" to quit): exit
```

Shells, such as Bash, use the fork and exec combination to run commands.

File access

You may have noticed the <STDIN> expression in various examples in this
chapter. That's Perl's way of reading from a file. In Perl, a *file handle,* also
known as an identifier, identifies a file. Usually, file handles are in uppercase
characters. STDIN is a predefined file handle that denotes the standard
input — by default, the keyboard. STDOUT and STDERR are the other two predefined file handles. STDOUT is used for printing to the terminal, and STDERR
is used for printing error messages.

To read from a file, write the file handle inside angle brackets (<>). Thus, <STDIN> reads a line from the standard input.

You can open other files by using the open function. The following example shows you how to open the /etc/passwd file for reading and how to display the lines in that file:

```
open (PWDFILE, "/etc/passwd"); # PWDFILE is the file handle
while (<PWDFILE>) { print $_;} # By default, input line is in $_
close PWDFILE;          # Close the file
```

By default, the open function opens a file for reading. You can add special characters at the beginning of the filename to indicate other types of access. A > prefix opens the file for writing, whereas a > prefix opens a file for appending. Following is a short script that reads the /etc/passwd file and creates a new file, named output, with a list of all users who lack shells (the password entries for these users have : at the end of each line):

```
#!/usr/bin/perl
# Read /etc/passwd and create list of users without any shell

open (PWDFILE, "/etc/passwd");
open (RESULT, ">output");    # open file for writing

while (<PWDFILE>)
{
    if ($_ =~ /:\n/) {print RESULT $_;}
}

close PWDFILE;
close RESULT;
```

After you execute this script, you should find a file named output in the current directory. Here's what the output file contains when I run this script on a Red Hat Linux system:

```
news:x:9:13:news:/etc/news:
```

Filename with pipe prefix

One interesting filename prefix is the *pipe character* — the vertical bar (|). If you call open with a filename that begins with |, the rest of the filename is treated as a command. The Perl interpreter executes the command, and you can use print calls to send input to this command. The following Perl script sends a mail message to a list of users by using the mail command:

```
#!/usr/bin/perl
# Send mail to a list of users

foreach ("root", "naba")
{
```

```
open (MAILPIPE, "| mail -s Greetings $_");
print MAILPIPE "Remember to send in your weekly report today!\n";
close MAILPIPE;
}
```

If a filename ends with a pipe character (|), that filename is executed as a command; you can read that command's output with the angle brackets (<...>), as shown in the following example:

```
open (PSPIPE, "ps ax |");
while (<PSPIPE>)
{
# Process the output of the ps command
# This example simply echoes each line
    print $_;
}
```

Subroutines

Although Perl includes a large assortment of built-in functions, you can add your own code modules in the form of subroutines. In fact, Perl comes with a large set of subroutines. Here's a simple script that illustrates the syntax of subroutines in Perl:

```
#!/usr/bin/perl
sub hello
{
# Make local copies of the arguments from the @_ array
    local ($first,$last) = @_;

    print "Hello, $first $last\n";
}

$a = Jane;
$b = Doe;

&hello($a, $b);      # Call the subroutine
```

When you run the preceding script, it displays the following output:

```
Hello, Jane Doe
```

Note the following points about subroutines:

✦ The subroutine receives its arguments in the array @_ (the at symbol, followed by an underscore character).

✦ Variables used in subroutines are global by default. Use the local function to create a local set of variables.

✦ Call a subroutine by placing an ampersand (&) before its name. Thus, the subroutine hello is called by typing &hello.

Book VIII
Chapter 4

Programming in Perl

If you want, you can put a subroutine in its own file. The `hello` subroutine, for example, can reside in a file named `hello.pl`. When you place a subroutine in a file, remember to add a return value at the end of the file — just type **1;** at the end to return 1. Thus, the `hello.pl` file appears as follows:

```
sub hello
{
# Make local copies of the arguments from the @_ array
    local ($first,$last) = @_;

    print "Hello, $first $last\n";
}
1;      # return value
```

Then, you have to write the script that uses the `hello` subroutine, as follows:

```
#!/usr/bin/perl
require 'hello.pl';   # include the file with the subroutine

$a = Jane;
$b = Doe;

&hello($a, $b);       # Call the subroutine
```

This script uses the require function to include the `hello.pl` file that contains the definition of the `hello` subroutine.

Built-in functions in Perl

Perl has nearly 200 built-in functions (also referred to as *Perl functions*), including functions that resemble the ones in the C Run-Time Library, as well as functions that access the operating system. You really need to go through the list of functions to appreciate the breadth of capabilities available in Perl. I don't have enough space in this book to cover these functions, but you can learn about the Perl built-in functions by pointing your Web browser to the following address:

```
http://www.perldoc.com/perl5.8.0/pod/perlfunc.html
```

This address connects you to the Perl 5.8.0 documentation page so you can get an overview of the Perl built-in functions. On that page, click a function's name to view more detailed information about that function.

You can also read the Perl function manual on your Red Hat Linux system by typing the following command in a terminal window:

```
man perlfunc
```

This command displays the text man page for the functions. I think you'll find the Web-based documentation much easier to use.

Understanding Perl Packages and Modules

A *Perl package* is a way to group together data and subroutines. Essentially, it's a way to use variable and subroutine names without conflicting with any names used in other parts of a program. The concept of a package existed in Perl since version 4.

The package provides a way to control the *namespace* — a term that refers to the collection of variable and subroutine names. Although you may not be aware of this, when you write a Perl program, it automatically belongs to a package named main. Besides main, there are other Perl packages in the Perl library (these packages are in the /usr/lib/perl5/X.Y.Z directory of your Red Hat Linux system where X.Y.Z is the version number of Perl such as 5.8.0), and you can define your own package, as well.

Perl modules are packages that follow specific guidelines.

Perl packages

You can think of a Perl package as a convenient way to organize a set of related Perl subroutines. Another benefit is that variable and subroutine names defined in a package do not conflict with names used elsewhere in the program. Thus, a variable named $count in one package remains unique to that package and does not conflict with a $count used elsewhere in a Perl program.

A Perl package is in a single file. The package statement is used at the beginning of the file to declare the file as a package and to give the package a name. For example, the file timelocal.pl defines a number of subroutines and variables in a package named timelocal. (Note that the timelocal.pl file has been superceded by the Time::Local module.) The timelocal.pl file has the following package statement in various places:

```
package timelocal;
```

The effect of this package declaration is that all subsequent variable names and subroutine names are considered to be in the timelocal package. You can put such a package statement at the beginning of the file that implements the package.

What if you are implementing a package and you need to refer to a subroutine or variable in another package? As you might guess, all you need to do is specify both the package name and the variable (or subroutine) name. Perl provides the following syntax for referring to a variable in another package:

```
$Package::Variable
```

Here *Package* is the name of the package, and *Variable* is the name of the variable in that package. If you omit the package name, Perl assumes you are referring to a variable in the `main` package.

To use a package in your program, you can simply call the `require` function with the package filename as an argument. For example, there is a package named `ctime` defined in the file `ctime.pl`. That package includes the `ctime` subroutine that converts a binary time into a string. The following simple program uses the `ctime` package from the `ctime.pl` file:

```
#!/usr/bin/perl -w

# Use the ctime package defined in ctime.pl file
require 'ctime.pl';

# Call the ctime subroutine
$time = ctime(time());

# Print the time string
print $time;
```

As you can see, this program uses the `require` function to bring the `ctime.pl` file into the program. When you run this program, it should print the current date and time formatted, as shown in the sample output:

```
Sat Oct 26 21:16:32 2002
```

Note that the first line of this script uses the `-w` option. That option causes the Perl interpreter to print warning messages about any bad constructs in the Perl script. It's a good idea to include the `-w` option on the line that invokes the Perl interpreter.

Perl modules

Perl 5 took the concept of a package one step further and introduced the *module,* a package that follows certain guidelines and is designed to be reusable. Each module is a package that is defined in a file with the same name as the package but with a `.pm` extension. Each Perl object is implemented as a module. For example, the `CGI` object (for use in Web servers) is implemented as the `CGI` module, stored in the file named `CGI.pm`.

Nowadays Perl comes with a many modules. You'll find these modules in the `/usr/lib/perl5/X.Y.Z` directory where `X.Y.Z` is the Perl version number.

For Perl Version 5.8.0, the Perl modules are in the `/usr/lib/perl5/5.8.0` directory. Look for files with names that end in `.pm` (that stands for Perl module).

Using a module

You can call the `require` function, or the `use` function, to include a Perl module in your program. For example, a Perl module named `Cwd` (defined, as expected, in the `Cwd.pm` file) provides a `getcwd` subroutine that returns the current directory. You can call the `require` function to include the `Cwd` module and call `getcwd` as follows:

```
require Cwd;  # You do not need the full file name
$curdir = Cwd::getcwd();
print "Current directory = $curdir\n";
```

The first line brings the `Cwd.pm` file into this program — you do not have to specify the full filename; the `require` function automatically appends `.pm` to the module's name to figure out which file to include. The second line shows how you call a subroutine from the `Cwd` module. When you use `require` to include a module, you must invoke each subroutine with the *Module::subroutine* format.

If you were to rewrite this example program with the `use` function in place of `require`, it would take the following form:

```
use Cwd;
$curdir = getcwd(); # no need for Cwd:: prefix
print "Current directory = $curdir\n";
```

The most significant difference is that you no longer need to qualify a subroutine name with the module name prefix (such as `Cwd::`).

You can call either `require` or `use` to include a module in your program. Just remember the following nuances when you use these functions:

✦ When you include a module by calling `require`, the module is included only when the `require` function is invoked as the program runs. You must use the *Module::subroutine* syntax to invoke any subroutines from a module you include with the require function.

✦ When you include a module by calling `use`, the module is included in the program as soon as the `use` statement is processed. Thus, you can invoke subroutines and variables from the module as if they were part of your program. You do not need to qualify subroutine and variable names with a *Module::* prefix.

You may want to stick to the use *Module*; syntax to include modules in your program, because this lets you use a simpler syntax when you call subroutines from the module.

Using Objects in Perl

An *object* is a data structure together with the functions that operate on that data. Each object is an instance of a class that defines the object's type. For example, a rectangle class may have the four corners of the rectangle as data; functions such as one that computes the rectangle's area; and another that draws the rectangle. Then, each rectangle object can be an instance of the rectangle class, with different coordinates for the four corners. In this sense, an object is an instance of a class.

The functions (or subroutines) that implement the operations on an object's data are known as *methods*. That's terminology borrowed from Smalltalk, one of the earliest object-oriented programming languages.

Classes also suggest the notion of inheritance. You can define a new class of objects by extending the data or methods (or both) of an existing class. A common use of inheritance is to express the IS A relationship among various classes of objects. Consider, for example, the geometric shapes. Because a circle IS A shape and a rectangle IS A shape, you can say that the circle and rectangle classes inherit from the shape class. In this case, the shape class is called a parent class or base class.

The basic idea behind *object-oriented programming* is that you can package the data and the associated methods (subroutines) of an object as a black box. Programmers access the object only through advertised methods, without having to know the inner workings of the methods. Typically, a programmer can create an object, invoke its methods to get or set attributes (that's another name for the object's data), and destroy the object. In this section I show you how to use objects in Perl. With this knowledge in hand, you'll be able to exploit objects as building blocks for your Perl programs.

Understanding Perl objects

Perl implements objects by using modules, which package data and subroutines in a file. Perl presents the following simple model of objects:

✦ An *object* is denoted by a reference (objects are implemented as references to a hash).

✦ A *class* is a Perl module that provides the methods to work with the object.

✦ A *method* is a Perl subroutine that expects the object reference as the first argument.

Object implementers have to follow certain rules and provide certain methods in a module that represents a class. However, you really don't need to know much about an object's implementation to use it in your Perl program. All you need to know are the steps you have to follow when you use an object.

Creating and accessing Perl objects

A useful Perl object is Lincoln Stein's `CGI` object, which is implemented by the Perl module `CGI.pm`. That module comes with the Perl distribution and is in the `/usr/lib/perl5/5.8.0` directory (for Perl Version 5.8.0).

As the name implies, the CGI object is meant for writing Common Gateway Interface applications for World Wide Web servers. A CGI program accepts queries submitted by a user and returns a HyperText Markup Language (HTML) document with a response (this is the document the user sees in the Web browser).

When you create a CGI object, it automatically parses a query string the user submits via an HTML form. (These are forms that you see on many Web pages; you can essentially fill in and submit information through these forms.) The CGI object provides methods for accessing the parameters the user enters on a form, creating headers needed for Web pages, and generating HTML code for the Web page the CGI program will send back.

To use the CGI object, follow these general steps:

1. **Place the following line to include the CGI module in your program:**

```
use CGI;
```

You must include this line before you create a CGI object.

2. **To create a CGI object, use the following syntax:**

```
$query = new CGI;
```

where `$query` is the reference to the CGI object. In the case of the CGI object, creating the object automatically parses the query and sets up the internal variables of the object.

3. **Invoke methods from the CGI object as the following examples illustrate:**

```
print $query->header;  // Send the HTTP header
print $query->start_html("Title of document");
print $query->end_html; // End HTML document
```

Here `$query->header` calls the header method of the `$query` CGI object. Similarly, `start_html` and `end_html` are methods in the CGI object. All of these methods return strings, which is why they are used as arguments to the print function.

Access the object's methods by using the arrow operator (->) and the object reference you obtain after creating the object.

How do you know which methods to call and in what order to call them? You have to read the object's documentation before you can use the object. The method names and the sequences of method invocation depend on what the object does.

Using the English module

Perl includes several special variables with strange names, such as $_ for the default argument and $! for error messages corresponding to the last error. When you read a program, it can be difficult to guess what a special variable means. The result is that you may end up avoiding a special variable that could be useful in your program.

As a helpful gesture, Perl 5 provides the English module (English.pm), which enables you to use understandable names for various special variables in Perl. To use the English module, include the following line in your Perl program:

```
use English;
```

After that, you can refer to $_ as $ARG and $! as $ERRNO (these "English" names can still be a bit cryptic, but they're definitely better than the punctuation marks).

The following program uses the English module and prints a few interesting variables:

```
#!/usr/bin/perl -w
# File: english.pl

use English;
if($PERL_VERSION ge v5.8.0)
{
    print "Perl version 5.8.0 or later\n";
}
else
{
    print "Perl version prior to 5.8.0\n";
}
print "Perl executable = $EXECUTABLE_NAME\n";
print "Script name = $PROGRAM_NAME\n";
```

Run this script with the following command:

```
./english.pl
```

When I run this script on Red Hat Linux, here's what I get as output:

```
Perl version 5.8.0 or later
Perl executable = /usr/bin/perl
Script name = ./english.pl
```

The English module is handy because it lets you write Perl scripts in which you can refer to special variables by meaningful names. To learn more about the Perl special variables and their English names, type **man perlvar** in a terminal window or, better yet, point your Web browser to

```
http://www.perldoc.com/perl5.8.0/pod/perlvar.html
```

Appendix: About the CDs

In This Appendix

✔ **System requirements**

✔ **CD installation instructions**

✔ **What you'll find on the CDs**

✔ **Troubleshooting**

System Requirements

Make sure that your computer meets the minimum system requirements shown in the following list. If your computer doesn't match up to most of these requirements, you may have problems using the software and files on the CDs.

◆ A PC with a Pentium or better processor running at 200 MHz or faster

◆ At least 64MB of total RAM installed on your computer; for best performance, we recommend at least 128MB

◆ At least 3GB of free space on your hard disk

◆ A CD-ROM drive

◆ A monitor capable of displaying at least 256 colors

◆ A sound card

◆ Ethernet network interface card (NIC) or modem with a speed of at least 56 Kbps

CD Installation Instructions

Installing Red Hat Linux from the CDs can be tricky, as some hardware on your PC is not supported by Red Hat Linux. Nevertheless, Red Hat Linux on the companion CDs already supports such a wide variety of hardware, so chances are good that all your PC's peripherals probably are supported.

To install Red Hat Linux from the companion CDs, follow these steps. (For the latest and greatest information, please refer to the README file located at the root of the CD-ROM.)

1. **Gather information about your PC's hardware, such as graphics card, network card, and SCSI card, before you install Linux.**

2. **Use a partitioning program such as PartitionMagic or the FIPS program to create room on your hard disk for Red Hat Linux. Skip this step if you plan to use Red Hat Linux as the sole operating system on your PC or if you plan to install it on an empty second hard disk.**

3. **If your PC cannot boot from the CD-ROM drive, create a Red Hat Linux boot disk.**

4. **Boot your PC with the first CD or by using the Red Hat Linux boot disk. This step automatically runs the Red Hat Linux installation program. From this point on, respond to the questions and choices in a number of windows as the Red Hat installation program takes you through the steps. Here are some of the key installation steps:**

   - Identify any SCSI adapters installed on your PC.

   - Prepare the hard disk partitions for Red Hat Linux. If you have created space by reducing the size of an existing DOS partition, this step enables you to create the partitions for Red Hat Linux.

   - Configure the Ethernet network, if any. You may have to specify parameters, such as the IP address and host name for your Red Hat Linux system.

   - Specify the local time zone and set the root password.

   - Install a boot loader program on your hard disk so that you can boot Red Hat Linux when you power up your PC after shutting it down.

   - Select the specific software packages that you want to install, such as the X Window System and the GNOME or KDE graphical desktop.

   - Configure the X Window System and enable the graphical login screen so that when you boot your Linux system, it displays a login dialog box and goes directly into the GNOME or KDE graphical desktop after successful login.

To install specific items from the CDs to your hard drive, follow these steps:

1. **Log in as root.**

2. **Insert the CD into your computer's CD-ROM drive.**

3. **If you are using GNOME or KDE GUI, wait for the CD to mount. Otherwise, open a terminal window and at the command prompt type**

```
mount /mnt/cdrom
```

4. **Browse the CD and find the RPM file you want to install. Then type the following command:**

   ```
   rpm -ivh packagename*
   ```

   Replace *packagename* with the name of the package you want to install.

5. **To remove the CD from your CD-ROM drive, type the following command at the command prompt:**

   ```
   umount /mnt/cdrom
   ```

What You'll Find on the CD

This section provides a summary of the software and other goodies you find on the CDs. If you need help with installing the items provided on the CDs, refer back to the installation instructions in the preceding section.

Shareware programs are fully functional, free, trial versions of copyrighted programs. If you like particular programs, register with their authors for a nominal fee and receive licenses, enhanced versions, and technical support. *Freeware programs* are free, copyrighted games, applications, and utilities. You can copy them to as many PCs as you like — for free — but they offer no tech support. *GNU software* is governed by its own license, which is included in the folder of the GNU software. There are no restrictions on distribution of GNU software. See the GNU license at the root of the CD for details. *Trial, demo,* or *evaluation* versions of software are usually limited by time or functionality (such as not letting you save a project after you create it).

You can find the following software on the CDs (for info on the directory organization of a CD, refer to the README file located at the root of the CD-ROM):

✦ Linux kernel 2.4.18 with driver modules for major PC hardware configurations, including IDE/EIDE and SCSI drives, PCMCIA devices, and CDs

✦ A complete set of installation and configuration tools for setting up devices and services

✦ A graphical user interface based on the XFree86 4.2.0 package, with GNOME 2.0 and KDE 3.0 graphical desktops

✦ Full TCP/IP networking for Internet, LANs, and intranets

✦ Tools for connecting your PC to your Internet Service Provider (ISP) using PPP, DSL, or dial-up serial communications programs

✦ A complete suite of Internet applications, including electronic mail (`sendmail`, `mail`), news (INN), TELNET, FTP, DNS, and NFS

- ✦ Evolution 1.0.8 e-mail and calendar application

- ✦ OpenOffice.org 1.0.1 office suite with word processor, spreadsheet, presentation software, and more

- ✦ Apache Web server 2.0.40, to turn your PC into a Web server; and Mozilla 1.0.1, to surf the Net

- ✦ Samba 2.2.5 LAN Manager software for Microsoft Windows connectivity

- ✦ Several text editors (for example, GNU Emacs 21.2; `vim`)

- ✦ Graphics and image manipulation software, such as The GIMP, XPaint, Xfig, Gnuplot, Ghostscript, Ghostview, and ImageMagick

- ✦ Programming languages (GNU C and C++ 3.2, Perl 5.8.0, Tcl/Tk 8.3.3, Python 2.2.1, GNU AWK 3.1.1) and software development tools (GNU Debugger 5.2.1, CVS 1.11, RCS 5.7, GNU Bison 1.35, flex 2.5.4a, TIFF, and JPEG libraries)

- ✦ Support for industry standard Executable and Linking Format (ELF) and Intel Binary Compatibility Specification (iBCS)

- ✦ A complete suite of standard UNIX utilities from the GNU project

- ✦ Tools to access and use DOS files and applications (`mtools` 3.9.8)

- ✦ Text formatting and typesetting software (`groff`, TeX, and LaTeX)

This book comes with the Publisher's Edition version of Red Hat Linux 8.0, provided by Red Hat. Unfortunately, the CDs don't include the DOSUTILS directory with the `rawrite.exe` and `fips.exe` programs you may need during installation. If you need these programs, download them from one of the mirror sites listed at `www.redhat.com/download/mirror.html`. Click on the *Distribution* link next to one of the listed FTP sites and look in the directory corresponding to the Red Hat Linux version number. For example, the DOSUTILS directory for Red Hat Linux 8.0 should be in the `8.0/en/os/ i386/dosutils` directory. Use a browser to download the `rawrite.exe` and `fips.exe` files.

Troubleshooting

If you have difficulty installing or using the materials on the companion CDs, consult the detailed installation and troubleshooting instructions in Book I.

If you have trouble installing items from the CDs, call Customer Service at 800-762-2974 (outside the U.S.: 317-572-3993) or e-mail `techsupdum@wiley.com`. Wiley Publishing Inc. will provide tech support only for installation and other general quality control items; for tech support on the applications, consult the program's vendor or author.

Index

X

Notes

Notes

Notes

Notes

Notes

Notes

GNU General Public License

Version 2, June 1991
Copyright © 1989, 1991 Free Software Foundation, Inc.
59 Temple Place - Suite 330, Boston, MA 02111-1307, USA

Preamble

The licenses for most software are designed to take away your freedom to share and change it. By contrast, the GNU General Public License is intended to guarantee your freedom to share and change free software — to make sure the software is free for all its users. This General Public License applies to most of the Free Software Foundation's software and to any other program whose authors commit to using it. (Some other Free Software Foundation software is covered by the GNU Library General Public License instead.) You can apply it to your programs, too.

When we speak of free software, we are referring to freedom, not price. Our General Public Licenses are designed to make sure that you have the freedom to distribute copies of free software (and charge for this service if you wish), that you receive source code or can get it if you want it, that you can change the software or use pieces of it in new free programs; and that you know you can do these things.

To protect your rights, we need to make restrictions that forbid anyone to deny you these rights or to ask you to surrender the rights. These restrictions translate to certain responsibilities for you if you distribute copies of the software, or if you modify it.

For example, if you distribute copies of such a program, whether gratis or for a fee, you must give the recipients all the rights that you have. You must make sure that they, too, receive or can get the source code. And you must show them these terms so they know their rights.

We protect your rights with two steps: (1) copyright the software, and (2) offer you this license which gives you legal permission to copy, distribute and/or modify the software.

Also, for each author's protection and ours, we want to make certain that everyone understands that there is no warranty for this free software. If the software is modified by someone else and passed on, we want its recipients to know that what they have is not the original, so that any problems introduced by others will not reflect on the original authors' reputations.

Finally, any free program is threatened constantly by software patents. We wish to avoid the danger that redistributors of a free program will individually obtain patent licenses, in effect making the program proprietary. To prevent this, we have made it clear that any patent must be licensed for everyone's free use or not licensed at all.

The precise terms and conditions for copying, distribution and modification follow.

TERMS AND CONDITIONS FOR COPYING, DISTRIBUTION AND MODIFICATION

0. This License applies to any program or other work which contains a notice placed by the copyright holder saying it may be distributed under the terms of this General Public License. The "Program", below, refers to any such program or work, and a "work based on the Program" means either the Program or any derivative work under copyright law: that is to say, a work containing the Program or a portion of it, either verbatim or with modifications and/or translated into another language. (Hereinafter, translation is included without limitation in the term "modification".) Each licensee is addressed as "you".

Activities other than copying, distribution and modification are not covered by this License; they are outside its scope. The act of running the Program is not restricted, and the output from the Program is covered only if its contents constitute a work based on the Program (independent of having been made by running the Program). Whether that is true depends on what the Program does.

1. You may copy and distribute verbatim copies of the Program's source code as you receive it, in any medium, provided that you conspicuously and appropriately publish on each copy an appropriate copyright notice and disclaimer of warranty; keep intact all the notices that refer to this License and to the absence of any warranty; and give any other recipients of the Program a copy of this License along with the Program.

You may charge a fee for the physical act of transferring a copy, and you may at your option offer warranty protection in exchange for a fee.

2. You may modify your copy or copies of the Program or any portion of it, thus forming a work based on the Program, and copy and distribute such modifications or work under the terms of Section 1 above, provided that you also meet all of these conditions:

a) You must cause the modified files to carry prominent notices stating that you changed the files and the date of any change.

b) You must cause any work that you distribute or publish, that in whole or in part contains or is derived from the Program or any part thereof, to be licensed as a whole at no charge to all third parties under the terms of this License.

c) If the modified program normally reads commands interactively when run, you must cause it, when started running for such interactive use in the most ordinary way, to print or display an announcement including an appropriate copyright notice and a notice that there is no warranty (or else, saying that you provide a warranty) and that users may redistribute the program under these conditions, and telling the user how to view a copy of this License. (Exception: If the Program itself is interactive but does not normally print such an announcement, your work based on the Program is not required to print an announcement.)

These requirements apply to the modified work as a whole. If identifiable sections of that work are not derived from the Program, and can be reasonably considered independent and separate works in themselves, then this License, and its terms, do not apply to those sections when you distribute them as separate works. But when you distribute the same sections as part of a whole which is a work based on the Program, the distribution of the whole must be on the terms of this License, whose permissions for other licensees extend to the entire whole, and thus to each and every part regardless of who wrote it.

Thus, it is not the intent of this section to claim rights or contest your rights to work written entirely by you; rather, the intent is to exercise the right to control the distribution of derivative or collective works based on the Program. In addition, mere aggregation of another work not based on the Program with the Program (or with a work based on the Program) on a volume of a storage or distribution medium does not bring the other work under the scope of this License.

3. You may copy and distribute the Program (or a work based on it, under Section 2) in object code or executable form under the terms of Sections 1 and 2 above provided that you also do one of the following:

   a) Accompany it with the complete corresponding machine-readable source code, which must be distributed under the terms of Sections 1 and 2 above on a medium customarily used for software interchange; or,

   b) Accompany it with a written offer, valid for at least three years, to give any third party, for a charge no more than your cost of physically performing source distribution, a complete machine-readable copy of the corresponding source code, to be distributed under the terms of Sections 1 and 2 above on a medium customarily used for software interchange; or,

   c) Accompany it with the information you received as to the offer to distribute corresponding source code. (This alternative is allowed only for noncommercial distribution and only if you received the program in object code or executable form with such an offer, in accord with Subsection b above.)

The source code for a work means the preferred form of the work for making modifications to it. For an executable work, complete source code means all the source code for all modules it contains, plus any associated interface definition files, plus the scripts used to control compilation and installation of the executable. However, as a special exception, the source code distributed need not include anything that is normally distributed (in either source or binary form) with the major components (compiler, kernel, and so on) of the operating system on which the executable runs, unless that component itself accompanies the executable.

If distribution of executable or object code is made by offering access to copy from a designated place, then offering equivalent access to copy the source code from the same place counts as distribution of the source code, even though third parties are not compelled to copy the source along with the object code.

4. You may not copy, modify, sublicense, or distribute the Program except as expressly provided under this License. Any attempt otherwise to copy, modify, sublicense or distribute the Program is void, and will automatically terminate your rights under this License. However, parties who have received copies, or rights, from you under this License will not have their licenses terminated so long as such parties remain in full compliance.

5. You are not required to accept this License, since you have not signed it. However, nothing else grants you permission to modify or distribute the Program or its derivative works. These actions are prohibited by law if you do not accept this License. Therefore, by modifying or distributing the Program (or any work based on the Program), you indicate your acceptance of this License to do so, and all its terms and conditions for copying, distributing or modifying the Program or works based on it.

6. Each time you redistribute the Program (or any work based on the Program), the recipient automatically receives a license from the original licensor to copy, distribute or modify the Program subject to these terms and conditions. You may not impose any further restrictions on the recipients' exercise of the rights granted herein. You are not responsible for enforcing compliance by third parties to this License.

7. If, as a consequence of a court judgment or allegation of patent infringement or for any other reason (not limited to patent issues), conditions are imposed on you (whether by court order, agreement or otherwise) that contradict the conditions of this License, they do not excuse you from the conditions of this License. If you cannot distribute so as to satisfy simultaneously your obligations under this License and any other pertinent obligations, then as a consequence you may not distribute the Program at all. For example, if a patent license would not permit royalty-free redistribution of the Program by all those who receive copies directly or indirectly through you, then the only way you could satisfy both it and this License would be to refrain entirely from distribution of the Program.

   If any portion of this section is held invalid or unenforceable under any particular circumstance, the balance of the section is intended to apply and the section as a whole is intended to apply in other circumstances.

   It is not the purpose of this section to induce you to infringe any patents or other property right claims or to contest validity of any such claims; this section has the sole purpose of protecting the integrity of the free software distribution system, which is implemented by public license practices. Many people have made generous contributions to the wide range of software distributed through that system in reliance on consistent application of that system; it is up to the author/donor to decide if he or she is willing to distribute software through any other system and a licensee cannot impose that choice.

   This section is intended to make thoroughly clear what is believed to be a consequence of the rest of this License.

8. If the distribution and/or use of the Program is restricted in certain countries either by patents or by copyrighted interfaces, the original copyright holder who places the Program under this License may add an explicit geographical distribution limitation excluding those countries, so that distribution is permitted only in or among countries not thus excluded. In such case, this License incorporates the limitation as if written in the body of this License.

9. The Free Software Foundation may publish revised and/or new versions of the General Public License from time to time. Such new versions will be similar in spirit to the present version, but may differ in detail to address new problems or concerns.

   Each version is given a distinguishing version number. If the Program specifies a version number of this License which applies to it and "any later version", you have the option of following the terms and conditions either of that version or of any later version published by the Free Software Foundation. If the Program does not specify a version number of this License, you may choose any version ever published by the Free Software Foundation.

10. If you wish to incorporate parts of the Program into other free programs whose distribution conditions are different, write to the author to ask for permission. For software which is copyrighted by the Free Software Foundation, write to the Free Software Foundation; we sometimes make exceptions for this. Our decision will be guided by the two goals of preserving the free status of all derivatives of our free software and of promoting the sharing and reuse of software generally.

NO WARRANTY

11. BECAUSE THE PROGRAM IS LICENSED FREE OF CHARGE, THERE IS NO WARRANTY FOR THE PROGRAM, TO THE EXTENT PERMITTED BY APPLICABLE LAW. EXCEPT WHEN OTHERWISE STATED IN WRITING THE COPYRIGHT HOLDERS AND/OR OTHER PARTIES PROVIDE THE PROGRAM "AS IS" WITHOUT WARRANTY OF ANY KIND, EITHER EXPRESSED OR IMPLIED, INCLUDING, BUT NOT LIMITED TO, THE IMPLIED WARRANTIES OF MERCHANTABILITY AND FITNESS FOR A PARTICULAR PURPOSE. THE ENTIRE RISK AS TO THE QUALITY AND PERFORMANCE OF THE PROGRAM IS WITH YOU. SHOULD THE PROGRAM PROVE DEFECTIVE, YOU ASSUME THE COST OF ALL NECESSARY SERVICING, REPAIR OR CORRECTION.

12. IN NO EVENT UNLESS REQUIRED BY APPLICABLE LAW OR AGREED TO IN WRITING WILL ANY COPYRIGHT HOLDER, OR ANY OTHER PARTY WHO MAY MODIFY AND/OR REDISTRIBUTE THE PROGRAM AS PERMITTED ABOVE, BE LIABLE TO YOU FOR DAMAGES, INCLUDING ANY GENERAL, SPECIAL, INCIDENTAL OR CONSEQUENTIAL DAMAGES ARISING OUT OF THE USE OR INABILITY TO USE THE PROGRAM (INCLUDING BUT NOT LIMITED TO LOSS OF DATA OR DATA BEING RENDERED INACCURATE OR LOSSES SUSTAINED BY YOU OR THIRD PARTIES OR A FAILURE OF THE PROGRAM TO OPERATE WITH ANY OTHER PROGRAMS), EVEN IF SUCH HOLDER OR OTHER PARTY HAS BEEN ADVISED OF THE POSSIBILITY OF SUCH DAMAGES.

END OF TERMS AND CONDITIONS

For more information, go to `www.gnu.org/copyleft/gpl.html`.

FOR DUMMIES®

A world of resources to help you grow

TRAVEL

0-7645-5453-0

0-7645-5438-7

0-7645-5444-1

Also available:

America's National Parks For Dummies
(0-7645-6204-5)

Caribbean For Dummies
(0-7645-5445-X)

Cruise Vacations For Dummies 2003
(0-7645-5459-X)

Europe For Dummies
(0-7645-5456-5)

Ireland For Dummies
(0-7645-6199-5)

France For Dummies
(0-7645-6292-4)

Las Vegas For Dummies
(0-7645-5448-4)

London For Dummies
(0-7645-5416-6)

Mexico's Beach Resorts For Dummies
(0-7645-6262-2)

Paris For Dummies
(0-7645-5494-8)

RV Vacations For Dummies
(0-7645-5443-3)

EDUCATION & TEST PREPARATION

0-7645-5194-9

0-7645-5325-9

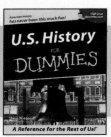

0-7645-5249-X

Also available:

The ACT For Dummies
(0-7645-5210-4)

Chemistry For Dummies
(0-7645-5430-1)

English Grammar For Dummies
(0-7645-5322-4)

French For Dummies
(0-7645-5193-0)

GMAT For Dummies
(0-7645-5251-1)

Inglés Para Dummies
(0-7645-5427-1)

Italian For Dummies
(0-7645-5196-5)

Research Papers For Dummies
(0-7645-5426-3)

SAT I For Dummies
(0-7645-5472-7)

U.S. History For Dummies
(0-7645-5249-X)

World History For Dummies
(0-7645-5242-2)

HEALTH, SELF-HELP & SPIRITUALITY

0-7645-5154-X

0-7645-5302-X

0-7645-5418-2

Also available:

The Bible For Dummies
(0-7645-5296-1)

Controlling Cholesterol For Dummies
(0-7645-5440-9)

Dating For Dummies
(0-7645-5072-1)

Dieting For Dummies
(0-7645-5126-4)

High Blood Pressure For Dummies
(0-7645-5424-7)

Judaism For Dummies
(0-7645-5299-6)

Menopause For Dummies
(0-7645-5458-1)

Nutrition For Dummies
(0-7645-5180-9)

Potty Training For Dummies
(0-7645-5417-4)

Pregnancy For Dummies
(0-7645-5074-8)

Rekindling Romance For Dummies
(0-7645-5303-8)

Religion For Dummies
(0-7645-5264-3)

Available wherever books are sold. Go to www.dummies.com or call 1-877-762-2974 to order direct

FOR DUMMIES®

Plain-English solutions for everyday challenges

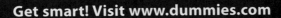

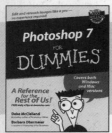